WESTMAR COLLEGE LIBRARY

D0213252

Volume 23: 1 January-May 1792

The documents in this volume concern a number of dramatic events in Thomas Jefferson's career as Secretary of State. They reveal for the first time the full extent of his role in securing Senate confirmation of Washington's controversial nominees as ministers to three major European capitals. The evolution of his last major effort as Secretary of State to achieve a comprehensive diplomatic settlement of America's differences with Spain is also evident. An important exchange of letters with the British minister helps to explain Jefferson's unsuccessful effort to settle longstanding disputes between the United States and Great Britain over enforcement of the Treaty of Paris. Other documents show his continuing interest in promoting closer commercial relations with France and the continuing intensity of his involvement in planning for the Federal District.

THE PAPERS OF
Thomas Jefferson

CHARLES T. CULLEN,
EDITOR

SECOND SERIES

THE PAPERS OF THOMAS JEFFERSON

SECOND SERIES

✝

Jefferson's Parliamentary Writings

"Parliamentary Pocket-Book" and
A Manual of Parliamentary Practice

EDITED

WITH AN INTRODUCTION BY
WILBUR SAMUEL HOWELL

✝

PRINCETON UNIVERSITY PRESS
PRINCETON, NEW JERSEY

88-196

Copyright © 1988 by Princeton University Press
Published by Princeton University Press, 41 William Street,
Princeton, New Jersey 08540
In the United Kingdom: Princeton University Press,
Guildford, Surrey

All Rights Reserved
Library of Congress Cataloging in Publication Data will
be found on the last printed page of this book
ISBN 0-691-04713-8

This book has been composed in Linotron Monticello

Clothbound editions of Princeton University Press books are
printed on acid-free paper, and binding materials are
chosen for strength and durability. Paperbacks, although
satisfactory for personal collections, are not usually
suitable for library rebinding

Printed in the United States of America by
Princeton University Press
Princeton, New Jersey

ADVISORY COMMITTEE

FRANCIS L. BERKELEY, JR.

WILLIAM G. BOWEN

HENRY STEELE COMMAGER

ROBERT F. GOHEEN

DATUS C. SMITH, JR.

IPHIGENE OCHS SULZBERGER

LUCIUS WILMERDING, JR.

CONTENTS

ILLUSTRATIONS

Following Page 50

PARLIAMENTARY POCKET-BOOK

Opening page of manuscript in Jefferson's hand (*Courtesy of the Massachusetts Historical Society, Coolidge Collection*)

PARLIAMENTARY POCKET-BOOK

Page of manuscript showing last paragraph, 145, numbered by Jefferson. The remaining paragraphs of the 105-page bound manuscript are unnumbered. (*Courtesy of the Massachusetts Historical Society, Coolidge Collection*)

MANUAL OF PARLIAMENTARY PRACTICE, 1801

Title page of the first edition printed in 1801 by Samuel Harrison Smith in Washington, consisting of 190 pages, unnumbered. (*Courtesy of the Library of Congress*)

MANUAL OF PARLIAMENTARY PRACTICE, 1812

Title page of the second edition printed in 1812 by Joseph Milligan and William Cooper in Washington, 183 pages. (*Courtesy of Princeton University Library*)

GUIDE TO EDITORIAL APPARATUS

1. TEXTUAL DEVICES

The following devices are employed throughout the work to clarify the presentation of the text.

[. . .], [. . . .]	One or two words missing and not conjecturable.
[. . .]¹, [. . . .]¹	More than two words missing and not conjecturable; subjoined footnote estimates number of words missing.
[ ]	Number or part of a number missing or illegible.
[roman]	Conjectural reading for missing or illegible matter A question mark follows when the reading is doubtful.
[*italic*]	Editorial comment inserted in the text.
⟨*italic*⟩	Matter deleted in the MS but restored in our text.

2. LOCATION SYMBOLS, OTHER SYMBOLS AND ABBREVIATIONS

CSmH 5986	Henry E. Huntington Library Manuscript described as "Apparently two fragmentary drafts of Jefferson's 'Manual of Parliamentary Practise' [sic]." For a photocopy, see TJ Editorial Files, 42624:1-53
MHi 41891	Manuscript of Parliamentary Pocket-Book in Massachusetts Historical Society, *Catalog*, IV, 164. See also TJ Editorial Files, 41891:1-54
PCC	Papers of the Contintental Congress, The National Archives
Rough Notes	Notes for A Manual of Parliamentary Practice. DLC: TJ Papers, v. 233:41793-41805. See also TJ Editorial Files, 32137; also same, 10541 (28 Feb. 1793-1798)
TJ	Thomas Jefferson
TJ Editorial Files	Photoduplicates and other editorial materials in the office of *The Papers of Thomas Jefferson*, Princeton University Library
TJ Papers	Thomas Jefferson Papers, Library of Congress

3. SHORT TITLES

ADB	*Allgemeine Deutsche Biographie*, Berlin, 1967-1971
Annals	*Annals of the Congress of the United States: The Debates and Proceedings in the Congress of the United States . . . Compiled from Authentic Materials by Joseph Gales, Senior*, Washington, D.C.: Gales & Seaton, 1834-1856, 42 vols.
Arber	Edward Arber, ed., *The Term Catalogues, 1668-1709* A.D., London, 1903-1906, 3 vols.

Aruego, *Philippine Government*	José M. Aruego, *Philippine Government in Action*, Manila, 1954
Bardsley	Charles Warren Bardsley, *A Dictionary of English and Welsh Surnames with Special American Instances*, Baltimore, 1968
Beckley *Catalogue*	[John James Beckley], *Catalogue of Books, Maps, and Charts, Belonging to the Library of the Two Houses of Congress*, Washington City, 1802
Bell, *Bench and Bar*	Charles H. Bell, *The Bench and Bar of New Hampshire*, Boston and New York, 1894
Bing	Geoffrey Bing, Introduction to Henry Elsynge, *The Manner of Holding Parliaments in England*, Shannon, Ireland, 1971
Biog. Dir. Cong.	*Biographical Directory of the American Congress, 1774-1949*, Washington, D.C., 1950
B.M.Cat.	British Museum, *General Catalogue of Printed Books*, London, 1931- ; also *The British Museum Catalogue of Printed Books, 1881-1900*, Ann Arbor, 1946
B.N.Cat.	Bibliothèque Nationale, *Catalogue général des livres imprimés. . . . Auteurs*, Paris, 1897-1955
Campion	Sir Gilbert Campion, *An Introduction to the Procedure of the House of Commons*, 2d ed., London, 1947
Catalog	*Catalog of Manuscripts of the Massachusetts Historical Society*, Boston, 1969, 7 vols.
Catalogus	*Catalogus Impressorum Librorum Bibliothecae Bodleinae*, Oxford, 1738, 2 vols.
Clarke	Maude V. Clarke, *Medieval Representation and Consent: A Study of Early Parliaments in England and Ireland, with Special Reference to the "Modus Tenendi Parliamentum,"* London, 1936
Clarkin, *George Wythe*	William Clarkin, *Serene Patriot: A Life of George Wythe*, Albany, N.Y., 1970
Cobbett's State Trials	Thomas Bayly Howell, ed., *Cobbett's Complete Collection of State Trials and Proceedings for High Treason and Other Crimes and Misdemeanors from the Earliest Period to the Present Time*, London, 1809, 33 vols.
Cokayne, *Peerage*	G[eorge] E[dward] C[okayne], *The Complete Peerage of England, Scotland, Ireland, Great Britain, and the United Kingdom*, ed. Vicary Gibbs and others, London, 1910-1940, 13 vols.
Collins, *Peerage*	Arthur Collins, comp., *The Peerage of England; or, an Historical and Genealogical Account of the present Nobility . . . Continu'd down to This Present Year, 1709*, London, 1709
Cowell, *Interpreter*	John Cowell, *The Interpreter: or Booke Containing the Signification of Words; Wherein is set foorth the true meaning of all, or the most part of such Words and Termes, as are mentioned in the*

Lawe Writers, or Statutes of this victorious and renowned Kingdome, Cambridge, 1607

Cushing — Luther Stearns Cushing, *Lex Parliamentaria Americana: Elements of the Law and Practice of Legislative Assemblies in the United States*, Boston, 1856

DAB — Allen Johnson and Dumas Malone, eds., *Dictionary of American Biography*, New York, 1928-1936; 1943

Davies and Keeler — Godfrey Davies and Mary Frear Keeler, eds., *Bibliography of British History, Stuart Period, 1603-1714*, 2d ed., Oxford, 1970

Davies, *Catalogue* — J. Conway Davies, *Catalogue of Manuscripts in the Library of the Honourable Society of the Inner Temple*, Oxford, 1972, 3 vols.

D'Ewes — Sir Simonds D'Ewes, *The Journals of All the Parliaments during the Reign of Queen Elizabeth, Both of the House of Lords and House of Commons*, London, 1682

DNB — Leslie Stephen and Sidney Lee, eds., *Dictionary of National Biography*, 2d ed., N.Y., 1908-1909

Evans — Charles Evans, comp., *American Bibliography*, Chicago, and Worcester, Mass., 1903-1959, 14 vols.

Flower — Milton E. Flower, *James Parton, The Father of Modern Biography*, Durham, N.C., 1951

Ford — Paul Leicester Ford, ed., *The Writings of Thomas Jefferson*, New York and London, 1892-1899, 10 vols.

Gray — Giles Wilkeson Gray, "Thomas Jefferson's Interest in Parliamentary Practice," *Speech Monographs*, 27 (November 1960), 315-322

Hare — Augustus J. C. Hare, *Walks in London*, 7th ed., Philadelphia, 189-?, 2 vols.

Harleian Miscellany — William Oldys, ed., *The Harleian Miscellany: or, a Collection of Scarce, Curious, and Entertaining Pamphlets and Tracts, as well in Manuscript as in Print, Found in the Late Earl of Oxford's Library*, London, 1744-1746, 8 vols.

Hatsell (1785) — John Hatsell, *Precedents of Proceedings in the House of Commons; with Observations*, 2d ed., London, 1785, 3 vols.

Hatsell (1796) — Ibid., 3rd ed., London, 1796, 4 vols.

Hatsell (1818) — Ibid., new ed., with additions, London, 1818, 4 vols.

History of Parliament Biographies 1439-1509 — Josiah C. Wedgwood with Anne D. Holt, eds., *History of Parliament Biographies . . . of the Members of the Commons House 1439-1509*, London, 1936

History of Parliament Register 1439-1509	*History of Parliament Register of the Ministers and of the Members of Both Houses 1439-1509*, Issued by the Committee of Both Houses, London, 1938
Holinshed, *Chronicles*	*Holinshed's Chronicles of England, Scotland, and Ireland*, London, 1807-1808, 6 vols.
Howell	Wilbur Samuel Howell, "The Declaration of Independence and Eighteenth-Century Logic," wmq, 18 (October 1961), 463-484
Index	*Index to the Thomas Jefferson Papers*, Manuscript Division, Reference Department, Library of Congress, Washington, D.C., 1976
Jacob	Giles Jacob, *A New-Law Dictionary*, 7th ed., [London], 1756
jcc	Worthington C. Ford and others, eds. *Journals of the Continental Congress, 1774-1789*, Washington, D.C., 1904-1937, 34 vols.
jep	*Journal of the Executive Proceedings of the Senate of the United States . . . to the Termination of the Nineteenth Congress*, Washington, D.C., 1828
jhc	*Journals of the House of Commons* [London, 1742-] (for a bibliographical note, see Jefferson's Abbreviations, s.v. Journ Com)
jhl	*Journals of the House of Lords* [London, 1767-]
jlc	*The Quarterly Journal of the Library of Congress*
Johnston	Richard Holland Johnston, "A Contribution to a Bibliography of Thomas Jefferson," in l & b, 20, supplement, p. 1-73.
js	*Journal of the Senate of the United States*, Washington, Gales & Seaton, 1820-1821, 5 vols.
Labaree, *Papers of Franklin*	Leonard W. Labaree and others, eds., *The Papers of Benjamin Franklin*, New Haven and London, 1959- , 25 vols. to date
l & b	Andrew A. Lipscomb and Albert E. Bergh, eds., *The Writings of Thomas Jefferson*, Washington, D.C., 1903-1904, 20 vols.
Lambert, *Bills and Acts*	Sheila Lambert, *Bills and Acts: Legislative Procedure in Eighteenth-Century England*, Cambridge, 1971
Latham, *Medieval Latin Word-List*	Ronald Edward Latham, *Revised Medieval Latin Word-List from British and Irish Sources*, London, 1965
MacDonagh	Michael MacDonagh, *The Speaker of the House*, London, 1914
Malone, *Jefferson*	Dumas Malone, *Jefferson and his Time*, Boston, 1948-1981, 6 vols.

SHORT TITLES

Manual (1801)	*A Manual of Parliamentary Practice, For the Use of the Senate of the United States*, by Thomas Jefferson, Washington City, MDCCCI
Manual (1812)	*A Manual of Parliamentary Practice, For the Use of the Senate of the United States*, by Thomas Jefferson, 2d ed., George Town and Washington, D.C., 1812
Marsden	Philip Marsden, *The Officers of the Commons 1363-1965*, London, 1966
May, *Treatise on Parliament*	Thomas Erskine May, *A Treatise on the Law, Privileges, Proceedings and Usage of Parliament*, ed. Sir Gilbert Campion, 14th ed., London, [1946]
McKechnie, *Magna Carta*	William Sharp McKechnie, *Magna Carta; A Commentary on the Great Charter of King John*, 2d ed., Glasgow, 1914
Menhennet	David Menhennet, *The Journal of the House of Commons A Bibliographical and Historical Guide*, London, 1971
Moore	Frank Gardner Moore, trans., *De Officio Hominis et Civis Juxta Legem Naturalem Libri Duo*, by Samuel von Pufendorf, New York, 1927
National Intelligencer	*The National Intelligencer, and Washington Advertiser*
Neale	J. E. Neale, *The Elizabethan House of Commons*, London, 1949
NUC	*The National Union Catalog*
OED	Sir James Murray and others, eds., *A New English Dictionary on Historical Principles*, Oxford, 1888-1933
Olsen	V. Norskov Olsen, *John Foxe and the Elizabethan Church*, Berkeley, Los Angeles, and London, 1973
Papers	Julian P. Boyd and others, eds., *The Papers of Thomas Jefferson*, Princeton, N.J., 1950- , 22 vols. to date
Parliamentary History of England	*Parliamentary or Constitutional History of England; Being a Faithful Account of All the Most Remarkable Transactions in Parliament, From the Earliest Times, Collected from the Journals of Both Houses* ... by Several Hands, London, 1751-1761, 24 vols.
Petyt	George Petyt, traditionally accepted author, *Lex Parliamentaria*, London, 1748
Petyt's *Jus Parliamentarium*	William Petyt, *Jus Parliamentarium: or, the Ancient Power, Jurisdiction, Rights, and Liberties of the Most High Court of Parliament, Revived and Asserted*, London, 1739
Pike, *House of Lords*	Luke Owen Pike, *A Constitutional History of the House of Lords*, London and New York, 1894
Pollard, *Evolution of Parliament*	A. F. Pollard, *The Evolution of Parliament*, 2d ed., London, New York, and Toronto, 1934

Powell and Wallis	John Enoch Powell and Keith Wallis, *The House of Lords in the Middle Ages*, London, 1968
Randall, *Life*	Henry S. Randall, *The Life of Thomas Jefferson*, New York, 1858, 3 vols.
Rapin-Thoyras	Paul de Rapin-Thoyras, *The History of England*, translated with additional notes, by N. Tindell, 2d ed., London, 1733-1751
Rivera, *Congress of the Philippines*	Juan F. Rivera, *The Congress of the Philippines: A Study of Its Functions and Powers and Procedures*, Manila, 1962
Roskell, *The Commons and Their Speakers*	J. S. Roskell, *The Commons and Their Speakers in English Parliaments 1376-1523*, Manchester, 1965
Rushworth	John Rushworth, *Historical Collections of Private Passages of State, Weighty Matters in Law, Remarkable Proceedings in Five Parliaments, Beginning the Sixteenth Year of King James, Anno 1618*, London, 1659-1701, 8 vols.
Sabin	Joseph Sabin, *A Dictionary of Books Relating to America, from Its Discovery to the Present Time*, New York, 1868-1936, 29 vols.
Sandford's *Genealogical History*	Francis Sandford, *A Genealogical History of the Kings of England, and Monarchs of Great Britain, &c. From the Conquest, Anno 1066 to the Year 1677* [London], 1677
Shaw & Shoemaker	Ralph R. Shaw and Richard H. Shoemaker, comps., *American Bibliography, a Preliminary Checklist for 1801-1819*, New York, 1958-1963, 22 vols.
Smith, *The First Forty Years*	Margaret Bayard Smith (Mrs. Samuel Harrison Smith), *The First Forty Years of Washington Society*, ed. Gaillard Hunt, New York, 1906
Smith, *Freedom's Fetters*	James Morton Smith, *Freedom's Fetters: The Alien and Sedition Laws and American Civil Liberties*, Ithaca, N.Y., 1956
Smith, *History of the English Parliament*	George Barnett Smith, *History of the English Parliament Together with an Account of the Parliaments of Scotland and Ireland*, London and New York, 1892, 2 vols.
Sowerby	E. Millicent Sowerby, comp., *Catalogue of the Library of Thomas Jefferson*, 1952-1959, 5 vols. Cited by the number assigned a given item in Sowerby and by volume and page numbers of that iten in her compilation.
Stone, *Crisis of the Aristocracy*	Lawrence Stone, *The Crisis of the Aristocracy 1558-1641*, Oxford, 1965

Strateman	Catherine Strateman, ed., *The Liverpool Tractate*, New York, 1937
Winfield	Percy H. Winfield, *The Chief Sources of English Legal History*, Cambridge, Mass., 1925
Wing	Donald Wing, comp., *Short-Title Catalogue of Books Printed in England, Scotland, Ireland, Wales, and British America and of English Books Printed in Other Countries 1641-1700*, New York, 1945, 3 vols.
WMQ	*William and Mary Quarterly*, 1892-
Woodbine and Thorne, *Bracton*	*Bracton De Legibus et Consuetudinibus Angliae*, ed. George Woodbine, trans. Samuel E. Thorne, Cambridge, Mass., 1968

4. JEFFERSON'S ABBREVIATIONS USED IN THE POCKET-BOOK AND *MANUAL* (1801, 1812)

Arcana parl (Arcan Parl, Arc parl)	R. C. [R. Corbin?], *Arcana Parliamentaria*, London, 1685
ass	See Lib ass
Atk (Atk' argum)	Sir Robert Atkyns, *Argument in the Great Case concerning Election of Members to Parliament*. See his *Parliamentary and Political Tracts*, 2d ed., London, 1741
Atk power of parl (powr. parl)	Sir Robert Atkyns, *Power, Jurisdiction, and Privilege of Parliament*. See his *Parliamentary and Political Tracts*, 2d ed., London, 1741
Bl (Blackst, Blackstone)	Sir William Blackstone, *Commentaries on the Laws of England, in Four Books*, Oxford, 1770
Boh deb (Bohun's coll, Bohun's deb)	William Bohun, *Collection of Debates, Reports, Orders, and Resolutions of the House of Commons*, London, n.d. (ca. 1700)
Bracton	Henry de Bracton, *Henrici de Bracton, De Legibus & consuetudinibus Angliae Libri Quinq*, London, 1569
Bro abr f edit (Bro abr tit parl, Brook, Brook tit Parl, Bro Par, Bro parl, Bro tit parl & Relat, Bro tit privilege)	Sir Robert Brooke, *La Graunde Abridgement*, [London], 1586
Burn (Reformn.)	Gilbert Burnet, *History of the Reformation of the Church of England*, 2d ed., London, 1681

[xv]

Chandl (Chandler)	Richard Chandler, *History and Proceedings of the House of Commons from the Restoration to the Present Time*, London, 1742-1744, 14 vols.
Clar hist reb	Edward Hyde, 1st Earl of Clarendon, *History of the Rebellion and Civil Wars in England, Begun in the Year 1641*, Oxford, 1702-1704, 3 vols.
Co (Cook)	Sir Edward Coke, *Reports . . . in English, Compleat in Thirteen Parts*, [London], 1738, 7 vols.
Co L	Sir Edward Coke, *First Part of the Institutes of the Laws of England; or, A Commentarie upon Littleton*, London, 1639
Com J (Com Jo, Com Journ)	*Journals of the House of Commons* (*See also*, Journ Com.)
Com p	Commons's Protest to James I, 18 December 1621
Constitution (Const U S, Constitution United States)	Constitution of the United States of America
Cotton's records	Sir Robert Bruce Cotton, *Exact Abridgement of the Records in the Tower of London, from the Reign of King Edward the Second, unto King Richard the Third, of All the Parliaments*, London, 1689
Croke	Sir George Croke, *First Part . . . [Second Part, Third Part] of the Reports*, London, 1683
Crompton' courts (Crompton's Iur, Crompton's jurisd)	Richard Crompton, *L'Authoritie et Iurisdiction des Courts*, London, 1594
Cursus Cancel	William Bohun, *Cursus Cancellariae; or, the Course of Proceedings in the High Court of Chancery*, 2d ed., London, 1723
Dallas's Rep	Alexander James Dallas, *Reports of Cases Ruled and Adjudged in the Courts of Pennsylvania*, Philadelphia, 1790-1807, 4 vols.
Declarn. of the Commons on the k's declaring Sir John Hotham a traitor	A Remonstrance; or the Declaration of the Lords and Commons, the 26th of May, 1642, in Answer to a Declaration under His Majesty's Name, Concerning the business of Hull (For this document, see Rushworth, Part III, Vol. 1, p. 577-88.)

D'Ewes
(D'ewes,
Dewes,
D'Ewes jour,
D'Ewes journ,
D'Ewes' journ,
Sr Simon
D'Ewes journ)
Sir Simonds D'Ewes, *Journals of All the Parliaments during the Reign of Queen Elizabeth, Both of the House of Lords and House of Commons*, London, 1682

Dier (Dyer)
Sir James Dyer, *Cy Ensvont Ascvns Novel Cases*, London, 1585 (This collection in law French went through later editions in 1592, 1601, 1621, 1672, and 1688. In 1794 it was translated into English by John Vaillant.)

Diurnal
occurrences
of parl
Diurnall Occurrences, or Dayly Proceedings of Both Houses, London, 1641

Doctor Cowel
John Cowell, *The Interpreter: or Booke Containing the Signification of Words; Wherein is set foorth the true meaning of all, or the most part of such Words and Termes, as are mentioned in the Lawe Writers, or Statutes of this victorious and renowned Kingdome*, Cambridge, 1607

Els (Elsyng,
Elsynge)
Henry Elsynge [the elder], *The Manner of Holding Parliaments in England*, ed. Thomas Tyrwhitt, London, 1768. (Under somewhat different titles this work had earlier editions at London in 1660, 1662, 1663, 1675, and 1679. Its latest edition was published at Shannon, Ireland, in 1971, with a Preface by Lord Hailsham of Saint Marylebone and an Introduction by Geoffrey Bing. The DNB, s.v. Elsynge, Henry the younger, errs in attributing this work to the son rather than the father. The son served as Clerk of the Commons during the Long Paliament, to be sure, but his father was Clerk of the House of Lords some years earlier, that is, from 1621 to 1635, and in that capacity he wrote two books on the parliamentary procedure of the Upper House, that under discussion here, and that listed next below. See Bing's Introduction to the 1971 edition, p. vii and ix.)

Elsynge
(Elsynge
Method of
passing bills,
Elsynge's
method of
passing bills)
Henry Elsynge [the elder], *Method of Passing Bills in Parliament*, London, 1685 (This work appeared as a separate small volume of thirty-six pages. See Wing, E649. See also *Harleian Miscellany*, v, 210-17.)

Elsynge's
memorials
Henry Scobell, *Memorials of the Method and Manner of Proceedings in Parliament in Passing Bills*, London, 1670. (In pars. [522], [523], [524], [525], and [526] of the Pocket-Book, TJ documents his passages by referring to Elsynge's *Memorials* when in fact those passages were derived from

[xvii]

Henry Scobell's *Memorials*. For an explanation of this seemingly curious but really understandable practice, *see* Mem).

Execut Journ June 25, 1795	*Journal of the Executive Proceedings of the Senate of the United States*, Washington, D.C., 1828, i, 187-8
FNB (FNB Fo A)	Sir Anthony Fitzherbert, *La Novel Natura Brevium*, London, 1534
Fost	Sir Michael Foster, *A Report of Some Proceedings on the Commission of Oyer and Terminer and Goal [sic] Delivery for the Trial of the Rebels in . . . 1746*, Dublin, 1767
Fox's book of martyrs	John Fox, *The Book of Martyrs, containing an Account of the Sufferings and Death of the Protestants in the Reign of Queen Mary the First*, London, [1761] (See Olsen, p. 224-6.)
Franklin's Historical Review of Pennsylva. Appendx.	Benjamin Franklin, *Historical Review of the Constitution and Government of Pennsylvania*, London, 1759 (TJ and many of his contemporaries believed that this work was written by Franklin. The actual author was Richard Jackson.)
Grey (Gray's deb)	Anchitell Grey, *Debates of the House of Commons, from the Year 1667 to the Year 1694*, London, 1769, 10 vols.
G W	George Wythe, TJ's mentor and friend.
Hakew (Hak, Hakewel, Hakewell)	William Hakewill, *Modus tenendi Parliamentum: or, The Old Manner of Holding Parliaments in England . . . Together with . . . the Manner and Method How Laws Are There Enacted*, London, 1671 (*See also* Mem.)
Hale on parl (Hale parl, Hales, Hales of parl, Hale's parl, Hale's parliaments)	Sir Matthew Hale, *The Original Institution, Power, and Jurisdiction of Parliaments*, London, 1707
Hale P C	Sir Matthew Hale, *Historia Placitorum Coronae. The History of the Pleas of the Crown*, [London], 1737
Hats (Hatsell, Hatsells)	John Hatsell, *Precedents of Proceedings in the House of Commons; with Observations*, London 1785, 3 vols; London, 1796, 4 vols; London, 1818, 4 vols. (TJ had not yet read Hatsell's fourth volume when his *Manual* was first published in 1801. But he read the fourth volume later, and he added passages from it to the edition that Milligan published in 1812. Thus passages cited by TJ from the first three volumes are identified here as belonging to the 1785 edition; and passages cited by TJ from the fourth volume are identified as belonging to the 1796 edition. For the convenience of the reader, the editor has supplemented TJ's documentation of his passages from Hatsell by noting where those passages may be located in the more available 1818 edition.)

Herbert's H 8	Edward Herbert, first Baron Herbert of Cherbury, *The Life and Reign of King Henry the Eighth*, London, 1683
Historl. essay on Engl Constn.	[Obadiah Hulme], *Historical Essay on the English Constitution; or, An Impartial Inquiry into the Elective Power of the People*, London, 1771 (Long attributed to Allan Ramsay, this treatise is now regarded as the probable work of a Yorkshireman, Obadiah Hulme. See Sowerby 2717; III, 124; v, 205.)
Hist Reform	Gilbert Burnet, *History of the Reformation of the Church of England*, London, 1681, 1715 (See Sowerby 624; I, 295.)
Hob	Sir Henry Hobart, *Reports of That Reverend and Learned Judge, the Right Honorable Sr. Henry Hobart*, London, 1671 (See Sowerby 2039; II, 331.)
Hollinshed	*Holinshed's Chronicles of England, Scotland, and Ireland, in Six Volumes*, London, 1807-1808 (According to Sowerby, TJ's library did not contain any edition of the *Chronicles*. Thus we do not know the date of the edition he used in the Pocket-Book, pars. [350] and [413]. The editor's notes on those paragraphs are based upon the six-volume edition cited above.)
Husbands collection	*An Exact Collection Of All Remonstrances, Declarations, Votes, Orders, Ordinances, Proclamations, Petitions, Messages, Answers, and Other Remarkable Passages betweene the Kings most Excellent Majesty, and His High Court of Parliament*, London, 1642 (On p. 956 of this book is a statement signed H. Elsynge Cler. Parl. Dom. Com. and dated "24 Martii 1642," noting that the Commons had this day ordered "that Edward Husbands Stationer, shall have the benefit of printing the Booke entitled, *An exact Collection. . . .*" No editor is mentioned. The Elsynge signing the statement is Henry Elsynge the younger. *See* Elsynge.)
Hutt	Sir Richard Hutton, *Reports . . . Written in French by His Owne Hand: and Now Faithfully Translated into English according to Order*, London, 1656
Inst (inst)	Sir Edward Coke, *Institutes of the Laws of England*, 4 pts., London, 1639, 1648, 1662, 1670, and 1681 (See Sowerby 1781, 1782, 1783, 1784; II, 217-19.)
Instit Leg	William Bohun, *Institutio Legalis: or, an Introduction to the Study and Practice of the Laws of England*, [London], 1732 (See Sowerby 1912; II, 281.)
Jac's L D by Ruffh (Jac's L D by Ruffhead)	Giles Jacob, *New Law-Dictionary*, ed. Owen Ruffhead and J. Morgan, 9th ed., London, 1772
Jones (W Jones)	Sir William Jones, *Les Reports*, London, 1675

Journ Com   *Journals of the House of Commons*, [London, 1742-] (Accord-
(Journ Comm,   ing to *B.M.Cat.*, s.v. England, II, col. 1151, the first volume of
Journ H C,   this long series was printed in 1742 at London but without in-
Journ of   dication of place or date. For information concerning the se-
Comm)   ries, see Menhennet, p. 19-30, 52-7, and *passim*.)

Journ Sen   *Journal of the Senate of the United States*, Washington, Gales &
          Seaton, 1820-1821, 5 vols.

Kelw rep   Robert Keilway, *Reports d'ascuns Cases*, 3d ed., London,
          1688 (Sowerby 2024; II, 324, notes that the first edition of this
          work was published in 1602. DNB spells its author's name
          Keilway, Kellway, and Kaylway.)

Lamb Arch   William Lambarde, *Arxaionomia sive de priscis Anglorum le-
          gibus libri, sermoni Anglico*, Cambridge, 1644 (Sowerby
          1767; II, 210-11, notes that this work was originally published
          in 1568.)

Lamb Just   William Lambarde, *Eirenarcha; or, Of the Office of the Justices
          of Peace*, London, 1599 (Sowerby 1964; II, 302, notes that
          TJ's library contained this edition.)

Laws of Honor [R. Gosling?], *Laws of Honour; or, A Compendious Account of
          the Ancient Derivation of All Titles, Dignities, Offices, &c.*,
          London, 1714 (The authorship of this work is uncertain.
          Sowerby 414; I, 183, treats it as an anonymous treatise. NUC,
          319, 560, attributes it on the authority of Cushing to R. Gos-
          ling. *B.M.Cat.* 132, col. 45, lists it under Laws without sug-
          gesting an author.)

Lev   Sir Creswell Levinz, *Les Reports . . . en Trois Parts*, London,
          1702 (Sowerby 2068; II, 343, says that TJ's copy of this work
          was part of the bequest he received from George Wythe.)

Lex   Giles Jacob, *Lex Constitutionis; or, The Gentleman's Law,
Constitution   Being a . . . Treatise of All the Laws and Statutes relating to the
          King, and the Prerogative of the Crown, the Nobility, and House
          of Lords, House of Commons*, [London, 1719]

Lex Parlia-   [George Petyt?], *Lex Parliamentaria: or, A Treatise of the Law
mentaria   and Custom of Parliaments . . . with an Appendix of a Case in
(Lex Parl,   Parliament between Sir Francis Goodwyn and Sir John Fortes-
lex parl,   cue, for the Knights Place for the County of Bucks, 1 Jac. I*, 3d
Lex parliam,   ed. London, 1748 (In all probability TJ, who made more use
L P, L Parl,   of this work than of any other parliamentary treatise, knew
L parl, l parl, that the question of its authorship had not been finally settled,
Append to   and that the scholarly course was for him to remain uncom-
L parl)   mitted on that subject. At any rate, TJ never cited the work
          except by the title or abbreviations listed here. The editor has
          chosen, however, to follow tradition in attributing the author-
          ship of *Lex Parliamentaria* to George Petyt. The first and sec-
          ond editions of *Lex Parliamentaria* (1690, 1740?) identified its
          author as G. P. Esq., and in 1738 the new *Catalogues* of the
          Bodleian Library declared that G. P. stood for George Petyt.

The same interpretation was given those initials in 1905 by the well-informed Edward Arber, II, 653. In recent times, almost without exception, *Lex Parliamentaria* has been listed in the catalogues of the leading libraries of England and America as the work of George Petyt, and this same designation has been endorsed by such qualified scholars as Strateman, p. ix, xi, and lviii; Lambert, *Bills and Acts*, p. 17-8, 27n.; and the editor of the reprint of *Lex Parliamentaria*, Wilmington, Delaware, 1974. Discordant voices have been raised to claim that G. P. stands for William Petyt. William Petyt did publish books on parliamentary subjects, one of which came out in 1680 and was cited by TJ in the Pocket-Book and *Manual—see* Pet misc. The attribution of *Lex Parliamentaria* to William Petyt was given some measure of substance by Sowerby, V, 205, in 1959, and again in 1972 by Davies, *Catalogue*, I, 13; II, 679. Sowerby based her argument on the recognition that William translates into Guillaume in French, and Davies based his in part upon the similar recognition that William is Gulielmus in Latin. Thus, they conclude, the G. P. affixed to the title page of *Lex Parliamentaria* when it was published in 1690 is to be construed as William Petyt, who is assumed on that occasion to have found it convenient to conceal his true identity not only under initials but also under Gallicized or Latinized forms of his English name. The very ease of this solution to a basically baffling problem tempts acceptance. But there are difficulties. The solution fails to recognize that William Petyt put his English name on his unquestionable works, and that it is difficult to see why in 1690 he would have chosen to identify himself under initials in Latin or French. Moreover, the anonymous editor of William Petyt's *Jus Parliamentarium*—a book that TJ purchased in 1769—wrote his Preface as one familiar with the whole body of his author's work, and did not mention *Lex Parliamentaria* in that or any other connection. Thus it seems wise to us to prefer George to William in the present stage of uncertainty.)

Lib Ass	[Johannes Rastell], *Liber assisarum & placitorum corone*, [London], [1514?], 1561, 1580, 1606, and 1679
Lords Journ (Lords Jo)	*Journals of the House of Lords*, [London, 1767-] (According to Menhennet, p. 23, the first volume in this long series was printed in 1767.)
magna charta	In his Pocket-Book, par. 87, TJ cites a Latin passage from this famous document.
Mar	John March, *Reports; or, New Cases; with Divers Resolutions and Judgements Given upon Solemn Arguments, and with Great Deliberation*, London, 1648. (See Sowerby 2054; II, 337. See also Pocket-Book, par. 138, n. 22, for TJ's misinterpretation of Petyt's reference to March's *Reports*.)

Mat Par (Matt Par, M Par) Matthew Paris, *Historia Major, Juxta exemplar Londinensi 1571, verbatim recusa*, London, 1640, 1639 (See Sowerby 343; I, 146-7.)

May's hist parl Thomas May, *History of the Parliament in England, Which Began November the third, M.DC.XL*, London, 1647

Mem (Mem in Hakew, Memor, Memorials, Memorials in Hakewell) [Henry Scobell], *Memorials of the Method and Manner of Proceedings in Parliaments in Passing Bills . . .*, London, 1670 (Sowerby 2879; III, 177, indicates that the initials on the title page (H. S. E. C. P.) designate Henry Scobell, Esquire, Clerk of the Parliament. Lambert, *Bills and Acts*, p. 18, notes that Scobell's *Memorials* was bound with the 1671 edition of Hakewill's *Modus*, and that these two volumes in one led George Petyt to cite "Memorials in Hakewill" when he meant Scobell's *Memorials* as combined with Hakewill's work. TJ adopted Petyt's way of referring to the *Memorials*. The twenty paragraphs between [189] and [208] of the Pocket-Book were ascribed by TJ to "Memorials in Hakewell" or an equivalent short title when in fact they were excerpts from Scobell's *Memorials*, as of course TJ would have known. His *Manual* contains many examples of the same type of reference. See also Pocket-Book, par. [492], n. 2.)

Mirr [Andrew Horne], *The Mirrour of Justices: Written Originally in the Old French, Long before the Conquest; and Many Things Added*, trans. by W. H. of Gray's Inn, Esq., London, 1768

Mod (Mod rep) [Anthony Colquitt and others], *Modern Reports; or, Select Cases Adjudged in the Courts of King's Bench, Chancery, Common-Pleas, and Exchequer, since the Restauration of . . . King Charles II to the Eleventh Year of George I*, London, 1757, 1781, and 1741, 12 pts. (Sowerby 2075; II, 346, indicates that only the tenth part of this collection was in TJ's library.)

Mod ten (Mod ten parl, Mod ten Parl, Mod t parl) William Hakewill, *Modus tenendi parliamentum* (*See* Hakew.)

Moor (Moore) [Sir Francis Moore], *Cases Collect & Report per Sr. Francis Moore Chevalier, Serjeant del Ley*, 2d ed., London, 1688 (Sowerby 2031; II, 328, places a copy of this edition in TJ's library.)

Nals (Nalson, Nalson's Col, Nalson's introdn.) [John Nalson], *Impartial Collection of the Great Affairs of State, from the Beginning of the Scotch Rebellion in . . . MDCXXXIX. to the Murther of King Charles I . . .*, London, 1682-1683, 2 vols.

Observans of France on Memorial of England Joseph Mathias Gérard de Rayneval, *Observations on the Justificative Memorial of the Court of London, . . . Paris . . .* Philadelphia, 1781

Ord H Com (ord H Commons)	*Orders, Essential, Fundamental and Standing Orders, Reports, Declarations, Memorandums, Rules, Agreements, and Resolutions of the House of Commons*, London, 1756 (Sowerby 2882; III, 178. The 1st edition of *Orders* came out in 1747.)
Parl hist	*Parliamentary or Constitutional History of England; from the Earliest Times, to the Restoration of King Charles II*, 2d ed., London, 1762-1761, 24 vols. (Sowerby 2925; III, 193.
Pet misc (Pet Misc parl, Pet misc parl, Pet Parl, Petyt misc parl, Petyts miscell parl, Petyt's misc parl)	[William Petyt], *Miscellanea Parliamentaria; Containing Presidents 1. Of Freedom from Arrests. 2. Of Censures. 1. Upon Such as Have Wrote Books to the Dishonour of the Lords or Commons, or to Alter the Constitution of the Government, 2. Upon Members for Misdemeanours, 3. Upon Persons Not Members, for Contempts . . . 4. For Misdemeanours in Elections . . .*, London, 1680 (*See also* Lex Parliamentaria.)
P J	Parliamentary Journals (*See also* Journ Com.)
Plowd (Pl R)	[Edmund Plowden], *Commentaries, or Reports of Edmund Plowden, of the Middle-Temple, Esq . . . Originally Written in French, and Now Faithfully Translated into English*, [London], 1761 (Sowerby 2027; II, 326. Sowerby notes that the Samuel Richardson whose name appears in the imprint of this publication was the author of *Pamela*.)
Protestation of Comm to Jac 1 1621	(*See* Com p.)
Prynne	In the *Manual*, Sec. xv, par. 2, TJ quoted a statement by Prynne as recorded in Grey's *Debates*, I, 52.
Puff Off hom et civis	Samuel Pufendorf, *De Officio Hominis & Civis, Juxta Legem Naturalem Libri Dvo*, Cambridge, 1682
Rapin	Paul de Rapin-Thoyras, *History of England, Written in French by Mr. Rapin de Thoyras, Translated into English by N. Tindal*, 2nd ed., London, 1733-1751 (TJ's quotation from this work in Pocket-Book, par. [215] came from Tindel's, that is, Tindal's translation, by way of *Lex Parliamentaria*, p. 303-4. TJ's own copy of Rapin was in French. See Sowerby 369; I, 156. Sowerby quotes Francis Calley Gray's reference to that copy in TJ's library as follows: "Rapin was here in French, though very rare in that language. Mr. Jefferson said that after all it was still the best history of England, for Hume's tory principles are to him insupportable. . . .")
Rast stat	William Rastell, *Collection in English, of the Statutes Now in Force*, London, 1611 (Sowerby 1816; II, 234, notes that the copy of this work in TJ's library was the 16th edition.)
Raym (T. Ray)	Sir Thomas Raymond, *Reports of Divers Special Cases Adjudged in the Courts of King's Bench, Common Pleas & Exchequer*, 2d ed., [London], 1743 (Sowerby 2064; II, 341)

Regist — Ralph de Hengham, *Registrum Brevium Tam Originalium, Quam Judicialium*, 4th ed., London, 1687 (Sowerby 1880; II, 268. Styled by Coke "the most ancient book of the law." See DNB, s.v. Hengham or Hingham, Ralph de.)

Resolution House Commons 1 Car. 1 — Adopted 22 April 1626. For its text, see George Petyt, p. 115; also JHC, I, 848; and Rushworth, I, 217

Ro rep — [Henry Rolle], *Les Reports de Henry Rolle . . . de divers Cases en la Court del' Banke le Roy, en le temps del' reign de Roy Jaques*, London, 1675, 2 vols. (Not mentioned by Sowerby as having been in TJ's library. But see her entry no. 1786; II, 219-20.)

Rot parl — *Rotuli Parliamentorum* (These extend from 1290 to 1503, says Winfield, p. 85. He adds: "They are entries of what occurred in Parliament from the opening to the close of the session." Sowerby does not list any of the printed volumes as having been held in TJ's library.)

Ruffh Jac's L D — Giles Jacob, *New Law-Dictionary . . . Now Corrected and Greatly Enlarged, by Owen Ruffhead and J. Morgan, Esquires*, 9th ed., London, 1772 (First published in 1729, this work went into its 10th edition in 1782. TJ cited the 9th edition on several occasions, but Sowerby does not place it or any other edition in TJ's library.)

Rush (Rush append, Rush Col, Rush Coll, Rush part 3, Rushw) — John Rushworth, *Historical Collections of Private Passages of State, Weighty Matters in Law, Remarkable Proceedings in Five Parliaments, Beginning the Sixteenth Year of King James anno 1618*, London, 1721-2, 8 vols. (See Sowerby 2723; III, 126-7.)

Rushw tr Straff — John Rushworth, *Tryal of Thomas Earl of Strafford . . . Upon an Impeachment of High Treason by the Commons Then Assembled in Parliament, in the Name of Themselves and of All the Commons in England*, London, 1680 (Sowerby 2723; III, 126-7, lists this work as Vol. VIII of the collection listed immediately above. It also was published as a separate volume in 1680 and 1700.)

Russel's Hist Mod Europe — William Russell, *History of Modern Europe, with an Account of the Decline and Fall of the Roman Empire and a View of the Progress of Society from the Rise of the Modern Kingdoms to the Peace of Paris, in 1763*, London, 1786, 5 vols. (Sowerby 161; I, 75.)

Sachev tr (Sachev trial, Sach tr) — *Tryal of Dr. Henry Sacheverell, before the House of Peers, for High Crimes and Misdemeanors; upon an Impeachment by the Knights, Citizens, and Burgesses in Parliament Assembled . . .*, Published by Order of the House of Peers, London, 1710 (Sowerby 1955; II, 297-8)

Sadler (Sadler's rights, Sadler's rights of the kingdom)   John Sadler, *Rights of the Kingdom; or Customs of Our Ancestours: Touching the Duty, Power, Election or Succession of Our Kings and Parliaments; our True Liberty, Due Allegiance, Three Estates, Their Legislative Power* . . . , London, 1649

Sax Chron   *Chronicon Saxonicum. Ex MSS Codicibus Nunc Primum integrum Edidit, ac Latinum fecit Edmundus Gibson*, Oxford, 1692 (Sowerby 4837; v, 111-12.)

Scob (Scobel)   Henry Scobell, *Memorials of the Method and Manner of Proceedings in Parliament in Passing Bills, Together with Several Rules & Customs, which by Long and Constant Practice Have Obtained the Name of Orders of the House, Gathered by Observation and out of the Journal Books from the time of Edward 6*, London, 1670 (Sowerby 2879; iii, 177-8. *See also* Elsynge's Memorials; Mem.)

Seld   [John Selden], *Joannis Seldeni Juris consulti Opera Omnia, Tam Edita quam Inedita*, ed. David Wilkins, London, 1726, 3 vols. (Sowerby 4920; v, 169-70.)

Selden judic (Selden's judicature, Seld jud, Seld judic, Seld judic in parl)   John Selden, *Of the Judicature in Parliaments, A Posthumous Treatise: Wherein the Controversies and Precedents Belonging to That Title, Are Methodically Handled*, London, n.d. [1681?] (Sowerby 2887; iii, 180. Sowerby suggests 1689 as the probable date of the 1st edition, which was contained in TJ's library. She bases her conjecture upon Arber, ii, 251, but an earlier entry in Arber, i, 443, indicates that the first edition probably appeared in 1681.)

Seym (Seymour)   When this abbreviation or this name figures in TJ's documentation of passages in the Pocket-Book, the reference is to the manuscript behind the first printed volume of *Journals of the House of Commons*. That particular manuscript was the work of John Seymour, Clerk of the House of Commons from 1548 to 1567. Neale says of him, p. 333, that he "deserves to be held in pious memory for inventing the Commons Journals—one of the salient landmarks in our constitutional development." Menhennet, p. 14, characterizes Seymour's invention in even more explicit terms: "The first manuscript volume in the official series . . . covers the period 8th November 1547 to 2nd January 1567. It is entitled 'Seimour,' after the compiler's name, and it begins as little more than a register of Bills such as Seymour's predecessors had been maintaining for some time [in the series now known as *Rotuli Parliamentorum*] . . . Seymour's successor as Clerk of the House was Fulk Onslow, and the second manuscript volume . . . is named 'Onslowe' after him." See also Marsden, pp. 30-1.)

Sid   Sir Thomas Siderfin, *Les Reports des divers special cases argue and adjudge en le Court del Bank le Roy et auxy en le Co. Ba. & l'Exchequer en les premier dix ans apres le restauration del son tres-excellent Majesty Le Roy Charles le II*, London, 1683, 1684 (Sowerby 2059; ii, 339.)

Smith's Common- wealth (Smyth's Commonw, Smyth's commth.)	[Sir Thomas Smith], *Common-wealth of England and the Maner of Gouvernement Thereof*, London, 1612
Smollet	Tobias George Smollett, *History of England from the Revolution to the Death of George the Second (Designed as a Continuation of Mr. Hume's History)*, London, 1790, 5 vols. (Not in Sowerby. But Sowerby shows that TJ's library contained copies of *Roderick Random* 4355 and *Critical Review* 4722; IV, 456; V, 50)
Spelm (Spelm glos, Spelm Glos)	[Sir Henry Spelman], *Glossarium Archaiologicum: continens Latino-Barbara, peregrina, obsoleta, & novatae significationis Vocabula*, London, 1664 (Sowerby 1809; II, 231)
S P Protest of the Commons to James 1, 1621	State Papers. Protest of the Commons to James I, 1621. Cited in Pocket-Book, par. [215] and in the *Manual*, Sec. III, par. 12. TJ would have seen its text in George Petyt, pp. 301-4 and no doubt also in Rapin-Thoyras, II, 211-12 and in Rushworth, I, 53. *See also* Com p.
Stamf P C (Stanf, Stanf Plc)	Sir William Stanford [also Stamford], *Les Plees del Coron, diuisee in plusors titles & comon. lieux*, London, 1583 (Sowerby 1945; II, 293-4.)
Stra	Sir John Strange, *Reports of Adjudged Cases in the Courts of Chancery, King's Bench, Common Pleas, and Exchequer*, 3d ed., Dublin, 1792 (Sowerby 2083; II, 350)
St tr (Sta Tr)	[Thomas Salmon and Sollom Emlyn, eds.], *A Compleate Collection of State-Tryals, and Proceedings upon Impeachments for High-Treason, and Other Crimes and Misdemeanours*, London, 1719-1730, 6 vols. (Sowerby 1951; II, 296.)
Torbuck's deb (Torbuck's Deb)	[John Torbuck], *Collection of the Parliamentary Debates in England, from the Year M,DC,LXVIII. to the Present Time*, Dublin and London, 1741-1742, 22 vols. (In leading libraries this collection is not catalogued under the name of John Torbuck. Torbuck's name appeared in the 3d edition, not as the editor but as the bookseller who sponsored the reprinting of the work. See also Davies and Keeler, p. 112, no. 789.)
Town (Town Col, Town Coll, Towns Col, Towns Coll)	[Heywood Townshend], *Historical Collections; or, An exact Account of the Proceedings of the Four Last Parliaments of Q. Elizabeth of Famous Memory, Wherein Is Contained the Compleat Journals Both of the Lords & Commons, Taken from the Original Records of their Houses ... Comprehending the Motions, Speeches, and Arguments of the Renowned and Learned Secretary Cecill, Sir Francis Bacon, Sir Walter Rawleigh, Sir Edw. Hobby, Divers Other Eminent Gentlemen*, London, 1680 (Sowerby 2920; III, 191-2.)

T. Ray   Sir Thomas Raymond (*See* Raym.)

Trials of the   [Heneage Finch, first Earl of Nottingham, comp.], *An Exact*
regicides   *and most Impartial Accompt of the Indictment, Arraignment,*
                       Trial, and Judgment (according to Law) of Twenty Nine Regi-
                       cides . . . , London, 1679

Vattel   Emmerich de Vattel, *Le Droit des Gens, ou Principes de la Loi*
                       Naturelle, Appliqués à la conduite & aux affaires des Nations &
                       des Souverains, Amsterdam, 1775, 2 vols. (Sowerby 1411; II,
                       71-2.)

Wilk   [David Wilkins], *Leges Anglo-Saxonicae ecclesiasticae & civ-*
(Wilk LL Sax)   *iles . . . Subjungitur Domini Henr. Spelmanni Codex Legum*
                       Veterum Statutorum Regni Angliae, quae ab ingressu Guilielmi
                       I. usque ad annum nonum Henr. III. edita sunt. Toti Operi prae-
                       mittitur Dissertatio Epistolaris admodum Reverendi Domini
                       Guilielmi Nicolsoni Episcopi Derrensis De Jure Feudali Ve-
                       terum Saxonum, ed. David Wilkins, London, 1721 (Sowerby
                       1768; II, 211. Sowerby notes that "the glossaries of Wilkins"
                       were referred to by TJ in his correspondence with Thomas
                       Cooper.)

W Jones   Sir William Jones (*See* Jones.)

Wms   [William Peere Williams], *Reports of Cases Argued and Deter-*
                       mined in the High Court of Chancery, and of Some Special Cases
                       Adjudged in the Court of King's Bench: Collected by William
                       Peere Williams, late of Gray's Inn, Esq; In Three Volumes, 4th
                       ed., Dublin, 1790 (Sowerby 1750; II, 204-5.)

Wood (Woodd,   [Richard Wooddeson], *A Systematical View of the Laws of*
Wooddeson)   *England; As Treated of in a Course of Vinerian Lectures, Read*
                       at Oxford, during a Series of Years, Commencing in Michealmas
                       Term, 1777, Dublin, 1792, 1794, 3 vols. (Sowerby 1808; II,
                       230.)

EDITOR'S ACKNOWLEDGMENTS

In acknowledging with warm gratitude the generous help I have received in preparing this volume, I should like to say that it owes its origin to Julian Boyd's having invited me in 1972, as I retired from the Department of English of Princeton University, to assume responsibility for this particular edition on behalf of its inclusion in his magnificent edition of *The Papers of Thomas Jefferson*. Thus it came about that my previous investigation of Jefferson's reading under the tutelage of William Small at the College of William and Mary became the background for a new investigation of Jefferson's parliamentary studies, activities, and writings. Julian considered this latter enterprise an important and necessary part of his project.

Well before my acceptance of his invitation, Julian had assembled in his editorial offices in Firestone Library every procurable facsimile and copies of all printed editions of Jefferson's letters, papers, and literary works; and these, under Julian's superbly informed guidance to me as I used them, have made my editorial duty more sensitive to its problems than it would otherwise have been. In fact, the TJ Editorial Files represent to our company of scholars a convenience unmatched elsewhere.

Charles T. Cullen, who was named Editor of the Papers after Julian's death in May 1980, has been a source of real support to me as this book has reached its present form. He supervised the process by which my manuscript, much of it handwritten, some of it typed, and one part already in print in an early edition, was put into final shape for the press. J. Jefferson Looney, Research Associate, assisted Charles in this taxing endeavor, and on several occasions caught errors that had gone undetected.

Ruth W. Lester, who has been on the Jefferson staff since 1962, is very familiar with the contents of the TJ Editorial Files, and she has given me cheerful and interested help at many times. Indeed, she once called my attention to an important item which in all probability I would have overlooked.

Mistakes and shortcomings still remaining in these pages are to be charged against me alone, not to any of the colleagues named above.

Wilbur Samuel Howell

THE PAPERS OF
Thomas Jefferson

SECOND SERIES

JEFFERSON'S PARLIAMENTARY STUDIES, ACTIVITIES, AND WRITINGS: A CHRONOLOGY

From 1760 to 1762 Thomas Jefferson pursued the course in liberal arts at the College of William and Mary in Williamsburg, his chief tutor being William Small, a graduate in 1755 of the Marischal College, Aberdeen. Small's double assignment at that particular time was that of professor of Moral Philosophy (Logic, Rhetoric, Ethics) and Natural Philosophy (Physics, Metaphysics, Mathematics). His influence upon Jefferson turned out to be profound. Jefferson later said of him that he "probably fixed the destinies of my life," and it has been argued convincingly that Small's course in Logic was responsible for the structure Jefferson chose for the Declaration of Independence.[1] Even under such favorable auspices, Jefferson decided in his second year to change the direction of his education. With Small's assistance, he was accepted in 1762 as an apprentice lawyer in the law office of George Wythe, not only a prominent, learned, and able lawyer in Williamsburg but also a member of Small's circle of friends.

Jefferson's studies under Wythe's tutelage were not confined solely to statutes and courtroom procedures. He found time and inclination, as he himself later testified, to embark upon a course of readings in parliamentary law. Speaking in 1800 of what he called "the Parliamentary branch of the law," he observed in a letter to George Wythe, "I had, at an early period of life, read a good deal on the subject, and commonplaced what I read. This common-place," he went on, "has been my pillar. But there are many questions of practice, on which that is silent."[2]

Along with that kind of reading and note-taking, Jefferson had at least one opportunity to observe the damaging effect of unparliamentary procedure upon the workings of a deliberative assembly. A letter written by Jefferson in Annapolis provides vivid details:

> But I will now give you some account of what I have seen in this Metropolis. The assembly happens to be sitting at this time. Their upper and lower house, as they call them, sit in different houses. I went into the lower, sitting in an old courthouse, which, judging from it's form and appearance, was built in the year one. I was surprised on approaching it to hear as great a noise and hubbub as you will usually observe at a publick meeting of the planters in Virginia. The first object which struck me after my entrance was the figure of a little old man dressed but indifferently, with a yellow queüe wig on, and mounted in the judge's chair. This the gentleman who walked with me informed me was the speaker, a man of very fair character, but who by the bye has very little the air of a speaker. At one end of the justices' bench stood a man whom in another place I should from his dress and phis

---

[1] For evidence of Small's great and lasting influence upon TJ's education and career, see TJ's Autobiography (Ford, i, 3-5); Malone, *Jefferson*, i, 49-61; and Howell, p. 463-84.

[2] TJ to George Wythe, 28 Feb. 1800. TJ repeated some of these same reflections in a letter to Edmund Pendleton, 19 Apr. 1800, quoted below.

have taken for Goodall the lawyer in Williamsburgh, reading a bill then before the house with a schoolboy tone and an abrupt pause at every half dozen words. This I found to be the clerk of the assembly. The mob (for such was their appearance) sat covered on the justices' and lawyers' benches, and were divided into little clubs amusing themselves in the common chit chat way. I was surprised to see them address the speaker without rising from their seats, and three, four, and five at a time without being checked. When [a motion was] made, the speaker instead of putting the question in the usual form only asked the gentlemen whether they chose that such or such a thing should be done, and was answered by a yes sir, or no sir: and tho' the voices appeared frequently to be divided, they never would go to the trouble of dividing the house, but the clerk entered the resolutions, I supposed, as he thought proper. In short every thing seems to be carried without the house in general's knowing what was proposed.[3]

An experience like this could only have reenforced Jefferson's early interest in parliamentary law. Following his admission to the bar in 1767 that subject continued to be of theoretical and practical concern to him as he extended the range of his readings and incorporated them into what at first he called his "commonplace" and later his Parliamentary Pocket-Book. Later, his studies helped him devise a system of rules for conducting the business of the Continental Congress; preside over the Senate of the United States as its second president; compile for the Senate its first rule book, the famous *Manual of Parliamentary Practice*; and finally provide textual additions to the *Manual* in its true second edition of 1812.

During the seven years between 1769 and 1776, Jefferson's service in the House of Burgesses and his attendance at the Continental Congress gave him his first opportunity to observe the day-to-day workings of parliamentary law in a legislative assembly. That experience alone would have invited him to continue the compilation of his Pocket-Book. But now he also was in the position to observe the parliamentary behavior of his erstwhile law teacher and admired friend George Wythe, who was a learned parliamentarian in his own right. Wythe held office as clerk of the House of Burgesses from 1769 to 1775, and in that capacity he ruled upon disputed questions of order and kept the Burgesses aware of procedural propriety.[4] In later years, when Jefferson was preparing himself to serve as president of the U.S. Senate during his Vice Presidency, he turned to Wythe as an authority upon parliamentary rules. "I know they have been more studied and are better known by you," he wrote, "than by any man in America perhaps by any man living."[5] In the late 1760s, Wythe had made a serious and methodical effort to master the regulations governing parliamentary practice, and Jefferson would certainly have known of that effort as he observed Wythe in action as clerk of the House of Burgesses. Wythe described that effort in reply to Jefferson's request for advice in 1797. He wrote thus: "I extracted, thirty years ago, from the journals of the british house of commons, the parliamentary rules of procedure, but left the copy of them among the papers belonging to the house of burgesses, among which a search for it at this day would be vain."[6] Thus the method used by Wythe in making his extract of parliamentary rules closely resembles that later followed by Jefferson in compiling his Pocket-Book, or, as he

[3] TJ to John Gage, 25 May 1766.
[4] Theodore S. Cox, s.v. "Wythe, George," in DAB.
[5] TJ to George Wythe, 22 Jan. 1797.   [6] George Wythe to TJ, 1 Feb. 1797.

occasionally characterized it, his "common-place." That method, it should be noted, was widely followed by eighteenth-century students in conducting their law studies.

Acquiring books for these studies often required purchases from London and solicitation of friends. In 1769, for example, Jefferson ordered and received from London copies of William Hakewill's *Modus tenendi Parliamentum* and William Petyt's *Jus Parliamentum* (that is, *Jus Parliamentarium*).[7] The purchase of these two works suggests a desire on his part to continue the study of parliamentary law as a necessary adjunct to his new duties as member of the House of Burgesses. Many references to Hakewill's treatise appear as excerpts in the Parliamentary Pocket-Book and *Manual of Parliamentary Practice*—proofs that Jefferson gave substantial study to Hakewill over the years. In the summer preceding his authorship of the Declaration of Independence Jefferson made a remark that calls attention to what he regarded as the incompleteness of his personal collection of classics and of books on parliamentary learning. Writing from Monticello to his friend John Randolph, who as a Loyalist was about to abandon Virginia for England, Jefferson attached the following postscript to a letter urging Randolph to do all he could to acquaint the English with the true temper of the Americans in that tense hour:

> P.S. My collection of classics and of books of parliamentary learning particularly is not so complete as I could wish. As you are going to the land of literature and of books you may be willing to dispose of some of yours here and replace them there in better editions. I should be willing to treat on this head with any body you may think proper to empower for that purpose.[8]

What came of this offer is not known.

Between June 20 and July 17 of 1776, while serving in the Continental Congress, Jefferson was called upon to put his parliamentary learning to work. He was named member of a three-man committee "to draw up rules and regulations" to guide the work of the Congress, his colleagues in that enterprise being Edward Rutledge and Robert Treat Paine. Jefferson drew up a set of ten rules.[9] Julian Boyd refers to them as Jefferson's "first jottings on a subject upon which he was to become a world-wide authority—parliamentary procedure." On July 10 the three-man committee submitted to the Congress a report containing seventeen rules for the guidance of its business, nine of them being expanded versions of Jefferson's original ten. The rules in the report were designated by Roman numerals in Jefferson's hand; and also in Jefferson's hand were 129 of the words appearing in them.[10] Seven days later, the Continental Congress adopted a set of twelve rules of procedure based in part upon the July 10 report of the three-man committee. Three of those rules can be traced back to Jefferson's original list.[11]

From October 1776 to June 1779 Jefferson served in the Virginia House of Delegates, the Revolutionary successor to the colonial House of Burgesses. That period in his life, remarks Dumas Malone, "comprised his most creative period as

[7] Perkins, Buchanan & Brown to TJ, 2 Oct. 1769.

[8] TJ to John Randolph, 25 Aug. 1775.

[9] Report of the Committee to Draw Up Rules of Procedure for Congress [Before 10 July 1776], printed in *Papers*, i, 458.

[10] *Papers*, i, 456-8. For the manuscript version, see PCC, No. 23, fols. 19-21.

[11] For the printed text of the twelve rules, see JCC, 573-4.

a statesman during the American Revolution. . . . A mere list of the motions he made, the bills he drafted, and the committees he served on in his first session is an index of his prominence."[12] Indeed, Malone's full account of Jefferson's legislative activity in those years indicates that parliamentary law and procedure were constantly associated with his participation in the legislative process.[13] As a matter of practical need and scholarly interest, he probably found time in the midst of everything else to continue his reading and note-taking for the Parliamentary Pocket-Book.

"It is now so long since I have acted in the legislative line," wrote Jefferson to George Wythe on January 22, 1797, "that I am entirely rusty in the Parliamentary rules of procedure."[14] These words were prompted by Jefferson's awareness that John Adams would probably be the next President of the United States, and that he himself, as runner-up, would become not only the Vice President but also the next presiding officer of the Senate. As he contemplated the latter prospect, he had reason to feel unprepared in any immediate sense. Between the end of his term as governor of Virginia in June 1781, and his resignation as President George Washington's Secretary of State in December 1793, he could count only six months of legislative experience—as delegate from Virginia to the Continental Congress in 1783-1784. In that short term, he distinguished himself, serving "on practically every committee of consequence," and drafting, as has been estimated, no fewer than thirty-one papers."[15]

Nevertheless, this eighteen-year interval was marked by his continuing interest in the study of parliamentary law, even if circumstances prevented him then from having had much legislative experience. In particular, he continued to order books related to his studies. During his diplomatic service in France, he wrote a letter from Paris to Thomas Payne, London bookseller, acknowledging the receipt of books that Payne had recently sent, and ordering one item that figured largely in Jefferson's parliamentary studies. "I will thank you," said the letter, "to send by the first Diligence such as can be immediately got and particularly Hatsell and the Irish debates, noting their cost in them because they are not for myself. This indeed would be a good general precaution because the books I write for are often for friends here." The two books mentioned so particularly were described in Jefferson's postscript as follows: "Hatsell's precedents of the H. of Commons 3v. 4to" and "Debates of the Irish house of Commons. 2. sets." Hatsell's *Precedents* was one of the most important sources of the Pocket-Book and of both editions of the *Manual*, and this letter to Payne establishes that source as being almost certainly in Jefferson's possession when he and his family sailed for home from France in the late autumn of 1789.[16]

In March 1789, while still in Paris, Jefferson addressed a point of parliamentary procedure in an exchange of letters between himself and François Soulés. Soulés had already published at London in 1785 a two-volume work entitled *Histoire des troubles de l'Amérique Anglaise*; and Jefferson had not only obtained a copy of it by 1786 but in that year had commented upon it in writing. A ver-

---

[12] Malone, *Jefferson*, I, 247-8.   [13] Same, p. 147-97.

[14] TJ to George Wythe, 22 Jan. 1797 (see above, note 5).

[15] Malone, *Jefferson*, I, 411.

[16] TJ to Thomas Payne, 28 Jan. 1789. Abundant details of Hatsell's influence upon TJ's parliamentary writings will be found in the editor's introductions and notes to these works in this volume.

sion of those comments reached Soulés somewhat later, and Soulés' reaction to them involved politeness to Jefferson and caustic disparagement to Jefferson's country.[17]

Earlier in 1789 Soulés had brought out in London and in Paris a work that in its British setting was entitled *Le Vade-Mecum parlementaire, ou The Parliamentary Pocket-Book* and, in its French setting, *Statuts, Ordre et Réglements du Parlement d'Angleterre*. Soulés' letter of March 21 and Jefferson's reply of March 23 dealt with this work and with Jefferson's similar work.[18] Soulés queried Jefferson on the requirements of membership in the House of Commons:

> In the parliamentary pocket-book I published, I find a note to that purport: *a member of the Commons is a Knight, a citizen or burgess. He must be resident within the same county the day of the writ of summons and ought to have 40 shillings of free hold within the said county, beyond all charges &c.*
>
> A person who has just published a book intitled, *les Comices de Rome &c.* maintains that to be a member for a county it is necessary to have five hundred pounds sterling a year, and 25₶ for a town or Borough; that to be elector for a county it is necessary to have 40 shillings a year. If he is in the right, I must certainly be in the wrong having followed the above note. Should be glad you would give me your opinion upon that subject.

Jefferson replied:

> I have had the honor of notifying to you before that the manuscript which I put into your hands contained notes which I had made, in the course of my reading for my own use as the member of a legislature in America. As such it was necessary for me to know not only the law of the moment but what it had been at other times. The qualifications of a knight of a shire have been different at different times. At present he must have £600. a year, and a member for a city or borough £300. a year in land. This is by the statute of the 9. Annae. chap. 5. The author of *les comices de Rome &c.* is mistaken in saying that £500. and £250. a year are the qualifications at present. I think the qualifications never stood at that sum, but was rather vague from the passing of the statute [23] H[enry VI. c. 15] till precisely fixed by that of An[ne. . . .].

The two letters reveal Jefferson as more widely informed about British parliamentary practice than his French rival; moreover, Jefferson's letter corrected the mistake of the writer whom Soulés had sought Jefferson's help in confuting.[19]

These two letters bring Soulés and Jefferson together as authors of works called the Parliamentary Pocket-Book. For Soulés, that title was a matter of record when he wrote to Jefferson, and Jefferson's title later became a matter of record when a manuscript under that name was catalogued in the library of the Massachusetts Historical Society. In other words, it is certain that the manuscript mentioned by Jefferson in his letter to Soulés on March 23 is to be posi-

[17] For a definitive account of that episode, see *Papers*, x, 364-8.

[18] Soulés to TJ, 21 Mch. 1789; TJ to Soulés, 23 Mch. 1789.

[19] The other French writer is anonymous, so far as these letters are concerned, but he can be identified as Paul-Philippe Gudin de La Banellerie. The full title of the work referred to by Soulés is *Essai sur l'histoire des Comices de Rome, des Etats-généraux de la France, et du parlement d'angleterre* (Philadelphia and Paris, 1789). The third volume of Gudin's three-volume work devoted a hundred pages to the British Parliament. For a laudatory contemporary review, see *Mercure de France* (Feb. 28, 1789), p. 175-7.

tively identified as the work that Jefferson himself later called the Parliamentary Pocket-Book. His description of the work in that letter—"notes which I had made, in the course of my reading for my own use as the member of a legislature in America"—recalls Jefferson's early note-taking when he was studying parliamentary law during his legal apprenticeship under George Wythe in the 1760s, and also his confrontation with his own parliamentary needs when he was a member in the 1770s of the House of Burgesses and House of Delegates in Virginia and of the Continental Congress in Philadelphia. Thus exemplary scholarly caution need no longer be maintained in respect to Boyd's saying that "The identity of the manuscript that TJ handed to Soulés has not been established with certainty. . . ."[20] But it is worth repeating with gratitude and endorsement what Boyd immediately added—that the document "was in all likelihood the remarkable volume of notes on parliamentary procedure drawn from English experience, to which TJ gave the title 'Parliamentary Pocket-Book' and which he employed not only as the member of a legislature but also as a source-book for his own *Manual of Parliamentary Practice. . . .* The extraordinary pains that TJ took to prepare himself for the responsibilities of a legislator are fully revealed in this manuscript (to be printed in Second Series), and the disciplined industry, as well as wide learning, that went into its compilation shows also why he was so successful as a law-maker."

On May 30, 1790, some six months after his return from Paris, and three months after he accepted appointment as President George Washington's first Secretary of State, Jefferson wrote a letter to his son-in-law, Thomas Mann Randolph, Jr., recommending books useful in the study of law, young Randolph's current preoccupation. Jefferson's letter avoided mention of narrowly specialized, highly technical works. For political economy he recommended Adam Smith's *Wealth of Nations*; for the science of government, Montesquieu's *Spirit of Laws*; for political essays, several by Hume. "Locke's little book on government," Jefferson added, "is perfect as far as it goes. Descending from theory to practice there is no better book than the Federalist." And then he recommended a book that had special meaning not only for the students of the law of parliaments but also for his own writings in that field: "For parliamentary knowledge the Lex parliamentaria is the best book."[21] Certainly no one work among the many openly or by implication cited in Jefferson's Parliamentary Pocket-Book was more frequently excerpted by him in quotation or paraphrase than was the *Lex Parliamentaria*, which has traditionally been ascribed to a shadowy author called George Petyt. Petyt's work stands as Jefferson's major parliamentary authority, along with Hatsell, Hakewill, and Scobell. Small wonder that Jefferson would recommend to his son-in-law a work that he himself greatly admired and must have productively used in the period between 1779 and 1797, and, for that matter, throughout the whole course of his self-conducted study of the procedures of the British House of Commons.

Another work that Jefferson acquired for his parliamentary studies in the period immediately preceding his term as Vice President was Richard Wooddeson's *Systematical View of the Laws of England*. This three-volume work, compiled from lectures read at Oxford by Wooddeson between 1777 and 1793 in his capacity as Vinerian professor, appeared in print in London in 1792–1793. Sowerby notes that Jefferson's library contained a copy of these volumes in the

---

[20] *Papers*, XIV, 691.
[21] TJ to Thomas Mann Randolph, Jr., 30 May 1790.

Dublin edition of 1792, 1794.[22] In all probability, Jefferson made use of them in his readings in parliamentary law during the later 1790s. In fact, Wooddeson's treatment of the procedures of impeachment in the British House of Commons figured largely in Jefferson's notes on that subject in the Parliamentary Pocket-Book and *Manual*.[23] During his Vice Presidency, Jefferson appears to have offered to lend his notes on impeachment to a colleague, Samuel Livermore, in connection with the Senate's first impeachment proceeding.[24] As late as February 26, 1821, Jefferson's opinion of Wooddeson's *Laws of England* remained clearly favorable. In a letter to a law student seeking advice on a good course of legal readings, Jefferson recommended the reading of Coke's "four Institutes," Matthew Bacon's abridgment, and Blackstone's *Commentaries*; and at that point Jefferson added: "Here too Woodeson should be read, as supplementary to Blackstone, under heads too shortly treated by him."[25] These words suggest that, in Jefferson's opinion, Wooddeson's treatise on the laws of England was in some respects superior to Blackstone's *Commentaries*—a verdict that later scholars in British law have shared.[26]

From March 4, 1797, to February 28, 1801, Jefferson presided over the Senate in his constitutional capacity as Vice President of the U.S.

As stated above, his previous experience with the actual workings of parliamentary law seemed to him in 1797 to have been too far in the past to offer him guidance for the task of presiding over the Senate. On January 22, 1797, he wrote to George Wythe for help, confessing that he was "entirely rusty in the Parliamentary rules of procedure," and asking Wythe as an acknowledged authority in that field to be so good as to send along on temporary loan any notes that he may have preserved from his own studies therein.[27] But Wythe's reply of February 1 pleaded his inability to satisfy Jefferson's present needs.[28] It is not surprising, then, that in his vice-presidential inaugural address on March 4, 1797, Jefferson made a special effort to prepare the Senate for what he feared to be his own inadequacies as a parliamentary leader:

> Entering on the duties of the office to which I am called, I feel it incumbent on me to apologize to this honorable House for the insufficient manner in which I fear they may be discharged. At an earlier period of my life, and through some considerable portion of it, I have been a member of legislative bodies, and not altogether inattentive to the forms of their proceedings; but much time has elapsed since that; other duties have occupied my mind, and in a great degree it has lost its familiarity with this subject. I fear that the House will have but too frequent occasion to perceive the truth of this acknowledgment. If a diligent attention, however, will enable me to fulfil the functions now assigned me, I may promise that diligence and attention shall be sedulously employed. For one portion of my duty I shall engage with more confidence, because it will depend on my will and not on my capacity.

[22] Sowerby, No. 1808 (II, 230).
[23] See present edition of Pocket-Book, pars. [539], [540], [542], [543], [544], [545], [548], [549], [550]; and the *Manual*, Sec. LIII, Impeachment, where the paragraphs just enumerated also appear.
[24] For details, see below, p. 11-12.
[25] TJ to Dabney Terrell, 26 Feb. 1821.
[26] See E. Irving Carlyle, s.v. "Wooddeson, Richard," in DNB.
[27] TJ to George Wythe, 22 Jan. 1797 (see above, note 5).
[28] For earlier reference to this letter, see above, note 6.

The rules which are to govern the preceedings of this House, so far as they shall depend on me for their application, shall be applied with the most rigorous and inflexible impartiality, regarding neither persons, their views, or principles, and seeing only the abstract proposition subject to my decision. If, in forming that decision, I concur with some and differ from others, as must of necessity happen, I shall rely on the liberality and candor of those from whom I differ, to believe that I do it on pure motives.[29]

Following this speech, the Senate resolved to assemble in the chamber of the House of Representatives, where, to a distinguished audience of legislators, diplomats, judges, wives, and social leaders, John Adams delivered the third presidential inaugural address in American history. Thereupon the Senate withdrew to its own chamber, where Jefferson presided over adjournment, it having been ascertained meanwhile that President Adams had no immediate legislative business to recommend. Thus Jefferson's apprehensions about his own parliamentary performance led that first day to no embarrassment for him or the Senate. It is plausible to assume that when Jefferson began to preside over the reassembled Senate on May 15, 1797, the Pocket-Book had reached its present form. Indeed, Jefferson's letter to George Wythe of February 28, 1800, referred to it as his "common place" and declared that, in supporting his conduct of Senate deliberations, it had been his "pillar."[30] By the end of his term as Vice President, and probably by its beginning, his Pocket-Book would have contained its many present excerpts from Hakewill, from the first three volumes of Hatsell, from Wooddeson, from Henrici de Bracton's classic *De Legibus*, from Sir Robert Brooke's *Abridgment*, from Sir Edward Coke's *Institutes*, from Sir Anthony Fitzherbert's *Natura Brevium*, from Edmund Plowden's *Commentaries*, from Giles Jacob's *New Law-Dictionary*, from Henry Scobell's *Memorials*, from the early volumes of the U.S. Senate Journals, and, above all, from the *Lex Parliamentaria*. No Vice President of the U.S. can be shown to have had the extent and depth of the parliamentary understanding that Jefferson brought to that office.

The first session of the Fifth Congress, assembled at a call from President Adams, provided Jefferson with his first opportunity to preside over the Senate for a longer period than he had had on the day of his inauguration. His democratic approach to the problem of ruling upon procedural issues is illustrated by an episode that occurred on June 28. The sixteenth rule of the Senate included a provision that "every question of order is to be decided by the President, without debate: but if there be a doubt in his mind, he may call for the sense of the Senate."[31] On June 24 the House of Representatives returned to the Senate a bill entitled "An act providing for the protection of the trade of the United States," to which the House had attached various amendments. The Senate on June 26 considered those amendments, voting then to agree to the ones affixed to three sections of the bill, but to disagree with all the others. A conference committee failed to reach a compromise upon the disagreements. Informed of this, the Senate decided to reaffirm its rejection of one of the amendments and to withdraw its opposition to three others. At this point a motion was made to amend those which had seemingly just been endorsed. Sensing that this motion might later be criticized as improper, the Vice President intervened. "Is it in order, in the

[29] JS, II, 398.   [30] TJ to Wythe, 28 Feb. 1800.
[31] See *Manual*, Sec. XVII, par. 30, editor's note; also *Manual*, Preface; also Pocket-Book, par. [442].

present case," he asked, "for the Senate to recede from their disagreement to an amendment of the House of Representatives, and agree to the same with an amendment?" The Senate thereupon answered the question in the affirmative.[32] Whether or not Jefferson thought this ruling proper, he did not settle the question by consulting only himself, as he would have been entitled to do. He allowed the Senate to decide it.

During his term as presiding officer of the Senate, the House of Representatives, for the first time in American history, forced the Senate to contemplate its constitutional procedures in a case of impeachment. The defendant, William Blount, a Senator from the recently admitted state of Tennessee, had been present in the Senate when Jefferson delivered his inaugural address as Vice President on March 4, 1797. In the summer of that year, President Adams released a letter from Blount to James Carey, an interpreter in Indian negotiations, outlining a scheme not only for the military use of Indians against Spanish territory to the south and west of the United States, but also for the subsequent ceding of that territory to the British. On July 7, 1797, the House of Representatives reacted to Blount's letter by proposing his impeachment,[33] and on the following day the Senate voted to expel him from his Senate seat.[34] Articles of impeachment against him were drawn up by the House on January 29, 1798, and in the course of the next two days the House agreed upon a panel of eleven members to manage the impeachment proceedings on the floor of the Senate.[35] Meanwhile, in anticipation of these actions, the Senate on January 23, 1798, gave a second reading to a bill "regulating certain proceedings in cases of impeachment" and assigned it, for further consideration and report, to a committee consisting of Messrs. Humphrey Marshall, Henry Tazewell, Uriah Tracy, James Ross, and Samuel Livermore.[36] The members of the committee would of course have been aware of their historic obligation to set a lasting precedent for the conducting of future cases of impeachment in the Senate.

An esteemed friend of Jefferson, the Senator from Virginia, Henry Tazewell, asked for his opinion upon a constitutional question sure to arise in impeachment proceedings, and Jefferson answered:

> As you mentioned that some of your committee admitted that the introduction of juries into trials by impeachment under the VIIIth. amendment depended on the question Whether an impeachment for a misdemeanor be a criminal prosecution? I devoted yester day evening to the extracting passages from Law authors shewing that in Law-language the term crime is in common use applied to *misdemeanors*, and that *impeachments*, even when for *misdemeanors* only are *criminal prosecutions*. These proofs were so numerous that my patience could go no further than two authors, Blackstone and Wooddeson. They shew that you may meet that question without the danger of being contradicted. The constitution closes the proofs by explaining it's own meaning when speaking of *impeachments*, *crimes*, *misdemeanors*.
>
> The object in supporting this engraftment into impeachments is to lessen the dangers of the court of impeachment under it's present form and [?] induce dispositions in all parties in favor of a better constituted court of im-

---

[32] For this whole episode, see JS, II, 376-9 (quotation at 379).
[33] *Annals*, I, 459.   [34] JS, II, 392.   [35] *Annals*, I, 948-57.
[36] JS, II, 428.

peachment, which I own I consider as an useful thing, if so composed as to be clear of the spirit of faction.

Do not let the inclosed paper be seen in my hand writing.[37]

The enclosed paper consisted of Jefferson's jottings on the question under inquiry, keyed either to some fifty-nine specified pages of Wooddeson's *Laws of England* or to about the same number of specified pages of Blackstone's *Commentaries*; while a few others are of Jefferson's own references to the Constitution of the United States. The manuscript version of many of these jottings and page numbers is now illegible or partly so, but in the aggregate it proves that Jefferson gave Tazewell a detailed answer to the question raised by the Senate committee, and that the answer was based upon the authorities which any constitutional scholar of the time would have considered impeccable.

Samuel Livermore was the other member of the impeachment committee to receive Jefferson's advice on that subject. Livermore had played a decisive part in 1788 in inducing New Hampshire to ratify the new Constitution, and had served as chief justice of the Superior Court of New Hampshire from 1782 to 1790.[38] As a member of the Senate in the Third Congress, he was chosen on February 20, 1795, as president pro tempore, in the absence of Vice President Adams, but on that occasion he declined the office.[39] As if to reaffirm their confidence in his parliamentary leadership, the Senate, again in the absence of Vice President Adams, chose Livermore as president pro tempore on May 6, 1796, for the remainder of the session (twenty-two legislative days).[40]

On January 28, 1798, Jefferson sent Livermore a letter volunteering to make available to him a summary of Jefferson's own notes on the impeachment process.[41] That letter is now badly faded and at first glance seems unintelligible. But a searching examination reveals that it refers to the impending impeachment proceedings confronting the Senate, and that it contains an offer to put into the hands of Livermore and his committee a digest of what Jefferson had gathered on that subject from his study of British constitutional law. Jefferson wrote:

> Having found it necessary, for my own governance, to [consult] the writers on Parliamentary law; a summary of their proceeding as to [formality] I have thought it might not be unuseful to put it into the hands of [one] of the committee to which a pretrial on impeachment [was referred]. I take [the] liberty therefore of inclosing it to you. It may serve to refresh your me[mory] on a subject in which you probably have not your books with you [and] is to [enable] you to judge on what point [the precedent] stands and to keep up analogies where changes [are necessary]. [In planning a] paragraph of a new law we should ask ourselves these questions: How [is the] law now? Is a change necessary? What changes [are the] best? [Do you want] it to be our guide in the im[peachment?] [If it] be upon us before the bill can be passed, that [warrants so]ber consider[ation]. That bill will probably undergo far [more discussion than others do. Considering] this, [it] would be advisable to be [careful ini]tially. These [situa]tions [always arise]. My pro[vince] being *order, [it should be accomplished by studying]* that subject.

[37] TJ to Henry Tazewell, 27 Jan. 1798.
[38] DAB, s.v. "Livermore, Samuel," 1732-1803.
[39] JS, II, 162.   [40] JS, II, 245, 250-88.
[41] TJ to Samuel Livermore, 28 Jan. 1798.

The "summary" mentioned toward the beginning of Jefferson's letter may without doubt be identified as his Parliamentary Pocket-Book, or, more particularly, as its paragraphs which dealt with the formalities of the impeachment process in the British parliament.[42] Those same paragraphs were to appear in Section LIII of the *Manual*, but the final manuscript of the *Manual* did not exist in early 1798, when Livermore's committee was asked to consider how impeachment proceedings should be conducted in the Senate. We do not know whether Livermore accepted Jefferson's offer or not, but the chances are excellent that he did.

In conducting two Senate executive sessions, Jefferson again demonstrated the prudent quality of his behavior as presiding officer. The first occasion was on May 3, 1797, when the Senate considered whether to give or withhold their consent to President Adams' appointment of his son to be minister plenipotentiary to the king of Prussia. The second occurred almost a year later, on March 14, 1798, in connection with President Adams' nomination of the same son to be commissioner plenipotentiary for negotiating a treaty of trade and friendship with the king of Sweden.[43] Fortunately Jefferson's own account of these sessions is extant. It is available in a lightly canceled passage of a manuscript in Jefferson's handwriting that marks one of the important preliminary stages in the evolution of the final copy text of the first edition of the *Manual of Parliamentary Practice*.[44] Jefferson's account reverses the chronological order of the two sessions:

74.1798.Mar.14. The President had nominated John Quincy Adams to be a commissioner plenipotentiary for making a treaty with the K. of Sweden; and the question of approbation being before the house, Mr. Tazewell moved to postpone the M.Q. [*i.e., Main Question*] in order to take up a motion that the Senate do not think it expedient to renew the treaty. This was declared to be out of order. It was observed that in the H. of R. they have a rule (derived from the old Congress) that no amendment to a resolution can be proposed which goes to defeat it, or to give a substitute for it. This is quite unparliamentary. In parliament resolutions are every day made to point even in an opposite direction, by striking out or inserting a negative by way of amendment; or by striking out the whole after the word 'resolved,' and inserting a proposition entirely different. This rule of the H. of R. is so inconvenient and embarrassing in practice that, in order to elude it's effect, they have been obliged to admit a practice of postponing the first proposition in *order to take up* another of a different tendency. But as the Senate have no such rule, they need no such evasion, and consequently have no such form of proceeding and entry as a postponement *in order to take up* a specified motion. But a general postponement might have been moved, and that being carried, the specific proposition might then have been made. After the debate a member shewed me the journals of the Senate of May 31. where the nomination of J.Q. Adams to Berlin being before the house, a motion to resolve the mission inexpedient was recieved and suppressd by the P.Q. [*i.e., Previous Question*]. I should suspect some error in this entry.

[42] See above, note 23.

[43] For the official record of these two sessions, see JEP, I, 240-2, 265-6.

[44] JLC, XXXII, No. 2 (1975), 94-102. CSmH 5986, p. 1-53. See below, Editor's Introduction to the *Manual*, "The Manuscript Problem."

The original message had been taken up the day before, and probably this motion was made as soon as the Senate the next day had resolved itself into it's Executive capacity, and before the house was repossessed of the M.Q. I cannot concieve as palpable an error could have been committed as that, the question of approbation being before the house, a motion entirely independent of it should have been recieved and voted on without any notice taken of it's irregularity either by the chair or by either party; and instead of rejecting it as not recievable, they should have resorted to the P.Q. to get rid of it.

Jefferson's original intention in putting this long passage into his preliminary manuscript of the *Manual* was doubtless to illustrate the Senate rule that a question duly seconded had priority over all others except privileged questions, and that an unprivileged question must not be allowed to intrude into procedure at such a point, lest it defeat or confuse orderly business. The next paragraph in the manuscript became the opening words of Section xxxvii of the printed *Manual*; that section, entitled "Co-Existing Questions," emphasized in its conclusion that "none but the class of privileged questions can be brought forward while there is another question before the House. . . ." Senator Tazewell's motion of March 14, 1798, had been ruled out of order by Jefferson, because, although it called for postponement of action on the main question, it simultaneously made postponement contingent upon the recognition of another main question quite distinct from the one already before the Senate. Thus it lost whatever privilege it might have claimed for its mention of postponement, and it became a violation of Senate Rule 8. The situation on May 31, 1797, involved the appearance of a second main question that should have been ruled out of order but was not. Jefferson felt that the disposal of it by the means recorded in the Journal was unparliamentary. Perhaps, he suggested, the clerk may have made an error in recording what had then been done, for certainly the chair or someone else would have called attention to the impropriety of introducing a second main question when the first was immediately pending. Jefferson's reference to the chair may indicate that he himself was not presiding at the early hour when that action occurred, with the result that the senator temporarily in the chair, having allowed a second main question to be introduced, had then accepted a call for the previous question, as if that were the proper procedure. Anyway, the call was defeated, and hence, with the second main question thereby disposed of, the way was clear for action upon the proper main question originally introduced. That question then passed.

A more detailed explanation of Jefferson's reason for ruling Tazewell out of order for his motion on March 14, 1798, occurs in the manuscript account, and that explanation sheds additional light not only upon Jefferson's parliamentary acumen, but also upon the endless efforts he made in assembling and organizing the notes from which he ultimately fashioned the copy text of the first edition of the *Manual*.

95.1798. Mar.14. The President nominated John Quincy Adams to be a commissioner with full powers to negotiate a treaty of amity and commerce with the K. of Sweden. This message, and the general question on it was before the house. A member moved that the President be informed that the Senate do not advise and consent to the appointment of *a* commissioner for the renewal of the treaty. On appeal to the chair whether in order? it was observed from the chair that the Senate have established no rule on this question, and there can be no parliamentary rule, because no such question can come before them. We must therefore resort to analogy; and from analogy it must be decided that on a message of appointment from the President, the Senate can answer only yea or nay, viz. that they do, or do not approve the appointment of J. Q. Adams. They cannot amend or modify, as by saying they do not approve the appointment of *a* commissioner &c. The legislature may originate bills in any form they please; and the constitution has given the President a simple affirmative or negative on them; but he cannot give a qualified one. So the President may originate an appointment, and the constitution gives the Senate a right to approve or reject simply.

So interested was Jefferson in the constitutional aspects of the question posed by J. Q. Adams' appointment as commissioner plenipotentiary to the king of Sweden that the next entry but one in this manuscript was a partial repetition of the passage just quoted. He seems in these two latter accounts to be testing his language against the version given already. What emerges from the three accounts is that in the first Jefferson ruled Tazewell's motion out of order from the point of view of parliamentary procedures, whereas in the other two the motion was ruled out of order from the point of view of American constitutional law. The change in emphasis is striking. It suggests Jefferson's dual capacity as a technician and as a philosopher—it calls attention to his concern for the mundane efficiency of legislative procedure as well as to his grasp of the problems involved in the constitutional functioning of the legislature and the executive in the newly established American government. Indeed, a student of Jefferson's parliamentary activities, studies, and writings comes to the conclusion that Jefferson must be regarded as a political philosopher in the field of parliamentary law, not just as a specialist in its intricate and abstract details. He could see these details as part of a grand innovative political design.

Another example of Jefferson's endeavors in 1798 to guide his senatorial colleagues toward the refining and improving of parliamentary law is afforded by a memorandum addressed to him by John Beckley on March 15. Beckley had served as clerk of the House of Representatives during the first four Congresses of the new nation, and he held the same office again in the Seventh, the Eighth, and the Ninth Congresses. The office of clerk in a parliamentary body tends irresistibly to induce its incumbent to master parliamentary rules and procedures, as in the case of George Wythe in the Virginia House of Burgesses, and as in various other cases in the British parliament, that of Hatsell, for example, or that of Scobell, or that of Henry Elsynge the elder. Beckley was no exception. His memorandum of March 15, 1798, showed his preoccupation with the laws that guide legislative conduct. He acknowledged that he was returning Jefferson's "parliamentary Notes," and that he had made comments upon some of them, asking that Jefferson permit him later to have a copy of those which he had not had time to inspect. He also asked that Jefferson send any other notes he might have made on "the law of parliament generally," to the end that Beckley might attempt to make "an attentive revisal of the whole subject" and have it ready before the next session of Congress.[45]

[45] John Beckley to TJ, 15 Mar. 1798. It was probably soon after this memorandum was sent to TJ that he received from Beckley a page headed "Extracts from Book of Minutes

From Beckley's references it is plain that the "parliamentary Notes" lent him by Jefferson had concerned privileged questions and conferences, and also an unspecified subject, called loosely "the first part." Jefferson's Pocket-Book contains paragraphs upon the first two of these subjects.[46] Thus it undoubtedly supplied the notes that Beckley's memorandum referred to. But, as in the case of Jefferson's letter to Livermore, it cannot be assumed that, in 1798, Jefferson had already prepared an early form of the manuscript which was to be printed in 1801 as A Manual of Parliamentary Practice, although the Manual does contain sections called "Privileged questions" and "Conferences." Beckley's indications toward the end of his memorandum that he himself was planning to make some kind of compilation on parliamentary law, based perhaps upon Jefferson's notes as well as upon his own experience, and that he wanted his compilation to be ready before the next session of Congress, suggest later exchanges between Jefferson and Beckley, but if they were realized, they have now been lost.

The record of Jefferson's attendance at the sessions of the Senate in the Fifth and Sixth Congresses, provides additional evidence that he took his parliamentary duties with real seriousness. On July 5, 1797, after presiding from its opening on May 15, Jefferson obtained a leave of absence from what remained of the first session of the Fifth Congress, which was to adjourn on July 10.[47] Thus he missed four legislative days in that session. He followed a somewhat less complete pattern of attendance in the second session, which began on November 13, 1797, and ended July 16, 1798.[48] For its opening eight legislative days, that session could not command a quorum, and, with Jefferson among the absentees, adjournment had to follow adjournment. A quorum was reached on November 22, whereupon the Senate chose Jacob Read as president pro tempore. Jefferson took the chair on December 13, 1797,[49] and he presided until the end of the legislative day on June 26, 1798, at which point on his own request he was excused from attendance for the remainder of the second session.[50] Thereupon, the Senate chose Theodore Sedgwick as president pro tempore, and the latter took the chair from June 27 to July 16, a total of seventeen legislative days. Thus Jefferson was not in attendance for forty-one legislative days of the second session of the Fifth Congress. The third session of that Congress convened on December 3, 1798, and adjourned without day on Sunday, March 3, 1799.[51] For its first three legislative days, lack of a quorum forced successive adjournments; but on December 6 a quorum brought the session into official existence, and, with Jefferson still absent, the Senate chose John Lawrance president pro tempore.[52] On

---

on parliamentary proceeding," calling attention to three instances in which the House of Representatives had either created a procedural precedent or had done something irregular and dangerous. These extracts proved interesting to TJ—he filed them away with his papers and took pains to make his future access to them easy. For the page containing them, see Extracts from Book of Minutes on Parliamentary Proceedings, 31 Jan. 1792 (DLC). See also RC in DLC: TJ Papers, 70: 12170; endorsed by TJ "Beckley, John"; not recorded in SJL. For the three instances of legislative action mentioned in the extracts, see Journal of the House of Representatives of the United States (Washington: Gales and Seaton), I, 482-3, 500, 362-5.

[46] For privileged questions, see pars. [166], [197], [202], [220], [442], [460], [466], [568]; for conferences, see pars. [167], [209], [513], [520], [583], [584], [585], [586], [587].

[47] JS, II, 386-93.   [48] JS, II, 405-554.   [49] JS, II, 414.   [50] JS, II, 519.

[51] JS, II, 557-611.   [52] JS, II, 557.

December 27, 1798—thirteen legislative days later—the *Journal* recorded that "The Honorable Thomas Jefferson, Vice President of the United States and President of the Senate, attended."[53] Jefferson presided until the end of the legislative day of February 28, 1799, at which time he gave notice that "he desired to be excused from attendance in Senate after this day, for the remainder of the session."[54] The Senate granted that request, with the result that Jefferson was absent for the four legislative days before adjournment.[55] These four absences, coupled with his sixteen earlier ones, made for twenty absences in Jefferson's part in the third session of the Fifth Congress.

The Sixth Congress, which brought an end to Jefferson's term as presiding officer of the Senate, consisted in two sessions, the first from December 2, 1799, to May 14, 1800, and the second from November 17, 1800, to March 3, 1801.[56] Jefferson was absent for the first eighteen legislative days of the first session, Samuel Livermore being president pro tempore. According to the *Journal* for December 30, 1799, "The Honorable Thomas Jefferson, Vice President of the United States and President of the Senate, attended,"[57] and from that time until the end of the legislative day of May 13, 1800, he occupied his official post. On that date, he expressed his desire in writing to be excused from further attendance in the Senate for that session, his reason being that adjournment was likely at the end of the next legislative day.[58] This prediction proved to be correct, and with Uriah Tracy as president pro tempore, the Senate, having completed its business on May 14, adjourned to "the third Monday of November next." Thus Jefferson was absent for nineteen legislative days in the first session of the Sixth Congress. In the second session, he missed ten legislative days at its outset (November 17 to November 28, 1800) and three at its close (February 28 to March 3, 1801). Jefferson resigned as president of the Senate on February 28, and James Hillhouse served as president pro tempore for that day and the next two.

Between May 13 and November 28, 1800, the copy text of Jefferson's *Manual* emerged from the various manuscript versions that he had successively drafted during the latter years of his Vice Presidency.[59] He began work upon that document well before February 28, 1800, and he took active steps to compile it during the months that followed. At first he intended to deposit a handwritten manuscript with the Senate at the end of his term as its president; but as time went on, thanks no doubt to the urging of his friends, particularly George Wythe, and to his awareness of the greater daily utility of a printed volume, he finally decided to have it committed to type.

A letter by Jefferson to George Wythe on February 28, 1800, plainly indicates that he had already started to prepare what later became the *Manual*, and that he was hoping to enlist Wythe's aid in carrying out the project. The letter also contains some important observations about the state of parliamentary conduct in the House of Representatives and the Senate. It reads in part:

> You recollect enough of the old Congress to remember that their mode of managing the business of the house was not only unparliamentary, but that the forms were so awkward and inconvenient that it was impossible sometimes to get at the true sense of the majority. The House of Repr. of the U.S.

[53] JS, II, 567.   [54] JS, II, 598.   [55] JS, II, 598-611.
[56] JS, III, 3-98, 105-144.   [57] JS, III, 15.   [58] JS, III, 96.
[59] For details, see below, p. 342-5.

are now pretty much in the same situation. In the Senate it is in our power to get into a better way. Our ground is this. The Senate have established a few rules for their government, and have subjected the decisions on these and on *all other points of order* without debate, and without appeal, to the judgment of their President. He, for his own sake, as well as theirs, must prefer recurring to some system of rules, ready formed; and there can be no question that the Parliamentary rules are the best known to us for managing the debates, and obtaining the sense of a deliberative body. I have therefore made them my rule of decision, rejecting those of the old Congress altogether; and it gives entire satisfaction to the Senate; insomuch that we shall not only have a good system there, but probably, by the example of it's effects, produce a conformity in the other branch. But in the course of this business I find perplexities, having for 20. years been out of deliberative bodies and become rusty as to many points of proceeding: and so little has the Parliamentary branch of the law been attended to, that I not only find no person here, but not even a book to aid me.[60]

At this point, Jefferson mentioned that his Pocket-Book, although helpful to him in the Senate, was silent upon many questions. He continued:

Some of them are so minute indeed and belong so much to every-day's practice that they have never been thought worthy of being written down. Yet from desuetude they have slipped my memory. You will see by the inclosed papers what they are. I know with what pain you write:[61] therefore I have left a margin in which you can write a simple negative or affirmative opposite every position, or perhaps, with as little trouble correct the text by striking out or interlining. This is what I have earnestly to sollicit from you: and I would not have given you the trouble if I had had any other resource. But you are in fact the only spark of Parliamentary science now remaining to us. I am the more anxious, because I have been forming a manual of Parliamentary law, which I mean to deposit with the Senate as the Standard by which I judge, and am willing to be judged. Tho' I should be opposed to it's being printed, yet it may be done perhaps without my consent; and in that case I should be sorry indeed should it go out with errors that a Tyro should not have committed. And yet it is precisely those to which I am most exposed. I am less afraid as to important matters, because for them I have printed authorities. But it is those small matters of daily practice, which 20. years ago were familiar to me, but have in that time escaped my memory. I hope under these circumstances you will pardon the trouble I propose to you in the inclosed paper. I am not pressed in time, so that your leisure will be sufficient for me.[62]

Written from Philadelphia, where books on the conduct of legislative assemblies apparently did not exist, this letter emphasizes that, as early as February 28, 1800, Jefferson had started to prepare a manual of parliamentary procedure, and that he intended ultimately to deposit it with the Senate. The "inclosed pa-

[60] TJ to George Wythe, 28 Feb. 1800 (see above, note 2).

[61] In a letter to TJ, 10 July 1788, George Wythe discussed his difficulties in writing, attributing them to "a gout" in his right thumb. See *Papers*, XIII, 329. See also Clarkin, *George Wythe*, pp. 185, 192.

[62] TJ to George Wythe, 28 Feb. 1800.

per" mentioned in the letter contained five handwritten pages of a list of questions on parliamentary doctrine.[63]

Wythe did not at once respond to Jefferson's letter, with the result that Jefferson sent him a similar letter and similar enclosure under the date of April 7, 1800, expressing his "vast reluctance" to do so and indicating that the points on which he was seeking Wythe's advice were "minutiae of practice, which are hardly to be met with in the books, and therefore can only be learned from practical men; and you know how destitute we are of such in Parliamentary reading at present."

> That science is so lost, and yet so important, that I am taking considerable pains, and shall pursue it through the ensuing summer to form a Parliamentary Manual, which I shall deposit with the Senate of the U.S. and may thence possibly get into the public possession. To this I shall not object, if I can be satisfied that what I shall prepare shall be correct. On the contrary it may do good by presenting to the different legislative bodies a chaste Praxis to which they may by degrees conform their several inconsistent and embarrassing modes of proceeding. But there is but one person in America whose information and judgment I have sufficient confidence in, to be satisfied that what I may put together, would be rigorously correct: and he is so absorbed in other useful duties, more peculiarly his own, that I have no right to trouble him with helping me through mine. I can ask it only on the score of charity, for which we are all bound to find time.[64]

Jefferson's unwillingness to have his *Manual* published is much less evident in this letter than it was in the one of February 28. Perhaps he had talked with colleagues about his plans for depositing a handwritten copy of the *Manual* with the Senate, and they had represented the desirability of its being ultimately printed. But he plainly was not planning on April 7, 1800, to publish it himself, despite his emerging conviction that a good printed guide issued by the Senate would help regularize parliamentary procedure in the House and throughout the legislatures of the various states.

Before the letter just quoted could have reached its destination, Wythe answered Jefferson's earlier letter, spelling out each word in meticulous hand-printed characters, severe pain in his right thumb having forced him to abandon his normal manner of handwriting.

> After the seventh decad of my years began I learned to write with the left hand, as you may see by this specimen, and that with ease, although slowly. Yet if to write were painfull, I should, before this time, have answered your letter of 28 of February: but I have been endeavouring to recollect what little of parliamentary procedings I formerly knew, and find myself unable to give information on the questions which you propounded.[65]

This letter reached Jefferson on April 18. Assuming that Wythe could not be expected to supply immediate information for the preparation of the manuscript of the *Manual*, Jefferson wrote to Judge Edmund Pendleton the next day, asking help of the kind he had twice solicited from Wythe. This time, however, he

[63] This important document, which contains TJ's original queries and George Wythe's comments upon them, came to TJ in a letter dated Dec. 7, 1800 (see below, note 72).

[64] TJ to George Wythe, 7 Apr. 1800. The enclosure resembled that sent with TJ's letter of 28 Feb. 1800.

[65] George Wythe to TJ, 10 Apr. 1800.

made no reference to his plan to prepare a manual of parliamentary practice for the use of the Senate. Instead, he presented his request for information as intended solely to improve his own present parliamentary work. This letter demonstrates once more the depth and seriousness of Jefferson's interest in parliamentary proceedings.

My duties here require me to possess exact knolege of parliamentary proceedings. While a student I read a good deal, and common placed what I read, on this subject. But it is now 20. years since I was a member of a parliamentary body, so that I am grown rusty. So far indeed as books go, my common place has enabled me to retrieve. But there are many minute practices, which being in daily use in parliament and therefore supposed known to every one, were never noticed in their books. These practices were I dare say the same we used to follow in Virginia: but I have forgot even our practices. Besides these there are minute questions arising frequently as to the mode of amending, putting questions &c. which the books do not inform us of. I have from time to time noted these queries, and, keeping them in view, have been able to get some of them satisfied and struck them off my list. But I have a number of them still remaining unsatisfied. However unwilling to disturb your repose I am so anxious to perform the functions of my office with exact regularity, that I have determined to throw myself on your friendship and to ask your aid in solving as many of my doubts as you can. I have written them down, leaving a broad margin in which I only ask the favor of you to write yea, or nay, opposite to the proposition, which will satisfy me. Those which you do not recollect, do not give yourself any trouble about. Do it only at your leisure; if this should be before the 9th. of May, your return of the papers may find me here till the 16th. If after that, be so good as to direct them to me at Monticello.[66]

On June 17, 1800, Pendleton complied with the above request by returning with marginal comments the list enclosed with Jefferson's letter of April 19. Apologizing for his delay in responding, Pendleton went on in his accompanying letter to suggest that the quality of his answers to Jefferson's queries compared unfavorably to Jefferson's trouble in forming them. "Another truth," he added, "is that I am not only rusty in Parliamentary Rules, but never read much on the subject; my small stock of knowledge in that way I caught from Mr. Robinson and Mr. Randolph, or was the result of my own reflections, dictated by the principle of having every question so put as to be well understood, and free as might be from embarrassment or complexity. My mite however is freely cast into your Treasury, and I wish it was of more value."[67]

The enclosure contained six pages of doctrinal statements and related queries in Jefferson's careful hand, and of replies to many of them set forth in the margins in a hand that is not now fully legible. The statements, the queries, and the replies concern themselves with procedures in committees, procedures on the floor of Commons, and procedures in dealing with privileged questions, equivalent questions, and the like. As a whole, the document exhibits a wide range of familiarity with "minute practices, which being in daily use in parliament and therefore supposed known to every one, were never noticed in their books."[68]

[66] TJ to Edmund Pendleton, 19 Apr. 1800 (see above, note 2).
[67] Edmund Pendleton to TJ, 17 June 1800.   [68] Same.

During the interval between Jefferson's letter to Pendleton and Pendleton's reply, George Wythe sent Jefferson a short note, dated April 23, 1800, which did not address itself to any of the questions posed by Jefferson's letters of February 28 and April 7, but which did reveal Wythe's playful fondness for classical learning and his lively interest in the progress being made by Jefferson in the preparation of the *Manual*. With its letters carefully printed by hand, the note said

"Whenever that εγχειριδιον π'ερι τ'ην συμ. βουλην νομοθετιχην, which thou art preparing, shall be published, as I anxiously hope it will be, reserve two or three copies for me."

The Greek title might be translated as "Manual concerning the Outside and the Inside of the Putting Together of the Laws of the Senate." And Wythe's hope that the *Manual* might be published certainly helped, it would appear, to dispose Jefferson toward allowing that possibility to be realized within the next ten months.[69]

On November 29, 1800, Jefferson wrote a letter to Wythe, but no copy of it is now available.[70] It may have informed Wythe that Jefferson was at last ready to deliver the manuscript of the *Manual* to the printer, and that there was now no urgency connected with Wythe's answering Jefferson's earlier requests for parliamentary information. But around that time a document containing Wythe's answers to Jefferson's first list of queries about parliamentary law reached Jefferson in Washington, D.C.

Dated December 7, 1800, that document, except for its opening and closing paragraphs, consisted in comments carefully keyed by Wythe to page numbers, line numbers, and paragraph numbers of the enclosure containing Jefferson's inquiries of February 28, ten months earlier.[71]

What Jefferson did upon receiving these contributions was to note them upon his own original handwritten copy of the queries sent with his letter to Wythe on February 28, 1800. Jefferson's paragraph on putting amendments to a vote in committee was followed by a list of questions dealing with particular cases:

Is it's statement exact as to the cases where questions are to be put on agreeing to the paragraph as amended or unamended? or
[The statement seemeth exact.]
In what cases is a question put Whether the paragraph is agreed to either as amended, or where no amendment has been made?
[The question is simply, that the committee do agree to it, if amendments be not made, or, if they be, that the committee do agree to it, with the amendments.]
And in what cases does he put a final question on the whole?
[The final question upon the whole I suppose to be in cases where the subjects upon which votes have passed are connected with one another.]
What is the form of the question? To wit, is it Whether they agree to the address, resolutions or bill in the whole, even where they have already past a vote of agreement on all it's parts? or is it Whether it shall be reported to the house?

[69] George Wythe to TJ, 23 Apr. 1800.
[70] Summary Journal of Letters, TJ Papers, DLC.
[71] Wythe to TJ, 7 Dec. 1800.

[That they do agree to the address &c. in the whole. If upon this a negative be put, I suppose the address, &c. which the committee have no power to reject, must be reported to the house, who if they do not pass it as it is, or recommit, may reject, it.][72]

On the second page of his enclosure, Jefferson took up similar questions about the reading of a bill or paper when it is ready for a final vote in the House. Wythe replied that he believed that the Speaker reads only the amended paragraphs, first in their original and then in their amended wording. If the bill is not amended at all by committee, Wythe said, "I suppose the bill is not read at all; and the question be that the bill be engrossed if it originated in that house, or, if not, that this house concur with the other house &c." Wythe concluded his comments on Jefferson's doubts about whether a bill was read and put to the question paragraph by paragraph by saying, "I remember nothing of reading them by paragraphs, or putting them to the questions by paragraphs."

In commenting upon page 3 of Jefferson's original enclosure, Wythe noted only that he could conceive of nothing more exact than the definitions given there, and that he had no additions to propose to them; and Jefferson allowed his copy of page 3 of the enclosure to remain unmarked, as if to remind himself that his mentor did not disagree with any of its statements. That page, by the way, referred to important parliamentary motions—to the previous question, indefinite postponement, adjourning a question to a definite day, tabling a bill or resolution, or committing it.

Keying his next comment to "page 4, paragr 1." of Jefferson's enclosure, which reads, "On a disagreement between the houses as to amendments to a bill, and a conference agreed on, can the conferees propose, or authorize either house to propose an amendment in a *new* part of the bill, having no *coherence* with the amendment on which they have disagreed," Wythe wrote that "the conferees cannot propose, or authorize either house to propose, an amendment in the new part, &c." For some reason this piece of advice was not recorded in Jefferson's notes on Wythe's letter. Its importance to Jefferson is emphasized by his inclusion of a query on the subject in the enclosure sent to Wythe with his letter of April 7.[73] And in the second edition of the *Manual*[74] he inserted a sentence declaring that members attending a conference may not "assent to any new thing there propounded." The omission of a similar sentence from the first edition of the *Manual* causes no problem to an editor—it can be explained by recalling that the copy text was already in the hands of the printer when Wythe's letter of December 7 arrived, and thus the insertion of new material would of course be difficult. But why Jefferson omitted from his notes on Wythe's letter any reference to that sentence is something of a puzzle, in view of his many other faithful recordings of his mentor's opinions.

Paragraphs 2 and 3 of page 4 of the enclosure read:

When the Previous question is moved, must the debate on the Main question be immediately suspended?

When a Previous question has been moved and seconded, may the Main quest. be amended *before* putting the Previous qu.? We know it cannot af-

[72] Queries sent to George Wythe, 28 Feb. 1800, and responses, bracketed herein by the Editors, from Wythe to TJ, 7 Dec. 1800.

[73] TJ to George Wythe, 7 Apr. 1800 (see above, note 64).

[74] Sec. XLVI, par. 2.

terwards; and that it is a vexata questio whether it may before. What is Mr. Wythe's opinion?

Mr. Wythe's opinion was yes to the first question and tentatively no to the second, although he added, "I might change it, if I knew what had been urged to the contrary."[75] These opinions became Jefferson's authority for par. [441] of the Pocket-Book.

There are no marks in Jefferson's copy to indicate a reaction on his part to what Wythe had said about the next two paragraphs of the enclosure. Perhaps from other sources Jefferson had already ascertained what the correct answers were, and thus he no longer needed to make note of Wythe's general agreement. For example, paragraph 4 concerned the difference between the procedure of the Speaker in putting the call of a member for the execution of an order of the House and the Speaker's procedure in putting into execution a member's call for an order of the day; and it hypothesized that the Speaker on his own authority required the former call to be carried out, whereas he asked for a vote on the execution of the latter call. Jefferson had already entered the correct formulations into the manuscript of Sec. 18, par. 4, and Sec. 33, par. 5, of the *Manual*. As for paragraph 5, it asked whether, when a motion was made to strike out an element in a bill, the advocates of that element have the right to propose amendments to it before action is taken on the question to strike it out. Jefferson did not note on the enclosure that Wythe's letter affirmed that right; and once again his failure to do so may have been occasioned by what was already entered into the manuscript of the *Manual* at Sec. 35, par. 5.

The remaining paragraphs on page 4 of Jefferson's enclosure had to do with amending bills. Wythe's comments were again transferred to Jefferson's copy:

> When a motion is made to strike out a paragraph, section, or even the whole bill from the word 'Whereas,' have not the friends of the paragraph a right to have all their amendments to it proposed before the question is put for striking out?
>
> After the question for striking out is negatived, can the section recieve any new amendment? . . .
> [Nay]
> 1. A motion is made to amend a bill or other paper by striking out certain words, and inserting others; and the question being divided, and put first on striking out, it is negatived, and the insertion of course falls.
> 2. After this a motion is made to strike out the same words and to insert others, of a different tenor altogether from those before proposed to be inserted. Is this not admissible?
> [I think the motion admissible.]
> 3. Suppose the 2d. motion to be negatived; would it not be admissible to move to strike out *the same words*, and to insert nothing in their place?
> [The same.]
> So if the 1st. motion had been to strike out the words and insert nothing, and negatived; might it not then have been moved to strike out the same words and insert other words?
> [Last paragr likewise.][76]

[75] Queries sent to George Wythe, 28 Feb. 1800, and Wythe to TJ, 7 Dec. 1800.
[76] Same.

Jefferson's last page of questions had to do with preambles to bills or resolutions before parliaments. "When a paper is under correction of the house," he wrote, "the natural order is to begin at the beginning, and proceed through it with amendments. But there is an exception as to a *bill*, the *preamble* of which is last amended." He goes on to ask, "Does this exception extend to any other form of paper? e.g. a resolution etc. or would the *preamble* of the resolution be first amended, according to the natural order?" Wythe replied that "the exception extends to any other form, to prevent a junctura cervicis equinae capiti humano." Jefferson next asks if a resolution brought in without a preamble can have a preamble attached by amendment before the body of the resolution is acted on. Wythe admits, "I suppose not," but adds, "My language is didactic. Yet am I confident of nothing that I have written." He concludes with a handsome compliment to the forthcoming *Manual* that deserves to be quoted in full: "I am persuaded that the manual of your parliamentary praxis will be more chaste than any extant, and, if you can be persuaded to let it go forth, that it will be canonized in all the legislatures of America."[77]

These expressions of encouragement from his respected advisor could not have triggered Jefferson's decision to deposit with the Senate a printed *Manual* rather than the manuscript originally contemplated, for, as already noted, that decision had already been made, and the copy text was even then in the printer's office. By a remarkably fortunate coincidence in which a memorable event found itself memorably recorded, Margaret Bayard Smith, who happened to be present when Jefferson brought his manuscript to the printer, makes us vividly experience what happened:

In December, 1800, a few days after Congress had for the first time met in our new Metropolis, I was one morning sitting alone in the parlour, when the servant opened the door and showed in a gentleman who wished to see my husband. The usual frankness and care with which I met strangers, were somewhat checked by the dignified and reserved air of the present visitor; but the chilled feeling was only momentary, for after taking the chair I offered him in a free and easy manner, and carelessly throwing his arm on the table near which he sat, he turned towards me in a countenance beaming with an expression of benevolence and with a manner and voice almost femininely soft and gentle, entered into conversation on the commonplace topics of the day, from which, before I was conscious of it, he had drawn me into observations of a more personal and interesting nature. . . . I knew not who he was, but the interest with which he listened to my artless details, induced the idea he was some intimate acquaintance or friend of Mr. Smith's and put me perfectly at my ease; in truth so kind and conciliating were his looks and manners that I forgot he was not a friend of my own, until on the opening of the door, Mr. Smith entered and introduced the stranger to me as *Mr. Jefferson.* . . .

The occasion of his present visit, was to make arrangements with Mr. Smith for the publication of his *Manual* for *Congress*, now called *Jefferson's manual*. The original was in his own neat, plain, but elegant hand writing. The manuscript was as legible as printing and its unadorned simplicity was

[77] Same. The Latin phrase joins with its opening English words to mean "a juncture of a horse's neck with a human head."

emblamatical of his character. It is still preserved by Mr. Smith and valued as a precious relique.[78]

Jefferson was presiding over the Senate on February 18, 1801, when a message arrived from the other House to announce that "the House of Representatives has chosen Thomas Jefferson, of Virginia, President of the United States, for the term commencing on the 4th. of March next."[79] Ten days later Jefferson resigned as president of the Senate. His speech on that occasion reads as follows:

> To give the usual opportunity of appointing a President, pro tempore, I now propose to retire from the chair of the Senate: and, as the time is near at hand when the relations will cease which have for some time subsisted between this honorable house and myself, I beg leave, before I withdraw, to return to them my grateful thanks for all the instances of attention and respect with which they have been pleased to honor me. In the discharge of my functions here, it has been my conscientious endeavor to observe impartial justice, without regard to persons or subjects; and if I have failed of impressing this on the mind of the Senate, it will be to me a circumstance of the deepest regret. I may have erred at times—no doubt I have erred: this is the law of human nature. For honest errors, however, indulgence may be hoped.
>
> I owe to truth and justice, at the same time, to declare, that the habits of order and decorum, which so strongly characterize the proceedings of the Senate, have rendered the umpirage of their President an office of little difficulty; that, in times and on questions which have severely tried the sensibilities of the house, calm and temperate discussion has rarely been disturbed by departures from order.
>
> Should the support which I have received from the Senate, in the performance of my duties here, attend me into the new station to which the public will has transferred me, I shall consider it as commencing under the happiest auspices.
>
> With these expressions of my dutiful regard to the Senate as a body, I ask leave to mingle my particular wishes for the health and happiness of the individuals who compose it; and to tender them my cordial and respectful adieu.[80]

Hardly had Jefferson retired from the Senate chamber after making this speech, and hardly had the Senate thereupon chosen James Hillhouse president pro tempore, when a motion was adopted to appoint a committee, to consist of Messrs. Gouverneur Morris, Jonathan Mason, and Jonathan Dayton, to prepare an address in reply to what Jefferson had just said.[81] On the next legislative day, Monday, March 2, 1801, Mr. Morris, as spokesman for that committee, read the following address for presentation to the retired president of the Senate:

> While we congratulate you on those expressions of the public will, which called you to the first office in the United States, we cannot but lament the loss of that intelligence, attention, and impartiality, with which you have

[78] Smith, *First Forty Years*, p. 6-8. For further discussion of this manuscript, see below, Editor's Introduction to the *Manual*, "The Manuscript Problem."
[79] JS, III, 127.   [80] JS, III, 134.   [81] JS, III, 135.

presided over our deliberations. The Senate feel themselves much gratified by the sense you have been pleased to express of their support in the performance of your late duties. Be persuaded that it will never be withheld from a Chief Magistrate, who, in the exercise of his office, shall be influenced by a due regard to the honor and interest of our country.

In the confidence that your official conduct will be directed to these great objects, a confidence derived from past events, we repeat to you, Sir, the assurance of our constitutional support in your future administration.[82]

A member of the Senate moved to amend the address by striking out the phrase "a confidence derived from past events," but that amendment was immediately voted down, 19 to 9.[83] The address was thereupon ordered to be presented to the President-elect by the committee which drew it up; and on the next day, in the midst of his concerns about not only his inauguration on March 4, 1801, as President of the United States, but also his inaugural address in particular, Jefferson responded in writing as follows:

I receive with due sensibility the congratulations of the Senate on being called to the first executive office of our government; and I accept, with great satisfaction, their assurances of support in whatever regards the honor and interest of our country. Knowing no other object in the discharge of my public duties, their confidence in my future conduct, derived from past events, shall not be disappointed, so far as my judgement may enable me to discern those objects.

The approbation they are so good as to express of my conduct in the chair of the Senate, is highly gratifying to me; and I pray them to accept my humble thanks for these declarations of it.[84]

These exchanges between Jefferson and the Senate should not be dismissed as mere formalities. Jefferson's valedictory speech is a reliable reaffirmation of his beliefs not only about the proper role of the presiding officer of a parliamentary assembly, but also about the proper conduct of the assembly itself, and the proper relationship to be developed between the presiding officer and his immediate constituents. To Jefferson, the presiding officer should conscientiously "endeavor to observe impartial justice;" the members of the assembly should cultivate at all times "the habits of order and decorum," as indeed the Senate had done; and the chairman and his immediate constituents should develop feelings of mutual respect. The reply of the Senate to Jefferson's valedictory speech, by lamenting "the loss of that intelligence, attention, and impartiality" which Jefferson had imparted to their deliberations, affirmed in striking terms the Senate's respect for their retiring officer. Jefferson's immediate reply reverted to the theme of mutual respect. As if he had been told of the defeated amendment he mischievously borrowed its language in suggesting that the confidence of the Senate in him, "derived from past events," would not be disappointed by what he did as President. Impartiality by the chairman, good order and decorum by the Senate, mutual respect on both sides—these, then, are the basic lessons to be learned from the courtesies surrounding Jefferson's resignation from the Presidency of the upper House.

On the day before he stepped down from that office, February 27, 1801, an event of some significance occurred in Washington that crowned Jefferson's ac-

[82] JS, III, 136.   [83] JS, III, 136-7.   [84] JS, III, 140.

complishments in parliamentary scholarship. *The National Intelligencer, and Washington Advertiser*, a triweekly newspaper, founded the preceding October, and strongly supportive of Jefferson's recent election as President, announced: "This day is published by Samuel H. Smith, Near the Capitol, *A Manuel Of Parliamentary Practice. For the use of the Senate of the United States.* By Thomas Jefferson. Washington. . . ." Thus the Senate acquired its first full parliamentary rule book, and the new American democracy a reliable guide to an altogether remarkable English parliamentary tradition.

Smith's recognition of Jefferson's *Manual* was not confined to the mere notice of its having been published on February 27. The first book review that it ever received appeared on April 13, 1801, written no doubt by Smith himself and printed perhaps in honor of Jefferson's fifty-eighth birthday. That review covered a little more than three full columns on the front page of *The National Intelligencer*. It began by emphasizing the importance of any work on parliamentary procedure that avoided the tediousness and incomprehensibility of European predecessors. It mentioned the practical value of such a work, and the contribution it can make to the efficient and fair transaction of public business. The rules governing those transactions, the review went on, must be valid, impartial, concise, and easy to grasp; and the author who lays down rules must show perspicuity of arrangement, simplicity of diction, and talent in condensing and generalizing. It concluded this introductory paragraph by affirming, "We do not hesitate to say that the author of this performance has successfully combined these many qualifications."

Later on, the review pointed out that the *Manual*, nominally for the Senate, would be found applicable to the House of Representatives, and to the deliberative bodies of the various state governments. And it then gave an insight into the *Manual*'s contents by quoting not only all of its preface, but also the whole of Section LII entitled "Treaties."

One paragraph of Smith's review evaluates the *Manual* in the terms that Jefferson would perhaps have found most gratifying of all. Those terms are a judicious outsider's estimate of the quiet value of a work intended more for its usefulness in an important activity than for the personal glorification of its author:

> About to leave the Senate of the United States, in presiding over whose deliberations his deportment had been so manly, so deft and enlightened as to receive even from his political opponents the palm of praise, it occurred to him that no more valuable legacy could be bestowed than a production, many of the materials of which had been collected from, and all of which applied to, its proceedings. Such a work may not be calculated to clothe with radiance the statesman or patriot or to increase by sudden accession of fame the weight of his popularity; but it establishes with the reflecting class of the community the more substantial claims derived from the performance of a useful act.

Evidence of Jefferson's continuing interest in parliamentary matters is scantier during his terms as chief executive. In 1802, however, his expert scholarly advice was solicited regarding selection of works for inclusion in the infant Library of Congress. Abraham Baldwin, senator from Georgia, whose initial term in the Senate had coincided with Jefferson's only term there, was chairman of a joint congressional committee appointed to draw up a plan for the purchase of books; and he wrote Jefferson on April 14 to ask his advice upon that matter.[85] In answer Jefferson supplied a catalogue for the Library. In doing so, he conformed to Baldwin's recommendation for the exclusion of "books of entertainment" and for the inclusion of books in other languages when translations of them were not available. Jefferson wrote that he had confined his catalogue "to those branches of science which belong to the deliberations of the members as statesmen," omitting many ancient and modern books "which gentlemen generally have in their private libraries, but which cannot properly claim a place in a collection made merely for the purpose of reference." In recommending histories, he stressed chronological works "which give facts and dates with a minuteness not to be found in narrations composed for agreeable reading." As for books on "the Laws of Nature and Nations," his catalogue, he said, included "every thing I know of worth possessing," while for books on law, it "set down only general treatises for the purpose of reference." Then Jefferson singled out a class of books for special mention:

> The Parliamentary selection I have imagined should be compleat. It is only by having a law of proceeding, and by every member having the means of understanding it for himself, and appealing to it, that he can be protected against caprice and despotism in the chair.[86]

Jefferson then made further references to what his catalogue included, and to what uses it might be put by Baldwin's committee in strengthening the Library each year "to the amount of the annual fund."

The catalogue still exists among Jefferson's manuscripts.[87] It lists some thirty-six entries under the heading "Parliamentary." All of them are standard works of their time. All of them were in Jefferson's great collection of books, which was to be sold to the nation in 1815, and was to help make the Library of Congress one of the world's largest and most distinguished libraries. Almost all of them had figured in the preparation of Jefferson's Pocket-Book and *Manual*. While this part of his catalogue cannot claim to be a complete list of the sources of Jefferson's writings on parliamentary law and procedure, it does enumerate the titles of the essential works, and if it were to be used as a supplement to works already held by the Library of Congress, it would justify Jefferson in using the word "compleat" to characterize it.[88] A sample of the titles contained in the catalogue that Jefferson sent to Baldwin on April 14, 1802, may indicate that the quality of Jefferson's parliamentary learning was still high after a year's preoc-

---

[85] JLC, XXXII, No. 2 (1975), 95.

[86] TJ to Abraham Baldwin, 14 Apr. 1802 (TJ Editorial Files, 14150; L & B, XIX, 128-9).

[87] A letterpress copy of the original document is in the Library of Congress. Its list of titles under various headings is not easily legible, except for certain items. See TJ to Abraham Baldwin, 14 Apr. 1802. The original document is in the Missouri Historical Society, St. Louis, Bixby Collection, under date of photocopy, see TJ Editorial Files, 19 July 1802. Preserved with this document are two lists of books drawn up by TJ to be purchased abroad by William Duane for the Library of Congress, both lists having been compiled from the latter list that TJ sent to Abraham Baldwin on the preceding April 14. Duane was directed by TJ to purchase in London the items on the longer of the two lists, and those items included works on history, law of nature and nations, maritime law, law, politics, geography, and some twenty-eight titles on the practices of parliaments.

[88] For a list of the holdings of the Library of Congress in 1802, see Beckley, *Catalogue*. See also JLC, XXXII, No. 2 (1975), 83-110.

cupation with the tasks and duties of his office as President: *Lex Parliamentaria*; Scobell's *Memorials*; Hakewill's *Modus tenendi Parliamentum*; C. R.'s *Arcana Parliamentaria*; Thurloe's *State Papers; Orders of the House of Commons*; Atkyns's *Power, Jurisdiction and Privilege of Parliament*; Selden's *Jurisdiction of Parliaments*; Rushworth's *Historical Collections*; D'Ewes's *Journals*; Hatsell's *Precedents of Proceedings in the House of Commons*; Townshend's *Historical Collections*; Bohun's *Debates; Journal of the House of Commons*; *Journal of the House of Lords*; Hale's *Jurisdiction of Parliaments*; *Debates in the Irish Commons*; and Petyt's *Jus Parliamentarium*. Baldwin's hope of strengthening the Library of Congress by the work of his committee could not have been served better than by Jefferson's catalogue of possible purchases in the parliamentary field and, indeed, in the fields of European history, American history, political arithmetic, commerce, geography, natural law, international law, maritime law, and foreign law.

On January 17 of 1810, in a letter to this son-in-law, John Wayles Eppes, Jefferson made some noteworthy observations based on his experiences as a parliamentarian. Eppes was then serving as Representative in Congress from Charles City, Virginia, and Jefferson's letter contained not only some sharp criticism of oratorical practices in the House but also a proposal for reform of its parliamentary conduct. Here is the passage bearing particularly upon those two points:

> I observe the house is endeavoring to remedy the eternal protraction of debate by setting up all night, or by use of the Previous Question. Both will subject them to the most serious inconvenience. The latter may be turned upon themselves by a trick of their adversaries. I have thought that such a Rule as the following would be more effectual and less inconvenient. 'Resolved that at [VIII.] aclock in the evening (whenever the house shall be in session at that hour) it shall be the duty of the Speaker to declare that hour arrived, whereupon all debate shall cease. If there be then before the house a Main question for the reading or passing of a bill, resolution or order, such Main question shall immediately be put by the Speaker, and decided by Yeas and Nays. If the question before the house be secondary, as for amendments, commitment, postponement, adjournment of the debate or question, laying on the table, reading papers, or a Previous question, such secondary question, [or any other which may delay the Main question] shall stand ipso facto discharged. And the Main question shall then be before the house and shall be immediately put and decided by Yeas and Nays. But a motion for adjournment of the house may once, and once only, take place of the Main question, and if decided in the negative, the Main question shall then be put as before. Should any question of order arise, it shall be decided by the Speaker instanter, and without debate or appeal; and questions of Privilege arising, shall be postponed till the Main question be decided. Messages from the President or Senate may be recieved but not acted on till after the decision of the Main question. But this rule shall be suspended during the [three] last days of the session of Congress.'[89]

On July 29, 1809, five months after the end of his second term as President, Jefferson received a letter from John W. Campbell of Petersburg, Virginia. Campbell, a publisher, wrote to propose "a complete Edition of your different writ-

[89] TJ to John Wayles Eppes, 17 Jan. 1810 (brackets in original).

ings, as far as they may be designed for the public; including the, 'Notes on Virginia.' " "The work should be executed in Philadelphia," the letter continued, "by the best publishers in the city, and in a stile, not inferior to any prose work yet published in our country."[90]

Responding to this proposal on September 3, 1809, Jefferson began by saying "that no writings of mine, other than those merely official have been published, except the Notes on Virginia, and a small pamphlet under the title of a Summary view of the rights of British America." Jefferson then said:

> The Notes on Virginia I have always intended to revise and enlarge, and have from time to time laid by materials for that purpose. It will be long yet before other occupations will permit me to digest them; & observations and enquiries are still to be made which will be more correct in proportion to the length of time they are continued. It is not unlikely that this may be through my life. I could not therefore at present offer any thing new for that work.
>
> The Summary view was not written for publication. It was a draught I had prepared of a petition to the king, which I meant to propose in my place as a member of the Convention of 1774. Being stopped on the road by sickness, I sent it on to the Speaker, who laid it on the table for the perusal of the members. It was thought too strong for the times and to become the act of the convention, but was printed by subscription of the members with a short preface written by one of them. If it had any merit it was that of first taking our true ground, and that which was afterwards assumed and maintained.

Up to this point, Jefferson had not mentioned his *Manual*, though it obviously belonged among his publications. But when he did so, his comments upon it indicate the two reasons why it should not be considered for inclusion in Campbell's projected collection. It was intended for a small, special audience, Jefferson made clear, and it was not so much his own work as that of other authors. His wording deserves quotation:

> I do not mention the Parliamentary manual published for the use of the Senate of the US. because it was a mere compilation, into which nothing entered of my own, but the arrangement, and a few observations necessary to explain that and some of the cases.

In the concluding paragraphs of this letter, Jefferson went on to say that many of his official papers had been published, and that these consisted of reports, letters, messages, resolutions, and declarations "such as the Declaration of Independance." But in general, he said, "I see nothing encouraging a printer to a republication of them. They would probably be bought by those only who are in the habit of preserving state-papers. . . . They belong mostly to a class of papers not calculated for popular reading, and not likely therefore to offer profit, or even indemnification to the republisher."[91]

Lest Jefferson's comments upon his *Manual* be taken to suggest that he held it in low esteem, unworthy of a place in a collected edition of his writings, we must take note of the context of these comments. Campbell had proposed publication of such of Jefferson's works as had been designed for the public, and it

[90] John W. Campbell to TJ, 29 July 1809.
[91] TJ to John W. Campbell, 2 Sept. 1809.

The true second edition of the *Manual* was now fully authorized.

The enclosure containing Jefferson's proposed supplements to Milligan's second edition of the *Manual* is no longer available, even though the letter quoted above refers to it as a printed document. But the supplements now exist as passages in Milligan's edition, and they may be identified easily by comparing Milligan's text with Samuel Harrison Smith's. They amount to approximately seventy-six lines of type. Since Milligan's text contains twenty-nine lines per page on the average, the additions increased the *Manual* by almost three pages.[100]

Joseph Milligan was not the only publisher interested in bringing out in 1812 a new and corrected edition of the *Manual*. On January 21 of that year, Mathew Carey, a prominent and successful journalist and publisher in Philadelphia, addressed to Jefferson the following letter:

> Your parliamentary Manual has been for a long time out of print, and in demand. I have written to the publisher, Mr. S. H. Smith, to enquire whether he has any objection to a republication of it. And wish to be informed by you, whether, if he consents to its being reprinted, you have any alterations or improvements to make in it.[101]

Jefferson's reply, dated from Monticello on January 27, contained an unexpected statement concerning his original intention in compiling the *Manual*, and it also contained evidence of a lapse of memory on his part in saying that he had not seen Hatsell's third volume when the *Manual* was first published. Otherwise, however, the letter resembled what Jefferson had told Joseph Milligan in answer to the latter's request of January 3:

> The Parliamentary Manual, originally compiled for my own personal use, was printed on the supposition it might be of use to others, and have some tendency to settle the rules of proceeding in Congress, where, in the lower house especially they had got into forms totally unfriendly to a fair extrication of the will of the majority. No right over it was therefore wished to be retained by myself, nor given to others. It's reimpression consequently is open to every one, nor have I any thing to add to it but what is contained in the inclosed paper. When I first printed it, I had never seen Hatsell's 3d. volume. A subsequent perusal of that suggested the inclosed amendments which should be incorporated with the text of the original in their proper places. I believe that Mr. Milligan of George town is now engaged in printing an 8vo. edition. I think he has erred in the size of the volume. Almost the essence of it's value is in it's being accommodated to pocket use.[102]

No copy of "the inclosed amendments" mentioned here by Jefferson is now available, but, as in the case of Jefferson's similar statement in his earlier letter to Joseph Milligan, the amendments may assuredly be deduced by comparing the text of the first edition of the *Manual* with that of Milligan's second edition. As for Jefferson's reference to Hatsell's third volume, there is indeed evidence of its

---

essary corrective to the lapse of memory suffered by TJ on that subject in his letter to Mathew Carey, 27 Jan. 1812. See below, note 102, for that letter.

[100] For further details, see Editor's Introduction to the *Manual* "The Basis of the Printed Text of 1812;" Editor's Notes on *Manual*, Secs. I, XIII, XXVI, XXXV, XLVI, and LIII.

[101] Mathew Carey to TJ, 21 Jan. 1812.

[102] TJ to Mathew Carey, 27 Jan. 1812. This letter was not printed by Ford or by Lipscomb and Bergh, but it is referred to and partly quoted by Sowerby 2894 (III, 183).

inaccuracy. In the first edition of the *Manual* there are twenty-three references to Hatsell's third volume but no references to Hatsell's fourth. On the other hand, Milligan's second edition of the *Manual* contains the twenty-three references just mentioned, and it also draws upon Hatsell's fourth volume for fourteen new references. Jefferson's mistake in his letter to Carey is not especially important in itself. But the unfortunate thing about it is that it came to light in a letter that reached the public under Sowerby's auspices at a time when Jefferson's correct statement on this matter in his letter to Milligan was not yet known. Thus what was doubtless a mere lapse of memory on Jefferson's part was accepted as fact by a normally respected authority, and that lapse is bound now and then to crowd the fact out.[103]

On February 15, 1812, Jefferson received from Joseph Milligan a letter under the date of February 2, indicating rapid progress on the publication of the second edition of the *Manual*. The letter reads thus:

> As you will see by the Enclosed proof of the first 12 pages of the Manual I have had it printed to meet your Idea as to size and think that it is certainly a great improvement as it may be bound like the Volume of the British Spy herewith sent so as to make an Elegant pocket Volume. I have not yet got the house of representatives to take a Vote on ordering a Certain Number for the house but I hope to have it brought before them in a week. I went this day to get *Mr. Burwell* to give me some instructions in what manner to bring it before the house but he had just set out for Baltimore but I hope he will be back in a few days. I have just been with our mutual friend Mr. John Barnes who is in good health, and desires his respects with the best wishes for your health and happiness.[104]

Milligan's mention of "the British Spy" is a reference to a popular contemporary book entitled *The British Spy or The Letters of the British Spy*, published anonymously in various editions at Richmond and elsewhere in the early nineteenth century, after having appeared serially in the *Virginia Argus*. It purported to be letters addressed to a member of the British parliament by a young Englishman of rank during his tour of the United States; but, as a matter of fact, its author was William Wirt, later to establish his literary reputation by a biography of Patrick Henry. In its edition of 1811, a copy of which may well have accompanied the above letter to Jefferson, *The British Spy* is indeed "an elegant pocket Volume," its dimensions being only slightly larger than those of Milligan's second edition of the *Manual*. Jefferson's previously mentioned letter of January 7 to Milligan suggested that the proper size for the *Manual* should be "5. by 3," and those measurements almost exactly fit Milligan's edition of 1812.

On March 16, Jefferson replied from Monticello: "I duly recieved your favor of Feb. 2. with a specimen of the size and type you proposed for the Manual, and think you have done prudently in accommodating it to the pocket rather than the shelf of a library." The rest of the letter concerned the payment of a bill owed by Jefferson to Milligan; and it included the request that, should Milligan reprint the *Scientific Dialogues*, Jefferson would "be glad of a copy," preferably in 8vo, so as to allow it to fit with his other like-sized volumes on the same subject.[105]

---

[103] Malone, *Jefferson*, III, 456, n. 49, for example, accepts Sowerby's authority on this matter.

[104] Joseph Milligan to TJ, 2 Feb. 1812.   [105] TJ to Joseph Milligan, 16 Mar. 1812.

Eight days after Jefferson wrote the above letter, Milligan's second edition of the *Manual* was published. The following notice heralded that event on March 24, 1812, in the columns of the *National Intelligencer*:

This day is published, And for Sale By Joseph Milligan George Town and William Cooper Washington A Manual of Parliamentary Practice for the Use of the Senate of the United States By Thomas Jefferson Second Edition With the Last Additions of the Author. To which are added, The Constitution of the United States of America with the Latest Amendments. Rules for Conducting Business in the Senate and in House of Representatives and the Joint Rules of Both Houses. In one total Pocket Volume.

Except for the first seven words and the last five, this notice, in serving to describe the makeup of the volume announced here, indirectly proclaims that a true second edition of the *Manual* is at last in existence. This second edition, complete with a table of contents, Jefferson's original Preface, the expanded text of its fifty-three sections, and an index, occupies 188 pages. The Constitution, with its own title page and imprint, has separate pagination and occupies 43 pages. The Senate Rules, also separately paged, run to 13 pages, while the House Rules and the Joint Rules are paged in sequence from 1 to 25. The "total Pocket Volume" thus contains 269 pages of information, and that information is presented readably, making it indispensable *pari passu* to Senators, Representatives, and their presiding officers.

A "third edition" of the *Manual* appeared in 1813, but, despite what it calls itself, it must be counted a second reissue of Smith's first edition. It has no connection with Milligan's second edition. Its title page reads thus:

A Manual of Parliamentary Practice For the Use of the Senate of the United States. By Thomas Jefferson. 3rd ed. Lancaster, Pa. Printed and published by William Dickson. 1813.

Very soon after the second edition was published, the *Manual* began to be translated into the major European languages. Not surprisingly, interest in the workings of American government was strongest among liberals, eager to educate their countrymen in republican ideals. Toward the end of 1814 the first French translation of Jefferson's *Manual* appeared in Paris. The translator, Louis-André Pichon, had served in the United States not only as secretary of the French legation (1794-1795) and as French consul general (1800-1805), but also as an unofficial but friendly supporter of Jefferson's successful efforts to purchase Louisiana from Napoleon.[106] Pichon's translation of the *Manual* was done several years after his return to his own country, and it unmistakably reflects his admiration for Jefferson and for America's having had the good fortune to choose parliamentary institutions as the center of their new government. The title page of Pichon's translation reads thus:

Manuel du Droit Parlementaire, ou Précis des Règles Suivies dans le Parlement d'Angleterre et dans le Congrès des États-Unis, pour l'introduction, la discussion et la décision des affaires; compilé a l'usage du Sénat des Etats-Unis, par Thomas Jefferson, Ancien Président des États-Unis. Traduit de l'Anglais, par L. A. Pichon, Ancien agent diplomatique; ancien conseiller

---

[106] Malone, *Jefferson*, III, 323, 327, 334.

d'état, et intendant-général du trésor en Westphalie. A Paris, chez H. Nicolle, a la Librairie Stéréotype, Rue de Seine, no 12. 1814.

Pichon's translation, as he himself said, was based upon Smith's first edition of 1801.[107] It consisted of his rendering of fifty-one of Jefferson's original fifty-three sections, with Section II (Legislature) and Section VIII (Absence) being omitted altogether because of their exclusive connection with American political realities. Before the beginning of his translation of the text of the *Manual*, Pichon appended an "*Avis du Traducteur*" and the "*Préface de l'Auteur*"; and at the end he listed forty Senate rules, eighty-two rules of the other House, and eleven rules common to both Houses. Pichon's translation omitted all of the notes that Jefferson had worked into his text, but as an informative supplement to his own work he gave to his French readers various explanatory comments upon the meaning of unfamiliar terms in the original.

On February 27 of 1815, Jefferson wrote a long letter to David Baillie Warden, whom he had successfully recommended to President Madison in 1810 for appointment to the consulship at Paris.[108] The letter contains much of interest. But what commends it to our attention is that it refers to the *Manual of Parliamentary Practice* and couples the reference to Jefferson's habits of acquiring books from abroad and giving sought-after books of his own in return. Warden had sent Jefferson a copy of Toulongeon's *Histoire de France*, and Jefferson responded thus: "According to your request, I send you a copy of my Parliamentary Manual, and am to acknolege the reciept of Toulongeon, whom I have read with great satisfaction and information." Jefferson went on to add that Toulongeon's history had brought significant order to the seeming chaos of the French Revolution up to the death of Robespierre, and had solved the riddle of the Jacobins. Perhaps it is not too much to comment upon Jefferson's observations by saying that his *Manual* would surely bring to Warden and its other readers the vision of a democratic government conducted with a decent respect for order, for uniformity of procedure, for impartiality, and for the rule of law. Thus what Jefferson did on this occasion for Warden would seem in basic philosophy to match what Warden had done for him.

A translation of the *Manual* into German occurred in 1819 under auspices that enhanced its value to the world of European learning. This time its translator was Leopold Dorotheus von Henning, a graduate of Heidelberg, his studies having been in jurisprudence, history, and philosophy. His first scholarly book, says his biographer,[109] was his translation of Jefferson's handbook of parliamentary law, which he stocked with annotations. The only copy of it in the United States seems to be that in the Library of Congress. Its title page reads thus:[110]

Handbuch des Parlamentarrechts; oder, Darstellung der Verhandlungsweise und des Geschäftsganges beim Englischen Parlament und beim Congress der Vereinigten Staaten von Nordamerika.

[107] See Pichon's edition just cited, p. viii.
[108] Malone, *Jefferson*, VI, 83. For the text of this letter, see TJ to David Baillie Warden, 27 Feb. 1815. See also Sowerby 240 (I, 104-5).
[109] See ADB.
[110] See NUC.

Ubers. und mit Aumerkungen begleitet von Leopold von Henning. Berlin, F. Dümmler, 1819.

Unlike Pichon, Henning had no personal contact with America, but his interest in jurisprudence suggests that he may have become interested in Jefferson's *Manual* when he was a student. He later turned to philosophy, participating with other scholars between 1832 and 1845 in producing an edition of Hegel's *Works*.

In 1826 the *Manual* received its first Spanish translation. The translator, Félix Varela y Morales, a Cuban-American, had fled to the United States in 1823 from the restrictive regime imposed upon Cuba and all other Spanish colonies by Ferdinand VII, newly restored to the Spanish throne by the French army. It may well have been, indeed, that Varela's own ordeals under Ferdinand VII's harsh colonial deputies prompted his later special interest in Jefferson's democratic philosophy. At any rate, he turned to the *Manual* upon his arrival in America and brought out his translation of it three years later. Its title reads thus:

> Manual de Practica Parlamentaria, para el Uso del Senado de los Estados Unidos. Por Tomas Jefferson. Al cual se han agregado el Reglamento de Cada Camara y el Comun a Ambas. Traducido del Ingles y Anotado por Felix Varela. Nueva-York: Por Henrique Newton, *Calle de Chatham*, No. 157. 1826.[111]

From 1820 to 1824, the *Manual* was published in three separate small volumes, and all of them would have to be counted as reprints of Samuel Harrison Smith's first edition. In other words, they bear no evidence of having been influenced by Milligan's second edition, "with the last additions of the author." Their titles follow:

> A Manual of Parliamentary Practice. For the Use of the Senate of the United States. By Thomas Jefferson. To which is added, the Rules and Orders of the Senate and House of Representatives of the United States, and Joint Rules of the two Houses. Washington city, Printed by Davis & Force, 1820.

> A Manual of Parliamentary Practice, Composed originally for the Use of the Senate of the United States. By Thomas Jefferson. To which are added, the Rules and Orders of Both Houses of Congress. Washington: Gales & Seaton, 1822

> A Manual of Parliamentary Practice. Composed originally for the Use of the Senate of the United States. By Thomas Jefferson. To which are added, the Rules and Orders of Both Houses of Congress. Concord: G. Hough & J. B. Moore, 1823

Jefferson's parliamentary activities and studies ended in 1826, and thus this Introduction, so far as it aims to trace those two aspects of his career, must now also end. He died July 4, 1826, on the fiftieth anniversary of his immortal work, the Declaration of Independence. His countrymen, who recognized that work as the charter of their nation's liberties and as the very essence of their nation's claim to a high destiny in human affairs, remembered its important words as they mourned his death. Certainly they did not think then or later of the impor-

---

[111] For other details, see List of Editions of the *Manual*, s.v. Editions in other languages (1826).

tance of his writings in the field of parliamentary procedure. But those writings are important, too, and in particular, the *Manual*. In fact, the *Manual* stands in relation to the Declaration as an enabling act stands to a general policy which it is designed to carry out. For example, the Declaration states that governments owe their just powers to the consent of the governed, and the *Manual* bends its energies to create the means by which consent may be obtained without tyranny or coercion. The *Manual* may be said to install the political machinery that transforms into prosaic realities the lofty and happily phrased ideals of the Declaration. Without that machinery the memorable words of the latter might not have been able, even with the help of the Constitution, to give lasting health to the American political experiment.

From 1801 to the present time, the *Manual* has received at least 143 editions. Certainly there have been other editions that the present search did not locate. Some of the editions in our list originally appeared as single volumes. Many others have appeared in collections containing related documents, such volumes having been mainly authorized for publication at intervals of two or more years by the Senate or the House of Representatives. All together they have exerted wide influence. They have taught basic parliamentary law to generation after generation of newly elected Representatives and Senators. They have helped to encourage orderly procedure in the meetings of state legislatures, local councils, professional organizations, governing bodies of all sorts, and private assemblies. In their total effect these editions have immeasurably contributed to the education of all classes of citizens in the unspectacular but indispensable lessons that have to be mastered if democratic principles are to become successful democratic government.

One special instance of the crucial influence of the *Manual* upon the democratic process deserves mention. Perhaps it might not be presumptuous to suggest that this instance would have given particular pleasure to Jefferson, could he have foreseen it. It occurred in Manila during the period that followed the annexation of the Philippine Islands by the United States in 1898.

The inevitable result of that annexation was the beginning of agitation on the part of the Philippines for political independence. On August 16, 1907, the United States inaugurated the Philippine Assembly, and the Assembly became the arena of parliamentary debate, as parties formed themselves around the independence issue. Within that context a Spanish translation of Jefferson's *Manual* was published at Manila in 1909; and that work, under its short title, took its place as a supplementary guide of the Senate and the House of Representatives of the Congress of the Philippine Republic.[112] The final story of Jefferson's *Manual*, if it is ever written, may show happier coincidences than it encountered when it played its part in fostering Philippine independence and self-government, after having taught important lessons of self-government in its own country. But if happier coincidences occur, they will fall beyond the limits of any record thus far uncovered.

[112] See List of Editions of the *Manual*, s.v. Translations (1909).

PARLIAMENTARY
POCKET-BOOK

EDITOR'S INTRODUCTION

The Original Manuscript
and Its Provenance

The present edition of the Parliamentary Pocket-Book, the first ever printed, is based upon the only existing manuscript, now held by the Massachusetts Historical Society (MHi 41891).

That document consists of 105 pages containing 588 distinct paragraphs in the small, readable characters of TJ's normal handwriting. As a general rule, each paragraph was transcribed verbatim or partly transcribed and partly paraphrased by TJ from one or more of his many sources. The first 145 paragraphs are numbered in TJ's hand, each number being placed in the indentation at the beginning of the paragraph's first line. The present edition continues the sequential numbering but encloses the added numbers in square brackets. TJ may have started the practice when he was considering the possibility of depositing the Pocket-Book with the Senate at the end of his term, and he may have abandoned it after becoming convinced of the impracticality of that idea.[1]

In the wide margins next to his paragraphs TJ often wrote words or phrases to identify the subject matter that stood opposite. On many occasions he placed asterisks alongside paragraphs, as if to call special attention to their contents. Elsewhere he gave paragraphs marginal numbers that differed from the ones placed at their beginning. He infrequently raised bracketed questions or made bracketed statements within the text of paragraphs or in their margins. At times he underlined words or sentences within paragraphs or called special attention to a word by making its letters resemble print. On one occasion he noted in the margin of a paragraph a cross-reference to the *Manual* by saying, "turn to the book."[2] These features of the original manuscript are preserved in the present edition.

The Massachusetts Historical Society received the original manuscript on June 9, 1898, as a gift from Thomas Jefferson's great-grandson, Thomas Jefferson Coolidge, a successful Boston businessman and public servant. Coolidge's mother, Ellen Wayles Randolph Coolidge, had been the "particularly valued" granddaughter of TJ.[3] Her brother, Colonel Thomas Jefferson Randolph, was the legatee of TJ's papers. Henry Randall, biographer of TJ, gives the following account of the manuscript:

> This original common-place book, entitled "Parliamentary Pocket Book" is before us, a leather bound duodecimo, one hundred and five pages of which, in a hand as compact as ordinary print, are covered with references. It takes a considerably wider range than the Manual which he codified from it while President of the Senate, because it traces down the parliamentary law from its origin, and therefore includes considerable that was obsolete, or which, being especially applicable to the English system of government, was not so to ours.[4]

[1] See p. 341.
[2] Par. [493].   [3] Malone, *Jefferson*, vi, 459.
[4] Randall, *Life of Jefferson*, ii, 356.

Earlier in his biography, Randall adds some details about the discovery of the manuscript:

> During a visit made to Edgehill by us in 1851, Colonel Thomas J. Randolph—Mr. Jefferson's oldest grandson, and the legatee of his *papers*, discovered in a long unthought-of receptacle, a pile of old books in manuscript, a part of which neither he nor any member of his family had any recollection of ever having seen before.[5]

The lucky discovery of those old books, among them, the Pocket-Book, explains how the manuscript would naturally have passed from Thomas J. Randolph to his sister Ellen and then to the Massachusetts Historical Society. Randall's brief outline of the contents of the manuscript did little to indicate its actual nature or its important place in TJ's parliamentary career, but Randall's words may have led TJ's great-grandson to see that the manuscript must be preserved for posterity. It has not received attention, however, in previous editions of TJ's collected works.

Title

The words "Parliamentary Pocket-Book," written in TJ's careful hand, are featured on a page of their own, as if TJ intended them to constitute the title page of the "leather bound duodecimo" deposited among his papers.

That particular title had not always been used by TJ to describe his compilation. In February 1800 he referred to the manuscript as "This common-place," adding that, in the course of discharging his duties as presiding officer of the Senate, the document thus casually mentioned "has been my pillar."[6] At the same time, he announced that he was beginning to think seriously of preparing a manuscript on parliamentary procedure for deposit with the Senate for future guidance when his term as Vice President had ended, and that he intended the document to be "a manual of Parliamentary law." There can be no doubt, of course, that those future plans were ultimately to produce what we now know as the *Manual of Parliamentary Practice*. But why did TJ come to give his "common-place" the title that it now possesses in its original manuscript?

That title may have been suggested to TJ from his contact in Paris days with François Soulés. Soulés and TJ exchanged letters in 1789 on parliamentary law, and Soulés mentioned on that occasion his having recently published a book with the bilingual title *Le Vade-Mecum parlementaire, ou The Parliamentary Pocket-Book*.[7] It could be that Soulés' title later came to TJ's mind as a most appropriate name for his own "common-place" when he decided to have it bound in leather for preservation among his personal records.

The first edition of TJ's *Manual* was of pocket size, and he himself may have influenced its publisher to give it that form.[8] Moreover, when Milligan was engaged in bringing out the authentic second edition, TJ laid considerable emphasis upon its not being an octavo but a smaller volume suitable for being carried in the pocket of a senator or representative.[9] TJ's recollection of Soulés' title

[5] Ibid., I, 16, n. 1.   [6] TJ to George Wythe, 28 Feb. 1800.
[7] See above, TJ's Parliamentary Studies, Activities, and Writings, p. 7.
[8] Ibid., p. 32.
[9] Ibid.

would have coincided neatly with his idea of the form he wanted for his own parliamentary writings, a "pocket-book."

Dates and Major Sources

The 588 paragraphs of the Pocket-Book were compiled by TJ between the late 1760s and the earlier 1800s. Those dates are conclusively established by his letters, one to George Wythe on February 28, 1800, and another on January 7, 1812, to Joseph Milligan.[10] Thus the preparation of the Pocket-Book occupied him at intervals from his student days in George Wythe's law office to his years of retirement at Monticello after his two terms as President.

As for individual sequences of paragraphs, some could have been compiled almost at the beginning, or at some early stage, of TJ's parliamentary studies. The *Lex Parliamentaria*, which TJ considered the best book for "parliamentary knowledge," was published in 1748. Indeed, it contributed more paragraphs to the Pocket-Book than did any other source.[11] In a letter dated from London on October 2, 1769, a bookseller sent an invoice to TJ for books he had ordered, and one of those books was Hakewill's *Modus tenendi Parliamentum*.[12] Hakewill's *Modus* stands in third place among the sources of the Pocket-Book in respect to the number of paragraphs it contributed. It is highly probable that TJ's parliamentary studies began with Hakewill's *Modus* and the *Lex Parliamentaria*, both of which were esteemed authorities, and both of which, moreover, through their citation of earlier works, would have led him to still other classics in the law of parliaments.

Second among the sources of TJ's Pocket-Book was a later, but more important treatise than the two just mentioned. This is Hatsell's *Precedents of Proceedings*. The second edition of that work appeared in three volumes at London in 1785, and TJ ordered and received a copy four years later.[13] When it became evident after the elections of 1796 that, as Vice President to John Adams, he would be presiding over the Senate during the next administration, TJ would have devoted himself to Hatsell with special care. Hatsell's work supplied more paragraphs to TJ's compilation than did any treatise except the *Lex Parliamentaria*—the first three volumes of Hatsell, that is. His fourth volume contributed much less.[14]

Two other portions of the Pocket-Book would in all likelihood have been compiled in the late 1790s under compulsions similar to those which made TJ's reading of Hatsell expedient. Paragraph [442], which records the twenty-eight rules for conducting business in the Senate, is based upon actions taken in that body on April 16, 1789, and on subsequent legislative days in that and later sessions of Congress.[15] The mastery of these rules would certainly have been regarded by TJ as essential to his preparation for presiding over the Senate, and his transcription of them in the Pocket-Book could accordingly have occurred in late 1796. A somewhat later date could be assigned to TJ's transcription of the passages that he entered into the Pocket-Book from Wooddeson's *Laws of Eng-*

---

[10] For details, see ibid., p. 3, 17-19, 34.
[11] Ibid., p. 8; also *Papers*, XVI, 449.
[12] Ibid., p. 5; also *Papers*, I, 33-4.
[13] Ibid., p. 6; also *Papers*, XIV, 511-12.
[14] Ibid., p. 32.   [15] See text of par. [442] and n. 1 thereon.

land. Those passages deal with the procedures of impeachment in the British Parliament, and it would seem logical to assume that they were transcribed in the late months of 1797, when action to impeach William Blount was looming in the Senate, and that body was studying ways in which such sensitive processes were to be conducted.[16] But aside from the paragraphs from Wooddeson, from Senate records, from Hatsell, and from Hakewill, the Pocket-Book could for the most part have been compiled at almost any time between 1766, or thereabouts, and 1812. Common sense might suggest that TJ's transcriptions from Coke's *Institutes,* Bracton's *De legibus,* Brooke's *La Graunde Abridgement,* Scobell's *Memorials,* Fitzherbert's *Natura Brevium,* Hengham's *Registrum Brevium,* Plowden's *Commentaries,* Rastell's *Liber assisarum,* and Sadler's *Rights,* seem closer to his earliest law studies than do many of the other works cited in the Pocket-Book, but there is no sure way of dating his actual transcriptions from them or from lesser sources not mentioned above.[17]

Main Subjects

The 588 paragraphs of the Pocket-Book are divided almost equally between two subjects, one of which concerns procedural matters incidental to the orderly conduct of a parliamentary assembly, and the other, constitutional matters that grew out of the confrontations between the British House of Commons and its rival centers of political power. Some paragraphs mix elements of these two subjects, but if we classify them by their predominant characteristics, we may say that procedural matters are represented by 286 paragraphs, and constitutional matters by 302.

The procedural paragraphs deal with such topics as these: voting practices in the two Houses; priorities among motions and among matters of business; procedures in the reading of bills; procedures in introducing, discussing, amending, and disposing of enactments; observances followed in breaking tie votes in each House of Parliament; uses of the call for the previous question; observance of the law of majority rule; regulations regarding quorums in committees; stipulations governing conduct during debates, courtesy toward members, propriety in dress; practices in choosing Speakers, and in following the Speaker's lead in discussing bills; actions on questions of adjournment; and so on.

As for the 302 paragraphs dealing with constitutional subjects, they are given a precise orientation at the very beginning of the Pocket-Book. The first paragraph reads:

> The three estates are. 1. the King. 2. the Lords. 3. the Commons. And the second estate includes the lords Spiritual as well as temporal, not as Spiritual persons, but by reason of the Temporal baronies annexed to their bishopricks. Parliaments may be held and have been excluso clero; agreed Trin. 7. H. 8. by all the judges of England: Lex Parliamentria. c. 1. Sadler's rights pa 79 to 93. Kelw. rep. 184. Stamf. P. C. 153. Bro. Par. 107. Hakew. 85.[18]

[16] For details, see p. 11-13.
[17] For a complete list of the sources cited by TJ in the Pocket-Book and *Manual,* see Jefferson's Abbreviations in the Guide to Editorial Apparatus.
[18] For an explanation of these references, see Editor's Notes, par. 1.

In its long history the British constitutional system worked by means of the interaction of these three estates, considered as the ascendant political powers. At first the House of Commons was an unimportant force under arbitrary kings and domineering nobles, but it gathered more and more authority as time went on, until it became ascendant, and its rivals in their turn unimportant. British constitutional history is the account of a gradual revolution in governmental affairs from a despotic to a democratic form—from the ascendancy of the king and nobles to the ascendancy of the Commons. TJ has often been called a revolutionary, and so indeed he was. But the American Revolution, which he did so much to support, and for which he expressed the immortal justification, was in fact anticipated by what had happened in Britain between the reign of King John and that of George III, or between Magna Carta and the Declaration of Independence. What the Commons did in those centuries in relation to the king and the nobles—that was one of TJ's major interests as he compiled his Pocket-Book; and that interest gave the Pocket-Book a philosophical import not often found in books devoted to parliamentary rules of order.

Editorial Procedures

The present edition of the Parliamentary Pocket-Book follows TJ's manuscript in an exact transcription, word for word, abbreviation for abbreviation, punctuation mark for punctuation mark, marginal note for marginal note. There are only three departures from a uniform adherence to this rule: a capital letter introduces each sentence in each paragraph of TJ's written text—a practice that TJ followed only now and then; "And" is substituted for an ampersand whenever an ampersand begins a sentence. TJ indicated contractions of words by placing a wavering line above letters he omitted. These lines are not retained in this edition, but are rendered periods after the words concerned in modern fashion. With these three exceptions differences between text and manuscript must be counted inadvertent errors on the part of the present editor, and he has endeavored to make them minimal, even if his care and patience may not have succeeded in eliminating them to the extent of his hopes.

In the Pocket-Book, and in the *Manual* as well, TJ often abbreviated authors' names and the titles of his sources. An alphabetical list of TJ's abbreviations appears in the front matter of this volume. The list also contains abbreviations borrowed by TJ from the source that he was quoting. For example, the opening paragraph of the Pocket-Book, quoted above, lists *Lex Parliamentaria* c. 1. as its first source. With one exception, that first source supplied TJ with the other titles or authors cited, and with the page or section numbers indicated for each. TJ's main source sometimes provided him with a reference which turns out to be incorrect, usually in a minor way—the *Lex Parliamentaria* affords several examples. These are corrected in the notes to the present edition whenever possible.

TJ sometimes added a source to the ones listed by his main authority. Paragraph 1 also affords an example of this. TJ's reference to "Hakew. 85." was not taken from Chapter 1 of *Lex Parliamentaria*. The indicated page in Hakewill lends support to what *Lex Parliamentaria* had been saying—that valid acts of parliament could be passed without the consent of the lords spiritual. TJ hence shows a scholar's interest in reaching beyond one authority for support from another, as some particular need may have suggested. Whenever this occurs, the present edition endeavors to point it out.

On occasion TJ wrote words or phrases into a paragraph and then crossed them out. The present edition prints the deleted material in italics, so far as it can be deciphered, and encloses it within angle brackets. The first example of this practice occurs in the third paragraph, where TJ was summarizing what the *Lex Parliamentaria* said about the court system that prevailed in Anglo-Saxon Britain. After recording that the Saxon government was arranged so as to provide the possibility of successive appeals from lesser courts to courts of greater and greater authority, TJ started a new sentence in such a way as to suggest that the course of such appeals began with the county courts. But even as he wrote these words, he realized that the simplest courts were those of the manors and tythings, and that an appeal, once originating in them, could then pass onward to the wapentakes or hundred courts before reaching the county courts or folkmotes. Hence TJ canceled out his original words and substituted for them a reference to the earlier links in the chain of appeals.

The manuscript frequently contains inserted abbreviations, words, or phrases. In the first paragraph, for example, "the" is inserted in the gap between "of" and "Temporal baronies." Thus too in the second paragraph, having inserted a caret between "to give" and "a right," TJ placed the phrase "to towns" above. And in referring almost at once to a statute passed in a parliamentary session spanning the thirty-fourth and thirty-fifth years of the reign of Henry VIII, TJ inserted a caret after "H.8." and wrote "c. 13." above to identify the statute as chapter 13 of that session. These interlineations are interesting, as they indicate TJ's concern for accuracy in the transcription of his source; but they are silently dropped into place in the present edition, on the theory that their physical position in the manuscript does not deserve special treatment. In some exceptional cases a footnote discusses the significance of an interlineation qua interlineation.

PARLIAMENTARY POCKET-BOOK

three estates.

1. The three estates are. 1. the King. 2. the Lords. 3. the Commons. And the second estate includes the lords Spiritual as well as temporal, not as Spiritual persons, but by reason of the Temporal baronies annexed to their bishopricks.[1] Parliaments may be held & have been excluso clero; agreed Trin.7. H.8.[2] by all the judges of England: Lex. Parliamentaria. c.1. Sadler's rights pa 79 to 93. Kelw. rep. 184. Stamf. P.C. 153. Bro. Par. 107. Hakew. 85.[3]

members for new boroughs rejected

2. It had been usual for the kings of England by their charters to give to towns a right of sending members to parliament.[1] Writ temp. Car.2.[2] the commons declared the elections void which were made by that prince's charters. By a stat. 34.35.H.8. c.13.[3] Chester was enabled to send members to parliament. The like right was given to Durham by stat.25. Car.2. c.9. The present number of the house of commons is 558.L.Parl. c.1. Spelm. voce 'Major.'[4]

Wittenagemote courts Saxon.

3. In the Saxon government there was an appeal from the lesser assemblies of the people to the greater.⟨Thus their County courts⟩[1] Thus there was an appeal from the courts of manors & Tythings[2] to the Wapentakes or Hundred courts. from these again to the Folkmotes or County cts. and from these to the Witenagemote[3] or Parliament. And all of these assemblies were held twice a year on stated days, so that there was no occasion for any Summons to them. The inferior courts were held about the end of September for electing their magistrates and officers, and about the end of March for the distribution of justice. So that all was over before the Witenagemote which by an express law commenced the first on the calends of October for constituting the Aldermen, Earls, Lord Lieutenants of the counties and other great officers; and the other

about the Calends of May for the distribution of justice. Wilk. LL. Sax. Lamb Arch. Spelm. 540. Mirr. c.5. s.1. Sadler. 50. Wilk. LL. Sax. 205. c.2. Spelm. glos. verb. 'manor' 'turnus' 'comitatus.' Law Edw. Conf. 32d Wilk. 205. c.1. Lex. Parl. c.1. pa.19.20.21.22. See post. 5.[4]

Officers Saxon elected & deprived.

4. Among the Saxons no officer Civil, Military or Ecclesiastical could be appointed without the free election of those over whom he was to preside. This election seems in some instances at least to have been subject to the confirmation of the King. Spelm. Glos. verb. 'Vicecom.' Sax. Chron. anno 1064. LL. Inae. c.8.36. LL. Edgari c.3. LL. Canuti c.13. 14.[1] Atk' power of parl. 32.[2] Lex. Parl. c.1. p.22.23. ⟨that⟩[3] Bishops were elected by the people even after the conquest. Sadler's rights of the kingdom. p.1178.133.134.140. And these officers were subject to deprivation and censure in their folkmotes & other conventions. Lex. Parl. c.1. p.25. Peace and war also were made by common consent of the people either in person or by their representatives. L. Parl. c.1. p.28. William the conqueror took upon himself the nomination of all officers. L. Parl. c.1. p.34. post 6.[4]

Parliaments ordinary and extraordinary

5. On the return of Robert, eldest son of W.1. from the holy land Henry 1. who had ascended the throne called a parliament. The words of the historian are 'Magnatibus EDICTO REGIO convocatis'[1] M. Par. p.42. This was one of those *extraordinary* parliaments called to consult 'de arduis negotiis regni'[2] and not one of those *ordinary* stated parliaments which were held twice yearly. These ordinary parliaments were reduced afterwards to one yearly by divers statutes. viz. 36. E.3. c.10. St.4. E.3. c.14. 4. Inst. 9. And they were to meet then certainly, or oftener if called by special Summons. L. Parl. c.1. p.39.[3] ante. 3.[4] And 16. Car.2. c.1. declares these statutes in force.[5]

Charter. Magna charta.

6. H.1. on the invasion of his brother Robert having called a parliament, promised them in these words 'Scripta subarata, si provediritis,[1] roborare, et iteratis juramentis confirmare, omnia videlicet

[48]

quae sanctus rex Edvardus sancivit.'² The charter granted on this promise was probably the one produced to k. John at Runny-mede, and not the one which Henry had granted at his coronation which had a restriction, viz 'lagam regis Edvardi vobis reddo *cum illis emendationibus quibus pater meus emendavit*'³ This is presumeable because it appears from history that for some years after the granting this new Charter by H.1. the people were restored generally to their right of chusing their magistrates and officers civil, military & ecclesiastical. Mat. Par. 167. 38.⁴ L. Parl. c.1. p.41.42. ante. 4. See several instances of the exercise of this right in chusing Bishops in England Scotland Ireland & France from ann. 1113. downwards. L. parl. c.1. p.44.45. The people originally chose Conservators of the peace who became out of date by the introduction of justices of the peace who are appointed by the king. This was brought about by stat. E.3. while that king was a minor & the queen and Mortimer ruled. all. Lamb. Just. 16.19.20.147. L. parl. c.1. p.47.⁵

officers elective.

Peace Conservators

Justices.

Parliamt. how to begin.

7. At the return of the writs the parliament cannot begin but by the presence of the king in person or by representation. 4 Inst. 6. L. Parl. c.2. p.55.¹ Hakew. 66.²

a Session, what?
*

8.a. When a parl. is called & doth sit and is dissolved without any act of parl. passed or judgment given it is no session of parl. but a convention. 4. Inst. 28. L. parl. c.2. p.55.¹

Parl. not subject to rules of Com. law.
*

8.b. Matters of parl. are not to be ruled by the Common law. 4. inst. 17. L. parl. c.2. p.56. Nor doth it belong to the judges to judge of any law, custom or privilege of parl. 1. inst. 50. L. parl. 56.¹

but one house of Parliament.

9. It is generally believed that the whole parl. sat together in one house before E.3. time, and the separation was at the desire of the commons. 1. Ro. rep. 18. L. parl. c.2. p.60.¹

*

10. What is done by either house according to the law and usage of parl. is in the judgment of the law the act of the whole parl. The house of Lords cannot exercise any power as an house of parl. or as

a court for error without the house of commons be in being at the same time. Both houses must be prorogued & dissolved together.[1] Atk. arg. 14.34.41.51.55.[2] L. parl. 57.61. c.2.

errors of parl.
how corrected.
*

11. The law has provided but one way to correct the errors of parl. that is by a subsequent parl. who may do it.[1] Atk. arg. 60.[2] L. parl. 62. Bro. parl. 16.[3]

12. A parliamt. may be holden at any place the king shall assign; but it ought not to {depart / be dissolved} as long as any bill remains undiscussed, and proclamation must be made in the parliamt. that if any person have any petition, he shall come in and be heard, and if no answer be given it is intended the public are satisfied.[1] Lex Constitution. 157.[2] Jac's L. D. by Ruffhead. voce parliamt. Mod. ten. parl. 28. 30. 4. Inst. 11.[3]

session, what.

13. ⟨When⟩ If a parliamt. is assembled & orders made and writs of error brought in the house of peers, & several bills agreed on, but none signed; this is but a Convention & no parliamt. or sessions of parl. But every session in which the king signs a bill is a parliamt., and so every parliamt. is a session.[1] Jac's L. D. by Ruffhead. voce. parliamt. 1 Ro. rep. 29. Hutt. 61.[2]

orders of parl.
when determd.
*

14. All *orders* of parliamt. determine by prorogation; and one taken by order of the parliamt., may after their prorogation, ⟨may⟩ be discharged on an habeas corpus, as well as after a dissolution: but the dissolution of a parliamt. doth not alter the state of impeachments brought up by the Commons in a preceding parliamt. Raym. 120. Jac's L. D. by Ruffh. Parl. And it hath been resolved that cases of appeals and writs of error, shall continue and are to be proceeded in statu quo &c as they stood at the dissolution of the last parl. Raym. 381. Ruffh's Jac's L. D. parl.[1] On return of a hab. corp. that the party was taken by order of the house of lords for a contempt, the house being now prorogued, per curiam their orders are all at an end & every other thing before them except writs of error & scire facias's upon them. 1. Lev. 165. Prichard's case.[2]

three estates. 1. The three estates are. 1. the King. 2. the Lords. 3. the Commons. & the second estates includes the lords Spiritual as well as temporal, not as Spiritual persons, but, by reason of their Temporal baronies annexed to their bishopricks. parliaments may be held & have been excluso clero; agreed Trin. 7. H.8. by all the judges of England. Lex. Parliamentaria. c.1. Sadler's rights pa.79 &g. Kelw.rep.184. Stamf.P.C.153. Pro.Par.107. Hakew.85.

members for new boroughs rejected
2. it had been usual for the kings of England by their charters to give to towns a right of vending members to parliament. 1mt temp. Car.2. the commons declared the elections void which were made by that prince's charters. by a stat. 34.35. H.8. c.13. Chester was enabled to vend members to parliament. the like right was given to Durham by stat. 25. Car. 2.c.9. the present number of the house of commons is 558. 2. Parl. c.1. Spelm. voce "Major".

Wittenagemote
3. in the Saxon government there was an appeal from the lesser assemblies of the people to the greater. there their county courts there

courts Saxon.
there was an appeal from the courts of manors & Tythings to the Wapentakes or Hundred courts from these again to the Folkmotes or County c.ts and from these to the Witenagemote or Parliament and all of these assemblies were held twice a year on stated days, so that there was no occasion for any Summons to them. the inferior courts were held about the end of September for electing their magistrates and officers, and about the end of March for the distribution of justice. so

affairs, & if there be cause, to resume the chair. Rush.
3. p. v. 1. p. 42. this day (20. Nov. 1640) the house ordered
the Speaker to sit in the afternoon. ib. 53. the Speaker
is the mouth, eyes, & ears of the house. hence when king
Charles I. commanded the speaker to discover certain
transactions, he justly replied that he had neither
eyes to see, ears to hear, nor mouth to speak, but as the
house should direct him. L. parl. c. 14.

    145. the Litany is read the first thing after the Spea-
-ker is set in the chair. 13. Eliz. 1571. Towns. 54.

memb. to sit.   when the Speaker is set in his chair, every member is
to sit in his place with his head covered. Scobel. 6.

not to pass between
nor to cross &c.   No member in coming into the house, or in removing
from his place, is to pass between the Speaker, & the member
then speaking; nor may cross or go overthwart the
house, or pass from one side to the other while the house
is sitting. Scobel. 6.

departure.   Mr Speaker & the residue of the house of the better sort
of calling alway at the rising of the house to depart, and
come forth in comely & civil sort, for the reverence of the
house, in turning about with a low courtesie, as they make
at their coming into the house, and not unseemly to thrust
& throng out. D'Ewes. 282. Col. 2.

covering.   no member is to come into the house with his head co-
-vered, nor to remove from one place to another with his hat
on, nor is to put on his hat in coming in, or removing, un-
-til he be set down in his place. Scobel. 6.

spurs.   none to enter the house with his spurs on; nor until
he prays the Serjeants fees. 39. Eliz. Town. 101.

whispering.   while the house is sitting, no man ought to speak or
whisper to another, to the end the house may not be interrup
-ted, when any are speaking; but every one is to attend unto what
is spoken. Scobel. 6. D'Ewes 487. Col. 1.

person speaking.   when any member intends to speak, he is to stand up
in his place uncovered, address himself to the Speaker; who
usually calls such person by his name "that the house may"

Parliamentary Pocket-Book: page with last numbered paragraph

A MANUAL

OF

PARLIAMENTARY PRACTICE.

FOR THE USE

OF THE

SENATE OF THE *UNITED STATES.*

BY THOMAS JEFFERSON.

WASHINGTON CITY.

PRINTED BY SAMUEL HARRISON SMITH.

MDCCCI.

Manual of Parliamentary Practice: title page, 1801 edition

A MANUAL

OF

PARLIAMENTARY PRACTICE:

FOR THE

USE OF THE SENATE

OF THE

UNITED STATES.

BY THOMAS JEFFERSON.

SECOND EDITION,

WITH THE LAST ADDITIONS OF THE AUTHOR.

GEORGE TOWN:

PUBLISHED BY JOSEPH MILLIGAN; AND BY
WILLIAM COOPER, WASHINGTON.

1812.

Manual of Parliamentary Practice: title page, 1812 edition

when a law
expires.

15. An act was to continue in force 3. years. and thence to the end of the next session of parl. Per curiam by the 'next session' the stat. intends the session which *begins* next after the expiration of the three years, and not one which, having begun during the three years, finishes after them. 1. Lev. 265. Man v. Cooper.[1]

3. estates.

16. The parl. consists of the king and of the three estates, viz. 1. the Lords spiritual in number 24. who sit in respect of their baronies. 2. the Lords temporal, in number 106. & 3. the Commons, in number 493. Of this court the king is caput, principium et finis. 4. Inst. 1. 3.[1]

Commons. who.

17. COMMONS, are in legal understanding taken for the frank tenants or freeholders of the counties. Thus in 28. E.3. c.6. it is provided that the coroners of counties shall be chosen in full county per les COMMONS de mesme les counties.[1] Regist. 177. F.N.B. 164.k. Pl. R. 232. Stanf. Pl. C.49.[2] 4. Inst. 2.[3]

when 2. houses.

18. Of antient times both houses sat together. Ld. Coke thinks they sat together 21.E.3. because to letters written to the pope the Common seal of England was put for the king et pro totâ *Communtate* regni [but qu. whether 'communitas' may not signify the 'community' as it does classically, & so include Lords & Commons; as well as 'Commonalty' which confines it to the Commons alone][1] whereas sais he if the Commons had had a SPEAKER at that time they would have appointed him to seal for them, as they did to an act of parl. 8.H.4. concerning the succession of the crown whereunto all the Lords severally sealed, and the Speaker in the name of the commons put to his seal. The Commons had no continual Speaker antiently, but after consultation had, they agreed upon some one or more of them that had greatest aptitude for the present business to deliver their resolution.[2] And. he thinks that on the separation of the two houses they for the first time chose a continual Speaker. 4. Inst. 2.[3]

peers how called

19. All the judges of the realm, barons of the Exchequer of the Coif,[1] the king's learned counsel &

the Civilians masters of the chancery are called by writ to attend in the house of lords 'super praemissis tracturi vestrumque consilium impensuri.'[2] But they have no vote. 4. Inst. 4.[3]

what a
dissolution.

20.a. It is enacted by 8.H.5 c.1., that if the king being beyond seas cause a parl. to be summoned by writ under the teste[1] of his Lieutenant, and afterwards the king arriveth in the realm, the parl. is not dissolved but shall proceed without New Summons. Quod nota, quia in praesentia majoris cessat potestas minoris.[2] 4. Inst. 7.[3]

Prorogation,
how.
4

20.b. When the parl. is not to begin at the return of the writ there must be a writ patent under the whole great seal reciting the summons & PROROGUING it to a certain day, which writ of prorogation being read in the upper house before certain of the Lords & Commons there assembled, the parl. is prorogued. 4. Inst. 7.[1]

opening of parl

21. The king or Chancellor most commonly (tho' any other person by his appointment & even in his presence may) declare the causes of calling the parl. to the Lords & commons. 4. Inst. 7.[1]

who chuse
Speaker.

22. The Commons have a right to chuse their Speaker;[1] yet seeing that the king may refuse him, the use is for the king to name (as in the Congé d'eslire in the bishop[2]) & the Commons to elect him; but without their election no Speaker can be appointed for them, because he is their mouth & trusted by them & so necessary that they cannot sit without him. Grievous sickness is good cause for removing a Speaker & chusing another. But it is no cause for removing a Burgess or Knight. Seymour. fol. 75. Hale parl. 116.[3] So note the diversity. For want of attending to this an erroneous opinion was begotten 38.H.8. Bro. Parl. 7. in which case a Burgess was discharged for sickness and a writ issued to elect another, who was received by the Commons.[4] The SPEAKER when chosen standing *in his place* [not in the chair][5] disables himself to undergo so weighty a charge & desires the house to proceed to a new choice. Which being denied, he is led to the chair by two members where being set ⟨*in the chair & then*⟩[6] he prayeth

162.

*

them to give him leave to disable himself to the king in the Lords' house. The Commons being called into the Lords' house, the Speaker is brought between two of them with low obeisance to the bar & presented to the king,[7] where after he hath disabled himself to speak before the king & for the whole body of the realm, and made humble suit to the k lest by his insufficiency the business of the realm may be hindred to be discharged & a more sufficient man to be chosen: if he be allowed by his majesty, then he maketh a protestation consisting on three parts: 1. that the Commons in this parliament may have free speech, as of right & by custom they have used. & all their antient & just privileges and liberties allowed to them. 2. that in any thing he shall deliver in the name of the Commons (if he shall commit any error) no fault may be arrected[8] to the Commons, and that he may resort again to the Commons for declaration of their true intent, & that his error may be pardoned. 3. that as often as necessity for his majesty's service & the good of the commonwealth shall require, he may by the direction of the house of Commons have access to his royal person.[9] This is in the Parl. rolls called a Protestation in respect of the first part, that the house of Commons be not concluded to speak only of those things which the k. or L. Chanc. delivers, but in a parliamentary course of all other arduous & urgent business. 4. Inst. 8. After return to their house he prays the Commons to assist him & promises all diligence. ib. 10.

freedom of speech. *

23. By 4.H.8. all suits, accusements, punishments &c. to be had on any member for any bill, speaking, reasoning or declaring of any matter or matters concerning the parliament to be communed or treated of, be utterly void. And this clause of the act is declaratory of the antient law and custom of parl. 4. Inst. 9.[1]

Committees.

24. The Commons being the general inquisitors of the realm appoint COMMITTEES of Grievances, of Courts of justice, of Privileges, and of advancement of trade; who when they meet, elect one of themselves to sit in the chair. They examine & vote the

qestions, and by one whom they appoint, their resolution is reported to the house. 4. Inst. 11.[1]

Proxy.

25. A Lord of parl. by license of the k. upon just cause of absence may make a proxy: but at this day he must do it to a Lord or Lords of parl. But a knight or Burgess cannot make a Proxy, because he is elected & trusted by multitudes. 4. Inst. 12. By the Lord's coming and sitting in parl. his proxy is revoked. ib. 13.[1]

freedom of parl.

26. By the antient law of parl. proclamation was made at the beginning of the parl. that no man upon pain to lose all that he hath, should during the parl. in London, Westminster or the suburbs &c wear any privy coat of plate, or go armed, or that games, pastimes, or strange shews should be used there during the parl. ib. 14.[1]

consult constituents 47.b.

27. It is the law & custom of parl. when any NEW DEVICE[1] is moved on the k's behalf, the Commons may answer that they tender[2] the k's estate and are ready to aid the same, only in this new device they dare not agree without CONFERENCE WITH THEIR COUNTIES: which shews that such conference is warrantable by the law & custom of parl. 4. inst. 14.34.[3]

representative ** 47.b.

28. Tho' one be chosen for one particular county yet when he is returned & sits in parl. he serveth for the whole realm. 4. inst. 14.[1]

law of Parl. 48 *

29. As every court hath laws & customs for it's direction,[1] some by the common law, some by the civil &c. so the high court of parl. suis propriis legibus et consuetudinibus subsistit.[2] It is lex & consuetudo parliamenti that all matters in parl. moved concerning the peers of the realm or commons in parl. assembled, ought to be determined by the course of the parl. & not by the Civil or Common law of this realm used in more inferior courts. And this is the reason that judges ought not to give any opinion of a matter of parl. because it is not to be decided by the Com. law but secundum legem et consuetudinem parliamenti. And some hold that every offence committed in any court punishable by that court, is punishable in the same, or some higher court only. And the court of parl. hath none

higher. In the 3.E.3.19. the bp. of Winton[3] was proceeded against in B.R.[4] by the Atty. Gen. for having absented himself from parl. without leave. To which he pleaded that he ought to be corrected in parliament & not elsewhere in a lesser court, and so concluded against the jurisdiction. Which plea after divers days given did stand & was never over-ruled. In the 1. & 2. Ph. & Mar.[5] informations were preferred in K.B.[6] by the Atty. Gen. against 39. of the house of commons for departing from parl. without license. 6. timorous Burgesses submitted to their fines. Edmd Plowden pleaded constant attendance & was acquitted. And nothing was ever done with the others.[7] 4. Inst. 15.-20.

notice of proceedings 49

30. The king cannot take notice of any thing said or done in the house of Commons, but by the report of the house. 4. inst. 15.[1]

31. Every member of the house of Commons[1] hath a judicial place, & can be no witness. 4. inst. 15.[1]

32. A privy counsellor is by his oath & the custom of the realm a privy counsellor for the life of the king who hath made choice of him, without any patent or grant. 4. Inst. 54.[1]

court of record *
6.H. comm.
act of recd.

mayor of Westbury

Long. Hall.

Muncton.*

33. The Lords in their house have power of judicature, the Commons in their house have power of judicature, & both houses together have power of judicature.[1] The book of the clerk of the house of Commons is a RECORD, as is affirmed by act of parl. 6.H.8. c.16. In the 8.El. the Maior of Westbury fined & imprisoned by the H. Com. for receiving a bribe to elect Long, & Long removed.[2] Hall a member of the H. Com. for discovering the conferences of the house & writing a book to it's dishonor, was by the House committed to the tower for 6. months, fined 500. marks, & expelled the house.[3] Muncton struck Johnson a burgess.[4] Resolved that every man must take notice of all the members of the house returned of record at his peril:[5] but otherwise of the servant of a member, for there he that strikes must have notice.[6] Munction sent to the tower. 8.H.6. If any Lord of parl. have committed any oppression, bribery, extortion or

the like, the H. Com. being the general inquisitors of the realm may examine the same, & if they find the charge true, may transmit the same to the Lords with the witnesses and proofs.[7] 4. Inst. 23.24.

34. A member of parl. has privilege not only for his servants but his goods.[1] In the 18.E.1. the prior of the holy trinity fined & imprisoned for serving the E. Cornwall during the parl. with a citation to appear before the archbp. of Cant. & also the person at whose suit he was cited.[2] And yet the serving the sd.[3] citation did not arrest the body or restrain. Same privilege in case of a spa.[4] or other process out of Chancery.[5] In the 8.E.2. the k. sent to the justices etc. not to proceed in their assises where those summoned to parl. were parties.[6] And generally privilege of parl. holdeth unless it be in treason, felony, or breach of the peace. 4. inst. 24.25.

35. All acts of parl must have the consent of the king Lords & commons: & whatsoever passeth in parl. with this threefold consent, hath the force of an act of parl.[1] The difference between an ACT and an ORDINANCE is that the ordinance wanteth the threefold consent and is ordained by one or two of them. In the 13.H.4.[2] there was a restitution of blood and estate[3] to Will. de Lasenby, by the king, Lords spiritual & Commons. This is but an ordinance. And when the clergy is omitted & the act made by the king, Lords temporal & Commons. All acts of parl. relate to the first day of the parl. if it be not otherwise provided by the act. 4. inst. 25.

36. Before printing was brought into England, it was usual for a copy of the stats passed at every. session to be sent to each sheriff[1] with the k's writ[2] commanding him to publish them at his court & see that they were observed. Yet this was not necessary to give them force: for as soon as the parl. hath done any thing the law intends that every person hath notice of it, for the parl. represents the body of the whole realm. It is convenient indeed

that the subjects should have express notice thereof & not be overtaken by an intendment in law. 4. Inst. 26. Bro. parl. 26.[3]

Session, what.
*

37. The passing of any bill or bills by giving the royal assent thereunto,[1] or the giving any judgment in parl. doth not make [i.e. end][2] a session, but the session doth continue until it be prorogued or dissolved. And produces[3] many instances of the parl. continuing to sit after some of it's acts had received the royal assent. By a prorogation there is a session, & then such bills as passed in either house & had no royal assent to them, must at the next assembly begin again. Every several session of parl. is in law a several parl. but if it be but adjourned or continued, then there is no session, and consequently all things continue still in the same state they were in before the adjournment or continuance. In the 18.R.2. a judgmt. given in the king's bench was reversed, but no act of parl. passed. But it is no question but it was a session of parl. for otherwise the judgmt. should be of no force: and many times judgments given in parl. have been executed, the parl. sitting, before any bill passed. 4. inst. 27.28. Hutton 61. Bro. abr. tit. parl. 86.[4]

Prorogation, how. *

38. The house of Commons is to many purposes a distinct court,[1] and therefore is not prorogued or adjourned by the prorogation or adjournment of the Lord's house:[2] but the Speaker upon signification of the k's pleasure by the assent of the house of Com. doth say this court doth prorogue or adjourn itself, & then it is prorogued or adjourned, and not before. But when it is dissolved they are sent for to the higher house & there the Lord Keeper dissolveth the parl. & then it is dissolved & not before. And the k. at the time of the dissolution ought to be there in person or by representation: so it cannot end or be dissolved without his presence either in person or by representation. Unumquodq. dissolvitur eo ligamine quo ligatum est.[3] By 33.H.8. c.21 the k's letters patents[4] under the his great seal & signed with his hand, & declared & notified in his absence to the *Lords & Commons assembled in*

the higher house of parl. is & ever was of as good strength & force as if the k. had been personally present. 4. Inst. 28.

who go forth.
*

39. The Commons give their voices by Yea & No:[1] and if it be doubtful which prevails, two are appointed to number them, one for the Yeas, & one for the No ⟨e⟩s,[2] the Yea going out & the No sitting; and thereof report is made to the house. In a Committee, tho' it be of the whole house, the Yeas go on one side of the house and the Noes on the other.[3] 4. Inst. 35.

40. The antient custom of parl. is to appoint in the beginning a select committee to consider of the bills in the two last parliaments that passed both houses or either of them. & such as had been preferred read or committed, & to take out of them such as are most profitable. 4. inst. 36.[1]

41. In 32.H.8[1] Thos. Cromwell E. of Essex,[2] & in 2.H.6. Sr. John Mortimer[3] were attainted by the parl. without being called to answer, tho' they were forthcoming: whereof Ld. Coke sais Auferat oblivio si potest; si non; utcunque silentium tegat.[4] 4. Inst. 37.38.

*

42. By the antient law & custom of parl. when any man was to be charged in parl. with any crime, offence or misdemeanor, a writ was directed to the sheriff to summon him to appear in parl. But if it was only de injuriis, gravaminibus aut molestationibus, the writ might be directed to himself.[1] See the forms.[2] 4. inst. 38.39.

43. Every lord & member of the H. Com.[1] shall come to parl. if he have no reasonable excuse, or be amerced[2] a lord by the lords & a Common by the Commons.[3] 5.R.2. stat.2. c.4. By the stat. 6.H.8. c.16. a member of ⟨either⟩ the lower house departing from parl. without licence of the Speaker & Commons entered of record in the book of the clerk of parl. shall lose his wages.[4] If a member of

*

either house depart from parl. he is fineable by his house independently of the stat. last mentd. 4. Inst. 43.44. Hakewell. 55.[5]

44. If the king by his writ calleth any knight or esquire to be a Lord of the parl. he cannot refuse to

serve the king there in communi concilio for the good of his country.[1] But an ecclesiastical person may, unless he hold *of the king* per baroniam:[2] because quoad secularia, he is mortuus in lege, & therefore incapable to have place & voice in parl.[3] By the law & custom of England it belongeth to the Archdeacon of Canterbury &c. the priors & other prelates, whatsoever, holding of the king per baroniam, to be personally present in parl. as peers of the realm.[4] King H.8. granted to the abbot of Tavestock & his successors to be one of the spiritual lords of parl. Which creation was void because the abbot was neither Baro, nor had Baroniam.[5] 4. Inst. 44.45.

45. The fees of a knight of a shire are 4/ a day to be levied by the sheriff de communitate comitatus excepting only the cities & boroughs which send members to parl.[1] The fees of Burgesses & Citizens are 2/ a day to be levied on their Cities or boroughs.[2] H.4. summd a parl. crastino purificationis & died 20th. March following whereby the parl. was dissolved without any thing passed in parl. And it became a question whether the members shd have their wages? Resolved if on view of the k's records any like precedents may be found their wages shall be allowed.[3] It seems that the Lords, their villeins, & masters in chancery who are attendent on parl. shall not contribute to the Commons wages. F.N.B. 229. F A.[4] The latter are exempted by 4.E.3.[5] 4. Inst. 46.

Who eligible.

46. Who eligible?[1] A baron is of the lowest degree of the Lord's house. A knight banneret is under that degree & is eligible to be knight, Citizen, or Burgess of the house of Commons. One under the age of 21. years cannot be elected, nor can a Lord under that age sit in parl. An alien, nor even a Denizen,[2] cannot be elected, because such an one can hold no place of judicature. But an alien naturalized may. A bishop elect may sit in Parl. as a Lord thereof. None of the judges of K.B.C.P. or Excheq.[3] can be chosen of the H. Com. (as it is now holden) because they be assistants in the Lords house. Yet 31.H.6. Thorp baron of the Excheq.

was Speaker of the parl.[4] But any that have judicial places in any other court (being no Lord of parl.) are eligible. None of the clergy are eligible because they are of another body, viz. of the Convocation.[5] Seymour. 75. Hale parl. 115.[6] A man attainted of treason or felony is not eligible. Maiors and bailiffs of towns corporate are eligible contrary to the opinion in of Brook tit. Parl.[7] 38.H.8. By special order of the H. Com. the Atty. Gen. is not eligible. At a parl. 1. Car. the sheriff of Buckingham was elected & allowed the privilege of parl. by the whole H. Com.[8] 4. Inst. 46.47.48. See post 102.[9] But it was for Norfolk that he was elected. 4. Inst. 48. L. parl. c.23.[10]

false return

*

47. No knight, Citizen or Burgess can sit in parl. till he hath taken the oath of Supremacy[1] by S. Eliz. c.1. If one be duly elected and the sheriff return another, the return must be amended by the sher. because the election & not the return is the foundation.[2] 4. Inst. 48.49.

*

48. No election can be made but between 8. & 11. o'clock in the forenoon. But if the election be begun within that time and not finished it may be made after. If a party or the freeholders demand the poll, the sheriff cannot deny the scrutiny, for he cannot discern who be freeholders by the view: & tho' the party would waive the poll, yet the sher. must proceed in the scrutiny. 4. Inst. 48.[1]

49. By original grant or by custom a selected number of burgesses may elect & bind the residue.[1] If the k. doth newly incorporate an antient borough which sent burgesses to parl. and granteth the right of election to certain selected burgesses, where all the burgesses elected before this charter doth not take away the election of the other burgesses. So if a city having power[2] to make ordinances they cannot ordain that a less number shall elect burgesses, 'for the parl then made the election before';[3] for free elections of members of parl are pro bono publico, & not like elections of maiors, bailiffs, &c. 4. Inst. 49 ⟨8⟩. 49.[4]

50. The k. cannot grant a charter of exemption to any man to be freed from being elected a mem-

ber of parl. as he may do of some inferior offices; because the election of them ought to be free, and his attendance is for the service of the whole realm. Nor can he by charter⟨s⟩ exempt a Lord from attendence. 4. Inst. 49.[1]

51. Any election or voices given before the precept[1] be read & published, are void. For the same electors after the precept read & published may make a new election & alter their voices by the law of parl. 4. Inst. 49.[2]

52. In the 33.H.6.17. the case was that Sr. J.P. was attaintd of a certain trespass by act of parl. with which the Commons were assenting that if he did not come in by such a day he should forfeit such a sum; & the lords give a longer day, and the bill was not delivered back to the Commons.[1] And by Kirbie[2] clerk of the rolls of parl. the usage of parl. is that if a bill comes first to the commons, & they pass it, it is the custom to endorse it in such form, 'soit baile as Seigniors'[3] and if the Lords nor *the king* will not alter the bill, then it is the usage to deliver it to the clerk of the parl. to be enrolled without endorsing it. And if it be a Common bill,[4] it shall be enrolled, & if it be a particular bill, it shall not be enrolled, but filed upon the file[5] and this suffices; but if the party will sue to have it enrolled, it may be enrolled 'deste suer.'[6] to be sure. Hakew. 81. And if the Lords will alter a bill in that which may stand with the bill, they may, without remanding it to the Commons. As if the Commons grant poundage for 4. years, and the Lords grant it but for 2. years, this shall not be redelivered to the commons, quaere inde.[7] But if the Commons grant but for 2. years. & the Lords for 4. years there it shall be redelivered to the Commons, & in this case the Lords ought to make a schedule of their intent, or to indorse the bill in this form 'the Lords assent to this to continue for 4. years,[8] and when the Commons have the bill back, & will not assent to this, it cannot be an act, but if the Commons will assent, then they indorse their answer upon the margin below within the bill on such form, 'the Commons are assenting to the schedule of the Lords, to this

same bill annexed,[9] and then it shall be delivered to the clerk of parl. as above. And if a bill be first delivered to the Lords, & the bill passes them, they do not use to make any endorsement, but to send the bill to the Commons, & then if the bill passes the Commons it is used to be thus endorsed 'the Commons are assenting.' And this proves that it has passed the Lords before, and their assent is to pass it after the Lords. And so this act abovementd. is not good, because it was not redelivered to the Commons. Bro. parl. 4.

53. Fawkes clerk of the parl. Every bill which passes the parl. shall have relation to the first day of the parl. altho' it be ⟨not⟩ brought in towards the end of the parl.[1] And it is not usual to make any mention what day the bill is brought in to the parl. And the justices 'eux aviseront'[2] for it comes in to them by writ as an act of parl. ideo quaere.[3] And the case was that the parl. commenced before Pentecost & continued after Pentecost, and the Commons agreed to the bill after Pentecost and gave a day at the *next pentecost* and the Lords gave a day at the *next pentecost save one* and all was one meaning: for because that the bill shall have relation to the first day of parl. therefore if it be not prevented, it shall be taken this pentecost which is passed at this session and so the Lords did well. quaere.[4] 33.H.6.17. Bro. parl. 4. [By this it should seem that the maxim 'no fiction of the law shall extend to work an injury' gives place here.][5]

54. At a parl. held 38.H.8. it was admitted[1] that if one burgess be made mayor of a town which hath judicial jurisdiction, & the other be sick, that these are sufficient causes for electing new ones.[2] And new members so elected were received in the Commons house. anno 7. & 38 Henrici 8. Bro. parl. 7. Mod. ten. Parl. 49.[3]

Privilege, breach of. *

55. J.S. having beaten the servant of a knight coming with his master to parl. in 8.H.4. it was enacted by parl. that proclamation should be made where the affray was and that if the sd. J.S. did not render himself before the justices of our Ld. the K.

the king 2/ a day unless he have some other office under him.[3] Mod. ten. parl. 17.

68. The order of deliberating business in parliamt should be as follows. 1st. concerning war: if there be any war, and concerning the other businesses touching the persons of the king, queen & of their children. 2ly. the common businesses of the kdom. as of making laws. 3ly. the business of particular persons.[1] Mod. ten. parl. 21.

50 *

69. Of right the door of the parl. ought not to be shut, but to be kept by porters or king's serjeants at arms assigned by the king. Mod. ten. parl. 23.[1]

70. The clerk of parl. shall not deny to any man a transcript or copy of his process, or process in parl.[1] if he do desire it: & the clerk shall take alwais for 10 lines but one penny. Mod. ten. parl. 30.[2]

71. The members being called,[1] they are willed to chuse a Speaker, which done he is presented to the king sitting in parl. where after his oration (the Ld Keeper approving in behalf of his majesty) he petitions the king in behalf of the house as ante 22.[2] which petition he concludes with 'promising a regardful respect as befitting loyal & dutiful subjects. M. ten. p. 35.[3]

72. Bills are to be thrice read on three several days. The same members to speak but once to a bill in the same day. Every one to speak standing and to address themselves to the Speaker. Their speeches to be free from taunts on their fellow members. If the two houses cannot agree, sometimes the Lords sometimes the Commons require a meeting of some of each house, whereby information may be had of each others minds. After a bill is twice read & engrossed, the Speaker asks if they will go to the question, & if agreed, holding up the bill in his hand he sais 'As many as will have this bill pass concerning such a matter, say Yea; and those that are against it, No.[1] And if it be a doubt which cry is bigger, the house divides, those that agree not to the bill sitting still, those who agree, going down[2] with the bill. Mod. t. parl. 36-38.[3]

Session what.

73. It hath been a question whether the royal assent given to any one bill doth not ipso facto conclude that session. But in 1.Jac.1 & 1 & 2.Ph. & Mar. the house resolved it did not. The king may give his assent by letters patent, and by the stat. 33.H.8. c.21. it is declared is and ever was of as good strength & force as if personally given. Mod. ten. parl. 40. Hakewell. 68. The king gives his assent in these forms, to wit, to a publick bill 'Le roy le veut.'[1] to a private bill 'soit fait come il est desire.'[2] If he rejects it 'Le roy se avisera.'[3] To the subsidy bill 'Le roy remercie ses loyaulx & ainsi le veult.'[4] Mod. ten. parl. 41.[5]

k's assent how given.

who eligible.

74. A knight chosen for a county must be a knight or such esquire or gentleman of the same county who may be a knight, and not one of the degree of yeoman.[1] He must be resident within the same county the day of the writ of summons, and ought to have 40ſ. of freehold within the sd. county beyond all charges. 7.H.4. c.12. 1.H.6. c.1. 8.H.6.13. 10.H.6. c.7.[2] 23.H.6. c.15. The election shall be between the hours of 8. & 9. before noon.[3] If a sheriff does not make a due return forfeits 100£ to the king & 100£ to the knight chosen if he will sue within 3. months after the parl. commenced, & prosecute his suit with effect & without fraud; if not any one who will may have the suit.[4] In a city or borough the forfeiture is £40. to the king & £40. to the Citizen or burgess.[5] If a knight, citizen or burgess be returned, & after such return [his name] be put out, and another be put in his place, if he that be put in take on him to be knight, citizen or burgess, he forfeits £100. to the king & £100 to the one put out. 23.H.6. c.15.[6] Hakew. 47.-54.

election how held.

*

75. Knights and burgesses for the parl. must take the oath of Allegiance before they enter the parliament house. 5.Eliz. c.1.[1] and also the oath of Supremacy made 7.Jac. c.6.[2] which oaths are taken before the Ld. Steward or his deputy. Hakew. 56.[3]

Convocation.

76. The Convocation[1] alwais hath been and ought to be assembled by the king's writ. 25. H. 8.

c. 19. Yet the clergy of the Convocation house are no part or member of the parl. as you may see resolved by the Ld. Richard, Ld Windsor and others in the beginning of the sixth examination of master Philpot, in the beginning of the reign of Q. Mary, in master Fox's book of martyrs fol. 1639.[2] contrary to the opinion of Doctor Cowel verbo Proclamation.[3] But by the ⟨8.H.⟩ stat. 8.H.6. c.1. all the clergy called to the Convocation-house by the king's writ and their servants and familiars shall have such liberty and defence in coming abiding and going as the great men and Commonalty of the realm called to the parl. shall have. Hakew. 57.59.60.[4]

77. If any assault or affray be made on a member of either house coming to parl. or the Counsel of the king proclamn. is to be made in the city or town where it was made, by three several days that the party yield himself before the k. & his bench within a quarter of a year if it be in term, or otherwise in the next day of the term following the sd. quarter. If he did not, that he be attainted & pay double damages to the party to be taxed at the discretion of the justices, or by inquest if it be needful & make fine and ransom at the king's will. And if he come and be found guilty by inquest or examination then to pay double damages and be fined ut supra. 11.H.6. c.11. Hakew. 60.[1]

Privilege of parl.
*

78. Every knight citizen or burgess has privilege during the sessions of parl. and if any arrest them he shall be imprisoned in the tower by the Nether house[1] of which he is, and shall be fined, and the Keeper also if he will not deliver him when demanded by the serjeant at arms by command of the house whereof he is.[2] Dyer. 60. Hakewell 62.

79. The servants tending on their masters who are necessary, and the officers attending on the parl. as the serjeant at arms, the porter, clerks & such like, and also their chattels and goods necessary shall not be arrested & taken by any officer unless in case of felony or treason, in the same manner as the judges and ministers of other courts for their

servants, goods, and chattels necessary. Crompton's courts. 11. Hakew. 62.[1]

80. The parl. doth not give privilege tempore
vacatonis sed sedente curia.[1] Bro. tit. privilege 56.
Hakew. 63.[2]

81. In 31.H.6. in the vacation Thos. Thorpe the
speaker was condemned in 1000. marks damages
in an action of Tresp. brought by the D. of York &
was committed in execution.[1] When the parl. met
the Commons made suit to the k. & Lords to have
their Speaker delivd up for the good exploit of the
parl. But it was concluded that he should still remain in prison, and the Commons were commanded to chuse another speaker.[2] Hakew. 63.[3]

82. In Thorpe's case 31.H.6. the judges certified
that if any member of parl. be arrested (not for treason, felony, surety of the peace, or condemnation
had before the parl.) he is released and may make
attorney so as he may have his freedom & liberty to
attend that parl. Hakew. 64.[1] It hath been much
questioned if a member taken in execution during
parl. may be set at liberty by writ of parl. as in
1.Eliz.4. fol.8.a. Dyer. 60.[2] 2 E.4. fol.8. Dyer 162.
arc. parl. 63.[3] But by stat. 1.Jac. c.13.[4] it is settled
and a new execution may be sued against any who
shall be ⟨so⟩ delivered by privilege of parl. Hakew:
64.[5]

83. In the case of the Lord Laware[1] 30.Eliz.
which was thus. His ancestors had sit in parl. from
3.H.8. when their first Summons was till 3.E.6.
when by an act of parl. his father was disabled during life to claim or enjoy any dignity &c. Afterwards however he was called to parl. by Queen
Eliz. and sat as youngest lord of parl. It was now
resolved by all the judges and confirmed by the
lords 1. that it was no attainder nor perpetual disability which would have corrupted the blood, but
only a personal and temporary disability for his life
only, after which his heirs may claim it as heir to
him. 2. that the acceptance of a new creation by his
father can not hurt the petitioner because his father
was at that time disabled, & in truth was no baron,

but only an esquire, so that when the old and new dignity descended together, the old should be preferred. Hakew. 76.-79.[2]

84. All the privileges which do belong to those of the Commons house, a fortiori appertain to the Lords, for their persons are not only free from arrests during parl. but during their lives. Nevertheless the original cause is that they have place and voice in parl. Hakew. 82.[1]

85. In the times of the antient Britons & Saxons the Archbps. & Bps. were called to parl. or other assemblies not so much in respect of their tenures which were in frankalmoigne[1] but because of their gravity, wisdom & learning. Wm. the Conqueror first altered their tenure Matt. Par. anno. 1070. ever since which they have no title or voice in parl. but in respect of their baronies. Hakew. 84.[2]

86. Tho of latter times the use is in the penning a stat. to say it is enacted by the *Lds. Spiritl.* & temporal & the commons, yet the antient form was not so; & good acts of parl. may be made though the Lords spiritual do not consent. 8.Co.19. and parliaments may be holden without them.[1] Hakew. 85.86.[2]

87. Nihil aliud potest rex quam quod de jure potest. Bracton. L. 2.[1] Every grant of the k. hath this condition expresed or implied as by the law annexed to it 'ita quod per donationem illam patria magis solito non oneretur seu gravetur.'[2] F.N.B. 222. Therefore resolved by the judges 4.Jac. that they who dig for saltpetre may not dig within the mansion house of any subject without his assent for the manifest inconvenience. 11.Co.82. Neither can the purveyers for timber for the king's use take timber trees on any man's freehold for that is prohibited by magna charta. c.21. 'Nec capiemus boscum alienum ad castra vel ad alia agenda nostra, nisi per voluntatem cujus boscus ille fuerit.[3] Haew. 87.88. A man attainted cannot be restored to his blood but by parl. for the king by his charter of pardon cannot alter the Com. law. The king may commit any one to prison during pleasure. Stanf. 72

[Aliter since the acts of hab. corp. & qu. before.][4] If a king and his subjects be driven out of his kingdom by his enemies, yet he is still k. over his subjects, & they are still bound by their bonds of allegiance wheresoever they be. Hakew. 88.-92.[5]

Majority binds.
51 *

88. In parl. if a majority assent to an act, it is good; for the law of Majoris partis[1] is so in all Counsels, Elections Etc. both by the rules of the Common law and the Civil. Hakew. 93.[2]

Journ. H. Com.

89. The journals of the h. of Commons are not extant farther back than 1.E.6. Hakew. 122.[1]

52 *

90. Upon motion for a law a committee is appointed by the house to draw the bill; which done, one of them presents it to the Speaker. Hakew. 132. Bills when sent from one house to the other are alwais sent in parchment fairly engrossed. Public bills are in due course to be preferred in reading and passing before private.[1] There have been often orders of the house that after 9. o'clock (when usually the house groweth full) they should not be troubled with the reading any private bill. Towards the end of the parl. when there remain many bills undispatched, there hath been a special committee appointed to take a survey of them and to marshall them in such order as they should be preferred to their passage, having respect to their importance. Hakew. 132.-135.[2]

* 53.a.

91. The Speaker is not precisely bound to any rules for the preferring of bills to be read or past, but is left to his own discretion unless the house specially direct the contrary: & howsoever earnestly pressed by the house for the reading some one bill, yet if he have not had convenient time to read the same over & to make a breviat[1] thereof for his memory, the Speaker doth claim a privilege to defer the reading thereof to some other time. Hakew. 136.[2]

92. Ordd that the committee which amends a bill should amend the breviat. temp. Jac.[1] Hakew. 138.[2] Scobel. 42.[3]

1st. reading
* 53.b.

93. Of the 1st. reading of bills. The clerk is usually directed by the Speaker, but sometimes by the

house, what bill to read; which done he delivers it to the Speaker who standeth up uncovered & holding the bill in his hand saith 'the bill is intituled &c & reading the title. Then he opens the substance to the house either trusting to his memory or using his breviat, or sometimes reading the bill itself, especially upon it's passage when it hath been much altered by the Committees so as to differ much from the breviat. Having opened the bill he declares 'it is the first reading of the bill' and delivereth it to the clerk. If it happen to be debated to & fro, & the house call for the question, if the bill originally begun in the Commons house, the question ought to be 'whether it shall be rejected' 43.Eliz.17. Nov. But if it came from the Lords, then out of respect the question should be 'whether it shall be secondly read' & if that be denied then for the rejection. But if the bill be not debated to and fro on the first reading, the question is for the second reading. Hakew. 137.141.[1]

bill of pardon.

bill of subsidies
*

94. The bill containing the king's pardon is read but once in each house because the subject must take it as the king will give it. So also of the bill of subsidies granted by the clergy. The morning should be spent in first readings till the house grow full. At the first reading it is not the course to speak to the bill, but rather to consider it & take time till the second reading. But where it is apparently inconvenient & so not fit to trouble the house any longer it is sometimes done. But in these cases no man should speak to any one part of the bill, or for any addition, for that implies that the body of the bill is good, which till the 2d reading doth not regularly come to trial. Bills are never read twice in the same day but upon motion & special order. Hakew. 138.-141.[1]

*

95. The day that the Speaker being approved by the king cometh down into the house the custom is to read some bill left unpassed in the last sessions (for that time & no more) to give him seisin[1] as it were of his place. 39.Eliz.27. Oct. Hakew. 138. Scobel 5. L. parl. 271. 23 May. 1.Jac.[2] Hale. parl.

[71]

133. But other business is sometimes taken up first. D'Ewes 43. L. parl. 271.[3]

96. It was the opinion of the Sollicitor general in K. William's time, that the Lords had no right to vote in the election of a Commoner because they were not contributors to the expences of a knight of the shire or a burgess; and they were not contributors to that expence because they were of another house. Franklin's Historic Review of Pennsylva. Appdx. 404.[1]

Session what.

97. A prorogation of parl. is alwais by the king, & in this case the Sessions must begin de novo; & if a parliment is prorogued upon return of the writ of Summons, it begins at the end of the prorogation: and adjournment is by each house & the Sessions continues notwithstanding such adjournment. 1.Mod.242. Jac's L. D. by Ruffhead voce Parliament.[1]

98. If at the time of an actual rebellion, or imminent danger of invasion, the parl. shall be separated by adjournment or prorogation, the king is empowered by the stat. 30.G.2. c.25. to call them together by proclamation, with fourteen days notice of the time appointed for their re-assembling. 1. Blackst. c.2.§.7.pa.187.[1]

99. A parl. may be summoned by proclamation to meet before the day to which they are prorogued.[1] Lex parliam. 354. [but qu. if this is not under authority of the stat. 30.G.2.?][2]

new baron how created.

100. The consent of parl. continued necessary for creating a baron of the realm about as low down as H.VII. which is the only title by which any man can obtain his seat in our house of lords; & not as duke, marquis, earl, viscount &c.[1] In all probability it will some time or other be a doubt whether the king's patent alone will be self sufficient to create a baron of the realm, without the consent of parliament; agreeably to the original institution, & confirmed by the custom and usage of so many ages. Historl. essay on Engl. Constn. 23.[2]

Prorogation, by whom.

101. The prorogation of parliaments hath been grafted into the prerogative of the crown though

[72]

formerly unknown to the constitution: but hath been used in modern times, where the case required to have two sessions in one year in order to gain a recess for a short period; but seldom or never to continue the same parliament longer than one year. However. as tyranny is always fertile in inventions, it hath since been made an instrument to subvert the elective power of the people; and reduce it to a meer shadow. ib. pa. 81.[1]

who eligible.

102. Charles the first, in order to exclude the most able men from parliament ordered them to be appointed sheriffs, that they might not be elected members:[1] however in that he was mistaken: for those popular members were elected for other places, and the parliament met the 6th. of Feb. 1626. ib. 86.[2] See ante 46.

*

103. If an offence be committed in parliament by a member, it is an infringement of privilege for any person or court to take notice of it, till the house has punished the offender, or referred him to a due course. L. parl. 63.[1]

* 53. C.

104. The right & privilege of parl. so far extends, that not only what is done in the very house, sitting the parliament, but whatever is done relating to them, or in pursuance of their order, during the parliament, is no where else to be punished, but by themselves or a succeeding parliament, tho' done out of the house. L. parl. 63.[1] Husband's collection. p. 61.[2]

*

105. Either house doth ever for the most part shew itself so careful to keep firm correspondence with the other, as that when a bill hath passed either of the said houses, and is sent to the other, it doth for the most part pass, and is neither dashed nor altered, without very great cause upon mature deliberation, & usually also not without conference desired & had thereupon; that so, full satisfaction may be given to that house, from which the bill so rejected, or altered, was sent. L. parl. 63.[1] D'Ewes journ. 186.[2]

*

106. The prerogative of parl. is so great, that all acts & processes coming out of any inferior courts,

must cease, & give place to that, the highest.[1] L. parl. 64.

*

107. The Commons declare it hath been the antient, constant, & undoubted right & usage of parliaments to question & complain of all persons of what degree soever, found grievous to the Commonwealth, in abusing the power & trust committed to them by the sovereign.[1] 1. Rushw. 245. L. parl. 67. The greater the persons are, the more proper for the undertaking & encounter of this High Court. It will not be impar congressus.[2] Atk's argum. 45. Lex Parl. 74. It is their proper work to deal with such delinquents as are too high for the court of King's bench or other ordinary courts.[3] Atk. arg. 50. L. parl. 75.

108. The Prelates, dukes, counts, barons & Commons resolved in the time of Edwd. 111. that neither the king nor any other could put the realm, nor the people thereof into subjection, sans l'assent de eux.[1] L. parl. 74. [This contradicts the position in the Law of Nations that the king in making peace may cede part of his kingdom.][2] Puff. Off. hom. et civis, L. 2.

2.

109. The king cannot by his proclamation alter the law. He may proclaim that he shall incur the indignation of his majesty, that withstands it. But the penalty of not obeying his proclamation, may not be upon forfeiture of his goods, his lands, or his life, without parliamt.[1] Hakew. 90. L. parl. 79.

110. The expounding of the laws doth ordinarily belong to the reverend judges; & in case of greatest difficulty or importance to the high court of parliament. Hakew. 94. Errors by law in the commonpleas are to be corrected in the King's bench; & of those in the king's bench in the parliament & not otherwise, i.e. where the proceedings are by Original writ. For if they are by bill they may be corrected in the Exchequer chamber by Stat. 27. El.c.8. from whence a writ of error lies to parliament. 4. Inst. 22. Instit. Leg. 171.172. L. parl. 81. Actions at Common law are not determined in this high court of parliament, yet com-

plaints have ever been received in parliaments, as well of private wrongs as public offences. And according to the quality of the person and nature of the offence, they have been retained, or referred to the Common law. Selden's judicature. 2. L. Parl. 81.[1]

111. The parliament hath three powers, a Legislative, in respect of which they are called the three estates; a Judicial, in respect of which they are called the High court of parliament, & a Counselling power, whence it is called, Commune Concilium regni.[1] Atk. arg. 36.[2] L. parl. 83.

112. The courts of Common law are guided by the rule of the Common law, but the proceedings of parliament are by the Custom & Usage of parliament. Atk. arg. 50.[1] Where by order of law a man cannot be attainted of High-treason, unless the offence be in law high treason, he ought not to be attainted by parl. by general words of high-treason, but the high treason ought to be especially exprest: for the parl. being the highest & most honorable court of justice ought to give example to inferior courts. 4. Inst. 39. L. parl. 76.[2]

113. When a Commee. of lords is selected out to meet with another Committee of the house of Commons, neither the judges, being but assistants, nor the queen's council, being but attendants of and upon the house, were ever nominated a joint Committees with the lords. But when the Lords among them selves do appoint a committee to consider of some ordinary bill, especially if it concern matter of law, it hath been used that the king's learned council, but especially the judges, may be nominated as Committees alone, or as joint committees with the lords.[1] Towns. Col. 9.[2] L. parl. 94.

114. When any bills or messages are brought from the lower house to be preferred to the upper house, the Lord Keeper, & the rest of the lords, are to rise from their places, and to go down to the bar, there to meet such as come from the lower house, and from them to receive in that place their messages or bills. Contrariwise, when any answer is to

be delivered by the Ld. Keeper &c. Towns. Col. 94. Sr. Simon D'Ewes' journ. L. parl. 95.[1]

Privilege, what breach of. *

115. Giving the lie to a peer is a breach of privilege. Nalson. 380. Hakew. 84. L. parl. 96.[1]

116. In judgments on delinquents in parliament, the Commons might accusare et petere judicium, & the king assentire, but the lords only did judicare. Selden's judicature. 132. L. parl. 98. The king's assent is requisite only in capital judgments, not in misdemeanors. Seld. judic. 141. L. parl. 98.[1]

117. An order of the H. of Lords was in 1640. that the Lords & widows & dowagers of Lords shall answer in Chancery &c upon protestation of honour only.[1] But altho' their honor may bind their conscience in Equity, yet evidence upon their honor ought not to be admitted in any court of law. Cursus Cancel. 112. L. parl. 99. In giving evidence to a jury, or in their depositions in Chancery &c they are to be examined on oath.[2] L. parl. 99.[3]

118. A peer of the realm shall be tried in an appeal by knights &c & not by his peers because it is at the suit of the party. Brook. 142. 153. But in an indictment of treason or felony he shall be tried by his peers, because it is at the suit of the king. Arcana parl. 71. L. parl. 98.[1] A Lord of parl. shall have knights upon his trial in every action. 27.H.8.f.27. A Ca. sa. does not lie against a Lord of parl. 27.H.8.f.27. for the law presumes that he has assets. An Attachment is not grantable by the Common law, Statute law, custom, or precedent against a Lord of parl. Dyer. 316. L. parl. 100.[2]

119. Resolved by the Lords (1692) that for the future when there shall be a division in the house upon any question the Contents shall go below the bar, and the Notcontents stay within the bar. Ordered by the Lords (1691.) that for the future upon giving judgment in any cases of appeals, or writs of error, the question shall be put for Reversing and not for affirming.[1] L. parl. 102.

120. When one sueth in parl. to reverse a judgmt. in R. B. he sheweth in his bill, which he

exhibiteth to the parliament, some error or errors, whereupon he prayeth a Scire facias.[1] 4. inst. 21. L. parl. 103.[2]

*

121. Upon complaints & accusations of the Commons the Lords may proceed in judgmt. against the delinquents of what degree soever, & of what nature soever the offence be, for where the Commons complain, the Lords do not assume to themselves trial at Common law. Seld. judic. 6.7. L. parl. 104.[1]

122. Judgments for life & death, are to be rendered by the Steward of England, or by the Steward of the king's house. At such arraignment the Steward is to sit in the Chancellor's place; all judgmts. for misdemeanors are by the Chancellor, or by him who supplies the Chancellor's place. Seld. judic. 176.177. L. parl. 106.[1]

123. In case of recovery of damages or restitution, the parties are to have their remedy, the parliament being ended, in the Chancery, and not in any other inferior court at the Common law. But the Lords, in parliament, may direct how it shall be levied. Seld. judic. 187.[1]

124. The judges, who are but assistants to the upper house, have leave from the Lord Chancellor or Keeper to sit covered in the house, but are alwais uncovered at a Committee. D'Ewes' journ. 527. Col. 2. L. parl. 107.[1]

*

125. The house of Commons is a house of information & presentment, but not a house of definitive judgment. Rush. Coll. 217. v.1. The H. of Comm. is a considble. grand jury, 'tis a good billa vera they return. Trials of the regicides. 53. L. parl. 114.[1]

126. The Stat. 6.H.8. c.16. says no Member shall depart from parl. nor absent themselves from the same without license of the Speaker & Commons assembled in parliament to be entred on record in the book of the clerk of parl. Rast. stat. 429. 4 inst. 23. Hales of parl. 213.215 L. parl. 114.[1]

H. Comm. act of recd. * 54

127. The Stat. 6.H.8. c.16. calls the journals of the Commons a *Record*. On the trial of Harrison

the regicide, Jessop clerk of the house was produced to attest[1] several orders of the Commons' house.[2]—Yet some judges have been of opinion, that the journals of the house of commons are no *records*, but only remembrances. Hob. 110. 111.[3] L. parl. 114.115.[4] Journ. H.C. Mar. 17. 1592.[5] Hale parl. 105.

55 *

128. 1. Car. 1. 1625. Resolved that common fame is a good ground of proceeding for this house, either by enquiry, or presenting the complaint (if the house find cause) to the king or Lords. Rushw. L. parl. 115.[1] But the Lords will not commit the person accused, on common fame: there must be special matters objected against him. Seld. judic. 29. L. parl. 115.[2] If any Lord of parl. have committed any oppression, bribery, extortion or the like; the house of Comm. being the general inquisitors of the realm may examine the same, & if they find by the vote of the house the charge to be true, then they transmit the same to the Lords with the witnesses and the proofs. 4. inst. 24. L. parl. 117.[3]

* Bp. of Bristol.
Dr. Cowel.
Dr. Manwaring
Dr. Montague
Dr. Burnet
Davenport.
Long.
Mayor of
Westbury.

Hall.

Darryel.
Rogers.
Muncton.
Williams.
Holland.
Long.

129. See the Bp. of Bristol's case,[1] Dr. Cowel's case, Dr. Manwaring's case, Dr. Montague's case, Dr. Burnet's case, who were punished for writing books; Pet. Misc. parl. 64.74.82. Rush. 4. Car.[2] Nalson's Col. p. 9.43.[3] Randolph Davenport's case for misinforming the house as a witness. Pet. misc. parl. 120. Long for bribing the Mayor of Westbury in an election.[4] 4. inst. 23. D'Ewes' journ. 182. Other cases of bribery in elections. Bohun's deb. 28.55.275.281.340. Journ. Comm. 1701. Mar. 6.7.13.17.18.20.30. Apr. 29. Arthur Hall for publishing the conferences of the house & writing a book.[5] Hale parl. 128. 4 Feb. 23. Eliz.[6] D'Ewes' journ. 212. Darryel for threatening a member's person. D'ewes 114.[7] Rogers for abusing a member. D'Ewes 114.[8] Muncton for striking a burgess.[9] Scobel. 113.—Williams for assaulting a member d'Ewes 251. Col. 2.[10] Holland for beating the servant of a member Scobel. 113.[11] Long, a justice, for setting a guard without consent of parl.

Aston.

Bland.
Drury.
Smalley &
Kirtleton.
Criketoft.
Tash.

Dr. Harris.
Burgess.
Wray.
Levet.

*

*

Nalson. 732.[12] Sr. Arthur Aston for not giving a Commee. that clear answer he ought. Rush. 656. Pet. misc. 108.[13] Bland for dishonorable reflections on the H. Com. 1584. 27. Eliz. Drury for the same. Journ. Com. 1588. 31. Eliz.[14] Smalley & Kirtleton for the same. Pet. misc. 16. 18.[15] Criketoft. for confederating in the escape of a prisoner from the tower. Pet. misc. 96. Tash, of his majesty's guards, for keeping the door of the lobby of the upper house agt several members of the H. of Com. Pet. misc. 98. Dr. Harris for misbehavr. in Preaching. Pet. parl. 104. Mr. Burgess in catechising. Pet. misc. 104. 105. Wray & others for violence at elections. Pet. parl. 105. 106. Levet for exercising a patent which had been adjudged a grievance by the house ib. 106.107. L. parl. 118.-135.[16]

130. Trussel, being in execution, was ordered to be brought before the Commee. with his keeper, without danger of an escape in the execution. Towns. Col. 20. D'Ewes 438. Col. 1.[1] Mr. W. Montague, being a prisoner in execution was elected a burgess for Stockbridge & discharged of his imprisonment by the house. Boh. deb. 275-281.[2] Several indentures for burgesses being returned for the borough of Bossinny, the house would not permit either to sit till the election was decided. Scobel. 16.[3] If the house is desirous to see a record the speaker sends a warrant to the Ld. Keeper to grant a Certiorari to have the record brought into the house. Towns. Col. 297.[4] L. parl. 123. 124.

131. If the Commons accuse a Commoner of misdemeanors, in such a state of liberty or restraint as he is in, when the Commons complain of him, in such he is to answer. Seld. jud. 101. Sr. Fr. Michel & Sr. John Bennet were both committed by the Commons before their complaint to the lords, & so they answered as prisoners. ibid. If the Commons impeach a man they are in loco proprio, & there no jury ought to be; only witnesses are to be examined in their presence, or they to have copies thereof &

the judgmt. not to be given till they demand it. ib. 124. They may require a rehearing. ib. 159. L. parl. 125.[1]

*

132. Issuing Quo Warranto's from K. B. &c. against boroughs are coram non judice, & void, & the right of sending members is questionable in parliamt. only; & the Occasioners, procurers & judges in such Quo warrantos are punishable in parl. Nalson 588.[1] When the Commons requested the king & Lords to restore their Speaker to them, the judges being advised with, after mature deliberation, answered, it was not their part to judge of the parl. which may judge of the law. Seld. jud. 55.[2] A parl. man cannot be compelled out of parl. to answer things done in parl. in a parliamentary course. Rush. V.1. 663.[3] In 27. Eliz. 1584. the serjeant was sent to the Com. pleas bar to charge the Recorder then pleading there to repair to the house for his attendance. D'Ewes 347. Col. 2.[4] And in 11. R. 2. all the judges, as they were sitting in Westminster hall were arrested by order of parl.[5] L. parl. 129.

56.

133. The king cannot take notice of what is done in the Commons' house, or delivered to them, but by the house itself. Seld. jud. 53.[1]

134. Resolved that no member of this house (of Com.) shall accept of any office or place of profit from the crown, without the leave of the house; nor any promise of any such office or place during his being a member. All offenders herein to be expelled. Journ. Com. 1680. Dec. 30. L. parl. 130.[1]

*

135. It was resolved 1680. that the discharge of the grand jury by the judges of B.R.[1] before they had finished their presentments was arbitrary & illegal; that a rule against printing a certain book was an usurpation of legislative power;[2] that the court had been arbitrary, illegal, & partial in the imposition of fines; that the refusing bail in bailable cases was illegal & a breach of the liberties of the subject; that some expressions of baron Weston in a charge to the grand jury were a scandal to the ref-

ormation & tended to the subversion of the antient constitution. Journ. Com. 1680. L. parl. 131.[3]

* 136. Resolved 28 & sq. Eliz. 1586. that the discussing & adjudging of differences about elections only belonged to the house: that tho' the Ld. Chancellor & judges were competent judges in their proper courts, yet they were not judges in parliament. D'Ewes' journ. 397. Col. 1. L. parl. 133.[1]

56.b.* 137. A member of the house stood indicted of felony. Adjudged, that he ought to remain of the house till he were convicted; for it may be any man's case who is guiltless, to be accused & indicted of felony or the like crime. 23. Eliz. 1580. D'Ewes' 283. Col. 1. L. parl. 133.[1]

57.* 138. Tho' freedom of speech be an undoubted privilege of the house, yet whatsoever is spoken in the house is subject to the censure of the house; & where they find cause, offences of this kind have been severely punished, by calling the persons to the bar to make submission, committing him to the tower, expelling the house, disabling him to be a member during that, & some time during any future parliament. Scobel. 72.[1] Peter Wentworth for wicked words of the queen was committed. Hale parl. 127.[2] 8. Feb. 1585.[3] Pet. misc. 12.73.[4] D'Ewes 244. Col. 1. Copley for the same. Seymour 178. Hale parl. 125.[5] Arthur Hall for publishing the conferences of the house & some matter of reproach agt particular members derogatory of the authority of the house & prejudicial to the validity of it's proceedings was committed to the tower for 6 months, fined £500. & disabled for ever to serve in parl. Pet. misc. 20.74. D'Ewes 296-298. Journ. Com. Nov. 21. 1586.[6] A bill passed against Jesuits. Dr Parry only gave a negative & after inveighed in violent speeches against the bill, affirming it to savour of treason, danger &c. Upon this he was sequestered into the outer room, & then to the bar on his knees & his reasons asked, he refused to give them and was committed; the next day he was brought again to the bar & kneeling made humble

Wentworth.

Copley.
Hall.

Dr. Parry.

confession of his ill-behavior &c whereupon he was again admitted to his seat. Pet. misc. 76.[7] D'Ewes 340-342. 17. Dec. 1584. 27 Eliz. Parry afterwards misbehaving himself was disabled to be a member of this house. 18. Feb. 1584. 27. Eliz. D'Ewes. 352. Col. 2.

Mompesson.

Sr. Giles Mompesson for being a monopolist & other oppressions was turned out of the house & committed. then impeached before the Lords who adjudged him to be degraded from his knighthood, be infamous, incapable of giving testimony, to be a perpetual outlaw, fined £10,000. forfeit his goods, & the profits of his lands for life, never to hold any office under the king nor be of any jury, to be imprisoned for life, & excepted out of all general pardons. 18.Jac.1. Pet. misc. 91.

Floyd.

Sr. Robert Floyd expelled the house for being a projector of a patent for a monopoly. 19.Jac.1. Pet. misc.

Bennet.
Barbour.

93. St. John Bennet for receiving bribes expelled & committed. 19.Jac.1. Pet. misc. 92. Barbour,[8] recorder of Wells, for signing a warrant for quartering of soldiers, suspended the house & sequestered till the pleasure of the house be known. 3.Car.1. Pet. misc. 94.95.

Piggot.

One of the knights of Buckinghamshire[9] behaved against order, sitting and calling out with a loud voice, & when called on to stand up & speak, rose and inveighed agt the Scots. The house being much engaged, his speech passed without censure; but on the Monday following it was remembered, & being absent, he was sent for & heard at the bar, and then committed & expelled. 13.Feb.1606. Pet. misc. 77-79. Hale parl. 130. A member inveighed against a bill and reflected on the member presenting it as savouring a Puritan and factious spirit. He was ordered to withdraw after explaining himself, then called to the bar on his knees, & discharged from the service of the house. 15. Feb. 18.Jac.1. Pet. misc. 79.[10] I.H. spoke words offensive to the house. He was first heard in explanation, then commanded to withdraw, called to the bar & suspended the house during that session. Apr. 26. 1641. Pet. misc.

Taylor.

80.[11] Mr. Taylor for words spoken of a bill of attainder, was first heard to explain & ordered to withdraw, then expelled made incapable of ever being a member of this house, committed to the tower during pleasure, & to acknolege his offence at the bar & at Windsor publicly. 27. May. 1641. Pet. misc. 80.[12] Indignities to Sr. Rob. Owen while in the chair of a Commee. offered by two members, they were obliged to acknolege their error. 13. May. 12. Jac.1. Pet. misc. 82.[13] Some speeches in the house privately between two members: one took offence, & going down the parliament stairs, struck the other, who thereupon catched at a sword to strike with it. Both were ordered to attend & heard & then withdrew. He who struck was brought to the bar on his knees & committed during pleasure. 19. Jac.1. Pet. misc. 82.[14]

Moor.

Mr. Moor sent to the tower for speaking out of season. 1626. Nalson's introdn. 61.[15] 2. Nalson. 513.

Conisby
Benson.

Conisby expelled for being a monopolist. Nov. 1641. 2. Nalson. 513.[16] Benson having granted protections for extortion was voted unfit to be longer a member of the house & sent for. 2. Nalson.

Hollis

596.[17] Hollis having been expelled the house for a speech made with great strength of reason & courage but more heat than the times would bear, was restored to his place. 2. Nalson. 710.[18] Sr. Wm.

Widdrington.
Price.

Widdrington & Sr. Herbert Price, sent to the tower for bringing in candles agt. the desire of the house. 2. Nalson. 272.[19] A resolution of 23. Eliz. 158. that every member who had been absent this whole session without excuse allowed by this house, shall have a fine set upon him to her majesty's use. D'Ewes. 309. Col. 2.[20] Mr. Lawrence

Hide.

Hide (pretend business of his clients) made known to the house that he would go out of town, & so took his leave in open audience, without the assent or leave of the house, which was censured & Mr. Speaker ordered to write to him, & also to other lawyers gone down in the same circuit, advising them to return & attend the house. Pet. misc. 147.149.[21] Several lawyers members of this house were committed for appearing as council in the

Trevor.

Hungerford

Speaker,
Election or
Removal of,
58.a

Speaker's
business.

case of Ashby & White. Mar. 1734.[22] Sr. John Trevor, Speaker, for receiving a gratuity from the city of London after passing a bill was resolved guilty of a high crime & misdemeanor & was expelled the house. 12. Mar. 1694. Bohum's deb. 331.[23] Hungerford expelled for a like cause. Boh. deb. 354.[24] L. parl. c.8.

139. Grievous sickness is a good cause to remove the speaker & chuse another. So in 1.H.4. Sr. John Cheyney discharged; & so William Sturton. So in 15.H.6. Sr. John Tyrell removed. So Mar. 14. 1694. Sr. John Trevor. 4. inst. 8. L. parl. 263.[1] Long use hath made it so material that without the king's commandment or leave the Commons cannot chuse their speaker. Sed aliter ab antiqua.[2] Elsyng. 154.[3] L. parl. 264. Surely the election of the speaker was antiently free to the Commons to chuse whom they would of their own house; which appears in this, that the king never rejected any whom they made choice of. Elsyng. 155. But contr. D'Ewes. 42. Col. 1. that in 28 H.6. Sr. John Popham was discharged by the king on his excuse, whereon the Commons chose & presented Wm. Tresham esq. who made no excuse. So of Paul Foley in Bohun's deb. 353.[4] If any man stand up & speak against the person who has been proposed for Speaker, alledging some reason, he ought to name another. Els. 152. Towns. Coll. 174. Boh. deb.[5] If more than one person be named, sometime one of the members standing in his place, doth by direction or leave of the house put a question for determining the same, or the clerk at the board. Scobel. 3.[6] L. parl. c.13.

140. The mace is not carried before the Speaker until his return after being allowed by the king Elsyng. 153. The Speaker's office is, when a bill is read, as briefly as he may, to declare the effects thereof to the house. Mod. ten. parl. 37. L. parl. c.14.[1]

141. Oftentimes on the first day of the meeting of the house, as soon as the Speaker hath been approved & sometimes before, such persons as have

been doubly returned have made their choice. Scobel. 18. L. parl. c.14.[1]

142. The Speaker is to be commanded by none, neither to attend any but the queen. per Sr. Edwd. Hobby. D'Ewes. 627. Col. 2. L. parl. 273.[1]

58.b.*

143. It is no possession of a bill except the same be delivered to the clerk to be read, or that the speaker read the title of it in the chair. L. parl. 274.[1]

Speaker's business *

144. The Speaker is not to deliver a bill of which the house is possessed to any without leave of the house but a copy only. May. 1604. Scobel 65. Pet. misc. 140.[1] It was resolved Apr. 16. 1640. 16.Car.1. that it was a breach of privilege of the house for the Speaker not to obey the commands of the house; & that it appeared the Speaker did adjourn the house by command of the king without the consent of the house which is also a breach of the privilege: it was therefore ordered that this should be presented to his majesty. Rush. 1137.[2] The speaker may deliver a copy of a bill, or shew it to the king. Pet. misc. 142.[3] Ordered 10. Nov. 1640. that mr. Speaker be intreated to be here this afternoon to sit by at the great Commee. of Irish affairs, & if there be cause, to resume the chair. Rush. 3.p. v.1. p.42. This day (20. Nov. 1640) the house ordered the Speaker to sit in the afternoon. ib. 53.[4] The Speaker is the mouth, eyes, & ears of the house. Hence when king Charles I. commanded the speaker to discover certain transactions, he justly replied that he had neither eyes to see, ears to hear, nor mouth to speak, but as the house should direct him.[5] L. parl. c.14.

145. The Litany is read first thing after the Speaker is set in the chair. 13. Eliz.1571. Towns. 54.[1]

memb. to sit.
* 59.a

[146].[1] When the Speaker is set in his chair, every member is to sit in his place with his head covered. Scobel. 6.[2]

not to pass between nor to cross &c. 59.b.*

[147]. No member in coming into the house, or in removing from his place, is to pass between the Speaker, & the member then speaking; nor may

[85]

cross or go overthwart the house, or pass from one side to the other while the house is sitting. Scobel. 6.[1]

departure. *

[148]. Mr. Speaker & the residue of the house of the better sort of calling, alway at the rising of the house to depart, and come forth in comely & civil sort, for the reverence of the house, in turning about with a low courtesie, as they make at their coming into the house, and not unseemly to thrust & throng out. D'Ewes. 282. Col. 2.[1]

covering.
60 *

[149]. No member is to come into the house with his head covered, nor to remove from one place to another with his hat on, nor is to put on his hat in coming in, or removing, until he be set down in his place. Scobel. 6.[1]

spurs. *

[150]. None to enter the house with his spurs on; nor until he pays the Serjeants fees. 39.Eliz. Town. 101.[1]

whispering.
61 *

[151]. While the house is sitting, no man ought to speak or whisper to another, to the end the house may not be interrupted, when any are speaking; but every one is to attend unto what is spoken. Scobel. 6. D'Ewes 487. Col. 1.[1]

person speaking.
62

[152]. When any member intends to speak, he is to stand up in his place uncovered, address himself to the Speaker; who usually calls such person by his name that the house may take notice who it is that speaks. ibid.[1]

who shall speak.
63

[153]. If more than one stand up at once, the Speaker is to determine who was first up; & he is to speak, & the other sit down, unless he who was first up sit down again, & give way to the other, or that some other member stand up & acquaint the house that another was up before him whom the Speaker calls, & the house adjudge it so. Scobel 7. D'Ewes. 434. Col. 1. 2.[1]

no interruption.
64

[154]. While one is speaking, none else is to stand up, or interrupt him, until he have done speaking, & be set down, & then the other may rise up & speak, observing the rules. ib. Town. Col. 205.[1]

mr. Speaker to be heard. 65.

[155]. When mr. Speaker desires to speak, he ought to be heard without interruption, if the house be silent, and not in dispute. 21. June. 1604. ibid. Hale parl. 133.[1]

do. 66

[156]. When the Speaker stands up, the member standing up ought to sit down. ibid.[1]

Questn. on a bill.

[157]. If any question be upon a bill the Speaker is to explain, but not to sway the house with arguments or dispute. Scobel. 8.[1]

hissing, coughing &c. 67

[158]. Whosoever hisseth or disturbeth any man in his speech, by coughing ⟨&c⟩ spitting, &c shall answer it at the bar. Scobel. 8. D'Ewes. 335. Col. 1. 640. Col. 2.[1]

departure at rising.

[159]. In going forth, no man shall stir, until mr. Speaker do arise & go before, & then all the rest to follow after him. 7. May 1607. ibid.[1]

Offensive words.

[160]. If in debate words be let fall that give offence, exceptions should be taken the same day, & before such member go out of the house: or he who is offended may move that such person may not go out of the house till he hath given satisfaction in what was by him spoken, and in such case after the present debate is over, the words must be repeated by the person excepting: and in case he desire, or the house command him, he is to explain himself, standing in his place; which if he refuse to do, or the house be not satisfied with such explanation, then he is to withdraw. Scobel. 81.[1]

when may enter.

[161]. After the names of the knights, citizens, & burgesses were read to the clerk of the crown & entered in his book, they entered into the house. Towns. ibid.[1]

Oath administd.

[162]. The house being set, the E. of Derby,[1] high steward for this parl. came into the house to take their oaths. All being removed into the court of Requests,[2] the Lord High-Steward sitting at the door, called the Knights & Burgesses of every county, according to the letters of their names in the alphabet. Every one answered as he was called & having answered, departed thence to the Parl. house door, & there took the oath of Supremacy,[3]

given him by one of the Queen's privy counsellors.[4] D'Ewes jour. passim.

Call of house.

[163]. Feb. 7. 1588. 31. Eliz. This day the house was called over and all those that did then sit in the house, and were present at the calling of the same, did thereupon severally answer to their names, & departed out of the house as they were called. Town. 15.[1]

publishing debates.

[164]. 31. Eliz. 1588. Speeches used in this house by the members of the same should not be made or used as table talk, or in any wise delivered in notes of writing to any person or persons whatsoever, not being members of this house, for that they are the common council of this realm. D'Ewes. 432. Col. 2.[1]

naming Commee.

[165]. 10. Nov. 1640. 16.Car.1. At the naming a Commee., if any man rise to speak about the same, the clerk ought not to write down any more names whilst the member standing up is speaking.[1] Rush, p.3. v.1. fol.41. Scob. 47. L. Parl. c.15.18.[2]

no new Motion till former determd.

[166]. 10. Nov. 1640. When a business is begun & in debate, if any man rise to speak to a new business, any member may, but mr. Speaker ought to interrupt him. Rush. p.3. v.1. fol.42.[1]

Reporters to Conferences. Messenger.

[167]. 11. Nov. 1640. The Reporters ought to go first to take their places at Conferences. Id. 44.[1]

[168]. 25. Nov. 1640. When any message is to go up to the Lords none shall go out of the house before the messenger. id. 60.[1]

right to a seat.

[169]. 26 Nov. Neither book nor glove may give any man title or interest to any place if they themselves be not here at prayers. id. 61.[1]

2d readg of bills.

[170]. Dec. 4. 1684. Ordered that no bills have their second reading but between nine & twelve. id. 84.[1]

who go forth.

[171]. Dec. 10. Declared for a constant rule, that those who give their votes for the preservation of the orders of the house, should stay in; & those who give their votes otherwise, to the introducing of any new matter, or any alteration, should go out. id. 92.[1]

heats.

Impertinencies.

personal
reflections 68

superfluous
motion
tedious speech

Offensive words.
69

impertinent
speakg. 70

motion to be
seconded. 71

no new motion,
till former
determd. 72

how often speak.

[172]. It is a rule of Order, that there ought to be no heats nor distempers within the house. id. 283.[1]

[173]. Mr. Speaker may stay impertinent speeches. Scobel. 32.[1]

[174]. Apr. 1604. He that digresseth from the matter, to fall upon the person, ought to be suppressed by the Speaker. Scobel. 31.[1] Hale parl. 133.[2]

[175]. Apr. 17. 1604. If any superfluous motion or tedious speech be offered in the house, the party is to be directed & ordered by the Speaker. ibid.[1] Hale. parl. 133.[2]

[176]. No reviling or nipping words must be used, for then all the house will cry 'it is against order.' And if any speak unreverently or seditiously against the prince or the privy council I (i.e. T. Smith) have seen them not only interrupted, but it hath been moved after in the house & they have sent them to the tower. Smith's Commonwealth. L. 2. c.3.[1]

[177]. If any man speak impertinently or beside the question in hand the speaker interrupts him, & asks the pleasure of the house. Whether they will further hear him. Scobel. 33.[1]

[178]. When a motion has been made, the same may not be put to the question, until it be debated, or at least seconded by one or more persons standing up in their places; & then the same may be put to the question, if the question be called for by the house, or their general sense be known, which the Speaker is to demand, unless any member stand up to speak. Scobel. 21.[1]

[179]. When a motion has been made & seconded that matter must receive a determination by the question, or be laid aside by the general sense of the house before another be entertained. ibid. 28. June. 1604. 4. Dec. 1640. Scobel. 22.[1]

[180]. If the matter moved do receive a debate pro et contra in that debate none may speak more than once to the matter: & after some time spent in that debate, the Speaker collecting the sense of the house upon the debate, is to reduce the same into a

question, which he is to propound, to the end the house in their debate afterward may be kept to the matter of the question, if the same be approved by the house to contain the substance of the former debate. Scob. 22.[1]

form of question. 73

[181]. After such question is propounded, any member may offer his reasons against that question in whole or in part: which may be laid aside by a general consent of the house, without a question put. Scob. 22.[1]

Qu. on Amendmt.

[182]. But without such general consent, no part of the question propounded may be laid aside or omitted; & tho' the general debates run against it, yet if any member before the question put (without that part) stand up, & desire that such words or clause may stand in the question before the main question is put; a question is to be put Whether those words, or that clause shall stand in the question. Scob. 23.[1]

speak to amendmt. 74.

[183]. The like method is observed when any other alteration is debated upon to be made in a question propounded: but upon putting a question for such addition, alteration or omission, any person, who hath formerly spoken to the matter of the question, may speak again, to shew his reasons for, or against such alteration, addition, or omission, before such question be put. ibid.[1]

speak before Negative. 75

[184]. When the Speaker (the house calling for a question) is putting the same, any member that hath not spoken before to the matter, may stand up before the Negative be put. ibid.[1]

Affirm & Neg. to be put 76

[185]. A bill having been formerly on a third reading recommitted, was returned: & a Proviso being tendered for Chester, which was twice read, the question was put for commitment in the affirmative, after which the Negative was put, which was admitted to be so, orderly, because it is no full question without the Negative part be put, as well as the Affirmative. ibid.[1]

every member vote. 77

[186]. Every question is to be put first in the Affirmative & then in the Negative: to which ques-

may call for
divisn.

tion every member ought to give his vote one way or other; & the Speaker is to declare his opinion whether the Yeas or Nos have it, which is to stand as the judgment of the house. But if any member, *before any new motion made*, shall stand up & declare that he doth believe that the Yeas, or the Noes (as the case shall be) have it, contrary to the Speaker's opinion then the Speaker is to give direction for the house to divide, declaring whether the Yeas or the Noes are to go forth. id. 24.[1]

who go forth.

[187]. Upon the dividing of the house, those are to go forth who are for varying from, or against the constant orders of the house (as that a question shall not be put, or not be now put; it being the course of the house that after a debate the same should be determined by a question or the like) or against any positive order made by the house, or for the passing any new thing, & for reading a petition, or bill, and committing, ingrossing, or passing such bills, or the like. Scobel. 25.[1]

who go forth.

[188]. Those that are for the new bill (if there be a question of voices) shall go out of the house; and those who are against the bill, and for the common law, or any former law, shall sit still in the house, for they are in possession of the old law.[1] Yet in 1604, those for the bill sate, & those against it went out. So. 7. Aug. 1641.[2] Scob. 52. Co. 12.116. D'Ewes 505. Col. 1. vid. contra Scob. 43.[3]

who go forth.

[189]. 24. Mar. 21. Jac. 25. The house being divided upon a question about election of members; it was overruled by the house that the Noes should go forth. This is also the course upon any question to agree with a report in favour of the opinion of a Committee.[1] Memorials in Hakewell. 25.[2]

Tellers.

[190]. Upon dividing the house the Speaker is to nominate two of those that are in the Affirmative, & two of the Negatives to count the house; which four, each of them having a staff in his hand, are to count the number of the persons who remain sitting in the house: & then to stand within the

door, two on the one side, & two on the other, & to count the number of them who went forth as they come in. id. 26.[1]

house in
division. 78

[191]. While the house is thus divided, or dividing, no member may speak, nor, unless it be to go forth upon the division, remove out of his place. ibid.[1]

Tellers.

[192]. When the house is thus told, those two of the Tellers, who are of the number of those who have the major votes, standing on the right-hand, and the two other on the left-hand at the bar, the rest being all set in their places, are to come from thence up to the table together, making the usual obeysance to the house three times, once at the bar, again in the middle of the house, and again when they are come to the table, & that person who stands on the right hand is to declare to the Speaker the number of the Yeas, who sat, or went out, as the case is, & of the Noes: & then with like reverence to depart into their places; after which Mr. Speaker is to report the same to the house. id. 27.[1]

Entry.

[193]. If the affirmative have the major votes by the judgment of the Speaker, or in case of Division, upon the division, the Clerk is to enter the vote 'Resolved.' If the Negatives, then he is to enter it thus—'the question being put' (setting down the words of the question) 'it passed in the Negative. ibid.[1]

Speaker's vote.

[194]. Upon the division, if the members appear to be equal then the Speaker is to declare his vote, whether he be a Yea, or a No, which in this case is the casting vote: but in other cases the Speaker gives no vote. ibid.[1]

Change opinion.
79

[195]. 1. May. 1606. Upon a question, whether a man saying Yea may afterwards sit & change his opinion, a precedent was remembered by the Speaker of Mr. Morris, Attorney of the wards, in 39. Eliz. that in like case changed his opinion. ibid.[1]

Previous Quest.
80

[196]. If upon a debate it be much controverted & much be said against the question, any member

may move that the question may be first made, whether that question shall be put, or whether it shall be now put; which usually is admitted at the instance of any member, especially if it be seconded & insisted on: & if that question being put it pass in the affirmative, then the main question is to be put immediately, & no man may speak any thing further to it, either to add or alter. But before the question '(whether the question shall be put') any person, who hath not formerly spoken to the main question, hath liberty to speak for it, or against it; because else he shall be precluded from speaking at all to it. id. 28.[1]

which Qu. first?

[197]. If in a debate there arise more questions than one & it be controverted which question should be first put; the question first moved & seconded is regularly to be first put unless it be laid aside by general consent. If the first question be insisted on to be put, & the major part seem to be against it, the Question is to be Whether that question shall be now put: if that pass in the Negative, then the other question may be put, if desired: nevertheless any person may speak to it again, before it be put. If in the affirmative, then it is to be put without any addition or alteration, as before: and after the question is put, if any member move to have the other question put, every one hath leave to speak to it again, as if it were a new question. ibid.[1]

who go forth.

[198]. If a matter be received into debate, & a question grow whether the house shall proceed in that debate at this time, & it fall out that the house be divided; in such case the Noes are to go forth, it being contrary to the course of the house that any business should be laid aside till it be determined by a question; if the question be for an adjournment of a debate, the Yeas are to go forth upon the same reason. id. 29.[1]

how often speak.
81

[199]. After a question is propounded, no man may speak more than once to the matter; but having spoken to the matter when the question comes to be put, he may speak to the manner or words of

[93]

the question, keeping himself to that only and not ravelling into the merits of it. ibid.[1]

divide question.
82.

[200]. If a question upon a debate contain more parts than one, & the members seem to be for one part, & not for the other, it may be moved, that the same may be divided into two, or more questions: as Dec. 2. 1640. the debate about the election of two knights was divided into two questions. ibid.[1]

none mentd by
name.
83

[201]. No member in his discourse in the house may mention the name of any other member then present, but to describe him by his title, or addition, or office, or place, or the like. id. 3. Smyth's Commonw. 85.[1]

speakg. to order.
84.

[202]. During any debate any member, tho' he have spoken to the matter, may rise up, & speak to the orders of the house, if they be transgressed, in case the Speaker do not: but if the Speaker stand up, he is first to be heard, & when he stands up, the other must sit down, till the Speaker sit down. Memorials in Hakewell. 30.[1]

speakg. to order.
85.

[203]. But if any person rise up to speak to the orders of the house in the midst of a debate, he must keep within that line & not fall into the matter itself: if he do, he may be taken down by the Speaker or any other member calling to the orders of the house. ibid. & 31.[1]

no interruption
while speaking.

[204]. While a member is speaking to a debate or question, he is to be heard out, & not taken down, unless by mr. Speaker (as in some cases he may) or that he speak of such matter as the house doth not think fit to admit. id. 31. Town. col. 205.[1]

no reconsidering.
86

[205]. A Question having been once made & carried in the Affirmative or Negative, cannot be questioned again, but must stand as the judgment of the house. Mem. in Hakew. 33.[1]

bar up, or down,
on examn. of
witness.

[206]. If a witness be brought to the house, the house sitting, the bar is to be down; otherwise if the house be in a Commee. id. 69.[1]

party concerned
to withdraw.

[207]. In a debate about an election, resolved that the party concerned shall be heard to inform the house, & then he is to go forth. id. 70.[1]

do. 87.

[208]. When any complaint is made against a

to the contrary) & tho' he be earnestly pressed by the house for the reading of some one bill, yet if he have not had convenient time to read the same over, & to make a breviat thereof for his own memory, the Speaker doth claim a privilege to defer the reading thereof to some other time. Hakew. 136.[1]

1st. reading of a Bill 91.

[222]. The clerk being usually directed by the Speaker (but sometime by the house) what bill to read, with a loud & distinct voice first reads the title of the bill, & then, after a little pause, the bill itself; which done, kissing his hand, he delivereth the same to the Speaker; who standeth up uncovered (whereas otherwise he sitteth with his hat on) and holding the bill in hand, saith, the bill is thus intituled, & then readeth the title; which done, he openeth to the house the substance of the bill, which he doth, either trusting to his memory, or using the help, or altogether the reading of his Breviat, which is filed to the bill. Hakew. 137.[1]
⟨sometimes.⟩ reading[2]

effect of vote on the Qu. of Rejection. 92.

[223]. If the question for rejection be made & the greater voice be to have it rejected, the clerk ought to note it rejected in his journal, & so to indorse it on the back of the bill; & it shall be no more read: if the voice be to have it retained, it shall have his second reading in course. Hakew. 141. Scob. 42.[1]

leave to bring in bill. 93

[224]. Any member of the house may offer a bill for publick good except it be for imposing a tax; which is not to be done, but by order of the house first had. Scob. 40. If any member desire that an act made and in force, may be repealed or altered, he is first to move the house in it, & have their resolution, before any bill to that purpose may be offered; & if upon the reasons shewed for repealing or altering such law, the house shall think it fit, they do usually appoint one or more of the⟨ir⟩ members to bring in a bill for that purpose. Scob. 40.[1]

Explanatory law.

[225]. All men of law know, that a bill which is only expository, to expound the common law doth enact nothing, neither is any Proviso good therein. Town. Col. 238.[1]

[97]

bill twice read in a day.

[226]. When special Committees, appointed for the drawing of some one special bill, present the same ready drawn to the house, it hath been often seen that the same bill hath not only been twice read, but ordered also to be engrossed the same day. Hakew. 142.[1]

bill thrice read in day.

[227]. It is not without precedent that a ⟨*precedent*⟩ bill hath been thrice read & passed in the same day. ibid.[1]

bill 4. times read.

[228]. A bill was read the fourth time, before it passed the house, & tho there want not other precedents, yet it is rare & worth the observation. D'Ewes. 90. Co. 1.[1]

Quest. on 1st. readg. 94.

[229]. A bill was put to the question upon the first reading & rejected, but it is not usual for a bill to be put to the question upon the first reading. D'Ewes 335. Col. 1.[1]

bill twice Committed. 95

[230]. 27. Eliz. 1584. A bill was committed upon the third reading, having been formerly committed upon the second; which is not usual. D'Ewes. 337. Col. 2. 414. Col. 2.[1]

2d. Reading of bills

[231]. A bill may be preferred to be secondly read the next day after the first reading; but the usual course is to forbear for two or three days that men may have more time to consider upon it, except the nature of the business be such that it requireth haste. Hakew. 143.[1]

.96

[232]. After the bill is secondly read, the Clerk, as before, in humble manner delivereth the same to the speaker, who again readeth the title & his Breviat, as he did upon the first reading; which done he declareth 'that it was a second reading of the bill.' And then he ought to pause a while, expecting whether any of the house will speak to it; for before the Speaker hath so declared the state of the bill, no man should offer to speak to it, & then & not before, is the time when to speak. Hakew. 143.[1]

Quest. on 2d readg 97

[233]. If after a pretty distance of time, no man speak against the bill for matter or form, he may make the question for ingrossing thereof, if it be a bill originally exhibited into the Commons house. ibid.[1]

[234]. So likewise if divers speak for the bill, without taking exception to the matter or form thereof, he may make the same question for the ingrossing. id. 144.[1]

[235]. The like question for the ingrossing ought to be made if the greater voice be 'that the bill should not be committed': for it were to end further delay in the proceeding of the bill, if there be no exception taken to the matter or form thereof: but upon the second reading & after the Speaker hath delivered the state thereof, the house doth usually call for committing of the bill; & then if any man will speak against it, either for matter or form, he ought to be heard. ibid.[1]

Quest. for Committg bill. 98

[236]. After the first man hath spoken, the Speaker ought to rest a while, expecting whether any other man will speak thereto: so ought he likewise to do after every speech ended: when he perceiveth that the debate is at an end, he ought then to make the question for the committing thereof, in this sort, 'as many as are of opinion that this bill shall be committed say Yea.' & after the affirmative voice be given, 'as many as are of the contrary opinion, say No.' & he ought by his ear to judge which of the voices is the greatest: if that be doubtful the house ought to be divided. id. 144.[1]

naming Commee. 99.

[237]. If it appear that the Affirmative voice be the greater then ought he to put the house in mind touching the naming of Committees, which is done thus.[1] Every one of the house that list may call upon the name of any one of the house to be a Committee, & the clerk ought in his journal to write under the title of the bill the name of every one so called on, at least of such whose names (in that Confusion) he can distinctly hear; & this he ought to do without partiality, either to those that name, or to the party named. He that speaketh directly against the body of a bill may not be named a Committee: for he that would totally destroy, will not amend it.[2] Hakew. 146. Town. Coll. 208. D'Ewes 634. Col. 2. Scob. 47.

appoint meetg. of Commee.

[238]. When a convenient number of Committees are named, then ought the Speaker to put the

house in mind to name time & place when & where the Committees may meet; which the Clerk ought likewise to enter into his Journal book: & when the house is in silence, he ought with a loud voice to read out of his book the Committees names, & the time & place of the Commitment, that the Committees may take notice thereof. Hakew. 146.[1]

quest. on 2d reading of a bill from the Lords. 100

[239]. After a bill which is sent from the Lords is twice read, the question ought to be for the Commitment: if it be denied to be committed, it ought to be read the third time, and the next question ought to be for the passage, & not for the ingrossing (as it is where the bill originally begins in the lower house) for bills which come from the Lords come alwais engrossed. ibid.[1]

Quest. on Passage

[240]. The question for the passage should in ordinary course be then made when the bill is denied to be committed; but not till the bill be read the third time. Hakew. 147.[1]

how often speak. 101.

[241]. In the debating of bills in the house, no man may speak twice in one day (unless some time by way of explication) except the bill be oftener read than once; and then a man may speak as often as the bill is read. Otherwise it is at Committees, or when in the house the debate ariseth upon some motion concerning the order of the house. Co. 12.116. Hakew. 148.[1]

Quest. for Ingrossg.

[242]. After the debate is ended, the Speaker ought to put the question for Ingrossing. Hakew. 250.[1]

bill Dashed.

[243]. If the greater number of voices be that the bill ought not to be engrossed, the clerk ought to make an entry in his journal, that the same was dashed: and so he ought likewise to note upon the back of the bill, & the day when. If the voice be to have it engrossed, it is the office of the clerk to do it. Hakew. 250.[1]

endorse title 101a

[244]. When the bill is engrossed the clerk ought to endorse the title thereof upon the back of the bill, & not within the bill in any case. Hakew. 250. So ought likewise such bills as come from the lords to have titles endorsed on the back of the bill & not within. ibid.[1]

Recommitment.
102

[245]. After a bill hath been committed & is reported it ought not in any ordinary course to be committed but either to be dashed or engrossed: and yet when the matter is of importance, it is sometimes for special reasons suffered; but then usually the recommittment is to the same Committee. Hakew. 151.[1]

3d reading.

[246]. About two or three days after the bill is thus ordered to be engrossed, and is accordly. engrossed, it is offered by the Speaker to be read a third time, for the passage thereof. Hakew. 152.[1]

Notice of 3d
readg.

[247]. For the most part, the Speaker putteth not any one bill to the passage by itself alone, but stayeth till there be divers bills ready engrossed for the third reading; & when he hath a convenient number (which may be 5, or 6, rather less than more) then he giveth notice to the house 'that he purposeth next day to offer up some bills for the passage, and desireth the house to give special attendance for that purpose.' And then the day following he doth accordingly put them to the third reading. first private bills, until the house be grown to some fullness; & then he offereth to be read the public bills, which are engrossed. Hakew. 153.[1]

hour of Quest. on
passage. 102.b.

[248]. It hath been sometimes ordered that for the preventing of carrying of bills with a few voices, no bills should be put to the passage until 9. o'the clock, at which time the house is commonly full, or shortly after. Hakew. 153.[1]

Report on
passage 103.

[249]. When the bill is read the third time, the clerk delivereth it to the speaker, who reads the title thereof & openeth the effect of the bill, & telleth them that the bill hath now been thrice read, & that with their favors he will put it to the question for the passing; but pauseth a while that men may have liberty to speak thereto; for upon the third reading the matter is debated afresh, and for the most part, it is more spoken unto this time, than upon any of the former readings. Hakew. 153.[1]

Quest. on
passage 104

[250]. When the argument is ended, the Speaker (still holding the bill in his hand) maketh a question for the passage, in this sort: 'as many as

are of opinion, that this bill should pass, say Yea,'
[&c.] Hakew. 154.[1]

entry in journal.
105

[251]. If the voice be for the passage of the bill,
the clerk ought to make a remembrance thereof in
his journal; if otherwise, then his remembrance
must be accordingly made. Hakew. 154.[1]

Notation on the
bill. ⟨Bro. abr. f.
edit. n. 4.⟩

[252]. Upon the bill thus passed (if it be originally exhibited in the house of Commons) the clerk
ought to write within the bill on the top toward the
right hand 'soit baille aux Seigneurs.' If the bill
passed be originally begun in the Lords house then
ought the clerk to write undeneath the subscription of the lords which always is at the foot of the
bill 'a cest bill les Commons sont assentus.'[1] Bro.
abr. f. edit. n.4.[2]

Endorsemt.
where.

[253]. Endorsements should be on the neither &
lower part not on the upper. D'Ewes jour. 344.
col. 2.[1]

Recommitmt. on
3d reading 106

[254]. No bill upon the 3d reading for the matter or body thereof, may be recommitted: but for
some particular clause or proviso it hath been
sometimes suffered; but it is to be observed as a
thing unusual after the third reading. Hak. 156.[1]

107

[255]. If a bill be rejected, the same bill may not
be offered to the house again the same session; but
if it be altered in any point material both in the
body & in the title, it may be received the second
time. Hakew. 158.[1]

no interruption
while bill readg.

[256]. In the time of the reading of a bill the
house should not be interrupted with any other
business & yet in 1. El. the house adjourned itself
till the next day after a bill was half read, only to be
present at the conference about religion in Westminster abby. Hakew. 158.[1]

bills ordd to be
torn.

[257]. Sometimes the house conceiving much
offence against some bills, doth not only order
them to be rejected, but to be torn &c. in the house.
Hakew. 158.[1]

bill not to be
altered after
passed. 108

[258]. When a bill is thrice read, & passed in the
house, there ought to be no further alteration
thereof in any point. Hakew. 159.[1]

bills to be sent to
the lords.

[259]. When the Speaker hath in his hands a
convenient number of bills ready passed, as 5. or 6.

or thereabouts,[1] he then putteth the house in mind of sending them up to the lords & desireth the house to appoint messengers; who accordingly do appoint some one principal member for that purpose; to whom the bills are delivered in such order, as he ought to present them to the lords; which is done by direction of the Speaker, except the house be pleased to give special direction therein. Hak. 175. The order which hath been usually observed in ranking them as 1st. those that came originally from the lords; 2dly those that having been sent up to the lords from the Commons, were sent back to be amended: 3dly. public bills originally coming from the Commons house & these to be marshalled according to their degrees in cosequence. lastly are to be placed private bills, in such order as the Speaker pleaseth. Hak. 176. Many times the house (with a purpose especially to grace some one bill) sendeth it alone with a special recommendation thereof: the messenger for this purpose is usually attended by 30 or 40 of the house, as they please & are affected to the business. Hakew. 176.[2]

bills, how delivd by Messenger.

[260]. The principal messenger, who delivers the bills to the lords, coming in the first rank of his company to the bar of the Lords house with three Congies[1] telleth the lords 'that the knights, citizens, & burgesses of the Commons house, have sent unto their Lordships certain bills; & then reading the title of every bill, as it lieth in order, he so delivereth the same in an humble manner to the Lord Chancellor; who of purpose cometh to receive them.[2]

bills by whom sent.

[261]. Bills sent from the Lords to the Commons house if they be ordinary bills, are sent down by Serjeants at law, or by two doctors of the Civil law being masters of the Chancery & attendants in the upper house, accompanied sometimes with the clerk of the crown. Hak. 177. Bills of greater moment are usually sent down by some of the judges assistants there, accompanied with some of the masters of the chancery; who being admitted entrance, do come up close to the table. where the clerk sits, making three Congies, & there acquaint-

ing the Speaker 'that the lords have sent unto the house certain bills' doth read the titles, and deliver the bills to the Speaker; and so departeth with three Congies.[1]

Speaker to report titles of bills sent. 109

[262]. When ⟨*bills*⟩ the messengers sent from the Lords with bills are out of the house, the Speaker holds the bills in hands & acquaints the house 'that the Lords by their messengers have sent to the house certain bills' & then reading the title of every bill, delivereth them to the Clerk to be safely kept & to be read when they shall be called for. Hak. 178.[1]

[263]. 39. Eliz. Feb. 9. 1597. Her majesty gave her royal assent to 24 public acts & 19 private, & refused 48 which had passed both houses. Towns. Coll. 127.[1]

private acts not enrolled

[264]. A private or particular act is always filed but not enrolled.[1] ⟨*Arc. Parl. 45.*⟩[2] Atk. arg. 57.[3]

time of Commencemt. of law.

[265]. Every bill that passeth the parliament shall have relation to the first day of the parliament, though it come in at the end of the parliament, unless a time be specially appointed by the statute for it's commencement. Arc. parl. 45.[1]

bill to be fairly written. 110

[266]. If a bill be admitted to be read, it is to be presented fairly written, without any razure or interlineation, together with a breviat of the heads of the bill; & unless it be so tendered, the Speaker may refuse it. Scobel 41.[1]

when may speak.

[267]. Until the bill be opened no man may speak to it. Scob. 42.[1]

effect of division. 111

[268]. It is the usual rule of the law, that where the numbers of the affirmative and negative are equal 'semper presumetur pro negante' the negatives by custom carry it; i.e. that the former law is not to be changed.[1] Towns. Coll. 134.[2] [But neither the house nor a committee can ever be divided.][3]

effect of a Vote.

[269]. When votes are digested into a bill, & that comes to be read, or passed, it is lawful to debate or argue against all, or any part thereof, to alter or reject it: because votes in order to a bill are no further binding, but that the bill is to be presented containing those votes; & because the bill

[104]

gives occasion of a more large debate, before it can pass into a law, every member hath liberty to offer his reasons against it, as well as to give his vote as often as it comes to a question. Scobel 45.[1]

how to move amendments. 112

[270]. When a bill has been read the 2d time & opened any member may move to have it amended, but must speak but once to it; & therefore must take all his exceptions to it, & every part of it, at one time; for in the debate of a bill, no man may speak but once the same day, except the bill be read more than once that day & then he may speak as often as it is read. Scob. 58.[1]

4th. reading.

[271]. A bill was read in the house of Lords four times. Quere if in one day? Hist. Reform. vol. 1. p. 144.[1] and have been read as far as a 6th. & 7th. time. Elsynge. 31.[2]

Committees 113

[272]. Committees are such as either house chuse to frame the laws upon such bills as are agreed upon and afterward to be ratified by the same houses. Symth's commw. 75.[1] Sometimes the house upon debate doth pass some votes to be the heads of a bill, or refer it to a Commee. of the whole house to prepare such heads. Scob. 44.[2]

cannt add members to a Commee. 113.b.

[273]. 43. Eliz. 1601. By order of the house it was agreed upon that a Commee. once made & agreed upon there shall not hereafter be more Commees. joined unto them for the same bill; but for any other there may. D'Ewes Col. 1. 190.[1]

Number upon Commee.

[274]. Commees. upon bills have not usually been less than 8, sometimes 20, seldom more in former times, which engaged them to attend it & speed it. Scobel. 47.[1]

how many to proceed

[275]. Apr. 12. 1604. Ordd. that if 8. of any Commee. do assemble, they might proceed to a resolution of any business of the house. Scob. 48. Five may adjourn. id. 48.[1]

who to be of Commee. 114

[276]. All who took exceptions at any particulars in the bill (but not those who spoke against the whole bill) are to be of the Commee. Scob. 47.[1]

who name Commee. 114.b.

[277]. Any member that pleases, may name one member apiece, but not more, to be of a commee. Scob. 47.[1]

who may be
present at a
Commee. 115

[278]. Any member of the house may be present at any select Commee; but is not to give his vote unless he be named to be of the Commee. Scob. 49.[1]

wherefore
committed.
116

[279]. If the exceptions to a bill be such, that it may not be amended at the table, then the question is for committing the bill; but no bill is to be committed without some exceptions taken to it. Scob. 46.[1]

what amendmts.
on 2d reading.

[280]. No proviso or Clauses are to be tendered to a bill upon the 2d reading; because if it be committed it is proper to offer them to the Commee., without troubling the house.[1] 16. Jun. 1604.[2] Scob. 46.

wherefore
committed.

[281]. Referring a bill to Commees. is chiefly for amendmt. or altern. thereof, after it hath been penned and put into the house by some one or more private men. Dewes. 186.[1]

when to be
committed.

[282]. 1592. 35.El. Held against the order of the house that a bill should be committed before it was read. Towns. Col. 61. Dewes. 476. Col. 1.[1]

wherefore
committed.

[283]. The proceeding in a Commee. is more honourable & advantageous to the king & the house; for that way leads most to the truth. And it is a more free & open way, where every man may add his reason, & make answer upon the hearing of other mens reasons & arguments. Rush. 557.[1]

bill to be delivd
to any of
Commee. 116.b.

[284]. In either house, after any bill is committed upon the 2d reading, it may be delivered indifferently to any of the said Commees. Towns. Col. 138.[1]

quest. on 2d
reading.

[285]. If the quest. for commitmt. pass in the negative, then the question is to be put for the ingrossing the bill. But if the question for ingrossing the bill pass in the negative then the question is to be put for rejecting the bill. Scob. 46.[1]

when Commee.
to proceed.

[286]. In some cases the house hath ordered a Commee. to withdraw into the Commee. chamber presently & to prepare & bring back the bill, sitting the house. Scob. 48.[1]

[287]. 1641. July 28. Declared by the house that no Commee. ought by votes to determine the

right or property of the subject without first acquainting the house therewith. Scob. 39.[1]

vote of Commee. not authoritative.

[288]. 1641. Aug. 6. Resolved that no vote passed at a Commee., & not reported nor confirmed by the house shall be any rule or direction for any court of justice to ground any proceedings thereon. Scob. 39.[1]

vote of Commee not authoritative. 117.

[289]. A Commee. of either house ought not by law to publish their own results, neither are their conclusions of any force without the confirmation of the house, which hath the same power of controuling them as if the matter had never been debated. Rush. part 3. vol. 2: p. 74.[1]

who speak first.

[290]. 1592. 35.El. Two or three stood up to speak, striving who might speak first. It was made a rule 'that the Chairman shall ask the parties that would speak on which side they would speak, whether with him that spake next before, or against him; and the party that speaketh against the last speaker is to be heard first. Dewes 493. Col. 2.[1]

to speak sitting or standg. 118

[291]. 1601. 43.Eliz. Sr. Walt. Raleigh speaking at a Commee., Sr. Edw. Hobby told him 'he should speak standing that the house might hear him.' To which Sr. Walt. Raleigh replied 'that being a Commee., he might speak sitting, or standing.' Dewes 630. Col. 1. 2. Hats. 77.[1]

Commee., in what order to proceed. 119

[292]. The Commee. are first to read the bill, & then to consider the same by parts. Scob. 49. The preamble, if any be, is usually considered after the other parts of the bill; because upon consideration of the body of the bill, such alterations may therein be made as may also occasion the alteration of the preamble; which will be best done last. Scob. 50.[1]

Commee. not to deface bill. 120

[293]. The Commee. may not raze, interline or blot the bill itself; but must in a paper by itself set down the amendments in this manner (in such a folio & such a line, between such a word and such a word, or after such a word, insert these words, or omit these words). Scob. 50.[1]

Commee. bound by their own vote. 121

[294]. 1607. 4. Jun. When a vote is once passed at a Commee., the same may not be altered, but by the house. Every question upon the voices of the

Commee. bindeth & cannot be altered by themselves.[1]

Commee. to amend Brief.

[295]. 1606. 3 Mar. Ordered 'that every Commee. when they proceed to the amendmt. of any bill committed to them shall also amend the Breviat annexed, & make it agree with the bill. Scob. 51.[1]

Commee. to attend house when sitting 122

[296]. June 1641. Ordered that so soon as the house sits, & that the Serjeant comes to any Commee. then sitting, to signify to them that the house is sitting, that the chairman shall immediately come away to attend the service of the house. 2. Nalson. 319.[1]

quest. to report. 123

[297]. When the amendmts. are all perfected every one being voted singly, all of them are to be read at the Commee. & put to the question, whether the same shall be reported to the house. When the vote is to be put, any member of the Commee. may move to add to those amendmts. or to amend any other part of the bill. Scob. 50.[1]

who to report. 124

[298]. If the vote of the Commee. pass for reporting the Amendmts. to the house, then he of the members of the Commee. (which is commonly the Chairman) who is best acquainted with the bill, is to be *appointed* to make the report; which being done, that Commee. is dissolved, & can act no more without a new power. Scob. 51.[1]

reports, when to be received.

[299]. Reports are usually to be received daily in the first place, after the house is full; except there be bills engrossed, which are to take place, & publick bills before private. Scob. 51.[1]

report, in what form to be made. 125

[300]. The reporter must first acquaint the house, that he is to make a report from such a Commee. to whom such a bill was committed; & standing in his place must read each of the amendments, with the coherence in the bill; & opening the alterations, & the reasons of the Commee. for such amendments, until he hath gone thro' all; & then must, if he sit not in the seat next the floor) come from his place to the bar, & so come up to the table, & deliver both the bill & the amendmts. to the clerk; by whom he is to stand while they are twice read; which is to be done by him (without reading

any words that are to be omitted but only such as are to be inserted) before any man speak to any of them; & then the bill with the amendmts., is to be delivd to the Speaker. Scob. 52. Hakew. 148. 1607. Jun. Agreed for a rule 'that every thing directed & agreed to be reported, ought accordingly to be reported: but not every thing spoken or debated at the Commee.' Scob. 39.[1]

amendmts. to be twice read.

[301]. 1601. 43. Eliz. By order of the house agreed 'when a bill is returned from commitment, the words must be twice read, which are amended, before the ingrossing thereof. Dewes 189.[1]

126

[302]. 1607. 4. Jun. The bill touching the Union between England & Scotland having been committed, when the amendmts. were reported, the whole bill was *by order of the house* read first, & then amendmts. by themselves. Which is a single precedent used only in a case of great weight. Scob. 52.[1]

amendmts. may be opposed.

[303]. After reading the amendments, any member may speak against all, or any of the amendments and desire the coherence to be read. But he is to make all his objections at once to all the amendmts., without speaking again. Scob. 52.[1]

[304]. Exceptions may be taken as well to what is omitted out of the bill by the Commee., as to what is amended. Scob. 53.[1]

who may oppose.

[305]. 1601. 43 El. Resolved upon the question if any Commee. speak against a bill at the Commitment he may speak again at the ingrossing thereof in the house, and have his free voice. Towns. 208. Dewes 135. Col. 1.[1] Same order 11 Nov. 1601. Memorials 60. 61. Towns. Col.[2]

Amendmts. how to be written.

[306]. Amendmts. in bills ought to be writ in paper not in parchment, without any indorsemt. Dewes 573.574.[1]

quest. on Report.
127

[307]. Upon any report from a Committee the first question ought to be for agreeing with the report, unless the house generally dislike it. Scob. 53.[1]

GRAND
COMMEES.

[308]. A Grand committee consists of as many members at least as constitute the house; less may not sit nor act as a ⟨*house*⟩ committee; who have

general power to consider of any matter touching the subject-matter referred, & to present their opinions therein to the house, the better to prepare matters of that nature or bills thereon for the house: which may better be prepared by the liberty that every member hath in a grand Commee., as well as in other Commees. to speak more than once to the same business, if there be cause, which is not permitted in the house. Scob. 35.[1]

what bills to Gr. Commee.

128

[309]. Bills of great concernment, & chiefly bills to impose a tax, or raise money from the people, are committed to a commee. of the whole house; to the end there may be opportunity for fuller debate: for that at a Commee. the members have liberty to speak as often as they shall see cause to one question: & that such bills being of general concernment, should be most solemnly proceeded in & well weighed. Scob. 49.[1]

what referrd to Gr. Commee.

[310]. The Commons upon debate of what fell from his majesty and the Lord Keeper, turned the house into a Grand Commee., ordered the doors to be locked, & no members to go forth; & that all proceedings in all other commees. shall cease till the house come to a resolution in this business.[1] Rushw. 225.[2]

manner of resolving into Gr. Commee.

[311]. When any great business is in agitation that requires much debate, or a bill for a public tax is to be committed, the house doth use to resolve into a Grand commee. of the whole house; which is done by a question; & then the Speaker leaves the chair; & thereupon the Commee makes choice of a Chairman. Scob. 36.[1]

who to put quest. for chairman.

129

[312]. If more than one be generally called to the chair, any member may stand up, & by consent of the Commee. put a question for one of those named to be the chairman. Scob. 36. 19 Jac. 1: A dispute being in the Commee., which of two members named should go to the chair, the Speaker was called to his chair & put the question 'that Sr. Ed. Coke (one of the persons named) should take the chair' & then the Speaker left his chair. Scob. 36.[1]

Chairman,
where to sit.

[313]. The Chairman of the Grand-Commee. is to sit in the clerk's place at the table & to write the votes of the Commee. id. ib.[1]

manner of
dividing.

[314]. If upon putting a question the Chairman (who is to judge the voices) have delivered his opinion that the yeas have it, & any member stand up & say he believes the Noes have it (or contrariwise) the Commee. is to divide within the house, the Chairman directing the Yeas to one side of the house & the Noes to the other, & then he is to appoint one of each to count the numbers & report them; which is to be done in the same order as in the house, saving that the obeisance is only twice in the Commee., thrice in the house.[1] If the number be equal, the Chairman hath the casting voice, otherwise he hath none in the Commee.[2] Scob. 38.[3]

Gr. Commee.
cannot adjourn.
130

[315]. If the Commee. cannot perfect the business at that sitting, they may not adjourn as other Commees.; but a question is to be made for reporting to the house & that leave be asked, that the Commee. may sit at another time on that business. Scob. 38.[1]

rising &
reporting.
131.

[316]. When the Commee. hath gone thro' the matter referred to them, the chairman having read all the votes, is to put the question 'that the same be reported to the house.' If that be resolved, he is to leave the chair, & the Speaker being again called to the chair (or at the next sitting of the house, if it be then adjourned) the chairman is to report what had been resolved at the Commee., standing in his usual place; from whence (if it be not in the seat next the floor) he is to go down to the bar, and so to bring up his report to the table. Scob. 38.[1]

rules in other
cases. 132

[317]. In other things the rules of proceedings are to be the same as are in the house. Scob. 39.[1]

Powers of Gr.
Commees.

[318]. Grand Commees. have their powers & rules in other circumstances given them in express words by the house as to send for witnesses, to hear counsel, or assign them on either part, to send for persons, papers and records. id. 35.[1]

[111]

disobedce. to Gr. Commees.

[319]. 15. May. 22, Jac. 1. Upon complaint from the Grand Commee. for Greivances that they had sent several warrants for divers persons to bring in their patents, which they had not done, the house ordered the Serjeant at arms to send for them. Scob. 36.[1]

house moved for order.

[320]. 8. & 13. March. 21. Jac. 1. Upon report from the Commee. for trade (which then was a grand commee., the house was moved for their order to the merchants adventurers to bring in their patents, & that the inventor of the pretermitted customs should attend the commee. Scob. 36.[1]

which are Gr. Commees.

[321]. The Commees. for religion, Grievances & courts of justice are always Grand Commees. of the house, which are to sit in the afternoon upon such days as the house doth appoint to them respectively. The Commee. for trade is sometimes made of a Grand Commee. of the whole house as in 21. Jac. 1. and is now usually so. Scob. 9.[1]

Standing Committees.

[322]. The Commons being the General inquisitors of the realm have principal care in the beginning of the parliament, to appoint days of Commees., viz. of Grievances (both in the Church & Commonwealth) of courts of justice, of Privileges, & advancement of Trade. 4. Inst. 11.[1]

how many?

[323]. In parliamt. there have usually been five standing Commees., appointed in the beginning of the parliament and remaining during all the session; other Commees are made occasionally, and dissolved after the business committed to them is reported. Scob. 9.[1]

what?

[324]. Standing Commees. are for Privileges & elections, Religion, Grievances, Courts of justice, Trade. id. ib.[1]

elect Chairman.
133

[325]. These Commees. when they meet elect one of them to sit in their chair, in likeness of the Speaker. The Commee. may examine, & vote the questions handled by them; & by one, whom they appoint, report their resolutions to the house; & the house sitting, the Speaker to determine the same by question. 4. Inst. 12.[1]

which are grand, which select.

[326]. The Commees. for Religion, Grievances, & Courts of justice, are always grand Commees. of the house; the Commee. for trade hath sometimes been a select Commee. particularly named; and all such members as should come to it to have voices, as in Nov. 1640. Sometimes a grand Commee. of the whole house as 21. Jac. 1. Scob. 9.[1]

Commee. of Privileges.

[327]. The Commee. for Privileges & elections hath always had the precedence of all other Commees., being commonly the first Commee. appointed, and ordinarily the first day after, or the same day the speaker doth take his place. Scob. 10.[1]

may admit Counsel.

[328]. Council may be admitted at that Commee. Scob. 11.[1]

is a select Commee.

[329]. This Commee. is constituted of particular numbers named by the house. Scob. 10.[1]

whether all who come shall have voices.

[330]. 21. Jac. 1. Upon naming a Commee. for Privileges & elections, a motion was made that all that come should have voices; but insisted to be contrary to all former precedents. A question was put, whether all that come should have voices at the Commee., and passed in the negative: another being put Whether the persons nominated only should be of the Commee. it was resolved in the affirmative. Scob. 10.[1]

power of the Commee.

[331]. In the journal 26. Feb. 1600. 42.El. the power antiently given to this Commee., is to examine & make report of all cases touching elections and returns, & all cases for privileges as may fall out during the parliamt. But in other parliaments both before & since, that power doth not appear to have been given them absolutely; but matters of privilege were, upon information to the house, there heard, & not in a committee, unless in some special cases wherein there was cause of examination or some preparation of a charge. Scob. 11. The power of this commee. usually was, as it is entered in Nov. 1640. to examine and consider all questions which shall grow & arise in that parl. about elections, returns, & other privileges. Or, as

in 1. Jac. 1. this Commee. are to examine all matters questionable touching privileges and returns, and to acquaint the house with their proceedings from time to time so as order may be taken according to the occasion, and agreeable with antient customs & precedents. Scob. 12.[1]

term to be fixed for disputing elections.

[332]. To the end these questions may be speedily determined, & the house may know their members days are usually assigned beyond which there shall be no questioning a former election.[1] The time allowed 21. Jac. 1. was 14. days; 16th Apr. 1640 ten days; 6. Nov. 1640 fourteen days, & the same time after any new return.[2] Scob. 12.13.

where a double return, neither member to take seat.

[333]. Some questions have been (where there have been double indentures returned for several persons for the same place) whether all, or any, or which shall sit. The general rule & practice hath been in such case, that neither one nor other shall sit in the house, till it were either decided or ordered by the house.[1] Scob. 13.14. 21. Jac. 1. Scob. 15.22. Mar. 21. Jac. 1. Scob. 15.[2]

petns. to be subscribed & delivered openly to Commee.

[334]. Apr. 17. 19. Jac. 1. Ordered that no petition shall be received by a Commee., but openly at a Commee., & read at the Commee., before the party go that preferred it, & the party's name that preferred it be subscribed. Scob. 16.[1]

affidavits taken in court not to be used.

[335]. In the parl. 21. Jac. 1. resolved that all affidavits to be taken in any court, concerning elections, returns, or anything depending thereupon, should be rejected, & not hereafter to be used. Scob. 17.[1]

punish untruths.

[336]. Though the Commee. examine not upon oath yet they may punish any that shall testify untruly, of which there was an instance in the case of one Damport. Scob. 17.[1]

what makes a Session.

[337]. What shall make a session of parl. See 1. Ro. rep. 29. Hutton 61. 4 inst. 27. 1. Sid. 457. 1. Mod. rep. 151, 155.[1]

from what time acts commence.

[338]. If several bills are passed at one and the same parl. none of them shall have priority of the other; for they are made all in one day and instant,

and each of them have relation to the first day of the parl. though in several chapters; & shall so be construed as if they had been all comprehended in one & the same act of parl.[1] W. Jones. 22. Hob. 111. Bro. tit. parl. 86. & Relat. 35. Plowd. 79.6. Lev. 9.[2] Croke says that tho' in fiction of law a statute shall have relation to the first day of the parl. yet reversa nothing is settled; nor is it a perfect stat. till the parl. is ended.[3] Jones 370. contr. ib: 371. L. parl. c.21. 1. Rush. 581.[4]

from what time acts commence.

[339]. Hales justice said, that if the parl. has several prorogations, & in the second or third session an act is made, this shall not have relation to the day of the beginning of the parl. that is to say to the first day of the first session, but only to the first day of the same session in which it is made. Plowd. 79.6. L. parl. c.21.[1]

Adjournmt. & Prorogation.

[340]. The adjournmt. or continuance of parliament is much more beneficial for the Commonwealth for expediting of causes, than a prorogation. 4. Inst. 28. L. parl. c.21.[1]

who may Adjourn.

[341]. The king may adjourn the parliament. Or the parl. may adjourn itself. Rush. 537.608.660. Resoln. of the house 12. & 18. Jac. 1. Dewes 318. Col. 2. L. parl. c.21.[1]

Commencemt., Prorogn., Dissolution.

[342]. See touching the Commencemt., Prorogn., & Dissoln. of several parliamts. from the beginning of E.3. to the end of R.3. in Cotton's records per totum; & from the beginning of E.6. in Hale's parliamts. 107. to 110. & 142. 143 &c. L. parl. c.21.[1]

Prorogation.

[343]. May. 15. 1540. 32. H. 8. Upon a prorogation of parl. for 10. days a vote passed that their bills should remain in the state they were in, & upon their next meeting they went on accordly. 1. Burn. Reformn. 276. Journ. Comm. L. parl. c.21.[1]

Adjournmt.

[344]. 1628. Apr. 10. 4. Car. A message from the king desiring the house not to ⟨adjourn⟩ make any recess these Easter Holidays, gave offence. 1. Rush. 537. L. parl. c.21.[1]

Adjournmt. by
the king, how to
be made.

[345]. The king may adjourn the house in person or under the great seal, but not by verbal message, for none is bound to give credit to such message. 1. Rush. append. p.48. L. parl. c.21.[1]

Ordinance.

[346]. If an Ordinance only be entered in the parl. roll & it hath the reputation & use of an act of parl. that makes it an act of parl. W. Jones. 104. L. parl. c.22.[1]

Act of parl.
Construction of.

[347]. If any doubt be conceived upon the words or meaning of an act of parl. it is good to construe it ccording to the reason of the Common law. 3. Rush. 77.78.[1]

who go forth?

[348]. 1597. Dec. 15. Resolved according to antient custom of the house, that all the members of the same, which did speak against passing of the bill should go forth of the house to bring the bill into the house again, together with the residue of the members which went out before with the passing of the said bill. All the members of the house being gone forth, except mr. Speaker & the Clerk, mr. Controller brought in the bill in his hand, accompanied with all the members of the house, and delivered the said bill to mr. Speaker. Dec. 17, 1597. The same ceremony on the like occasion omitted upon a motion of the Speaker, & ordered accordingly upon the question. Towns. col. 116.117. Dewes 505. Col. 1. 574. Col. 2. L. parl. c.22.[1]

Money bill.

[349]. The custom & privilege of the house of Comm. hath always been, first to make offer of the subsidies from hence, then to the Upper house except it were that they present a bill to this house, with desire of their assent thereto, and then send it up again. And reason it is that we should stand upon our privilege, seeing the burden resteth upon us as the greatest number. per Francis Bacon. 35.El. 1592. Dewes. 483. Col. 2. L. parl. c.22.[1]

Delivery of
member, how to
be.

[350]. The Ld. Chancellor in parl. offered the Commons a writ to deliver their burgess; but they refused it, as being clear of opinion that all their commandments and acts were to be done and exe-

cuted by their Serjeant without writ. Pet. misc. parl. 4. in marg. L. parl. c.22.[1]

reasons for Disagreement by one house to be given to the other.

[351]. Mar. 19. 1677. It was conceived by the Comm. that according to the antient course & method of transactions between the two houses, when a bill with amendments is sent from either house to the other by messengers of their own, the house that sends them gives no reasons of their amendments but the house to whom it is sent, if they find cause to disagree do use to give reasons for their dissent to every particular amendment. Every one of them is supposed to carry the weight of it's own reason with it until it be objected against. Journ. Com.[1] ⟨364⟩ L. parl. 364.[2].

Petition agt. bill.

[352]. May 28. 1678. A paper of reasons against a bill (viz. for wearing woollen) being printed & delivered at the door, was committed, it being irregular for reasons to be printed & published against a publick bill, before a petition be exhibited to the house against the bill. ib.[1]

Privilege in parl.

[353]. If offences done in parl. might have been punished elsewhere it shall be intended that at some time it would have been put in ure. 4. inst. 17. L. parl. c.22.[1]

Non-usage.

[354]. As Usage is a good interpreter of laws so Non-usage, where there is no example, is a great intendment that the law will not bear it. Not that an act of parl. by Non-user can be antiquated or lose it's force, but that it may be expounded or declared how the act is to be understood. Co. L. 81. b. L. parl. c.22.[1]

Dissolution.

[355]. A parl. cannot be discontinued or dissolved but by matter of record, & that by the king alone. Hutton. 62. L. parl. c.22.[1]

Vote by lords, how given.

[356]. In the Lords' house, the Lords give their voices from the puisne lord seriatim by the word 'Content' or 'Not Content.' 4 inst. 34.35. L. parl. c.22.[1]

Vacation of seat.
Vice.-delegate.

[357]. 18. El. 1575. Resolved by the house that, any member, being either in service of ambassage, or else in execution, or visited with sickness, shall

not in any ways be amoved from their place in this house nor any other to be during such time of service, execution or sickness, elected. Dewes. 244. Col. 2. L. parl. c.22.[1] Hale parl. 116.[2]

Absence without leave.

[358]. 31. El. 1588. Assented to by the whole house that none after the house is set do depart before the rising of the same house, unless he do first ask leave of mr Speaker on pain of paying 6d. to the use of the poor. Dewes. 439. L. parl. c.22.[1]

Cognisance of it's laws is in parl. alone.

[359]. It doth not belong to the judges to judge of any law custom or privilege of parl. 4. inst. 50. Rot. parl. 31. H. 6. n. 27. L. parl. c.22.[1]

Strangers not to debate.

[360]. Cardinal Wolsey coming to the lower house of parl. told them that he desired to reason with them who opposed his demands. But being answered that it was the order of that house to hear & not to reason but among themselves, the Cardinal departed. Herbert's H. 8. 136.[1]

Strangers intruding.

[361]. If any sit in the house who are not returned by the clerk of the crown in Chancery it is accounted a great crime & severely punished. Scobel. 84.[1] Sometimes committed to the custody of the Serjeant ib. Dewes 156. Col. 1. 2. id. 248. Col. 1. id. 334. Col. 1.[2] Sometimes stripped & searched & sworn to secrecy. Scob. 86. Dewes. passim. id. 334. Col. 1.[3]

Call of house. 134.

[362]. 1562. 9 Jan. For that it seemed to the house, being very full that there were a greater number than was returned, therefore the names were immediately called over, & as they were called, departed out of the house. Scob. 85.[1] Chiefly the calling of the house is to discover what members are absent without leave of the house or just cause in which case, fines have been imposed. If the house be called, the manner has been to call over the names:[2] if the person be present, he riseth up bare headed & answereth; if absent, he is either excused (& so entered 'licentiatur per speciale servitium' 'excusatur ex gratiâ' or 'aegrotat') or if none excuse him he is entered 'deficit,'[3] having been called over again the same day; sometimes the day

after; sometimes he is summoned & sometimes sent for by the Serjeant. ib.[4]

Petitions.
134.b

[363]. Petitions are usually presented by members of the same county.[1] If they be concerning private persons, they are to be subscribed; & the persons presenting them called in to the bar, to avow the substance of the petition, especially if it be a complaint against any. 18. Nov. 1640. One Vivers presenting a petition in the name of the Mayor, Aldermen, burgesses & other inhabitants of Banbury, was called in, & did acknolege the hand to the petition to be his, & that he did deliver it by order & on behalf of the town of Banbury; & thereupon it was committed.[2] The like in the same parl. upon reading the petition of one Ward of Salop; & likewise on reading the petition of Henry Hogan. Scob. 87.[3] L. P. c.22.

Freedom of
speech.
135

[364]. Though freedom of speech & debates, be an undoubted privilege of the house, yet whatsoever is spoken in the house is subject to the censure of the house. Scob. 72. L. P. c.22.[1]

Contributions to
Knights by
whom?.

[365]. Tenants of antient baronies are discharged from contribution to the wages of knights of parl. because their lords serve for them in parl. Moor. 768. L. P. c.22.[1]

member retd. for
two places.

[366]. Apr. 1640. Ordd. that if any sit in that house that are returned by more indentures than usual they should withdraw till the Commee. for privileges had farther ordered. Scob. 14.[1].

Commee. for
expiring laws.

[367]. In the beginning of every parl. some persons have been appointed to consider of such laws as had continuance to the present session, whether they were fit to be continued or determined; as also of former statutes repealed or discontinued, whether fit to be revived & what are fit to be repealed. Scob. 40.[1]

who may offer
public bill.

[368]. Any member of the house may offer a bill for public good, except it be for *imposing a tax*; which is not to be done, but by order of the house first had. Scob. 40.[1]

public bill when
offered, to be
opened.

[369]. If any public bill be tendered, the person who tenders the bill must first open the matter of the bill to the house, & offer the reasons for admitting thereof; & thereupon the house will either admit or deny it. Scob. 41. [1]

Private bill.

[370]. A private bill that concerns a particular person is not to be offered to the house till the leave of the house be desired & the Substance of such bill made known either by motion or petition. Scob. 41.[1]

who to be of
Commee.
136

[371]. 7. Mar. 1606. Mr. Hadley being assigned of a Commee. to confer with the lords, desired to be spared, he being in opinion against the matter itself. And it was conceived for a rule 'that no man was to be employed in any matter that had declared himself against it; & the question being put, it was resolved mr. Hadley was not to be employed. Scob. 46.[1]

Power of parl.

[372]. The privileges of parl. consist in three things; 1st. as they are a *council* to advise; 2ly. a *court* to judge; 3ly. a representative body of the realm to make, repeal, or alter laws. May's hist. parl. l. 3. p.27. Atk. powr. parl. 36.[1]

Priv. of parl.

[373]. The rights & privileges of parliament are the birthright & inheritance of the whole kingdom wherein every subject is interested. 3. Rush. p. 1. 458.[1]

Priv. of parl.

[374]. The violating the privileges of parl. is the overthrow of parl. 3. Rush. p. 1. 475.[1]

Cognisance of
rights of parl.
where?
137

[375]. Upon some questions propounded to the judges in 1629. 5.Car.1. all the judges agreed that regularly a parliament man cannot be compelled, out of parliament, to answer things done in parl. *in a parliamentary course*. 1. Rush. 663.[1]

Words punished.

[376]. May. 27. 1641. Mr. Tayler, a barrister & burgess for old Windsor was brought upon his knees in the house of Commons for speaking some words in disparagement of the whole house about the E. of Strafford's death, to wit, 'that they had committed murder with the sword of justice. & that he would not for a world have so much blood lie on his conscience as did on theirs, for that sen-

tence.' He was expelled the house, voted incapable of ever being a parliament-man committed to the tower during pleasure; to be carried down to Windsor, there to make recantation, & to return back to the house of Commons, to receive further sentence: & it was ordered that a writ should presently issue out for a new election in his room. The 2d of June he petitioned to be restored on submission; but his petition would not be hearkened unto. Diurnal occurrences of parl. from Nov. 3. 1640. to Nov. 3. 1641. pa. 111. Rushw. p. 3. v. 1. fo. 278, 280.[1]

Divulging debates.

[377]. Mr. Nevill of Yorkshire, a member in the parl. which met Apr. 13. 1640. discovered to the k. & council what words some members did let fall in their debate in the house, whereupon Mr. Bellasis & Sr. John Hotham were committed by the Council board. Nevill in the succeeding parl. Feb. 4. 1640. 16. Car. 1. was by the house committed to the tower, & Sr. Wm. Savil, touching the same matter was ordered to be sent for in custody. Rush. p.3. v.1. fo.169.[1]

to take notice of members 138

[378]. Every man must take notice of all the members of the house returned of record, at his peril. 4. inst. 23.24. lex parl. c.23.[1]

but not of servants. 139

[379]. Otherwise it is of the servant of any of the members of the house. 4. inst. 24.[1]

servts & goods.

[380]. A member of parl. has privilege not only for his servants, but for his horses &c or other goods distrainable. 4. inst. 42. Hakewel. 62.[1] Memor. 102. Hale on parl. 28.[2]

privilege, how long? & to what?

[381]. The privilege is eundo, morando, et redeundo, for the persons of members & their necessary servants & in some cases for their goods & estates also during the time. Scob. 88.[1] Memorials. 97. 98. Dewes 85. col. 1. 251. col. 1. 688. col. 1.[2]

privilege from what?

[382]. For their own persons they have been privileged from suits, arrests, imprisonmts., attendance on trials, serving on juries, & the like, yea from being summoned or called to attend upon any suit in other courts by subpoena. Scob. 88.[1] 4. Inst. 24.[2]

breach of
privilege how
punished?

[383]. He who arrests a member during session shall be imprisoned in the tower by the house of which he is and shall be fined; & the keeper also if he will not deliver him when the Serjt at arms doth come for him by command of the house. Hakew. 62. Dyer. 60.[1] 61. pl. 28.[2] ante 78.[3]

who privileged?

[384]. The servants tending upon their masters during parl. who are necessary, as also of such officers as attend the parl. as the Serjt at arms, porter of the door clerks & such like & also their chattels & goods necessary are privileged, so that they shall not be taken but for treason and felony. Hakew. 62. Crompton's jurisd. 11.[1] Or breach of the peace.[2] ante 79.[3] 4. inst. 25. 2 Nals. 450. Dyer 60. pl. 19. As the king & his whole realm have an interest in the body of every one of it's members, the private commodity of any particular man ought not to be regarded. Dyer. ibid.[4] The bag bearer to the clerk of the house had privilege. Memorials. 98.[5]

privilege, when
arises?

[385]. If after judgment in Debt or Trespass, a man be elected a burgess, he may notwithstanding be taken in execution. Moor. fol. 57. n. 163. Crompton's Iur. p. 7.8.9.10.11. 34. H.8. Petyt's misc. parl. 1. &c So if after arrest one be elected, he shall not have privilege. Fitzherbert's case. Moore 340. n. 461.[1]

privilege, when
arises?

[386]. But [April 12 Jac. 1. S]r Wm. Bampfeild, committed by the Chancell[or for a cont]empt after the writ of Summons but before [the electi]on, had his privilege by Hab. corp. Scob. 96.[1]

privilege, from
what?

[387]. Service of a Citation is breach of privilege. Towns. Col. 255. Dewes Journ. 655. 4. inst. 24. Hale parl. 29.[1] So is an information in the Starchamber. Dewes 688. Col. 1.[2]

[388]. So also is service of a subpoena. ib. Scob. 89.90.91. Towns. col. 213.246. Dewes. 438. col. 1.2. 651. 656 Col. 1. id. 257. Rush. 653. Petyt misc. parl. 107. Hale parl. 29.[1]

[389]. So also of a spa. ad testificandum. Towns. col. 109. Dewes. 546. col. 2. id. 212.213.214.[1] ⟨Or of a commission.⟩[2]

[390]. So is the service of a privy seal. Dewes. 655. col. 1.2. Or the awarding Outlawry. Scob. 92. Or attamt. for contempt. ib. Or a return on an attaint. Scob. 96.[1]

[391]. A member shall be privileged from serving on a jury. Dewes 560. col. 2. Or from being chosen sheriff. Scob. 96. Or from executing a Commission out of chancery. Memor. 103.[1]

privilege, how obtained?

[392]. If any member require privilege for himself or his servant, on declaration thereof to the Speaker he shall have a warrant signed by the Speaker to obtain the writ. 22. Feb. 6.Ed.6. Scob. 110. Dewes. 249. Col. 1.[1] Which warrant is directed to the Chancellor to award a writ of Supersedeas. Scob. 94. Dewes. 436. col. 1. 2. 21. Feb. 1588.[2] But upon an order Mar. 2. 1592. that the Speaker move the Ld Keeper for a hab. corp. cum causa to bring up a member who was confined, the Ld Keeper returned that in regard of the antient liberties and privileges of the house, the Serjt at arms be sent by order of the house, so that he may be brought without peril of further arrest by the way. Scob. 112.113. Moor. 340. n. 461. Fitzherbert's case. Dewes 479.480.490. col. 2. [3] In 18. Jac. 1. Mar. 3. a Commee. appointed to consider of a way for staying trials against members reported that by precedents the custom was that on motions & orders in the house letters were written by the clerk to the justices of assize to stay trials against members; which lres. were entered in the journal book. which course was therefore resolved to be held.[4]

privilege, how waived?

[393]. It hath been questioned whether a member may wave privilege, as it is not so much his own privilege as that of the house, but not doubted but the house may give leave to wave privilege. Scob. 95.[1]

privilege, when arises?
140

[394]. The privilege takes place by force of the election & before a return be made. for a servant of Lanckton (reported to the house to be elected tho' not returned) having been arrested, had privilege.

Memor. 107. Dewes 642. col. 2. 643. col. 1. Pet. misc. parl. 119.[1]

privilege, to whom?

[395]. Privilege was allowed to Sr. Nicholas Sandys's Solicitor it being proved that he lay in the house of Sr. Nicholas solicited his causes, & received wages. & similar precedents produced. Mem. 101.102. Towns. coll. 225.226,[1]

privilege, from what?

[396]. Darrell was committed for having threatned the person of mr. Lovell a member & that for a speech spoken by him in the house he should be sent to the Tower during parl. or presently after. Memor. 114.[1] Rogers for abusing a member in slanderous & unseemly terms upon his proceedings at a Commee., was called to answer it at the bar. 16. Jun. 1604.[2] A page brought to the bar for offering to throng a member as he went down stairs. Towns. coll. 195. Dewes 629. col. 1.[3]

how far privileged? 141.

[397]. The parl. shall not give privilege to any member contra morem parliamentarium, to exceed the bounds & limits of his place & duty. Though a man cannot be compelled out of parl. to answer things done in parl. in a parliament[ary course]; but it is otherwise where things are done [exorbitantly], for those are not the acts of the court. R[ush. Col. 663.][1]

privilege in what?

[398]. No [privilege is a]llowable in treason, felony or breach of t[he peace. 2] Nalson 450.[1]

parl. not restrained by privilege. 142.

[399]. All privilege of parl. is in the power of parl. & is a restraint to the proceeding of other inferior courts; but is no restraint to the proceedings of parliamt. 2 Nalson 450.[1]

privilege, what breach of?

[400]. The lords voting the propounding & declaring matters of supply, before it was moved in the house of Commons is a breach of privilege. 16.Car.1. Rush. 2. vol. 2 part. 1147.[1]

privilege, what breach of?

[401]. 1641. Dec. the setting any guards about this house without the consent of the house is a breach of privilege, & such guards ought to be dismissed. 2. Nals. 729.823.[1]

privilege, what breach of. 143

[402]. His majesty's taking notice of the bill for suppressing soldiers being in agitation in both houses & not agreed on, was a breach of privilege. 2 Nals. 743.[1]

privilege, what
breach of.
144

[403]. His majesty in propounding a limitation and provisional clause to be added to the bill before it was presented to him by the consent of both houses was a breach of privilege. 2 Nals. 743.[1]

privilege, what
breach of.
145

[404]. His majesty expressing displeasure against some persons for matters moved in parl. during the debate & preparation of a bill was a breach of privilege. 2. Nalson. 743.[1]

[405]. See stat. 12. & 13. W.3. for preventing any inconveniences that may happen by privilege of parl.[1]

no privilege as
trustee, or
officer.

[406]. 1700. Feb. 13. no member has privilege in any case where he is only a trustee. Bohun's collection pa. 27. nor where he acts as a publick officer. ib. 230.[1]

privilege, how
long?

[407]. Declared as a standing order that no member have privilege, except for his person only, against any commoner, in any suit or proceeding for any longer time than the house shall be actually sitting for the dispatch of business in parl. Bohun's coll. 27.[1]

disability of
member, what
is?

[408]. Outlawry in personal actions is no cause to disable any person from being a member of parl. So resolved by parl. 39.H.6. Again 1.El. Again in Fludd's case 23.El. So in Fitz-Herbert's ca. & Killegrew's case, & Sr. Walter Harcourt's case in 35.El. And so again 1.Jac. in Goodwyn's & Fortescue's case. But in this last case the judges denied the position & e contrario gave it as their opinion that a person outlawed could not be a member & cited 35.H.6. & 1.H.7. So adjudged in parl. & further that the party outlawed was not discharged by paiment of the debt, but must sue out a Sci. fa. against the creditor. But the house of Commons presevered in their resolution & admitted Goodwyn.[1] See Arc. parl. 65.[2]

returns, when
should be?

[409]. The returns of writs ought not to be made till the first day of the parl. Goodwyn & Fortescue's case. Append to L. parl. 427.[1]

returns, who
may examine?

[410]. All writs for the election of members of parl. were returned into the parl. house till 7.H.4. as appears by the records from the time of E.1. till then when it was enacted that all such returns

ought to be made into the chancery. But yet this did not take away the jurisdn. of the house to inquire into the returns. & accordingly the clerk of the crown attends the parl. every day till the end of it with all the writs & returns. and in the 29.El. it was resolved that the Chancellor had no right to meddle with returns. The case of Goodwyn & Fortescue. Append. to L. parl. 428.[1]

146

[411]. Privilege takes place by force of the election & before the return be made. 19. Nov. 1601. On information to the house that Roger Boston, servant to ____ Lanckton baron of Walton, who (upon *credible report of divers members* of the house was affirmed to be chosen a burgess for Newton, but *not yet returned by the clerk of the crown*) had been during that session arrested in London, the plaintiff & officer were sent for to the bar & committed three days, & the servant allowed privilege & discharged from his arrest. L. parl. c.23. Memorials 107.108. Dewes 642. Col. 2. 643. Col. 1. Petyts miscell. parl. 119.[1]

privilege in
Treason felony,
breach of peace
how to be taken
away.
147.

[412]. Though the privileges of parl. do not extend to cases of Treason, felony, & breach of the peace, so as to exempt the members of parl. from punishment, nor from all manner of process or tryal, as it doth in other cases, yet it doth privilege them in the way & method of their tryal & punishment; & that the parl. should have the cause first brought before them, that they may judge of the fact & of the grounds of the accusation, & how far forth the manner of their tryal may concern, or not concern the privilege of parl; otherwise it would be in the power, not only of his majesty, but of every private man, under pretensions of treason, or those other crimes, to take any man from his service in parl. & so as many, one after another, as he pleaseth; & consequently to make a parl. what he will, & when he will; which would be a breach of so essential a privilege of parl. as that the very being thereof depends upon it. Declarn. of the Commons on the k's declaring Sr. John Hotham a trayter in 16[42]. 4. Rushw. 586.[1]

[413]. Ferrers, a member of parl. was taken in execution in going to the parliament house anno 34. H. 8. but he was discharged by privilege, & could not be again taken by law whereby the party was without remedy. Arcana parliamentaria. 53. This is the case Dier. 275. & Hollinshed 1584. See ante 82. 130. &[1]

[414]. In Ferrers' case the H. of Comm. were clearly of opinion that all commandments & other acts proceeding from the nether house, were to be done & executed by their Serjeant without writ, only by shewing of his mace, which was his warrant. Arc. parl. 57.[1]

[415]. Persons attainted of treason cannot resume their seats in parl. till the act of attainder be repealed. 1. H. 7. 4. Arc. parl. 65.[1]

[416]. The book called Arcana Parliamentaria was written temp. Eliz. as appears ibid 68.[1]

[417]. Where a man hath an elder title to land by one entail, & after the same land is given to him by parl. his heir shall not be remitted, for by the act all other titles are extinct, for that the act is the Common judgment & an estoppel to every one that is privy to the act. Bro. parl. 73. 29 H.8. 21.E.4.57. Arc. parl. 69. If the King gives land to me, that is mine already, I shall not be remitted 21.E.4.57. But if the king recites my former right & gives it to me, I shall be remitted. ib. & Lib. Ass. 28. Arc. parl. 77.[1]

majority of commee. may proceed. 148 who may be present at Commee. hearing counsel. 148.b.

[418]. The Committees being met, though not all, yet if the better half, they may proceed. Elsynge Method of passing bills. 11. Any other member of the house [of lords] may be present at a Commee. [to whom bill is refered] but they may not vote: and must give place to all of the Commee. & sit below them. id. 12.[1]

[419]. When Counsel is heard before a commee., the counsel which speaks agt the bill is to be first heard, because it is already understood what the bill desires. ib. So also when counsel is heard before the house: which is allowed even in case of a publick bill. If it concern any officer, corporation,

or particular person, or any artificers, they are usually sent for to attend the Commee. ib.[1]

who Tellers.

[420]. In Dom. Procerum on a division one lord who said content & another who said not content are appointed to number them by the poll, the one party standing the other sitting. ib. 19.[1]

bill read more than thrice.

[421]. Temp. H. 8. & E. 6. bills were frequently read a 4th. 5th. & even a 6th. time, & then might be recommitted after the 3d reading, but it is now constantly observed to read bills but thrice. id. 31.[1]

Privilege.

[422]. Suits wherein members of parl. are parties, are not to be proceeded in during privilege time. Hale parl. 29.[1]

Privilege how obtaind.

[423]. Resolved in Thorp's case 31. H. 6. who was chosen Speaker while in execution, that every member of the H. of Comm. may have a special Supersedeas to enjoy his privilege except in treason, felony or surety of the peace for a condemnation before the parliament. Hale parl. 30.[1]

148.b.

[424].[1] Jan. 17. 1744/5 a disputed election & counsel thereon heard at the bar of the house. The counsel for the petitioner was first heard. The papers they produced were brought up & read. Journ. H. C. The counsel were always ordered to withdraw when any question was about to be put. ib.[2]

149

[425]. A member, *in his place*, informed the house of what he knew concerning an election then under hearing at their bar. Journ. H. C. Jan. 22. 1744/5.[1]

[426]. On a disputed election, the petitioner proposing to prove or disprove certain matters, the counsel for the sitting member objected to the admission of that kind of evidence, and was heard to it; then the petitioners' counsel was heard in answer to the objections; then the counsel for the sitting member in reply. Journ. H. C. Jan. 18. 1745.[1]

[427]. Where a person is chosen by two different counties he makes his election for which he will appear, and a writ issues for the other. Seymour 58.

9. Apr. 13. El. 19. Mar. 1. Jac.[1] Hale parl. 110. ante 141.[2]

[428]. Every member of the house is to be returned by warrant or the book of the clerk of the crown. Seymour. 128.[1]

[429]. Mace. seems to be derived from the Ital. Mazza. a club.[1]____The Satellites Caesaris, or Emperor's guard were sometimes called Macerones[2] from whence probably the word Mace might be used which the Serjeants at arms carry before the king &c. Laws of Honor. 391.[3]

bribery.

[430]. A member confessing he had given to the bailiff & some others of a borough £4. for burgesship, they were ordered to repay the £4. & the corporation fined £20. to the queen. Hale parl. 112. 10. May 13. Eliz.[1]

[431]. A member indicted of felony retains his till he be convicted. 21. Jan. 23. Eliz. Hale parl. 113.[1]

150

[432]. A burgess was returned dead, & another chosen, & returned. The party returned dead appeared; he was admitted & the second rejected.[1] 24. El. Hale parl. 114. ante 137.[2]

who eligible.

[433]. 25. Jun. 1 Jac. Resolved for a rule that after this parliament, no Mayor of a town shall be a member; & if returned a new writ to issue. This was on view of the resolution in Bro. abr. tit. Parl. 38. H. 8. Hale's parl. 114.[1] see ante 46.[2]

[434]. A resolve that being in Embassage, in execution, or sickness is no cause for removing a member & electing another.[1] Yet in another instance Christopher Perne a member being reported lunatick a new writ was issued. Seymour 263.[2] And again it was resolved that persons employed by the crown on patents for life had vacated their seats & new writs issued.[3] Hale. parl. 116.117. Onslow Sollicitor general was notwithstanding adjudged a member of the house & chosen Speaker on the death of Williams 8. Eliz. tho' the Lords urged his incapacitation by office & his writ of attendce. on their house.[4] Hale par. 120.

Popham Sollicitor was chosen speaker in like manner. 7 Jan. 23. Eliz.[5] Hale parl. 122.

if person
proposed for
Speaker be
absent he may be
sent for.

[435]. In the case of Onslow chosen Speaker 8. Eliz. & Popham 23. Eliz. who were Sollicitors general & as such attending the house of lords, a Member declared to the house he had seen them in the house of lords, & that they were members of the Commons' house. Whereupon there being opinions that one absent could not be chosen, they sent to the Lords for them, & on their being restored they were elected. Hale parl. 122.123.[1]

[436]. Perne affirming himself returned burgess for Plimton, but having no warrant nor being returned by the clerk of the crown, was committed to the Serjeant till further considered by the house. Seymour. 178. Hale parl. 126.[1]

[437]. Taking fee or reward by a member for his voice in furtherance or hinderance of a bill punishable. 17. May. 13 Eliz. Hale parl. 126.[1] Sr. Francis

Hall.

Hall for lewd speeches in & out of the house called to the bar, and charged with them by the speaker; upon submitting himself he was exhorted & remit-

Paine.

ted. Hale parl. 126.[2] Paine for an unreverent speech against reading a bill, called to the bar & sequestered. 3. Apr. 1. Jac. Hale parl. 129.[3] The Speaker at the return of himself & others from the queen, took exception to a speech used to the

Story.

queen by Story a burgess, in which he was touched of neglect & prayed the advice of the house. It appearing that it was done of good zeal, & Story asking pardon of the house & Speaker it was remitted. Seymour. 153. Hale. parl. 132.[4]

[438]. 4. June. 1. Jac. Resolved that no man is or ought to be concluded in his opinion by any subscription, but hath and may have his free liberty in the house to assent and disassent as he shall see just cause the next session of parl. Hale parl. 137.[1]

[439]. It seems that those who by their office are to attend the upper house, may yet be members of the lower. egr. the attorney & solicitor general. Seymour. 27.127.160.280. 24 Jac. 3. sess. Jac.[1] So the king's serjeant. 17. Feb. 14. Eliz.[2] So the

Master of the rolls. Seym. 243.[3] So the Deputy of Ireland 1. May. 13 Eliz.[4] Yet there seems to be some doubt about it. Hale. parl. 140.141.[5] A member of the lower house may be of counsel before a committee of the upper.[6] Seymour. 187. 205. Hale parl. 141.

[440]. A bill brought down from the lords was rejected on the first reading. The lords sent messengers to demand a reason of their judgment, it was denied to yeild any reason. 17. Eliz. [1] Hale's parl. 145.

[441]. Who go forth.[1]

That a bill be read a 2d. time[2]	Yeas go forth.	
That it be committed...................	Yeas. G.W.[3]	
that a bill with amendmts. be ingrossed	Yeas.	
	30. P.J.395.	
that a bill be *now* read a third time.	Noes.	398.
that a bill pass	Yeas.	259.
to receive a Ryder........................	Yeas.	260.
for receiving a clause	Yeas.	334.
for printing a bill........................	Yeas.[4]	
for taking a report into considn. in 3. months.	Yeas.	251.
that house agree with Commee. in amendmt.	Noes.	400.
that house now resolve into Commee.	Noes.	291.
for amendmt. Shall such words stand...	Noes.[5]	329.
for further examining a witness....	Yeas.	344.
for reading orders of the day	Noes.[6]	269.
that no member be absent without leave	Noes.	380.
on filling blank with sum qu. on largest	Yeas. G.W.[7]	

2. Hats. contra.

[442]. Rules for conducting the business in the Senate of the U.S.[1]

I. The President having taken the chair & a Quorum being present, the Journal of the preceding day shall be read, to the end that any mistake may be corrected that shall have been made in the entries.

II. No member shall speak to another, or otherwise interrupt the business of the Senate, or read any printed paper while the journals or public papers are reading, or when any member is speaking in any debate.

III. Every member, when he speaks shall address the chair, standg. in his place, & when he has finished shall sit down.

IV. No member shall speak more than twice in any one debate, on the same day, without leave of the Senate.

V. When two members rise at the same time, the Presidt. shall name the person to speak. But in all cases the member first rising shall speak first.

VI. No motion shall be debated until the same shall be seconded.

VII. When a motion shall be made & seconded, it shall be reduced to writing if desired by the President or any member delivered in at the table & read by the President before the same shall be debated.

other exceptions.
case of order.
privilege reading
papers.

VIII. While a question is before the Senate, no motion shall be recieved unless for an amendment, for the previous question, or for postponing the main question, or to commit it or to adjourn.

IX. The Previous question being moved & seconded, the question from the chair shall be 'Shall the main question be now put?' and if the Nays prevail, the main question shall not then be put.

X. If the question in debate contain several points, any member may have the same divided.

XI. When the Yeas & Nays shall be called for by one fifth of the members present, each member called upon shall, unless for special reasons he be excused by the Senate, declare openly and without debate, his assent or dissent to the question. In taking the Yeas & Nays, and upon the call of the house, the names of the members shall be taken alphabetically.

XII. One day's notice at least shall be given of an intended motion for leave to bring in a bill.

XIII. Every bill shall recieve three readings previous to it's being passed, & the President shall give notice at each whether it be the first, second, or third, which readings shall be on three different days, unless the Senate unanimously direct otherwise.

XIV. No bill shall be committed or amended, until it shall have been twice read, after which it may be referred to a committee.

XV. All committees shall be appointed by balot, & a plurality of votes shall make a choice.

XVI. When a member shall be called to order, he shall sit down until the President shall have determined whether he is in order or not, & every question of order shall be decided by the President without debate, but if there be a doubt in his mind, he may call for the sense of the Senate.

XVII. If a member be called to order for words spoken, the exceptional words shall be immediately taken down in writing, that the President may be better enabled to judge of the matter.

XVIII. When a Blank is to be filled, and different sums shall be proposed, the question shall be taken on the highest sum first.

XIX. No member shall absent himself from the service of the Senate without leave of the Senate first obtained.

XX. All bills on a second reading shall first be considered by the Senate in the same manner as if the Senate were in a Committee of the whole, before they shall be taken up and proceeded on by the Senate agreeably to the standing rules, unless otherwise ordered.

XXI. Before any petition or memorial addressed to the Senate shall be recieved and read at the table, whether the same shall be introduced by the President or a member, a brief statement of the contents of the petition or memorial shall verbally be made by the Introducer.

XXII. When a question has been once made & carried in the affirmative or negative, it shall be in order for any member of the majority, to move for the reconsideration of it.

XXIII. All bills passed in Senate, shall, before they

are sent to the H. of Representatives be examined by the committees respectively who brought in such bills, or to whom the same have been last committed in Senate.

XXIV. Every vote of Senate shall be entered on the journals, and a brief statement of the contents of each petition, memorial or paper presented to the Senate be also inserted on the journals.

XXV. The proceedings of Senate, when they shall act in their Executive capacity shall be kept in separate & distinct books.

XXVI. The proceedings of the Senate, when not acting as in a Committee of the house, be entered on the journals as concisely as possible, care being taken to detail a true & accurate acct. of the proceedings.

XXVII. That the titles of bills and such parts thereof only as shall be affected by proposed amendments be inserted on the journals.

XXVIII. That on a motion made & seconded to shut the doors of the Senate on the discussion of any business which may in the opinion of a member require secresy, the President shall direct the gallery to be cleared, & that during the discussion of such motion, the doors shall remain shut.

[443]. The Scots, antenati, not naturalized, were deemed by the H. of Commons not capable of a seat in their house. 2. Hatsell. 2. Ld. Coke says that Minors are incapable by law, and so says Blackstone. 1. 162. But Hatsell quotes a decision of the Commons in 1690, in the case of Trenchard a minor, declared duly elected, and he says the practice was against Coke's opinion. But he adds that the stat. 7.8. W.3. c.25. has made their election void. 2. Hats. 6. The clergy were deemed not eligible because they were, by themselves or their representatives, of the Convocation.[1]

[444]. The clergy taxed themselves till 1663. In 1664 the parliamt. for the first time included them in the assessment bill and have done it ever since. In consequence of this the clergy have assumed, & without objection have enjoyed the privilege of

voting for members of the H. of Com. by virtue of their ecclesiastical freeholds, & two acts of parl. 10. Ann. 23. & 18. G. 2. 18. suppose it to be now a right. Yet it is not founded in any express law. 2. Hats. 10.[1]

[445]. Ambassadors & others employed abroad are eligible, for absentia ejus qui reipublicae causa abest, non obest. 2. Hats. 16.[1] The Atty. genl. tho' an assistant to the H. of Lords, and the Sollicitor genl. King's Serjeants & Masters in Chancery. who are but attendants to them, may all be of the H. of Commons. 2. Hats. 23.[2]

[446]. Sr. Edward Coke sheriff of Buckinghamshire, returned de facto member for Norfolk, tho the matter of right was not decided & he never took his seat, yet had his privilege. 2. Hats. 22.[1] It seems that a sheriff is eligible for any county or town where the election does not proceed by virtue of his own precept. 2. Hats. 25.[2]

[447]. Members once chosen are not to be discharged but by operation of law. 2. Hats. 27.[1]

[448]. Outlaws, and persons in execution may be elected,[1] & and [sic] Asgyll in 1707, under execution, was ordered by the house to be delivered out of custody by the Serjeant with the mace. 2. Hats. 30.[2]

[449]. It seems to be in consequence merely of certain acts of parl. from the 5 W. & M. C. 7. downward, that certain placement & pensioners cannot be of the H. of commons, while others may. 2. Hats. 43.[1]

[450]. A person actually a member already is ineligible for any other county, borough &c. At a general election indeed, persons elected for several places may chuse for which they will serve, because all the writs are returnable on the same and a distant day, till which day the law does not notice the return (for this purpose) even if made. But where several particular writs issue during a parl. as all of these are returnable *immediately*, ⟨*that which is first*⟩[1] the indenture which is first executed by the returning officer makes the person a member, and

from that moment ineligible for any of the other places. 2. Hats. 52. The reason further is that though elected by one county he becomes thereby the representative of the whole state, and consequently is already so of any county or borough which would elect him a second time ib.[2]

[451]. A person, after he is duly chosen, cannot relinquish. Yet a quaker chosen and refusing to take the *oaths*, a new writ was issued.[1]

[452]. On report that a member was dead, a new writ was issued but a doubt of the fact arising afterwards, it was ordered not to be delivered till further directions; and it turning out that the member was not dead, a Supersedeas ordered to be made out. ib. 57.[1]

[453]. The reading a bill at the opening the session is only a claim of right to proceed on any matter they please, without being confined or giving preference to those in the k's speech. ib. 59.[1]

[454]. Notwithstanding the laws requiring a member to be sworn he is to all intents a member, except as to the right of voting. e.g. he has his privileges, & may be chosen of a commee. ib. 62.[1]

[455]. Orders for calls of the house on different days may exist at the same time. 2. Hats. 71.[1]

[456]. A member who had spoken before, permitted to speak again merely to explain himself. 2. Hats. 73. in some material point of his speech. ib. 75. and it is the duty of the Speaker to maintain the observance of this rule, without waiting the interposition of the house: as also to interrupt a member speaking beside the question 75.77. as well as to keep the house quiet while a member speaks 78. A member may speak from the gallery. ib. 78.[1]

[457]. Members indisposed may be *indulged* to speak sitting. 2. Hats. 75.77.[1]

[458]. If two stand up at the same time he against the bill is to be heard first. A member may speak after the question for the affirmative has been taken: because no full question without the part negative. 2. Hats. 73.[1]

[459]. The question for adjourning a debate ap-

1

2.

3.a.

3.b.

4.a

4.b

5

pears to be a common one.[1] 2. Hats. 81. And those who have spoken before may not speak again when the adjourned debate is resumed. 74.[2]

6.

VIIIth. rule of Senate

contra.

3. Hats. 133.

[460]. It is a general rule that the question first moved & seconded is to be first put. The following are exceptions to it. 1. A motion *simply* to adjourn. This takes place of all questions, and can neither be amended nor debated 2. To read the orders of the ⟨house⟩ day, *generally*, & not a *particular* order, & if carried, the orders must be proceeded on in the course in which they stand. This takes place of all except questions of adjmt. 3. To amend. This is necessarily put before the main question. 4. On a question between a greater & lesser sum, or longer or shorter time, the least sum & longest time to be first put. 5. The previous question, which puts off the main question *for that day.* If a motion be superseded by moving for adjmt. or for the orders of the day, the original motion is not printed in the votes, because it has neither been a vote nor introductory to a vote. But on the previous question it is different; as the first question must be stated to introduce and make intelligible the previous question. [So on an amendment, postponement, or commitment.] A question on an amendment cannot be prevented by the previous question. 2. Hats. 81-83, because deciding that the words shall not be inserted, has all the effect of the Previous question. ib. 84. A motion to adjourn simply, cannot be amended, as by adding 'to a particular day.' but must be put simply 'that this house do now adjourn.' & if carried in the affirmative it is adjd to the next sitting day, unless it has come to a previous resolution 'that at it's rising they will adjourn to a particular day.' and then the house is adjourned to that day. 2. Hats. 82.[1]

7.a.

7.b.

[461]. A motion made and seconded is in possession of the house & cannot be withdrawn but by leave of the house. ib. 82.[1]

8.a

[462]. Amendments may be made so as totally to alter the nature of the proposition, and it is a way of getting rid of a proposition by making those who

[137]

moved it join in the vote against it. 2. Hats. 82.84.[1]

[463]. If the question for adjmt. takes place before 4. o'clock, the Yeas go forth. 2. Hats. 82.[1]

8 b

[464]. Where amendmts. are made to a question, they are not printed separately from the question, but only the question as finally agreed to by the house. id. 85.[1]

[465]. When a question is moved & seconded, if complicated, it may be divided by *order* or *consent* of the house.[1] but no member has a *right* to have it

9 a

divided.[2] The only mode by which he can separate it is by moving amendments to it.[3] The only case where a member has a *right* to insist on any thing is where he calls for the execution of a subsisting order of the house. Here there having been already a resoln., any member has a right to insist that the Speaker or any other whose duty it is, shall carry it into execution, & no debate or delay can be had on it, as on the admission of strangers into the gallery, clearing the lobby of footmen, telling the house (when it has been noticed) that there are not 40. members present. &c.[4] 2. Hats. 87.

[466]. Tho' a question is moved & seconded, if any matter of privilege arises, either out of it, or from a quarrel between members or any other cause, this supersedes the considtn. of the original question, & must be first disposd of. So if a question of order arises, or to read a paper. id. 88.[1]

9.b.

[467]. The right of moving for the orders of the day to be read in the midst of any other proceeding does not hold when they are actually proceeding on one of the orders. id. 88.[1]

10

[468]. When you have amended the latter part of a question, you cannot recur back & ⟨amend⟩ make any alteration in the former part. id. 90.[1]

[469]. Hatsell is of opinion that after the previous question is proposed from the chair, no amendment can be proposed to the main question. but that the same effect may be obtained by voting that the main question shall not *now* be put, and the amender then moving the main question as altered by his amendment & consequently made a

are understood in law to be in custody of the Serjeant, whether standing by them or not, ⟨&⟩
whether standing with the mace or not. 105. &
whether attended by the keeper of the jail from
which they are, or not.[3]

[478]. A person may be before the house 1. as a
witness. 2. attending, as on some petition, charge
or other case of their own when they may be heard
at the bar. 3. to be examined on some charge. 4. as
a delinquent.[1] 1. Witnesses are not to be produced
but where the house has previously instituted an
enquiry. 2. Hats. 102.[2] Before a select committee
they are to be within the bar, but before the House,
or Commee. of the whole, they must be without
the bar. 105.[3] A Lord of parl. however, a judge, or
Ld. Mayor appearing *as a witness* is to be within
the bar & to have a chair. 108.[4] If the mace is to be
off the table, the Speaker, before the witness enters, is to ask to what points he is to examine him.
107.[5] & the questions are all to be settled in writing, & to be put by the Speaker. 106.[6] If the Mace
is to be *on* the table, questions may, while the witness is at the bar, be proposed by a member to the
Speaker. & by him to the witness. For convenience
sake the member is often permitted to put the
question himself at short hand, but this leads to irregularities. 106.[7] But when *prisoners* are brought
to the bar only for examination, whether as witnesses or on a charge, it would be more convenient
always to dispense with the practice of the mace
being *off* the table: because tho' the members cannot debate while any body is at the bar, they may
suggest to the Speaker such questions as arise out
of the examination.[8] Persons in custody whether
witnesses, or for examination, ⟨or as delinquents⟩
may be brought by the keeper of the jail from
which they are, or by the Serjeant.[9] If as delinquents, they must be brought in by the Serjt. with
the mace, & he is to stand by them with the mace.
102.107.[10] The person is to recieve his judgment
standing, unless otherwise ordered. 104. or his
censure. 102.103.[11]

[141]

[479]. If the propriety of a question be objected to, the Speaker without taking the sense of the house, direct the witness, counsel or party to retire; for no question can be moved, or put, or debated, while they are there. 108.[1]

[480]. Where papers are laid before the house or referred to a commee., every member has a right to have them once read at the table before he can be compelled to vote on them. But it is a great tho' common error to suppose that he has a right to his question to have acts, journals, accounts or papers on the table read independantly of the will of the house. The delay & interruption which this might be made to produce, evince the impossibility of the existence of such a right. There is indeed so manifest a propriety of permitting every member to have as much information as possible on every question on which he is to vote that when he desires the reading, if it be seen that it is really for information & not for delay, the Speaker directs it to be read without putting a question, if no one objects. But if objected to, a question must be put. 2. Hats. 117.118.[1]

[481]. It is equally an error to suppose that any member has a right, without a question put, to lay a book or paper on the table & have it read on suggesting that it contains matter infringing on the privileges of the house. id. 117.118.[1]

[482]. No member may be present when a bill or any business concerning himself is *debating*, nor is any member to speak to the merits of it till he withdraws. 2. Hats. 219.[1] The rule is that if a charge against a member arise out of a report of a commee., or examination of witnesses in the house, as the member knows from that to what points he is to direct his exculpation, he may be heard to those points before any question is moved or stated against him. He is then to be heard & withdraw before any question is moved.[2] But if the question itself is the charge, as for breach of order, or matter arising in the debate, there the charge must be stated, i.e. the question must be moved, himself heard, & then to withdraw. 2. Hats. 121.122.[3] A

15

16

17

18

member's vote disallowed even after a division because he appeared somewhat concernd in interest. 119.[4]

[483]. When a quorum does not *assemble*,[1] the Speaker waits till 4. aclock, then takes the chair & adjourns the house without any question put, to the next sitting day.[2] He cannot adjourn over a sitting day unless the house have has previously resolved it.[3] If on the return from the H. of L. there be not a quorum present, the Speaker may still report what has passed. When it is observed that a quorum is not present, the Speaker is to be called on to count the house.[4] When there is a division in the house on some question, and it appears from the report of the tellers that there is not a quorum, the matter continues exactly in the state in which it was before the division, & must be resumed at that period on any future day.[5] 2. Hats. 126.

[484]. When a defect of quorum arises during a committee of the whole, the Speaker resumes the chair & the chairman reports the cause of their dissolution. When a message from the *king* is announced during a commee., the Speaker takes the chair & recieves it, & this even if there be no Quorum. for the message may be to adjourn prorogue or dissolve them, and they should not have it in their power to defeat a prorogative of the king. 2. Hats. 126.[1]

[485]. An order is made at the beginning of every session for the Serjeant to take strangers into custody, who are found in the house while it is sitting. and this he is to carry into execution without any order of the house. and when a member takes notice to the Speaker that there are strangers in the house, it is the Speaker's duty without delay or debate, immediately to order the Serjeant to execute the orders of the house & to clear it of all but members. and this the Speaker must do if any one member insists on it. 2. Hats. 129.[1]

[486]. The Speaker's declaration which voice has it by the sound may be contradicted by any one till some member comes into the house. It is too late after that. 2. Hats. 140.[1]

19

20

21

[487]. No member can withdraw who is in the house when the question is put. nor can be told in the division if not in when the question was put. Passages & rooms having no avenue to them but thro' the house are in the house. as Solomon's porch & the Speaker's *room*. But the Speaker's *chamber* is not in the house. If, being in the porch or room, they did not hear the question put they have a right to demand of the Speaker what was the question? But if in the body of the house, they did not hear it thro' inattention or other circumstance, & so failed to go forth, they must be told in the house, tho' against their inclination. So must those who get into a passage &c (but within the house) to avoid being counted. 2. Hats. 140.1.2.[1]

22.a

[488]. There must be silence while the tellers are telling, for if any one of them thinks there is a mistake, or if they are not all agreed, they must tell again. No member to remove from his place when they have begun telling. 143.[1]

22.b.

[489]. If any difficulty arises in point of order during the division the Speaker is to decide peremptorily, subject to the future censure of the house if irregular. He sometimes permits old experienced members to assist him with their advice, which they do sitting in their seats, covered, to avoid the appearance of debate. But this can only be with the Speaker's leave, else the division might last several hours. 2. Hats. 143.[1]

[490]. The right which a single member has to call for a division is only when *he thinks* the contrary voice has the question, but of this he is himself the judge. 2. Hats. 144.[1]

[491]. If a mistake is made in reporting the numbers to the Speaker, it may be corrected after the report made. id. 145.[1]

[492]. Who go forth?[1] The general rule is that those who give their votes for the preservation of the orders of the house shall stay in. and those who are for introducing any new matter or alteration, or proceeding contrary to the established course are to go out.[2] But this rule is subject to many exceptions & modifications.[3] 2. Hatsell. 134. as follows

Rushw. p. 3. vl. 1. fol. 92. Scob. 43. Co. 12. 116.
D'Ewes. 505. col. 1. Scob. 52. Mem in Hakew.
25. 29.[4]

Who go forth.

Petition.[5] that it be recieved ..	Noes.
	9 Grey 365.[6]
read	ayes.
lie on the table	
rejected (after refusal to lie on table)	Noes.
for referring to a commee. or farther proceedg	ayes.
Bills. that it be brought in[7]	
read 1st. or 2d. time	
engrossed or read 3d time .	ayes.
proceedg on in every other stage	
Committed	
to commee. of whole	noes
to select commee	ayes.
report of bill lie on table[8]	noes.
be *now* read	ayes.
be takn into considn. 3. months hence[9]	ayes.
	30 P.J. 251.
Amendmts. be read a 2d. time[10]	noes.
clause offered on report of bill. be read 2d time.........	ayes.
for recieving a clause[11]	ayes. 334.
with amendments be ingrossed	ayes. 395
that bill be *now*	
read a 3d. time............	Noes. 398
recieve a rider	260
pass..................	ayes. 259
be printed	
Committees. that A. take the chair[12]	
〈 〉[13]	noes.
to agree to whole or any part of report[14]..........	

[145]

that the house do *now*
resolve into commee.[15] .... ⎫
Speaker.[16] that he do *now* leave ⎬ noes.   291.
the chair (aftr. ord. to go
into commee) ⎭
that he issue warrant for
new writ[17] .... noes.
Member. that none be absent
without leave .... noes.
Witness. that he be further
examined[18] .... ayes.   344.
Previous question. *(those against*
putting the main one go forth.)[19] .. noes.
Blanks. question on filling
with the largest sum[20] .... ayes.
Amendmts. that words stand
part[21] .... ayes.
Lords. that their amendmt. be
read a 2d. time[22] .... noes.
    messenger be recieved .... ayes.
orders of day. that they be now
    read.
    if before 2. aclock[23] .... ayes.
    if after 2 .... noes.
Adjournmt. till the next sitting
    day,
    if before 4. aclock.[24] .... ayes.
    if after 4 .... noes.
    over a sitting day (unless a
    previous resoln.) .... ayes.
    over the 30th. of January ..... noes.
for sitting on a Sunday or any
other day, not a sitting day[25] .... ayes.

[493]. It is more material that there should be a
rule to go by, than what that rule is; that there may
be an uniformity of proceeding in business, not
subject to the caprice of the Speaker, or captiousness of the members. It is very material that order,
decency & regularity be preserved in a dignified
public body. 2. Hats. 149.[1]

[494]. Though the Mace belongs to the House,
yet it attends the Speaker's person only, and if he

23
turn to the book

be sick, it is kept at his house, and the house adjourn without it.[1] The Clerk puts questions, by order of the house, when the Speaker is absent, or there is none. 2. Hats. 160. But no question can be put but of adjournment. ib.[2]

24   [495]. No member is to speak against ⟨any⟩ or reflect upon any prior determination of the house unless he means to conclude with a motion to rescind it.[1]

25   [496]. Members speaking twice or oftner in the same debate, speaking impertinently or beside the question, using unmannerly or indecent language against the proceedings of the house, or against particular members, using the king's name irreverently, or to influence the debate, hissing or disturbing a member in his speech, walking up & down in the house, standing on the floor, in the gangways or gallery, taking papers or books from the table, or writing there, crossing between the chair & a speaking member or the mace when it is off the table are offenses against order. id. 170.[1]

26   [497]. The orders of 1641. & 1693. direct the Speaker to call on a member by name, or present his name to the house who makes noise or disturbance in the house. The house may then call on the member to withdraw, on which he must be heard in explanation and withdraw. The Speaker will then state to the house the offence & they will consider what punishment to inflict. 167.172.[1]

[498]. The Speaker adjourning the house without authority, or refusing to put a question is a breach of privilege. The Speaker had formerly a right to adjourn the house himself. In 1678 it was ordered that he shall not do it without putting a question if it be insisted on. Ever since it has been the practice to put a question tho' not insisted on, unless when no quorum, in which case his antient power is exercised. If it be before 4 oclock he is not to adjourn till 4. or till it is probable there will not be 40. members that day. 2. Hats. 175.[1]

[499]. The Speaker is but a private member of committees of the whole house. He is not compell-

able to be at them as other members are. When in the house he gives the casting vote it has been sometimes usual to give his reasons, because the possibility of swaying the house is then past. 2. Hats. 177.[1]

27

[500]. The duty of the clerk is to make true entries of the things done, of the orders & proceedings, 'under the direction of the Speaker.' He is also to let no journals, records, accounts or papers be taken from the table, or out of his custody. 2. Hats. 194.5.[1]

28

[501]. The form of proceeding on disorderly words spoken is this. The member objecting to them & desiring them to be taken down by the clerk at the table must repeat them. The Speaker then *may* direct the clerk to take them down in his minutes. but if he thinks them not disorderly he delays the direction. If the call becomes pretty general he orders the clerk to take them down as stated by the objecting members. They are then part of his minutes. & when read to the offending member, he may deny they were his words, & the house must then decide by a question whether they are his words or not. Then the member may justify them, or explain the sense in which he used them, or apologize. If the house is satisfied no further proceeding is necessary. But if ⟨a question be moved & seconded⟩ two members still insist to take the sense of the house, the member must withdraw before that question is stated, & then the sense of the house is to be taken. 2. Hats. 199.[1] When any member has spoken, or other business intervened, after offensive words spoken, they cannot be taken notice of for censure. And this is for the common security of all & to prevent mistakes which must happen if words are not taken down immediately. Formerly they might be taken down any time in the same day. 2. Hats. 196.[2]

[502]. The not paying fees to the Serjeant &c is a contempt of the house and so dealt with. 2. Hats. 202.[1]

29

[503]. The house which has recieved a bill and

passed it *may* present it for the royal assent, &
ought to do it, tho' they have not by *message* notified to the other their passage of it. Yet the notifying by message is a form which ought to be observed between the two houses from motives of
respect & good understanding. 2. Hats. 242. Were
the bill to be witheld from being presented to the
king it would be an infringemt. of the rules of parl.
ib.[1]

[504].[1] On passing the bill of attainder against
the Ld. admiral Seymour, in 1548. the Commons
resolve that the Lords which affirm that evidence
may come hither & deliver it vivâ voce' & accordingly require it by message.[2] [qu. if the bill had
come to them from the Lords?][3] 3. Hats. 2.

30

[505]. Either house may request, but not command the attendance of a member of the other.
They are to make the request by message to the
other house, and to express clearly the purpose of
the attendance. that no improper subject of examn.
may be tendered to him. The house then gives
leave to the member to attend if he chuse it, waiting first to know from the member himself whether
he chuses to attend, till which they do not take the
message into considn. 3. Hats. 17.[1] But when the
peers are sitting as a court of criminal judicature
they may *order* attendance, unless where it be a
case of impeachmt by the commons. There it is to
be a request. ib.[2]

31

[506]. A message is recieved from the lords during a debate without adjourning the debate. 3.
Hats. 22.[1]

[507]. The Lords return a bill because the title
is not ingrossed, and it is without the usual words
importing a direction for sending it. 3. Hats. 22.[1]

[508]. If a message require an answer, the messengers should wait in the lobby to carry it back. If
the message be immediately agreed to, the answer
is delivered them. but if it be disagreed to or require consideration, they are called in again & told
that the house will send an answer by messengers
of their own. ib. 25.[1]

32

[509]. It is not the usage for one house to inform the other by what numbers a bill has passed. Yet they have sometimes recommended bills, as of great importance, to the considn. of the house to which it is sent. 3. Hats. 25.[1]

[510]. The Serjt. informs the Speaker & he reports to the house that there is a message from the Lords, & a question must be put for calling in the messengers. 3. Hats. 26.[1]

[511]. When a bill is sent by one house to the other & is neglected, they may send a message to remind them of it. 3. Hats. 25.[1]

33.

[512]. The Commons appoint a commee. to inspect the journals of the Lords, to report to them what they have done in any particular case. because the journal of the Lords is a record, open to every subject. But a printed vote of one house is sufficient ground for the other to notice it.[1] The journal of the commons is also a record, because the house of commons ⟨is a court⟩[2] having a judicature in some things is therefore a court of record.[3] 3. Hats. 27-30. 2. Hats. 261.

34

[513]. A conference is to be desired by that house which is possessed of a bill on which the conference is to be & not by the other. 3. Hats. 31.[1]

35

[514]. Neither house can exercise any authority over a member or officer of the other, but should complain to the house of which he is and leave the punishment to them.[1] Where the complaint is of words disrespectfully spoken by a member of another house, it is difficult to obtain punishment because of the rules supposed necessary to be observed (as to the immediate down of words) for the security of members.[2] Therefore it is the duty of the house & more particularly of the Speaker to interfere immediately, & not to permit expressions to go unnoticed which may give a ground of complaint to the other house, & introduce proceedings & mutual accusations between the two houses which can hardly be terminated without difficulty & disorder.[3] 3. Hats. 51.

36.

[515]. When bills passed in one house & sent to

the other are grounded on special facts requiring proof, it is usual either by message or at a conference to ask the grounds & evidence, & this evidence, whether arising out of papers or from the examination of witnesses, is immediately communicated. id. 48.[1]

37.

[516]. If either house have occasion for the presence of a person in custody of the other, they ask the other their leave that he may be brought up to them in custody. 3. Hats. 52.[1]

38.

[517]. A bill passed by the H. Comm. with blanks. these filled up by the Lords as amendments, returned to the Commons as such & passed. 3. Hats. 83.[1]

39.

[518]. Cases of riders mentioned 3. Hats. 121.122.124.126.[1]

40

[519]. He that hath once spoken to a bill, may not speak to it again on that day though he would change his opinion.[1] Arcana Parliamentaria. 17.

qu?

[520]. When a conference is required it is always granted. ib. 18.[1]

[521]. Ferrers (34.35. H. 8. 1584)[1] being in execution under a judgment for debt, was enlarged[2] by privilege of parl. by the Serjeant with his mace without any written warrant. He could not by law be brought again into execution, & so the party without remedy for his debt. See Arcan. Parl. 59. A very full report of this case which was a very solemn one, the king, Lords, commons & judges concurring.[3] Elsynge. 104.[4]

[522]. All the amendments to a bill reported by a commee. are to be proceeded in before any new amendment or Proviso be admitted, unless it be amending the amendments reported. Elsynge's memorials. 53. After the amendments reported are done with, other amendments, provisos or additional clauses may be offered. ib. 54. But regularly these amendments &c should be offered to the Commee. to be first considered & prepared, to save the time of the house. ib.[1]

41

[523]. When a clause is offered to be added to a bill after the 3d. reading the clause ought to be read

& put to the question 3. times. Elsynge's memorials 59.[1]

[524]. An apparent mistake has been amended by the house the day after the bill had passed, the amendments being thrice read & the bill again passed. ib. 62.23. Eliz.[1]

42

[525]. It is no possession of a bill unless it be delivered to the clerk or that the Speaker read the title. ib. 95.[1] ord. H. Commons. 64.[2]

[526]. A precedent 6. Edw. 6. a burgess claiming his privilege to the Speaker, the Speaker issues his warrant to obtain the writ. ib. 110.[1] to wit a writ of Habeas corpus from the house. Ord. H. Com. 122.[2]

43

[527]. When a bill from the one house is passed by the other with amendments the first house may propose amendments to the amendments. Elsinge's method of passing bills. 23-27.[1]

44

[528]. An essential order that amendments be twice read. Ord. H. Com. 67. A Proviso from the other house to be thrice read,[1] and on each new reading the members may speak again. id. 68.[2]

[529]. When ⟨a⟩ messengers come⟨s⟩ from the other house they are to be admitted as soon as the business then then in agitation is finished. Ord. H. Com. 73.[1]

45

[530]. When a conference is asked the subject of it must be expressed or the conference not agreed to. Ord. H. Com. 89.[1]

46:

[531]. On a call of the house the absentees are noted, but no excuse to be made till the house be fully called over. Then on a second call of the absentees, excuses are to be heard. Ord. H. Com. 92.[1]

[532]. In case of arrest or other breach of privilege of a member a letter shall issue under the Speaker's hand for the party's relief therein, as if the parliament were sitting, & the person disobeying to be censured at next meeting. Ord. H. Com. 110.[1]

[533]. Witnesses and sollicitors, constables attending parliament have the privilege of parl. ib. 119.[1]

[534]. The wife of a member def. to a bill of review brought by her husband to reverse a decree for alimony cannot have privilege as the wife of a member against her husband. nor can the servt of a member against the member. ib. 121.[1]

1625. Feb. 15.
1666. Dec. 20.
1550. Feb. 20.

1749. Jan. 22.

[535]. On an arrest of a member or servant it seems the Speaker may issue a warrant for an Habeas corp. or an Order for the discharge and to stay all proceedings in the suit. Ord. H. Com. 122.[1] or an order for a writ of privilege out of the chancery. Ord. H. Com. 129.[2] These orders must of course be directed to the officer from whom such writs issue in the ordinary course of law, as may be inferred from ib. 254.[3]

[536]. No member has privilege against paimt of taxes, aids, supplies or parish duties. Ord. H. Com. 131. nor where he is trustee, or a public officer & for any matter done in execution of his office, nor as a copartner in any trade or undertaking. Ord. H. Com. 133.134.[1]

[537]. The printing the names of the members, & reflecting on them is a breach of privilege. id. 140. So is the misrepresenting their proceedings.[1] The aspersing the last house of Commons or any member thereof with recieving French money, voted to be scandalous &c & the party committed to Newgate. ib. 141. [1701.][2] The breaking open a letter to a member is a breach of privilege. ib. 162.[3]

[538]. The proper officer (except in cases of impotency or sickness) ought to amend in the house all returns of elections, where, upon an error committed in the return, the house shall see cause to order an amendmt. ib. 223.[1]

Impeachmt.
Jurisdiction.

[539].[1] The Lords cannot impeach any to themselves, nor join in the accusation because they are the judges. Seld. Judic. in parl. 12.63.[2] Nor can they proceed against a Commoner but on complaint of the Commons. id. 84.[3] The lords may not by the law try a commoner for a capital offence, on the information of the king, or a private person; because the accused is entitled to a trial by his peers

generally: but on accusation by the H. of Commons they may proceed against the delinquent of whatsoever degree, & whatsoever be the nature of the offence: for there they do not assume to themselves trial at Common law. The Commons are then instead of a jury, and the judgment is given on their demand, which is instead of a verdict. So the Lords do only *judge*, but not *try* the delinquent. id. 6.7.[4] But Wooddeson[5] denies that a Commoner can now be charged capitally before the Lords, even by the Commons: & cites Fitzharris's case 1681. impeached of High treason, where the Lords remitted the prosecution to the inferior court. 8. Grey's deb. 325.-7.[6] 2. Wooddeson 601.576. 3. Seld. 1610.1619.1641. 4. Blackst. 257. 3. Seld. 1604.1618.7.1654.[7]

Accusation.

[540].[1] The Commons as the Grand inquest of the nation become suitors for penal justice. 2. Woodd. 597.[2] 6. Grey. 356.[3] The general course is to pass a resolution containing a criminal charge against the supposed delinquent, & then to direct some member to impeach him by oral accusation at the bar of the H. of Lords in the name of the Commons. The person signifies that the Articles will be exhibited, & desires that the delinquent may be sequestered from his seat, or be committed, or that the peers will take order for his appearance.[4] Sachev. trial. 325. 2. Woodd. 602-605. Lords Journ. 3. June 1701. 1. Wms. 616. 6. Grey. 324.[5]

Process.

[541].[1] If the party do not appear, Proclamations are to be issued giving him a day to appear. On their return they are strictly examined. If any error be found in them, a new Proclamation issues giving a short day. If he appear not, his goods may be arrested, & they may proceed. Seld. Jud. 98.99.[2]

Articles.

[542].[1] The Accusation [articles] of the Commons is substituted in place of an indictment.[2] Thus by the usage of parl. in impeachment for writing or speaking, the particular words need not be specified.[3] Sach. tr. 325. 2. Woodd. 602.-605. Lords Journ. 3. June 1701. 1 Wm. 616.[4]

Appearance.

[543].[1] If he appears, & the case be capital, he answers in custody. (tho' not if the accusation be general. He is not to be committed but on special accusations.) If it be for a misdemeanor only, he answers, a lord in his place, a Commoner at the bar, & not in custody, unless, on the answer, the lords find cause to commit him till he find sureties to attend, & lest he should fly. Seld. Jud. 98.99.[2] A copy of the Articles is given him & a day fixed for his answer. T. Ray. 1. Rushw. 268. Fost. 232. 1. Clar. hist. reb. 379.[3] On a Misdemeanor, his appearance may be in person, or he may answer in writing, or by attorney. Seld. Jud. 100.[4] The general rule, on an accusation for a misdemeanor is that in such a state of liberty or restraint as the party is when the Commons complain of him, in such he is to answer. id. 101.[5] If previously committed by the Commons, he answers as a prisoner. but this may be called, in some sort, judicium parium suorum. ib.[6] In Misdemeanors the party has a right to Counsel by the Common law; but not in capital cases. Seld. Jud. 102-5.[7]

Answer.

[544].[1] The Answer need not observe great strictness of form. He may plead guilty to part, & defend as to the residue, or, saving all exceptions, deny the whole, or give a particular answer to each article separately.[2] 1. Rush. 274. 2. Rush. 1374. 12. Parl. hist. 442. 3. Lords Journ. 13. ⟨Apr⟩ Nov. 1643. 2. Woodd. 607.[3] But he cannot plead a pardon in bar to the impeachment. 2. Woodd. 615. 2. St. tr. 735.[4]

Replication.
Rejoinder.

[545].[1] There may be a Replication, Rejoinder &c. Seld. Jud. 114. 8. Gray's deb. 233. Sachev. tr. 15. Com. Jo. 6. Mar. 1640. 1.[2]

Witnesses.

[546].[1] The practice is to swear the witnesses in open house, and then examine them there: or a committee may be named, who shall examine them in committee, either on interrogatories agreed on in the house, or such as the committee in their discretion shall demand. Seld. Jud.[2] 120. 123.

Jury.

[547].[1] In the case of Alice Pierce 1. R. 2. a jury was empannelled for her trial, before a committee.

Seld. Jud. 123. but this was on a complaint, not on impeachment by the Commons. Seld. Jud. 163. It must also have been for a misdemeanor only, as the Lords spiritual sat in the case, which they do on misdemeanors but not in capital cases. id. 148. The judgment was a forfeiture of all her lands & goods. id. 188. This, Selden says, is the only jury he finds recorded for misdemeanors in parl. but he makes no doubt, if the delinquent doth put himself on the trial of his country,[2] a jury ought to be empanelled: & he adds that it is not so on impeachment by the Commons; for they are in loco proprio,[3] & there no jury ought to be empannelled. id. 124. The Lord Berkeley 6. E. 3. was arraigned for the murder of E. 2. on an information ex parte regis, & not on impeachment of the Commons; for then they had been patria sua.[4] He waived his peerage, & was tried by a jury of Gloucestershire & Warwickshire. id. 125.[5] In 1. H. 7. the Commons protest that they are not to be considered as parties to any judgment given or hereafter to be given in parliament. id. 133.[6] [They have been generally & more justly considered, as is before stated, as the Grand jury; for the conceipt of Selden is certainly not accurate that they are the patria sua of the accused, & that the Lords do only *judge*, but not *try*. It is undeniable that they do try, for they examine witnesses as to the facts, & acquit or condemn, according to their own belief of them. And Ld. Hale says 'the peers are judges of law as well as of fact.' 2. Hale. P. C. 275. consequently of fact as well as of law.][7]

presence of Commons.

[548].[1] The Commons are to be present at the examination of witnesses. Seld. Jud. Seld. Jud. 124. Indeed they are to attend throughout, either as a committee of the whole house, or otherwise at discretion appoint managers to conduct the proofs. Rushw. tr. Straff. 37. Com. Jo. 4. Feb. 1709.10. 2. Woodd. 614. And judgment is not to be given till they demand it. Seld. Jud. 124. But they are not to be present on impeachment when the Lords consider of the answer or proofs, & determine of their

judgment. Their presence however is necessary at the answer & judgment in cases capital. id. 158.159. as well as not capital. 162. The Lords debate the judgment among themselves. Then the vote is first taken on the question of guilty or not guilty: and if they convict, the question or particular sentence, is out of that which seemeth to be most generally agreed on. Seld. Jud. 167. 2. Woodd. 612.[2]

Judgment.

[549].[1] Judgments in parliament for death have been strictly guided per legem terrae,[2] which they cannot alter; & not at all according to their discretion. They can neither omit any part of the legal judgment, nor add to it. Their sentence must be secundum, non ultra legem.[3] Seld. Jud. 168-171. This trial, tho' it varies in external ceremony, yet differs not in essentials from criminal prosecutions before inferior courts. The same rules of evidence the same legal notions of crimes and punishments prevail, for impeachments are not framed to alter the law, but to carry it into more effectual execution against too powerful delinquents. The judgment therefore is to be such as is warranted by legal principles or precedents. 6. Sta. tr. 14. 2. Woodd. 611. The Chancellor gives judgments in misdemeanors, the lord High Steward formerly in cases of life and death. Seld. Jud. 180. but now the Steward is deemed not necessary. Fost. 144. 2. Woodd. 613. In misdemeanors the greatest corporal punishment hath been imprisonment. Seld. Jud. 184. The king's assent is necessary in capital judgments. [but 2. Woodd. 614. contra.] but not in misdemeanors. Seld. Jud. 136.[4]

Continuance.

[550].[1] An impeachment is not discontinued by the dissolution of parliament, but may be resumed by the new parliament. T. Ray. 383. 4. Com. J. 23. Dec. 1790. Lords Jo. May 16. 1791.[2] 2. Wood. 618.

[551]. 'The Senate shall have the sole power[1] A13.[2]

[552]. On complaint of a breach of privilege the party may either be sent for in custody of the Ser-

jeant, or simply summoned. 1. Grey's deb. 88.95.[1]

[553]. A new bill engrafted by way of amendment on the words 'be it enacted by the Lords & Commons.' 1. Grey's deb. 190.192.[1]

Privile qu.

[554].[1] A conference after a 1st. reading of a bill. ib. 194.[2] On a motion to put a smaller sum to the question first it was observed not to be fair to put a question which all agree to. The fair question is whether there shall be addition to the question. 1. Grey. 365.[3]

[555]. Journal of Lords denied to be a record. 1. Grey. 368.[1]

[556]. The king can no more raise men in England than he can money without an act of parl. 1.E.3. 7.E.3. 4.E.4. But others said the contrary. 6. Grey. 44. Some thought he might raise men for foreign countries but not for England. ib.[1]

[557]. Counsel are to be heard only on private, not on public bills, and on such points of law only as the house shall direct. 10. Grey. 61.[1]

[558]. Three of Coleman's letters were entered on the Journ. of the commons by order of the house. 1. Chandler. 300.[1]

[559]. The king having sent original letters to the commons, afterwards desires they may be returned that he may communicate them to the lords. 1. Chandler. 303.[1]

[560]. The H. of com. ⟨pro⟩ has adjourned itself de die in diem for 14. days together without a Speaker. the clerk putting the question. 1. Chandler. 331.[1] Again for 6. days. ib. 335.[2]

[561]. The first order for printing the votes of the H. of Commons was Oct. 30. 1680. 1. Chandler. 387.[1]

[562]. Mr. Prynne having at a Commee. of the whole ⟨corrected⟩ amended a mistake in a bill without order or knowledge of the commee. was reprimanded. 1. Chandl. 77.[1]

[563]. When a commee. is charged with an enquiry, if a member prove to be involved, they cannot proceed against him, but must make a special

report to the house, whereupon the member is heard in his place, or at the bar, or a special authority is given to the Comee. to enquire concerning him. 9. Grey. 523.[1]

[564]. In the ordinary parliamentary course there are two free conferences at least before an adherence. 10. Grey. 147.[1]

[565]. It appears that on joint committees of the Lords & Commons each commee. acted integrally in the following instances. 7. Grey 261.278. 285.338. 1. Chandler 357.462. In the following instances it does not appear whether they did or not. 6. Grey 129. 7. Grey. 213.229.321.[1]

[566]. It seems implied that standing commees. are never adjourned. 7. Grey. 353.[1]

[567]. A member, on the 1st. reading of a bill, moved it might *lie on the table*, as he had not made up his mind for throwing it out or giving it a 2d. reading. But the Speaker said he never saw an instance of that. The proper question was whether it should be read a 2d. time. Whereupon they adjourned the consideration of it to a fixed day. 9. Grey 176.[1] But amendments to a bill from the other house were laid on the table. 9. Grey 346.[2]

[568]. A motion of privilege has preference over others. 7. Grey. 433.[1]

[569]. The house in commee. of the whole on the king's speech. A bill from the lords interposed in the debate, was read the 1st. time debated on that reading, then read a 2d time, debatd & committed, & then the Comme. of the whole was resumed. 9. Grey 150.[1]

[570]. The granting of money is never referred to the consideration of a private committee. 9. Grey 199.[1]

[571]. Two bills, the one from the lords, the other of the H. of Com: on the same subject, seem to have been both taken up & read, at the same time. 9. Grey 252.[1]

[572]. Petitions are not recieved against a bill before it is brought in. 9. Grey 438.[1]

[573]. Speakers.
Sr. Job Charlton ill. Seymour chosen
1673. Feb. 18.
Seymour being ill Sr. Rob. Sawyer
chosen 1678. Apr. 15
Sawyer being ill, Seymour chosen Apr. 29
$\left.\right\}$ not merely pro tem.
See 1. Chandler. 169.276.277.
Thorpe in execution, a new speaker chosen. 31. H.
VI. 3. Grey. 11.[1]

[574]. A bill on the 1st. reading resolved to be
withdrawn, & a commee. appointed to bring in a
new one on the same subject. 3. Grey. 10.[1]

[575]. Debates, or rather conversation, often
goes off without any question put. 3. Grey. 45.[1]

[576]. Orders for the attendance of witnesses are
not given blank. 3. Grey. 51.[1]

[577]. The Serjeant at arms may appoint ⟨men⟩
deputies to aid him. ⟨3. Grey. 59.⟩ who are then the
servants of the house. 3. Grey. 59.147.255.[1]

[578]. A Member of the H. of Lords was committed to the tower in vacation time. When the
parliament met, the lords presented petition after
petition to the king, to preserve the privilege of
parliament, and no cause of his commitment being
expressed they refused to sit until he was restored
to them, which was not done till 3. months after.
ib. 127.[1]

[579]. It would seem that the house of whom a
conference is asked cannot get at a free conference
unless asked by the other. 3. Grey. 145.151.[1]

[580]. Neither house can judge of the privileges
of the other. ib. 280.[1]

[581]. It is understood that a Previous question
cannot be put in a committee. Yet see instances of
it. 3. Grey. 377.384.[1]

[582]. When the H. commands it is by an 'Order.' But ⟨the⟩ facts, principles, their own opinions
and purposes are expressed in the form of 'Resolutions.'[1]

[583].[1] When either house make amendments to
a bill they do not ask a Conference. But if the other

house disagree to any of them, they may ask a conference. 4. Hats. 4.223.[2]

[584]. Conferees may argue at a Conference in support of any thing done or passed in their house, but not against it, nor assent at such a conference to any new thing there propounded till their house be informed and agree to it. 4. Hats. 31.33.[1]

[585]. At a conference (not a free one) asked by the Commons the Lords come only to hear, & not to propound, and no reporters ⟨being⟩ therefore being appointed no report of any thing propounded by the Lords can be made. 4. Hats. 32.[1]

[586]. A free conference cannot be asked till there have been two conferences. 4. Hats. 37. 40.[1]

[587]. During the time of a conference the house can do no business. As soon as the names of the managers are called over, & they are gone to the Conference, the Speaker leaves the chair, without any question, and resumes it on the return of the managers. It is the same whilst the managers of an impeachment are at the H. of Lords. 4. Hats. 47.209.288.[1]

[588]. The commons affirm that it is usual to have two free conferences, or more, before either house proceeds to adhere; because before that time the houses have not had the full opportunity of making replies to one another's arguments: and to adhere so suddenly & unexpectedly excludes all possibility of offering expedients. 4. Hats. 330.[1]

EDITOR'S NOTES

PARAGRAPH 1

1 On this point, see below, par. 44, n. 2.

2 In the Pocket-Book and in the sources upon which it is based, law cases decided in the courts of King's Bench, Common Pleas, and Exchequer are identified by a formula which places them in the appropriate court term of the appropriate year of the appropriate sovereign's reign. Thus the case mentioned here was decided in Trinity Term of the seventh year of the reign of Henry VIII. In connection with references to court terms, it is helpful to remember that before 1873 there were four successive terms in an English legal year: Hilary Term (from January 23 to February 12); Easter Term (from the Wednesday which coincided with the end of the fortnight after Easter to the first Monday after Ascension Day); Trinity Term (from the Friday after Trinity Sunday to the Wednesday which fell a fortnight later); and Michaelmas Term (from October 23 to November 28). See Jacob, s.v. terms. See also OED, s.v. term. *sb.* 5.

3 The *Lex Parliamentaria*, ch. 1, p. 3-4, provided TJ with the substance of this paragraph and with all of its sources as listed here except for the reference to "Hakew. 85." This reference points to an instance in which the king, the barons, and the Commons had passed a statute against the wishes of the archbishops and bishops, that is, *excluso clero*. The *Lex Parliamentaria*, p. 4, line 6, uses this same Latin phrase and in a marginal note indicates that the statute to which the phrase applied was passed at Bury St. Edmunds in the 24th year of the reign of Edward I. Hakewill's account adds some additional details about the whole transaction, and thus it has value beyond Petyt's account, even when we recognize that Hakewill inadvertently dated the transaction a hundred years too early. As for TJ's interest in citing Hakewill at this point, it seems to originate in his desire to confirm his regular sources whenever he could.

PARAGRAPH 2

1 This entire paragraph consists of condensed versions of George Petyt, *Lex Parliamentaria*, p. 5, lines 9-15, and p. 7, lines 3-19.

2 TJ drew these abbreviations from a marginal note in Petyt, p. 7, referring to a resolution adopted in Parliament on February 6, 1672/73, "That all Elections upon Writs issued since the last Session, are void." The writs concerned had been issued by the clerk of the Crown at the command of Charles II and thus were not in conformity with the established practice requiring the issuance of such writs only after the Commons had authorized them by express warrants. See JHC, IX, 248.

3 Statutes, as distinguished from court decisions, were identified in early legal writings by a formula specifying not only the year or years in which they were passed in a sovereign's reign but also their chapter numbers within the parliamentary acts of those sessions. Thus the act enabling Chester to send members to Parliament was identified as being chapter 13 of the statutes passed during the session divided between the 34th and 35th years of Henry VIII's reign; and the statute giving the same right to Durham was chapter 9 of the statutes passed

in the 25th year of Charles II. Sometimes, however, the chapter number in one of these references designates only a section of the specified statute, as, for example, in a reference to 34 Edward I, St. 5, c. 2, the "c. 2." designates, not a separate bill, but the second section of Statute 5. I take these explanations and examples from Winfield, p. 77.

4 In Spelman's *Glossarium Archaiologicum*, p. 380-1, there is a Latin disquisition upon the term *Maior*, one passage in which reads thus (Editor's translation): "Following his [Richard I's] example, King John in the 6th year of his reign (A.D. 1204) also named as mayor the bailiff of Lenni Episcopalis (today called King's Lynn), whereas the very famous city of Norwich did not obtain a magistrate under that title before the 7th year of the reign of Henry V, that is, the year of grace 1419."

PARAGRAPH 3

1 See above, p. 46.

2 Tythings were originally companies of ten men and their families who had obliged themselves to behave peaceably within their own group, each group being presided over by a Teothungman or Tithing-man and having its own court. See Jacob, s.v. tithing.

3 In TJ's marginal notation, but not in his text, he doubled the "t" in the first syllable of this word.

4 In deriving this paragraph from George Petyt, p. 19-22, TJ paraphrased p. 19, lines 16-24; p. 20, lines 1-8; p. 21, lines 11-32; and p. 22, lines 1-14. TJ compiled his list of sources from marginal references in Petyt. His final reference is of course to par. 5 of the Pocket-Book.

PARAGRAPH 4

1 TJ's references to Ine (688-726), Edgar (944-975), and Cnut (1016-1035) were taken from a marginal note in Petyt, p. 23.

2 This reference came to TJ from Petyt, p. 47. Atkyns' *Power of Parliament*, p. 32 (or p. 61-2 of the 1741 edition), expressed disapproval of the modern practice of allowing justices of the peace to be appointed by the king instead of elected by freeholders, as had anciently been done. The change from the ancient to the modern practice, said Atkyns, had been authorized by parliament when Edward III was still a minor, and his mother and Mortimer were exercising and extending the royal power. TJ's insertion of this reference at this particular point in the Pocket-Book shows that, as he took notes upon what Petyt was discussing at a given moment, he would bring to mind Petyt's later observations upon the same matter and would thus put material from one page of his source into a context with material from later pages. In other words, TJ seems here to have been an alert and resourceful reader—a characteristic repeatedly shown by his use of similar procedures elsewhere in the Pocket-Book.

3 See above, p. 46.

4 In specific terms, this entire paragraph was derived from the following passages in Petyt: p. 22, lines 15-22; p. 23, lines 27-32; p. 25, lines 11-15; p. 28,

lines 3-8; and p. 34, lines 20-1. Except for the reference to Atkyns, the sources listed by TJ are also listed in Petyt, p. 23, 25. The final reference is to par. 6 of the Pocket-Book.

PARAGRAPH 5

1 That is, "the magnates having been convened by royal edict" (Editor's translation). Henry I's speech to this parliament is given by Petyt in Latin, p. 36-7, and in English, p. 37-8. Petyt derived his Latin text from "Mat. Paris old Edicon p. 83. and in Watts, p. 42." In the Watts edition, as published at London in 1640, the *Oratio Regis Henrici* appears on p. 62.

2 That is, "concerning the difficult matters of the kingdom" (Editor's translation).

3 Up to this point, TJ based the paragraph upon the following specific passages in Petyt: p. 35, lines 16-23; p. 36, lines 6-7; p. 38, lines 30-2; and p. 39, lines 9-12.

4 A cross reference to par. 3, above.

5 This concluding sentence originated in Petyt, p. 62, lines 10-14, where Petyt spoke thus: "By 16 *Car.* 2.c.1. these Acts are declared to be in Force: And further, it is declared and enacted, *That the holding of* Parliaments *shall not be discontinued above three Years at the most.*" Once again TJ brought a later passage from Petyt into relation with earlier passages.

PARAGRAPH 6

1 TJ has *provediritis*, whereas Petyt, p. 36, line 29, and Matthew Paris, p. 62, line 18, have *provideritis*, the correct form.

2 TJ's Latin sentence is a somewhat condensed version of Petyt's. As translated in *Parliamentary History of England*, I, 10, the entire sentence reads thus: "If you desire it, I will strengthen this Promise with a written Charter, and all those Laws which the holy King Edward, by the Inspiration of God, so wisely enacted, I will again swear to keep inviolable."

3 "I restore to you the law of King Edward, along with those changes by which my father amended it" (Editor's translation). The italics are of course TJ's. Petyt, p. 42, lines 2-5, gave the Latin passage which TJ transcribed. As this passage appears in Matthew Paris, Watts edition of 1640, p. 56, lines 27-8, Henry added that his father had amended Edward's law "with the advice of his barons."

4 These two references may be traced to Matthew Paris, p. 252, 56, in the Watts edition of 1640.

5 TJ's major source for this entire paragraph is Petyt, p. 36, lines 29-32; p. 37, lines 1-2; p. 41, lines 27-32; p. 42, lines 1-5, 8-14; p. 43, lines 30-2; p. 44-5; p. 47, lines 18-32; p. 48, lines 1-2. TJ took from Petyt the references to Matthew Paris and Lambarde. The cross-reference is to par. 4, above.

PARAGRAPH 7

1 In transcribing this sentence from Petyt, p. 55, lines 18-21, TJ omitted two of Petyt's words, "royal" before "presence" and "either" before "in person,"

while adding "by" before "representtion." But he followed Petyt in attributing the passage to Coke.

2 The reference to Hakewill is not in Petyt. TJ supplied it on his own.

PARAGRAPH 8a

1 Except for differences in style, this sentence exactly parallels that in Petyt, p. 55, lines 27-31. In turn, Petyt transcribed this exact sentence from Coke, *Institutes*, IV, 28, lines 7-9.

PARAGRAPH 8b

1 See Petyt, p. 56, lines 10-11, 16-18, for this exact passage somewhat differently styled. Petyt condensed Coke's similar passage, *Institutes*, IV, 17 (lines 22-3) and 50 (lines 5-6). Petyt's imperfect documentation, attributing this passage to Vol. I of the *Institutes*, was adopted by TJ without checking it.

PARAGRAPH 9

1 The first part of this sentence is a verbatim transcript of Petyt, p. 60, lines 9-11; and the second part is TJ's translation of a French passage in Petyt, p. 60, lines 4-5. Petyt provided TJ with the reference to Rolle's *Reports*, I, 18.

PARAGRAPH 10

1 In respect to wording, not to style, these three sentences closely parallel or exactly reproduce the following passages in Petyt: p. 57, lines 3-7; and p. 61, lines 26-30, 30-1.

2 In citing Atkyns' *Argument* as authority for these sentences, Petyt was in error. He should have cited Atkyns' other influential work, *The Power, Jurisdiction, and Privilege of Parliament*, p. 24, 99-100. Petyt was familiar with both of these treatises, and he cited each of them on various occasions in the *Lex Parliamentaria*: see p. 8, 42, 46, 47, 48, 57, 61, 73, 74, 75, 83, 84, 89. But in the present instance he seems carelessly to have referred to the wrong one, and TJ did not bother to check the reference.

PARAGRAPH 11

1 This sentence is a paraphrase of Petyt, p. 62, lines 25-9.

2 As in the preceding paragraph, Petyt has once again confused one of Atkyns' works with another. The reference here should be to the latter's *The Power, Jurisdiction, and Privilege of Parliament*, p. 98.

3 On his own TJ supplied this reference to §16 of the article on Parliament & Statutes in Brooke's *La Graunde Abridgement*.

PARAGRAPH 12

1 The second of TJ's notes enables his readers to discover that this paragraph is a verbatim transcription of a passage in the article entitled "Parliament" in Owen Ruffhead's edition of Giles Jacob's *A New Law-Dictionary*, sig. 7 G [1], except that TJ added and bracketed "depart" above "be dissolved," and dropped out "that" before "the public."

2 TJ took this reference from Jacob, the work concerned being by Jacob himself.

3 In his *Institutes*, IV, 11, Coke cited what he called "the ancient Treatise, *De modo tenendi Parliamentum*," to support the doctrines stated in the present paragraph, whereas Jacob made no such reference. Thus TJ must be credited here with having sought wider authority for these doctrines than Jacob had supplied. And it should also be noticed that the two page numbers which TJ here recorded after the title of "the ancient Treatise" came not from Coke, but from TJ's own reading of that treatise in Hakewill's translation.

PARAGRAPH 13

1 The two sentences making up this paragraph are an exact transcription of a passage from the article on parliament in Ruffhead's edition of Jacob's *A New Law-Dictionary*, sig. 7 G [1], except that TJ omits "several" and "are" as these words respectively occur just before and just after "orders."

2 TJ took these two references from Jacob.

PARAGRAPH 14

1 Up to this point TJ's text exactly parallels a passage in Ruffhead's edition of Jacob, sig. 7 G [1], with two exceptions: TJ corrected and improved Jacob's style by altering the position of "may" in relation to "be discharged"; and he dropped Jacob's phrase, "by the Lords Spiritual and Temporal" after "hath been resolved." The two references to Raymond TJ borrowed from Jacob.

2 The final sentence of this paragraph, with its reference to Prichard's case, and with its Latin words, is paraphrased by TJ from Levinz's *Reports*, I, 165. *Per curiam* means "by the Court." *Scire facias* was a judicial writ which a sheriff served upon a specified person. The writ said, in effect, to a sheriff, "You should make so-and-so know *(scire facias)* that he is to appear in court and respond to the following legal actions contemplated against him." TJ may have made *scire facias* into a plural so that the phrase would agree grammatically with "writs"— a nicety Levinz did not observe. As for the case mentioned here, it concerned a man named Prichard who was ordered imprisoned by the Lords on the charge that he had shown contempt for them. When Parliament was prorogued, he sought release under a writ of habeas corpus. The Lords objected to the writ and cited their order as the reason why Prichard should not be freed. But the court held (1665) that the Lords' order had no legal standing after a parliamentary prorogation, inasmuch as that order was not in the same class as a writ of error or a *scire facias*. And so Prichard won his point.

PARAGRAPH 15

1 The case of *Man vs. Cooper*, as summarized by Levinz at the point specified in TJ's note, became the source of this paragraph, TJ being concerned only to present the case in its essentials. From Levinz's own meager account of those essentials, it appears that Man sued Cooper for money which Cooper had failed to pay as he had promised to do upon the expiration of a certain act of parliament. It also appears that Man's claim was sustained by the lower court. On appeal, however, the verdict in Man's favor was reversed on the ground that the parlia-

mentary act cited by Man had not legally expired when Man's suit was filed. The act had indeed provided that its life was to be a three-year period from its enactment plus a period made up of the next full parliamentary session; and indeed Man had instituted his suit after the three-year period had ended and after the subsequent end of the parliamentary session which began in that period; but the judges argued that the filing of the suit should have been postposed, so that the complete new parliamentary session specified in the act could have had time to run its course and thus render the act inoperative.

PARAGRAPH 16

1 The first sentence of this paragraph summarizes eighteen lines of the opening passage in the chapter which Coke entitled, "Of the High and most Honourable Court of Parliament," TJ's statistics as to the makup of the three estates being taken directly from that source. The second sentence stands in Coke (IV, 3, line 18) as follows: "Of this Court of Parliament the King is *Caput, principium & finis*."

Coke's figures on the size of Parliament apply only to the period before 1644. The figures given above in par. 2 of the Pocket-Book apply to the period after 1707, when the union of England and Scotland had finally been made fully effective. George Petyt said (p. 7) that the act of union added 45 Scottish members to Parliament for a new total of 558.

PARAGRAPH 17

1 The phrase in law French came to TJ from Coke. In context it means that coroners were elected in a countywide vote "by the commons of those very same counties."

2 TJ borrowed these references from a marginal note in Coke. Coke had "164k" in his reference to FNB, that is, to Fitzherbert. In the 1718 edition of Fitzherbert, the passage indicated by Coke is on p. 163k.

3 TJ reversed the order in which the sentences in this paragraph stand in Coke, IV, 2, lines 9-12, but TJ's wording is largely Coke's.

PARAGRAPH 18

1 TJ's bracketed query refers not only to the Latin phrase which precedes it but also to a longer Latin passage in Coke's *Institutes*, IV, 2, lines 20-2, where Coke spoke thus: "In cujus rei testimonium sigilla nostra tam pro nobis quam pro tota Communitate praed. Regni Angliae praesentib. sunt appensa." ("In witness whereof our seals are now appended as much on our own behalf as on behalf of the whole commonalty of the aforesaid kingdom of England." Editor's translation.) Coke argued from this passage that, in the 21st year of the reign of Edward III (1348), the Commons must have had no Speaker, and that both Houses of Parliament must then have been sitting together, else the Speaker would have affixed the Commons' seal upon the letters to the pope, and the king would have affixed his seal on behalf of himself and the nobles. TJ's query seems in the first instance designed to call attention to two meanings which "communitas" had in early English legal parlance, where it referred interchangeably either to the entire body politic, thus including Lords and Commons, or to one part of that body, the Commons; and in the second instance, the query seems intended to

question Coke's assumption that "communitas," as Edward III used the term in 1348, referred to the Commons alone at a time when, according to Coke, they were sitting together with the Lords in the same house. TJ may have raised this query by way of reminding himself to inquire for his own information into the precise extent to which the House of Commons had developed in Edward III's time. So far as the bold outlines of the question are concerned, Coke was right in saying that both Houses of Parliament were sitting together in 1348. In this connection, Smith observes (*History of the English Parliament*, I, 196): "The knights of the shire, who had previously acted with the barons, joined the citizens and burgesses, and in the first parliament of Edward III. they were found sitting together as 'the Commons.'" But whether the word "communitas" meant "the Commons" in Edward III's statement of 1348 is a more difficult question. "By the end of the fourteenth century the term *communitates* or *communes*," says A. F. Pollard (*Evolution of Parliament*, p. 114), "implies both the knights of the shires and the representatives of the cities and boroughs; but this usage expresses the result of a gradual amalgamation, and before 1350 the word is used in different senses." Thus Coke's assumption that in 1348 the term *communitas* meant Commons would appear to be shaky, as TJ suspected.

2 The first Speaker of the Commons is now acknowledged to have been Sir Peter de la Mare, who served in the next to the last parliament of Edward III (1376). In Edward III's last parliament (1377), the Speaker was Sir Thomas Hungerford. See Roskell, *The Commons and Their Speakers*, p. vii, 10-15, 119-21. See also MacDonagh's *Speaker of the House*, p. 115, and Hakewill's *Manner and Method*, p. 199-200.

3 Except for the bracketed query, this entire paragraph came from Coke's *Institutes*, IV, 2, lines 15-33, in direct quotation or in paraphrase.

PARAGRAPH 19

1 The coif was a "white cap formerly worn . . . by a serjeant-at-law as part of his official dress." See OED, s.v. coif, *sb.* 3. Judges of the Court of Exchequer were barons, and those who were also serjeants-at-law belonged to the degree of the coif.

2 The writ summoning judges to attend the House of Lords, as quoted by Coke, reads in part thus: "Quod intersitis nobiscum . . . super praemissis tractaturi, vestrumque consilium impensuri." ("That your advice may be pondered and may be applied along with our own to intervening matters brought up before us." Editor's translation.) TJ condensed *tractaturi* to *tracturi* as if the original verb were *traho* instead of *tracto*; but he did not thereby alter Coke's basic meaning. Both verbs may mean "ponder" or "reflect."

3 In its first twenty-six words this paragraph is an almost exact quotation, and in its remaining words a paraphrase, of Coke's *Institutes*, IV, 4, lines 23-9. TJ condensed Coke's "but they have no voices in Parliament" into "But they have no vote."

PARAGRAPH 20a

1 Jacob defined this term as "A Word generally used in the last Part of all Writs, wherein the Date is contained; which begin with these Words, *Teste meipso, &c.* if it be an original Writ; or *Teste* the *Lord Chief Justice, &c.* if judicial."

2 "Note this—that in the present instance the greater power yields to the lesser" (Editor's translation). TJ added *Quod* to the *Nota* which began Coke's presentation of this Latin passage. The passage itself is to be interpreted in relation to events in the reign of Henry V. Henry V was abroad from late July 1417 to late December 1420, carrying on a war which ended in his being proclaimed heir to the throne of France. On the eve of his return to England, he ordered his regent, the Duke of Gloucester, to call a session of Parliament. The session began on December 2, 1420, and lasted about a fortnight. One of the resolutions passed on that occasion provided, "That, if a Parliament should be summoned by the King's Lieutenant, and the King arrive soon after the Writs were issued out of Chancery, yet that Parliament should not be dissolved, nor new Summons made; but that it should meet by Virtue of the former." See *Parliamentary History of England*, II, 165. The authors of that work said of this resolution that it was "the first cautionary Act that was made for Security against any Inconvenience that might arise from the uniting of *England* to *France*." No doubt Parliament in 1420 was beginning to fear that Henry V's brilliant success at Agincourt in 1415, and his subsequent position as heir to the throne of France, were fraught with the ugly possibility that he was now in the position to subvert the English parliamentary system and to nullify English liberties by his power to dissolve Parliament and to refrain from summoning it again. Coke's epigrammatic Latin comment stated the principle behind the parliamentary action of 1420—that, in cases of possible misuse of the royal prerogative, the power to keep Parliament in session rested with the lesser authority, Parliament, rather than with the greater authority, the king.

3 The entire paragraph is a condensed transcript of Coke's *Institutes*, IV, 7, lines 3-8, the Latin passage and the reference to Henry V being taken by TJ from Coke's marginal notes.

PARAGRAPH 20b

1 A paraphrase of Coke's *Institutes*, IV, 7, lines 34-8, 41-5. The number in the left-hand margin of TJ's manuscript is smudged. It appears to be "4."

PARAGRAPH 21

1 Closely paraphrased from Coke's *Institutes*, IV, 7-8.

PARAGRAPH 22

1 This clause, and a large part of the ensuing paragraph, represent condensed quotations or paraphrases from Coke's *Institutes*, IV, 8 (lines 19-25, 32-5, 38-55), 9 (lines 1-6), and 10 (lines 12-6). The paragraph also owes something to Brooke's *La Graunde Abridgement* and to George Petyt, as noted below. The references to Seymour and Hale provide no contribution to the wording of TJ's text.

2 Coke wrote "Conge de eslier of a Bishop." TJ slightly altered that wording and added the accent mark and the apostrophe. The modern phrase is usually written *congé d'élire*.

3 The reference to Seymour TJ borrowed from Hale. Neither of these authorities is mentioned at this point by Coke. TJ cited both of them on his own.

4 The two clauses that follow the reference to "Bro. Parl. 7." represent TJ's translation of a law French passage in that source. The law French passage is not in Coke, although at that point Coke referred to an error made by Parliament in the time of Henry VIII, and for details concerning it he referred his readers to §7 of the article on Parliament in Brooke. Evidently curious as to what the error was, TJ took occasion to read and to translate what Brooke said of it, thus giving increased substance to Coke's text.

5 TJ put this phrase in brackets to lend emphasis, no doubt, to Coke's statement that the Speaker-elect disabled himself while "standing in his place." TJ had already emphasized the latter phrase by underscoring its last three words.

6 What probably led to the cancellation of this phrase was that TJ, after transcribing it from Coke, decided to insert some details from George Petyt, p. 267, lines 4-5, 9, 11-12, and, having done so, he scored out the earlier phrase as being no longer necessary.

7 This wording, beginning with "The Commons being called into the Lords' house," and ending with "presented to the king," is very close to a direct quotation from George Petyt, p. 268, lines 5-9.

8 TJ's word "arrected" is in Coke. It is a later corruption of "areted," meaning "imputed." See OED, s.v. arrect, aret.

9 TJ closely followed Coke's text in phrasing these three parts of the Protestation.

PARAGRAPH 23

1 A condensed quotation from Coke, *Institutes*, IV, 9, lines 41-50.

PARAGRAPH 24

1 A condensed quotation from Coke, *Institutes*, IV, 11 (lines 50-2), 12 (lines 1-4).

PARAGRAPH 25

1 Partly condensed, partly paraphrased, from Coke, *Institutes*, IV, 12 (lines 7-13), 13 (lines 5-8). For a brief account of the use of proxies in the Upper House, see Pike, *House of Lords*, p. 243-5.

PARAGRAPH 26

1 A condensed and slightly paraphrased quotation from Coke, *Institutes*, IV, 14, lines 32-7.

PARAGRAPH 27

1 Within the present context, a device "moved on the king's behalf" would mean "an expedient for raising money for the crown."

2 That is, "have a tender regard for." (OED, s.v. tender, v.[2] 3.)

3 The entire paragraph represents condensed quotations from Coke, *Institutes*, IV, 14 (lines 41-6) and 34 (lines 5-8). On the latter page, Coke mentioned a case in which the Commons notified Edward III of their intention to confer with

"their several Countries and places" in connection with the king's request for a "new kind" of subsidy. TJ changed "Countries" to "counties."

PARAGRAPH 28

1 These twenty-three words were transcribed from a passage of thirty-one words in Coke's *Institutes*, IV, 14, lines 47-9. After "County" Coke placed "or Borough," and TJ deleted the latter phrase. But otherwise his deletions amounted only to the removal of six needless words in Coke's sentence.

PARAGRAPH 29

1 The wording of this entire paragraph depends upon quotations or paraphrases from the text of Coke's *Institutes*, IV, 15 (lines 1-9, 16-23, 30, 37, 42-3, 49-52), 16 (lines 1-4), and 17 (lines 1-3, 24-34). But, as TJ indicated, the three following pages in Coke (18, 19, and 20) cast further light upon the accusation made against the thirty-nine members of the Commons and so needed to be mentioned in the documentation given here.

2 According to this Latin passage, Parliament "stands upon its own laws and customs." The two subsequent Latin phrases relate to the same sentiment—that the conduct of Lords and Commons within the boundaries of their parliamentary function can be called to question only before the high court of Parliament acting under laws and procedures determined by itself.

3 TJ's brief account of the case of the bishop of Winton (Latin for Winchester) is made up of TJ's own translation of selected parts of the Latin account in Coke, IV, 15-16. The principal in the case was John de Stratford (d. 1348), who served as bishop of Winchester between 1323 and 1333, and as archbishop of Canterbury between 1333 and 1348. In both of these capacities he was of course a member of the House of Lords. In October 1328, he withdrew without the king's permission from the parliamentary session sitting at that time in Salisbury, and his action was construed as a violation of the royal decree against nonattendance in Parliament. But when an attempt was made in the court of King's Bench to hold him accountable for his alleged offense, he argued that Parliament alone had jurisdiction in his case. The court of King's Bench agreed with his argument, with the result that his case became one of the first precedents invoked in later times to support the supremacy of Parliament above all other courts in matters pertaining to its jurisdiction over its own procedures. See Pike, *House of Lords*, p. 159; also Powell and Wallis, p. 339; also Charles Lethbridge Kingsford in DNB, s.v. Stratford, John de.

4 That is, *Bancus Regis* or King's Bench.

5 Philip of Spain and Queen Mary of England, married in 1554, appear in English parliamentary history from 1554 to 1558 under the initials Ph. and Mar., or Phil. and Mar., or P. and Mar. See JHC, I, 37-52.

6 That is, King's Bench.

7 Coke's text, p. 17, lines 31-4, reads thus: "And *Edmond Plowden* the learned Lawyer pleaded, that he remained continually from the beginning to the end of the Parliament, and took a Travers full of pregnancy: and after his plea was *sine die per demise la Roign*." ("Travers" means "legal exception," and the Latin

phrase is an official way of saying "without consideration of date even unto the death of the king.")

PARAGRAPH 30

1 Except for differences in style, this sentence is an exact transcription of the central part of a sentence in Coke's *Institutes*, IV, 15, lines 13-15.

PARAGRAPH 31

1 The major words in a clause in Coke's *Institutes*, IV, 15, lines 15-16, are here exactly transcribed, except that Coke had "Parliament" for TJ's "house of Commons" and the regular conjunction for TJ's ampersand.

PARAGRAPH 32

1 A rearranged and somewhat condensed version of a statement in Coke's *Institutes*, IV, 54, lines 44-6, where Coke was in the second chapter of part IV and was speaking "Of the Councel Board, or Table." It will be remembered that his first chapter, from which TJ had previously been quoting, treated "Of the High and most Honourable Court of Parliament." Thus this paragraph shows TJ's concern for the functioning not only of Parliament but also of the executive arm of the British government. This note is also a further indication that the Pocket-Book is more than a manual of parliamentary rules—it is rather a compilation of passages having to do with British constitutional law. The Council, that is, the Privy Council, owed its origins, as did Parliament itself, to an ancient institution, the Curia Regis. See Pike, *House of Lords*, p. 23-6, 27-56, 251-2.

PARAGRAPH 33

1 This entire paragraph is made up of slightly condensed quotations from Coke, *Institutes*, IV, 23 (lines 19-21, 25-6, 41-4, 46-50, 51-4), and 24 (lines 1-8).

2 Coke wrote "Maior of Westbury," as did TJ, but in his margin TJ has "mayor." For the case of the Mayor of Westbury, see D'Ewes, p. 182, col. 2. D'Ewes identified the mayor as Anthony Garland, and his accomplice in receiving the bribe as "one . . . Wats." D'Ewes also identified Long as Thomas Long, Gentleman, "a very simple man of small capacity," who gave Garland and Wats £4 in return for Long's being elected to Parliament. See also below, pars. 129, [430].

3 A mark was a unit of currency originally valued in terms of a mark weight (eight ounces) of pure silver, and thus it represented two thirds of a pound sterling, the latter unit being valued in terms of an amount of pure silver weighing a twelve-ounce pound. As for the case of Arthur Hall, who published a book reflecting in derogatory terms upon the House of Commons, it occupied the Commons for some little time. See D'Ewes, p. 291-2, 295-8, 308-9; also JHC, I, 122-3, 125-7, 136; also below, pars. 129, 138.

4 Without apparently recognizing his victim as a member of Commons, Muncton, also called Monyngton, came one day to the House and assaulted William Johnson for taking "a Net out of Mr. *Bray's* House in *Bedfordshire*." Johnson explained to the Commons during the ensuing inquiry that what he took from Bray's house was a net belonging to Lord Mordaunt, and that he was acting at

the time as undersheriff. See JHC, I, 35, under April 23, 1554; also below, par. 129.

5 For a similar entry, see below, par. [378].

6 For a similar entry referring to servants of members, see below, par. [379].

7 For a repetition of this rule, see below, par. 128.

PARAGRAPH 34

1 This paragraph is wholly made up of condensed excerpts from Coke's *Institutes*, IV, 24 (lines 16-18, 19-22, 28-30, 31-3) and 25 (lines 6-8).

2 The case involving the prior and the Earl of Cornwall is translated and summarized by TJ from Coke's brief Latin description. The prior, it appears, had served the citation at the instigation of Bogo de Clare in "Anno 18 E.I." (1290). From other sources we know that Bogo de Clare lived in Oxfordshire, and that his name appeared on the Hundred Rolls for the year 1273. See Bardsley, s.v. Clare.

3 Coke has "said."

4 Coke has *Subpoena.*

5 Coke has "process out of any Court of Equity."

6 A free translation of Coke's Latin passage.

PARAGRAPH 35

1 TJ formed this paragraph by quoting, abridging, or paraphrasing passages from Coke's *Institutes*, IV, 25, lines 10-13, 14-16, 20-4, 40-1.

2 This reference came to TJ from a marginal note in his source.

3 A restitution of this kind was based upon a writ issued by Parliament for the return to a person of certain rights and properties taken from him as a result of his having been unlawfully convicted of a crime. See Jacob, s.v. restitution. See below, case of Baron Stourton, par. [440], n.

PARAGRAPH 36

1 The wording of this entire paragraph represents a condensed version of Coke's *Institutes*, IV, 26, lines 16-17, 21-6, 10-13, 18-19.

2 "And this Writ," said Coke, lines 28-30, "was sometime in Latin and sometime in French, as in those days the Statutes were enacted in Latin or in French." To illustrate the point, Coke then gave the text of an eight-line Latin writ of the reign of Edward III, and of a fourteen-line French writ of Richard II's reign.

3 TJ inserted this reference on his own. The paragraph cited reads thus in *La Graunde Abridgement*, s.v. Parliament & Statutes: "26 Nota que statut ou acte de parliament ne besoigne deste proclaime, car le Parliament represent le corps de tout le realme, quar la sont gents come Chiuallers et Burgeises de chescun Countie ou Pais."

1 This entire paragraph is a close transcription of Coke's *Institutes*, IV, 27 (lines 3-5, 44-9) and 28 (lines 10, 12-17).

2 The brackets and the enclosed phrase are of course TJ's.

3 "Coke" is understood as the subject of this verb.

4 These two references do not appear in Coke. Paragraph 86 of Brooke's article on Parliament & Statutes deals with the legal concept of a session of Parliament.

1 Transcribed with some deletions but otherwise word for word from Coke's *Institutes*, IV, 28, lines 19-36. TJ eliminated some fifty-three words of Coke's text; his abbreviations stand for full words in his source; he did not always follow Coke's punctuation; and moreover he disencumbered Coke's style on two occasions—he substituted "they" for "the House of Commons" before "are sent for," and he wrote "as if the k. had been personally present" for Coke's "as if the Kings person had been there personally present."

2 Coke had "the Lords House."

3 The Latin *sententia* from which TJ fashioned his present maxim reads thus in Coke: "Nihil enim tam conveniens est naturali aequitati, unumquodq; dissolvi eo ligamine quo ligatum est." ("Nothing indeed is more in accord with natural law than that a thing be dismembered by the bond which held it together." Editor's translation.) TJ changed Coke's *dissolvi* into *dissolvitur* because for his context he seems to have preferred a passive present indicative to a passive infinitive, but he did not thereby lessen the applicability of the *sententia* to his own paragraph. And is it not better that the *sententia* be expressed in Latin rather than in English? For in English how could one express the basic irreconcilability between *dissolvi* and *ligatum est* in such a way as to suggest by the enigmatic presence of *eo ligamine* that the binding agent between dismemberment and wholeness may be that which ultimately reduces wholeness to dismemberment? One could say, of course, that "the tie which binds a political community together may ultimately destroy it," but even so one has used eleven words to TJ's seven, and one has failed to convey the apocalyptic overtone of the Latin maxim.

4 "Letters Patents," ordinarily to be considered a plural noun, is treated by TJ and Coke as singular.

1 A slightly abridged transcript of Coke's *Institutes*, IV, 35, lines 18-22.

2 Coke had "one for the Yea, another for the No."

3 Coke had "the Yeas go of one side of the House, and the Noes on the other."

1 A slightly abridged transcript of Coke's *Institutes*, IV, 36, lines 10-13. Coke wrote "ancient" for TJ's "antient," and he added "for the Commonwealth" after "profitable."

PARAGRAPH 41

1 This paragraph represents fragments from Coke's *Institutes*, IV, 37 (lines 38-9, 41-2, and marginal note b) and 38 (lines 24, 26, 33-4, and marginal note e).

2 Thomas Cromwell (1485?-1540) was created Earl of Essex on April 17, 1540, after having played a conspicuous part in arranging the marriage of Henry VIII and Anne of Cleves. But when the king's marriage proved unsuccessful, Cromwell lost the royal favor and was subsequently accused of high treason by the Duke of Norfolk on June 10, 1540. Both the Lords and Commons passed a bill of attainder against him, and he was beheaded on July 28 of that year, Henry VIII having refused to heed his plea for mercy. See *Parliamentary History of England*, III, 134, 163; also James Gairdner, "Cromwell, Thomas, Earl of Essex," in DNB.

3 Sir John Mortimer's case is vividly described by Coke, and TJ would have had that description in mind in his present reference. Said Coke: "And as evil was the procéeding in Parliament against Sir John Mortimer, third son of Edmond the second Earl of March, . . . who was indicted of High Treason for certain words, in effect, that Edmond Earl of March should be King by right of Inheritance, and that he himself was next rightful heir to the Crown after the said Earl of March, wherefore if the said Earl would not take it upon him, he would: and that he would go into Wales, and raise an army of 20000 men, etc. which Indictment (without any arraignment or pleading) being méerely faiyned to blemish the title of the Mortimers, and withall being insufficient in Law, as by the same appeareth, was confirmed by Authority of Parliament: and the said Sir John being brought into the Parliament without arraignment or answer, Judgment in Parliament was given against him upon the said Indictment, That he should be carried to the Tower of London, and drawn through the City to Tyburn, and there hanged, drawn and quartered, his head to be set on London-Bridge, and his four quarters on the four gates of London, as by the Report of Parliament appeareth." The date of Sir John's indictment and execution was 1423, the second year of the reign of Henry VI. See Sandford's *Genealogical History*, p. 222-3. For a brief note concerning Sir John Mortimer, see T. F. Tout, "Mortimer, Edmund (II) de, third Earl of March," in DNB.

4 Coke's sardonic comment upon the treatment of Thomas Cromwell may be rendered thus (Editor's translation): "Forgetfulness taketh away, if it is able. But if it does not, silence can hide."

PARAGRAPH 42

1 These two sentences are slightly abridged transcriptions of Coke's *Institutes*, IV, 38 (lines 40-3) and 39 (lines 15-17).

2 Coke provided a Latin example of each of the two writs mentioned in this paragraph. The first example (Coke, p. 38-9) represented the kind of document sent to the sheriff of the county in which the accused party lived, and it directed that sheriff to require the accused "to appear before the King in the next parliament." Writs of this sort were issued when the accusation involved a serious crime. The second kind of writ (Coke, p. 39) was issued for less serious offenses—Coke's Latin phrases, which TJ transcribes, would be englished as "in-

juries, physical inconveniences, and harrassments"—and such writs summoned the accused "to appear in his proper person before the King and his councel."

1 This full paragraph is partly quoted and partly paraphrased from Coke, *Institutes*, IV, 43 (lines 47-54), 44 (lines 1-3).

2 "Amerced," that is, fined. The money thus collected went to the Crown. D'Ewes, p. 309, col. 2.

3 Coke wrote "one of the Commons by the Commons."

4 A member of the Commons received wages from his constituents for his services as their representative. The usual procedure was for the clerk of the Commons to present to the clerk of the Crown in Chancery a record of the attendance of members of the Lower House at sessions of Parliament, and for the clerk of the Crown to issue writs *de expensis* to the members concerned. Those writs were put into the hands of the sheriffs for collection, and from the sheriffs the members ultimately received their wages. See Pollard, *Evolution of Parliament*, p. 113-14, 317-19, 387-428; also D'Ewes, p. 309, col. 2; also Neale, p. 74, 142, 155-7, 321-31.

5 TJ added this latter reference on his own.

1 Based upon Coke, *Institutes*, IV, 44 (lines 48-52) and 45 (lines 1-2, 14-17, 32-6, 38-40), this paragraph represents editorial procedures varying from an almost literal transcription of Coke's text to abridgment and paraphrase, with TJ's translation of Coke's Latin included at one point.

2 *Per baroniam*, that is, "by virtue of a barony." "Barony, (*Baronia*) Is that Honour and Territory which gives Title to a *Baron*; comprehending not only the Fees and Lands of Temporal *Barons*, but of Bishops also who have two Estates; one as they are spiritual Persons, by Reason of their spiritual Revenues and Promotions; the other grew from the Bounty of our *English* Kings, whereby they have *Baronies* and Lands added to their spiritual Livings and Preferments." Jacob, s.v. barony. Ecclesiastics per *baroniam* were bishops "who by Virtue of *Baronies* annexed to their Bishopricks, always had Place in the Lords House of Parliament, as *Barons* by Succession." Jacob, s.v. baron.

3 As TJ's Latin phrases indicate, an ecclesiastic who does not also hold title as a temporal baron is "in respect to worldly matters . . . dead in the eyes of the law," and thus he is prevented from holding a seat in Parliament.

4 This sentence is translated from the following Latin passage in Coke, *Institutes*, IV, 45, lines 14-17: "De jure & consuetudine Angliae ad Archidiaconatum Cantuariensem, &c. Abbates, Priores, aliosq; Praelatos quoscunque per Baroniam de domino Rege tenentes pertinet in Parliamentis regiis quibuscunque ut Pares regni praedicti personaliter interesse, ibiq."

5 According to Coke, *Institutes*, IV, 45, lines 31-42, this abbot of Tavestock was Richard Banham, and the episode mentioned here occurred in the 5th year of Henry VIII's reign (1514). See Pike, *House of Lords*, p. 163-4.

PARAGRAPH 45

1 Paraphrased in part from the English text and in part from Latin quotations in Coke's *Institutes*, IV, 46, lines 14-15, 24-7. *De communitate comitatus* means "from the political community of the county."

2 Based upon the same source, lines 21-2, 27-8.

3 A paraphrase of the same source, lines 37-42. Coke wrote, "H.4.An.14. of his Reign summoned a Parliament Cro. Purificationis," and TJ expanded the Latin phrase into *crastino purificationis*, that is, "the morrow of the festival of the Purification." The festival, popularly called Candlemas, is celebrated on February 2. Thus Henry IV summoned that Parliament for February 3 of 1412/13. See *Parliamentary History of England*, II, 124.

4 Based partly upon Coke's text and partly upon his footnote reference to "F.N.B. 229.a." TJ looked that reference up and incorporated into this sentence some of what he found there. The letters "F A" following "229" refer to William Hughes' translation of Fitzherbert's work in which the passage consulted by TJ is partly marked F in the margin, and partly A. See *The New Natura Brevium*, 6th ed. (1718), p. 507.

5 See *Institutes*, IV, 46, line 47.

PARAGRAPH 46

1 This entire paragraph, as TJ indicated in a general way, is derived from the following specific sources: 1) Coke's *Institutes*, IV, 46 (lines 51, 53-4, 52-3), 47 (lines 3-5, 6-7, 10-12, 41, 43-53), 48 (lines 3-4, 23, 25-6, 28-30); 2) Hale's *Jurisdiction of Parliaments*, p. 115, from which TJ borrowed the reference to Seymour; and 3) George Petyt, p. 405-6.

2 "An Alien enfranchised." See Jacob.

3 In place of these abbreviations Coke wrote "Kings Bench or Common Pleas, or Barons of the Exchequer." (p. 47, lines 43-4). See also George Petyt, p. 182-3.

4 Thomas Thorpe, who died in 1461. See Roskell's *The Commons and Their Speakers*, p. 248-54, 366-7. See also below, pars. 81, 82, [423], [572].

5 "Convocation, . . . the Assembly of all the Clergy, to consult of Ecclesiastical Matters in Time of Parliament: And as there are two Houses of Parliament, so there are two Houses of *Convocation*; the one called the *Higher or Upper House*, where the Archbishops and all the Bishops sit . . . ; and the other the *Lower House* . . . , where all the Rest of the Clergy sit." Jacob.

6 The references to Seymour and Hale are not in Coke. TJ evidently added them in order to confirm Coke's statement that members of the clergy are ineligible for Parliament by virtue of their being members of the Convocation. Hale's citing of Seymour in this connection is in fact a reference to JHC, I, 27.

7 Coke wrote, "the opinion in Brook" (IV, 48, lines 3-4). TJ wrote "of" at first, and then inserted "in" above the line, without deleting the other preposition.

[178]

8 The case of the sheriff of Buckingham is explained by Coke, IV, 48, lines 25-30, as follows: "At the Parliament holden 1 *Caroli Regis*, the Sheriff for the County of *Buckingham* was chosen Knight for the County of *Norff.* and returned into the Chancery: and having a *Subpoena* out of the Chancery served upon him at the suit of Lady *C. pendente Parliamento*, upon motion, he had the priviledge of Parliament allowed unto him by the Judgment of the whole House of Commons."

9 A reference to par. 102 below, where the events just recited are mentioned again.

10 TJ's reference takes us to George Petyt's virtual transcript of Coke's account of the sheriff of Buckingham as set forth above, n. 8. Had Petyt or Coke named the sheriff, they would have identified him as Sir Edward Coke himself. Sir Edward had been an outspoken opponent of James I's arbitrary behavior toward Parliament; and Charles I, determined to prevent similar opposition, appointed Sir Edward sheriff of Buckingham, thus making him ineligible under parliamentary rules for a seat in Commons. In the parliamentary election of early 1625/26, however, Sir Edward was returned to the Commons from Norfolk. Charles I at once requested the Commons to authorize a writ calling for a new election to replace the ineligible Sir Edward. The Commons took this request under advisement and even on one occasion debated whether their ancient rule allowing sheriffs membership in Commons should be restored or declared still inoperative. Without deciding that particular question, the Commons finally resolved in the closing days of the session to declare Sir Edward a *de facto* member and to grant him privilege in response to a suit filed against him by the Lady Cleare, said to be his wife, Lady Hatton. See JHC, I, 817, 825, 829, 869. See also G. P. Macdonell in DNB, s.v. Coke, Sir Edward.

PARAGRAPH 47

1 The Oath of Supremacy was made mandatory by an act passed in the Parliament held during the first year of the reign of Elizabeth I; and it was first administered in Elizabeth I's second Parliament, which began January 11, 1562/63. See D'Ewes, p. 39, 78-9. See also Neale, p. 351.

2 These two sentences are slightly altered versions of Coke's *Institutes*, IV, 48 (lines 37-8) and 49 (lines 4-7).

PARAGRAPH 48

1 A somewhat condensed version of Coke's *Institutes*, IV, 48, lines 42-8. TJ wrote "and not finished" as a replacement for Coke's clumsy phrase, "and cannot be determined within those hours." And for Coke's "wave" TJ has "waive."

PARAGRAPH 49

1 This entire paragraph is made up of a largely verbatim transcription of Coke's *Institutes*, IV, 49 (lines 8-9), 48 (lines 49-54), and 49 (lines 1-3).

2 Coke's text reads "hath power."

3 Coke's text did not set this clause off with quotation marks.

4 The MS rather clearly reads, "4. Inst. 49.,49.," but the first "9" appears to have been superimposed upon an "8." Perhaps TJ meant to show that these quotations began and ended on p. 49, whereas the submerged "8" may have marked an initial impulse on his part to credit some of them to p. 48. At any rate, the quotations stem from these two pages, not from p. 49 alone.

PARAGRAPH 50

1 This paragraph rests upon Coke's *Institutes*, IV, 49, lines 11-18, 28-9, where Coke spoke thus: "The King cannot grant a Charter of Exemption to any man to be fréed from election of Knight, Citizen, or Burgess of the Parliament (as he may do of some inferior Office or places) because the elections of them ought to be frée, and his attendance is for the service of the whole Realm, and for the benefit of the King and his people, and the whole Commonwealth hath an interest therein: and therefore a Charter of exemption that King H.6. had made to the Citizens of *York* of exemption in that case, was by Act of Parliament enacted and declared to be void . . . *a fortiori*, he cannot grant any exemption to a Lord of Parliament."

PARAGRAPH 51

1 In its present context, a precept is a notice by a sheriff to a borough or city directing it to hold an election.

2 This paragraph is exactly transcribed from Coke, *Institutes*, IV, 49, lines 44-7, except for two changes: TJ omitted Coke's phrase, "and of no force" after "void"; and TJ's final phrase was his translation of Coke's *secundum legem & consuetudinem Parliamenti*. According to the law and custom of Parliament, said Coke, the sheriff must see to it that a convenient interval elapses between the issuing of a precept for an election and the holding of the election itself; and he must also see that advance notice is given those who have votes.

PARAGRAPH 52

1 This entire paragraph is TJ's translation of a law French passage in Brooke's *La Graunde Abridgement*, s.v. Parliament & Statutes, par. 4. The passage begins thus: *Case fuit que Sir J.P. fuit atteynt de certen tréspas per acte de Parliament, dont les commons fueront assentes que sil ne vient eins per tiel iour que il forfeytera tiel summe.* On his own responsibility TJ added the reference to Hakewill's *Modus*, p. 81, where "Kirbie's" explanation of the parliamentary point under discussion is set forth more briefly than in Brooke. Brooke did not identify "Sir J.P.," and Hakewill made no mention of him.

2 Thomas Kirby, keeper of the rolls of Chancery, 1456. Another Thomas Kirby or Kyrkeby was member of Parliament from Dorchester, 1491-1492. See *History of Parliament Biographies 1439-1509*, p. 517. Brooke called the clerk of the rolls "Kyrbye."

3 Brooke wrote, *Soit bayle as Seigniors*, and Hakewill, *Soyt bayle à Seigneures.* TJ preferred *baile* to *bayle*, but otherwise he followed Brooke. In either case, the phrase meant, "Let it be delivered to the Lords."

4 That is, a public bill affecting the community, as distinguished from a partic-

ular bill affecting persons named in it. Brooke noted in his margin: "Particuler byll. & comon. byll."

5 A translation of Brooke's *mes file sur les filass.* Hakewill wrote, p. 82, "then it shall be filed upon *filaces.*" A filace was a string or wire used in a court of law to hold the papers needed in trying the case at hand, and by extension it came to mean any appliance for holding documents. See OED, s.v. filace; also s.v. file, *sb.*[2] 3b.

6 The phrase *deste suer* means "to that suer," that is, "to the person instituting that petition or suit." Hakewill did not use the law French expression. The sentence in which it would have appeared, had he used it, reads thus in his text, p. 82: "unless the party whom it particularly concerneth will sue to have it inrolled, that it may be inrolled to be sure." The last three words of Hakewill's sentence found their way into TJ's text just after *deste suer.*

7 That is, "to inquire thereupon." Brooke had *quere inde.*

8 TJ did not close the quotation at this point, as he normally would have done.

9 Once again TJ did not close the quotation at this point.

PARAGRAPH 53

1 This entire paragraph is translated by TJ from the source indicated for par. 52, and the clerk mentioned here is John Fawkes, who held office from May 23, 1447, to November 25, 1470. See *History of Parliament Register 1439-1509*, p. xlix.

2 Brooke's text reads, *& les Justices eux aviseront . . .*, that is, "And the justices advise themselves accordingly."

3 "To inquire into judicially in those terms."

4 That is, the Lords did well "to question the matter."

5 TJ's bracketed query appears to mean that the Lords, in acting as they did in this instance, set aside a protective maxim of the law and replaced it with a protective expedient of their own devising, so as to have become guilty of legislative redundancy. That is to say, the Lords amended a bill so as to postpone its enforcement until a year from its fictitious date of passage, and thus they guaranteed that the fictitious date would in this case be inoperable. But had they not passed their amendment, the enforcement of the bill from its fictitious date would still not have been possible if someone had legally proved that he was injured thereby. The maxims of the common law are themselves safeguards against injustice, TJ seems to be saying here, and had the Lords recognized that truth, they would perhaps not have felt the need to accomplish the same result by legislative means.

PARAGRAPH 54

1 This paragraph continues TJ's translation of passages from "Parliament & Statutes" in Brooke's *La Graunde Abridgement,* TJ's aim at this point being to give the gist of the first four lines of article 7.

2 TJ's interpretation of this passage in Brooke seems to lack accuracy. Brooke's text indicates that there were three classes of burgesses who, as members of the Commons, could be removed and replaced by a new election; 1) those who while serving became mayors of towns; 2) those who while serving were appointed judges; and 3) those who while serving became ill. Perhaps these three classes were not made utterly clear by Brooke but at any rate TJ's translation appears to obliterate Brooke's intended distinction between the second and the first.

3 TJ added this reference to Hakewill, p. 49, by way of calling attention to Hakewill's translation of the paragraph recorded here. On that page Hakewill made no mention of Brooke as the source of the passage concerned, but even so he appears to have been following Brooke, and he noted, as did Brooke, that the parliament under discussion was held in the 38th year of Henry VIII's reign. Later he added the reference to Henry VIII's 7th year, and TJ borrowed it although it was not authorized by Brooke.

PARAGRAPH 55

1 TJ's translation of the first five lines of article 11 of Brooke's account of Parliament. Brooke identified the servant's assailant only as "Jo.S.," the servant only as "Rich.C.," and the knight only as "C.B." The proclamation was dated by Brooke "8.H.4.13, & 20."

PARAGRAPH 56

1 Article 12 of Brooke's account of Parliament is here abridged and translated. The full article reads thus in Brooke's text: *12 ¶ Quare impedit, acte de Parliament fuit plede que le Roy ne presente in aut droyt, nisi de voydance in tempore proprio, que ne fuit mise in use deuant, & uncore Curia contra Regem, que il serra myse in use a ore.* ("Asking an impedance. An act of parliament was pled that the king does not participate in any right except in the case of a vacancy at the proper time—which law had never been put to use before, and now the court holds against the king that the law may nevertheless be put to use from now on." Editor's translation). The court's verdict referred to a situation in which Parliament had issued a writ saying that the king had no right to appoint anyone to a benefice except when the benefice had become vacant in normal course. But the king appointed someone to a benefice which had not become normally vacant, and a rival claimant filed suit to upset the appointment. Although the original writ had never been put to use, the court decided against the king's appointee and held that the original writ should be observed from then on.

PARAGRAPH 57

1 Articles 35 and 54 of Brooke's account of Parliament are here abridged and translated. Article 35 reads thus in the part translated by TJ: *que ou matter est econter reason, et le partie nad remedy al comon ley, il suera pur remedy in parliament, & nota que a ceo iour plures de ceux suets sont in le court de Chaunc.* To this article TJ added his translation of the following observation in article 54: *la ceo sera aid p acte de pliament.* Brooke's reference at this point was to "4.E.4.41."

EDITOR'S NOTES

1 Up to this point TJ's paragraph is an abridged translation of the five lines making up article 35 in Brooke. The "thus" between "So" and "that" is partly illegible in the manuscript.

2 This sentence is a translation of the last three lines of article 38 in Brooke, and TJ added a reference to article 60 as being helpful in distinguishing private or particular from general statutes.

3 TJ took this reference from the margin of article 35.

PARAGRAPH 59

1 A legal phrase meaning "Having the status of a legal person . . . , and as such competent to maintain a plea in court, or to take anything granted or given." OED, s.v. personable, 2. The OED adds: "1660 Sheringham *King's Suprem*. VII. (1682) 68 All agreed that the King was Personable, and discharged from all attainder in the very act that he took the Kingdom upon him."

2 This paragraph is a somewhat abridged translation of the five lines comprising article 37 in Brooke.

PARAGRAPH 60

1 A slightly abridged translation of the two lines making up article 42 in Brooke. J.S. was not further identified in Brooke's text. TJ's "Por" is an expansion of Brooke's "*p*," and it represents an old form of "pour."

PARAGRAPH 61

1 Article 86 of Brooke's account of Parliament contains five lines of text, and the present paragraph is a faithful and accurate translation of those lines, except for TJ's omission of the last three words of his source—*qd nota diuersitatem* ("Take note of the diversity"). The first three lines of this passage were often quoted in translations similar to TJ's. See George Petyt, p. 352-3.

PARAGRAPH 62

1 John Vavasour (died 1506?) was king's serjeant during the reigns of Edward V, Richard III, and Henry VII; after August 14, 1490, he was puisne justice of the common pleas. See E. Irving Carlyle in DNB, s.v. Vavasour, John.

2 Article 107 in Brooke's account of Parliament (there are 109 articles in all) contains three lines, all of which are here translated by TJ, except for Brooke's concluding clause, *qd non contradicitur* ("which cannot be denied"). For a somewhat abridged transcription of article 107 in Brooke's law French, see Hale's *Jurisdiction of Parliaments*, p. 83-4.

3 Article 76 mentions the various formulas used to indicate the status of laws at the end of the parliamentary process. One formula says that the king with the assent of the Lords and Commons grants or establishes, etc.; another, that the law is enacted at the request of Lords and Commons, and that the king gives his assent; still another (the most usual) is that the law is enacted by the king with the assent of Lords and Commons; and yet one more (the briefest) is that the law

is enacted by authority of Parliament. These formulas are to be understood in connection with TJ's cross-reference at this point.

PARAGRAPH 63

1 This passage falls within Hakewill's translation of the medieval Latin treatise, *Modus tenendi Parliamentum*, p. 9.

PARAGRAPH 64

1 This paragraph represents TJ's condensation of a somewhat longer passage in Hakewill's translation of the *Modus tenendi Parliamentum*, p. 9-10.

2 The Cinque Ports (that is, the five ancient ports of Hastings, Romney, Hythe, Dover, and Sandwich) formerly supplied a large part of the English navy, and thus they enjoyed political and commercial privileges of a special kind. They were represented in Parliament by the so-called "barons of the Cinque Ports." These barons, however, were not peers of the realm but members of the House of Commons. See OED, s.v. Cinque Ports. See also Pollard's *Evolution of Parliament*, p. 141.

3 For an explanation of these units of currency, see above, par. 33, n. 3.

PARAGRAPH 65

1 In constructing this paragraph, TJ made use of the following somewhat fuller passage in Hakewill's translation of the *Modus tenendi Parliamentum*, p. 11: "In the First day Proclamation ought to be made in the Hall, or in the Monastery, or in some publick place, where the *Parliament* is to be held, and afterwards publickly in the City or Town, *That all those who would deliver Petitions or Bills to the Parliament, that they may deliver them the First day, and so other five days next following.*" The references in this quotation to "the Hall" and "the Monastery" are intended respectively to designate Westminster Hall and the Chapter House of Westminster Abbey, the latter location being the customary meeting place of early London parliaments. Says Pollard, *Evolution of Parliament*, p. 36-7: "The first step towards the holding of a parliament, after its summons had been decided, the writs issued, and the representatives, if any, elected, was to make public proclamation in the great hall of Westminster Palace (for Westminster Hall was the 'aula' in which the king, like every feudal lord, held his court), in the chancery, in the court of common pleas, in the exchequer, in the guildhall, and in Westcheap that all who wished to present petitions at the approaching parliament should hand them in by a certain date."

PARAGRAPH 66

1 According to Hakewill's translation of the *Modus*, p. 12-13, this speech was delivered by the king, or the chancellor, or the lord chief justice, "or some other fit, honest, and eloquent Justice or Clerk chosen by the Chancellour, or chief Justice"; and the purpose of the speech was to announce the reasons why Parliament had been called into session. The stipulation that the speaker stand as he spoke was supposed to guarantee "that all of the *Parliament* might hear him. . . ." But should Parliament not hear him, even so, as would be the case if he spoke "darkly" or talked "in a low voice," then, added the translation, "let him speak again, and speak louder also, or let another speak for him."

[184]

PARAGRAPH 67

1 These two sentences state the gist of Hakewill's translation of a part of the paragraph which the ancient Latin *Modus* devotes to "the principal Clerks of the *Parliament*" (p. 15-16). For the Latin paragraph, which is entitled "*De Principalibus Clericis Parliamenti*", see Clarke, p. 379.

2 TJ's bracketed observation calls attention to a point not fully clarified in the *Modus*. The clerk of the Parliaments originally sat in the House of Lords, and it is altogether probable that he had one or more underclerks to aid him as the duties of his office expanded in the course of time. Shortly after the beginning of the reign of Edward III (1327-1377), an underclerk was assigned to take care of the affairs of the Lower House, and he came to be called the clerk of the *domus communis* in response to the demands of his new post. The two principal clerks mentioned in the *Modus* can thus be identified as the clerk of the parliaments and the clerk of the Commons. Both of these officers were paid by the king, but the primary loyalty of each was to the House which he served and in which he sat. Each was instrumental in founding the Journals of his own House during the middle years of the sixteenth century, the Journals of the Lords having been started in the reign of Henry VIII, and of the Commons in that of Edward VI. See Pollard's *Evolution of Parliament*, p. 73-4, 113-114, 125, 271-2; also Neale, p. 333-5, 338-9; also Pike, *House of Lords*, p. 127, 323.

3 The final two sentences of this paragraph represent a shortened version of the section headed "*Touching the five Clerks of the Parliament*," in Hakewill's translation of the *Modus*, p. 17. Hakewill has "every one of them," not "every of them," in the last sentence. The Latin passage is entitled, "*De Quinque Clericis Parliamenti*." See Clarke, p. 380. Pollard, *Evolution of Parliament*, p. 125, comments thus: "The *Modus Tenendi Parliamentum* speaks of each of the five 'gradus' of parliament having its own clerk; but the fusion of estates reduced the number of clerks to two, or three if the clerk of convocation be included."

PARAGRAPH 68

1 Hakewill's translation of the *Modus* contains a section headed "*Touching the Order of deliberating business in the Parliament*," p. 20-1, and TJ's present paragraph represents a condensed verbatim transcript of that heading and of the three numbered clauses which follow it. For the Latin paragraph, which is entitled "*De Ordine Deliberandi Negotia Parliamenti*," see Clarke, p. 381.

PARAGRAPH 69

1 This sentence is a verbatim transcript of the last four lines of Hakewill's translation of a section of the *Modus* entitled "*Touching the Cryer of the Parliament*," p. 23, except that TJ's final four words were adapted from an earlier part of Hakewill's paragraph. For the Latin paragraph, entitled "*De Clamatore Parliamenti*," see Clarke, p. 382.

PARAGRAPH 70

1 In a legal or parliamentary sense, *process* is a term for the whole course of proceedings in a given action in court or in a legislative body.

2 This paragraph is a verbatim transcript of the first six lines of Hakewill's translation of a section of the *Modus* headed: "*Touching the Transcript or Writing out of Records, and Process made in Parliament,*" p. 30-1. The translation added that if the man who required the transcript was not able to pay the fee, the clerk should take nothing for his labors. For the Latin paragraph, which is entitled "*De Transcriptis Recordorum et Processuum in Parliamento,*" see Clarke, p. 383-4. According to Neale, p. 339, the cost to members of Parliament for a transcription of a private bill was still one penny for ten lines in 1571.

PARAGRAPH 71

1 On the first day of Parliament, Hakewill explained, the roll is called and each member answers to his name and identifies the place that he represents.

2 Par. 22 above had dealt with the events at the opening of Parliament, and that account was largely based upon Coke's *Institutes*, IV, 8, 9, and 10.

3 Although a transcript of selected sentences from a longer passage in Hakewill's *Modus*, p. 35, this paragraph falls outside of Hakewill's translation of the medieval work upon which TJ had based his preceding eight paragraphs. TJ's unclosed final quotation represents Hakewill's exact words, except that TJ inserted "a" after "promising."

PARAGRAPH 72

1 TJ did not close the quotation.

2 The usual phrase is "going out," or "going forth." See Coke, *Institutes*, IV, 35, line 20; Scobell, *Memorials*, p. 24-6; George Petyt, p. 289-90.

3 TJ constructed this paragraph by paraphrasing or transcribing sentences from Hakewill's *Modus*, p. 36 (lines 21-2, 25), 37 (lines 1-9, 20-5), 38 (lines 10-23).

PARAGRAPH 73

1 "The King approves it." Hakewill has *Le Roy le voet*, his last word being a typographical error, which TJ corrects to *veut*, in line with modern usage. The old form was *veult*. See George Petyt, p. 324.

2 That is, *soit fait comme il est désiré*, "let it be as he wishes."

3 "The King apprises himself." This formula for a royal veto "is said to be due to the need of the 14th-century kings to temporize with the Commons, and to leave the fate of their petitions for legislation open until supplies had been voted—which was not till the end of the session." Campion, *Procedure of the House of Commons*, p. 230. Campion adds that this formula came in time "to mean final dissent."

4 TJ followed Hakewill in stating this formula. The correct form should be *Le roy remercie ses Loyaux sujets, accepte leur benevolence, et ainsi le veult*, "The king thanks his loyal subjects, accepts their benevolence, and accordingly approves." See Campion, p. 230; also Strateman, p. 91.

5 This entire paragraph is derived from Hakewill's *Modus*, p. 39 (lines 8-11, 20-2), 40 (lines 8-9, 14-15, 22-4, 29), 41 (lines 1-3, 11-12, 20-8), and 68 (lines 1-12).

PARAGRAPH 74

1 Part paraphrase, part condensed transcript of Hakewill's *Modus*, p. 54, lines 9-10.

2 Condensed transcript of Hakewill, p. 47 (lines 25-9), 48 (lines 1-7). The symbol stands for shillings. Hakewill said, "40 s. of Free-hold within the said County beyond all charges." A parallel passage in George Petyt, p. 156, reads: "No Person shall be an Elector of the Knights for the Parliament, except he hath Freehold Lands or Tenements within the same County, to the value of Forty Shillings *per Annum* at the least, above all charges." Hakewill made the forty shillings a requirement for the knights to be elected, Petyt, for the electors of the knights.

3 A condensed transcript of Hakewill, p. 48, lines 13-16.

4 Partly paraphrased and partly condensed from Hakewill, p. 48 (lines 22-7), 49 (lines 1-7). Hakewill has "a true return" instead of TJ's "a due return."

5 A paraphrase of Hakewill, p. 52, lines 6-15.

6 A paraphrase of Hakewill, p. 53, lines 14-25. The bracketed phrase is TJ's, of course.

PARAGRAPH 75

1 A person taking the oath of allegiance sincerely promised and swore that he would "be Faithful and bear true Allegiance" to the reigning sovereign. See Jacob, s.v. Oaths *to the Government*. This oath had its origins in Magna Carta, and it was taken by the king's counsellors, sheriffs, mayors, bailiffs, judges, bishops, etc.

2 The oath of supremacy was a solemn declaration of abhorrence of the doctrine that rulers excommunicated by the pope could be deposed or murdered by their subjects; and it was also an affirmation of the principle that no foreign authority had jurisdiction in Britain. See Jacob, s.v. oaths. . . . This oath was first taken by Lords and Commons on January 12 or 15, 1562/63, pursuant to an act of Parliament in the first year of Elizabeth I's reign. See D'Ewes, p. 39 (col. 2), 78-9; also *Parliamentary History of England*, IV, 7, 13; also JHC, I, 418, 426, 442, 445, 448.

3 This paragraph is an abridged transcription and paraphrase of Hakewill, p. 56, lines 12-24. Hakewill added that all citizens and barons of the Cinque Ports, on entering Parliament as members, must take the oath of allegiance and of supremacy. For a gloss on the Cinque Ports, see above, par. 64, n. 2.

PARAGRAPH 76

1 See above, par. 46, n. 5

2 In strict bibliographical terms, Hakewill knew this work as Fox's *Acts and Monuments*, but he cited it here in the familiar title that would one day become

official. See above, Jefferson's Abbreviations, s.v. Fox, John. The sixth examination of John Philpot occurred on November 1, 1555. Early editions of *Acts and Monuments* were published in two or three volumes paged in a single sequence. Hakewill's reference to "fol. 1639" indicates the place of the Philpot episode in the third volume of one of the early editions, of course, but I have not located the episode on that particular page of the editions of 1563, 1583, and 1641.

3 It should be noted that Hakewill, from whom TJ borrowed this reference to Cowell's *Interpreter*, erred in attributing to Cowell's entry on "Proclamation" the opinion expressed here. In actual fact, that opinion was part of Cowell's entry for "Proctors of the clergie," where he said that churchmen, "howsoever the case of late dayes is altered, had place and suffrage in the lower house of Parlament, as well as the knights, citizens, Barons of the Cinque ports, and Burgesses." Cowell's opinion reflected the early practices of the Commons. In what has been called the first full Parliament in English history, that of 1295, the clergy attended as representatives of various ecclesiastical constituencies, but during the fourteenth century they ceased to attend altogether. See Smith, *History of the English Parliament*, I, 155-7.

4 The first sentence of this paragraph is an almost verbatim transcript of Hakewill's *Modus*, p. 57, lines 6-8. The other sentences are a close approximation of the text of a passage beginning in the same source at line 11 of p. 59 and ending at line 6 of p. 60.

PARAGRAPH 77

1 This entire paragraph is made up of sentences quoted nearly verbatim or paraphrased or condensed from a continuous passage beginning in Hakewill, p. 60, line 18, and ending at the bottom of p. 61.

PARAGRAPH 78

1 In the reign of Henry VIII, the House of Commons was prevailingly called the Nether House, and that term in that sense continued in occasional use during the seventeenth century. See OED, s.v. nether 2b.

2 A ninety-word passage in Hakewill, p. 62, lines 1-14, is here condensed into sixty-one words without sacrificing essential meaning.

PARAGRAPH 79

1 A condensed and at times slightly paraphrased quotation from Hakewill, p. 62, lines 15-29. Those lines in Hakewill were a close translation of a French passage from Crompton's *Courts*, p. 11, which Hakewill acknowledged as his source.

PARAGRAPH 80

1 That is, parliamentary privilege does not extend to vacations, but only to actual sittings of the court.

2 TJ's sentence and reference were taken with slight abridgment from Hakewill, p. 63, lines 1-4.

PARAGRAPH 81

1 For an account of this case, see Roskell, *The Commons and Their Speakers*, p. 248-54. Thomas Thorpe was elected Speaker of the Reading Parliament of 1453. The action against him was brought by Richard, 3rd Duke of York (1411-1460), and Thorpe's "trespass" consisted in his having impounded certain possessions of the Duke at a London inn on Henry VI's order.

2 The Duke argued that the trespass had been committed during a session of Parliament, but that his action against Thorpe had been started and terminated during a parliamentary vacation. The Lords, who heard the case, held that Thorpe should not be freed until he had paid the damages levied against him, and that a new Speaker should be elected by the Lower House.

3 TJ uses words, phrases, and sentences from Hakewill, p. 63 (lines 5-17) and 64 (lines 12-24) to construct this entire paragraph. It turns out that his next paragraph was to contain part of what this paragraph omitted from the two pages just specified.

PARAGRAPH 82

1 For this sentence, see Hakewill, p. 64, lines 2-11, TJ's editorial method being to paraphrase at times, to condense at other times, and at still other times to transcribe verbatim.

2 TJ took the references to "Dyer. 60" and to "1.Eliz.4. fol. 8.a.," along with the sentence which immediately precedes them, from Hakewill, p. 64-5.

3 The references to "2.E.4. fol.8," to "Dyer 162," and to "arc. parl. 63.," written above the line in TJ's text, and keyed so as to follow "Dyer. 60.," do not appear in Hakewill and are undoubtedly inserted here as TJ's own supplementary documentation. Inasmuch as the third item in this supplement, the *Arcana Parliamentaria*, contains the other two, we may assume that it provided TJ with his entire three-part extension of Hakewill's original references. This may be yet another example of TJ's interest in adding confirmatory citations to the notes given by his major authorities.

4 TJ originally followed Hakewill in writing "c.19" at this point, but he then crossed out that figure and entered "13" above it. What led him to make his correction is of course conjectural, but he may have found that Hakewill's figure was not in line with that of other authorities, and was hence suspect. For example, Hatsell, I, 160, in discussing the statute here cited by Hakewill, referred to it as "the general law of the first of James I. Ch.13," and TJ may well have chosen Hatsell as the preferred authority on this occasion.

5 This final sentence is partly paraphrased and partly transcribed verbatim from Hakewill's italicized quotation (p. 65, lines 2-8) of the James I statute. TJ apparently canceled the word in angle brackets as being unnecessary in the light of his decision to omit the phrase, "out of prison," which the statute had inserted after "be delivered." In short, the canceled word had no answering referent in TJ's amended text.

[189]

PARAGRAPH 83

1 That is, Thomas West, Lord De La Warr, whose second son not only inherited his father's ancient title but also became captain general and governor of the colony of Virginia in 1610 and gave his name to the Delaware River, Delaware Bay, and the State of Delaware. Thomas West, the subject of TJ's paragraph, entered the House of Lords in 1595, upon his having inherited the title of Baron De La Warr from his father William, who died that same year. William had had a checkered career. Born before 1520, he succeeded to the estate of his father George in 1538, and he also became in that era the adopted heir of his uncle, with every prospect of one day assuming the uncle's ancient title. But William coveted that title beyond his ability to wait for it to come in normal course, and he accordingly laid plans to hasten his uncle's death by poisoning him. His dark plot was discovered before he could carry it out, and the discovery led to his being deprived by act of parliament, February 1, 1549/50, of all honors and privileges that belonged to his hereditary rank. Thus when his uncle died in 1554, the title fell into abeyance, and William had to seek other ways to improve his fortunes. An opportunity to do so came in the religious turmoil of Queen Mary's reign. William associated himself with the Protestant opposition to the queen and in 1556 was even found guilty of conspiring against her, but the good will which this conviction won for him among his coreligionists saved him and even gave him favorable standing with Queen Elizabeth when she came to the throne. In 1569 he was made joint lieutenant of Sussex and later dubbed knight and by patent created Baron Delaware—a dignity that was not as highly esteemed as his uncle's title would have been, even though it gave its bearer a seat as junior baron in the House of Lords. That junior seat William's son Thomas inherited in 1595, and Thomas, thinking back upon the ancient title that William had coveted, took legal action to have it bestowed upon himself. The result of that action is described in TJ's paragraph. The judges resolved, and the Lords confirmed, that the deprivations imposed upon William for the duration of his life applied only to his own person, not to that of his son; and that Thomas' inheritance of his father's new barony did not impair his right to assume the dignity of the ancient barony to which his father had once been the declared heir. On November 14, 1597, Thomas' right to possess the ancient barony was affirmed by the Lords, and Thomas was assigned a much more prestigious seat in the Upper House than he had had, being now "next below the Lord Willoughby of Eresby, and next above the Lord Berkeley." Cokayne's *Peerage*, IV, 158-60, upon which my account of Thomas and his father relies.

2 What Hakewill's *Modus*, p. 76-9, explained as "The Case concerning priority of place in the upper House of *Parliament*" is here presented at times in summary and paraphrase, and at times in almost verbatim quotation. Hakewill did not mention the reason why William West was deprived of his title, nor did he refer to William's activity against Queen Mary, but he indicated that Queen Elizabeth had summoned William back to Parliament as "youngest Lord," and he dwelt at some length upon the deliberations of the Lords in connection with Thomas West's petition for the restoration of his ancient title. Hakewill even went so far as to specify that the deliberation ended in Thomas' being escorted to his new seat "next after the Lord *Berkley*." TJ omitted this latter detail, but he would have been aware of it, while making sure that in other respects his paragraph

stated the gist of Hakewill's parliamentary doctrine in the accurate yet sketchy manner of a scholar taking notes.

PARAGRAPH 84

1 See Hakewill, p. 82, lines 9-18. TJ's paragraph represents a verbatim quotation from that source, except that TJ removed nine words which clarified what was already clear, and he otherwise gained conciseness by writing "that they have place" instead of "by reason they have place."

PARAGRAPH 85

1 Hakewill wrote "*Francki Almonage*," and TJ amended the two words and combined them as traditional usage would often allow. See OED, s.v. almoign, 2; see also Jacob, s.v. frankalmoign. The term literally meant "free alms," and it usually designated lands granted to an ecclesiastical corporation for use only in behalf of charity.

2 TJ's paragraph of sixty-eight words made use of verbatim quotations and paraphrase from 200 words in two paragraphs of Hakewill, p. 83-4.

PARAGRAPH 86

1 See above, pars. 1, 35, 62.

2 This entire passage is in part a verbatim quotation, and in part a paraphrase, of Hakewill, p. 84 (lines 27-9), 85 (lines 1-9), and 86 (lines 13-18).

PARAGRAPH 87

1 TJ condensed Bracton's Latin aphorism, which Hakewill, and TJ as well, attributed to Bracton's second book. As a matter of fact, the aphorism is in Bracton's third book (see *De Legibus*, Liber III, Cap. 9, fol. 107**r-v, of the London edition of 1569). Thorne translated the full aphorism thus: "For the king, since he is the minister and vicar of God on earth, can do nothing save what he can do *de jure*." Woodbine and Thorne's *Bracton*, II, 305.

2 That is, "on account of which grant, a person's home may therefore not be burdened or overladen more than usual" (Editor's translation). This regulation was called "*Ad quod Damnum*," and Jacob defined it as "a Writ which ought to be issued before the King grants certain Liberties, as a Fair, Market, &c. which may be prejudicial to others." TJ followed Hakewill in attributing the Latin version of the regulation to Fitzherbert's *Natura Brevium*, fol. 222.

3 TJ did not add the final quotation mark. His Latin sentence is a condensed transcription of Hakewill, p. 88, lines 25-8, and Hakewill attributed the passage to "*Magna Charta* cap. 21." As translated by McKechnie, *Magna Carta*, p. 336, the full text of the passage which TJ here shortened reads thus: "Neither we nor our bailiffs shall take, for our castles or for any other work of ours, wood which is not ours, against the will of the owner of that word." See also Smith's *History of the English Parliament*, II, 554.

4 TJ's bracketed comment and query may be taken to mean that the preceding rule no longer applied as a result of the Habeas Corpus Act of 1679, and that it

probably did not apply before that date to the full extent of Stanford's (and Hakewill's) expressed understanding of it. The rule as stated by Hakewill, p. 91, lines 1-4, reads thus: "And by his absolute authoritie, the King may commit any one to prison during his pleasure." TJ's immediate comment indicated the precise way in which Hakewill's statement of this rule was far too sweeping, and TJ's subsequent query may well suggest his awareness of King John's promise of 1215 in Magna Carta that "No freeman shall be taken or imprisoned or disseised or exiled or in any way destroyed, nor will we go upon him nor send upon him, except by the lawful judgment of his peers or by the law of the land." McKechnie's *Magna Carta*, p. 375. See also Barnett Smith's *History of the English Parliament*, II, 554.

5 All of the sentences in this paragraph, except for the bracketed passage, are present either as almost verbatim or somewhat reduced statements in Hakewill, p. 87-92.

PARAGRAPH 88

1 That is, "The law of the major part." Jacob, s.v. majority, had this to say: "The only Method of determining the Acts of many, is by a *Majority*: The major Part of Members of Parliament enact Laws, and the *Majority* of Electors chuse Members of Parliament; the Act of the major Part of any Corporation, is accounted the Act of the Corporation; and where the *Majority* is, there by the Law is the whole."

2 TJ's paragraph uses thirty-six words to express everything that Hakewill, p. 93, lines 7-16, said in sixty-nine words. The final twenty-three words of the two texts correspond exactly, as if TJ did not want to trust a paraphrase in stating the terms of the law being there set down.

PARAGRAPH 89

1 TJ based this observation upon testimony provided in Hakewill's Preface to the fourth part of the work usually cited as his *Modus tenendi Parliamentum*. The year in which the Commons began the practice of keeping a record of their doings from day to day was 1547, and the person credited with this important step in British constitutional development was John Seymour, who served as clerk of the Commons in the reigns of Edward VI and Mary. See Pollard's *Evolution of Parliament*, p. 113, n.

PARAGRAPH 90

1 For previous references to these two kinds of bills, see above, pars. 52, 58, 68, 70, 73. The bill concerning Thomas West (par. 83) is a good example of the private bill.

2 The sentences making up this paragraph are from the fourth part of Hakewill's treatise, as follows: sentence 1 is a reduced transcription of p. 132, lines 17-23; sentences 2-3 closely parallel p. 134, lines 3-6, 13-15; and sentences 4-5 are shortened versions of p. 135, lines 1-15.

PARAGRAPH 91

1 That is, a breviate, an abridgment, a summary, akin to a lawyer's brief. See OED, s.v. breviate, *sb*.

2 This paragraph is nearly a verbatim transcript of Hakewill, p. 136, lines 17-30.

PARAGRAPH 92

1 Hakewill, p. 138, lines 5-6, dated the order "*Tertia Sessione 1. Parliament. Jac. Reg.*," that is, March 3, 1606/07. See JHC, I, 346.

2 TJ used twelve words to Hakewill's twenty-seven in stating the order.

3 This reference is not in Hakewill. If TJ added it on his own authority, he must be held responsible on this occasion for failing to cite the correct page (p. 51) in Scobell's *Memorials*.

PARAGRAPH 93

1 This entire paragraph was drawn in sequence from the following passages in Hakewill: p. 137 (lines 6, 7-9, 12-20, 21-5), 138 (lines 1-4, 11-15), and 140 (lines 1-5, 8, 16-26, 6-8). The reference to "43.Eliz.17. Nov." stands in TJ's text as an interlineation. TJ took the phrase from Hakewill, p. 140, lines 13-14.

PARAGRAPH 94

1 This paragraph is entirely made up from the following passages in Hakewill: p. 138 (lines 16-20, 25-6), 139 (lines 6-10, 11-29), 141 (lines 15-17), and 142 (lines 4-5).

PARAGRAPH 95

1 That is, possession. A common law term, says Jacob, s.v. seisin.

2 This date must be a mistranscription for "23 Mar. I.Jac." James I came to the throne March 24, 1602/03, and the first session of his first parliament opened March 19, 1603/04. Thus only five days of James' first year as king fell within that first session, and TJ's date of 23 May would belong to the second month of James' second year when the first session would no longer be concerned with its opening business. Hale's *Jurisdiction of Parliaments*, p. 133, to which TJ referred after he set down the date of 23 May, mentioned "23 Mar. I Jac." in connection with his recording of the opening events in a session of Parliament, and it is possible that TJ inadvertently mistranscribed Hale's date while intending to preserve the substance of that part of Hale's documentation. See JHC, I, 139, 142-52.

3 This entire paragraph is of composite origin. Most of its content and wording come from Hakewill, p. 138 (lines 27-9) and 139 (lines 1-5). The other authorities mentioned here were cited not by Hakewill but by George Petyt, p. 271, except for the reference to Hale, which TJ added on his own. The final sentence of the paragraph is based upon Petyt.

PARAGRAPH 96

1 This paragraph is nearly an exact quotation from *An Historical Review of the Constitution and Government of Pennsylvania*, p. 403-4. That work was often attributed to Benjamin Franklin in TJ's time, and TJ himself regarded Franklin as its author or reputed author. The best modern opinion is that, while Franklin

and his son William contributed many materials to the work, "the actual writer was Richard Jackson." See Labaree, *Papers of Franklin*, VIII, 361.

PARAGRAPH 97

1 An almost verbatim transcription of a passage from the article on Parliament in Jacob's *New Law-Dictionary*. TJ borrowed from Jacob the reference to "1. Mod. 242," and he followed Jacob's text in writing "the Sessions continues."

PARAGRAPH 98

1 An exact copy of the indicated passage in Blackstone's *Commentaries*, with the following exceptions: 1) TJ omitted the "And" which opened Blackstone's sentence; 2) TJ abbreviated "parliament"; and 3) TJ worked into his text Blackstone's footnoted reference to "Stat. 30 Geo.II. c.25."

PARAGRAPH 99

1 A verbatim transcription of George Petyt, p. 354, lines 6-8.

2 TJ's bracketed query appears designed to remind himself to explore Petyt's statement in depth. Did the statement mean that the rule announced by Petyt had to be construed in the light of the limitations imposed by the statute passed in the 30th year of the reign of George II (1757)? In other words, did the realm have to be threatened by domestic rebellion or invasion from abroad before the king had the right to summon a meeting of Parliament by proclamation at a time when Parliament was prorogued and a date had already been set for their return? And did the fourteen-day restriction imposed by the statute have to be observed, even if such a procedure might postpone the return of Parliament beyond the date already set and thus defeat the purposes which the statute was intended to serve? Questions like these arise when Petyt's rule and the statute set forth in TJ's preceding paragraph confront each other, and TJ may well have wanted to remind himself at this point to come back to these questions later.

PARAGRAPH 100

1 For an authoritative account of the extent to which the peerage alternately shrank and expanded from the reign of Henry VII (1485-1509) to the eve of the Civil War (1641), see Stone, *Crisis of the Aristocracy 1558-1641*, p. 97-128, 755, 758.

2 Once considered the work of Allan Ramsay, this treatise, which TJ admired but did not identify by author, is now believed to have been written by Obadiah Hulme of Yorkshire. See Sowerby, v, 205.

PARAGRAPH 101

1 See p. 81 of the work cited in par. 100.

PARAGRAPH 102

1 One of the most eminent victims of Charles I's attempt to exclude able men from Parliament by this particular expedient was Sir Edward Coke. See above, par. 46, n. 10.

2 See p. 86 of the work cited in par. 100.

EDITOR'S NOTES

PARAGRAPH 103

1 Without departing from the vocabulary of his source, TJ expressed here in forty words the basic meaning of a fifty-six-word passage in George Petyt, p. 63, lines 3-10.

PARAGRAPH 104

1 A nearly verbatim transcript of George Petyt, p. 63, lines 14-21.

2 This reference, which TJ copied exactly from Petyt's marginal notes, should in fact read p. 67, not p. 61.

PARAGRAPH 105

1 An exact transcript of a passage in George Petyt beginning at line 22 of p. 63 and ending at line 2 of p. 64.

2 This reference was taken from Petyt, who transcribed his own passage almost verbatim from D'Ewes, p. 186, col. 2, lines 44-54.

PARAGRAPH 106

1 Transcribed word for word from George Petyt, p. 64, lines 26-9.

PARAGRAPH 107

1 Transcribed with minor deletions from George Petyt, p. 67, lines 15-23. Petyt indicated that the passage was part of the "Remonstrances" of the Commons to Charles I in 1626, and he located its text in "*Rushw.* Coll. vol. l, p. 245." In more specific terms, the passage came from the Remonstrance submitted to Charles I on April 5, 1626. For its full text, see Rushworth, I, 243-6; for the excerpt quoted by Petyt and TJ, see p. 245, lines 22-6; and for details concerning the parliamentary background of this Remonstrance, see JHC, I, 843-4. We should emphasize that the Pocket-Book here presents the actual words of the Commons in asserting their right to complain against the king's advisers whenever the latter abused the power entrusted to them. In this case the adviser was the Duke of Buckingham, Charles I's unpopular chief counselor, who was later murdered by a disaffected naval officer.

2 The Latin phrase means "an unequal match." This and the preceding sentence are a condensed transcription of Petyt, p. 74, lines 8-13, and it is Petyt who said that he based them upon "*Atkyns* Argument, p. 45." The actual source, however, is Atkyns' *Power, Jurisdiction, and Privilege of Parliament*, p. 88. See above pars. 10, 11.

3 An almost verbatim transcript of Petyt, p. 75, lines 3-6. Once again Petyt referred the sentence to "Atkyn's [sic] Arg. p. 50," whereas the true source is the latter's *Power, Jurisdiction and Privilege of Parliament*, p. 71. See above, pars. 10, 11.

PARAGRAPH 108

1 A somewhat condensed, slightly rearranged transcript of George Petyt, p. 74, lines 18-25. Petyt quoted the French phrase and translated it as "without their Assent."

2 This bracketed observation raised a constitutional point which the subsequent reference to Pufendorf would clarify for anyone wishing additional information on the subject. The reference and the observation TJ added on his own. At this point he had in mind that in Bk. II, Ch. IX, of Pufendorf's celebrated *De Officio Hominis & Civis*, a student of constitutional law would find a discussion of two theories of monarchy, both of which involved the question of a king's right to cede part of his realm to another. Said Pufendorf, II, ix, §7: "Finally, in kingdoms we often meet with a distinction in the method of holding the royal power—a method which is not found to be uniform in all cases. For some kings are said to hold their kingdom as a patrimony, so that, at their caprice they can divide it, alienate and transfer it to anyone they please. This is particularly the case with those who have gained a kingdom for themselves by arms, and have acquired a people of their own. But the other kings, who have been chosen by the will of the people, although they have the highest right to exercise authority, are nevertheless unable to divide the kingdom at their pleasure, to alienate or transfer it. On the contrary, they are bound to follow the fundamental law, or established practice of the nation, in handing on the kingdom to their successors; and for this reason some compare them in a way with usufructuaries." (Moore's translation.)

PARAGRAPH 109

1 TJ's paragraph is for the most part a verbatim transcription of George Petyt, p. 79, lines 9-17, and Petyt's paragraph is for the most part a verbatim transcript of Hakewill's *Modus*, p. 90-1, as indeed Petyt indicated in a general way.

PARAGRAPH 110

1 This entire paragraph is a verbatim transcript of three successive paragraphs in George Petyt, p. 81, except for two minor deletions of definite articles and one minor clarifying prepositional phrase. Petyt supplied TJ with the reference to Hakewill's *Modus*, to Coke's *Institutes*, to Bohun's *Institutio Legalis*, and to Selden's *Judicature*.

PARAGRAPH 111

1 Except for the omission of two brief elaborative phrases, the addition of one coordinate conjunction, and the slight alteration of two idioms, this sentence exactly duplicates lines 6-12 of George Petyt, p. 83. The Latin phrase is readily construed as Common Council of the Realm.

2 Petyt himself attributed this passage to Atkyns' *Argument*, despite his having copied it verbatim from that author's *Power, Jurisdiction, and Privilege of Parliament*.

PARAGRAPH 112

1 TJ silently borrowed this reference from George Petyt, p. 83, line 19, and from the same source, lines 19-24, he borrowed the sentence to which the reference is here affixed. Once again, Petyt should have cited Atkyns' *Power, Jurisdiction and Privilege of Parliament*, not his *Argument*.

2 For this sentence, and the reference to Coke's *Institutes*, IV, 39, see George Petyt, p. 76, lines 21-31. Petyt's text and Coke's are virtually identical.

PARAGRAPH 113

1 With minor variations, this paragraph corresponds to a passage in George Petyt, p. 94-5.

2 TJ relied upon Petyt for this reference to Townshend's *Historical Collections*, but Petyt's reference should have been to p. 7-8, not 9. Petyt's text is a somewhat abbreviated replica of Townshend's.

PARAGRAPH 114

1 TJ transcribed this paragraph verbatim from George Petyt, p. 95, lines 18-28, and Petyt, who indicated that it came originally from D'Ewes' *Journals*, transcribed it almost verbatim from an indicated second source, Townshend's *Historical Collections*, p. 94. For the same passage in D'Ewes, see p. 585. As set forth by D'Ewes, the circumstances behind this passage involved what Sir Walter Raleigh considered an affront by the Lords to himself and the Commons. It happened that Sir Walter and other members of a committee of the Commons delivered to the Lords on Saturday, January 14, an answer to a message previously sent from the Upper House to the Lower, and that the Lords received the answer without rising from their places. This behavior seemed insulting to Sir Walter and his committee. Upon being apprised of the committee's attitude, the Lords took the alleged insult under advisement, and they concluded that their conduct had been strictly in accord with traditional etiquette. They went on to say that, when a committee of the Commons delivered a bill or message to the Lords for action, the Lords arose and went down to the bar of their House to receive the communication, but that it was their ancient custom not only to remain seated whenever they received an answer to a communication sent to them by the Commons, but also to have the answer read by the Lord Keeper, himself seated and covered, while the Commons waited outside the bar. D'Ewes did not record whether this declaration mollified Sir Walter, but it satisfied the Commons, and it became the standard pattern for similar behavior in the future.

PARAGRAPH 115

1 TJ took this sentence without change from George Petyt, p. 96, lines 13-14, and he also took from the same source the references to Nalson and Hakewill. Petyt's reference to Hakewill was intended to define the posture of bishops and archbishops in Parliament. It was his reference to Nalson, however, which provided the wording of TJ's present paragraph. See Nalson, *Impartial Collection*, II, 380.

PARAGRAPH 116

1 This paragraph is intended to say that, in performing its several functions as a high court, the Parliament must proceed as follows: the Commons must bring charges (*accusare*) against delinquents subject to parliamentary legal action, and must request that such delinquents be tried by legal process (*petere judicium*); the king in capital cases must give his consent to the trial (*assentire*); and the Lords must be given sole responsibility for rendering judgment (*judicare*) in the trial itself. TJ stated this doctrine as he found it stated by George Petyt, p. 98, lines 8-11, and it was the latter whom TJ followed in referring it to Selden's *Judicature*, p. 132, 141.

PARAGRAPH 117

1 This order, which reaffirmed an ancient procedure, was adopted by the Lords on December 31, 1640, and it asserted the right of all members of the Upper House, and the right of all widows and dowagers of Lords, "to answer in all Courts, as Defendants, upon Protestation of Honour only, and not upon the common Oath." For the entire text of this order, see JHL, IV, 120.

2 The case was different, however, when members of the nobility appeared as witnesses for or against a person charged with a crime. On those occasions, they took the oath prescribed for everybody. In the proceedings against the Earl of Strafford in the House of Lords, for example, all members sworn as witnesses from either House took the same oath under God to "speak the Truth, the whole Truth, and nothing but the Truth." See JHL, IV, 104.

3 TJ transcribed this paragraph from George Petyt, p. 99 (lines 20-30), and 100 (lines 1-3), keeping close to the exact wording of his source. He took the reference to "Cursus Cancel. 112" from Petyt.

PARAGRAPH 118

1 The first of these two sentences is an exact transcript of George Petyt, p. 98, lines 28-31, and the second, a somewhat expanded version of Petyt's next sentence. TJ borrowed the three references from that source. For the references to Brooke, see *La Graunde Abridgement*, s.v. trialles, £142, and s.v. corone, £152 (not "153" as Petyt had it). Petyt's wording in these two sentences is a verbatim copy of *Arcana Parliamentaria*, p. 70, as he correctly indicated. TJ's "71" is incorrect.

2 The three sentences that conclude this paragraph are close transcripts of Petyt, p. 100, lines 4-5, 12-15, 16-18. TJ's legal abbreviation is written out by Petyt as *Capias ad Satisfaciendum*, that is, "you may seize for purposes of satisfying," and it refers to a writ addressed to a sheriff to command him to seize the body of a defendant and bring him safely to court to satisfy there a plaintiff's claim for payment of debt or damages. See Jacob, s.v. capias ad satisfaciendum. TJ followed Petyt in citing Dyer and the two identical references to Henry VIII's reign.

PARAGRAPH 119

1 The two parliamentary resolutions which constitute this paragraph were transcribed almost verbatim from George Petyt, p. 102, lines 7-13, 17-23. Petyt dated the first resolution "*Die Mercurij* [that is, *Mercurii Dies*, Mercredi, Mercury's Day, Wednesday], 25 *Novembris*, 1692," and the second, "*Die Lune* [that is, *Lunae Dies*, Lundi, Moon's Day, Monday] 7. *Decembris*, 1691." For the voting conventions observed by the Commons, see above, pars. 39, 72, 88.

PARAGRAPH 120

1 For the meaning of this term, see par. 14, n. 2.

2 This sentence and the attribution to "4. inst. 21.," are transcribed verbatim from George Petyt, p. 103, lines 26-30, except that Petyt wrote "King's Bench" for "R.B."(*Regis Bancus*). As for Petyt's wording of the entire passage, it exactly parallels that in Coke's *Institutes*, IV, 21, lines 49-52.

PARAGRAPH 121

1 Transcribed word for word from George Petyt, p. 104-5. Petyt indicated that his passage was taken from Selden's *Judicature*, p. 6, 7, but in fact he took it almost exactly from that source, p. 6, lines 15-22.

PARAGRAPH 122

1 An exact transcription of the two chief parts of a longer passage in George Petyt, p. 106, lines 18-21, 24-9. Petyt's wording is in turn copied almost verbatim from the same two parts of his acknowledged source, Selden's *Judicature*, p. 176-7.

PARAGRAPH 123

1 Attributed by TJ to Selden's *Judicature*, p. 187, this passage was in reality exactly transcribed from George Petyt, p. 106-7. Although Petyt indicated that his passage came from p. 187 of Selden's work, he altered the latter's first six words, and TJ followed Petyt's alterations, not Selden's original wording.

PARAGRAPH 124

1 For this passage almost exactly as given here by TJ, see George Petyt, p. 107, lines 5-9. It was the latter who identified his source as a loosely similar passage in D'Ewes, p. 527, col. 2.

PARAGRAPH 125

1 These two sentences, together, with the references to their confirmatory sources, were transcribed verbatim from George Petyt, p. 114, lines 3-8, except for TJ's use of abbreviations in place of Petyt's corresponding words. The legal expression *billa vera* means true bill. Said Jacob, s.v. bill: "In Criminal Cases, when a Grand Jury upon a Presentment or Indictment find the same to be true, they indorse on it *Billa vera*; and thereupon the Offender is said to stand indicted of the crime, and is bound to make answer unto it." Petyt's use of that term in his text was not expressly authorized in *Trials of the Regicides*, p. 53, as he said it was, but that work, in its London edition of 1679, p. 3, 58-60, 86, 99-102, 118, 232, 289, offers abundant evidence that the Commons could be said to have acted as "a considerable grand jury" in their indictment of Charles I.

PARAGRAPH 126

1 The text and annotations of this paragraph were transcribed with a few minor textual changes from George Petyt, p. 114-115. Petyt's reference to Rastell's *Statutes* was intended not only to lend authority to the regulation governing absenteeism in Parliament but also to establish parliamentary absences as part of an official record in respect to their having been entered in the book of the clerk. The citation of Coke's *Institutes* and of Hale's *Jurisdiction of Parliaments* offered support not to the question of absenteeism but to the doctrine that the journals of the Commons were legal records.

PARAGRAPH 127

1 This word in the manuscript is clear enough in its final four letters, but its first letters are definitely problematical. In the source being used here by TJ—

George Petyt, p. 114, line 18—the text reads "attest" at this point, and the manuscript legibly reproduces the second syllable of this word, while seeming to precede it with "at" written over a somewhat longer word beginning with "p" and possibly ending with "y." Under the circumstances I have unhesitatingly allowed the word to stand as Petyt has it.

2 In the trial of Thomas Harrison, the regicide mentioned here, William Jessop, Clerk of the Commons, testified that two documents bearing the signature of Harrison were an actual part of what Jessop referred to as "*Books, and Records, Papers*, and other things" belonging to the Lower House. One document was the summons which convened the High Court of Justice in 1648 to try Charles I under the indictment that the Commons had brought against him. The other document was the warrant for the execution of Charles I after the High Court of Justice had pronounced him guilty of the charges stated in the indictment. See *Trials of the Regicides*, p. 18, 20, 52-3.

3 This reference is from Petyt, p. 115, lines 4-5. In his *Reports*, p. 110-11, Hobart said: "Now Journals are no Records, but Remembrances for Forms of Proceedings to the Record, they are not of Necessity, neither have they always been: They are like Dockets of the Pronotaries, or the Particular to the King's Patents. ... The Journal is of good use for the Observation of the Generality and Materiality of Proceedings and Deliberations as to the three readings of any Bill, the Intercourses between the two Houses, and the like, but when the Act is passed, the Journal is expired."

4 The three sentences making up this paragraph are partly paraphrased and partly transcribed almost verbatim from George Petyt, p. 114 (lines 6-9, 16-20) and 115 (lines 4-7).

5 This reference and the next were supplied by TJ himself. The first was to D'Ewes, p. 502, where, under the date of March 17, 1592/93, the following passage was recorded: "On *Saturday* the 17th day of *March*, Mr. *Richard Toptliffe* and Mr. *William Basset* Esquires, Sheriffs of the County of *Darby*, with Mr. *Moore* being of Councel with Mr. *Basset* were heard at large at the Bar of this House touching the Case of *Thomas Fitzherbert* Esquire, returned a Member into this House, and now Prisoner in the Custody and Charge of the said Sheriffs; and after long hearing of the said Parties, it was in the end resolved by this House, that this House being a Court of Record would take no notice of any matter of fact at all in the said Case, but only of matter of Record." As for the second of TJ's references, it pointed to a fractured declaration, "The House of Commons a Court of Record," in Hale's *Jurisdiction of Parliaments*, p. 105. A marginal note in Hale dated the declaration "17 Mart. 1592."

PARAGRAPH 128

1 This sentence is exactly transcribed from George Petyt, p. 115, lines 20-4, except that Petyt put its text in italic type to indicate its status as a parliamentary order, and he obliquely referred it to "Rush. ib.," that is, to Rushworth, I, 217. Rushworth's wording is virtually identical with Petyt's.

2 In part a paraphrase and in part a quotation from George Petyt, p. 115, lines 28-32. Petyt took the statement almost verbatim from Selden.

3 In respect to text and documentation, this sentence of fifty-eight words is made up from a sixty-seven-word passage in George Petyt, beginning on p. 117, line 28, and ending on p. 118, line 6. Petyt's sentence is taken verbatim from Coke's *Institutes*, IV, 24.

PARAGRAPH 129

1 This case, and all of the others touched upon in this paragraph, together with all the accompanying annotations save that to Hale's *Jurisdiction of Parliaments*, were noted by TJ from his reading of George Petyt on the following pages: p. 118, lines 7-19, for the Bishop of Bristol; p. 118, lines 20-8, for Dr. Cowel; p. 118, lines 29-30, for Dr. Manwaring; p. 118, lines 31-2, for Dr. Montague; p. 119, lines 1-12, for Dr. Burnet; p. 119, lines 13-20, for Randolph Davenport; p. 120, lines 6-15, for Long and the Mayor of Westbury; p. 120, lines 16-20, for other cases of bribery in elections; p. 120, lines 21-30, for Arthur Hall; p. 121 (lines 30-2), and 122 (lines 1-7), for Darryel; p. 122, lines 9-11, for Rogers; p. 120 (lines 31-2), and 121 (lines 1-8), for Muncton; p. 121, lines 13-17, for Williams; p. 121, lines 20-3, for Holland; p. 124, lines 21-4, for Justice Long; p. 122, lines 16-32, for Sir William Aston (TJ's "Arthur" is an error); p. 132 (lines 29-32), and 133 (lines 1-2), for Bland; p. 133, lines 16-20, for Drury; p. 133 (lines 28-32), and 134 (lines 1-11), for Smalley and Kirtleton; p. 134, lines 12-15, for Criketoft; p. 134, lines 16-24, for Tash; p. 134, lines 25-31, for Dr. Harris; p. 135, lines 1-5, for Mr. Burgess; p. 135, lines 6-17, for Wray; p. 135, lines 18-23, for Levet.

2 Petyt's full citation, p. 118, lines 20-2, reads, "Vide *Rush*. Hist. Col. 4 Car.," and it points to Rushworth, I, 585-6 (Dr. Manwaring's case).

3 This reference occurred in Petyt, p. 119, lines 10-12, but it was ambiguously placed, and it did not belong to its context, although it might at first be assumed to document the case of Dr. Burnet, which Petyt outlined, p. 119, lines 1-8. As a matter of fact, however, Petyt confused Dr. Burnet's *An Exposition of the Thirty-nine Articles of the Church of England* (1699) with Charles Blount's *King William and Queen Mary, Conquerors* (1693). The latter work was censured by Parliament, the former by the Lower but not the Upper House of Convocation. See DNB, s.v. Burnet, Gilbert (1643-1715); also s.v. Blount, Charles (1654-1693). Nalson's *Impartial Collection*, I, 9, 43, does not refer to Dr. Burnet or to the other cases thus far mentioned here.

4 For the case of Long and the Mayor of Westbury, see Coke, *Institutes*, IV, 23; also D'Ewes, p. 182, col. 2; also above, par. 33, n. 2; also below, par. [430].

5 In describing the case of Arthur Hall, and in referring it to D'Ewes, p. 212, TJ followed George Petyt, p. 120, lines 21-30, but Petyt's reference was once again unreliable. D'Ewes, p. 207, 212, told of Arthur Hall's censure by the Commons, to be sure, but on that occasion Hall was censured for having delivered "sundry lewd Speeches." What Petyt had in mind was D'Ewes' account of Hall's fine and expulsion from the Commons at another time for having published a book in disparagement of that chamber. This latter story is told by D'Ewes, not on p. 207, 212, but on p. 291-2, 295-8, and 308-9. See also JHC, I, 122-3, 125-7, 136.

6 This date and the antecedent reference to Hale's *Jurisdiction of Parliaments* did not appear in Petyt, but they were correctly seen by TJ as confirming Petyt's mention of the Hall case. For the action involving Hall on February 4, 1580/81, see D'Ewes, p. 291, not p. 212. See n. 5 above.

7 The case of Darryel is not in D'Ewes, p. 114, but in Scobell's *Memorials*, p. 114. At that point, Petyt's documentation could be construed to mean either of these two sources, but Petyt himself seemed to intend the former rather than the latter, with the result that TJ was led into error. As for the case, it grew from an episode on February 12, 1620/21, when Lovel, a member of Commons, complained that Darryel had threatened him with imprisonment for a speech which he delivered in the Parliament. Lovel's complaint was substantiated by investigation, and Darryel was punished. See also JHC, I, 517-18, 520.

8 The story of Thomas Rogers and his abuse of a member of the Commons, Sir John Savil, for the latter's conduct in a committee toward a bill involving tanners, is told in Scobell's *Memorials*, p. 114, not in D'Ewes, p. 114. But Petyt's ambiguous documentation of the episode could have tied it to either of these sources, and once again TJ chose the wrong one. Sir John's complaint against Rogers was filed in the Commons on June 16, 1604, and thus it occurred beyond the final date recorded in D'Ewes' *Journals*. See JHC, I, 993.

9 For a brief account of the case of Muncton (Monyngton), see above, par. 33, n. 4.

10 Petyt indicated that on February 29, 1575/76, an unnamed member of the Commons complained to the House of having been assaulted by "one Williams." When sent for, Williams was brought to the bar of the House and "committed to the Serjeant's Ward." In D'Ewes, p. 251, col. 2, Williams is given the first name of Walter, and the member assaulted, Mr. Bainbrigge. The offense is specified not only as a blow by Williams against Bainbrigge, but also as a threat by him to use a dagger next time. The same episode, somewhat condensed, is told in Scobell's *Memorials*, p. 113, as Petyt recorded. TJ chose to refer the case to D'Ewes rather than to Scobell. See also JHC, I, 109.

11 Holland, a scrivener, and his servant, Brooks, inflicted a beating upon the servant of Mr. Fleetwood, the latter being a member of the Commons. Holland and Brooks were brought before the bar of the House and punished by confinement for five days in the custody of the serjeant.

12 Long, a justice of the peace, was examined by the Commons in December 1641 for his having signed a warrant authorizing that armed guards be stationed at the Lower House. Angry at this seeming attempt at intimidation by unidentified parties, the Commons investigated and found that the warrant signed and acted upon by Long had been issued by the Lord Keeper at the direction of the Lords and with the advice of the judges. The Commons refused to strip Long of his commission as justice of the peace, but they voted that he be sent to the Tower, "*For that He the said Mr.* Long *in his Warrant, had exceeded the Authority given him by the Writ; and had directed Constables, and Sitting the Parliament had sent down Armed Men to the Parliament, never acquainting the Parliament with it.*" This account is in Nalson's *Impartial Collection*, II, 732, as TJ and Petyt partly noted. The italics are Nalson's. Petyt reduced Nalson's account of this case to twenty-two words, and TJ condensed to eleven words what he found in Petyt.

13 George Petyt identified the principal in this case as Sir William Aston, Sheriff of London, as did Rushworth, I, 656. The *Miscellanea Parliamentaria*, p. 108, which George Petyt also cited, identified the principal as Sheriff Acton of London but gave him no title or first name. Entries in JHC, I, 928-9, indicate not only that the principal, "Mr. Sheriff *Acton*," was sent by the Commons to the Tower on February 10, 1628/29, after the Speaker had successfully accused him of contemptuously replying to a parliamentary committee when it sought to question him, but also that he was freed two days later upon acknowledging his misconduct. As for his true names, the first seems to have been William, despite TJ's unsubstantiated preference for Arthur, and the second seems officially weighted toward Acton rather than Aston.

14 For the cases of John Bland and Thomas Drury, see D'Ewes, p. 366-7, 448-9, 451. These references merely particularize those given less fully by George Petyt and TJ.

15 Edward Smalley was the servant of Arthur Hall, whose troubles with the Commons were mentioned above, n. 5. Matthew Kirtleton was "Schoolmaster to Mr. *Hall*." In addition to George Petyt's and TJ's citations of *Miscellanea Parliamentaria* on these two cases, see JHC, I, 106, 112-113.

16 George Petyt briefly identified Criketoft, Tash, Dr. Harris, Mr. Burgess, Wray, and Levet; and he cited his source as *Miscellanea Parliamentaria*, p. 96, 98, 104, 105, 106, 107. In each case, George Petyt's account is much longer than TJ's, and with one exception much shorter than that in his source. The *Miscellanea Parliamentaria* is careful to refer each of these cases to the JHC by date of occurrence. For the page references to these cases in Vol. I of the latter work, see as follows: for Criketoft, 21-2; for Tash, 142, 150, 152, 933-4; for Dr. Harris, 694, 695, 745, 779, 781; for Burgess, 889, 894, 896, 898, 900, 902, 904, 908, 918; for Wray, 886, 895-7; for Levet, 886, 906, 912, 916, 921.

PARAGRAPH 130

1 This sentence, quoted in respect to its text and annotations from George Petyt, p. 123, lines 1-5, reduced to twenty-three words the thirty-one words of its source. The phrase "being in execution" means "undergoing punishment ordered legally."

2 TJ transcribed this sentence, together with its annotation, from George Petyt, p. 123, lines 6-13, reducing Petyt's fifty-one words to twenty-six.

3 Condensed by TJ from George Petyt, p. 123, lines 14-25. By "several Indentures" Petyt meant two, one of which was returned by the mayor of Bossinny for Sir Charles Harbord. The Committee on Privileges of the Commons declared Sir Charles legally returned, so far as his indenture was concerned; but he was not allowed to take his seat until his election had been decided. Petyt's lines are exactly transcribed from Scobell's *Memorials*, p. 16.

4 The wording of this sentence was taken almost exactly from George Petyt, p. 123, lines 26-31. As his source, Petyt cited Townshend's *Historical Collections*, p. 297. According to the latter authority, the words recorded by TJ were uttered by Mr. Cary in a debate in 1601 on a procedural question before the Commons.

PARAGRAPH 131

1 This entire paragraph was transcribed almost verbatim by TJ from George
Petyt, p. 124, lines 29-31; p. 125, lines 1-15; p. 126, line 3. TJ's three references to Selden's *Of the Judicature in Parliaments*, p. 101, 124, 159, designate
in Petyt the sources from which he took this paragraph virtually word for word.
The phrase "*in loco proprio*," that is, "in their own special rank," is intended to
emphasize that, in regard to impeachments, the Commons are the sovereign authority—they are above any other court of the realm. See Pollard's *Evolution of
Parliament*, p. 78-9, 112, 239.

PARAGRAPH 132

1 This sentence was condensed from George Petyt, p. 127, lines 14-27; and the
passage in Petyt was transcribed exactly from Nalson's *Impartial Collection*, II,
588, lines 12-19. Petyt's reference to Nalson, like TJ's, contains no volume
number. *Quo Warrantos* were writs formerly issued by the Court of King's
Bench (K.B.) against a person or persons to require them "to show by what warrant he or they held, claimed, or exercised an office or franchise." See OED, s.v.
quo warranto. Writs of this sort, however, when filed against boroughs to question their right to send members to the Commons, were *coram non judice*, that
is, "not before the judge" [of the court concerned]. Only the Commons could
rule upon such a matter.

2 TJ produced this sentence by abridging a somewhat similar sentence from
George Petyt, p. 128, lines 23-30. In a marginal note at that point, Petyt indicated his source as Selden's *Judicature*, p. 55, and TJ made note of that reference. In actual fact, however, Selden's *Judicature*, p. 55, did not deal with any
aspect of the case under discussion here. What Petyt did was to draw these materials from Bohun's *Collection of Debates*, p. 276-7, and to acknowledge later
that he had done so. The Speaker mentioned here is Thomas Thorpe. See above,
pars. 46, 81, 82; below, pars. [423], [572].

3 Exactly transcribed from George Petyt, p. 129, lines 9-12, where it is cred-
ited to Mr. Justice Crook (Croke) as well as to Selden's *Judicature*, p. 58, to
Rushworth, I, 663, and to Sir Robert Atkyns' *Argument*, *per Totum*, this sentence was unhesitatingly referred by TJ to Rushworth, perhaps because the latter authority gave it a particularly detailed explanation. In the spring of 1629,
Charles I dissolved Parliament and arrested nine of its members, among them
Sir John Eliot, on charges of sedition and contempt. On April 25 of that year,
Charles convened a panel of judges at Sergeants Inn and asked them to respond
to certain questions about parliamentary privilege. One of his questions was
"whether a Parliament-man, committing an offense against the King or Council
not in a Parliament way, might, after the Parliament ended, be punish'd or not?"
The judges answered that he might be, if Parliament had not already done so.
But the judges all agreed "That regularly he cannot be compelled out of Parliament to answer things done in Parliament in a Parliamentary course." This latter ruling was to find its way not only into the Pocket-Book but also into the
Constitution of the United States, Art. I, Sec. 6, and into TJ's *Manual*, (1801,
1812), Sec. III. In connection with TJ's preference for Rushworth rather than
Selden or Atkyns as authority for this important point, we should take notice
that Selden's *Judicature*, p. 58, and Atkyns' *Argument*, do not contain it, despite

Petyt's indication to the contrary. As a matter of fact, if Petyt had been more careful about the second of these references, he would have cited Atkyns' *Power, Jurisdiction, and Privilege of Parliament*, not the *Argument*. See Atkyns' *Tracts*, p. 113.

4 Condensed and quoted in part verbatim and in part by paraphrase from George Petyt, p. 129, lines 20-5. TJ took the reference to D'Ewes from Petyt. From the account in D'Ewes, it appears that the Recorder sent for on this occasion had earlier introduced into Commons a resolution requiring its members who were practicing law during a parliamentary session to leave their courtroom and return to Parliament if they were officially summoned. In short, the Recorder himself stood in violation of the resolution which he had sponsored. But the Commons on this occasion did not cite him for contempt. They merely notified him that his attendance was required.

5 Transcribed almost verbatim from part of a longer sentence in George Petyt, p. 129-30. Petyt recorded that the Parliament which took this action was called "The Wonder working Parliment."

PARAGRAPH 133

1 Taken word for work from George Petyt, p. 128, lines 18-20, where it is erroneously attributed to Selden's *Judicature*, p. 53. In actual fact, Petyt transcribed this passage from some other source—perhaps from Atkyns' *Power, Jurisdiction, and Privilege of Parliament*. See Atkyns' *Tracts*, p. 102.

PARAGRAPH 134

1 George Petyt, p. 130, lines 24-32, cited this passage in slightly expanded form, and gave as his authority *Journals of the House of Commons* for December 30, 1680. TJ consulted both of these sources and used each on occasion as a guide in evolving his own final wording. The parenthetical comment is TJ's. Cf. JHC, IX, 695-6.

PARAGRAPH 135

1 That is, *Bancus Regis* or the King's Bench.

2 The book here mentioned was Henry Care's *The Weekly Pacquet of Advice from Rome*, a collection of issues of a journal published between 1678 and 1680, attacking the Church of England for its alleged inclination toward Roman Catholicism. Care was also called Carr. For a brief account of his life by Thompson Cooper, see DNB, s.v. Care, Henry (1646-1688). See also George Petyt, p. 131, lines 21-2; JHC, IX, 688.

3 TJ condensed into eleven handwritten lines the forty-one lines of print used by George Petyt, p. 131-2, in stating these five resolutions. According to Petyt, the resolutions appeared in the "Report and Censure of the Proceedings of divers of the Judges of *Westminster-Hall, viz.* Sir *Francis North*, Sir *W. Scroggs*, Justice *Jones*, and Baron *Weston*." TJ followed Petyt in tracing the resolutions to the *Journals* of the Commons, 1680, that is, December 23, 1680. See JHC, IX, 691-2.

PARAGRAPH 136

1 Transcribed almost verbatim from George Petyt, p. 133, lines 8-15, where this passage is ascribed to the Commons' *Journal*, 397, Col. 1. TJ properly corrected Petyt by construing this reference to mean "D'Ewes' journ. 397. Col. 1."

PARAGRAPH 137

1 This paragraph rests almost word for word upon George Petyt, p. 133, lines 21-7. Petyt credited it to the Commons' *Journal*, p. 283, col. 1, but in reality it should be assigned, as TJ indicated, to that same page and column in D'Ewes. In this particular instance, TJ's correction of Petyt is not to be regarded as an example of overconscientiousness. The JHC, I, 118, (for January 21, 1580), contains an account of the episode behind TJ's paragraph more or less as D'Ewes gave it, but without the important words, "for it may be any mans case who is guiltless to be accused, and thereupon indicted of Felony or a like Crime." Had TJ adhered to the formal reference used by Petyt, the modern reader of the Pocket-Book would not have been able to find these words in the official account and only then would perhaps have turned to D'Ewes in search of their possible source. In short, Petyt's scholarly procedure is here quite helter-skelter, while TJ's is entirely disciplined. It should be added, however, that neither the JHC nor D'Ewes identified the indicted member mentioned in this episode. But D'Ewes did record that one Mr. Broughton, a companion of the indicted member, moved that day to have his colleague's case judged at once.

PARAGRAPH 138

1 The passage which precedes this reference to Scobell's *Memorials* was transcribed by TJ almost verbatim from George Petyt, p. 136, lines 1-13. Petyt used the passage as the opening sentence of his eighth chapter, which is entitled "Of the Power of the House of Commons over their own Members." Upon this eighth chapter TJ based almost all of the text and the references in this long paragraph, as his final note indicates in a general way. The few exceptions to this statement of indebtedness are pointed out in subsequent notes below. The following table lists the names of the cases mentioned by TJ and opposite each case is given its page and line location in Petyt:

Peter Wentworth	p. 137, lines 8-19.
Arthur Hall	p. 137, lines 20-32, p. 138, lines 1-32.
Dr. Parry	p. 139, lines 1-32, p. 140, lines 1-24.
Sir Giles Mompesson	p. 140, lines 25-33, p. 141, lines 1-25.
Sir Robert Floyd	p. 142, lines 1-6
Sir John Bennet	p. 141, lines 26-31.
Barbour	p. 142, lines 7-11.
One of the Knights	p. 142, lines 19-32, p. 143, lines 1-20.
A member inveighed	p. 143, lines 21-32, p. 144, lines 1-7.
J.H.	p. 144, lines 16-32.
Mr. Taylor	p. 144, lines 23-32, p. 145, lines 1-8.
Sir Robert Owen	p. 145, lines 9-24.
Some speeches in the house	p. 145, lines 25-32, p. 146, lines 1-18.
Mr. Moor	p. 146, lines 19-20.
Conisby	p. 146, lines 21-7.
Benson	p. 146, lines 28-32, p. 147, lines 1-6.

Hollis	p. 147, lines 7-12.
Widdrington & Price	p. 147, lines 13-16.
A resolution of 23. Eliz.	p. 147, lines 17-24.
Mr. Lawrence Hide	p. 147, lines 25-32, p. 148, lines 1-6.
Several Lawyers	p. 148, lines 7-12.
John Trevor	p. 148, lines 13-19.
Hungerford	p. 148, marginal note

2 References in the Pocket-Book to Hale's *Jurisdiction of Parliaments* are not in George Petyt. TJ inserted them on his own, as if to add authority to his text. See above, pars. 22 (nn. 1, 3), 127 (n. 5), 129 (n. 6).

3 TJ transcribed this date from Petyt, who cited D'Ewes, p. 244, col. 1, as his authority. But D'Ewes, p. 236-44, dated the case of Wentworth February 8, 1575.

4 The case of Wentworth is not discussed in William Petyt's *Miscellanea Parliamentaria*, p. 73, despite the reference by George Petyt to the contrary. Petyt is correct, however, in assigning the case also to D'Ewes. See that work, p. 236-44.

5 The case of Copley is not mentioned by George Petyt in Chap. 8, but it is mentioned in Hale's *Jurisdiction of Parliaments*, p. 125, where Seymour, p. 178, is also referred to, as TJ noted.

6 For the full sources of George Petyt's and TJ's account of the Hall case, see William Petyt's *Miscellanea Parliamentaria*, p. 12-13, 20-54, 55-63 (but not p. 74); see also D'Ewes, p. 291-2, 295-8, 308-9; also JHC, I, 122-3, 125-7, 136. George Petyt dated the case "21 *Nov.* 1586," as did TJ. In the JHC, however, the dates are February 4, 6, 14, and March 18, 1580.

7 This reference is not in George Petyt, p. 139-40. TJ inserted it on his own. It dealt with Dr. Manwaring's case, which was quite similar to that of Dr. Parry.

8 Identified by George Petyt as John Barbour. William Petyt's *Miscellanea Parliamentaria* said that Barbour was a lawyer who attributed his conduct in signing the warrant to fear of losing his post as recorder if he did not do so. The Commons decided that any man must be adjudged unfit to serve as a lawmaker in Parliament if out of fear of losing some other office he chose to violate the law rather than to see justice done.

9 This knight was Sir Christopher Piggott (or Piggot), as we learn from Hale's seven-line account of the case in *Jurisdiction of Parliaments*, p. 130. George Petyt's account was considerably longer, but it left the knight unnamed, and it did not mention Hale. TJ followed George Petyt in attributing this case to William Petyt's *Miscellanea Parliamentaria*, p. 77-9, but that source is incorrect. In JHC, I, 1012, 1014, it appears that the Commons took action against Piggot only after James I had heard of Piggot's denunciation of the Scots and had taken offence at it. See also *Parliamentary History of England*, v, 178-81.

10 In dating this case, TJ followed George Petyt, and like Petyt he referred it to William Petyt's *Miscellanea Parliamentaria*, p. 79. In respect to the latter reference, however, George Petyt was once again in error. The member concerned

was a Mr. Sheperd, who on February 15, 1600/01, rose to object to a bill introduced to prohibit dancing on Sunday. Mr. Sheperd contended that the bill had an improper title, so far as it used the term "Sabaoth-day," not "Sunday." Then he went on to argue that the bill savored of Puritanism, and that its sponsor was "a Sectary" bent upon disturbing the peace of the kingdom. These remarks occasioned an immediate debate, during which Mr. Shephard was required to withdraw. The debate was resumed next day. The final verdict of the Commons was that, although Mr. Sheperd's offence was great and unprecedented (so far no doubt as it imputed bad faith to the sponsor of the bill), Mr. Sheperd should be discharged from the House rather than imprisoned or punished in some other way. See JHC, I, 521-2, 524-5.

11 I.H., that is Mr. Jervis Hollis, who, on the date mentioned by TJ and George Petyt, gave great offense to the Commons by saying of the Scots "That some of them were dishonourable; and that this House hath not only entertained them half way, but embraced them." See JHC, II, 128. For a fuller account, see Nalson's *Impartial Collection*, I, 726-7 [incorrectly numbered 804, 805]. Hollis' suspension was lifted December 2, 1641. William Petyt's *Miscellanea Parliamentaria*, p. 80, does not contain an account of this case, despite George Petyt's and TJ's references to the contrary. See below, n. 18.

12 Mr. Taylor (William Taylor), a barrister, was a member of the Commons from Windsor, and the punishment he received on this occasion came about as aftermath of a debate and vote in the Commons April 21, 1641, on the question whether a bill of attainder should be voted against Thomas Wentworth, first Earl of Strafford, the chief adviser of Charles I. The Commons decided that day 204 to 59 to pass the attainder. Some weeks later, Taylor declared off the floor of the house that, for the Commons to have passed the attainder "before the Lords had finished the Trial upon the Articles of Impeachment exhibited by the Commons against him [Wentworth], was to commit murther with the Sword of Justice." These remarks were made in the presence of three men after Wentworth had been put to death May 12, 1641, under the authority of the attainder. The three men drew up a document attesting to what Taylor had said, and that document was introduced into Commons on May 27. TJ's account lists all of the punishments meted out to Taylor for his condemnation of the Commons' action. Despite the seeming severity of the sentence against him, however, Taylor was released from the Tower on June 12. It should be noted that the words which caused the Commons to punish Taylor were a close paraphrase of part of a speech made in Commons on April 21 by Lord Digby in opposing the bill of attainder. Lord Digby, a foe of Wentworth, had at first supported the impeachment proceedings against him. But when the Commons sought to supersede the judicial process while it was still in course, and to substitute for it a political attainder, Digby thought that politics were being used to thwart justice. The choice before the Commons, Digby argued, was either justice under the impeachment proceeding or murder under the proposed attainder; and he concluded by saying, "he that commits Murther with the Sword of Justice, heightens that Crime to the utmost." These were the words that brought punishment upon Taylor when he repeated them later outside the House of Commons. But they brought punishment upon Digby, too, on the ground that they degraded parliamentary procedures and that Digby, in making them public in manuscript, violated a rule of the Commons that speeches made before them could not

be published except by their permission. Digby's punishment consisted in his having all copies of his speech burned, and in his being declared unworthy of receiving further honor or employment at the hands of Charles I. For Taylor's remarks on the attainder bill, see Nalson's *Impartial Collection*, II, 257; also JHC, II, 158-9, 172-3. For Lord Digby's speech and its aftermath, see Nalson, II, 157-60; also JHC, II, 125, 127, 136, 207-9. TJ follows George Petyt in incorrectly attributing the case of William Taylor to *Miscellanea Parliamentaria*, p. 80.

13 George Petyt incorrectly attributed this episode to *Miscellanea Parliamentaria*, p. 82, as did TJ. For an account of it, see JHC, I, 483, under the proceedings for Wednesday, May 13, 1614. The abused committeeman was Sir Roger Owen (not Robert). The two members who subjected Sir Roger to the indignities mentioned were Sir William Herbert and Sir Robert Killigrew. It appears that Sir William accused Sir Roger of partiality in his conduct of committee deliberations, and that Sir Robert seized Sir Roger's hand and threatened to pull him from the chair in which he was acting as presiding officer.

14 Incorrectly attributed by George Petyt and hence by TJ to *Miscellanea Parliamentaria*, p. 82, this episode, as fitfully set forth in JHC, I, 606, 611-13, 615-16, 619, 621, began on Monday, April 30, 1621, when a committee consisting of Mr. Glanvill, Sir Charles Morrison, Mr. Clement Coke (Sir Edward Coke's son), Sir Samuel Sands, and others, were considering a glass patent. In an aside addressed to those nearest him, one of whom was Clement Coke, Sir Charles Morrison began to quote an old rhyme, and when he forgot what came next, he asked for help. Thereupon Mr. Glanvill repeated the last two verses of "Asses and Glasses." At this point some words which are now lost to history were exchanged between Clement Coke and Sir Charles. One of the witnesses, Sir Samuel Sands, later observed, however, that Clement Coke understood Sir Charles' verses to picture judges riding upon asses, whereas Clement Coke remembered the verses as having judges ride upon mules. Thus the lost words may have concerned this seemingly benign difference of opinion. But at any rate, for whatever reason, Clement Coke seized someone else's sheathed sword and struck Sir Charles twice with it as the Commons later filed down the Parliament stairs; and Sir Charles responded by getting his own sword from his servant but not by unsheathing or using it. At a hearing of the case of May 8 and 9, Clement Coke was adjudged guilty of showing contempt for the Commons by his hostile action, and he was sentenced to the Tower for an interval that turned out to be brief. As for Sir Charles Morrison, the Commons decided that he was not to be punished for having displayed his sword when he was attacked on this occasion.

15 Nalson's *Impartial Collection*, I, 59 (not 61, as George Petyt and TJ have it), tells us that Mr. Moor's speech "out of season" was made during the impeachment proceedings brought against the Duke of Buckingham, adviser of Charles I. These proceedings were initiated May 8, 1626, and while they were in progress, Sir John Eliot and Sir Dudley Digges appeared before the Lords with a request from Commons that Buckingham be confined to prison while his trial was being held. Charles I took deep offense at the language used in this request, and he had Sir John and Sir Dudley imprisoned. The Commons voted May 12 to suspend all business until their two imprisoned members were released, and in the ensuing battle of wills it was Charles I who suffered defeat. Sir Dudley was released May 16, and Sir John, May 19. Meanwhile, the proceed-

ings against Buckingham were going on, and they continued until Charles halted them for good by dissolving Parliament on June 15. In the interval between the release of Sir Dudley and Sir John, on the one hand, and the dissolution of Parliament, on the other, the relations of the king to the Commons were extremely uneasy, and in that sort of atmosphere, Mr. Moor, a member of Commons, speaking at a meeting of the committee of the whole on June 3, said to his associates that "we were born free, and must continue free, if the King would keep his Kingdom." And then he added, "As, Thanks be to God, we have no Occasion, we having a just and pious King." The Commons decided that these words were spoken without evil intention but nevertheless could not be considered acceptable parliamentary language. Accordingly, Mr. Moor was sent to the Tower during the pleasure of the Commons. He was released June 7, at the request of Charles himself. For other accounts of this episode, see JHC, I, 857-62, 866, 867; also Rushworth, I, 371.

16 Mr. Fitzwilliam Connisby was expelled from the Commons on October 30, 1641, for having sought to establish a monopoly of the manufacture of soap, in defiance of an order passed by the Commons on November 9, 1640, making participation in monopolistic practice incompatible with membership in their body. See JHC, II, 24, 299. George Petyt and Nalson did not mention what product Connisby's monopoly involved.

17 The case of Mr. Hugh Benson arose from a practice which citizens found even more objectionable than monopolies. It consisted in having a member of the Upper or Lower House sell to the public so-called "protections of parliament," which in the first instance were documents issued by members of the two Houses to their servants so as to provide the latter with a means of identifying themselves to the police or to merchants or to anyone seeking to question their status. Under certain restrictions these protections were an extension of the privileges enjoyed by a member of Parliament during a parliamentary session. It is obvious, of course, that these protections would be useful commodities for certain unauthorized citizens to have, and for certain unscrupulous Commoners or Lords to sell. Mr. Hugh Benson sold these protections as widely as he could. He prepared or had a scrivener prepare forms which were signed by himself and left open to the name of the bearer. He sold perhaps as many as twenty-nine of them through his own servants or his son-in-law at prices ranging from 17 to 40 shillings. But at last his profitable scheme came to grief. On November 2, 1641, the Commons took notice of a detailed report upon his brisk sale of protections, and he was given the punishment recorded here by TJ from George Petyt and Nalson. See also JHC, II, 301.

18 George Petyt and TJ were apparently unaware that they had already mentioned this case and had identified it as that of J.H. See above, n. 11. It should be noted, however, that the earlier reference concerned J.H.'s (that is, Jervis Hollis') suspension on April 26, 1641, whereas the present reference concerns his restoration the following December 2. In addition to Nalson, II, 710, see JHC, II, 329.

19 The episode involving Sir William Widdrington and Mr. (apparently not Sir) Herbert Price occurred on June 8, 1641, during an evening meeting of the Commons as the House was debating the propriety of some harsh words previously directed by George Digby against his colleague Colonel Goring. The hour

was late, and some members requested that candles be brought in and lighted. Other members, hoping for adjournment, opposed this request. At this point the serjeant, without waiting for the House to decide what to do, came in with the candles, as if they had been called for. Thereupon the House ordered the candles removed. As the serjeant was complying with this order, Sir William Widdrington and Mr. Herbert Price violently snatched the candles from the serjeant's hands. At its meeting on June 9, the Commons debated the propriety of what these two members had done, and committed them both to the Tower. They were released on June 14. In addition to Nalson's account (II, 272), see JHC, II, 171, 175. See also Rushworth, I, 282-3, and *Parliamentary History of England*, IX, 373-4. See also below, par. [172].

20 According to D'Ewes, p. 309, col. 2, this resolution fixed at £20 the fine to be levied upon knights, and at £10 the fine to be levied upon citizens, burgesses, and barons, for absence during "this whole Session of Parliament." George Petyt omitted the amount of the knight's fine, and set the date at "23 *Eliz.* 1580." TJ omitted the cypher in writing the latter date.

21 TJ followed George Petyt in giving the details of this case, and in ascribing them to William Petyt's *Miscellanea Parliamentaria*, p. 147, 149. These references are entirely correct, and in this important respect they differ from George Petyt's many other citations of the work of his namesake. The case of Lawrence Hide and the other lawyers occurred in the first year of James I's reign (1603).

22 This reference is apparently intended by TJ to be a date (March 1734) affixed to the case involving the imprisonment of the several lawyers mentioned. If so, TJ's reference is incorrect. In fact, TJ seems to have misconstrued his source George Petyt, p. 148, lines 7-12, at this point. Petyt referred this case to "*March* 173-4," that is, to John March, *Reports; or New cases* (1675), p. 173-4.

23 George Petyt allowed two errors to creep into his account of Sir John Trevor, and they emerge uncorrected here. First of all, Sir John was expelled by the Commons on March 16, 1694. And secondly, Bohun's version of the expulsion falls on p. 347-54 of his *Collection of Debates*. See also JHC, XI, 274. As for the grounds of this action of the Commons, Petyt said that the gratuity offered Sir John by the city of London amounted to 1,000 guineas, and that the occasion prompting it had been Sir John's effort in behalf of the passage of the Orphan's Bill. Petyt then went out of his way to add that Sir John's punishment was far too lenient for so great a crime—he should have been sentenced to death for his corrupt practices, as was Judge William de Thorp in Edward III's time.

24 In a marginal note on the case of Sir John Trevor, George Petyt mentioned Mr. Hungerford and implied that his expulsion resembled Sir John's in respect to time and circumstance. That is to say, Mr. Hungerford's expulsion occurred ten days after Sir John's, and his specific offense was that he accepted 20 guineas for "his Pains and Service, as Chairman of the Committee of this House, to whom the Orphan's Bill was committed." Petyt cited Bohun's *Collection*, p. 354, as his authority. See also JHC, XI, 283.

PARAGRAPH 139

1 Transcribed almost verbatim by TJ from George Petyt, p. 263, lines 18-24. Note that Petyt repeats here the erroneous date of Sir John Trevor's dismissal.

See above, par. 138, n. 23. Note also that TJ's reference to Coke's *Institutes*, IV, p. 8, is taken from Petyt.

2 For this sentence as TJ wrote it here, see George Petyt, p. 264, lines 20-3. TJ made two changes in his source: 1) he substituted "the Commons" for Petyt's "they"; and 2) he changed Petyt's "Antiquo" to "antiqua." The Latin phrase means, "But it was otherwise in ancient times."

3 TJ's references to Elsynge's *Manner of Holding Parliaments* are taken from George Petyt, and they designate passages on p. 154, 155, and 152 of one of the early editions of Elsynge's work. These passages also appear in Tyrwhitt's authoritative edition of 1768, p. 162, 163-4, and 160.

4 The text and notes of the passage beginning, "Surely the election of the speaker," and ending with the reference to Paul Foley, are transcribed almost verbatim by TJ from a continuous passage in George Petyt, p. 264-5.

5 For this sentence and its documentation, see George Petyt, p. 265, lines 18-28.

6 See George Petyt, p. 266, lines 6-12.

PARAGRAPH 140

1 The text and documentation of these two sentences were transcribed almost word for word by TJ from George Petyt, p. 272, lines 1-3, 9-11, at the beginning of Petyt's fourteenth chapter, entitled *"Business of the Speaker."* Petyt's reference to "Elsyng. 153" would point to Elsynge's *Manner of Holding Parliaments*, p. 161, if Tyrwhitt's edition of 1768 were being consulted.

PARAGRAPH 141

1 A verbatim transcription of the text and documentation of a passage in George Petyt, p. 273, lines 12-17, except that TJ silently eliminates a printer's error in the guise of a duplicated line of type in his source. Scobell's *Memorials*, p. 18, carried the information that certain members of the Commons sometimes found themselves elected from two or more constituencies, and that, under those circumstances, the member concerned would chose which constituency he wished to represent, and would waive his right to the other or others, so that new elections could be held therein. If a member did not make this choice himself, the house would make it for him. Scobell wondered whether the Commons had ever been forced to take the latter action.

PARAGRAPH 142

1 Transcribed by TJ almost verbatim in respect to text and documentation from George Petyt, p. 273, lines 29-32. This sentence had its origin in a speech in Commons by Sir Edward Hoby on November 5, 1601. D'Ewes quoted Sir Edward as having said on that occasion, "Only this proposition I hold, That our Speaker is to be commanded by none, neither to attend any, but the Queen only." At that time the Speaker was Mr. John Crooke, Recorder of London. See D'Ewes, p. 621.

1 A word-for-word transcription of George Petyt, p. 274, lines 8-12, but without the inclusion of Petyt's documentation. Petyt correctly referred this sentence to Scobell's *Memorials*, p. 65, and to William Petyt's *Miscellanea Parliamentaria*, p. 140. See also JHC, I, 223, where the passage copied by TJ appears anonymously in somewhat truncated form in the course of a debate in Commons, May 23, 1604. For further details, see below, par. 144, n. 1.

1 Transcribed by TJ in slightly altered wording but with documentation intact from George Petyt, p. 274, lines 4-8. The episode to which this sentence and that in par. 143 referred began on May 15, 1604, and ended eight days later. On the earlier of these dates, the Speaker of the Commons, Sir Edward Phelips, when on his way to the House, was given a legislative bill by William Jones, a printer. From his chair in the House, Sir Edward later read the title of the printer's bill, and he intimated not only that it had been drawn up by a minister, one Mr. Erbury, but also that it alleged an act of treason on the part of A.B., a magistrate, who was not further identified. The Commons pressed Sir Edward to read the entire bill, but he urged them to let him read it first himself. His motion to this effect was reluctantly approved, but with the understanding that he would soon present the bill to the Commons in full. The next day James I sent for the bill, and the Speaker, seeing that it amounted to an allegation that A.B. had uttered treasonous words against the king, decided that the king was entitled to retain and act upon it. When the Speaker brought the bill before the House on May 23, in line with his promise to let the Commons see it, several questions arose. One of them concerned the constitutional issue as to whether the original reading of the title of the bill by the Speaker on May 15 meant that the bill passed at that moment into the possession of the House. Another one, also constitutional in nature, grew out of the action of the Speaker in handing over to the king a document which belonged arguably to the Commons and had not been specifically authorized by their vote to be given to anyone else. After debate upon these two and other issues, the Commons finally resolved, "That, for this time, all Questions should cease touching these Matters; with this Caution and Care, proceeding from a tender Regard of the Privilege of this House, that it should be precisely registred as the Judgment of the House, That no Speaker from henceforth should deliver a Bill, whereof the House standeth possessed, to any whosoever, without Allowance and Leave as aforesaid; but that he had Liberty, and might either shew it, or deliver a Copy, if it seemed so meet unto him." JHC, I, 223-4.

2 Transcribed by TJ without major change in wording or documentation from George Petyt, p. 275, lines 7, 17-26.

3 Condensed by TJ from George Petyt, p. 276, lines 1-6, with Petyt's documentation intact.

4 From "Ordered 10. November 1640" to "ib. 53," TJ's words are a somewhat rearranged but prevailingly verbatim transcript of the text and documentation in George Petyt, p. 277, lines 1-8. The order of Nov. 10, 1640, however, should have been dated November 12. See JHC, II, 27. For the order of November 20,

1640, see JHC, II, 33. It appears that the date of the first of these orders, as indirectly given by Rushworth, is incorrect, and that Petyt accepted it without seeking verification elsewhere.

5 This famous declaration by Speaker Lenthall was uttered on January 4, 1641/42, as he confronted Charles I in the course of the latter's unprecedented invasion of the House of Commons. Charles had come to the House on that occasion accompanied by a force of soldiers to demand that five members of the Commons, to wit, Denzill Hollis, Sir Arthur Hesslerig, John Pym, John Hampden, and William Stroud, be surrendered to him for punishment as traitors. Speaker Lenthall left his chair and went forward to meet the king striding into the House, and the king repaid this courtesy by proceeding to occupy the Speaker's chair and to start to call out the names of his five intended victims. When his call produced no answer from the Commons, the king asked Lenthall whether any of the members named were present and could be pointed out or accounted for, and Lenthall answered thus while kneeling: "May it please your Majesty, I Have neither Eyes to see, nor Tongue to speak in this place, but as the House is pleased to direct me, whose Servant I am here, and humbly beg your Majesties Pardon, that I cannot give any other Answer than this, to what your Majesty is pleased to demand of me." With these words in his ears, the king left the House, and the question whether he would prevail or not over the Commons remained to be settled by other means than verbal clashes. George Petyt did not document Speaker Lenthall's words, nor did TJ. Indeed, they are not given in JHC, II, 368. But Rushworth, who was present that day in Commons, recorded them in his *Historical Collections*, Part III, Vol. 1, p. 478. See also MacDonagh, p. 215-17. Petyt obviously relied upon Rushworth's account, and he seems to have quoted it from a somewhat inaccurate memory.

PARAGRAPH 145

1 The text and documentation of this passage were transcribed verbatim by TJ from George Petyt, p. 278, lines 1-4. This particular reading of the Litany is a matter of parliamentary record for April 4, 1571, as Petyt's dating allows us to gather, and as JHC, I, 82, clearly confirms. Petyt's reference to Townshend's *Historical Collections*, p. 54, concerned a Litany reading which occurred on February 26, 1591/93, but was not preceded by a motion of the Speaker, as Petyt said the earlier one had been.

PARAGRAPH [146]

1 From this point onward, the numbers placed in the paragraph indentations are double bracketed to indicate that they are supplied by the editor as a continuation of the numerical sequence established by TJ for the first 145 paragraphs of the manuscript.

2 This sentence was transcribed word for word in text and documentation from George Petyt, p. 278, lines 5-7, and Petyt in turn had transcribed it from Scobell's *Memorials*, p. 6, lines 1-3.

PARAGRAPH [147]

1 For this sentence in its entirety, see George Petyt, p. 278, lines 8-14, and Scobell's *Memorials*, p. 6, lines 4-9. Both of these authors used "overthwart."

Scobell had "between the Speaker and any Member," whereas Petyt, like TJ, had "the member"—an indication that TJ followed Petyt's text rather than Scobell's in making his transcription.

PARAGRAPH [148]

1 TJ transcribed this paragraph almost verbatim from George Petyt, p. 278, lines 17-25, but with an uncharacteristic disregard of syntax he changed Petyt's wording by omitting "do" before "alway" and by adding "to" before "depart." On the other side, Petyt made five distinct changes in the wording that he found in D'Ewes, p. 282, col. 2, lines 30-8. There can be no doubt that Petyt, not D'Ewes, was TJ's source on this occasion. D'Ewes and Petyt both indicated that this paragraph was based upon a motion made by Sir James Croft, Comptroller of her Majesty's Household, on January 21, 1580/81, and approved by the whole House.

PARAGRAPH [149]

1 Text and documentation transcribed verbatim from George Petyt, p. 279, lines 1-6. Scobell's *Memorials*, p. 6, lines 10-15, contains this same passage, but it has "sate" for "set" in the last clause, and thus it can hardly be accepted as TJ's primary source.

PARAGRAPH [150]

1 This sentence was transcribed word for word by TJ from George Petyt, p. 279, lines 7-9, except that the latter had "pay" for "pays." Petyt attributed the sentence to Townshend's *Historical Collections*, p. 101, 181, and to D'Ewes, p. 550, col. 1, and TJ made note of the first of these references. According to D'Ewes, the sentence was part of a motion and admonishment made to the Commons on October 27, 1597, by the Chancellor of the Exchequer, "before Mr. Speaker went up to her Majesty in the Upper House." The fees mentioned here were collected from members of the Commons in return for their being registered in the serjeant's book so as to be assured of admittance by him to the daily sessions of the House. For the amounts involved in these fees during the reign of Elizabeth I, see Neale, p. 345.

PARAGRAPH [151]

1 For this exact sentence and its documentation, see George Petyt, p. 279, lines 10-14. Following in turn the exact wording of Scobell's *Memorials*, p. 6, lines 16-20, Petyt attributed the ruling to D'Ewes, p. 487, col. 1, whereas Scobell did not. Thus it is certain that TJ's primary authority on this occasion was Petyt. D'Ewes' entry was part of his records for March 3, 1592/93, and it reads thus: "Mr. Speaker perceiving some men to whisper together, said, that it was not the manner of the House, that any should whisper or talk secretly, for here only publick Speeches are to be used." The Speaker at that time was Edward Coke, later distinguished as author of *Institutes of the Lawes of England*. See D'Ewes, p. 469. See also MacDonagh, p. 189-92.

PARAGRAPH [152]

1 This sentence and its documentation are verbatim transcriptions of George Petyt, p. 279, lines 17-22. Petyt used "Ibid." at that point to refer to Scobell's

Memorials, p. 6-7, and the passage thus indicated in the latter work parallels what Petyt and TJ were to copy, except that Scobell inserted "and" between "uncovered" and "address."

PARAGRAPH [153]

1 See George Petyt, p. 280, lines 3-11, for this passage and its documentation. The reference to Scobell contains the passage exactly as Petyt and TJ gave it, except that Scobell made no mention of D'Ewes. The reference to D'Ewes takes us to February 18, 1588/89. On that date the Speaker, Serjeant-at-Law Snagg, having remarked upon the great disorder occasioned in the Commons by several speakers demanding recognition and refusing to give way to any of their competitors for the floor, proceeds then to remind the House of their own rule against this kind of thing, and of their own obligation as members of the highest court in the land to repudiate procedures that would never be tolerated in any other court.

PARAGRAPH [154]

1 This sentence and its documentation were transcribed verbatim from George Petyt, p. 280, lines 12-16. Petyt indicated that the sentence came from Scobell's *Memorials*, p. 7, and from Townshend's *Historical Collections*, p. 205. The latter reference, which Scobell did not note, records that, on Monday, November 9, 1601, the Speaker of the Commons, Mr. John Crook, admonished the House for its conduct in humming, laughing, and talking at the conclusion of a statement by Serjeant Heale to the effect that her Majesty had as much right to all the lands and goods of her subjects as to any royal revenue of her Crown. Of the disruptive behavior among the Commons on that occasion, Speaker Crook spoke thus: "*It is a great Disorder, that this should be used; for it is the Antient Use of this House, for every Man to be Silent when any one Speaketh; and he that is Speaking, should be suffer'd to deliver his Mind without Interruption*" (italics are Townshend's). See also D'Ewes, p. 633, col. 1.

PARAGRAPH [155]

1 Transcribed verbatim from George Petyt, p. 280, lines 17-21, where the wording adopted by TJ was identified as a rule of order passed on June 21, 1604. Petyt cited "Ibid.," that is, Scobell's *Memorials*, p. 7, as his authority for this rule, but he made no mention of Hale's *Jurisdiction of Parliaments*, p. 133. This latter reference TJ added on his own, but he did not notice that Hale's pagination at that point should have read "p. 134." The rule owes its ultimate authority to JHC, I, 244.

PARAGRAPH [156]

1 Transcribed verbatim from George Petyt, p. 280, lines 22-3, who in turn transcribed verbatim from a source identified, as "Ibid.," that is, Scobell's *Memorials*, p. 7. In its full extent, Scobell's passage reads thus: "12 *Jacobi*, It was vouched by Sir *Dudley Diggs*, (a person of much experience in Parliaments) *That when the Speaker stands up, the Member standing up ought to sit down*" (italics are Scobell's). Sir Dudley's observation was made in a session of the Commons on May 10, 1614. See JHC, I, 479.

PARAGRAPH [157]

1 TJ's wording here corresponds exactly with that in George Petyt, p. 280, lines 24-8. Petyt made it plain that his passage was a rule of order adopted April 27, 1604, and he cited "Scobel. 8" as his authority. Scobell's wording of the passage differs from TJ's and Petyt's only by preferring "Argument" to "Arguments." According to JHC, I, 187, this rule would come into use "If any Doubt arise upon a Bill."

PARAGRAPH [158]

1 This passage in its exact wording and documentation was transcribed by TJ from George Petyt, p. 280, lines 29-34, and Petyt in turn adapted it from Scobell's *Memorials*, p. 8, and from D'Ewes, p. 335, col. 1. Scobell omitted "by coughing, spitting,&c." from the passage as he gave it, after having identified it as a rule of order adopted in Commons on June 4, 1604. By drawing upon D'Ewes' account of a debate in Commons on December 2, 1584, Petyt added the words which Scobell had omitted. According to D'Ewes' account, a bill then under consideration had produced some unpopular speeches, with the result that "divers of the House had endeavoured by coughing and spitting to shorten them." This discourteous conduct led Sir Francis Hastings to remind the House of its previous attempts to prevent offensive names from being applied to speakers; and he urged "that in respect of the gravity and honour of this House, when any Member thereof shall speak unto a Bill, the residue would forbear to interrupt or trouble him by unnecessary coughing, spitting or the like." As for Petyt's (and TJ's) second reference to D'Ewes, it also had to do with Sir Francis Hastings, but now with his protest to the Commons on November 16, 1601, against their disruptive conduct in hawking and spitting during a tiresome and indistinct speech by "an old Doctor of the Civil Law." It should be noted that the date affixed by Scobell to these practices is not supported by the record of the Commons for June 4, 1604. See JHC, I, 231-2.

PARAGRAPH [159]

1 This sentence and its documentation were transcribed verbatim by TJ from George Petyt, p. 281, lines 2-5, the "ibid." being intended to refer to Scobell's *Memorials*, p. 8. Both Petyt and Scobell identified the sentence as an order of the Commons dated May 7, 1607. Scobell's wording of the order had "should" rather than "shall" before "stir." For the official version, see JHC, I, 371.

PARAGRAPH [160]

1 For the verbatim text and documentation of this passage, see George Petyt, p. 281, lines 9-23. As he partly indicated, Petyt transcribed the passage verbatim from the inner portion of a paragraph in Scobell's *Memorials*, p. 81, except that Scobell had "until" for "till."

PARAGRAPH [161]

1 TJ transcribed this sentence and its documentation from George Petyt, p. 282, lines 3-7. Petyt dated the sentence "*Febr.* 19. 1592. 35 *Eliz.*," and authenticated it by referring to "*Towns.* Coll. Ibid." See Townshend's *Historical Collections*, p. 51. Townshend worded the sentence thus: "*Munday, Feb.* 19. This day the Knights and Burgesses met, and at this day appeared: after that their

Names were declared to the Clerk of the Crown, and there entered into his book, they entred into the House." Inasmuch as TJ's wording differs from Townshend's, while being a verbatim transcript of Petyt's, there can be no doubt about TJ's primary source on this occasion. The sentence recorded a circumstance at the very beginning of Elizabeth I's eighth Parliament. See Neale, p. 433. See also D'Ewes, p. 468, col. 2.

PARAGRAPH [162]

1 That is, Henry Stanley, who became fourth Earl of Derby, October 26, 1572, and died on September 25, 1593. He served in several important political capacities in Elizabeth I's reign, and was distinguished also as patron of the actors' company which performed before the Queen, 1579-1580. See A. F. Pollard, "Stanley, Henry," in DNB.

2 The room in which this court carried out its functions was also White Hall. See Neale, p. 351.

3 For previous mention of the Oath of Supremacy, see above, pars. 47 (n. 1), and 75 (n. 2).

4 This entire paragraph is a verbatim transcription of George Petyt, p. 282, lines 8-21, except that TJ omitted "Alphabetically" before "Every one answered." Petyt himself credited the paragraph to "Sir *S. d'Ewes. Jour. pas.*," but in reality Petyt transcribed it from Townshend's *Historical Collections*, p. 51, with some omissions and changes. Cf. D'Ewes, p. 468, col. 2.

PARAGRAPH [163]

1 Text and documentation exactly transcribed from George Petyt, p. 282 (lines 27-31), and 283 (lines 1-2, except that Petyt substituted "Id." for "Town." As for the reference to Townshend's *Historical Collections*, p. 15, it pointed to this passage in the exact wording used here by TJ and Petyt, but with the elements of its date distributed between a preceding paragraph and the margin of its page.

PARAGRAPH [164]

1 This entire passage was transcribed verbatim in text and documentation from George Petyt, p. 283, lines 3, 6-13, except that TJ deleted three words of his source and added one. For his part, Petyt composed the passage by drawing much of it word for word from D'Ewes, p. 432, col. 2, and by proceeding then to give a drastic condensation of the concluding stage of D'Ewes' remarks. Said D'Ewes: "On *Saturday* the 15th day of *February*, Sir *Edward Hobby* moved (he said) upon good cause, that Mr. Speaker [i.e., Serjeant Snagg] do give admonition unto this whole House, that Speeches used in this House by the Members of the same be not any of them made or used as Table talk, or in any wise delivered in notes of writing to any person or persons whatsoever not being Members of this House, as of late (is thought) hath been done in this present Session: And thereupon by consent of this House admonition was given by Mr. Speaker in that behalf accordingly, shewing unto them that they are the Common Council of the Realm." These admonitory words were addressed to the Commons less than seven months after the defeat of the Spanish Armada, and they have to be understood as reflecting the apprehensions of the British about the possibility of

renewed aggression against them by Philip II of Spain. Even speeches in the Commons, said Sir Edward Hobby in effect, must be kept from the ears of the enemy. And eleven days before he uttered this warning, a note similar to his had been sounded by Sir Christopher Hatton. Addressing a joint session of the Lords and Commons in the presence of Queen Elizabeth I on February 4, Sir Christopher declared in part that "though the Spanish late Wonderful Fleet had been lately defeated, yet there wanted not still power and malice in him against this Nation and her Majesty: and so much the more implacable it may be conjectured he now remains, because of his late defeature and loss before-mentioned." D'Ewes, p. 428, col. 2.

PARAGRAPH [165]

1 Transcribed verbatim from George Petyt, p. 283, lines 14-19, except that the passage as given by Petyt is prefaced by "It was declared in the House in 10 *Nov.* 1640. 16 *Car.* 1. that. . . ." As Petyt partly noted, his own wording was taken verbatim from Rushworth, Part III, Vol. 1, p. 41, except that Rushworth omitted "in 10 *Nov.* 1640. 16 *Car.* 1."

2 TJ rightly indicated that this paragraph made two appearances in *Lex Parliamentaria*, one in Ch. 15 and one in Ch. 18. The first of these appearances is identified above. For the second, see p. 331, lines 7-10. The latter reference documents the paragraph as having come from Scobell's *Memorials*, p. 47—a fact TJ noted. Scobell's wording was more condensed than Rushworth's, but it was nevertheless an almost verbatim transcription of an order of the Commons dated November 10, 1640. See JHC, II, 25.

PARAGRAPH [166]

1 Transcribed verbatim in text and documentation from George Petyt, p. 283, lines 20-4, except that Petyt had "the same day" for TJ's "10. Nov. 1640" and "was begun" for TJ's "is begun." See also JHC, II, 25.

PARAGRAPH [167]

1 Transcribed verbatim in text and documentation from George Petyt, p. 283, lines 27-8, except that Petyt placed the date at the end of the sentence. In actual fact, that date, as given by Petyt and TJ, should have read "12 Nov. 1640." See JHC, II, 28. The reporters mentioned in the sentence were members appointed by the Commons to attend a conference between the Commons and the Lords and to bring back to the Commons a report of what had transpired. JHC, II, 27.

PARAGRAPH [168]

1 Text and documentation transcribed word for word from George Petyt, p. 283-4, except that Petyt identified the sentence as an order of the Commons and put its date last. See also JHC, II, 36.

PARAGRAPH [169]

1 Text and documentation transcribed verbatim from George Petyt, p. 284, lines 3-6. The date of this order of Commons was November 26, 1640, as neither Petyt nor Rushworth fully specified. See JHC, II, 36. As for the words "book" and "glove," they are to be respectively understood as metaphors for a

deed of purchase of land or an insignia of office—two proofs of eligibility for a seat in Commons. The order here stated would mean that, even with these two proofs of eligibility, a member could not take his seat if he had not been present at prayers that day.

PARAGRAPH [170]

1 TJ silently transcribed the date, the wording, and the documentation of this order from George Petyt, p. 284, lines 17-19, and Petyt declared for his part that the order was derived from *"Rush. Coll.* p. 3. v.1. fol.84." It must be pointed out, however, that Rushworth himself plainly dated the order Saturday, December 5, 1640, with the result that Petyt's (and TJ's) date is incorrect by forty-four years and one day. See JHC, II, 45.

PARAGRAPH [171]

1 For this rule and its documentation, exactly as stated here, see George Petyt, p. 284, lines 20-6. In borrowing the rule from Rushworth, Part III, Vol. 1, p. 92, Petyt followed Rushworth's wording, except for his using "those who" on the two occasions when Rushworth wrote "those that." See also JHC, II, 49.

PARAGRAPH [172]

1 See George Petyt, p. 284, lines 27-9, for this exact rule and its documentation. And for almost the same words, ordered somewhat differently, see Rushworth, Part III, Vol. 1, p. 283. According to Rushworth, this rule figured as part of a speech in Commons by Denzil Holles on June 9, 1641, in protest against George Digby's having implied in a debate the preceding evening that his colleague, Colonel Goring, had been guilty of perjury when he disclosed to the House an army plot which he had sworn not to reveal. For an account of the disorderly behavior of William Widdrington and Herbert Price during that evening's debate, see above, par. 138, n. 19. For another summary of Denzil Holles' speech, see Nalson's *Impartial Collection,* II, 272. See also JHC, II, 171-3, and *Parliamentary History of England,* IX, 373-4.

PARAGRAPH [173]

1 In stating this rule and attributing it to Scobell, TJ drew word for word upon George Petyt, p. 285, lines 4-5. Petyt and Scobell attached the rule to the proceedings of the Commons on May 2, 1610. See also JHC, I, 423. See also below, par. [177].

PARAGRAPH [174]

1 For the exact wording of this sentence, and for its attribution to Scobell, see George Petyt, p. 285, lines 18-20. In Petyt's wording, the sentence did not identify itself as "a Rule of the House," but Scobell did so identify it. TJ would in all likelihood have preferred Scobell to Petyt in respect to this detail, had he been following Scobell's text.

2 On his own initiative, and without any prompting from Petyt or Scobell, TJ gave this sentence added authority by his reference to the work here noted, in which Hale spoke as follows: *"Qui digreditur Amateriâ [A materiâ] ad Personam [what strays from subject matter to personalities]* Mr. Speaker ought to suppress."

Hale's wording, which in fact came from p. 134 of his work through the printer's error in pagination, was derived ultimately from an action in the Commons on April 19, 1604. See JHC, I, 177.

PARAGRAPH [175]

1 This reference was meant to refer to Scobell's *Memorials*, p. 31, where the passage here cited is to be found. But TJ's true source on this occasion was George Petyt, p. 285, lines 21-4. Petyt attributed the passage to "Ibid.," and in quoting it, he failed to preface it with the phrase, "Agreed for a general Rule." Had TJ been following Scobell rather than Petyt, his sentence would not have contained the word "Ibid." and would in all likelihood have preserved the phrase which Petyt omitted. For the circumstances attending the passage of that "general Rule," see JHC, I, 175.

2 This reference to Hale, p. 133 [i.e., p. 134] is not in Petyt or Scobell. TJ seems to have intended it to call attention to other episodes in which the Speaker was authorized to interrupt irrelevant speeches. For those episodes, which Hale dates on April 14 and April 19, 1604, see JHC, I, 172, 177. For previous reference to the second of these episodes, see above, par. [174], n. 2.

PARAGRAPH [176]

1 These two sentences and their documentation were transcribed from George Petyt, p. 286, lines 1-8, except that TJ omitted "the" before "order" and not only added the parenthetical identification after "I" but also changed the page numbers to book and chapter numbers in the reference to Smith. Petyt's text followed Smith's verbatim, except that Petyt omitted the parenthetical identification and put "in the House" for "to the House." Petyt's failure to identify "I" leads of course to the conclusion that he was speaking of himself, and TJ wanted to correct that impression.

PARAGRAPH [177]

1 Partly a verbatim transcription and partly an adaptation of the text and documentation of George Petyt, p. 286, lines 9-14. Petyt drew the passage verbatim from Scobell's *Memorials*, p. 32-3, except that Scobell had "besides" for "beside" and "them" for "him" at the end. Both Scobell and Petyt began the main clause with "it stands with the Orders of the House for Mr. Speaker to interrupt him, and to know the Pleasure . . ."—a construction which TJ simplified and changed. This order was adopted May 2, 1610. See above, par. [173], n. 1.

PARAGRAPH [178]

1 Transcribed verbatim in text and documentation from George Petyt, p. 286, lines 21-30. Petyt in turn deleted four words and changed two verb forms in drawing his text from lines 1-11 of page 21 of Scobell's text. Scobell's text constitutes the first paragraph in his Ch. VII, which is entitled, "Rules and Method of Debates in the House."

PARAGRAPH [179]

1 Text transcribed verbatim from George Petyt, p. 286, lines 31-2, and p. 287, lines 1-3. Petyt, p. 287, quoted parliamentary precedents of June 28, 1604, and

December 4, 1640, to authorize the rule that he had just stated, and he indicated that he drew the text of the rule and its documentation from Scobell, p. 21-2. For the parliamentary precedents merely dated by TJ, and quoted more at large by Scobell and Petyt, see JHC, I, 247-8; II, 45. The first of these precedents grew out of an episode involving an injury to James I. On June 28, 1604, Sir Edward Hobby informed the Commons that the king had been hurt in the foot "by the Stroke of a Horse" and was confined to bed. Sir Edward proceeded to move that a delegation be selected and sent in the name of the House to visit the injured king. But before action was taken, Sir Lewys Lewknor interposed a speech on the necessity for the House to answer a recent letter of the king on the matter of a subsidy. When Sir Lewys had finished, a member objected to his speech as having no claim to action until the pending motion of Sir Edward had been disposed of. Accordingly the House did not act on Sir Lewys' proposal but on Sir Edward's motion instead, and a delegation was dispatched to the king at once. That afternoon, the vice chamberlain, who had headed the delegation, reported back to the House that the king's injury, which consisted in a swelling on his instep, had been inflicted by a stroke of the queen's horse while he was hunting. The vice chamberlain added that James I had very graciously received the delegation of the Commons, and that he wanted them not only to have his thanks in return but also his assurances that "he would ever be as careful of any Sore or Grievance that should come to this House, as they were of his Hurt."

PARAGRAPH [180]

1 A verbatim transcript of George Petyt, p. 287, lines 17-28, except that TJ puts "Scob. 22" for Petyt's "Ibid." The same passage in Scobell differs in four minor ways from TJ's and Petyt's.

PARAGRAPH [181]

1 This passage was transcribed word for word from George Petyt, p. 287, lines 29-31, p. 288, lines 1-2, except that Petyt had "Ibid." in place of "Scob. 22." In turn Petyt transcribed his passage verbatim from Scobell's *Memorials*, p. 22.

PARAGRAPH [182]

1 This entire paragraph was transcribed verbatim from George Petyt, p. 288, lines 3-13. For his part, Petyt made a few minor textual changes in transcribing it from Scobell's *Memorials*, p. 22-3.

PARAGRAPH [183]

1 For this paragraph exactly as it stands here in wording and documentation, see George Petyt, p. 288, lines 14-23. As for Petyt's text, it is a verbatim transcript of Scobell's *Memorials*, p. 23, lines 6-15, except that, in the second clause, Scobell's "where" became Petyt's "when."

PARAGRAPH [184]

1 See George Petyt, p. 288, lines 24-8, and Scobell's *Memorials*, p. 23, lines 16-20, for the exact wording of this sentence as TJ gave it here.

PARAGRAPH [185]

1 The text and documentation of this passage were transcribed verbatim by TJ from George Petyt, p. 288, lines 29-32, p. 289, lines 1-7, with three exceptions: l) Petyt opened the passage by giving the date, "13 *Junij* 1604"; after "A bill," Petyt added the phrase, "touching a Subsidie of Tunnage and Poundage"; and Petyt wrote "upon" rather than "on" before "a third Reading." Petyt acknowledged by an "Ibid." that he had transcribed the passage from Scobell's *Memorials*, p. 23-4. Scobell's text and Petyt's are identical in their wording, except that Scobell added three clauses of his own between "affirmative" and "orderly." Those three clauses read thus; "but before the Negative was put, one stood up and spake to it, which was admitted for Orderly." As for the parliamentary rule involved in the wording adopted by Petyt and TJ, it would seem to differ from Scobell's. Scobell appears to define "orderly" in terms of the propriety of speaking to a motion after those in favor had voted and those opposed had not. On the other hand, Petyt and TJ appear to define "orderly" in terms of the necessity of registering the negative as well as the affirmative votes on a motion before it can be accepted as having attained full legal status. Both of these interpretations are bound up in the language describing the action of the Commons on June 13, 1604. See JHC, I, 237-8.

PARAGRAPH [186]

1 In text and documentation, this paragraph is a verbatim transcription of George Petyt, p. 289, lines 8-22, except for TJ's special way of writing the term for negative votes, of inserting a preposition in one of Petyt's phrases, and of omitting the definite article in another. On the other hand, Petyt omitted some twenty-six words of Scobell's text when he copied the paragraph given here by TJ. The italics were not suggested to TJ either by Petyt or Scobell.

PARAGRAPH [187]

1 TJ exactly transcribed this paragraph and its documentation from George Petyt, p. 289 (lines 23-32), and 290 (lines 1-2). The same paragraph in Scobell's *Memorials*, p. 24-5, differs in four minor details from Petyt's and TJ's text.

PARAGRAPH [188]

1 Up to this point, the text of the paragraph is a verbatim transcript of George Petyt, p. 290, lines 3-11. Petyt's wording was in turn a verbatim transcript of a passage in Sir Edward Coke's *Reports in thirteen Parts*, 12, 116, except for Coke's omission of "still" after "sit." Coke, Petyt, and TJ had in mind the following rule of the Commons as stated on March 20, 1592/93, by the Speaker, who happened to be none other than Edward Coke himself: "the Order of the House is, that the I [Yea] being for the Bill must go out, and the No against the Bill doth always sit. The reason is, that the Inventor that will have a new Law, is to go out and bring it in; and they that are for the Law in possession must keep the House, for they sit to continue it." D'Ewes, p. 505, col. 1. In other words, the opponents of the status quo went out, and the proponents stayed in.

2 But in certain cases the opponents of the status quo stayed in, while the proponents went out, and the two precedents mentioned here show why. In each of them, the question called for the rejection of the bill before the House, not for its

adoption, and thus an affirmative vote on the question required proponents of the status quo to behave against their usual practice, as indeed the opponents of the status quo had likewise to do. That is to say, the proponents went out, and the opponents stayed in. See Scobell's *Memorials*, p. 43. See also JHC, I, 152; II, 244.

3 TJ transcribed this documentation from Petyt.

PARAGRAPH [189]

1 The two preceding sentences and the date given before them were taken word for word from George Petyt, p. 290, lines 19-26, except that Petyt wrote "*Mart.*" for "Mar." What "25" stands for in Petyt's and TJ's opening phrase is not clear. The parliamentary episode to which the first sentence refers took place on March 24, 1623/24, and it concerned the question whether Sir Thomas Holland and Sir John Corbett had been properly elected from Norfolk. After debate, the question was brought to a division of the House, and at this point, a contest arose between those who believed that the Noes should stay in their places, and those who wanted the Noes to go forth. The House proceeded thereupon to overrule the latter proposition, on the principle, no doubt, that the Noes were somewhat in the position of defending the status quo and should thus be required to play the role assigned them by tradition. In the later vote on the main question, the House decided that Sir Thomas and Sir John had been properly elected. See Scobell's *Memorials*, p. 25; also JHC, I, 749.

2 This reference, which TJ borrowed from Petyt, is to be construed here and elsewhere in the Pocket-Book and *Manual* as Petyt's way of designating Scobell's *Memorials* as that work appeared in a volume also containing Hakewill's *Modus tenendi Parliamentum*. See above, p. xxii.

PARAGRAPH [190]

1 Transcribed verbatim in text and documentation from George Petyt, p. 290 (lines 27-32), and 291 (lines 1-5). The documentation referred to Scobell's *Memorials*, p. 26, where the identical passage appeared.

PARAGRAPH [191]

1 For a passage identical in wording and documentation, see George Petyt, p. 291, lines 6-9. Petyt borrowed the selfsame passage from Scobell's *Memorials*, p. 26, as his reference to "ibid." indicated.

PARAGRAPH [192]

1 See George Petyt, p. 291, lines 10-27, for the paragraph that exactly equals TJ's in text and documentation. Petyt's paragraph exactly equals one in Scobell's *Memorials*, p. 26-7, with three insignificant exceptions.

PARAGRAPH [193]

1 TJ's text and documentation were transcribed verbatim from a passage in George Petyt at the bottom of p. 291 and the top of p. 292. Petyt did not use quotation marks. TJ's MS omitted the mark at the end of his final quotation. As for Petyt, he transcribed his passage verbatim from Scobell's *Memorials*, p. 27.

PARAGRAPH [194]

1 Transcribed word for word from George Petyt, p. 292, lines 4-9, except that Petyt wrote "the casting Voice." Petyt's passage was taken from an exactly similar passage in Scobell's *Memorials*, p. 27.

PARAGRAPH [195]

1 George Petyt, p. 292, lines 10-15, provided TJ with the exact wording and documentation of this passage, except that Petyt wrote "afterward" without an "s" and "*Maij*" for "May." Petyt's wording was in part an adaptation and in part an exact copy of a passage in Scobell's *Memorials*, p. 27. Scobell identified "the Speaker" as Sir Edward Phelips, and the JHC, I, 303, indicates that it was he who on May 1, 1606, converted the invoked precedent into a present rule.

PARAGRAPH [196]

1 For the exact precursor of the wording of the text and documentation of this paragraph, see George Petyt, p. 292-3. Petyt's text was a verbatim transcript of a passage in Scobell's *Memorials*, p. 27-8. The punctuation of the parenthetical clause is partly Petyt's and partly TJ's.

PARAGRAPH [197]

1 Transcribed verbatim in text and documentation from George Petyt, p. 293, lines 3-22. Petyt made five slight textual changes in transcribing this passage from Scobell's *Memorials*, p. 28-9

PARAGRAPH [198]

1 Transcribed verbatim in text and documentation from a paragraph in George Petyt, p. 293-4. Petyt in turn transcribed the paragraph verbatim from Scobell's *Memorials*, p. 29.

PARAGRAPH [199]

1 Transcribed verbatim in text and documentation from George Petyt, p. 294, lines 3-10. Petyt in turn transcribed the passage from Scobell's *Memorials*, p. 29.

PARAGRAPH [200]

1 Transcribed exactly in text and documentation from George Petyt, p. 294, lines 11-18. Petyt transcribed the passage from Scobell's *Memorials*, p. 29-30, in part keeping to Scobell's wording and in part condensing it measurably. Scobell identified the two knights as from Warwick, but he did not add that their names were Mr. Coomes and Lord Compton, and that the election of each was declared void when the Commons voted separately upon the two. See JHC, II, 43.

PARAGRAPH [201]

1 See George Petyt, p. 294, lines 19-29, for the eighty-seven-word paragraph upon which TJ based the forty words of the text and documentation represented here. Petyt transcribed his paragraph almost verbatim from Scobell's *Memorials*, p. 30—a page reference which TJ incorrectly noted. The forty-seven words that TJ omitted from Petyt's text consisted largely of a parenthetical enumeration of concrete expressions to be used in designating a member by title, addition, of-

fice, place, and so on. According to OED, a condition described by a word annexed to a person's title to characterize his quality was formerly known as an "addition." For example, noble lord, worthy knight, wise judge, distinguished gentleman. As for "office," it identified a person by his professional status or dignity, and "place," by his habitual location in, say, the House of Commons—"near the Chair," "near the Bar," "on the other side."

PARAGRAPH [202]

1 For the exact duplicate of this paragraph, see George Petyt, p. 294-5. Petyt's paragraph exactly duplicates Scobell's *Memorials*, p. 30, lines 21-8; but the latter source seems once more not to have been TJ's primary authority, if we may argue that TJ, like Petyt, made the paragraph independent of its surroundings, whereas Scobell did not. TJ's manuscript placed an *e* above the *r* in *Memorials*—an interlineation perhaps intended to remind himself in his own shorthand that Scobell's wording and Petyt's are identical on this occasion, as they had not always been.

PARAGRAPH [203]

1 For this paragraph in the exact wording that TJ here used, see George Petyt, p. 295, lines 6-12. Petyt in turn transcribed the paragraph verbatim from Scobell's *Memorials*, p. 30-1, and indicated as much by a marginal note reading *"Ibid. & 31."* TJ followed the identical form of that note, and in addition he followed Petyt in giving this paragraph independent status—two sure indications that the latter was his primary authority.

PARAGRAPH [204]

1 For its exact wording and documentation, this paragraph relied upon George Petyt, p. 295, lines 13-18, even as Petyt drew his wording almost verbatim from Scobell's *Memorials*, p. 31. The differences between these two authorities, particularly in the wording of the parenthetical observation, indicate once again that TJ followed Petyt. The reference to Townshend's *Historical Collections*, p. 205, involved the episode in which the Speaker, Mr. John Crook, on Monday, November 9, 1601, admonished the Commons about their disruptive conduct during and after a member's speech. See above, par. [154], n. 1. Also D'Ewes, p. 633, col. 1.

PARAGRAPH [205]

1 Transcribed almost verbatim from George Petyt, p. 298, lines 9-13. Petyt's indicated source for this passage was "Id. 71.," that is, *Memorials* in *Hakewel*, p. 71, and TJ properly corrected the latter page reference to 33, while preserving Petyt's ambiguous title. See above, par. [189], n. 2. Both Petyt and Scobell identified the passage as a rule of the commons, and they indicated that it was adopted April 2, 1604. The case which gave rise to this rule concerned a contested election for one of the eight seats assigned to Buckinghamshire in the first Parliament convened by James I, and the king's intervention on that occasion led to a tense confrontation between him and the Commons. See JHC, I, 149, 151, 156-66, 168-9, 171, 934, 937-44. See also *Parliamentary History of England*, v, 7, 11, 56-86. The lasting result of this case was that it greatly helped to establish beyond challenge the right of the Commons to be sole judges of the election of their members.

EDITOR'S NOTES

PARAGRAPH [206]

1 See George Petyt, p. 296, lines 15-20. Said Petyt: "11 *Nov.* 1640. It is declared, as a constant Order of the House, *That if a Witness be brought to the House, the House sitting, the Bar is to be down; otherwise, if the House be in a Committee.*" Italics are Petyt's. As for his source, Petyt cited "Id. 69.," that is, *Memorials* in *Hakewel*, p. 69. Scobell's wording corresponds verbatim to Petyt's, and Scobell found his in JHC, II, 26.

PARAGRAPH [207]

1 Transcribed almost verbatim in text and documentation from George Petyt, p. 296, lines 21-4. Petyt based his version of the passage upon Scobell's *Memorials*, p. 70, where Scobell made the following note: "18 *Jacobi*, Upon the Report from the Committee for Priviledges, touching Election for *Gatton*, Sir *Henry Brittain* being concerned, and offering to speak in his own Case; it was resolved upon long Debate, *he should be heard to inform the House, and then go forth.*" See also JHC, I, 512 (February 7, 1620).

PARAGRAPH [208]

1 A verbatim transcript of a passage and its documentation in George Petyt, p. 296-7. Petyt indicated that his source was Scobell's *Memorials*, p. 71. Had he chosen to do so, he could have added that he followed his source exactly, but that he omitted Scobell's final sixteen words, which cited cases in support of his doctrine.

PARAGRAPH [209]

1 For the source of this exact wording, see George Petyt, p. 297, lines 3-6. Petyt rightly indicated that he based his wording upon Townshend's *Historical Collections*, p. 311, but TJ, apparently missing that reference, while assuming that Petyt's preceding reference still applied, wrongly attributed the passage to "id. 71.," that is, to p. 71 of Scobell's *Memorials*. Petyt's wording, and of course TJ's as well, make the passage sound cryptic, unfinished, trivial. But in Townshend it is part of an episode of some interest to a student of British constitutional history. It seems that a conference between committees of the two Houses had been arranged for December 11, 1601, in the Painted Chamber, on a bill dealing with letters patent. The committee from the Commons numbered Secretary of State Robert Cecil among its members. When it arrived at the meeting place, the committee from the Lords had already taken seats at the conference table. Cecil opened the meeting by making a speech to the effect that, if the Lords had come with their course of action agreed upon advance, or if they had agreed in advance upon amendments or alternatives, then the committee from the Commons was not authorized to proceed further; but that, if the Lords had done neither, and were intent only upon conferring to resolve whatever doubts the bill may have given them, then the meeting could proceed. These words were in one sense merely a statement of the conventions governing any conference between Lords and Commons upon legislative matters; but as Cecil uttered them, they seemed to imply that the Lords were about to confer in bad faith. This unpleasant, perhaps unintended, imputation led Lord Buckhurst to enter into a whispered consultation with his colleagues on the Lords' committee, after which he made a speech himself in condemnation of the Commons for their apparent desire to dic-

tate the agenda of the conference, and of Cecil's speech for being strange, improper, and preposterous. Now it was the Commons who held a consultation, and when it was finished, Cecil spoke again. He denied that the three disparagements leveled against his earlier speech were applicable to it, and he went on to stress that the Lords and Commons were members of one body, each dependent upon the other for existence, while his earlier speech had been designed to carry out a constitutional function and to separate what could be discussed in a conference from what could not. After he finished, the Lords consulted together again, and then, through Lord Buckhurst, they expressed their satisfaction with what Cecil had just said. Thus did a tense confrontation between the two Houses ease into continued harmony. See D'Ewes, p. 679, cols. 1-2, for a similar account of this episode.

PARAGRAPH [210]

1 For this passage in the same wording that it has here, see George Petyt, p. 297, lines 7-11. Earlier in the work just cited, p. 95, lines 18-28, Petyt gave an almost identical version of this passage, and that version had become the text of TJ's 114th paragraph, above. The historical situation to which both of Petyt's passages refer is sketched above, par. 114, n. 1.

PARAGRAPH [211]

1 A word-for-word transcript of George Petyt, p. 297, lines 15-24.

2 This reference is of course to Townshend and D'Ewes, as in par. [210].

PARAGRAPH [212]

1 Transcribed verbatim from George Petyt, p. 298, lines 17-20.

2 Petyt documented this passage by noting that it came from "Id. 38.," and TJ interpreted the reference to mean p. 38 of what he called "Mem. in Hakew.," that is, Scobell's *Memorials*. But in fact TJ overlooked Petyt's other reference at that juncture to Rushworth, Part III, Vol. 1, p. 38 (not Vol. III, Part I, as Petyt misstated it), and those numbers direct the reader to the true source of the passage. Said Rushworth on that page under the date of November 9, 1640: "*Ordered*, That the General Order for those that are double returned, shall not bind Mr. *William Herbert*, now *Extra Regnum*." (The Latin phrase means "outside the kingdom.") Why Petyt left a black space for Herbert's name, when Rushworth did not, is odd. The "General Order" mentioned by Rushworth was a rule of the Commons that any member elected simultaneously from two or more constituencies had soon to decide which constituency he preferred to represent, and thereupon the House would order a new election in the vacated district or districts. See Scobell, *Memorials*, p. 18-19. In the parliamentary session which began November 3, 1640, the Commons, on an action taken November 6, ordered that all double returns be reported the following Monday, November 9; and on that day several double returns were announced. But, in view of William Herbert's absence from the country, he was excused from making his choice. See JHC, II, 20-2. That particular session began what came to be called the Long Parliament. On November 11, 1640, the Commons sent up to the Lords a message impeaching Thomas Wentworth, Earl of Strafford, of high treason, and in less than two years the Civil War broke out.

PARAGRAPH [213]

1 Transcribed verbatim from George Petyt, p. 299, lines 17-23. Petyt copied the passage word for word from Rushworth, Part III, Vol. 1, p. 66, but TJ, in line with the error in his previous paragraph, misconstrued the reference as being to Scobell's *Memorials*. November 28, 1640, was a Saturday, and the order recorded here was intended to guarantee that any Commoner whose full membership in the House had not yet been finally completed would nevertheless be able to attend services next day in St. Margaret's Church, the official church of the Commons, located just north of Westminster Abbey. Seats in that church were reserved each Sunday for members of the Commons, and four times a year the Commons attended it in state. On occasion they specified who the preacher was to be. See JHC, II, 38-9, 244. See also Hare, II, 427-35.

PARAGRAPH [214]

1 For this sentence exactly as it is worded here, see George Petyt, p. 300, lines 15-16.

2 This reference should properly designate Rushworth, Part III, Vol. 1, p. 392. Scobell's *Memorials*, to which TJ mistakenly assigned the paragraph, contains only 116 pages. And besides, the paragraph is fully sustained by an episode recounted by Rushworth on the page just indicated. That episode involved a speech by Sir Edward Deering (Dering), on October 21, 1641, questioning whether an order promulgated by the Commons on the preceding September 8 could be regarded as binding when it had not yet had the concurrence of the Lords, and when its own possible authority had been undermined by a subsequent resolution declaring the order temporarily optional.

PARAGRAPH [215]

1 Using the exact words of his source, while omitting certain elaborations and certain parallel details, TJ transcribed this important paragraph from George Petyt, p. 303 (lines 12-13, 21-32), 304 (lines 1-2). As his own documentation made amply clear, Petyt transcribed the paragraph in its full extent from what he himself called "The Commons Protestation in Vindication of their Privileges," as that famous document of December 18, 1621, appeared in Rapin-Thoyras, Vol. 2, No. 54, p. 211-12. Petyt printed the document in italics to indicate that the words were those of the Commons themselves. For the record of the action taken in passing the Protestation, see JHC, I, 668, where we are told that James I himself, in the presence of his Council, later tore the Protestation from the *Journal*. For a further reference to the Protestation, see *Manual* (1812), p. 23.

PARAGRAPH [216]

1 These two sentences were transcribed verbatim by TJ from George Petyt, p. 305, lines 17-18, 23-6, except that TJ added "Resolved" to the wording. Petyt indicated that his source, which he followed verbatim in the second but not in first sentence, was "*Journal Dom. Com.*," that is, JHC, XIII, 400-1. In that work the two sentences figured respectively as resolutions 6 and 8 of a report designed at William III's request to set forth guidelines governing the next succession to the crown of England. The report later became "An Act for the further Limita-

tion of the Crown; and better securing the Rights and Liberties of the Subject"; and under that title it was passed by the Commons on May 14, 1701. See JHC, XIII, 463, 465, 475, 487, 515, 524-5, 540.

2 This word, which TJ added on his own, was widely used in eighteenth-century Britain as a pejorative term. Perhaps "political stooges" would be a close modern equivalent. See OED.

PARAGRAPH [217]

1 For the verbatim text and documentation of this entire paragraph, see George Petyt, p. 306, lines 16-25. Petyt's wording closely but not exactly follows that in Townshend's *Historical Collections*, p. 209, except that Townshend identified the man who stood up as "One Mr. *Brown*, Clerk, Comptroller to the Queens Household."

2 That is, John Croke. See MacDonagh, p. 195-8.

3 For an earlier reference to this rule, see above, par. 144.

PARAGRAPH [218]

1 Transcribed word for word by TJ from George Petyt, p. 307, lines 1-4, and by Petyt from Edward Coke's *Reports in thirteen Parts*, Pt. 12, p. 115, except that Coke's text, in the 5th edition, at least, reads "does," not "doth." For further observations on the Speaker's conduct in reading bills, see above, par. 140, and below, par. [222].

2 TJ copied this reference from Petyt, who had mistakenly assigned the paragraph to "Cook 22.115." Coke's *Reports* has only thirteen major divisions.

PARAGRAPH [219]

1 Text and documentation transcribed by TJ from George Petyt, p. 307, lines 5-7, except that Petyt had "first passed" instead of "past." For the verbatim source of Petyt's text, see Hakewill's *Manner and Method*, p. 134.

PARAGRAPH [220]

1 TJ transcribed the exact text and documentation of this passage from George Petyt, p. 307, lines 8-21; and Petyt drew his text almost verbatim from Hakewill's *Manner and Method*, p. 134, except for the last clause, which came to Petyt from Townshend, p. 270. That clause figured in Townshend as a statement made by Sir Robert Wroth in Commons on December 1, 1601.

PARAGRAPH [221]

1 See George Petyt, p. 308, lines 5-17, for the exact text and documentation which TJ followed here, except that he put "directed" before rather than after "specially"; and see Hakewill, p. 136, for the text which Petyt used with slight modifications as his source.

PARAGRAPH [222]

1 For the verbatim text and documentation of the paragraph as given here by TJ, see George Petyt, p. 308 (lines 18-32), 309 (lines 1-2); and for Petyt's source, worded not quite as he himself had it, see Hakewill, p. 137.

2 At this point the manuscript contains two words, the first of which is a partly obliterated "sometimes" with an indistinct "93" superimposed upon it, and the second, a clearly legible "reading." For the source of these words, see George Petyt, p. 309, line 3. It evidently happened that TJ started to transcribe them as if they belonged with the passage just finished, and that he stopped short when he realized his mistake. As for the number superimposed upon the first of the two words, it can perhaps be said to be an abandoned designation for this paragraph, later numbered "91" in the margin to the left.

PARAGRAPH [223]

1 This paragraph and its documentation were transcribed almost word for word by TJ from George Petyt, p. 311, lines 7-14, and by Petyt with slight modifications from Hakewell, p. 141. See also Scobell's *Memorials*, p. 42-3.

PARAGRAPH [224]

1 As written here, this entire paragraph and its documentation were printed word for word as two consecutive paragraphs in George Petyt, p. 307, 308; and Petyt in turn transcribed the two paragraphs from Scobell's *Memorials*, p. 40, where they figure unchanged as the opening words of Ch. ix, entitled, "Publique Bills, and manner of Proceeding on them." In his last clause TJ originally wrote "their" and then, under the dictates of Petyt's text, drew a line to change the pronoun into the definite article.

PARAGRAPH [225]

1 TJ transcribed this sentence verbatim from George Petyt, p. 309, lines 28-31, and Petyt transcribed it almost verbatim from Townshend, p. 238. In the latter source, it figures as part of a speech by Sir Francis Bacon on Saturday, November 21, 1601, at an afternoon meeting of the Committee for Monopolies of the Commons. The committee was considering a bill to reform the abuses caused by royal grants of monopolies to various importers, manufacturers, and sellers of widely used commodities. Sir Francis believed that the best way to reform those abuses would be to petition the queen as the occasion might demand, but not to pass the proposed bill, which contained a proviso excluding grants to corporations. Of the proviso, Sir Francis spoke scornfully: "That is a gull to sweeten the Bill withall, it is only to make Fools Fond. All men of the Law know, that a Bill which is only Expository to Expound the Common-Law, doth Enact nothing, neither is any *Proviso* good therein." See also D'Ewes, p. 648, col. 1.

PARAGRAPH [226]

1 For the exact text and documentation of the sentence given here, see George Petyt, p. 311, lines 26-32. Petyt made two slight changes in wording, and omitted the citing of two relevant precedents, in transcribing what Hakewill had said on this matter. For further details concerning those precedents, see D'Ewes, p. 298, 302.

PARAGRAPH [227]

2 TJ reproduced the exact text and documentation of this passage by making use of George Petyt, p. 312, lines 1-3. Petyt's source was Hakewill, p. 142,

where the sole precedent supporting the action described in the passage was declared to have occurred in the first session of James I's first Parliament. On that occasion—the date was March 29, 1604/05—the Commons received a bill from the Lords, had it read three times, and adopted it, under the title, "An Act of a most joyful and just Recognition of the immediate, lawful, and undoubted Succession, Descent, and Right of the Crown." See JHC, I, 158, 938. To that sole precedent recorded by Hakewill, Petyt added another, which occurred on June 15, 1685, and involved the bill of attainder against James, Duke of Monmouth, for high treason. That bill was given three readings and adopted *nemine contradicente* in one day. The Duke, illegitimate son of Charles II, had landed four days earlier at Lyme Regis and was attempting to raise an army to drive James II from the throne, under the pretext that he wanted to free England from James' tyranny and from the alleged threat of Catholicism. See JHC, IX, 737.

PARAGRAPH [228]

1 This sentence and its documentation were transcribed verbatim by TJ from George Petyt, p. 312, lines 6-9, after D'Ewes, p. 90, col. 1, had furnished Petyt with a similar but enlarged account of the precedent mentioned here. Said D'Ewes under the date of March 30, 1563: "The Bill also for the School-House at *Guildford*, was read the fourth time, and passed the House. *Nota*, That here a Bill was read the fourth time, before it passed the House (having had its third reading on *Thursday* the 25th day of this instant *March* foregoing) of which, though there want not other Presidents, yet it is rare and worth the observation."

PARAGRAPH [229]

1 TJ followed George Petyt, p. 312, lines 10-13, in wording this sentence exactly as it stands here, and in citing D'Ewes, p. 335, col. 1, as its authority. According to the latter, the bill mentioned here provided for "a Bank of general Charity to be appointed for the relief of common necessity," and its unusual rejection upon the first reading occurred December 3, 1584.

PARAGRAPH [230]

1 For TJ's exact wording of this sentence and documentation, see George Petyt, p. 312, lines 14-17; and for the source of the wording upon which Petyt based his slightly modified version of the sentence, see D'Ewes, p. 337, col. 2. Petyt's other reference was to D'Ewes, p. 415, col. 2, which TJ mistranscribed in respect to its page number. These two references by Petyt pointed to instances in which bills had been sent back to committee upon third readings, after having been committed upon second readings; and in each instance D'Ewes had called the procedure unusual. The first instance was on Wednesday, December 9, 1584; the second, on March 15, 1586/87.

PARAGRAPH [231]

1 Transcribed verbatim by TJ in text and documentation from George Petyt, p. 312, lines 18-24, and by Petyt almost verbatim from Hakewill, p. 143, where it stands as the first paragraph of Section IV of that author's *Manner and Method*.

EDITOR'S NOTES

PARAGRAPH [232]

1 See George Petyt, p. 312-13, for the exact source of this wording and documentation; and for almost the same wording that Petyt used, see Hakewill, p. 143.

PARAGRAPH [233]

1 See George Petyt, p. 313, lines 6-10, for the exact source of this wording and documentation; and see Hakewill, p. 143-4, for the exact source of Petyt's wording, except that Hakewill wrote "for the engrossing thereof."

PARAGRAPH [234]

1 TJ transcribed this sentence and documentation word for word from George Petyt, p. 313, lines 11-14, but he did not follow Petyt in placing parentheses around "matter or." Petyt transcribed the sentence word for word from Hakewill, p. 144, lines 5-8, except that Petyt inserted "matter or" before "form" and then parenthesized the insertion. The purpose of his insertion was to make Hakewill's text conform on this point to its own later practice. See below, par. [235].

PARAGRAPH [235]

1 Transcribed verbatim by TJ in text and documentation from George Petyt, p. 313, lines 15-27. The clause enclosed in quotation marks in TJ's text is italicized in his source. Petyt's text was taken almost word for word from Hakewill, p. 144, where it figured as the continuation of a paragraph begun with the sentence given above by TJ as par. [234].

PARAGRAPH [236]

1 The text and documentation given here were taken verbatim by TJ from George Petyt, p. 313-14, except that TJ added "be" after "affirmative voice." As for Petyt, he transcribed the passage verbatim from Hakewill, p. 144-5, without having made the addition just noted. After "divided," Hakewill inserted twelve rather ambiguous words which Petyt omitted.

PARAGRAPH [237]

1 This sentence and the entire following paragraph were transcribed verbatim by TJ from three consecutive paragraphs of George Petyt, p. 314-15, except that TJ added to Petyt's documentation the two references to D'Ewes and Scobell. So far as Petyt was concerned, he derived his three paragraphs almost verbatim from Hakewill, p. 145-6, but he attached on his own the reference to Townshend's *Historical Collections*.

2 Petyt's reference to Townshend, and TJ's references to D'Ewes and Scobell, pointed to a parliamentary action which on November 11, 1601, ambivalently reaffirmed the doctrine that the opponent of a bill before the Commons could not serve on a committee appointed to consider that bill. The date just specified had witnessed a debate upon an act designed to shorten Michaelmas Term, and the debate had resulted in the passing of a motion to refer the act to a committee. At this point it was ruled that the committee must not contain any of the London burgesses, inasmuch as they had opposed the bill in the debate. The ruling was

at once warmly contested, with Sir Edward Hoby speaking to have it upheld, and Sir Robert Cecil, to have an exception made to it in this case, in view of its importance to the London burgesses. The contest ended in a delightful British compromise—the ruling against the London burgesses was reaffirmed, but a special resolution was then passed to allow an exception to be made to the rule on the present occasion. Thus did the Commons show that with a little caution they could have the best of both worlds. Perhaps the conspicuous successes of Britain as a political power in history owed something to its capacity for that kind of compromise, even as its conspicuous failures owed something to its opposite capacity.

PARAGRAPH [238]

1 Transcribed by TJ word for word in text and documentation from George Petyt, p. 315, lines 10-21, and by Petyt word for word from Hakewill, p. 146.

PARAGRAPH [239]

1 Transcribed by TJ word for word in text and documentation from George Petyt, p. 315, lines 22-31. Petyt's transcription of this same passage from Hakewill, p. 146-7, is word for word, with four minor exceptions.

PARAGRAPH [240]

1 Transcribed by TJ word for word in text and documentation from George Petyt, p. 316, lines 1-4, and by Petyt with not quite the same exactitude from Hakewill, p. 147.

PARAGRAPH [241]

1 Transcribed verbatim by TJ in text and documentation from George Petyt, p. 316, lines 5-13, and by Petyt verbatim from Hakewill, p. 148, except for the parenthetical phrase, which Petyt borrowed intact from Coke's *Reports in thirteen Parts*, Pt. 12, p. 116.

PARAGRAPH [242]

1 Transcribed verbatim by TJ in text and documentation from George Petyt, p. 316, lines 14-16, and by Petyt almost verbatim from Hakewill, p. 150. Petyt's reference to p. 250 is incorrect.

PARAGRAPH [243]

1 Transcribed verbatim by TJ in text and documentation from George Petyt, p. 316, lines 17-24, and by Petyt nearly verbatim from Hakewill, p. 150. Petyt's reference to p. 250 is again incorrect.

PARAGRAPH [244]

1 Transcribed verbatim by TJ in text and documentation from George Petyt, p. 316-17, except that TJ drops seven needless words from the beginning of Petyt's first sentence, and substitutes "on" for "upon" after "endorsed." As for Petyt's version of this passage, it has the seven words that TJ omitted, and it came verbatim from Hakewill, p. 150, except that Hakewill wrote "ingrossed" instead of "endorsed." Petyt's reference to p. 250 is once again incorrect.

PARAGRAPH [245]

1 Transcribed verbatim by TJ in text and documentation from George Petyt, p. 317, lines 3-10, except that TJ's spelling of "recommittment" differs from Petyt's. The similar passage, which Petyt copied almost verbatim from Hakewill, p. 151-2, called attention to actions in the Commons on April 30, 1607. Those actions involved a bill which *"was committed and reported, and Counsell heard at the bar."* "Whereupon it was recommitted," Hakewill went on, "and other Committees added who altered the former proceedings; and it was agreed that the former proceedings were waved, and the latter good." For further details, see JHC, I, 365.

PARAGRAPH [246]

1 Transcribed verbatim by TJ in text and documentation from George Petyt, p. 317, lines 11-15, except that TJ's contraction with a period in our text did not appear in his source. Petyt transcribed his passage nearly verbatim from Hakewill, p. 152.

PARAGRAPH [247]

1 Transcribed verbatim by TJ in text and documentation from George Petyt, p. 317, lines 16-32, and by Petyt almost verbatim from Hakewill, p. 152-3.

PARAGRAPH [248]

1 Transcribed with minor changes by TJ in text and documentation from George Petyt, p. 318, lines 1-6. Petyt wrote, "It hath at some times been order'd," and he placed a redundant "that" after "Voices, but in other respects his wording and TJ's are alike. As for Petyt, he inserted the redundancy on his own, and he placed "a" before "few Voices," while conforming otherwise to Hakewill, p. 153.

PARAGRAPH [249]

1 Transcribed verbatim by TJ in text and documentation from George Petyt, p. 318, lines 7-19, and by Petyt in text from Hakewill, p. 153-4.

PARAGRAPH [250]

1 Transcribed verbatim by TJ in text and documentation from George Petyt, p. 318, lines 20-5, except that TJ's manuscript seems only to suggest the probability of "&c." after "Yea." The "&c.," however, is in Petyt's text, which in this and all other respects exactly followed Hakewill's, p. 154.

PARAGRAPH [251]

1 Transcribed verbatim by TJ in text and documentation from George Petyt, p. 318, lines 26-30, and by Petyt from Hakewill, p. 154, except that Hakewill made "bill" plural and placed "accordingly" at the end of the last phrase.

PARAGRAPH [252]

1 Transcribed verbatim by TJ in text and documentation from George Petyt, p. 318-19, except that TJ omitted 1) the page number "119" from Petyt's reference to Brooke's *La Graunde Abridgement* and 2) the translations which Petyt

attached to the two Latin notations. Petyt worded those translations thus: "Let it be deliver'd to the Lords"; and "To this Bill the Commons have assented." Petyt based his text almost word for word upon Hakewill, p. 154, but his translations and his reference to Brooke owed nothing to that source.

2 TJ seems originally to have put this reference into the left-hand margin above and then to have reinserted it here, after having superimposed upon its earlier formulation a different phrase. At any rate, the marginal note given above to the left is almost illegible in the manuscript.

PARAGRAPH [253]

1 For the source upon which TJ based his own wording of this sentence and its documentation, see George Petyt, p. 319, lines 12-20. Petyt's lines were condensed and paraphrased from D'Ewes, p. 344, col. 2. According to D'Ewes, the Lords had on one occasion sent certain bills to the Commons and had had the Commons indignantly return them with the request that they be properly endorsed. After complying with this request, the Lords sent them back to the Commons through the good offices of "Mr Doctor *Ford* and Mr Doctor *Barkeley*." D'Ewes' next entry read thus: "*Nota*, That on *Saturday* the 19th day of *December* last past [1584] the House of Commons taking exceptions at this last mentioned matter about indorsing of Bills in the upper parts of them, whereas it ought to be done at the nether and lower part, the Lords did very respectively both then and now take away their said grievance by the alteration of the indorsements aforesaid according to the usual and ancient form." As for TJ's use of "neither" in locating the place where the endorsement is made, we should notice that it did not result from his carelessness in reading D'Ewes, but from his accuracy in reading Petyt.

PARAGRAPH [254]

1 Transcribed verbatim by TJ in text and documentation from George Petyt, p. 319, lines 21-6, and by Petyt from Hakewill, p. 156, except that Petyt dropped sixty-four words and slightly altered a phrase in making an otherwise accurate reproduction of his source. Petyt's omissions involved two parliamentary actions in which bills were altered after they had had a third reading and had become presumably immune to further change before the final vote. See JHC, I, 372-3; 397, 398, 409, 418, 424.

PARAGRAPH [255]

1 Transcribed verbatim by TJ in text and documentation from George Petyt, p. 320, lines 10-15, and by Petyt from Hakewill, p. 158.

PARAGRAPH [256]

1 Transcribed verbatim by TJ in text and documentation from George Petyt, p. 320, lines 16-23, except that Petyt wrote "the Bill for Sealing Clothes was half read," whereas TJ condensed the five opening words of that clause to "a bill." Petyt's text followed Hakewill's verbatim, except that, after "1. Eliz.," Hakewill added "24. Maii." For the sake of the record, however, Hakewill's date is incorrect. The bill for "Sealing Clothes" was half read on April 3, 1559, and thereupon the Commons adjourned to attend the conference in Westminster Abbey. See JHC, I, 59; see also D'Ewes, p. 53, col. 1.

[236]

1 Transcribed verbatim by TJ in text and documentation from George Petyt, p. 320, lines 24-7 and by Petyt from Hakewill, p. 158, except that Hakewill did not authorize Petyt's "&c." To the passage as given by Petyt and TJ, Hakewill added, "as it was done in the Bill *to avoid Aliens not being here for Religion*, I Eliz. 23. Jan." Hakewill's identification of the bill just mentioned was correctly stated in its title as he gave it, but not in the date. That particular bill had its first reading on January 18, 1562/63 (Elizabeth I's fifth year), and after its second reading on January 23, it was rejected and torn. See JHC, I, 63; see also D'Ewes, p. 80, col. 1.

1 Transcribed verbatim by TJ in text and documentation from George Petyt, p. 320, lines 28-30, and by Petyt from Hakewill, p. 159.

1 For similar wording in another connection, see above, par. [247].

2 This entire paragraph was transcribed verbatim by TJ from George Petyt, p. 321, lines 1-31, except that TJ dropped out six of Petyt's needless words, changed the word order in one of Petyt's clauses, and converted from a present to a perfect participle one of Petyt's verbs. TJ's paragraph, which in Petyt occupied a full page divided into three paragraphs, spaced its three references to Hakewill at the points where Petyt's paragraphs ended. Petyt's text is a verbatim transcript of six consecutive paragraphs in Hakewill, p. 175-6, with three unimportant exceptions, not one of which coincides with TJ's above-mentioned changes in Petyt.

1 That is, three bows. *Congy* (later *congee*), a word of Latin origin, means in one of its senses, a bow given in leave-taking or in greeting.

2 TJ transcribed this paragraph verbatim from George Petyt, p. 322, lines 1-12; and Petyt transcribed it with minor variations of wording from Hakewill, p. 176-7. Petyt italicized the opening announcement by the messenger to the Commons, and, since those italics end with the words, "certain bills," it is to be assumed that TJ would have closed his own quotation marks at that point, and that he failed to do so only because he forgot. At any rate, he left that quotation unclosed in his manuscript, as the present text also does. Then, too, at the end of this paragraph and the next, TJ, against his almost invariable practice, omitted Petyt's citation of Hakewill as the authority on the matters being discussed. There is no need, however, to construe this particular omission as forgetfulness on his part. He would no doubt have assumed that his references to Hakewill in the preceding and the following paragraphs would suffice for his own guidance if he wanted to identify the source of the materials here being presented. Beyond that he would not expect himself to have to go. After all, he was not preparing the Pocket-Book for the public but for himself.

PARAGRAPH [261]

1 Transcribed verbatim by TJ in text and documentation from George Petyt, p. 322, lines 13-31, except that TJ dropped out Petyt's phrase identifying the clerk of the crown as an attendant of the Upper House. Petyt transcribed this entire passage not quite verbatim from Hakewill, p. 177-8.

PARAGRAPH [262]

1 TJ added eight words, and omitted one, in transcribing the text and documentation of this sentence from George Petyt, p. 322-3. Petyt had begun the sentence with the phrase, "When they," after having opened the preceding sentence with "Bills." To TJ the pronoun in Petyt's first words must have seemed ambiguous. At any rate, he wrote "bills" into his text at that point, and then, perceiving, no doubt, the illogic in his own construction, he crossed out his word and substituted for it eight other words, so as to identify Petyt's "they" beyond question. As for the word which TJ omitted from Petyt, it was the pronoun "his" before "hands." On Petyt's side, he transcribed the whole sentence verbatim, ambiguity and all else, from Hakewill, p. 178.

PARAGRAPH [263]

1 Except for his rearrangement of the units in the date, TJ transcribed this sentence verbatim in text and documentation from George Petyt, p. 324, lines 5-9. And Petyt transcribed it verbatim from Townshend's *Historical Collections*, p. 127, after having deleted its one definite article and assembled its date from scattered indications in its source.

PARAGRAPH [264]

1 Transcribed verbatim by TJ in text and documentation from George Petyt, p. 325, lines 4-5, except that Petyt has "never" where TJ has "not."

2 Although this reference was placed by Petyt so as to invite the assumption that it might belong where TJ originally put it, it has in fact nothing to do with private acts being filed but not enrolled. See *Arcana Parliamentaria*, p. 45. Thus TJ was right to have canceled it.

3 In Petyt this reference stood unambiguously as the source of the sentence transcribed here by TJ, and to Petyt that source was Atkyns' *Argument*, p. 57, as TJ duly noted. Actually, however, Petyt cited the incorrect source. He should have cited Atkyns' *Power, Jurisdiction, and Privilege of Parliament*, where Atkyns spoke thus of a bill passed in the time of Henry VIII: "And this Act of 4 H. 8. is enrolled as general Acts use to be. But a private or particular Act is always filed, but never enrolled." See Atkyns, *Tracts*, p. 111.

PARAGRAPH [265]

1 TJ transcribed this sentence verbatim in text and documentation from George Petyt, p. 325, lines 6-11, except that his last three words of text stand for Petyt's clause, "when it shall commence." Petyt transcribed the passage almost verbatim from *Arcana Parliamentaria*, p. 45, except that he omitted some thirty words of historical comment designed to trace back to Henry VI's reign the practice of not mentioning the day when a bill was introduced into Parliament.

PARAGRAPH [266]

1 TJ transcribed this sentence verbatim in text and documentation from George Petyt, p. 325, lines 12-17, and Petyt transcribed it verbatim from Scobell's *Memorials*, p. 41, except that Scobell had "the same" rather than "it" at the beginning of the first main clause.

PARAGRAPH [267]

1 Transcribed verbatim by TJ in text and documentation from George Petyt, p. 325, lines 18-19, and by Petyt from Scobell's *Memorials*, p. 42, lines 9-10, except that Scobell wrote "no Member" as subject of the main clause.

PARAGRAPH [268]

1 This sentence was transcribed verbatim by TJ in text and documentation from George Petyt, p. 325, lines 25-30, except that Petyt put "are to" before "carry." Petyt adapted the sentence in part verbatim and in part by paraphrase from Townshend's account of an action of the Lords on Nov. 21, 1601, in dividing equally upon the question whether a bill for the assurance of lands, having been read a third time and engrossed, should be recommitted for certain improvements before it was put to a final vote. In any division of their House, the Lords allowed the Speaker to vote, and thus he necessarily could have no part in breaking a tie. What the Lords did in case of a tie was to dispose of it by invoking the old rule of law that an equally divided vote was always presumed to be negative (*semper presumetur pro negante*). See Townshend's *Historical Collections*, p. 134. See also D'Ewes, p. 605, col. 2.

2 This reference and a paraphrase of the principle which it here supports are in TJ's *Manual* (1801), Sec. XLI. See also the *Manual* (1812), p. 137.

3 TJ's bracketed observation was quite obviously meant as a reminder to himself that the Commons, whether in full session or in committees, did not allow an equally divided vote to stand legally as a negation without further action on their part. Their way of dealing with an equal division was to prohibit their Speakers or presiding officers from voting upon questions except for the purpose of breaking a tie. Thus their final decisions were always by majority vote one way or the other, and ultimate responsibility for the action rested with them, not with a face-saving convention. See George Petyt, p. 276 (lines 7-10), 342 (lines 11-13). See also Scobell's *Memorials*, p. 27, 38; and Hatsell (1818), II, 244-5.

PARAGRAPH [269]

1 This entire paragraph was transcribed verbatim in text and documentation by TJ from George Petyt, p. 325-6, except that TJ inserted "to" before "give" in the last main clause, no doubt to make that infinitive stand forcefully in parallel structure against its earlier counterpart, "to offer." Petyt transcribed the paragraph nearly verbatim from Scobell's *Memorials*, p. 44-5. The important point behind the somewhat technical concepts in this paragraph is that votes for or against piecemeal provisions of a bill on its way to assuming the form needed for final passage or rejection are not to be construed as binding upon members when they vote at last upon the fate of the bill as a whole. In other words, readying a bill for final consideration is one thing, and voting upon it in its final wording is another; and voting behavior during the first process does not impose the same

[239]

behavior during the second. Without such a principle to guide it, deliberation itself would be unable to change minds or to avoid ending in sterile inflexibility.

PARAGRAPH [270]

1 Text and documentation transcribed exactly from George Petyt, p. 326, lines 12-21, except for TJ's omission of "any" before "more than once that day." Petyt's own passage was transcribed verbatim, except for one omission, two substitute wordings, and one addition, from Scobell's *Memorials*, p. 45 (not p. 58, as Petyt mistakenly had it).

PARAGRAPH [271]

1 The text and documentation of this part of TJ's passage was transcribed verbatim from George Petyt, p. 326, lines 26-8, except that Petyt opened the passage with "Note." Petyt drew the facts behind his first sentence from Burnet's *History of the Reformation*, I, 144, where an account is given of a bill which, having provided for the discharge of all English subjects from allegiance to Rome, was read four times in the Lords between March 13 and 20, 1534/35, whereupon "it passed without any protestation." The bill had been sent up from the Commons on March 9. Petyt's query was obviously intended to suggest to himself an area for further research. For details concerning the fourth reading of bills before the Commons, see above, par. [228]. See also D'Ewes, p. 90, col. 1.

2 Petyt's query may well have led TJ to do some research of his own upon the attitude of Parliament toward four or more readings. At any rate, without prompting from Petyt, he called to mind Elsynge's *Method of Passing Bills*, p. 31, where there was a statement that the Lords, in the sixth year of Henry VIII, not having agreed upon a bill after its third reading, requested it to be "read again the fourth Time, yea, and the sixth and seventh Times, and at last . . . [they] appointed a new Bill to be drawn." For the text of this statement, see *The Harleian Miscellany*, v, 217.

PARAGRAPH [272]

1 TJ transcribed this sentence in text and documentation from George Petyt, p. 327, lines 8-13, being careful to follow Petyt's wording exactly, except for his having preferred "either house" to Petyt's thirteen-word enumeration of the units within that two-word phrase. As for Petyt, he transcribed his sentence almost verbatim from Smith's *Common-wealth of England*, p. 75 (p. 38 of the 1612 edition).

2 The text and documentation of this sentence were transcribed verbatim by TJ from George Petyt, p. 330, lines 3-6. On his side, Petyt transcribed its text verbatim from Scobell's *Memorials*, p. 44. In the latter work, this sentence immediately precedes that given above in par. [269].

PARAGRAPH [273]

1 Transcribed verbatim by TJ in text and documentation from George Petyt, p. 328, lines 19, 24-9, and by Petyt in text from Townshend's *Historical Collections*, p. 190. Petyt incorrectly attributed this sentence to D'Ewes, p. 190, col. 1. Had it fallen anywhere in D'Ewes, it would have appeared upon p. 626-8 of that work, where the events of November 5, 1601, are enumerated.

EDITOR'S NOTES

PARAGRAPH [274]

1 For this exact sentence and its documentation, see George Petyt, p. 331, lines 19-22; for the identical sentence without documentation, see Scobell's *Memorials*, p. 47-8. Petyt and Scobell wrote "then" for TJ's "than."

PARAGRAPH [275]

1 TJ transcribed these two sentences verbatim in text and documentation from George Petyt, p. 331 (lines 23, 28-31), 332 (lines 9-10), and Petyt took their text verbatim from Scobell's *Memorials*, p. 48, lines 4, 9-11, 24-5. Petyt wrote the date "12 *April*, 1604," and Scobell, "12° *Aprilis*, 1604." For the original order governing the quorum of a committee, see JHC, I, 169.

PARAGRAPH [276]

1 This sentence of twenty-eight words stands for a sentence of forty-two words in George Petyt, p. 331, lines 1-6. TJ was careful to preserve in his shortened version a form of the reference that Petyt more heavily abbreviated in marking his own source. Petyt's longer version is a nearly exact transcription of a sentence in Scobell's *Memorials*, p. 46-7, where no source was mentioned.

PARAGRAPH [277]

1 TJ transcribed here almost verbatim in text and documentation the words which he had omitted in forming the twenty-eight-word sentence annotated immediately above (par. [276]). His source was George Petyt, p. 331, lines 4-6, and Petyt's source was Scobell's *Memorials*, p. 47, lines 3-6.

PARAGRAPH [278]

1 Exactly transcribed by TJ in text and documentation from George Petyt, p. 332, lines 15-18. Petyt took his version word for word from Scobell's *Memorials*, p. 49, lines 21-4, except that he wrote "not to give his Vote" as a substitute for Scobell's "not to have any Vote."

PARAGRAPH [279]

1 Exactly transcribed by TJ in text and documentation from George Petyt, p. 330, lines 7-11. Petyt's version was closely but not exactly made up from a sentence in Scobell's *Memorials*, p. 45-6. That is, Petyt edited and changed the text of his source by adding three words at one point, by changing a connective at another point, and by deleting two needless words elsewhere.

PARAGRAPH [280]

1 Transcribed verbatim by TJ in text and documentation from George Petyt, p. 330, lines 17-21, except for TJ's omission of "as" before the date. Petyt transcribed the passage verbatim from Scobell's *Memorials*, p. 46, lines 8-12, except for his substituting "the" for "a" before "2nd reading."

2 Having noted this date, Scobell and Petyt added thirteen words which pointed to a motion passed that day in Commons. TJ failed to add those words, and thus he deprived the date of its context. See JHC, I, 994. The omitted words merely recommended that various provisos offered for a certain bill be referred to its committee.

PARAGRAPH [281]

1 Transcribed verbatim by TJ in text and documentation from George Petyt, p. 328, lines 1-5, except that TJ, by omitting two needless words, restored the true subject and true verb of the main clause to their primary function in the sentence, as Petyt had not done. Petyt transcribed his sentence verbatim from D'Ewes, p. 186, col. 2.

PARAGRAPH [282]

1 Transcribed verbatim by TJ in text and documentation from George Petyt, p. 328, lines 15-18, except that TJ omitted two words before and two after "held" and changed the order of units in the date. Petyt transcribed the passage verbatim from the pages indicated in Townshend and D'Ewes. The passage had to do with an occurrence in the Commons on February 27, 1592/93, during the speakership of Sir Edward Coke. A bill introduced that day by Mr. Morrice occasioned a debate before it had been given a first reading. Taking formal notice that the bill could not be assigned to a committee if it had not been read, the Commons heeded the Speaker's request and assigned the bill to him, the practice being that he could be allowed time to consider it before a first reading was decided upon. See above, pars. [221], [222].

PARAGRAPH [283]

1 Transcribed by TJ without change in text or documentation from George Petyt, p. 327, lines 14-21, and by Petyt with minor changes from Rushworth, I, 557. The passage came ultimately from a speech by Sir John Eliot in the Commons on May 6, 1628. The Commons in committee of the whole were debating that day whether on the one hand to trust Charles I's promise that he would henceforth govern according to the laws and customs of the realm or on the other to declare their own understanding of the liberties which his subjects expected the king to observe in exercising his prerogatives. Speaking for Charles I, Secretary of State Cook urged reliance upon the king's promise rather than upon a bill adopted in Commons, and he also urged that the issue be debated in regular session, not in committee of the whole. At this point Sir John Eliot uttered the words recorded in TJ's paragraph, and his advocacy of proceeding in committee of the whole carried the day. Thus his speech was not mentioned in the Journals of the Commons—proceedings of such committees never are—but it was recorded by Rushworth, whose great contribution consists in his having preserved parliamentary items of that kind. As a result of immediate deliberations following Sir John's speech, the Commons completed on May 8, 1628, the document which they called the Petition of Right (Rushworth, I, 558); and it contained a statement of their own understanding of their liberties under the king. Charles I approved of this document on the following June 7. It ranks with Magna Carta and the later Bill of Rights as a great step toward bringing the royal prerogatives in Britain under parliamentary control.

PARAGRAPH [284]

1 Transcribed verbatim by TJ in text and documentation from George Petyt, p. 330, lines 12-16, except that TJ's three-word opening phrase is a condensation of twelve words in his source. Petyt drew his passage verbatim from Townshend's *Historical Collections*, p. 138, except that Townshend's opening phrase

consists of eighteen words, not twelve. Townshend drew his passage from the records of the House of Lords. See D'Ewes, p. 610, col. 2. The passage means that, when a bill had been given a second reading in the whole house, it could then be delivered to any one member of the committee designated to consider it. In other words, it need not be delivered to the first member, although, upon appointment, persons assigned to a committee for a specific bill were designated members in numerical sequence, as if to establish their priority in later procedural matters.

PARAGRAPH [285]

1 See George Petyt, p. 330, lines 25-30, for the exact source of TJ's passage and its documentation. For Petyt's source, see Scobell's *Memorials*, p. 46. The parliamentary actions on which the passage is based occurred on February 25, 1623/24, as Scobell indicated in a passage somewhat longer than Petyt's. See also JHC, I, 673, col. 2.

PARAGRAPH [286]

1 Transcribed verbatim by TJ in text and documentation from George Petyt, p. 332, lines 11-14, except that TJ made a conspicuous grammatical improvement by substituting "bring back the bill" for Petyt's "bring it back." As for Petyt, he transcribed his passage verbatim from Scobell's *Memorials*, p. 48, except that he added "to prepare and" before Scobell's "bring," thus enriching the context of the latter word.

PARAGRAPH [287]

1 Transcribed verbatim by TJ in text and documentation from George Petyt, p. 336, lines 1-5, except that TJ rearranged the units in the date and put into English the Latin word for the month. Petyt's text exactly reproduced that in Scobell's *Memorials*, p. 39, except for Petyt's substitution of "Votes" for "Vote." Scobell's passage ultimately came from the following record in JHC, II, 227:

> The Petition of *Theophilus Man* read; touching the Resolution of the Committee where Mr. *King* hath the Chair, and signed by him, whereby Mr. *Man* is voted not to take any Fees by virtue of his Office as Searcher, till further Order &c.
> Declared by the House, that no Committe ought, by Vote, to determine the Right and Property of the Subject without first acquainting the House therewith.

PARAGRAPH [288]

1 Transcribed verbatim by TJ in text and documentation from George Petyt, p. 336, lines 6-10, and by Petyt in text from Scobell's *Memorials*, p. 39, except that Petyt omitted "*in* Westminster-Hall" after Scobell's "*any Court of Justice.*" For Scobell's source, see JHC, II, 240, col. 2.

PARAGRAPH [289]

1 Transcribed verbatim by TJ in text and documentation from George Petyt, p. 327, lines 1-7, and by Petyt nearly verbatim from Rushworth, as indicated. The admonition stated in TJ's paragraph came from a protest by Charles I against an ordinance of the Lords and Commons on November 29, 1642, giving

nine specified men authority to appoint a six-member committee in each London ward to collect from each of its citizens a tax of 20 percent of the value of his estate for the support of the parliamentary army being raised to resist Charles I's gathering forces. Each six-man committee was to enforce its assessments without having to get higher authority. Charles I's full protest expressed his concern not only that Parliament should be delegating to committees a power legally belonging only to itself, but also that committees thus empowered could raise money for a parliamentary army without having to get the king's assent as well as that of the Lords and Commons. Moreover, the full protest expressed Charles I's conviction that the king's presence in any act of government would do more than could any other influence to protect the lives, liberties, and estates of all the people of England. Six-member committees unchecked by the king and by Parliament would inevitably become in Charles I's calculation instruments of tyranny and oppression.

PARAGRAPH [290]

1 Transcribed word for word by TJ in text and documentation from George Petyt, p. 332, lines 19-26, except that TJ rearranged the units in the date and left unclosed the quotation marks that he opened to mark Petyt's use of italics. Petyt adapted his version of the passage from D'Ewes, as indicated, noting that the rule was styled "an Order" by the Speaker at a time when the Commons were meeting in committee of the whole, and the Speaker by custom was not in the chair himself, even though he was allowed in that situation to give parliamentary advice.

PARAGRAPH [291]

1 Transcribed verbatim by TJ in the text and in the reference to D'Ewes from George Petyt, p. 328-9; and adapted by Petyt from D'Ewes and Townshend's *Historical Collections*, p. 198. Although TJ did not follow Petyt by citing Townshend, he did something more up-to-date—he cited Hatsell (1785), II, 77. For this citation in a more recent edition, see Hatsell (1818), II, 107, n.

PARAGRAPH [292]

1 Transcribed verbatim by TJ in text and documentation from George Petyt, p. 332 (lines 27-32), 333 (lines 1-3), and by Petyt in text from Scobell's *Memorials*, pp. 49-50, except that Petyt made two slight changes in Scobell's word order.

PARAGRAPH [293]

1 Transcribed verbatim by TJ in text and documentation from George Petyt, p. 333, lines 4-10, and nearly verbatim by Petyt from Scobell's *Memorials*, p. 50.

PARAGRAPH [294]

1 TJ transcribed this sentence word for word from George Petyt, p. 333-4, except that he made two changes: 1) he omitted Petyt's two references to sources; 2) and he rearranged and modernized the units of the date. Petyt drew the sentence from Scobell's *Memorials*, p. 50-1, and JHC, I, 379. Scobell himself cited only the latter source.

EDITOR'S NOTES

PARAGRAPH [295]

1 Transcribed verbatim by TJ in text and documentation from George Petyt, p. 334, lines 13-17, except for TJ's omission of two introductory words before "Ordered." The quotation which TJ opened but did not close was printed by Petyt in italics. Petyt transcribed the sentence verbatim from Scobell's *Memorials*, even as he modified its wording in three insignificant ways. For its official text, see JHC, I, 346.

PARAGRAPH [296]

1 This order and its documentation TJ transcribed verbatim from George Petyt, p. 328, lines 6-14, except that he omitted after the date the following statement: "In the Afternoon, it being a considerable Time before there were forty Members to make a House." Petyt slightly altered the introductory wording of the order in transcribing it from Nalson's *Impartial Collection*, II, 319. See also JHC, II, 191, under June 28, 1641.

PARAGRAPH [297]

1 Transcribed verbatim by TJ in text and documentation from George Petyt, p. 333, lines 11-19, and by Petyt nearly verbatim from Scobell's *Memorials*, p. 50.

PARAGRAPH [298]

1 Transcribed verbatim by TJ in text and documentation from George Petyt, p. 334, lines 4-12, except that TJ's underscoring was not in his source. Petyt transcribed his text verbatim from Scobell's *Memorials*, p. 51, except for his inserting "he of the Members" in place of Scobell's "one of the Members."

PARAGRAPH [299]

1 The text and documentation of this paragraph were drawn verbatim by TJ from George Petyt, p. 334, lines 18-22; and the text was drawn verbatim by Petyt from Scobell's *Memorials*, p. 51.

PARAGRAPH [300]

1 This entire passage and its documentation were transcribed verbatim by TJ from two separate paragraphs in George Petyt, p. 334 (lines 23-32), and 335 (lines 1-10, 27-31), except that TJ Englished Petyt's date, added a definite article before one of Petyt's nouns, and used a comma instead of a round bracket to indicate the opening of Petyt's first parenthesis. Petyt transcribed almost verbatim in text the first of his paragraphs from Scobell's *Memorials*, p. 51-2, and the second from the same source, p. 39, where Scobell dated the rule "4 *Junii*, 1607." See JHC, I, 379. Petyt must have intended the Hakewill reference to support the substance, not the wording, of the first paragraph.

PARAGRAPH [301]

1 Transcribed verbatim in text and documentation from George Petyt, p. 328, lines 19-23, except that TJ not only rearranged the units of Petyt's date but also indicated by incomplete quotation marks what his source had printed in italics. As for Petyt's reference to Dewes, it is incorrect in this case. Petyt should have

referred to D'Ewes, p. 626, col, 2, or, more exactly, to Townshend's *Historical Collections*, p. 189.

PARAGRAPH [302]

1 Transcribed verbatim by TJ in text and documentation from George Petyt, p. 333, lines 20-7, except that TJ changed the order of units in the date, put "read" before "first," and added the marks of emphasis. Petyt's transcription exactly followed the text in Scobell's *Memorials*, p. 52, except for Petyt's having dropped Scobell's "the" after "then." The parliamentary practice recorded in this paragraph was made into a rule of order as the result of a recommendation to the Commons by Sir Francis Bacon on the date indicated. According to JHC, I, 379, Bacon, as reporter for the committee considering the bill "For the Continuance and Preservation of the blessed Union," said that the committee would propose many alterations to the original proposal, and that in "a Matter of such Weight and Consequence, it might well enough stand with Order" for "the whole Bill to be read first, as it is, and then the Alterations by themselves."

PARAGRAPH [303]

1 Transcribed verbatim by TJ in text and documentation from George Petyt, p. 335, lines 11-16, except that TJ omitted "of" after "reading." These lines in Petyt conform to an identical passage in Scobell's *Memorials*, p. 52, except that in the latter text "reading" is preceded by "such." Scobell added that, when amendments are considered and voted on, one by one, in a matter of importance, a member may speak on each of them.

PARAGRAPH [304]

1 For TJ's exact passage and its documentation, see George Petyt, p. 335, lines 17-19. For Petyt's exact source, see Scobell's *Memorials*, p. 53.

PARAGRAPH [305]

1 Transcribed verbatim by TJ in text and documentation from George Petyt, p. 329, lines 24-8, except that Petyt indicated the date by "*Eodem*," and TJ by the referent of that word on Petyt's preceding page. Petyt was quite correct in specifying his source as Townshend's *Historical Collections*, p. 208, but he should have cited as his secondary source D'Ewes, p. 634, col. 2, not p. 135, col. 1.

2 For what TJ correctly called the "same order," see George Petyt, p. 329 (lines 29-32), p. 330 (lines 1-2). For the text of this order, Petyt gave the two references that TJ noted here: Scobell's *Memorials*, p. 60-1, and "Towns. Col.," that is, Townshend's *Historical Collections*.

PARAGRAPH [306]

1 This rule and its documentation were transcribed by TJ from George Petyt, p. 335, lines 20-2. Petyt's reference to D'Ewes involved an episode in which the Commons on December 20, 1597, received one of their own engrossed bills from the Lords with the latter's amendments and endorsement written in parchment, not in paper, against "the Ancient and usual Order of the Parliament in both Houses." On this occasion the Commons protested the violation of preced-

ent and returned the offending bill to the Lords. It turned out that the Lords had not intended to break the rule. Their new clerk, Thomas Smith, had broken the rule inadvertently. And so this minor crisis ended in a tacit agreement by both parties that the ancient practice, which is stated in TJ's paragraph, was still in force. See D'Ewes, p. 573-7.

PARAGRAPH [307]

1 Transcribed verbatim by TJ in text and documentation from George Petyt, p. 335, lines 23-6. Petyt's text was taken verbatim from Scobell's *Memorials*, p. 53, except that Petyt dropped three of the five opening words in that source.

PARAGRAPH [308]

1 TJ's exact transcription of the text and documentation of George Petyt, p. 336 (lines 14-22), 337 (lines 1-6). This paragraph in Petyt constitutes the opening words of his chapter entitled *"The Order and Power of Grand Committees."* TJ evidently wrote "house" at first, and then struck it out, after noticing that it did not appear at that point in his source. Petyt transcribed his text almost verbatim from Scobell's *Memorials*, p. 35, making only two slight changes in wording. It should be noted that TJ's text contains those changes.

PARAGRAPH [309]

1 Transcribed verbatim by TJ in text and documentation from George Petyt, p. 337, lines 7-17. Petyt's text is a verbatim transcription of a large part of a paragraph in Scobell's *Memorials*, p. 49, except that Scobell inserted two unimportant words that Petyt dropped.

PARAGRAPH [310]

1 This paragraph and its documentation were transcribed verbatim by TJ from George Petyt, p. 341, lines 1-8.

2 The parliamentary events shadowed forth in this paragraph occurred in late March 1625/26, during the second Parliament of Charles I. At the beginning of that Parliament the king and the Commons were not on good terms, thanks to Charles' previous arbitrary conduct and to the disastrous failure of his favorite, the Duke of Buckingham, in the expedition against Cadiz the preceding year. On March 27 the Commons voted in favor of various subsidies to Charles, but they said openly that those actions would become final only after Charles had heard and responded to their grievances. Charles summoned the two houses to a joint meeting on March 29, and at that time, after thanking the Lords for their support, and after causing the lord keeper to enumerate the offenses that the Commons had committed, he ended by threatening to do without Parliament altogether, if the Commons held to their present course. Next day the Commons met to consider what the king and lord keeper had said, and it was at this meeting that they passed the resolution contained in TJ's paragraph. According to their journals, they asserted at that time that the committee of the whole would have "Power to call for the Key, to keep any from going out from the Committee, without Leave." See JHC, I, 843. See also Rushworth, 221-5. Petyt drew his text verbatim from the latter source, p. 225.

PARAGRAPH [311]

1 Transcribed verbatim by TJ in text and documentation from George Petyt, p. 337, lines 24-32, and by Petyt verbatim from Scobell's *Memorials*, p. 36-7, except that Petyt deleted eighteen of Scobell's words and changed one of them from "his" to "the."

PARAGRAPH [312]

1 Transcribed verbatim by TJ in text and documentation from two consecutive paragraphs in George Petyt, p. 338, lines 1-5, 6-12. Petyt drew his text from Scobell's *Memorials*, but he erred in placing it on p. 36, the correct page being 37. Scobell's text differs from Petyt's in two matters of wording: 1) Scobell, whose *Memorials* appeared first in 1656, did not know that there would be a second James, and hence he wrote "19 Jacobi," which Petyt changed to "19 *Jac.* 1"; 2) Scobell's parenthetical phrase reads "who was one of the persons named." For the episode involving Sir Edward Coke, see JHC, I, 650.

PARAGRAPH [313]

1 Exactly transcribed by TJ in text and documentation from George Petyt, p. 338, lines 13-16, and by Petyt in text from Scobell's *Memorials*, p. 37.

PARAGRAPH [314]

1 See above, par. [192], where this practice is also mentioned.

2 See above, par. [194], where this rule is stated as it applies to the whole house. For the practice of the Lords in this matter, see above, par. [268], nn. 1, 3.

3 This paragraph was transcribed verbatim by TJ in text and documentation from George Petyt, p. 338-9. Petyt drew his text from Scobell's *Memorials*, p. 37-8, deleting a total of fifteen words from his source, reducing two of Scobell's words to one, changing a plural noun to a singular, and substituting a definite for an indefinite article.

PARAGRAPH [315]

1 Transcribed verbatim by TJ in text and documentation from George Petyt, p. 339, lines 17-23. In turn, Petyt's text conforms exactly to a paragraph in Scobell's *Memorials*, p. 38.

PARAGRAPH [316]

1 Transcribed verbatim by TJ in text and documentation from George Petyt, p. 339, lines 3-16, except that TJ silently corrected Petyt's omission of "it" before "be then adjourned" and substituted "had" for "hath" before "been resolved." Petyt's transcription of this paragraph from Scobell's *Memorials*, p. 38, is fully accurate, except that Scobell's text contains the pronoun that Petyt omitted by editorial inadvertence.

PARAGRAPH [317]

1 Transcribed verbatim by TJ in text and documentation from George Petyt, p. 339, lines 29-31, and by Petyt in text from Scobell's *Memorials*, p. 39, except that Scobell wrote "then as aforesaid" after "things."

PARAGRAPH [318]

1 Transcribed verbatim by TJ in text and documentation from George Petyt, p. 337, lines 18-23, except that Petyt made "papers" singular. Petyt drew his paragraph verbatim from Scobell's *Memorials*, p. 35, except that he omitted Scobell's opening "But," and he inserted "Persons, Paper, and" before "Records." As for Scobell, he acknowledged his authority to be parliamentary motions in the 21st year of James I. See JHC, I, 719, 769.

PARAGRAPH [319]

1 Transcribed verbatim by TJ in text and documentation from George Petyt, p. 340, lines 9-15, except that TJ anglicized the word for the month and changed the spelling of two of Petyt's nouns. Petyt's text exactly duplicated that in Scobell's *Memorials*, p. 36, except that Scobell wrote "*Jacobi*" instead of "*Jac. I*" and closed his sentence with the words "*to be sent for them.*" For the parliamentary episode behind TJ's paragraph, see JHC, I, 704, where the Commons ordered the serjeant at arms to bring in a Mr. Wood, a Mr. Withers, and several others, who had ignored requests by the grievances committee to appear with their patents. A patent was a document issued by the king for the purpose of conferring upon some person or persons some right or privilege. Mr. Wood's patent was for "Printing of Briefs, and other Things, on one Side." Failure to adhere to the terms of his patent rendered the patentee liable to the kind of summons mentioned above and to subsequent punitive action.

PARAGRAPH [320]

1 This order was transcribed verbatim by TJ in text and documentation from George Petyt, p. 340, lines 25-31, except that TJ anglicized the word for the month and did not close the parentheses at the end of the first clause. Petyt's text exactly followed that in Scobell's *Memorials*, p. 36, except that Scobell treated the dates by saying "8. *Martii* and 13. *Martii* in the same Parliament." See JHC, I, 686, (March 13, 1623/24), for the source of Scobell's text.

PARAGRAPH [321]

1 The two sentences in this paragraph were transcribed verbatim by TJ in text and documentation from George Petyt, p. 340, lines 19-24, 16-18, except that TJ reversed the order in which Petyt presented them, and he put an "is" before "now" in the last clause. As for Petyt, he drew his two sentences from Scobell's *Memorials*, p. 9, but he reversed the order in which Scobell presented them, and, while following Scobell's text almost verbatim in the account of the committee for religion, grievances, and courts of justice, he omitted fifteen words from Scobell's account of the committee for trade. Thus it is plain that TJ's real source was Petyt rather than Scobell, although Scobell and TJ agreed on the order to be followed in presenting the two sentences. See below, par. [326], for an entry partly similar to par. [321]. For occasions when the committee for trade functioned as a select committee, see JHC, I, 680, 681, 686, 689. For its functioning as a grand committee, see *ibid.*, I, 672; II, 21.

PARAGRAPH [322]

1 Transcribed verbatim by TJ in text and documentation from the opening paragraph of George Petyt's twentieth chapter, headed "*Of Standing Commit-*

tees," (p. 341). TJ's capitalized marginal note seems to have been derived from Petyt's chapter title. Petyt drew his wording verbatim from Coke's *Institutes*, IV, p. 11-12, except that he omitted the "of" before "advancement."

PARAGRAPH [323]

1 Transcribed verbatim by TJ in text and documentation from George Petyt, p. 341-2. Petyt's text is copied verbatim from Scobell's *Memorials*, p. 9, except that Scobell had a "were" before "made," an "unto" after "committed," and a "was" before "reported."

PARAGRAPH [324]

1 Transcribed verbatim by TJ in text and documentation from George Petyt, p. 342, lines 5-10. The first four words in Petyt's text run toward a brace within which the terms for the five committees appear as a vertical list. In format and language Petyt's text is identical to that in Scobell's *Memorials*, p. 9, except that Scobell began his sentence with "The."

PARAGRAPH [325]

1 Transcribed verbatim by TJ in text and documentation from George Petyt, p. 342, lines 11-19, except that Petyt repeated "they" after "meet." Petyt drew his text verbatim from Coke's *Institutes*, IV, 12, except that Coke wrote "Chair," not "their Chair," and "Resolution," not "Resolutions."

PARAGRAPH [326]

1 Transcribed verbatim by TJ in text and documentation from George Petyt, p. 342 (lines 20-2, 26-30), 343 (lines 1-2). Petyt drew his text verbatim from Scobell's *Memorials*, p. 9, except that Scobell dated the episode involved in the last sentence as "21. *Iacobi*." See above, par. [321], for an entry that partly duplicates the present paragraph. It should be noted that par. [321] was based by TJ upon Petyt, p. 340, and that the present paragraph upon Petyt, p. 342-3. Petyt seems not to have been aware of the partial duplication of his second entry by the first, but TJ noticed the duplication, and took steps to lessen it. For example, Petyt noted in both entries that the same three committees usually sat in the afternoon, whereas TJ omitted reference to that detail in the present paragraph, after having recorded it earlier.

PARAGRAPH [327]

1 Transcribed verbatim by TJ in text and documentation from George Petyt, p. 343, lines 3-8, and by Petyt in text from Scobell's *Memorials*, p. 10, except that Scobell's initial word is "But," his ninth word is "alway," and his last auxiliary verb is "did."

PARAGRAPH [328]

1 Transcribed verbatim by TJ in text and documentation from George Petyt, p. 344, lines 4-5, where this sentence stands as a paragraph. Petyt adapted it from Scobell's *Memorials*, p. 11, where it stands as a paragraph and reads, "It was then also agreed, That *Council should be admitted at that Committee*." Scobell indicated that his source was an action in Commons "21. *Jacobi*," that is, February 23, 1623/24. See JHC, I, 671.

PARAGRAPH [329]

1 Transcribed verbatim by TJ in text and documentation from George Petyt, p. 343, lines 9-10, and by Petyt in text from Scobell's *Memorials*, p. 10, except that Scobell wrote "Members" instead of "Numbers."

PARAGRAPH [330]

1 Transcribed verbatim by TJ in text and documentation from George Petyt, p. 343, lines 11-20, except that Petyt inserted "on" after "insisted." In drawing upon Scobell's *Memorials*, p. 10-11, for this paragraph, Petyt reduced to 70 words what Scobell expressed in 112. Scobell's source was JHC, I, 671. See above, par. [328], n.

PARAGRAPH [331]

1 Transcribed verbatim by TJ in text and documentation from George Petyt, p. 343-4, except that TJ changed Petyt's spelling of "anciently" and "ancient," and did not insert "so" before "absolutely." Petyt's text is a somewhat reduced version of Scobell's *Memorials*, p. 11-12. Scobell referred the first part of his passage to "the Journal Book 26. *Feb.* 1600. in 39 *Eliz.*," a date which Petyt changed to "42 *Eliz.*" But in reality the correct date should have been entered by both authors as February 26, 35 Eliz. (1592/93). See D'Ewes, p. 471, col. 1. As for the other two dates in the present paragraph, the first referred to November 6, 1640 (JHC, II, 20-1), and the second to March 22, 1603/4 (JHC, I, 149-50).

PARAGRAPH [332]

1 Transcribed verbatim by TJ in text and documentation from George Petyt, p. 344, lines 19-23, except that TJ omitted Petyt's opening "And." Petyt drew the sentence verbatim from Scobell's *Memorials*, p. 12, except that he twice changed Scobell's "might" to "may."

2 These dates and figures were abstracted by TJ from somewhat longer sentences by George Petyt, p. 344 (lines 24-9, 30-2), 345 (lines 1-5). Petyt transcribed those longer sentences almost verbatim from Scobell's *Memorials*, p. 12-13. Scobell's sources for the figures and dates were JHC, I, 673; II, 3; II, 21.

PARAGRAPH [333]

1 These two sentences were transcribed verbatim by TJ from George Petyt, p. 345, lines 6-13.

2 TJ's documentation was taken from Petyt, p. 345-6. It reveals among other things that Petyt transcribed the two sentences verbatim from Scobell's *Memorials*, p. 13, except that he deleted two words from Scobell's text, changed "should" to "shall" on two occasions, and wrote "till" for "until."

PARAGRAPH [334]

1 Transcribed verbatim by TJ in text and documentation from George Petyt, p. 345, lines 14-19, except that TJ slightly rearranged the units in the date. In transcribing this passage from Scobell's *Memorials*, p. 16, Petyt adhered to Scobell's text, with four unimportant exceptions, one of which consisted in his adding "I" after the Latin name for James.

PARAGRAPH [335]

1 Transcribed verbatim by TJ in text and documentation from a separate paragraph in George Petyt, p. 345, lines 20-4, and by Petyt almost verbatim from parts of two paragraphs in Scobell's *Memorials*, p. 16-17. Scobell's source was JHC, I, 678.

PARAGRAPH [336]

1 Transcribed verbatim by TJ in text and documentation from George Petyt, p. 345, lines 25-9, and by Petyt from Scobell's *Memorials*, p. 17, with one slight change in wording and one unimportant condensation in the last clause. The case of Damport involved a statement given by him to the committee for the courts of justice in the Commons. On the basis of that statement, the Commons charged the bishop of Landaph with corrupt practices, and they requested that the Lords bring him to trial on that charge. Summoned to testify against the bishop before the Lords, Damport contradicted his earlier testimony, whereupon the Commons called him to account and judged him to have testified falsely before them. Damport was punished June 4, 1621, by being sentenced to the Tower for one month. See JHC, I, 560-1, 621, 632, 635, 639.

PARAGRAPH [337]

1 Transcribed verbatim by TJ in text and documentation from George Petyt, p. 347, lines 1-4, except that TJ made slight changes in two of the abbreviations used by Petyt to designate his sources.

PARAGRAPH [338]

1 Text transcribed verbatim by TJ from George Petyt, p. 347, lines 5-13.

2 TJ took these annotations from Petyt, p. 347, slightly altering three of Petyt's abbreviations. The latter's reference to "*Levintz.* 9." (TJ's "Lev. 9.") is incorrect—it should read in full Creswell Levinz, *Les Reports*, I, 296.

3 Transcribed verbatim by TJ from George Petyt, p. 348, lines 1-5. Petyt did not specify where this sentence can be found in Sir George Crooke's (i.e., Croke's) *Reports*.

4 TJ took the first two of these annotations from George Petyt, p. 348, lines 5-6, but he added the final two on his own. In many preceding paragraphs, as these notes show, TJ took his text and documentation from Petyt, without openly specifying as much. But here he reverted to his earlier practice of citing Petyt as occasion demanded, and here, too, he went beyond Petyt in citing Rushworth. On the page specified, Rushworth recounted that Sir Henry Martin, in a speech to a conference of Lords and Commons on May 23, 1628, made the following observations: "Now Your Lordships well know, that the House of Commons is not ignorant, that in a Session of Parliament, though it continue so many weeks, as this hath done days, yet there is nothing *prius & posterius*, but all things are held and taken as done at one time." These words confirm Petyt's paragraph, of course, as TJ knew they would when he cited Rushworth, I, 581. But this reference also calls our attention to TJ's almost certain awareness that Sir Henry Martin was speaking on that occasion to pave the way for the Lords and Commons to adopt and send to Charles I the historic Petition of Right, which was

meant to assert the rights and privileges of Parliament against the monarch in the conduct of public affairs. Could it be that this Petition of Right, and the other remonstrances addressed by Parliament to the Stuarts, were not only made familiar to TJ in the course of his preparation of the Pocket-Book but were also to become his guides at a later date in his own life when he wrote the Declaration of Independence, itself a protest against George III's violation of the rights and privileges of the American colonies? The latter possibility is by no means remote.

PARAGRAPH [339]

1 Transcribed verbatim by TJ from George Petyt, p. 348, lines 7-14, as the final annotation partly indicates. Petyt's source was an observation by Sir Matthew Hale as quoted in Plowden's *Les Commentaires*, fol. 79v, in law French. It is highly probable that Hale's observation, as given here, was Petyt's own translation of Plowden's law French text. At any rate, Petyt's translation is faithful to that original, and it could not have been taken from the standard translation of Plowden, which did not appear until thirteen years after the date of the third and last edition of Petyt's work.

PARAGRAPH [340]

1 Transcribed verbatim by TJ in text and in first annotation from George Petyt, p. 350, lines 22-5, except that, after "continuance," TJ added "of parliament." Petyt drew his text verbatim from Coke's *Institutes*, IV, p. 28, lines 2-4, except that, after "continuance," Coke added "as before it appeareth," and after "causes," "then."

PARAGRAPH [341]

1 TJ gathered the substance and part of the documentation of these three sentences from George Petyt, p. 351 (lines 20-2), 350 (lines 31-2), and 351 (line 1). Petyt based the sentences upon D'Ewes, p. 318, col. 2, and Rushworth, I, 537. To Petyt's references TJ on his own added the two others to Rushworth, both of which involved instances of Parliament's being adjourned by Charles I. See also below, par. [344].

PARAGRAPH [342]

1 Transcribed verbatim by TJ in text and in first two annotations from George Petyt, p. 353, lines 7-14, except that TJ abbreviated the names of the monarchs and omitted "pag." in Petyt's references to Hale's *Jurisdiction of Parliaments*.

PARAGRAPH [343]

1 The last twenty-three words of the text of this paragraph, and the references to Burnet's *History of the Reformation* and to JHC were transcribed verbatim by TJ from George Petyt, p. 353, lines 17-20. TJ condensed the earlier part of his text from the preceding lines of that same passage. The printed JHC begins with November 8, 1547, and thus does not include events in Henry VIII's reign. Burnet, I, 276, gave May 14, 1540, as the date of the prorogation to which Petyt here referred. At that time Parliament had just passed a bill suppressing the knightly order of the Hospitallers on the grounds that it was controlled by the pope and the Emperor Charles V of Spain, and was thus under hostile foreign

domination. As the ten-day prorogation was about to take place, Parliament voted "that their Bills should remain in the State they were in." They met next on May 25, and as they were going on with their interrupted business, the Duke of Norfolk, speaking on June 13, 1540 for Henry VIII, accused Cromwell of high treason and ordered him to the Tower.

PARAGRAPH [344]

1 As TJ transcribed it, this passage is partly a paraphrase and partly a verbatim text of George Petyt, p. 354, lines 9-19. As he copied it, TJ wrote "adjourn" and then canceled it, proceeding thereupon to adhere for the next six words to the text of his source. TJ's reference to Rushworth is taken from Petyt. On the page indicated in that reference, Rushworth reported that, on April 10, 1628, Charles I expressed the desire that the Commons not take a recess for the coming Easter holidays. "This Message for non-recess," said Rushworth, "was not well pleasing to the House." And he added: "Sir *Robert Phillips* first resented it, and took notice, 'That in 12 and 18 *Jac.* upon the like intimation, the House resolved it was in their power to adjourn or sit.' "

PARAGRAPH [345]

1 Transcribed verbatim by TJ in text and in first annotation from George Petyt, p. 357, lines 17-21, except that TJ dropped "himself" after "King." Petyt's source (Rushworth, I, Appendix, p. 48) reveals that the exact sentence which Petyt copied was contained in a speech made in the Court of King's Bench by Robert Mason of Lincoln's Inn in defense of the defiant conduct of Sir John Eliot in the Commons. One of the charges upon which Sir John was being tried asserted that he had conspired with other defendants "to detain Mr. Speaker in the Chair." That action had been taken to prevent the Speaker not only from rising to move an adjournment but also from thereby halting Sir John's speech in denunciation of the arbitrary conduct of Charles I. Mason argued that Charles I had the right to appear in person and command an adjournment, or to command an adjournment in writing under the great seal. But, said Mason, the king did not have the right to adjourn Parliament by the process of a verbal command given by him to the Speaker. In a word, the Commons did not consider themselves obliged to accept a message of that sort as authentic. For an account of the famous episode in which the Speaker, Sir John Finch, was prevented on March 2, 1628/29, from leaving the chair, see *Parliamentary History of England*, VIII, 377.

PARAGRAPH [346]

1 Transcribed verbatim by TJ in text and in first annotation from George Petyt, p. 359, lines 1-5. The only source cited by Petyt is William Jones' *Les Reports*, p. 104.

PARAGRAPH [347]

1 Transcribed verbatim by TJ in text and documentation from George Petyt, p. 359, lines 6-10. Petyt referred this paragraph to the designated volume and pages of Rushworth, but that source does not at those points support the declaration made here. It is, however, a familiar precept. Says Jacob, s.v. statute: "*Statutes* consist of two Parts, the Words, and the Sense; and 'tis the Office of an

Expositor, to put such a Sense upon the Words of the *Statute*, as is agreeable to Equity and right Reason." See also Jacob, s.v. acts of Parliament, and Coke's *Institutes*, I, p. 381v.

PARAGRAPH [348]

1 Transcribed verbatim by TJ in text and in first two annotations from George Petyt, p. 361, lines 4-21, except that TJ changed the order of units in each of the dates, omitted one of the definite articles, and preferred "antient" to Petyt's more modern form of that word. Petyt's text was in some parts transcribed word for word, and in other parts paraphrased, from Townshend's *Historical Collections*, p. 116, 117. D'Ewes also covered these incidents, as Petyt indicated; but Petyt's first reference at this point to D'Ewes should read p. 573, col. 2. The ceremonial procedure outlined in the first part of TJ's paragraph was given a rather full treatment by D'Ewes, p. 451, col. 1, in connection with his account of the doings of the Commons on March 21, 1588/89. On that date, a bill calling for a new way of providing relief for the city of London was given a third reading and then passed by a vote of 118 to 65. Inasmuch as this bill involved a change in the traditional way of accomplishing its objective, those favoring it had to register their yeas by going forth (they were after all for quitting the old way) and those opposing it had to register their noes—their resistance to change—by remaining inside. When the absent yeas were declared winners, the losers had to pass a motion declaring their intention of going forth and bringing back the winners and the victorious bill. While this motion was being carried out, the Speaker and the Clerk remained behind alone in the house. Upon the return of the losers and the winners, the new bill, now in the custody of the vice chamberlain or the controller, was delivered to the Speaker, and this latter act signified that the bill was at last a part of the regular procedures of the Commons. Highly respected as this ceremony was in a nation given to ritual and display, it was very time-consuming, and thus, as TJ's paragraph recorded, it was omitted on December 17, 1597. But that omission was declared then to imply no prejudice to future observances of the ceremony.

PARAGRAPH [349]

1 Transcribed verbatim by TJ in text and in first two annotations from George Petyt, p. 363, lines 10-20, with the following exceptions: 1) Petyt had "of this House" before "hath always been"; 2) Petyt had "unto this House" after "Bill"; and 3) Petyt had "and then to send" after "thereto." Petyt drew his text almost verbatim from D'Ewes' transcript of a passage in a speech by Sir Francis Bacon in Commons on March 2, 1592/93. D'Ewes makes it clear that Sir Francis' speech that day had followed a speech by Sir Robert Cecil. Sir Robert revealed that a committee of which he was a member had met the day before with a committee of the Lords, and that the Lords, after characterizing as inadequate a grant by the Commons to the queen, had threatened not to approve of the next grant, unless the Commons increased it by a specified amount. Sir Francis, a member of the same committee, followed Sir Robert by saying that he approved of the grant as specified by the Lords, but that he did not favor proceeding in such a way as to make the grant appear to be a joint action of the Commons and the Lords. The Commons must insist, said Sir Francis, that they proceed by themselves. Citing a precedent from the reign of Henry VIII, Sir Francis declared "that the Lords might indeed give notice unto the said House of Com-

mons, what need or danger there was, but ought not to prescribe them what to give, as at the meeting of the former Committee the Lord Treasurer had done." After Sir Francis' speech, the Commons discussed the needs of the queen for higher defense subsidies, but they finally voted 217 to 128 not to accept a proposal by the Lords for a joint conference to determine how large the subsidies might ultimately be.

PARAGRAPH [350]

1 Transcribed verbatim by TJ in text and in first annotation from George Petyt, p. 363, lines 21-7, and by Petyt to a large extent verbatim from William Petyt's *Miscellanea Parliamentaria*, p. 4. According to this latter authority, the burgess referred to here, named George Ferrers, was arrested in London on his way to the Commons as the result of a process initiated in the Court of King's Bench by one White, who alleged that Ferrers owed him 200 marks. The arrest was reported to Sir Thomas Moyle, Speaker of the Commons, and to the rest of the House; and they at once dispatched their serjeant to the prison in Breadstreet, where Ferrers was being held. The clerk of the prison refused to release Ferrers and openly resisted the serjeant's attempt to take the prisoner away. Two sheriffs of London appeared on the scene during this altercation, and they refused to help the serjeant or even to listen to him. The Commons were angry when the serjeant told them what had happened. Rising in a body, they went to the House of Lords and demanded that the prison officials and the two sheriffs be cited for contempt. This demand was immediately honored by the Lords, who then ruled that the Commons should take charge of punishing the culprits. Upon their return to their own House, the Commons ordered their serjeant to go to the sheriffs and require them to release Ferrers; and when the lord chancellor offered to supply the serjeant with a writ to advertise his authority to carry out the order, the Commons refused, indicating *"that all Commandments and other Acts proceeding from the Nether House, were to be done and executed by their Serjeant, without Writ, only by shew of his Mace, which was his warrant."* This display of parliamentary determination became public knowledge at once. Confronted by the serjeant upon his second mission, the sheriffs released Ferrers with alacrity, and they obeyed the serjeant's summons to appear next day before the Commons and to explain their conduct, bringing with them the prison officials and White. That appearance, conducted without benefit of counsel, resulted in the citation of the culprits for contempt of Parliament. The two sheriffs and White were sentenced to the Tower, and the other culprits to Newgate. Ferrers was declared exempt from paying the 200 marks, inasmuch as he had acquired the debt by having acted as surety for a man named Weldon, the principal debtor. The Commons later passed a bill requiring Weldon to assume responsibility for the debt. When Henry VIII received word of this whole affair, he summoned to a conference the chief parties involved—the lord chancellor, the judges, the Speaker, and other influential Commoners—and he expressed his gratification that the Commons had properly maintained their privileges. He added that, by virtue of his being head of Parliament, all of its members had privileges as his servants performing duties for him. William Petyt concluded his account of this case by remarking that it was a precedent in the development of parliamentary privilege. For a similar account of this case, see Holinshed's *Chronicles*, III, 824-6. See also below, par. [413].

PARAGRAPH [351]

1 Transcribed verbatim by TJ in text and in first annotation from George Petyt, p. 364, lines 7-20, and by Petyt with several minor changes in wording and word order from JHC, IX, 457.

2 TJ placed the number in angle brackets immediately after his reference to "Journ. Com." and then placed it where it is now, superimposing across the earlier number the letter "L." Petyt had here given no page reference for what he cited as "*Journal, Dom. Com.*"

PARAGRAPH [352]

1 Transcribed verbatim by TJ in text and documentation from George Petyt, p. 364, lines 21-7, and developed by Petyt partly verbatim and partly in paraphrase from "*ibid.*," that is, JHC, IX, 484.

PARAGRAPH [353]

1 Transcribed verbatim by TJ in text and in first annotation from George Petyt, p. 365, lines 5-8; and by Petyt verbatim from Coke's *Institutes*, IV, p. 17, lines 35-6. The phrase, "in ure," when it applies to statutes, means, "In or into effect, force, or operation." See OED, s.v. ure, *sb.*[1] c. See also Coke's *Institutes*, I, fol. 81 (Sec. 108).

PARAGRAPH [354]

1 Transcribed verbatim by TJ in text and in first annotation from George Petyt, p. 365, lines 9-16, except that Petyt's text read "lose his Force," and it designated his source as "*Coke Lit.* 81.b." Here is certainly an instance of TJ's use of George Petyt as his primary source, and of his correction of Petyt's text after testing it against Coke's. TJ's wording of this passage followed Coke's verbatim in preferring "lose its force" to Petyt's "lose his Force." And in other respects TJ exactly paralleled Coke, except that he, like Petyt, omitted Coke's twenty-three-word quotation from Littleton between "not bear it" and "Not that an act." See Coke's *Institutes*, I, fol. 81v.

PARAGRAPH [355]

1 An exact transcript by TJ of the text and the first annotation of George Petyt, p. 366, lines 27-9. Petyt's source, as he indicated, was Hutton's *Reports*, p. 62.

PARAGRAPH [356]

1 Exactly transcribed by TJ in text and in first annotation from George Petyt, p. 367, lines 19-21, except that TJ omitted Petyt's "of" before "Content." TJ also omitted Petyt's next sentence: "The Commons give their Voices upon the Question, by *Yea*, or *No*." This latter sentence Petyt transcribed without change from Coke's *Institutes*, IV, p. 35, even as his former sentence came verbatim from Coke's preceding page. TJ jotted down both page numbers, but the second had no reference to his own text. The "puisne lord" is the youngest sitting lord.

PARAGRAPH [357]

1 Transcribed verbatim by TJ in text and in first annotation from George Petyt, p. 368, lines 11-19, except that TJ dropped out seven words which in Petyt

served no purpose except to create redundancy. Petyt transcribed his text almost verbatim from D'Ewes, p. 244, col. 2, preserving the seven needless words, and making a very few minor changes, one of which consisted in replacing D'Ewes' "in any wise" with "in any ways."

2 TJ added on his own this reference to Hale's *Jurisdiction of Parliaments*, p. 116, where the resolution under discussion here is stated in twenty-six words, as compared with fifty-seven words in the parliamentary wording recorded by D'Ewes.

PARAGRAPH [358]

1 Transcribed verbatim by TJ in text and in first annotation from George Petyt, p. 368, lines 20-6, except that TJ dropped Petyt's "It was" before "assented." Petyt's text was in part a verbatim transcription, and in part a condensed version, of a motion presented by Mr. Wroth on February 25, 1588/89. See D'Ewes, p. 439, col. 1.

PARAGRAPH [359]

1 Transcribed verbatim by TJ in text and in the first two annotations from George Petyt, p. 369, lines 1-3, and by Petyt almost verbatim from Coke's *Institutes*, IV, p. 50, lines 5-6.

PARAGRAPH [360]

1 Transcribed verbatim by TJ in text from George Petyt, p. 369, lines 4-10. Petyt attributed the passage to "*Hebert's* Hen. 8. 136," but TJ silently and properly corrected the first word in this reference to "Herbert's." Petyt based his text almost verbatim upon Herbert's *The Life and Reign of King Henry the Eighth* (London, 1672), p. 136. As Herbert described this mission of Cardinal Wolsey to the Commons, it came about in the spring of 1523, when Wolsey, in his capacity as Henry VIII's prime minister, had gone to the Commons in person to request that the fifth part of every man's estate be committed to the war of Henry VIII and Charles V against Francis, the French king. The Commons raised objections to this request, but they ultimately agreed to a lesser amount. "The Cardinal hearing no more was intended, seemed much troubled," said Herbert; "and therefore, coming to the Lower House of Parliament, he told them, that he desir'd to reason with those who oppos'd his Demands; but being answer'd, that it was the Order of that House to hear, and not to reason, but amongst themselves, the Cardinal departed." Quoted from Herbert in *Parliamentary History of England*, III, 33. Perhaps somewhat taken aback by their own parsimony toward the king in his request for aid against the French, the Commons then voted to increase the amount of their previous subsidy, but even so they thereby met only about half of Wolsey's original request.

PARAGRAPH [361]

1 Transcribed verbatim by TJ in text and documentation from George Petyt, p. 369, lines 11-14, and by Petyt almost verbatim from Scobell's *Memorials*, p. 84.

2 This fragmentary sentence and its four annotations were TJ's jottings from George Petyt, p. 369 (lines 15-31), 371 (lines 9-32). Petyt drew the materials for these jottings from the sources indicated in TJ's annotations.

3 This fragmentary sentence and its three annotations were compiled by TJ from George Petyt, p. 371 (lines 1-8), 372 (lines 1-11). For Petyt's sources, see the three works indicated by TJ's annotations.

PARAGRAPH [362]

1 Transcribed verbatim by TJ in text and documentation from George Petyt, p. 370, lines 3-8, except that TJ rearranged the units of the date. Petyt's text followed that in Scobell's *Memorials*, p. 84-5, except that, after giving the date as Scobell had it, Petyt omitted Scobell's phrase, "In the second Parliament of Queen *Elizabeth*."

2 This clause and the preceding sentence constitute TJ's verbatim transcript of one paragraph and its immediate predecessor in George Petyt, p. 370, lines 13-18. Petyt drew these materials almost verbatim from Scobell's *Memorials*, p. 85.

3 These three conditional clauses were transcribed verbatim by TJ from George Petyt, p. 370, lines 25-31, and by Petyt almost verbatim from Scobell's *Memorials*, p. 85-6. The Latin phrases may be translated respectively as follows: "He is freed for special service; he is excused out of courtesy; he is ill; he is absent without leave."

4 These four concluding phrases and clauses were transcribed by TJ almost verbatim in text and annotation from George Petyt, p. 370, lines 22-4, and by Petyt verbatim from Scobell's *Memorials*, p. 85.

PARAGRAPH [363]

1 As TJ's later notes at the end of this paragraph show in a preliminary way, this sentence was transcribed verbatim by him from George Petyt, p. 372, lines 21-7, and by Petyt verbatim from Scobell's *Memorials*, p. 87.

2 This sentence belongs in the pattern mentioned in the preceding note. For its exact wording as TJ gave it, see George Petyt, p. 372 (lines 28-32), 373 (lines 1-3), except that Petyt wrote "acknowledge." Petyt's wording and that in Scobell's *Memorials*, p. 87, are identical, except that Scobell put "So" before the date, "presented" before "a Petition," and "*Bambury*" instead of "*Banbury*." In JHC for November 18, 1640, there is no record of the presentation of Vivers' petition. But on November 28, 1640, a "humble Petition of the Mayor, Aldermen, Burgesses, and other Inhabitants of the Town and Borough of *Bambury* in the County of *Oxon*" was read in the Commons and referred to the Committee for Religion, after a man named Viners had been called in and had acknowledged not only that the handwriting in the petition was his but that he was delivering it "by Order, and on the Behalf, of the Town of *Banbury*." See JHC, II, 30-1, 38.

3 Transcribed verbatim by TJ in text and annotation from George Petyt, p. 37, lines 4-7, and by Petyt verbatim from Scobell's *Memorials*, p. 87, except that Scobell has "Hoogan."

PARAGRAPH [364]

1 Transcribed verbatim by TJ in text and first annotation from George Petyt, p. 373, lines 8-12, and by Petyt verbatim from Scobell's *Memorials*, p. 72, except that Scobell put "another" instead of "an" before "undoubted."

PARAGRAPH [365]

1 Transcribed verbatim by TJ in text and first annotation from George Petyt, p. 373, lines 29-32. Petyt's text is an English translation of law French as stated in Sir Francis Moore's *Cases Collect & Report*, p. 768. Petyt preceded his translation by a paragraph giving an almost verbatim version of Sir Francis' French passage.

PARAGRAPH [366]

1 Transcribed verbatim by TJ in text and documentation from George Petyt, p. 374, lines 1-6, except that Petyt, after giving the date, wrote, "It was ordered by the Commons." Petyt's text was a verbatim transcript of Scobell's *Memorials*, p. 14, except that Scobell wrote "further" and had a longer introductory clause than Petyt did. For the order stated here, see JHC, II, 3.

PARAGRAPH [367]

1 An exact transcript by TJ in text and documentation from George Petyt, p. 374, lines 7-14, and by Petyt in text from Scobell's *Memorials*, p. 40.

PARAGRAPH [368]

1 An exact transcript by TJ in text and documentation from George Petyt, p. 374, lines 15-18, except that Petyt wrote "publick" and did not italicize "imposing a tax." Petyt's wording exactly follows that in Scobell's *Memorials*, p. 40, except that Scobell wrote "Publique."

PARAGRAPH [369]

1 Transcribed verbatim by TJ in text and documentation from George Petyt, p. 375, lines 4-9, except that Petyt wrote "publick." Scobell's *Memorials*, p. 41, had "Publique," but otherwise it provided Petyt's exact wording.

PARAGRAPH [370]

1 Transcribed verbatim by TJ in text and documentation from George Petyt, p. 374, lines 19-23. Petyt drew his text verbatim from Scobell's *Memorials*, p. 41.

PARAGRAPH [371]

1 An exact transcript by TJ in text and documentation from George Petyt, p. 375, lines 10-18. TJ's single quotation mark falls at the start of a clause which Petyt italicized. Petyt drew his text verbatim, italics and all, from Scobell's *Memorials*, p. 47 (not 46 as Petyt and TJ had it), except that Scobell, before "It was resolved," wrote "whether Mr. *Hadley* were to be employed." For the circumstances attending the rule set forth here, see JHC, I, 350, where the excused member was called Hedley.

PARAGRAPH [372]

1 Transcribed verbatim by TJ in text and annotations from George Petyt, p. 376, lines 25-9, except that TJ added the underscoring. Petyt drew his wording almost verbatim from the indicated page of Bk. III of May's *History of the Parliament*, and, in a confirmatory sense, from Atkyns' *Power, Jurisdiction, and Privilege of Parliament*, p. 36. See Atkyns' *Tracts*, p. 69-70.

PARAGRAPH [373]

1 This twenty-word sentence and its annotation were transcribed by TJ with a trivial omission from a twenty-three-word passage and its annotation·in George Petyt, p. 377, lines 4-7. Petyt drew his wording largely verbatim from a thirty-word passage on the indicated page of Rushworth, Part III, Vol. 1 (not Vol. 3, Part I, as Petyt's note had declared). Rushworth drew the passage from a document headed "The humble Petition of the Lords and Commons in Parliament, concerning His Majesties Speech, of the 14th of *Decemb.* 1641." For this petition as it appears in the proceedings of the Commons for December 16, 1641, see JHC, II, 345-6.

PARAGRAPH [374]

1 Transcribed verbatim by TJ in text and documentation from George Petyt, p. 377, lines 8-9, except that TJ dropped Petyt's "of" after "Violating." Petyt took his text verbatim from Rushworth, his reference to that source being correct if we read his "Vol." as "Part," and vice versa. In JHC, II, 366, under the date of January 3, 1641, the sentence reads thus: "That the Violating the Privileges of Parliament is the Overthrow of Parliaments." Expressed in this way, with the final word a plural, the declaration has the status of a constitutional law, and the Commons intended it so. On that very day, Charles I theatened one of their most cherished privileges by demanding that they consent to the arrest of five of their members, including Pym and Hampden, on a charge of high treason. In short, the king commanded the Commons to surrender their power of impeachment, and this intrusion upon their privileges seemed to both Lords and Commons to put the very existence of Parliament into the most serious jeopardy. The imminent Civil War was to be fought to determine whether the basic law articulated here by the Commons was to endure or to lapse as a constitutional principle, and thus TJ's paragraph captures the main issue in a momentous political crisis.

PARAGRAPH [375]

1 Transcribed verbatim by TJ in text and annotation from George Petyt, p. 376-7, except that TJ added the underscoring, whereas Petyt had "*Anno*" rather than "in" before the date. Petyt drew his wording almost verbatim from Rushworth, Part I, Vol. 1, p. 663. That is to say, Petyt's three opening phrases were not transcribed verbatim from Rushworth, but the rest of his sentence was, although Rushworth did not put "the judges" after "all" and did put "he" where Petyt had "a Parliament man." A reduced version of the paragraph given here figures as part of pars. 132 and [397].

PARAGRAPH [376]

1 Transcribed verbatim by TJ in text and documentation from George Petyt, p. 377 (lines 23-30), 378 (lines 1-18), except that Petyt had "saying" where TJ had "to wit, that," and TJ omitted some twenty-nine words and one page reference from scattered parts of Petyt's text. As for Petyt, he drew his wording almost verbatim from *The Diurnal Occurrences*, p. 111, 116, and from Rushworth, Part III, Vol. 1, p. 278, 280. For another mention of this case and its content, see above, par. 138, especially nn. 1, 12. On that earlier occasion, TJ's account rested upon George Petyt, p. 144-5, where Petyt incorrectly based his statements upon William Petyt's *Miscellanea Parliamentaria*, p. 80. In other

words, George Petyt covered William Taylor's case twice, but only his second account rested upon relevant authorities. For the official version, which confirms and supplements those authorities, see JHC, II, 158-9, 172, 173.

PARAGRAPH [377]

1 TJ based the wording of this paragraph in text and documentation upon George Petyt, p. 378-9, but he omitted parts of that source, and slightly altered the arrangement and phraseology of other parts, so as to reduce Petyt's text of 101 words to 81. Even so, TJ did not sacrifice any substance, except for his omission of Petyt's mention that Nevill's first name was Francis. Petyt transcribed his passage almost verbatim from Rushworth, Part III, Vol. 1, p. 169. According to the official record of the Commons for February 4, 1640/41, Nevill had been summoned at the end of the preceding Parliament to appear before the king and his council, and "was there demanded, whether, when Sir *Wm. Savile*, a Member likewise of this House, spake in the House something for the King's Service, Two Members of the said House did not rise up immediately after him, and contradict that which he had so said for the King's Service." Upon Nevill's having given an affirmative answer to this demand, the king and his council committed the two members to prison. It is Rushworth who identified them as Bellasis and Sir John Hotham. To the Commons, Nevill, in having caused the imprisonment of his two fellow members by revealing what they said in refuting Sir William, became guilty of a "great offence, and Breach of Privilege of Parliaments," and was accordingly committed to the Tower. Sir William was next placed in custody for having testified before the king and his council that Nevill's account of the episode just mentioned was accurate. See JHC, II, 78, 149, 161, 173.

PARAGRAPH [378]

1 Transcribed verbatim by TJ in text and first annotation from George Petyt, p. 379, lines 17-19, and by Petyt verbatim in text from Coke's *Institutes*, IV, 23-4. According to Coke, and also to JHC, I, 35, a man named Muncton, likewise called Monyngton, was brought before the Commons for having struck one of their members, William Johnson. Not being told of Johnson's parliamentary status, Muncton confessed to striking him for his having stolen a net out of the house of a man named Bray of Bedfordshire. Johnson replied by testifying that, as undersheriff at the time, he had removed the net from Bray's house because the net belonged to Lord Mordaunt. The Commons ordered Muncton to be committed to the Tower, not because he had falsely accused Johnson of being guilty of robbery, but because he had shown contempt for the Commons by assaulting one of their members without bothering to find out who the victim was or what special privilege might belong to him if he turned out to have status in Parliament.

PARAGRAPH [379]

1 Transcribed verbatim by TJ in text and documentation from George Petyt, p. 379, lines 20-1, and by Petyt verbatim from Coke's *Institutes*, IV, 24, except that Petyt dropped Coke's initial word "but." Coke intended that word to call attention to the difference between an assault upon a member of Commons and an assault upon a member's servant. As par. [378] shows, a member need not

proclaim himself a Commoner as a safeguard against physical attack. It is up to the would-be assailant to find that out or suffer the consequences. But the servant of a member must proclaim what his position is, if he expects to have immunity. In that case, as Coke put it, "he that striketh, &c., must have notice."

PARAGRAPH [380]

1 Transcribed verbatim by TJ in text and annotations from George Petyt, p. 380, lines 1-4, except that Petyt has "shall have Privilege of Parliament" for TJ's "has privilege." Petyt drew his wording verbatim from Coke's *Institutes*, IV, 24 (not 42 as he noted it), except that Petyt used twenty-three words to express what Coke expressed in thirty-one. The passage to which Petyt pointed in Hakewill confirmed but did not duplicate Coke's wording.

2 To Petyt's citations of Coke and Hakewill TJ added those to Scobell's *Memorials*, p. 102, and to Hale's *Jurisdiction of Parliaments*, p. 28-9, both of which support the substance but not the exact wording of TJ's paragraph.

PARAGRAPH [381]

1 Transcribed verbatim by TJ in text and annotation from George Petyt, p. 380, lines 5-9, except that Petyt inserted "due" between "is" and "eundo." The Latin gerunds without the accompanying influence of "due" mean "for going," "for staying," and "for returning." Petyt drew his text almost verbatim from the final twenty-nine words of a somewhat longer sentence in Scobell's *Memorials*, p. 88. For TJ's later use of these Latin gerunds, see *Manual* (1801), Sec. III, par. 3; *Manual* (1812), Sec. III, par. 4.

2 The two references to Scobell's *Memorials* and the three to D'Ewes were added by TJ to point to cases involving the protection of Commoners and their servants against interference by the law during the various phases of their attendance at Parliaments.

PARAGRAPH [382]

1 Transcribed verbatim by TJ in text and annotation from George Petyt, p. 380, lines 10-16, except that Petyt added "served on them" after "Subpoena." Petyt drew his text verbatim from Scobell's *Memorials*, p. 88, except that Scobell preferred "in" to "on" before "Juries."

2 This reference TJ added on his own perhaps to remind himself that a passage in Coke's *Institutes*, IV, 24, supported in general terms the privileged exemptions enumerated by Petyt and Scobell.

PARAGRAPH [383]

1 The final twenty-four words and the first two annotations of this sentence were transcribed verbatim by TJ from George Petyt, p. 380, lines 21-4. The other twenty-four words represent a condensed version of the other half of Petyt's sentence, p. 380, lines 17-21. As for Petyt's entire text, it proceeded largely verbatim from the last part of a paragraph in Hakewill's *Modus*, p. 62, where Hakewill cited "Dyer. 60.," that is, Dyer's *Novel Cases*, p. 60, as his source.

2 These two numbers and the accompanying abbreviation were added by TJ to Petyt's reference to Dyer, and they designate page 61, paragraph 28, of that

author's *Novel Cases*, with "pl." standing for "place," that is, locus or topic. The paragraph numbered 28 in Dyer, p. 61, dealt with penalties inflicted upon sheriffs for failing to release members of Parliament from custody, when the serjeant at arms appeared without writ and demanded their release. TJ's procedure in pointing to paragraph 28 would appear to indicate that, far from taking Petyt and Hakewill on faith in their references to Dyer, he went beyond them and consulted Dyer on his own, with the result that he found evidence to confirm and extend what they had said.

3 TJ's cross-reference is of course to par. 78 above.

PARAGRAPH [384]

1 Transcribed largely verbatim by TJ in text and annotations from George Petyt, p. 380 (lines 25-32), 381 (line 1). Petyt followed Hakewill's *Modus*, p. 62, almost verbatim in phrasing these lines and in making the reference to Crompton's *Courts*, p. 11.

2 TJ drew this phrase and the following references to Coke and Nalson from George Petyt, p. 381, lines 2-7. Petyt's wording of these lines was based upon Coke's *Institutes*, IV, 25, and upon Nalon's *Impartial Collection*, II, 450.

3 This cross-reference to par. 79 above really belongs to the first sentence of the present paragraph, and it is obviously intended by TJ to remind himself that that first sentence and a large part of par. 79 are quite similar in wording. Par. 79, as TJ's notes indicated, was framed from Hakewill and Crompton. The first sentence of the present paragraph was framed from the indicated lines in George Petyt, who followed Hakewill's wording, but did not add what Hakewill took from Crompton's *Courts*, p. 11, even though Petyt acknowledged both of these authorities. In other words, the present paragraph represents Petyt's reduced version of Hakewill, whereas par. 79 represents TJ's larger version of Hakewill and Crompton.

4 Transcribed verbatim by TJ in text and annotations from George Petyt, p. 382, lines 27-31, except for Petyt's having "it seems that" before "the private Commodity." Petyt's lines were translated from his quotation of a passage in law French from Dyer's *Novel Cases*, p. 60, pl. 19.

5 This sentence and its annotation represent TJ's note upon a longer passage in George Petyt, p. 398, lines 7-11. Petyt drew these lines verbatim from Scobell's *Memorials*, p. 98. The bag carrier was Valentine Syre.

PARAGRAPH [385]

1 Paraphrased by TJ in text and annotation from four paragraphs in George Petyt, p. 383 (lines 19-32), 384 (lines 1-3, 23-31). Two of those paragraphs were in law French and two in Petyt's English translation; and all together they represent Petyt's sources to be Moore's *Cases Collect*, p. 57 (n. 163), 340 (n. 461), Crompton's *Courts*, p. 7-11, and William Petyt's *Miscellanea Parliamentaria*, p. 1 (&c.) Fitzherbert's case took its name from Thomas Fitzherbert, who was arrested by the sheriff two hours after his election as member of Parliament had occurred, but several hours before his election was formally certified to the sheriff. Two questions arose in connection with the sheriff's action: Was Fitzherbert a member of the Commons at that moment? And, if he were, should he

have privilege, despite his having incurred a previous legal judgment, which had led the sheriff to arrest him? The Commons decided that, although Fitzherbert would have to be counted a member when he was arrested, he was not entitled to privilege for three reasons: 1) he was arrested before his election had been formally certified; 2) he had previously been declared an outlaw by the court for having refused to pay a debt which he legally owed; and 3) his arrest had occurred under circumstances which did not permit him to claim that he was then staying at, or going to, or returning from Parliament ("neither *sedente Parliamento*, not *eundo*, nor *redundo*," as D'Ewes, p. 518, col. 1, phrased it). See also D'Ewes, p. 479-82, 514-16; and Moore's *Cases Collect*, p. 340, n. 461.

PARAGRAPH [386]

1 In TJ's manuscript the spaces enclosed here in brackets contain words made illegible by a coin-shaped impression of an object presumably falling upon TJ's ink when it was wet. The words placed here within those spaces are not authenticated by the indistinct and almost invisible marks in TJ's text, but they are largely the same as those in George Petyt's text, p. 392, lines 25-31, and in Scobell's *Memorials*, p. 96, lines 16-21. There is no record of Sir William's arrest and release in the JHC for any April 12 falling within James I's Parliaments (1604-1624).

PARAGRAPH [387]

1 This sentence and its annotations represent TJ's note upon a paragraph in George Petyt, p. 385, lines 24-30, except for TJ's adding on his own the reference to Hale's *Jurisdiction of Parliaments*, p. 29. Petyt's paragraph recalled the case of Bogo de Clare and the Prior of Trinity, who were confined to the Tower for serving a citation upon the Earl of Cornwall when Parliament was in session. In addition to Hale, see Townshend's *Historical Collections*, p. 255; D'Ewes, p. 655, col. 1; and Coke's *Institutes*, IV, 24.

2 TJ based this sentence and its annotation upon George Petyt, p. 396, lines 4-10, and Petyt based upon D'Ewes, p. 688, col. 1, the paragraph from which the sentence emerged. According to D'Ewes, a member of Commons named George Belgrave, during a session of Parliament, was accused in the court of Starchamber by the king or one of his agents of having violated parliamentary proprieties and obligations. Such an accusation from such a source was known as an Information, and it had the approximate status of a grand jury indictment. See Jacob, s.v. information. Belgrave protested that the Information had been filed while Parliament was sitting *(sedente Curiâ)*, and he asked the Commons to investigate it. The Committee for Returns and Privileges did so, and the Commons subsequently voted that Belgrave was free of any imputation of misconduct within the terms of the Information.

PARAGRAPH [388]

1 TJ drew this sentence and all but two of its accompanying annotations from George Petyt, p. 386-96. The two annotations not cited by Petyt stemmed from Townshend's *Historical Collections*, p. 246, and Hale's *Jurisdiction of Parliaments*, p. 29, both of which, we may be sure from their content, were added by TJ as supplemental evidence concerning the immunity of members of Parliament to subpoenas during a parliamentary session. Two of the other annotations

taken by TJ from Petyt on the present occasion were incorrect in their source—that to D'Ewes, p. 438, should read p. 348, and that to William Petyt's *Miscellanea Parliamentaria*, p. 107, should have been deleted, since that page contains no reference to subpoenas.

PARAGRAPH [389]

1 This sentence and the accompanying annotations were taken by TJ from George Petyt, p. 388, lines 13-14, 19-20. Petyt's reference to D'Ewes, p. 546, col. 2, was incorrect—the page number should have been 564—and thus TJ here borrowed an error. In Petyt, "id." referred to Townshend's *Historical Collections*, as it would in TJ's paragraph, and the following page numbers were to that work. The *subpoena ad testificandum* was a writ summoning a person to testify in court, the other chief subpoena being a writ requiring a person to appear in court to answer a complaint against himself. See Jacob, s.v. subpoena.

2 In TJ's manuscript the bracketed words were partially obliterated by a smudge, perhaps with the intent of cancelling them out at this point, so that they could appear in a more proper setting in par. [391].

PARAGRAPH [390]

1 TJ drew his descriptive phrase and annotation for each of these legal processes from George Petyt, as follows: 1) service of a privy seal, p. 389, lines 5-11, D'Ewes, p. 655, cols. 1, 2; 2) awarding Outlawry, p. 389, lines 28-33, Scobell's *Memorials*, p. 92; 3) attachment for contempt, p. 390, lines 1-6, Scobell's *Memorials*, p. 92; 4) return on an attaint, p. 392, lines 11-18, Scobell's *Memorials*, p. 96. Each of Petyt's descriptive phrases proceeded from the annotation that he was then recording.

PARAGRAPH [391]

1 These three exemptions from parliamentary duty, as mentioned and annotated by TJ, represent the following passages and annotations in George Petyt: 1) from serving on a jury, p. 392, lines 19-24, D'Ewes, p. 560, col. 2; 2) from being chosen sheriff, p. 393, lines 1-5, Scobell's *Memorials*, p. 96; 3) from executing a Commission out of chancery, p. 404, lines 6-14, Scobell's *Memorials*, p. 103. The third of these exemptions involved Sir Edmund Ludlow and his son Henry, who were summoned to appear at the court of chancery before a commission appointed to hear a case pitting the two Ludlows against the provost and scholars of Queen's College, Oxford. Being a member of Commons, and scheduled to be in a parliamentary session at the time set for the hearing in chancery, Sir Edmund asked the Speaker of Commons to write a letter to the commission explaining that a rule of Parliament would prevent Sir Edmund, without prejudice to his case, from obeying the summons. The Speaker's subsequent letter is given as part of the record of the proceedings of the Commons for March 31, 1607/08. See JHC, I, 363.

PARAGRAPH [392]

1 Transcribed almost verbatim by TJ in text and annotations from George Petyt, p. 386, lines 15-20. Petyt recorded that this sentence was based upon an order adopted in Commons on the date indicated, (February 22, 1549/50), but his wording of it was taken almost verbatim from Scobell's *Memorials*, p. 110,

rather than from JHC, I, 18. Petyt's reference to D'Ewes concerned the procedure recommended on February 22, 1575/76, for obtaining the release of a member's servant during a parliamentary session.

2　This sentence represents TJ's condensed note upon the text and annotations of the final words of a paragraph in George Petyt, p. 390, lines 21-8. In turn, Petyt transcribed its text almost verbatim from Scobell's *Memorials*, p. 94, while citing the indicated page in D'Ewes as official confirmation. A writ of *supersedeas* would legally establish the priority of one thing above another. For example, it could be used to declare the superiority of parliamentary duty to that of responding to, say, a writ of *nisi prius*, as Petyt, Scobell, and D'Ewes pointed out.

3　The text and annotations of this sentence were taken almost verbatim by TJ from a paragraph in George Petyt, p. 393 (lines 16, 21-31), 394 (lines 1-2), except that TJ referred to Fitzherbert's case less specifically than Petyt did. Petyt's paragraph was an almost verbatim transcript of Scobell's *Memorials*, p. 111 (lines 25-9), 112 (lines 1-5), 113 (lines 1-9), the references to Moore and D'Ewes being confirmatory. For a preceding reference to Fitzherbert's case, see above, par. [385].

4　TJ transcribed this sentence so as to make it stand at first as a condensed version, and later as an almost verbatim copy, of George Petyt, p. 390 (lines 29-33), 391 (lines 1-10). Contrary to his uniform practice, TJ did not annotate the sentence, but Petyt not only assigned it to Scobell's *Memorials*, p. 94, but also made his own wording of it conform quite faithfully to that source. Note that, in TJ's text, and in Petyt's and Scobell's as well, the task of writing letters to justices of assizes for the purpose of deferring trials against members of Parliament during a session belongs to the clerk. But note also that the writing of similar letters to the officers of higher courts is the task of the Speaker of the Commons. See above, par. [391], n. 1.

PARAGRAPH [393]

1　In framing this sentence and providing it with an annotation, TJ relied upon George Petyt, p. 391 (lines 24-9), 392 (lines 7-10); and Petyt's more verbose wording was drawn almost verbatim from Scobell's *Memorials*, p. 95. TJ achieved in his version a stylistic distinction not found at this point in either of those sources. For example, compare the economy of the wording that he chose for himself with the prolixity of the following parallel sentences from Petyt: "The Privilege of the House is so much insisted on, that it hath been a Question, *Whether any Member of the House could consent, that himself might be sued, during the Session; because the Privilege is not so much the Person's, as the House's* . . . There was a Question, *Whether the House should give Leave for a Breach of Privilege*; and it was resolved, *The House might give Leave*" (italics are Petyt's). For the parliamentary action behind the second of Petyt's sentences, see JHC, I, 378. That action occurred on June 3, 1607, in response to Sir Thomas Holcroft's request that, during the session then current, he be allowed to answer a suit that had been filed against him, and to file a suit against the suer, despite his being restricted by parliamentary privilege from taking either of those steps. A countersuit on Sir Thomas' part would imply that, as a Commoner on official duty, he was acknowledging the formal propriety of the other party's suit, as well as the emptiness of his own claim to special privilege, with the inevitable result that he was compromising the very notion of parliamentary privilege itself. The Commons gave him the right that day to proceed on his requested course, but there was a note of reluctance in the manner in which their consent was phrased for posterity.

PARAGRAPH [394]

1 In part transcribed by TJ almost verbatim in text and annotations, and in part condensed in text, from George Petyt, p. 400, lines 9-11, 14-29. Petyt's text was transcribed almost verbatim from Scobell's *Memorials*, p. 107-8. On the indicated pages in D'Ewes, the servant is called Roger Buston, and the Baron, Langton, while D'Ewes' text is somewhat more expansive than Scobell's. Petyt's reference to William Petyt's *Miscellanea Parliamentaria*, p. 119, did not concern Lanckton, Baron of Walton, but Sir Robert Philips, also titled Baron of Walton, whose servant is identified as the Baron's solicitor. His case, however, resembled that of Lanckton's servant, and thus it has some relevance to its present context. For TJ's longer entry using much of the wording and documentation given here to this subject, see below, par. [411].

PARAGRAPH [395]

1 What TJ did here was to condense into 30 words a 143-word paragraph in George Petyt, p. 403, lines 4-25. Like TJ, Petyt identified Scobell's *Memorials*, p. 101-2, as the source of this paragraph, and indeed its wording in Petyt is almost exactly that in Scobell. TJ added on his own the reference to Townshend's *Historical Collections*, p. 225-6, where the case of Lanckton's servant, who was also his master's solicitor, was discussed. See above, par. [394]. As for the case mentioned in the paragraph now before us, it concerned Sir Michael (not Sir Nicholas) Sandys and his solicitor, Thomas Finch, an attorney at law, who lived in Sir Michael's household and received regular wages for handling his employer's legal affairs. On February 6, 1606/07, Finch was arrested by Harrison, a serjeant at law, upon the allegation of a Longon fishmonger, Thomas Knight, that Finch owed him £40. At the moment, Parliament was in adjournment until February 10, but an adjournment did not mean that the privileges of its members were in abeyance. When Parliament reassembled, Sir Michael reported to the Commons what had happened to Finch. Thereupon the Commons decided not only that Finch be freed on a writ of habeas corpus, but also that Harrison and Knight be summoned to a hearing on February 13. At the hearing, Harrison and Knight declared that, at the time of the arrest, they had not known of Finch's affiliation with a member of the Commons. Sir Michael then testified that Finch slept in his house, tended to his legal business, received wages, and as his servant was entitled to parliamentary privilege. The hearing having ended, the Commons voted that Harrison and Knight were not guilty of wrongdoing, but that Finch should have privilege from arrest, even as former solicitors in the employ of members of the Commons had had. See JHC, I, 332, 334.

PARAGRAPH [396]

1 In compiling this sentence and its annotation from George Petyt, p. 405, lines 7-12, TJ made use of paraphrase and verbatim transcription. Petyt's wording of his passage followed Scobell's *Memorials*, p. 114, almost word for word. Scobell

and Petyt dated the case February 12, 18 Jacobi, that is, 1620/21. See JHC, I, 517, 518, 520.

2 This sentence and the date given here were transcribed in large part verbatim by TJ from George Petyt, p. 405, lines 19-26. The passage in the latter source was transcribed verbatim from Scobell's *Memorials*, p. 114.

3 The twenty-four words which make up this sentence and its two annotations represent TJ's partly verbatim and partly paraphrased condensation of George Petyt, p. 406, lines 4-8. Petyt drew his text from Townshend's *Historical Collections*, p. 195-6, and from D'Ewes, p. 629, col. 2 (not col. 1, as Petyt said). In D'Ewes' account, the page was identified as Rowland Kendall, and the affronted member as Sir Francis Hastings. What happened was that, on November 6, 1601, as he was descending the outer stair near the entrance into the Commons, Sir Francis and other members were subjected to abuse and lewd suggestions by some pages and their companions. Sir Francis seized one of the pages, a long haired-youth with the name just mentioned, and took him into the presence of the Speaker. And the Speaker, on the strength of Sir Francis' complaint, committed Kendall to the custody of the serjeant at arms. At the meeting of Commons on the next day, Sir Francis presented the details of his encounter with the pages, but his attitude was no longer hostile. Admitting that Kendall had committed no specific offense against him, he expressed the belief that Kendall was innocent of any lewd intent and was quite unwilling to perform the acts which the demeanor of his companions had implied. Sir Francis then urged that Kendall's further punishment be confined to his kneeling at the bar and indicating his submission to the House. This recommendation was carried out, and Kendall was discharged after being given a sharp reprimand by the Speaker. It should be added that, according to Townshend's account, some members of Commons, acting before Kendall's reprimand, introduced a resolution that Kendall be taken to the barber shop for a haircut. That resolution lost, however, because it was thought "unfit, for the Gravity of the House to take notice of so light a fault." All of these circumstances have to be mentioned if the modern reader is to find a context into which the verb "throng" would fit, as TJ, Petyt, and Townshend used it. D'Ewes described the abuse heaped upon Sir Francis by the pages as "lewd misdemeanors." The notions of lewdness and illegality might shed light, however, on the off-color meaning sometimes attached to "throng." The OED indicates that it can signify "squeeze," or "press," or "force one's way against obstacles." Thus the offer of the pages, couched in such language, or in D'Ewes' blunter phrase, cannot be devoid of sexual implications.

PARAGRAPH [397]

1 Transcribed verbatim by TJ in text and annotation from George Petyt, p. 406 (lines 29-32), 407 (lines 1-6), except that Petyt's second sentence began with "And all agreed, *That regularly he*," whereas TJ reduced those six words to three, as indicated. Both TJ and Petyt put the word "member" before the Latin phrase, and "the" before "court," whereas Rushworth, whom Petyt otherwise followed verbatim, did not. Thus it is certain that in this paragraph Petyt was TJ's true but unacknowledged source, and Rushworth was Petyt's. The textual units in brackets, as in the following paragraph, are here copied into TJ's text from the corresponding units in Petyt, inasmuch as a smear has made TJ's

manuscript illegible at those precise points. It should be noted that the first sentence of this paragraph was paraphrased in part, and in part copied verbatim, into TJ's *Manual* and there attributed to "*Com. P.*" For an explanation, see Jefferson's Abbreviations in the front matter. For references by TJ to the opening clause of the second sentence of this paragraph, see above, pars. 132, [375]. According to Rushworth, I, 662-3, this entire paragraph represents the opinion of a panel of judges assembled by Charles I in April 1629, to define the boundaries of the Commons' right to debate. The king had just arrested Sir John Eliot and three other members of the Commons for what they had said in the Lower House, and he obviously wanted the judges to approve of his action. But the approval he received from them here was more noncommittal than positive.

PARAGRAPH [398]

1 In wording and documentation, this sentence was drawn by TJ from George Petyt, p. 381, lines 2-7, whereas Petyt drew his similar but not identical sentence from "2. *Nalson*. 450." and "4. Inst. 25." Earlier (see above, par. 79), TJ recorded that the rule here given included only felony and treason; and he based that limitation of its whole scope upon Crompton's *Courts*, p. 11, and Hakewill, p. 62. On a later occasion (see above, par. [384]), TJ broadened the rule so as to make it embrace breach of the peace as well as treason and felony; and there he relied upon Petyt, p. 380-1, while taking not of Petyt's references to Hakewill, p. 62, Crompton's *Courts*, p. 11, Coke's *Institutes*, IV, 25, Nalson's *Impartial Collection*, II, 450, and Dyer's *Novel Cases*, p. 60, pl. 19.

PARAGRAPH [399]

1 Transcribed verbatim by TJ in text and documentation from George Petyt, p. 407, lines 18-22, except that TJ made the seventeenth word singular, whereas Petyt made it plural. So far as his passage goes, Petyt transcribed it almost verbatim from a longer passage in Nalson's *Impartial Collection*, II, 450.

PARAGRAPH [400]

1 Transcribed verbatim by TJ in text and documentation from George Petyt, p. 407, lines 23-7, except that Petyt placed the date at the beginning of the paragraph, inserted two words immediately thereafter, wrote "matters" as a singular noun, put the main verb into the past tense, and added "of the House" after "privilege." Petyt's version is stated in the form of a parliamentary resolution, and he indicated its source as "*Rush*, 2 vol. 2d Part. 1147," that is, Rushworth, Part II, Vol. 2, p. 1147. The resolution itself (see JHC, II, 13-14), which was adopted on April 27, 1640, had grown out of the longstanding struggle between Charles I and the Commons on the subjects of money, supply, and parliamentary privilege. In the preceding eleven years, Charles had conducted the government without bothering to convene Parliament. But his ultimate need for parliamentary revenue finally became greater than his capacity to run affairs from his other resources, and at that point, April 13, 1640, to be exact, he summoned Parliament into session. The Commons met in a rebellious mood, as Charles I knew full well, thanks to their having been treated with contempt for eleven years, and to their having been subjected to arrest and persecution in the earlier part of his arbitrary reign. But warlike tensions between England and Scotland were threatening English security in 1640, and, in the light of them, Charles assumed

that English patriotism would lead the Commons to submerge their grievances against him and give priority to his military requirements. On that occasion, however, Charles took a step which made the Commons think less of the dangers from Scotland than of their own resentments against their king. Appearing before the Lords on April 24, Charles urged them to use their influence to get the Commons to give financial support to his plans to arm England, and the Lords thereupon complied by voting that the Commons should do as the king wished. But instead of directly notifying the Commons of their action, the Lords asked instead for a conference between the two houses, thinking that, in a small meeting, they could explain the reasons behind their vote while disclaiming any intention on their part of interfering with the right of the Commons to originate money bills. On Monday, April 27, the conference committee of the Commons reported back to their house. Out of respect for the king and the Lords as historic partners of the Commons in the English political system, the Commons voted to make the Lords' recommendation a matter of record in their own journals; but they also voted that the Lords, merely by making that recommendation, had interfered with the ancient right of the Commons to handle those particular matters by themselves, and thus had been guilty of a breach of privilege. So it is that TJ's paragraph has behind it the undiplomatic behavior of the king, the unconstitutional practice of the Lords, and a new occasion for resentment among the Commons.

PARAGRAPH [401]

1 This paragraph is a somewhat condensed version not only of a passage and its documentation in George Petyt, p. 407, lines 28-32, but also of a marginal reference in the same source, p. 408, lines 21-2. Petyt based his passage upon Nalson's *Impartial Collection*, II, 729; and a page later, in connection with another matter, he added a marginal reference to p. 823 of the same volume of Nalson's work. These citations by Petyt and TJ respectively designate two episodes in which attempts were made to use troops to influence the parliamentary procedures of the Commons. The first episode occurred on December 10, 1641, when halberdiers, who had been stationed in Westminster to discourage public outcries against unpopular votes registered by the bishops in the House of Lords, were ordered to surround the Lower House, as if to place it under military duress. The Commons passed an immediate resolution declaring it a breach of their privilege for armed guards to be stationed around their house without their consent; and later the Commons conducted an investigation which revealed that the order behind the action of the guards had passed along a chain of command involving a bailiff, an undersheriff, a sheriff, a high constable, a justice of the peace, the lord keeper, and the House of Lords, acting under the advice of judges. The investigation also revealed that the justice of the peace, one George Long, had neglected to pass down from the lord keeper a stipulation that the Commons should receive prior notice of the stationing of armed guards around their house. Long was not deprived of his justiceship by the Commons, but he was sent to the Tower for "an Offence committed against the Privilege of this House." See JHC, II, 338, 339, 340. See also above, par. 129, n. 12. As for the second abovementioned episode, it occurred on January 4, 1641/42, less than a month after the case of the halberdiers. For a previous account of it, and for the famous rebuke which Speaker Lenthall administered to Charles I on that occasion, see above, par. 144, n. 5. With Charles I's unconstitutional behavior in mind, the

Commons met next day and passed a resolution which George Petyt, p. 408-9, reduced to two parts. Its first part recorded that Charles I had come to the House of Commons on January 4, accompanied by armed men, and had demanded that five Commoners be surrendered to him. Its second part not only denounced the king's conduct as "a high Breach of the Rights and Privileges of Parliament," but also requested that, as the price of their willingness to continue to perform their parliamentary function, they should be fully vindicated and given a sufficient guard to ensure their future security. Five days after this disastrous confrontation between the king and the Lower House, Charles I left London with his family, never to return, except as a prisoner, and the Civil War began at Nottingham August 22, 1642. In addition to the references cited above in par. 144, n. 5, for this second episode, see Nalson's *Impartial Collection*, II, 820-3, and *Parliamentary History of England*, x, 161-8, 196-7. See also JHC, II, 368-9.

PARAGRAPH [402]

1 See below, par. [404].

PARAGRAPH [403]

1 See below, par. [404].

PARAGRAPH [404]

1 This paragraph and the two immediately preceding consist of TJ's almost verbatim transcription of the key import and documentation of each of three one-sentence paragraphs in George Petyt, p. 408, lines 2-6, 8-13, 15-20. The three paragraphs were transcribed by Petyt from three resolutions adopted by the Lords and Commons on December 16, 1641, and recorded in Nalson's *Impartial Collection*, II, 741 (not 743, as Petyt's mistaken reference led TJ to believe). See also JHC, II, 345, where the paragraphs are presented, not as separate resolutions, but as statements in what the Commons called "A declaratory Protestation, and a petitionary Remonstrace." This remonstrance had been occasioned by Charles I's behavior on December 14, only four days after the Commons had objected to the stationing of an armed guard around their house (see above, par. [401], n. 1). What Charles I did on December 14 was to summon the Lords and Commons to a joint meeting that very day in the House of Lords, where he called their attention, not only to the need to send troops to Ireland to reduce that nation to its "true and wonted Obedience," but also to his request that the Commons refrain from attaching to a current bill any infringement upon the royal prerogative, and from allowing a certain unnamed one of their members to prolong debates by making the royal prerogative an issue. After this speech by the king, the Commons returned to their own house and immediately summoned a conference with the Lords to consider whether Charles I, in taking notice of a bill while it was under deliberation in both houses, had violated ancient custom, and whether he, in speaking of infringements of the royal prerogative, had implied that the sphere of activity of the Commons was to be reduced to the king's definition of what it ought to include. In the conference that followed between the Commons and the Lords, a third grievance against the king was added to the two previously suggested by the Lower House—that it had been a breach of privilege for the king to "*express his displeasure against some Person or Persons, which had moved some Doubt or Question concerning the Bound of Prerogative.*"

(Italics are Nalson's, p. 739.) These three protests were incorporated into a petition to the king from the Lords and Commons, and were adopted by both houses on December 16, in somewhat the form that they have in TJ's paragraphs. See Nalson's *Impartial Collection*, II, 738-41; and JHC, II, 342, 345-6; and *Parliamentary History of England*, x, 98-100.

PARAGRAPH [405]

1 The final eleven words of this sentence were transcribed verbatim by TJ from George Petyt, p. 409, lines 26-9, and TJ's earlier wording, except for "See," came to him from Petyt's accompanying marginal note. Petyt went on to explain that, in Statute 12 & 13, as passed in the reign of William III, members of the House of Lords or the House of Commons, and other privileged persons, could be prosecuted in the interval between the dissolving or prorogating of one Parliament and the assembling of the next. Thus parliamentary privilege was clarified so as to remove important inconveniences that might occur to an aggrieved party seeking the earliest possible settlement of his claim against a Lord or a Commoner. For the parliamentary actions taken to pass the statutes mentioned here, see JHC, XIII, 510, 511, 515, 522, 531, 533, 540, 559, 567-70, 625.

PARAGRAPH [406]

1 TJ transcribed these two rules from the somewhat expanded wording in which they were expressed by George Petyt, p. 414, lines 5-7, 20-1. Petyt transcribed them almost verbatim from Bohun's *Collection of Debates*, p. 27, 230. The first rule was adopted February 13, 1700/01, and the second, November 28, 1699. See JHC, XIII, 326, 8.

PARAGRAPH [407]

1 Transcribed verbatim by TJ in text and documentation from George Petyt, p. 414, lines 12-18, except for TJ's omission of "for" after "sitting" and of eight elaborative but not strictly necessary words. Petyt's transcription of this rule followed almost verbatim the wording that he found in Bohun's *Collection of Debates*, p. 27. See also JHC, XIII, 326, under the date of February 13, 1700/01.

PARAGRAPH [408]

1 This paragraph was compiled by TJ from words, phrases, complete sentences, numerals, etc., as they appear in the Appendix of George Petyt's *Lex Parliamentaria* in Petyt's account of the struggle between James I and the Commons over the case of a disputed election involving Sir Francis Goodwyn and Sir John Fortescue. The following list shows where key units in TJ's text are to be found in Petyt:

"Outlawry in personal actions . . . ," Petyt, p. 417, lines 29-31.
"39.H.6.," p. 417 (lines 31-2), 418 (lines 1-4).
"Again 1.El.," p. 419, line 20-1.
"Again in Fludd's case 23.El.," p. 419, lines 24-5.
"So in Fitz-Herbert's ca. & Killegrew's case, & Sr. Walter Harcourt's case in 35.El.," p. 419 (lines 30-2), 420 (line 2).
". . . Goodwyn's & Fortescue's case," p. 415, lines 3-6.
"But in this last case the judges denied the position," p. 420, lines 9-13.
". . . a person outlawed could not be a member & cited 35.H.6. & 1.H.7. So

adjudged in parl.," p. 424 (lines 31-2), 425 (lines 6-11).

". . . & further that the party outlawed . . . but must sue out a Sci. fa. against the creditor," p. 425, lines 19-21.

"But the house of Commons persevered . . . Goodwyn," p. 427, lines 5-6.

2 Petyt's Appendix contains no reference to *Arcana Parliamentaria*, p. 65, but that work on the designated page discussed the question whether outlawry disqualified anyone from serving in the Commons. TJ added this reference to draw attention to a source which supplemented what Petyt said. For TJ's previous mention of the Goodwyn-Fortescue case, see above, par. [205], n.

PARAGRAPH [409]

1 See below, par. [410].

PARAGRAPH [410]

1 As his notes partly indicate, TJ based this and the preceding paragraph upon George Petyt, p. 427, 428-30, as follows:

"The returns of writs . . . parl.," p. 427, lines 27-9.
"All writs . . . chancery," p. 428, lines 11-25.
"But yet . . . returns," p. 428, lines 25-7.
". . . & accordingly . . . returns," p. 429, lines 13-15.
". . . and in the 29.Eliz. . . . returns," p. 429 (lines 20-1), p. 430, lines 1-3.

In transcribing verbatim or paraphrasing these passages, TJ made one interesting change in Petyt's wording. Petyt said, "but yet that did not take away the Jurisdiction of the Parliament, to meddle with . . ." (p. 428, lines 25-7). TJ changed "meddle with" to "inquire into," but he later followed Petyt's use of "meddle" when Petyt recorded (p. 430) Parliament's characterization of the chancellor's interference with election results.

PARAGRAPH [411]

1 As its first note indicates in part, this paragraph and its secondary documentation were transcribed largely verbatim by TJ from George Petyt, Ch. 23 (p. 400, lines 9-26, 29-32). The italics are TJ's. For a thirty-five-word condensation of the ninety-two-word paragraph and secondary documentation given here, see above, par. [394]. The shorter version contains no italics. Petyt recorded that the plaintiff was "one *Muscle*" and that Muscle and the officer making the arrest were brought by the Serjeant to the bar and "there charged by Mr. Speaker, in the Name of the whole House. . . ."

PARAGRAPH [412]

1 As TJ's final note indicated without full details, this passage was transcribed almost verbatim from Rushworth, ɪᴠ, 586 (that is, as the 1692 edition identifies it on its title page, from "The Third Part; In Two Volumes [volume the First]," p. 586). The passage, as transcribed by Rushworth, is part of a document entitled *A Remonstrance; or the Declaration of the Lords and Commons now assembled in Parliament, the* 26th *of* May, 1642, *in Answer to a Declaration under his Majesty's Name, concerning the business of* Hull. As TJ's own title pointed out, this document may with equal propriety be called Declaration of the Commons on the king's declaring Sir John Hotham a trayter. Had TJ gone on to transcribe

[274]

the sentence given next in Rushworth's text, he would have recorded the following words: "And therefore we no ways doubt, but every one that hath taken the Protestation, will, according to his Solemn Vow and Oath, defend it with his Life and Fortune." TJ would have read this sentence, of course; and its final phrase may have been in a corner of his memory when, in penning the Declaration of Independence, he vowed, in the name of those who were to risk all by signing it, that to its support "we mutually pledge to each other our lives, our fortunes, & our sacred honour." As for the king's declaring Sir John Hotham a traitor, that name-calling took place on April 23, 1642, just four months before the Civil War became a military reality. On January 11, 1641/42, both houses of Parliament had resolved that some companies of trained troops were to be moved into Hull to protect the munitions stored there, and that those troops would be commanded by Sir John Hotham, a member of Commons (JHC, II, 371). What Parliament feared was that the Hull munitions would be seized by Charles I for the use of his forces, if the threatening war actually broke out. Having established his court that spring at York, Charles I was incensed to hear that a plan was afoot to transfer the Hull munitions to London for safekeeping, and so he acted at once. With 400 armed horsemen behind him, he marched to the gates of Hull on April 23, and, in the name of his royal authority, he demanded admission. Sir John refused the king's request on the ground that Parliament had ordered no one to be admitted except by its approval. Charles I then asked Sir John to produce that order. Sir John declined. Charles I next proposed that he be admitted to Hull with 20 armed horsemen, and that he be granted one night's lodging. Sir John accepted this offer, but only under restrictive conditions. Thinking himself humiliated by the mere idea of having conditions imposed upon him, Charles I called Sir John a traitor. To his credit, however, the king did not start a fight, he elected rather to withdraw with his men. In the Remonstrace which the Lords and Commons voiced against the king's behavior in this episode, they protested that his words of condemnation took Sir John's guilt for granted in advance and thus deprived him of his right to be regarded as innocent until the customary trial by the Lords had found otherwise. And behind their protest was the recognition that, if a man guilty of treason may not serve in Parliament, and if his guilt could be established only by the say-so of the king or some other person, then Parliament itself in any given session could be deprived of its membership merely by a series of unproved accusations. For the sources of this account of the Hotham episode, see the following: Rushworth, IV, 577-88; JHC, II, 132, 371, 542-89; *Parliamentary History of England*, IX, 292-3; X, 417, 439-42, 454-8, 465-9; XI, 89-115; *Papers*, I, 427.

PARAGRAPH [413]

1 This paragraph would seem at first to have been based by TJ upon the *Arcana Parliamentaria*, p. 53, as the initial unit of his documentation suggests. Certainly that source contains a short account of the case of Ferrers, and it refers its readers to "*Hollinshed*, in his Chronicle, *Fol.* 1584," and to "*Dier, Fol.* 275." But three details in TJ's paragraph are not in the *Arcana Parliamentaria*, namely, that Ferrers was arrested "in going to the parliament," and that, after he was discharged "by privilege," he "could not be again taken by law whereby the party was without remedy." These phrases are recognizable parts of Hollinshed's rather full account, whereas Dyer's one-sentence account does not mention them. What may have happened was that TJ's paragraph started off from the

Arcana Parliamentaria, and ended with Holinshed, after TJ had found the former source too sketchy. His concluding cross-references were doubtless intended to remind him that he had previously made oblique references to Ferrers' case, and that those references were part of pars. 82, 130, and another one not specified, except as it is hinted at by the blank space following the final ampersand. Perhaps, if TJ had himself numbered more than the first 145 paragraphs of the Pocket-Book, and had he chanced to adopt the numbering system used in the present edition, he would have added [350] after his final ampersand to round out his documentation. At any rate, par. [350] deals with Ferrers' case, as the note affixed to it shows in detail above, and reference to it here would not have been out of order.

PARAGRAPH [414]

1 As TJ's documentation indicated in part, this paragraph was taken from the *Arcana Parliamentaria*, p. 56-7, the final 33 words having been transcribed verbatim. George Petyt's somewhat similar paragraph, p. 363, lines 21-7, was based upon William Petyt's *Miscellanea Parliamentaria*, p. 4, and its omission of TJ's final ten words is silent evidence that it could not have been TJ's source on the present occasion.

PARAGRAPH [415]

1 The passage condensed by TJ in forming this sentence is in *Arcana Parliamentaria*, p. 65-6, as his note partly indicated.

PARAGRAPH [416]

1 The author of *Arcana Parliamentaria*, who identified himself on his title page as "R.C. *of the Middle Temple*," gave TJ authority for making this statement by saying (p. 68): "The Queen may under the great Seal assign two or three Lords of Parliament to supply her place in Parliament, . . . as it was done *Anno* 31 *Eliz.* the Queen that now is. . . ."

PARAGRAPH [417]

1 Transcribed verbatim by TJ in text and secondary documentation from *Arcana Parliamentaria*, p. 69 (lines 5-14) and 77 (lines 7-12), except that TJ substituted "hath" for "had" in the first sentence, and he omitted "by Patent in Fee" after "mine already" in the second. The word "remitted" as it appears in this paragraph means "restored," and it indicates here that an older title to land cannot be restored to an heir if he inherits that land under a later title conferred by Parliament or by the king. But, in the latter case, if the king acknowledges that he is giving land to a person who already possesses it under an earlier title, then that earlier title may be restored to that person or his heirs at their request. See Jacob, s.v. remitter.

PARAGRAPH [418]

1 As his notes indicated, TJ transcribed this passage verbatim from Elsynge's *Method of Passing Bills*, p. 11, 12, except that TJ himself supplied the bracketed words and in the second sentence wrote "a" before "Commee." See *The Harleian Miscellany*, v, 213.

EDITOR'S NOTES

PARAGRAPH [419]

1 TJ compiled this passage in part by transcribing exact phrases and sentences from Elsynge's text and in part by summarizing or changing the wording that Elsynge had used to join them together. See *The Harleian Miscellany*, v, 213.

PARAGRAPH [420]

1 For the passage which supplied TJ with the substance and part of the wording of this paragraph, see *The Harleian Miscellany*, v, 215, col. 2, lines 9-22. *Domus Procerum* has been the Latin name of the House of Lords throughout much of its history, *procer* being the Latin term for noble, chief, leader. See Pike, *House of Lords*, p. 25, 113, 318.

PARAGRAPH [421]

1 TJ's wording was in part a paraphrase and in part a verbatim transcript from two paragraphs in Elsynge's *Method of Passing Bills*, p. 31. See *Harleian Miscellany*, v, 217, col. 2, lines 24, 35-7, 41-3, 45-6. For an earlier reference by TJ to these passages in Elsynge, see above, par. [271].

PARAGRAPH [422]

1 The rule here stated was derived by TJ from a Latin account of the case of Bogo de Clare in Hale's *Jurisdiction of Parliaments*, p. 29. Bogo de Clare and the prior of Trinity served a citation on the Earl of Cornwall during a session of Parliament, Bogo being the instigator of the action. Bogo was fined 3,000 marks, and he and the prior were confined to the Tower, for this violation of the privilege of a member of Parliament. Two-thirds of the fine went to the king, and one third to the Earl. See also George Petyt, p. 385-6, and Coke's *Institutes*, IV, 24. For earlier reference to Bogo de Clare, see above, par. 34, n. 2.

PARAGRAPH [423]

1 The final thirteen words of this paragraph were transcribed verbatim by TJ from Hale's *Jurisdiction of Parliaments*, p. 30, except that TJ added "or" before "surety." The other thirty-three words TJ transcribed from the same source, but he condensed Hale's phraseology somewhat. For previous mention and further explanation of the case of Thomas Thorpe, see above, pars. 81, 82.

PARAGRAPH [424]

1 The marginal number attached by TJ to this paragraph repeats the number in the margin of par. [419], as if TJ may have intended by this repetition to keep himself reminded that both paragraphs dealt with the procedures used in Commons when each party to a dispute among members was allowed counsel to represent him. These procedures were also the subject of pars. [425] and [426], and thus the reminder just mentioned would of course extend to them.

2 For comment upon TJ's sources and interests in this paragraph and the two following, see below, par. [426].

PARAGRAPH [425]

1 See below, par. [426].

PARAGRAPH [426]

1 In all likelihood, TJ derived this and the two preceding paragraphs from JHC, XXIV, 709-11, 714, 715, as his own citations would indicate in part. Those pages record the doings of the Commons on January 17, 18, 22, and 23, 1744/45; and TJ's three paragraphs turn upon those doings as they were confined at that time to a dispute concerning which one of two would-be members had been legally elected to represent in Commons the borough of Great Marlow in Bucks. One party to the dispute, Mr. Ockenden, had been adjudged winner after the election was held; the other party, Henry Conyngham, complained that some of the ballots cast for him had been improperly disqualified and should rightfully have given him the victory. Each party was represented by counsel when the dispute was heard before the bar of the Lower House. The JHC records what principles and facts were involved, how the Commons, the disputants, and their counsel conducted themselves, and which party came out victorious. (Because he withdrew his complaint at the end, the loser was Mr. Conyngham.) With these materials at his disposal, TJ chose to confine his notes to the procedral side of the question, his use of underscoring in par. [425] being a reflection of his main interest throughout. For the presence of pars. [424], [425], in the *Manual*, see that work (1801), Sec. XIII, pars. 3, 5; (1812), p. 45-6.

PARAGRAPH [427]

1 Up to this point, TJ's paragraph and its documentation represent a slightly expanded version of a passage in Hale's *Jurisdiction of Parliaments*, p. 110. As his authorities, Hale cited Seymour and the two specified parliamentary precedents. For the precedents, see D'Ewes, p. 159, col. 2, and JHC, I, 83, 141. The second precedent involved Sir Francis Bacon, who, having been elected from St. Albans in Hertford and from Ipswich in Suffolk, chose to represent Ipswich, in apparent unawareness that he was destined later to become Viscount St. Albans. The reference by Hale and TJ to "Seymour 58" involves an earlier precedent than the two just mentioned. The earliest on record would seem to be that of March 11, 1552/53. See JHC, I, 24.

2 A revealing aspect of this cross-reference is that it points back from information based upon Seymour and Hale's *Jurisdiction of Parliaments* to similar information based upon George Petyt, p. 273, lines 12-17, and on Scobell's *Memorials*, p. 18. TJ would thus seem to be engaged in keping himself reminded of the developing interconnections among his notes and of the composite strands of learning that he acquired from his sources.

PARAGRAPH [428]

1 This rule was transcribed verbatim by TJ in text and documentation from Hale's *Jurisdiction of Parliaments*, p. 111, although TJ did not mention that source. Hale based his wording of the rule upon "Seymour, Fol. 128." During Seymour's tenure as clerk of the Commons (1547-1567), the only recorded instance of the application of the rule to a claimant to membership occurred on March 5, 1557/58. The claimant was Christopher Perney (see below, par. [436]), but he was unable to prove "by warrant or the book of the clerk of the crown" that his claim was valid. See JHC, I, 50-1.

PARAGRAPH [429]

1 The OED traces the English word "mace" to the Old French *masse* and relates it to the Italian *mazza*, etc. For its late Latin forms, see Latham's *Medieval Latin Word-List*, p. 284.

2 According to Pliny the Elder's *Naturalis Historia*, 6.11.29., the Macerones were a people living along the southeastern shore of the Black Sea. They might have been recruited by one or more Roman emperors to serve in the emperor's bodyguard, and the arms carried in that capacity would of course have resembled maces. But even so the tribal name of an emperor's guards would not have been likely to become the term used for the weapons they bore. It is more probable that the English word "mace" came from the Latin *matea*, which is related to *mateola*, meaning mallet. See OED.

3 TJ's library contained a copy of this anonymous work, which has often been attributed to R. Gosling. See Sowerby 414 (I, 183).

PARAGRAPH [430]

1 TJ transcribed the substance of this paragraph, and some of its wording, from Hale's *Jurisdiction of Parliaments*, p. 112; and Hale indicated in a marginal note that he had based his text upon the record of the action taken by the Commons "10 May, 13 Eliz.," that is, May 10, 1571. See D'Ewes, p. 182, col. 2. D'Ewes related that the briber was Thomas Long, Gent.; that he had been lawfully elected to his seat in Parliament; that he was considered "a very simple man and of small capacity to serve in that place"; and that, for some reason, he confessed in open Parliament to having given to Anthony Garland, mayor of Westbury, and to a Mr. Wats, a bribe of £4, if they would name him to the Commons. After Long's confession, the Commons voted to penalize Garland and Wats "for their said lewd and slanderous attempt," and to release Long and his heirs from any obligations Long may have assumed in getting his seat in Parliament. D'Ewes did not mention whether Long received any penalty for his part in bringing those transactions into effect. But Coke's *Institutes*, IV, 23, lines 44-5, noted that Long was removed from the Lower House "for this corrupt dealing was to poyson the very fountain it self." For other references to this case of bribery, see above, pars. 33, 129.

PARAGRAPH [431]

1 In fashioning this sentence from the text of Hale's *Jurisdiction of Parliaments*, p. 113, lines 10-14, TJ condensed the thirty-two words of his source into fifteen words and bettered the syntax. Hale's original sentence declared it to be a rule of the Commons that, if a member is indicted of felony during a parliamentary session, "he shall remain until he be Convict thereof." TJ changed "Convict" to "convicted" and "remain" to "retains," while dropping out "thereof" altogether. But then he tended to nullify these stylistic improvements by failing to add "seat" after "his" so as to give the possessive pronoun something definite to possess. Hale acknowledged in a marginal note that his text rested upon the record of proceedings in Commons on "21 Jan. 23 Eliz.," that is, January 21, 1580/81. For that record, see D'Ewes, p. 283, col. 1. For TJ's other version of the parliamentary rule given here, see above, par. 137.

[279]

PARAGRAPH [432]

1 These two sentences state in twenty-two words the substance and much of the wording of a thirty-three-word passage in Hale's *Jurisdiction of Parliaments*, p. 114. Hale identified his source as "24 Eliz.," but in that year no session of Parliament occurred, and the episode mentioned here seems not to have been recorded in earlier or later parliamentary sessions in Elizabeth I's reign. A member was reported dead and a new member elected in the dead man's place in the parliamentary session of 1610, but that dead man seems not to have been found later to be alive. See JHC, I, 417-18. For the case of a member reported dead but later found to be alive before a new member was elected, see below, par. [452].

2 TJ mistakenly placed this cross-reference here. But it belongs to par. [431], since that paragraph and par. 137 deal with the same subject.

PARAGRAPH [433]

1 In transcribing this rule, its date, and the first two units of its documentation from Hale's *Jurisdiction of Parliaments*, p. 114-15, TJ borrowed much of the phraseology of his source but condensed it measurably without loss of essential meaning. Hale drew a large part of his text almost verbatim from the recorded proceedings of the Commons, but the date as he gave it was wrong. It should have been "25 Junii, 2 Jac." See JHC, I, 246. The rule owed its original authority to a precedent in the 38th year of Henry VIII's reign, as recorded by Brooke's *La Graunde Abridgement*, s.v. Parliament, par. 7.

2 This cross-reference was plainly intended by TJ to keep himself reminded that the rule just stated had not always been observed—that par. 46 above denied it on the authority of Coke's *Institutes*, IV, 48, lines 3-4, and on the precedents which Coke's legal learning would probably have included.

PARAGRAPH [434]

1 As his later note indicated without giving details, TJ transcribed this sentence verbatim from Hale's *Jurisdiction of Parliaments*, p. 116, lines 13-16, except that TJ's three final words accurately condense the meaning expressed by Hale at that point in nine words.

2 This sentence and its documentation were based by TJ upon a differently arranged sentence and marginal note in Hale's *Jurisdiction of Parliaments*, p. 116, lines 3-6. The reference to "Seymour 263" must be construed as the citation of the manuscript version of what was to appear in JHC, I, 75, as an entry under the date of October 29, 1566, when John Seymour was clerk of the Commons. That entry read as follows: "A Warrant granted for a Burgess for *Grampond* in *Cornub'*, in Place of *Christopher Perne*, reported to be lunatick."

3 TJ compiled these twenty-three words from a sentence of thirty-three words in Hale's *Jurisdiction of Parliaments*, p. 117, lines 1-6, as TJ's note made certain.

4 TJ constructed this sentence by accurately summarizing a much longer sentence and its documentation in Hale's *Jurisdiction of Parliaments*, p. 120, lines 3-29. For further details concerning Richard Onslow's election as Speaker of the Commons, see below, par. [435]. For authorities not mentioned by Hale, see JHC, I, 73, and D'Ewes, sig. A 4v and p. 120-1, 277-8.

5 Hale's *Jurisdiction of Parliaments*, p. 122-3, supplied TJ with the materials upon which he here based his mention of the circumstances of John Popham's election as Speaker. For a source not cited in this connection by Hale or TJ, see D'Ewes, sig. A 4v and p. 280-1. For further details of Popham's case, see below, par. [435].

PARAGRAPH [435]

1 The two cases discussed here and in Hale's *Jurisdiction of Parliaments*, p. 120-3, were so closely parallel as to make the earlier one an inevitable precedent for the later. In 1566, Richard Onslow, who was sitting at that time with the Lords in his capacity as the queen's solicitor general, was brought back to the Lower House to participate as a duly elected Commoner in the choosing of a new Speaker; and when he arrived there, he found himself the victorious candidate for that office. Almost the same set of circumstances prevailed in 1581, when John Popham, a Commoner serving as solicitor general, came down from the Lords and was chosen Speaker of his own house. But in his case the Commons openly made his eligibility for the Speakership depend upon his being present at the election. Thus a basic requirement for him had not received special application to Onslow. This slight difference between the two elections is indicated in the accounts of them by D'Ewes and Hale, but TJ ignored it altogether. And indeed, in view of the process by which two or more parliamentary cases merge over the years into a single precedent, TJ's interpretation seems valid enough.

PARAGRAPH [436]

1 TJ's text and first article of documentation were transcribed partly verbatim and partly by paraphrase from Hale's *Jurisdiction of Parliaments*, p. 126, except that TJ changed Hale's probable misprint, *"Perue,"* to "Perne." Hale's source was "Seymour, Fol. 178," in the manuscript he was using, but to us that same source would be indicated as JHC, I, 51. There the name of the self-proclaimed member is given as "Christopher Perney." The connection between him and the "Christopher Perne" mentioned above in par. [434] goes no farther than a similarity of names.

PARAGRAPH [437]

1 Transcribed verbatim by TJ in text and first unit of documentation from Hale's *Jurisdiction of Parliaments*, p. 126, except that TJ dropped "of the House" after "Member." Hale said that he based his text upon an act of the Commons on "17 May, 13 Eliz.," but he should have given the date as May 28 of that year (1571). See JHC, I, 93. On that day, the Commons appointed a distinguished committee to investigate rumors that certain members of the Commons had sold their votes "in the Furtherance or Hindrance" of bills before the House. The committee reported next day "That they cannot learn of any, that hath sold his Voice in this House, or any way dealt unlawfully or indirectly in that Behalf." See also D'Ewes, p. 189-90.

2 The thirty-one words of this sentence represent TJ's condensed version of a paragraph of 110 words in Hale's *Jurisdiction of Parliaments*, p. 126-7. Hale's source, which he did not indicate, was JHC, I, 95, 96. See also D'Ewes, p. 207, 212. The offending member was Arthur Hall, Esq., not the Sir Francis of Hale's account. For TJ's previous references to Hall, see above, pars. 33, 129, 138. See

also Hale's *Jurisdiction of Parliaments*, p. 128-9, where Hall's first name was given correctly.

3 Condensed by TJ in text and first unit of documentation from Hale's *Jurisdiction of Parliaments*, p. 129. As Hale indicated in part, but not with complete accuracy, his source was JHC, I, 162, under the date of April 3, 1604, in the second, not in the first, year of James I's reign. The speaker was Griffin Payne, a caterer; his "unreverent speech" attacked the Commons for sponsoring a bill that would regulate caterers; and, when called to the bar of Commons to explain the bitter invectives in his speech, he incidentally revealed that he was mayor of his borough, Wallingford. Thus two charges were in order against him—that of his unparliamentary language, and that of his serving in Commons as a mayor; and he was suspended until a decision could be made on these matters. The decision came on June 25, 1604, and it affirmed that, from the end of that very Parliament to the end of time, no mayor would be eligible to serve in the Lower House. See JHC, I, 245-6. The authority behind that decision was cited in Commons as "Brook's Abridgment," that is, Brooke's *La Graunde Abridgement*, s.v. Parliament, par. 7. For TJ's earlier mention of that decision as a parliamentary rule, see above, par. [433], n. 1.

4 These two sentences and the first unit in their documentation were transcribed by TJ in part verbatim and in part by close paraphrase from Hale's *Jurisdiction of Parliaments*, p. 131-2. Hale's source, "Seymour. 153," is of course equivalent to JHC, I, 44-5. The episode to which these sentences refer occurred on November 20 and 21, 1555. On November 19, a meeting had taken place between Queen Mary and the Speaker of Commons accompanied by some fifty of his colleagues; and on November 20 the Speaker gave to the Commons a report of that meeting. The queen, he said, had expressed her views on the question of profits from the first year of spiritual livings and on that of tributes from spiritual benefices; and he indicated that he and the Lord Cardinal had then made some observations to the queen. At that point, he went on, Mr. John Story, a member of the group from Commons, claimed attention and, kneeling before the queen, declared that the Speaker had neglected to tell her of the desire of the Commons to restrain the royal practice of issuing licenses to certain persons to permit them to ignore the laws of the land. Story's words amounted to a breach of parliamentary etiquette. For one thing, he had spoken to the queen on behalf of the Commons when only the Speaker could do that. Moreover, he had revealed to an outsider what the Commons were discussing among themselves in legislation not yet enacted. Still again, he had implied that the Speaker was at fault in not telling the queen what was going on in his own bailiwick. Small wonder that the Speaker, having reported Story's words to the Commons, should ask them what they would want next to do. The Commons decided that Story had acted, not to humiliate the Speaker, or to violate parliamentary proprieties, but to emphasize his zeal for the issues involved. Thus the Commons fixed no penalty upon him; and on the next day, when he himself confessed to his faults and promised to be discreet in the future, they voted a second time not to punish him. For these details, see JHC, I, 44-5; also see *Parliamentary History of England*, III, 346-8.

PARAGRAPH [438]

1 As his note partially indicated, TJ transcribed this passage verbatim from Hale's *Jurisdiction of Parliaments*, p. 137, except that Hale put "4 June. I Jac."

in the margin. Hale's source was JHC, I, 224-5, but the date he gave was incorrect. It should be May 24 of the second year (1604) of James I's reign. The original resolution in its context was designed to guarantee a member of Commons the freedom not only to subscribe to the wording of a treaty that he had helped to formulate in a special commission, but also to oppose that wording, if he chose, when the treaty came up later for consideration by Parliament. The same freedom already applied to member's conduct on the floor of the house toward a bill which he had endorsed in committee. Like TJ and Hale, the Commons in their resolution used "concluded" to mean "precluded," as it sometimes did up to the early eighteenth century.

PARAGRAPH [439]

1 In text and documentation this sentence appears to be the end result of TJ's attempt to resolve an inconsistency between three earlier and two later paragraphs in Hale's *Jurisdiction of Parliaments*, p. 140 (lines 14-18, 21-4) and 141 (lines 13-14, 24-6). The first three of those paragraphs definitely declared that the attorney general and the solicitor general were attendants of the House of Lords but were not simultaneously members of the Commons. Hale rested that declaration upon Seymour, fols. 27, 280, 127, and 160. Hale's last two paragraphs, however, cited instances in which the solicitor general and attorney general were simultaneously members of the Commons and attendants upon the Lords, the solicitor general being Onslow in 1566, and the attorney general, Sir Henry Hobart in 1606. See JHC, I, 73, 324. See also above, par. [435]. Note that, in transcribing Hale's citation of this latter case, TJ wrote "24 Jac. 3. sess. Jac.," when the date as Hale gave it was "3 Sess. Jac. 24 Nov." In other words, TJ omitted Hale's "Nov." and placed "24" before "Jac.," as if Sir Henry's case came much later than it did, and as if James I's reign had not ended in its 23rd year. The facts were, of course, that, on November 24, 1606, in the third session of James I's first Parliament, Sir Henry Hobart, a member of the Commons, was appointed attorney general, and the question immediately arose among the Commoners whether Sir Henry could remain in the Lower House and simultaneously fill his new office. Precedents were consulted, and it was found that that particular question had never been confronted. Nevertheless, the Commons voted at once to refrain from making a question of the matter, and thus Sir Henry was left with official status in two jobs, but without positive action to back up his right to both. In consulting the precedents that led to this ambiguous solution, the Commons took notice that Onslow and Jeffereys were members of the Lower House in their day and had also sat with the Lords, the former as solicitor general, and the latter as queen's serjeant. And those two cases must have caused the Commons to hesitate about voting to make the new attorney general an exception to what seemed the rule in similar situations. But, even so, the Commons did not vote to make that rule apply to the attorney general. They simply refused to vote upon its applicability, thereby allowing it to apply by default. Thus TJ's reluctance, as implied in the first sentence of this paragraph, to consider the rule completely firm, is understandable.

2 TJ condensed this note and took its documentation from Hale's *Jurisdiction of Parliaments*, p. 141, lines 17-23. Hale's true source, however, should have been given as "17 Feb. 18 Eliz.," that is, 1575/76; and Hale's "King's Serjeant" should have been "Queen's Serjeant." See D'Ewes, 249, col. 1.

[283]

3 This note and the main part of its documentation were drawn by TJ from a nine-word jotting and its marginal note in Hale's *Jurisdiction of Parliaments*, p. 141. For other mention of the Master of the Rolls, see JHC, I, 9, 16, 25, 83.

4 See Hale's *Jurisdiction of Parliaments*, p. 141, for the source of TJ's note and documentation. For Hale's source, see JHC, I, 87.

5 TJ's doubt could have originated from the uncertainty that he felt as he was transcribing the first sentence of the present paragraph. Or it could have originated, not from Hale's unambiguous statement about the Deputy of Ireland, but from a sentence that Hale inserted in the *Jurisdiction of Parliaments*, p. 141, just prior to his remark about the Deputy. That sentence read thus: "*Note*, That in the whole Book of *Seymour*, the Attorney or Sollicitor was not of the House; *Onslow* sent for purposely to be chosen Speaker." Hale would surely have known that "the whole Book of *Seymour*" covered the period from 1547 to 1567, and that it therefore covered the year 1566, when, by Seymour's own record, Onslow, a member of the Commons serving as solicitor general, was called back to the Lower House and elected its Speaker. Confronted by this contradiction in Hale, TJ's skepticism at this point toward Hale was by no means unexpected. At the same time, the skepticism tends to show that TJ read his sources carefully and preferred doubt to certainty if they contradicted themselves.

6 TJ based this sentence and its documentation upon Hale's *Jurisdiction of Parliaments*, p. 141 (lines 2-8, 27-30), 142 (lines 1-4). For the source of Hale's second reference, see JHC, I, 373 (under the date of May 15, 1607).

PARAGRAPH [440]

1 In text and documentation this passage was transcribed verbatim by TJ from Hale's *Jurisdiction of Parliaments*, p. 145, except that TJ changed Hale's "upon" to "on," while transposing the last two grammatical units in Hale's first sentence and the two vowels in Hales "yield" as well. Hale gave his source merely as "17 Eliz." but in reality he should have cited "18 Eliz.," and if he had wanted to specify the date more accurately, he should have cited March 7-14, 1575/76. See JHC, I, 111, 113, 114, 115; also D'Ewes, p. 254, 258, 260, 261, 262, 263, 264, 265. The bill that occasioned this constitutional tension between the Lords and the Commons was intended "for Restitution in Blood of the Heirs of the Lord *Sturton*." Lord Sturton had been convicted by the Lords on February 26, 1556/57, and hanged a week later, for the murder of William Hartgill and Hartgill's son in a feud involving Hartgill's service as land steward for Lord Sturton's father. Lord Sturton's son John suffered legal penalities as a result of his father's conviction, and it was to remove those penalties that the Lords introduced the bill mentioned above. See Cokayne's *Peerage*, Vol. XII, Part I, p. 307-9.

PARAGRAPH [441]

1 For TJ's various other references to this question, see pars. 39, [171], [187], [188], [189], [190], [191], [192], [198], [314], [348], [492], and Sec. XLI of his *Manual*. The first eleven of these references contain TJ's notes upon the following topics: the occasions when a division of the Commons is called for; the principle behind going out and staying in; the mechanics of appointing tellers and reporting results of a division; the procedure of division when the Commons are meeting as a committee of the whole; the proper use of division in stopping

[284]

debate; the need for the Noes to go forth when the question concerns the election of new members; and the requirement that speeches are out of order when a division is in progress. The last two of the numbered paragraphs listed above, and the additional paragraph now under discussion, are devoted to lists of the motions involved, and of the kind of procedure that occurs for each when the Commons vote by the method indicated here. The list in the present paragraph contains sixteen motions and their voting arrangements. The list in paragraph [492] below is made up of forty-two similar motions, sixteen from the present paragraph, and twenty-six from TJ's other resources. As for the list in Sec. xli of the *Manual*, it is identical in substance and style to the list in par. [492]. Thus the present paragraph may be considered an early draft, and par. [492] a final draft, of what the *Manual* has to say about this means of determining the will of the majority in Commons.

TJ's three lists are to be hailed as a genuine contribution to the parliamentary science of his day. Such lists were not abundant in the eighteenth century. Hatsell published one in the 1780s, and his major reason for doing so may well have been identified in part at least with his personal awareness that, more than a hundred years before, the Commons had appointed a committee "to search into precedents, in what cases the Yeas and Noes are to go forth." And another of his reasons may have been that he could not find out whether that committee had ever reported. See Hatsell (1818), ii, 186-211, especially p. 187. In the years that followed the publication of Hatsell's list, it became the basic authority on its subject, and TJ's reference to it in the present paragraph is hardly unexpected. There is every reason to believe, nevertheless, that, so far as the sixteen items here under scrutiny are concerned, TJ used Hatsell as primary authority solely for two items, while recording Hatsell's dissent from another, and that, for the rest, TJ relied not only upon his own researches into jhc, xxx, for twelve items, but also upon an American authority for two others, one of which may also have involved Hatsell. See below, nn. 2, 3, 4, 5, 6, 7. Thus we can say that Hatsell's list stood in TJ's present paragraph as a known but little-used reference. The best evidence for this statement is that Volume xxx of jhc records the proceedings of the Commons from January 10, 1765, to September 16, 1766, and that TJ backed up every item in his list, except for the four just mentioned, from that particular volume; and then, too, Hatsell's list contained in its entirety only two items dated in 1765 and 1766. To be sure, the latter two items are also in TJ's list; yet they appear there, not under Hatsell's, but under TJ's characteristic style of documentation, and thus in all likelihood they came directly to TJ from his own researches into the thirtieth volume of the jhc.

2 TJ's source for this item may well have been Hatsell (1785), ii. See also Hatsell (1818), ii, 189-90.

3 These initials, and those below in the last item, may confidently be said to stand for George Wythe. In the middle 1760s, TJ studied law at Williamsburg under Wythe, participating in Wythe's considerable legal learning, benefiting by the use of Wythe's extensive law library, profiting by Wythe's friendship, and gaining respect for parliamentary law through Wythe's presumable willingness to discuss his own experiences in that field during his membership and later his clerkship in the House of Burgesses. Wythe himself testified that during the late 1760s he extracted from the Commons' *Journals* the rules of parliamentary procedure, and that he left his copy of those rules with the Burgesses for their guid-

ance. See Jefferson's Parliamentary Studies, p. 4. Thirty years later, when TJ faced the problem of presiding over the Senate, and still later when he was intent upon the task of editing the manuscript of his *Manual* for deposit with the Senate as he left that body to become President, he sought Wythe's advice on certain points of parliamentary procedure, sending to Wythe on the latter occasion two considerable lists of queries for Wythe's personal attention. See Jefferson's Parliamentary Studies, p. 19. Each of those lists was accompanied by a letter expressing TJ's great respect for Wythe's learning in the parliamentary science. On December 7, 1800, Wythe replied to TJ's first list, not by returning it with marginal annotations, as TJ had suggested, but by keying his comments upon its separate items to the page numbers and line numbers of TJ's original text. When TJ received that letter, he wrote upon his original text, still in his possession in his own handwritten copy, the comments that Wythe's letter contained. See Jefferson's Parliamentary Studies, p. 21-4. In so doing, TJ placed the initials "G.W." after several of Wythe's comments, as if to give them distinctive authority. Thus there can be no doubt that the same initials in the present paragraph represent TJ's formal way of identifying what his mentor had said. As for TJ's use of these initials as the authority for saying that the yeas go forth when the question is on the committal of a bill, a special problem seems involved. Hatsell (1818), II, 190, noted that it was usual practice to have the yeas go forth in voting on that question; but at the same time he indicated that, on April 23, 1735, the opposite procedure had been followed. Faced with these conflicting precedents, TJ may well have appealed to Wythe for a final ruling, and may well have recorded that Wythe then cast his vote in favor of regarding the usual practice as the rule to be adhered to. Thus Wythe and Hatsell were in all probability TJ's authorities for that rule.

4 In TJ's manuscript the space is blank where the authority for this procedure would have been cited; but the faint vestige of what may once have been written there remains. In any event, p. 329 of Vol. XXX of the JHC may appropriately be understood to have been once intended, or perhaps once actually written, to mark the source of the division recorded here.

5 TJ's own reading of JHC, XXX, 329, led him to record that the Noes went forth on this motion. But he carefully noted in his left-hand margin that Hatsell's second volume took the opposite position. See (1818), II, 192-3, 207. It may be that TJ decided against following Hatsell on this occasion for the reason that Hatsell expressed some doubts about the position that he finally felt constrained to endorse.

6 On this occasion, TJ appears to have followed Hatsell rather than the Commons' *Journals*, despite his having cited the latter. Cf. Hatsell (1818), II, 194, and JHC, XXX, 269. What may have happened is that TJ found the *Journals* to be in conflict with Hatsell on the division indicated here, and that he decided to follow Hatsell's three supporting precedents for the Noes going forth rather than the *Journals'* single precedent for the Yeas; but, if things turned out that way, TJ did not remember to change his original documentation.

7 If "G.W." stood for George Wythe in TJ's estimation, as n. 3 above would seem to establish beyond doubt, then it is fair to say that TJ gave Wythe special credit in the history of parliamentary law, not only for opposing British tradition in the matter here under inspection, but also for endowing American parliamen-

tary practice *pari passu* with a rule befitting its own political preferences. That TJ was aware of a nationalistic dimension in the difference between Wythe's rule and its opposite may be gathered from the following passage in his later treatise on parliamentary law: "*In filling a blank with a sum, the largest sum shall be first put to the question by the 18th rule of the Senate,* contrary to the rule of Parliament which privileges the smallest sum and longest time. 5 *Grey* 179. 2 *Hats.* 81, 83. 3 *Hats.* 132, 133." See *Manual* (1801), Sec. xxxiii, par. 28; (1812), p. 102. Italics are TJ's. Now, the nationalistic dimension itself, as taught to TJ by Wythe, might conjecturally be rationalized as the difference perceived by both men between the British and the American concepts of parliamentary government. The Commons achieved their historical dominance in the British constitution by having to work within an aristocratic society regulated by the universal conviction that opulence was the most desirable mark of distinction. Always intending that their periodic grants of money to the crown would reach toward but perhaps never quite achieve opulence, the Commons adopted the practice of beginning with a vote upon the smallest possible grant, and of continuing with votes upon progressively larger grants, until their final sum, in comparison to its predecessors, would be opulent in their own eyes and perhaps on occasion in the eyes of royalty. On the other hand, the U.S. Senate, after having been modeled upon centuries of British parliamentary experience, and after having been taught by the Commons to treat monarchy as an unwelcome form of government, realized at the outset that America's political climate was antiaristocratic, and that frugality was for American society one of the most visible and most popular marks of political, even of personal, distinction. Seeing frugality as the characteristic virtue of the community which they served, Wythe and TJ would have been likely to advise the U.S. Senate to conduct their deliberations upon a money bill by beginning with the highest acceptable amount, and by inching down from there, so that their growing concern for frugality would be apparent in the record, and would end in a final sum which, by comparison with its predecessors, would show to the fullest extent its repudiation of ancient royal predispositions. See below, par. [554].

PARAGRAPH [442]

1 Upon his becoming aware in late December 1796 of the strong possibility that he would be the next Vice President of the United States, and that he would therefore be the presiding officer of the Senate in the first session of the Fifth Congress and thereafter for four years, TJ turned his attention to preparing himself for that new post. On January 22, 1797, he wrote to his respected mentor and good friend, George Wythe, asking whether Wythe, in the course of acquiring his own widely recognized learning "in the Parliamentary rules of procedure," had made notes upon them, and, if so, whether he would entrust them temporarily to TJ, however few or many they might have been. As we mentioned above in n. 3 of par. [441], Wythe replied on February 1 that thirty years before he had extracted a set of parliamentary rules from the jhc, but that, although he had left them with the House of Burgesses, it would now be vain to seek to recover them. Wythe then added that his memory of them was now too imperfect to enable him to supply any which TJ would find useful. (See Jefferson's Parliamentary Studies, p. 19.) We may be sure that the dates of those two letters marked a continuation of research by TJ into the basic rules governing the procedure of law-making bodies; and we may certainly take for granted that

his research would have led him to the *Journal* of the Senate as the source of a working knowledge of that body's rules. At any rate, the first nineteen of the twenty-eight rules given in par. [442] "for conducting the business in the Senate of the U.S." were transcribed almost verbatim by TJ from the list of nineteen rules adopted by the Senate on April 16, 1789, during the first session of that Congress. The only exceptions to this statement are these: that, in Rule viii, in Rule x, and in Rule xvii, the versions given in the *Journal* respectively read "received," "a question," and "exceptionable." See js, i, 13. As for Rules xx-xxviii in TJ's list, they are also to be found in various places in the *Journal*, some numbered differently there, some not numbered at all, and some differently worded in unimportant ways. See js, i, 28, 14, 116, 398, 27, 407, 408; and ii, 34. But TJ transcribed these nine rules almost verbatim, not from the *Journal*, but from a seven-page pamphlet entitled *Rules for Conducting Business in the Senate*, probably published at Philadelphia by John Fenno in 1797. A copy of that pamphlet is in The New York Public Library, and the Editor has examined a reproduction of it in the Princeton University Library in a series called Early American Imprints. Evans (xi, 319) numbered that pamphlet 33043 and called it the "first publication" of TJ's *Manual*. Perhaps on the strength of Evans' authority, Campion, in his *Procedure of the House of Commons*, p. xvii, identified the *Manual* as having been first published in 1797. But so early a date for the latter work is inadmissible. See above, Jefferson's Parliamentary Studies, p. 27. Moreover, the pamphlet mentioned by Evans was devoted exclusively to a list of Senate rules, whereas the *Manual* contained ever so much more than that, as Evans and Campion would have seen, had they inspected it on the inside.

PARAGRAPH [443]

1 This paragraph consists of TJ's notes on the first three sections of the first chapter of Hatsell's second volume where the status of Aliens, Minors, and Clergy is discussed in relation to membership in the Commons. "On the 10th of March, 1623, a question arose," noted Hatsell (1785), ii, 2; (1818), ii, 2, "on the eligibility of Mr. William Stewart, a Scotchman, and not naturalized; and on the 28th of May following, it is resolved, That the election of Mr. Stewart, being no natural-born subject, is void. . . ." And on the same page Hatsell added, "On the 18th of February, 1625, a new writ issued in the room of a Scotchman 'antenaturs,' and not naturalized." As for Minors, TJ recorded that Hatsell had declared them ineligible on the authority of Coke and Blackstone but eligible on the authority of the Commons, when they acted in the case of Trenchard. Even so, Hatsell noted, in the 7th and 8th years of William III, Parliament made void "the election of any person who is not 21 years of age." Hatsell (1785), ii, 6; (1818), ii, 9-10. TJ's final sentence proceeded accurately to summarize Hatsell's discussion of the ineligibility of the Clergy for seats in Parliament.

PARAGRAPH [444]

1 TJ constructed this paragraph by making a precise abstract of a quotation by Hatsell (1785), ii, 10; (1818), ii, 15-16, from a lengthy opinion of the learned Arthur Onslow, widely respected as the foremost British constitutional authority of his time, and well known as having been Speaker of the House of Commons in five successive Parliaments from 1728 to 1760. Much of his constitutional learning has come down to us, not from his own publications, but from

references to him, and quotations of his opinions, in Hatsell. See Hatsell (1818), II, vi-vii, 15-16, 27-8, 45, 49, 50, 51, 62, 76, 80, 85, 150, 166, 171, 174, 202, 205, 222, 228, 233-4, 236-8, 241, *et passim*.

PARAGRAPH [445]

1 Drawn by TJ from the 5th section of Hatsell's chapter on members of Parliament, this particular observation stemmed from Hatsell's quotation of the following remark by Sir Edward Coke in a parliamentary debate in 1620-1621: "Those who are employed abroad are without question eligible, though absent when they are chosen; for absentia ejus qui reipublicae causa abest, non obest." (1785), II, 16; (1818), II, 23-4. The Latin phrase would translate thus: "The absence of him who is abroad on public business does no injury."

2 This sentence represents TJ's summary of the text and notes in the 6th section of Hatsell's chapter on members, (1785), II, 23; (1818), II, 26-8. Hatsell's notes recalled the cases of Richard Onslow and John Popham, both of whom, while serving in the Upper House as solicitors general, were recalled to their own chamber, the Lower House, to assist it in electing a new Speaker. For TJ's previous mention of these cases, see above, pars. [434], [435], and [439].

PARAGRAPH [446]

1 TJ's single sentence summarized Hatsell's account of Charles I's attempt to exclude Sir Edward Coke from membership in the House of Commons. See (1785), II, 22; (1818), II, 31-3. Aware of Sir Edward's opposition to James I and to himself, Charles I appointed Sir Edward sheriff of Buckinghamshire, thus giving him an innocuous share of the royal power while making him *pari passu* ineligible under the Commons' own rule for a seat in their house. But the king's scheme for disposing of his enemy ran into difficulties, and those difficulties came to public attention when, upon the assembling of Charles' second Parliament on February 6, 1625/26, Sir Edward presented his credentials to it as a duly elected member for Norfolk. The king sent a message at once to the Commons, questioning Sir Edward's right to his seat, and demanding a new election in his district. The Commons referred the king's request to their Committee of Privileges, and the Committee reported upon it three weeks later without making any recommendation. Debate upon the report followed on that very day and was then postponed until March 3; and on March 3 it was postponed again for a week, only to be ignored then and later. Sir Edward never took his seat in that Parliament, thanks to the inaction of the Commons upon the king's request. A few days before that Parliament was dissolved, however, the Commons took unexpected action, not to do what their sovereign wanted, but to guarantee that their conduct toward Sir Edward could not be used to damage their own institutional rights. On June 9, 1626, the Commons voted that "Sir *Edw. Coke*, standing *de facto* returned a Member of this House, to have Privilege against a Suit in Chancery, commenced against him by the Lady *Cleare*." So runs the account in Hatsell and in Hatsell's own source, the JHC, I, 817, 825, 829, 834, 837, 869. Neither account identified Lady Cleare, who was of course none other than Coke's second wife, Lady Elizabeth Hatton. See George Paul Macdonell on Coke, Sir Edward (1552-1634), in DNB. For Coke's own third-person reference to his being granted privilege, see his *Institutes*, IV, 48. For the whole episode, see *Parliamentary History of England*, VI, 412, 421-2, 424-5.

2 This sentence represents TJ's frugal and accurate abstract of a passage in which Hatsell mentioned two cases involving parliamentary action on the question of the propriety of a sheriff's serving as member of the Commons. See (1785), II, 25; (1818), II, 34. "The conclusion to be drawn from these instances," said he, "particularly that of Abingdon, seems to be, that a Sheriff of a County is not eligible for any Town or Borough within that County, where the election proceeds by virtue of his own precept."

PARAGRAPH [447]

1 For this rule, in the language which TJ followed in compiling it, see Hatsell (1785), II, 27; (1818), II, 36, lines 7, 25-6. Hatsell was there discussing whether members who proclaimed themselves ill could for that reason be excused from parliamentary duty. It appears that some members pleaded illness when they did not feel that they could take the oaths, and others, when they were genuinely disabled. In every case, however, removal of a duly chosen member had to be accomplished only by the Commons' deciding that the member's personal situation justified it. Outside suits for the removal of members did not fall within the jurisdiction of the outside courts concerned.

PARAGRAPH [448]

1 The first independent clause in this passage represents TJ's statement of the gist of Hatsell's conclusions as to whether outlaws or persons in execution were entitled to election to the Commons. See (1785), II, 30; (1818), II, 37-9. In the accepted meaning of the terms, an outlaw was a person deprived of legal rights and of the king's protection by reason of his having failed to comply with a legal judgment pronounced upon him; and a person in execution was someone in the process of having his goods seized and himself imprisoned through his having failed to perform one or more of his legal obligations.

2 For the case of John Asgyll, as summarized here by TJ, see Hatsell (1785), II, 30, or (1818), II, 39. The case was brought to the attention of the Commons on November 10, 1707, by a letter from Asgyll (also called Asgill) to the Speaker saying that he was a prisoner in the Fleet under two legal convictions. The Commons considered his case on November 15 and again on December 16; and on the latter date they authorized the "Serjeant with the Mace" to go to the warden of the Fleet and demand the deliverance of Asgyll out of custody. The serjeant did so on December 17, and Asgyll was promptly released. For the source of Hatsell's account, see JHC, XV, 396, 466-71. Asgyll's convictions had resulted from decisions against him in two suits, one by John Holland, and the other by Thomas Mathews and John Wetton.

PARAGRAPH [449]

1 Section X of Hatsell's chapter on Members discussed the question whether members after having been awarded pensions or appointed by the king to government office should be eligible to serve in the Commons. As TJ briefly noted, eligibility or ineligibility under those circumstances depended, not upon a fixed rule, but upon what the Commons deemed appropriate for each case. See Hatsell, (1785), II, 43; (1818), II, 58-72.

PARAGRAPH [450]

1 The phrase in angle brackets is a conjectural reading for words obliterated by TJ after he had perhaps come to realize that his next phrase expressed more exactly the meaning to be conveyed at this point.

2 This entire paragraph presents an economical summary by TJ of the text and notes of Section XI of Hatsell's chapter on membership. In addition to affirming that a member already elected as representative of one place, and already assigned to that place by his own choice, cannot be eligible to represent another place unless he resigns his other seat, Hatsell drew a distinction between the possibility of a member's choosing an alternative seat immediately after a general election and the possibility of his doing so after his election to fill a vacancy during an existing session. In the former case, membership began only when a member elected for two or more places had decided early in the parliamentary session which place he would serve. In the latter case, membership began at the moment when a special election had determined what candidate had won and should therefore be certified winner by the officer in charge. The chief reason why this second case differed from the first, said Hatsell, was that, at the instant of his victory in the special election, the member became the representative, not only of his own district, but of all districts in the country; and in this double capacity, for that session of Parliament, he had no legal choice but to stay where he was, no matter what other district might want him for their nearly simultaneous vacancy. See Hatsell (1785), II, 52; (1818), II, 73-7.

PARAGRAPH [451]

1 Although TJ did not so specify, this passage came to him from Hatsell. See (1818), II, 78-9. "On the 2d of March 1623," said Hatsell, "it is agreed, That a man, after he is duly chosen, cannot relinquish." And Hatsell added later, "On the 3d of January, 1698, Mr. Archdale, a Quaker, being returned for Chipping Wycomb, is ready to serve, if the House will accept his declarations of fidelity, &c. instead of the oath; but on the 6th of January, Mr. Archdale coming into the House, but declining to take the oaths from a principle of his religion, the House order a new writ to issue in his room."

PARAGRAPH [452]

1 The fifth paragraph of Section XII of Hatsell's chapter on members was here paraphrased by TJ. That paragraph pointed out that, on April 29, 1765, the Commons ordered a new writ to be issued for a special election to replace a Mr. Willey, who had been reported dead; and that, on April 30, having been led to doubt the report, they ordered the delivery of the writ to be postponed "till further directions." It was not until May 6, however, said Hatsell, that they ordered a supersedeas to the writ, after having learned that Mr. Witley was still alive. See Hatsell (1785), II, 57; (1818), II, 79-80. Hatsell's account of this case was based upon that in JHC, XXX, 386, 391, 404. For mention of a somewhat similar case, see above, par. [432].

PARAGRAPH [453]

1 Using many of the words of his source, and supplying some of his own, TJ compiled this passage from Hatsell (1785), II, 59, where the latter, in discussing

[291]

the opening of a parliamentary session on November 15, 1763, introduced his very important chapter on the rules governing the procedures of the Commons as a deliberative assembly. Hatsell's own words in describing what the Commons did in that opening session were as follows: ". . . the custom of reading a Bill immediately on the return from the House of Lords, is probably nothing more than a claim of right on the part of the Commons, that they are at liberty to proceed, in the first place, upon any matter which they think material, without being limited to give a preference to the subjects contained in the King's speech." See also (1818), ii, 82-3. In using these words as a basis for his own paragraph, TJ would inevitably have noticed that they occurred in connection with Hatsell's discussion of three topics which vied with each other for priority in a long, opening-day debate at the time in question. One of the topics that day was a complaint by John Wilkes that he had been unjustly imprisoned. The second was a communication addressed by George III to the Commons and read by George Grenville, chancellor of the exchequer. And the third was a bill made ready by the clerk for presentation as the first business of an opening session. After the debate, the Commons voted to give their bill its customary priority. When TJ was taking notes in the 1790s upon this episode in Hatsell, the names of Grenville, Wilkes, and George III would certainly have stirred special memories in him as he recalled their role in the history of the American Revolution. And Hatsell's account of the failure of George III to obtain a first hearing in the opening session of the Commons in 1763, and of the success of the Commons in establishing their own priorities on that occasion, would surely have emphasized for TJ what his own study of British parliamentary practice had repeatedly taught him—that the Commons deserved a large share of credit in British history for their part in making the royal command subservient to popular preferences. For the source of Hatsell's account of the opening session of 1763, see JHC, XXIX, 667.

PARAGRAPH [454]

1 TJ compiled this passage from a somewhat longer one in a footnote to Hatsell's enumeration of precedents governing the introduction and swearing in of new members of the Commons. See (1785), ii, 62; (1818), ii, 88. Hatsell's footnote reads thus: "Notwithstanding all these laws, which are introductory to a Member's taking his seat in the House, a person, when returned, is, though he should not have taken his seat, to all intents a Member, except as to the right of voting, and is entitled to the same privileges as every other Member of the House. Insomuch, that upon the 13th of April, 1715, the House determine, 'That Sir Joseph Jekyll was capable of being chosen of a Committee of Secrecy, though he had not been sworn at the Clerk's Table.' "

PARAGRAPH [455]

1 TJ's note briefly records a footnote in Hatsell (1785), ii, 71, to the effect that, in the parliamentary session beginning in November 1781, a roll call of the Commons had been appointed for the following January 31, but that, just before adjournment for Christmas recess, another roll call was appointed for January 21, without any provision for a discharge of the call already authorized. The change of date, Hatsell remarked, was caused by the expectation of the Commons that business of great importance would arrive earlier than they had previously anticipated. See also (1818), ii, 101.

1 Given below are the successive passages in Hatsell (1785), II, 73, 75, 77, 78, from which TJ compiled this paragraph:

"No man is to speak twice to a Bill at one time of reading it, or to any other proposition, unless it be to explain himself in some material point of his speech." See also (1818), II, 105n. Quoted from an order of the House of Lords, May 9, 1626.

". . . and it is the duty of the Speaker to maintain the observance of this rule, without waiting for the interposition of the House." See also (1818), II, 105, lines 10-12.

"If a Member speaks beside the question, it is the duty of the Speaker to interrupt him." See also (1818), II, 107, lines 8-10.

"So Mr. Speaker stood up and said, 'It is a great disorder that this [hemming and laughing] should be used; for it is the antient use of every man to be silent when any one speaketh.' " See also (1818) II, 107, n. Quoted by Hatsell from *Parliamentary History of England*, IV, 447.

"A Member may speak, and often does, from the gallery . . ." See also (1818), II, 108, line 15.

1 TJ indicated that the rule given here was based upon the following two passages in Hatsell (1785), II, 75, 77:

"On the 1st of December, 1669, Lord Orrery . . . was admitted to give in his answer to articles, sitting in the House, being infirm, and unable to stand." See also (1818), II, 104, lines 19-22, and n.

"I remember two instances of the House's permitting Members to speak sitting; one was Mr. Pitt, in his very long speech against the Peace of 1763; the other the Lord Mayor Crosby, before he was sent to the Tower; both on account of indisposition." See also (1818), II, 107, lines 4-8. Hatsell was speaking here from his own personal experience in the Commons, where he served as clerk assistant in the last years of George II's reign, and as chief clerk from 1768 to 1797.

1 These two sentences represent TJ's accurate condensation of two consecutively numbered passages in Hatsell (1785), II, 73, in his chapter on rules of proceeding, Section V, "As to Members speaking." Hatsell worded the passages thus:

"4. On the 4th of June, 1604, agreed for a rule, That if two stand up to speak to a Bill, he against the Bill (being known by demand or otherwise) to be the first heard." See also (1818), II, 102.

"5. On the 13th of June, 1604, a Member offers to speak after the question put, and the voice given in the affirmative; which was admitted for orderly, because no full question without the part negative." See also (1818), II, 102.

Hatsell's sources for these passages were JHC, I, 232, 237-8. The second passage grew out of a debate on the designated day as a subsidy bill was being considered after its third reading, and an amendment to it was made the subject of a motion of referral to a committee, after having been given two readings. Those in favor of that motion voted, but, before those against it were polled, a member on that side of the question spoke. When his right to speak between the two votes was questioned, he was ruled in order, on the ground that, if opposition to a question were not allowed to be expressed, the resulting vote would not be a full question and would hence be illegal.

PARAGRAPH [459]

1 Using data provided by Hatsell (1785), II, 81, TJ concluded in his own words that motions to adjourn debates were frequent in the Commons. Hatsell's data consisted of an enumeration of five such motions dated April 22, 1712, June 14, 1712, May 7, 1713, November 17, 1742, and February 9, 1677. Hatsell indicated that the last of these dates, so far as he knew, provided the first instance of the introduction of a motion to adjourn a debate. See also (1818), II, 109.

2 TJ based his wording of this rule upon a passage in Hatsell (1785), II, 74; (1818), II, 103. Hatsell's passage reads thus: "6. On the 23d of June, 1604, agreed for a rule, That if a Bill be continued in speech from day to day, one man may not speak twice to the matter of the same Bill. So on the 21st of April, 1610." Hatsell's wording of the rule adopted on June 23, 1604, exactly paralleled that in JHC, I, 245. But Hatsell's note on that rule cited dates when exceptions had occurred; and later, (1818), II, 104, he cited two other exceptions.

PARAGRAPH [460]

1 As he himself indicated, TJ based the notes making up this entire paragraph upon Hatsell (1785), II, 81-4, where Hatsell discussed the rules governing original and privileged motions in parliamentary procedure. Each one of TJ's separate topics, as listed in the left-hand column below, finds its source in the designated pages and lines of Hatsell (1818), II:

Priority among original motions	111, lines 12-13
Exceptions to that rule	112, n. lines 2-4
Motion to adjourn	113, lines 3-7; 113 n.
Orders of the day	115, lines 9-19
Motion to amend	112, line 15; 117, lines 1-2
Greater or lesser sum, etc.	111, n.
Previous question	112, lines 14-15; 115, lines 22-4
Printing original question, 2 cases	115, lines 6-9, 16-19
Printing original question, 1 case	115, lines 19-22
Preventing an amendment	116, lines 6-13
Amending motion to adjourn	113-14

It should be added that the bracketed observation in TJ's text was apparently inserted by him as an extension of what Hatsell was saying at that point. And the same remark applies to TJ's two marginal notes and to his observation that the simple motion to adjourn is undebatable. The reference to "3. Hats. 133" in one of the marginal notes was meant by TJ to call attention to the rule regarding lesser or greater sums, shorter or longer times, as that rule was reaffirmed by the Commons on November 3, 1675. See also Hatsell (1818), III, 166, in connection with his discussion of the rules of the Commons in matters of supply. In a footnote at that point Hatsell recalled a Commons debate in which the principle behind this rule was stated as follows: "That the charge may be made as easy upon the people as possible." There is an alternative principle behind this rule, and it suggests that the Commons, when they adopted it, may have been also conscious of its conciliatory effect upon the king. See above, par. [441], n. 7.

PARAGRAPH [461]

1 TJ compiled this rule in part by paraphrasing and in part by quoting a somewhat longer passage in Hatsell (1785), II, 82. See also (1818), II, 112, lines 4-10.

PARAGRAPH [462]

1 As TJ's notes indicated, he compiled this sentence from two passages in Hatsell (1785), II, 82-4. See also (1818), II, 112-13, 117.

PARAGRAPH [463]

1 This rule, which TJ avowedly transcribed from Hatsell (1785), II, 82, was credited by Hatsell to Arthur Onslow, the Speaker. See also (1818), II, 113 n.

PARAGRAPH [464]

1 As recorded here by TJ, this rule was in large part a verbatim transcript and to some extent a paraphrase of Hatsell (1785), II, 85. See also (1818), II, 118, lines 3-6. Hatsell indicated that the rule represented what the Speaker of the Commons had said when commenting upon a sequence of events in the session of January 29, 1765. In that session Sir William Meredith had been given leave after 3 P.M. to introduce a motion condemning the issuance of general warrants for the arrest of authors, printers, and publishers of seditious libel. Sir William's motion was debated, and its opponents succeeded at last in getting the House to amend it in such fashion as to force the House to lay down the law for the issuance of general warrants in seditious libel cases whenever cases of that sort were actually pending in a court of law. In other words, the amendment partly, or perhaps fully, nullified the effect of the motion to which it was attached. The amendment in itself was approved in the Commons by a vote of 224 to 185; but, when the amendment and the main motion were presented together in a single resolution, without differentiation between its two parts, the obvious contradiction of one part by the other led to a change of mind among some of those who had been beguiled into supporting the amendment in the first place. As a result, the single resolution failed. But the Commons decided that, while the single resolution should stand on the books as the customary, undifferentiated amalgam of main motion and amendment, Sir William should be allowed, against the usual practice of the House, to have his original motion entered on the books by itself. Thus the parliamentary record did not expose Sir William to the future charge of having presented a more or less nonsensical motion. Nor did it expose the Commons to the future charge of having acted irresponsibly in allowing a nonsensical resolution not only to be created in the amending process but also to receive their approval at the end. It is inconceivable that TJ, as he compiled par. [464] from Hatsell, would not have noticed Hatsell's account of the circumstances which produced it, and would not have seen in those circumstances an example of the way in which the opponents of a bill can use the amending process rather than open hostility to defeat what the bill aims to accomplish. For the source of Hatsell's account of the parliamentary fate of Sir William Meredith's motion, see JHC, XXX, 70.

PARAGRAPH [465]

1 TJ formulated this rule from two precedents mentioned by Hatsell (1785), II, 87. See also (1818), II, 119 (lines 19-20 and n.), 120 (lines 1-2).

2 Hatsell noted that George Grenville repeatedly claimed the right of any individual member of the Commons to call for the division of a motion into its parts, whenever it was susceptible to such treatment. But Hatsell then added that the Commons, on February 19, 1770, finally decided against Grenville's claim. See (1785), II, 87; (1818), II, 118-19. TJ's rule was, of course, based upon that action by the Commons.

3 For Hatsell's nearly identical statement of this rule, see (1785), II, 87; (1818), II, 119, lines 20-1.

4 This passage, from "The only case" to the final "&c.," was based by TJ upon the substance and in part the wording of Hatsell (1785), II, 87; (1818), II, 120, n.

PARAGRAPH [466]

1 TJ compiled this passage from Hatsell (1785), II, 88, using many of the words of his source, while omitting others, and altering a few in unimportant ways. See also (1818), II, 121, lines 2-13. The final phrase condensed into four words the following thirty-one-word sentence in Hatsell: "Or if it is desired to have an Act of Parliament, or extract from the Journal, or any paper before the House, read, and the House acquiesce, this may be read."

PARAGRAPH [467]

1 A nearly verbatim transcription by TJ of a passage in Hatsell (1785), II, 88. See also (1818), II, 121, lines 21-4.

PARAGRAPH [468]

1 The word in angle brackets represents what TJ first wrote when he was transcribing this sentence verbatim from Hatsell (1785), II, 90. See also (1818), II, 123, lines 27-30. But when TJ checked his text against that of his source, he noticed Hatsell as having written "make" instead of "amend," and thus he superimposed Hatsell's word upon his own without totally obliterating the final "d" in the latter. At that point the manuscript, however, is not fully legible.

PARAGRAPH [469]

1 This paragraph presents TJ's summary of part of a long argument set forth by Hatsell (1785), II, 88, in support of the traditional rule of the Commons that, when the consideration of a main question has been interrupted by a call for the previous question, and that call has been set before the House by the chair, no amendment to the main question can at that point be entertained. See also (1818), II, 121-4. Hatsell's final judgment was that this rule worked no hardships upon the legislative process because: 1) The call for the previous question could be defeated, whereupon amendments to the main question could then be proposed and voted upon; and 2) the call for the previous question could be withdrawn from consideration in the interval between its being moved and seconded, on the one hand, and its being presented by the chair as a fully sponsored

motion, on the other. This latter maneuver could possibly restore amendments to further consideration, subject to the approval of the mover and seconder of the call for the previous question, and subject also to the approval of the House. Such a strategem was carried out by the Commons on March 16, 1778, as TJ's paragraph noted and Hatsell's authority confirmed. See JHC, XXXVI, 825. That March 16 date intervened between the signing on February 6, 1778, in Paris, by three American commissioners, and the ratifying on May 4 by the Continental Congress in Philadelphia, of three separate Franco-American treaties of alliance and friendship. And it was between those dates that the Commons voted to amend a motion dealing with the three treaties, after having allowed a call for the previous question to be withdrawn so as to give proper parliamentary status to the rival move. It should be added, not only that the Commons then defeated the main question as amended, even though the amendment had been given their approval, but also that the passing of the amendment favored the antiadministration party in Parliament, whereas the defeat of the main motion as amended favored the king. TJ would have had a personal interest in the work of the three American commissioners who negotiated those treaties, and thus the date of the action on them by the Commons would have had special significance to him. For, after all, he had been originally appointed as one of those three commissioners, the two others being Benjamin Franklin and Silas Deane; so it is unthinkable that he would not have been reminded of what they had done, and of the British reaction to their mission in France, when in the 1790s he transcribed from Hatsell the date of the action taken by the Commons some dozen years earlier. For TJ's refusal to be one of the commissioners, see *Papers*, I, 521-4. See also Malone, *Jefferson*, I, 245.

PARAGRAPH [470]

1 In Section VII of his chapter on the rules and proceeding of Commons, Hatsell devoted himself to discussing the rule that a question once carried or rejected may not be brought up again in the same session. TJ's present paragraph summarized important parts of Hatsell's observations on this matter. See (1785), II, 92, 98, 100, 101, 99, 97. For those same observations, see (1818), II, on the pages and lines indicated in the following notes.

2 TJ abridged this sentence from p. 125, lines 2-5, 13-14.

3 A nearly verbatim transcription of p. 132, lines 20-2.

4 For TJ's words, see p. 133 (lines 2-4), 135 (lines 15-16).

5 In the manuscript the words in angle brackets were canceled out, presumably because TJ wanted to enter them more or less in the same form below. See n. 7.

6 For the source of these words, see p. 135, n., col. 2, TJ's transcription being largely verbatim, with the word order changed somewhat.

7 This cryptic sentence represents TJ's summary of Hatsell's account of a proceeding in the Commons on December 9 and 10, 1762. See Hatsell (1818), II, 134-5. That particular proceeding began when the Commons formulated an address to the king on the subject of the preliminaries of the peace being negotiated at that time to end the war between Britain and France over the suzerainty of French Canada. By a vote of 319 to 65, the address to the king expressed the

gratitude of the Commons that what they called this "long, bloody, and expensive War" was being brought to a close. Next day, when the same address was presented to the Commons by a committee that had been appointed to report upon its final wording, Lord Midleton started to argue about what the committee had written, and Sir John Philips called him to order for doing so, on the ground that the rules did not permit him to speak against a resolution already passed. But it was decided that the address to the king was before the House for adoption in the form given it by the committee, and that a vote upon it in that form would require each member to decide whether he approved of it or not. Thus, he would be free, if he chose, to give the reasons behind the vote that he would cast. In the debate that followed this decision, a single amendment to the address was proposed and adopted. And, no doubt to the king's ultimate satisfaction, that amendment consisted in adding the phrase "though glorious and successful" to what the original formulation had called a "long, bloody, and expensive War." These historical details should help to convey to the modern student of the Pocket-Book the meaning which TJ's fragmentary notes were assuredly capable of conveying to him. For the official account of the episode narrated by Hatsell, see JHC, XXIX, 393-6.

8 TJ based this note on p. 133, lines 4-5. By reference to the passing of an order by the Commons on January 14, 1766, and to the cancelling of that order the next Friday, Hatsell illustrated how orders by the House could be discharged. In that particular sequence, the order had concerned the printing of certain American documents for the information of the Commons, and the discharge of the order simply meant that the Commons had not thought it necessary to have the documents printed after all. See JHC, XXX, 451, 463. Those documents were in many cases the expression of American anger toward the Stamp Act, and all together they would have added up to many pages of print, had the Commons' order not been rescinded.

9 TJ's manuscript shows a square bracket before "being" but no closing bracket. The missing punctuation has been inserted after "natura," where it seems reasonably to belong. The enclosed phrase appears to be TJ's explanation of the special status of an order of the House. Such an order was not to be treated as if it were a bill, for in that case it could not be introduced a second time in the session which had passed or rejected it. In short, an order was not *"legibus natura,"* that is, not within the class of laws by origin. Thus it could be passed without going through the process of first reading, second reading, referral to committee, etc. And it could be reconsidered and rejected in the session that had passed it.

10 The seventy-nine-word passage preceding this footnote was compiled by TJ from a much longer passage in Hatsell's footnote on p. 134. According to Hatsell, a parliamentary resolution, which TJ on his own responsibility identified in the square brackets as "the address on the preliminaries of peace in 1782," was introduced into Commons on February 22 by General Henry Seymour Conway, and it failed by one vote (193 to 194) to command the assent of those voting. This defeat would normally mean that the resolution could not be introduced again in the same session. Nevertheless, it was introduced a second time on February 27, the sponsor being this time none other than General Conway himself. General Conway justified his formal violation of the rules by three arguments.

His resolution, he said, was on a subject of very great importance, involving as it did the question whether the British Empire was to be dismembered into two parts or was to be kept together by reconciliation. So fateful a subject, he went on, should be decided by the full House of Commons, not by the small number voting upon it before, and certainly not by the small number that had divided almost equally upon it. And finally, he concluded, "he had introduced, in the second question, some words which were not in the first; and which, to some persons, might make, in their opinion upon the subject, an essential difference." "These arguments," remarked Hatsell, "were thought to be of such weight that the objection of form was never made." And so it came about that General Conway's resolution was allowed reconsideration. Here is what it said: "That it is the Opinion of this House, that the further Prosecution of offensive War on the Continent of *North America*, for the Purpose of reducing the revolted Colonies to Obedience by Force, will be the Means of weakening the Efforts of this Country against her *European* Enemies; tends, under the present Circumstances, dangerously to increase the mutual Enmity so fatal to the Interests both of *Great Britain* and *America*; and, by preventing an happy Reconciliation with that Country, to frustrate the earnest Desire graciously expressed by His Majesty to restore the Blessings of Public Tranquillity." The debate which followed the reading of General Conway's motion was interrupted by an attempt to adjourn the debate for a fortnight; but a division of the House on the latter question lost by 215 to 234 votes. When the main question was then voted upon, it passed in the affirmative. On this occasion, there was a voice vote, and the record does not accordingly show the size of the margin of victory for the measure previously defeated so narrowly. But the vote on the question of adjournment may be taken to represent more or less accurately what the vote on the main question was. Thus reconciliation may have won by as many as nineteen votes of February 27, 1782, as TJ would probably have known soon after that time from his own sources of information. Hatsell's account did not cover that final action. For the official record, see JHC, XXXVIII, 814, 861.

11 TJ's partly indecipherable notes seem to originate on p. 125, n., where Hatsell quoted from an entry for May 17, 1606, in JHL, which said in part that, "if a Bill begun on one House, be disliked and refused in the other, a new Bill of the same matter may be drawn and begun again in that House whereunto it was sent . . ." That is to say, although the general rule prevents either House from renewing in a given session a bill which that House in the same session had rejected, it does not prohibit either House from rejecting and then renewing in the same session a bill that the other House had originated and passed in the first place.

12 TJ compiled this sentence from two passages in Hatsell, p. 130-1. The first (p. 131) recorded that, "On the 11th of April, 1753, a Bill from the Lords for settling Lord Ashburnham's estate, read once, and laid aside; and another Bill, with the very same title, ordered immediately." The second (p. 130-1) read: "On the 30th of May, 1739, the Lords having amended a Bill about gaming, which had passed the Commons; the consideration of these amendments is put off for a month, and leave is immediately given to bring in another Bill to the same effect, but with a different title; which Bill passes." For details concerning the Lord Ashburnham matter, see JHC, XXVI, 740, 743, 757-8, 763, 778, 802, 838, 839. For details concerning the bill to regulate gaming, see JHC, XXIII, 376-7.

1 This paragraph lists various expedients used by the Commons to prevent any bad legislative effects from the applying of the rule stated in the first sentence of the paragraph immediately above. What TJ did was to compile his list of expedients from Hatsell and to locate them by noting the pages on which they were to be found in (1785), II, 94-8, 194, 196. For those passages in (1818), II, see the footnotes below.

2 See p. 127, n., where Hatsell recorded from JHL, under the date of May 25, 1689, that it is "the common course of Parliament, to pass explanatory Acts if any thing has been omitted, or ill-expressed, in any other Act passed in the same session."

3 See p. 128, par. 15, where Hatsell noted that, "On the 26th of July, 1715, a Bill is ordered for enforcing and making more effectual an Act of the same session."

4 On p. 127, par. 12, Hatsell pointed to two occasions when the Commons ordered bills to be introduced "for rectifying mistakes in Acts passed in the same session."

5 On p. 127-8, par. 13, Hatsell noted that, on May 9, 1711, a committee of the Commons was instructed to receive into a bill then under the committee's auspices a clause that would rectify a mistake in a previous bill of supply. That mistake, which Hatsell did not fully or accurately explain, arose from what seems to have been an oversight in transcribing figures in an act of the Commons. That is to say, on February 1, 1710/11, the Commons voted a duty of 1 shilling on every chaldron (36 bushels) of coal mined in Wales or west England and exported to Ireland or the Isle of Man; but, in entering into the bill the amount of that duty, someone failed to notice that the proper figure for it should have been 2 shillings, not 1, and that the committee originally recommending the bill to the Commons had stipulated the larger amount. On April 13, 1711, under pressure from dealers and carriers, the Commons assigned to an existing committee the task of studying how the mistake had occurred. That committee, having traced the history of the mistake, reported on April 30 the facts as given above. The report was then tabled, but the error identified by it was corrected on May 9 by the expedient mentioned by Hatsell and TJ. For the correct details in this sequence of events, see JHC, XVI, 594, 620, 656, 662-3.

6 TJ's sentence rested upon p. 129 (lines 8-9), and 127 (lines 8-10). A prorogation of Parliament terminates the session then under way, and parliamentary acts being considered at that time must either be reintroduced at a later session or dismissed as legislatively dead. Thus the rule under discussion here never hinders a bill's reappearance in another session of the same Parliament. For the distinction between prorogation and adjournment, see Hatsell, II (1818), 335-7. See also above, pars. 10, 12, 14, 20b, 37, 38, 97, 98, 99.

7 TJ transcribed this sentence almost verbatim from Hatsell on the indicated pages. See also p. 266, lines 15-17.

1 This sentence originated from Hatsell (1785), II, 95, 96, as TJ noted. See also (1818), II, 128 (lines 20-1), and 131 (lines 15-17, 22-4).

PARAGRAPH [473]

1 See above, par. [470], n. 12.

PARAGRAPH [474]

1 TJ's condensed notation was based upon Hatsell (1785), II, 96. See also (1818), II, 130, lines 7-11. The clause mentioned in TJ's note was cut off from the bill on May 2, 1733, when it was discovered that the same clause had been previously canceled by a duly passed amendment.

PARAGRAPH [475]

1 The angle brackets shown here were used to indicate that, in TJ's manuscript, this paragraph had first been written out and then canceled by a line slanting through it from top left to bottom right. The cancellation occurred, it would seem, because TJ, having transcribed the passage from the indicated page of Hatsell, and having commented then upon its opposition to the practice of the U.S. Senate, became suddenly doubtful of the validity of his comment, and thereupon turned to another page of Hatsell, as identified by the marginal note, where he found that his doubt had indeed been justified. In the former place, Hatsell's example would lead to the supposition that the form to be followed in calling for the previous question should be phrased negatively; and, in two latter places, that it should be phrased positively. See (1818), II, 123, lines 5-12, and compare with p. 111, n., and 115-16. In such a call, the positive phraseology is of course more characteristic of British parliamentary usage than is the negative. See JHC, I, 226, *et passim*. As for the Latin phrase "at econtra," it here means "and [or but] on the contrary."

PARAGRAPH [476]

1 As his own documentation indicated, TJ compiled this paragraph from Hatsell (1785), II, 106-7, his procedure being to rely almost exclusively upon wording attributed by Hatsell to Onslow. See also (1818), II, 141, n.; 142, lines 16-17. For other references to the mace, see above, par. [429], and below, pars. [477], [478], [494].

PARAGRAPH [477]

1 The manuscript shows that TJ entered these eleven words here, and then canceled them out in the apparent conviction that they would figure more advantageously in the next paragraph.

2 The person mentioned here was Mr. Howard, who on October 26, 1675, was allowed a chair to sit in, "on account of his infirmity." See Hatsell (1785), II, 102. See also (1818), II, 138, lines 3-5.

3 TJ pieced this whole sentence together from various pages of Hatsell, but particularly from (1785), II, 105. See also (1818), II, 138 (lines 6-14), 140-1.

PARAGRAPH [478]

1 This sentence was certainly intended by TJ to stand in his own notes as a summary of Section VIII of Hatsell's chapter entitled "Rules of Proceeding," that section being organized as a discussion of persons summoned before the Commons as witnesses or as delinquents. As for what follows immediately, TJ's sen-

tences refer to Hatsell (1785), II, 102, 105, 108, 107, 106, 104, 103; also to (1818), II, on the pages and lines indicated in the following notes.

2 See p. 127, n., col. 2.

3 See p. 127, lines 5-7; 140, lines 4-9.

4 See p. 143, n., col. 1. See also above, par. [477].

5 See p. 142, lines 8-18.

6 See p. 142, lines 5-8.

7 See p. 141, lines 8-18.

8 See p. 143, lines 2-5; 144, lines 3-7.

9 See p. 138, lines 6-14.

10 See p. 127, lines 3-4; 139, lines 2-4; 140, lines 17-23.

11 See p. 139-40; 137, lines 8-10; 144, lines 13-22.

PARAGRAPH [479]

1 In basing this forty-word paragraph upon a sixty-four-word passage located at the specified page of his source, TJ did not sacrifice Hatsell's essential meaning, but he allowed his notes to waver from strict grammatical propriety when he omitted the "must" that Hatsell had placed before his form of the verb "direct." TJ's notes, however, were not for public scrutiny. See (1785), II, 108. See also (1818), II, 144, lines 7-12.

PARAGRAPH [480]

1 In part transcribed by TJ almost verbatim, and in part committed by him to condensation and paraphrase, this paragraph, as its documentation makes clear, is to be found in Section XI of Hatsell's chapter entitled "Rules of Proceeding," that section being devoted to the rights of members to call for the reading of papers or journals during a session. TJ rearranged the order in which Hatsell presented these sentences. See (1785), II, 117, 118; also (1818), II, 163-4.

PARAGRAPH [481]

1 TJ based this passage upon Hatsell's spirited denial of a claim by Mr. George Grenville "That, if any Member complained of any book or paper, as containing matter which infringed on the privileges of the House, he had a right, without any question put, to deliver it in at the Table, and to have it read." Hatsell concluded his refutation of Grenville's claim as follows: "Indeed, this right of delivering in a paper—or the other, of having papers read at any time—or one mentioned before of separating a question—or any other right claimed by a Member, to be exercised by him against the opinion of every other Member of the House, is so extraordinary, that it is a matter of wonder how such a doctrine ever came to be advanced." See (1785), II, 117, 118; (1818), II, 165. As to the alleged right of one member to have a question separated, and to George Grenville's assertion of the validity of that right, see above, par. [465], n. 2.

PARAGRAPH [482]

1 TJ constructed this sentence from the first and third footnotes in Section xii of Hatsell's chapter entitled "Rules of Proceeding," that section being headed "*On Questions where Members are interested.*" See (1785), ii, 219 n.; (1818), ii, 167, n.

2 The preceding two sentences represent TJ's somewhat condensed version of a continuous passage in a long footnote on Hatsell (1785), ii, 121-2 n. See also (1818), ii, 171, n., col. 1.

3 The long footnote just referred to in Hatsell supplied TJ with this sentence.

4 As TJ's documentation indicated, this sentence is based upon an earlier note in the same section of Hatsell (1785), ii, 119 n. See also (1818), ii, 169, n., col. 2, lines 12-14.

PARAGRAPH [483]

1 This sentence and those which follow in the present paragraph were compiled by TJ from sentences scattered here and there in Section xiii of Hatsell's chapter on rules of proceeding, that section being headed "*When the Speaker may take the Chair.*" See (1785), ii, 126. For the precise location of each of these sentences as they appear in (1818), ii, 176-8, see the following notes.

2 See p. 177, lines 16-20. The manuscript had "aclock," Hatsell, "o'clock."

3 See p. 176, lines 7-10. In transcribing Hatsell, TJ first made "house" plural and so followed Hatsell by making the verb plural. But then, without canceling what he had written, he entered the verb in its singular form, thus creating an uncharacteristic and certainly unintended duplication of words in his style.

4 For this and the preceding sentence, see p. 177, lines 1-4, 10-12.

5 See p. 177, lines 20-1; 178, lines 1-2, 9-12.

PARAGRAPH [484]

1 As his documentation indicated, this entire paragraph was compiled by TJ from scattered passages in Hatsell (1786), ii, 126; (1818), ii, 176 (lines 14-23, 27-33).

PARAGRAPH [485]

1 TJ compiled this paragraph from scattered passages in Section xiv of Hatsell's second chapter, the section being headed, "*For not admitting Strangers into the House.*" See (1785), ii, 129; (1818), ii, 180 (lines 10-13, 18-19, 26-7), 181 (lines 1-3, 10-11).

PARAGRAPH [486]

1 This paragraph, and the following six, represent TJ's notes on various passages in Section xvi of Hatsell's second chapter, the section being headed, "*On a Division of the House.*" The passage upon which the present paragraph is based was attributed by Hatsell to Arthur Onslow, and its full text reads thus: "After the Speaker has put a question, and declared who have it, the Ayes or the Noes, any Member is at liberty to contradict him, until some Member comes into the

House, but after a Member is come in, it is too late. Mr. O." See (1785), II, 140; (1818), II, 194, n., col. 2.

PARAGRAPH [487]

1 TJ compiled this paragraph from scattered sentences and words in Hatsell (1785), II, 140, 141, 142. See also (1818), II, 195 (lines 6-11), 196 (lines 1-7, 10-19). TJ's notes do not follow the exact sequence established by Hatsell in his observations upon these details of voting procedure.

PARAGRAPH [488]

1 In compiling these sentences, TJ closely followed Hatsell (1785), II, 143. See also (1818), II, 198, lines 12-16, which read thus: "Whilst the Tellers are telling, Members should be silent, that they not be interrupted; for if any one of the Tellers thinks there is a mistake, or if they are not all agreed, they must begin and tell again. No Member must remove from his place, when they have begun telling . . ."

PARAGRAPH [489]

1 In compiling this paragraph of 69 words from a passage of 142 words in Hatsell (1785), II, 143, TJ used his sources in such a way as to preserve much of its vocabulary and its arrangement of ideas while avoiding its pronounced redundancy. For example, Hatsell wrote that "the Speaker must take upon himself to decide it, 'peremptorily,' " and "subject however to the future censure of the House, if that determination appears to be irregular or partial," whereas TJ's parallel notes reject many of Hatsell's needless words. See also (1818), II, 198-9.

PARAGRAPH [490]

1 This sentence represents TJ's greatly compressed rendering of a closely reasoned footnote in Hatsell (1785), II, 144. That footnote was written to reassert the traditional rule of the Commons in regard to the right of a single member to call for a division of the House whenever he believed that the Speaker had made a mistake in judging the results of a voice vote. Hatsell took notice of abuses of this rule in cases where the Speaker's judgment was called into question only to force a division, for its own sake, and not for the sake of a more accurate count of the Commons. Hatsell admitted discontent with the traditional rule. He even mentioned that some members wanted two, three, or more persons, not one, to be able to force a division and thus to prevent abuses in cases like this. But Hatsell apparently did not feel that the abuses constituted a standard practice or that a single member could not be trusted to behave honorably for the most part in calling the Speaker's judgment to account. TJ's note on this matter reflected Hatsell's balanced optimism. See also (1818), II, 199-200.

PARAGRAPH [491]

1 TJ's source for this sentence is of course Hatsell (1785), II, 145, where the sentence reads thus in context: "See in the Lords Journals of the 11th of January, 1689, a very extraordinary proceeding, where, upon a division, the Speaker reports from the Tellers, that the Contents were 17, and the Non-contents 18. After which declaration, one of the Tellers acquainted the House, 'that he had

mistaken in his report to the Speaker, for that the Contents were 18, and the Non-contents 17.'—Upon debate whereof, it was resolved, 'That, after a mistake in a report, the mistake may be rectified after the report made.' " For the text of this quotation as just given, see (1818), II, 201 n., col. 1.

PARAGRAPH [492]

1 This entire paragraph, including the list of forty-two directions for voting by division upon the indicated parliamentary questions, appears almost verbatim in TJ's *Manual*, Sec. XLI. Sixteen of these directions are also contained in par. [441] above, the accompanying notes to which indicate that TJ based twelve of the directions upon his own research into JHC, Vol. XXX, while two came to him from George Wythe, and two from Hatsell. The other twenty-six directions, together with the statement of the general rule, the warning that it has exceptions, and TJ's enumeration of the major sources upon which this paragraph relies, significantly extend what par. [441] had accomplished in its earlier form. Thus it seems right to conclude that TJ was here intent upon combining the results of his own independent investigations with what he had later acquired from other authorities, and was now confident of his being able to give his own work on the subject of this paragraph sufficient distinction to establish its claim to scholarly excellence among its outstanding competitors. The following notes, so far as they trace TJ's present dependence upon Hatsell, refer to the 1818 edition, II.

2 See Hatsell, p. 187, lines 1-5, where the following passage occurs: "On the 10th of December, 1640, it was declared for a constant rule, That those that give their votes for the preservation of the orders of the House, should stay in; and those that give their votes otherwise, to the introducing of any new matter, or any alteration, should go out." The phrase which follows the word "alteration" in TJ's text came to him no doubt from Scobell's *Memorials*, p. 29, which TJ often designated as Mem. in Hakew. See below, n. 4; see also above, pars. [189]-[208]; see also Jefferson's Abbreviations, s.v. Mem.

3 TJ adapted this clause from Hatsell, p. 202 (lines 19-20). Hatsell proceeded then (p. 203-10) to explain the exceptions under the following heads: petitions, bills, committees, reports from committees, Speaker and members, question moved and amended, Lords, adjournment, orders of the day. These heads provide TJ with the framework of his own present treatment of the procedures of voting by division.

4 This list may be taken as TJ's bibliographical note upon the sources of his own information upon the matter here under discussion. Hatsell (1785), II, has first place on the list, of course, and the other items are familiar from the earlier pages of the Pocket-Book.

5 The five questions and the accompanying votes listed at this point were noted by TJ from Hatsell, p. 188 (lines 2-3, 7-8, 9-10, 19-20) and 203 (lines 4-20, and n.). Hatsell recorded, however, that the Ayes go forth on the question whether a petition "be brought up," whereas TJ, without changing the voting procedure, transcribed the verb as "be recieved."

6 TJ carefully noted that Grey's *Debates*, IX, 365, authorized the Noes to go forth on the question here mentioned.

7 This item and the six which immediately follow were transcribed by TJ from Hatsell. See p. 189-90; 203 (lines 22-8); 204 (lines 1-2).

8 For this item and the next, TJ went to Hatsell. See p. 190 (lines 9-10, 13-14); 204 (lines 2-12).

9 This item, which is not in Hatsell, was supplied by TJ from JHC, xxx, 251, as he noted here, and also above, par. [441].

10 For this item and the next, TJ drew upon Hatsell. See p. 190 (lines 18-22).

11 This item and the following five were not mentioned in Hatsell's list of the procedures followed in parliamentary division, but they were authenticated here by TJ from his own researches into JHC, xxx. Even the procedure followed in voting whether or not a bill be printed was noted in the latter source, not in Hatsell. See above, par. [441], n. 4.

12 TJ's authority for this item was Hatsell, p. 191 (lines 3-4); 204 (lines 14-17).

13 The manuscript shows that TJ wrote some words here and then obliterated them so completely as to make mysteries of his original intention and of the nature of his erasure.

14 This item TJ transcribed from Hatsell, p. 191 (lines 14-15); 205 (lines 4-8).

15 As TJ indicated in the margin, this item came to him from JHC, xxx, 291, where, on March 21, 1765, an order of the day required the House to resolve itself into a committee of the whole, and, if the resulting voice vote had been inclusive, as in this case it was not, the following vote by division would have forced the Noes to go forth. See above, par. [441]. See also Hatsell, p. 191-2, 205 (lines 16-19).

16 It could be that this item also came to TJ from JHC, xxx, 291, although in the manuscript the latter reference may have been intended to apply only to the item opposite it. At any rate, page 291 of Volume xxx of the Journals records that, after the order of the day had been read, the question was put "That Mr. Speaker do now leave the Chair," and, in voting upon it, the Noes went forth. See also Hatsell, p. 191 (line 30), 205 (line 15).

17 TJ's source for this item and the next was Hatsell, p. 192 (lines 5-6, 9-11) and 206 (lines 1-2, 2-5).

18 As TJ's marginal note indicated, this item depends upon JHC, xxx, 344. On that page, under the date of April 4, 1765, a motion was made that a witness named Captain Palliser, who had testified the preceding day, be summoned to testify again in the same connection. In the subsequent division, the Ayes went forth. See also above, par. [441].

19 For TJ's source, see Hatsell, p. 192 (lines 23-5).

20 As a source for this item, TJ turned away from the practice recommended by Hatsell, p. 111, n., col. 2, and recommended the one authenticated by George Wythe. See above, par. [441], n. 7.

21 For TJ's source, see Hatsell, p. 192 (lines 26-7); 206 (lines 17-19); 207 (lines 1-3).

22 TJ's source for this item and the next was Hatsell, p. 193 (lines 19-23), 208-9.

23 This item and the next were based by TJ upon Hatsell, p. 210 (lines 13-19).

24 This practice and the subsequent three were based by TJ upon the respective following pages of Hatsell: 1) p. 210 (lines 1-4); 2) p. 210 (line 5); 3) p. 210 (lines 8-11); 4) p. 194 (lines 6-7).

25 For TJ's source, see Hatsell, p. 209 (lines 11-12).

PARAGRAPH [493]

1 This paragraph of fifty-seven words captures the essence of a 120-word passage in Hatsell (1785), II, 149. See also (1818) II, 207 (lines 28-9), 208 (lines 1-9). TJ omitted the first ten words of Hatsell's text; he exactly transcribed the next eighteen words; he kept to the basic philosophy but left out unnecessary amplifications in the following thirty-five words; the next twenty-seven words he did not include; and he brought his excerpt to an end by using what was essential, and rejecting what was peripheral, in Hatsell's final twenty words. In his last sentence, TJ substituted "dignified public body" for Hatsell's "numerous, and consequently sometimes tumultuous assembly." TJ's marginal note, "turn to the book," is a reference to his *Manual*, Sec. I, where the present paragraph appears almost verbatim in the form given it here.

PARAGRAPH [494]

1 This sentence was framed by TJ from a longer passage in Hatsell (1785), II, 160. See also (1818), II, 223, n., col. 1, where the following quotation is to be found: "On the 18th of November, 1763, upon Sir John Cust, the Speaker's, being ill, and sending a message to the House by the Clerk, there was some doubt, whether the Mace ought not to have been in the House, and under the Table; but upon consideration, it was determined that it ought not: the Mace, though belonging to the House, is in the custody of the Speaker; and until he declines to act as such, the Mace must be kept by him. Accordingly, in this and several other similar instances, the House adjourned themselves without the Mace." For previous references on the mace, see above, pars. [429], [476], [478].

2 TJ based these final two sentences upon Hatsell (1785), II, 160. See also (1818), II, 222 n., col. 2. For brief notes upon same two sentences, see the *Manual* (1801), Sec. IX, par. 4; (1812), p. 36.

PARAGRAPH [495]

1 Although TJ did not document this sentence, it came to him from Hatsell (1785), II, 169-70. See also (1818), II, 233 n., col. 2, where Hatsell spoke thus: "The antient practice, and which in my memory was strictly adhered to by Mr. O. was, That no Member had a right to speak against, or reflect upon, any determination of the House, unless he meant to conclude with a motion for rescinding such determination." (The word given in the angle brackets is probably

"any," but TJ's cancellation is here so effective in the manuscript that an attempt to penetrate beneath it is speculative.) For a paraphrase of this sentence in TJ's later work, see *Manual* (1801), Sec. XVII, par. 12, or (1812), p. 54.

PARAGRAPH [496]

1 The individual items in this list of seventeen offenses against parliamentary decorum were taken by TJ from Hatsell's similarly arranged and worded list of twenty-three items (1785), II, 170. See also (1818), II, 233-6. Thirteen of TJ's items were later given a place in the *Manual* (1801), Sec. XVII; (1812), p. 51-62. The six items which TJ did not transfer from Hatsell to the Pocket-Book comprised the rule against a member's reading a printed book or letters, against his taking tobacco in the gallery or at the table or in committees, and against his crossing between the Chair and table. The three rules against tobacco were also excluded by TJ from the *Manual*, as was the warning that the king's name must not be used to influence debate. But the *Manual* did record that "In parliament to speak irreverently or seditiously against the king is against order." (1801), Sec. XVII, par. 22; (1812), p. 59.

PARAGRAPH [497]

1 TJ compiled this paragraph from passages in Hatsell (1785), II, 167, 172. See also (1818), II, 231 (lines 8-26), 238 (n., col. 1). In the last of these references, Hatsell spoke thus: "I should suppose, that, if the Speaker is compelled *to name a Member*, from his persisting obstinately in any irregularity, after having been frequently admonished from the Chair, the House ought to support the Speaker in his endeavours to enforce obedience to their orders, and should call upon the Member so named, to withdraw.—When he is heard, and withdrawn, the Speaker will then state to the House the offence committed; and the House will consider what punishment they ought to inflict upon the offender." The offenses mentioned in TJ's paragraph would be punishable in the U.S. Senate and House under the powers given those bodies to protect themselves against injuries inflicted upon them by their own members. See TJ's *Manual*, Sec. III.

PARAGRAPH [498]

1 TJ compiled this paragraph from three passages in Hatsell (1785), II, 175. See also (1818), II, 240 (lines 3-8, 14-16, and n., col. 2, lines 16ff.)

PARAGRAPH [499]

1 This paragraph represents TJ's paraphrase of two passages in Hatsell (1785), II, 175. See also (1818), II, 243 (n. cols. 1 and 2), 244 (lines 3-7), 245 (lines 1 and 2), as follows: 1. "The Speaker is not obliged to be at Committees of the whole House. When he is at a Committee, he is considered as a private Member, and has a voice accordingly: He is supposed, whilst the House is in a Committee, to be in his private room, and is not, upon a division, compellable to come out of it, as other Members are, who may happen to be there." 2) "If, however, as has frequently happened, the numbers upon a division should be equal, and it thereby becomes the Speaker's duty to give a casting voice, it has been sometimes usual, in giving this vote, to give, at the same time, the reasons which induce him to it; but, at that moment, all possibility of his swaying or influencing the House by these reasons is past." The first of these passages is credited by Hatsell to Arthur Onslow.

PARAGRAPH [500]

1 TJ documented these two sentences by citing Hatsell (1785), II, 194-5, where Hatsell discussed the duties of the clerk of the Commons. See also (1818), II, 267 (lines 9-11), 268 (line 3), 265 (lines 22-7), 266 (lines 22-5).

PARAGRAPH [501]

1 In compiling the passage that makes up the preceding part of this paragraph, TJ condensed a long footnote in Hatsell (1785), II, 199, where Hatsell spoke in his own person upon the subject discussed. At one point, TJ's manuscript seems to show that he wrote "farther" and then changed the word to "further," as if in conformity with Hatsell's text. Within the angle brackets, TJ, having written the words as shown, canceled them out and entered above them "two members still insist," thus bringing his final text toward conformity once more with the wording of his source. For that source, see also Hatsell (1818), II, 273, n., cols. 1 and 2.

2 These two sentences, as TJ indicated, were derived from Hatsell (1785), II, 196. See also Hatsell (1818), II, 268 (n., col. 2, lines 7-14), 269 (n., col. 1, lines 1-5, 26-9). TJ varied the order in which elements of these sentences were presented in the text of his source, his purpose having apparently been to improve sequence as well as to shorten wording.

PARAGRAPH [502]

1 TJ drew this sentence from a passage in Hatsell (1785), II, 202. For the same passage, see Hatsell (1818), II, 276 (lines 20-2), where Hatsell spoke thus: "On the 11th of July, 1625, a warrant for Mr. Wood, to answer his contempt to the House, in not paying fees for his Bill, to the Speaker, Serjeant, &c." Mr. Wood, and all other beneficiaries of private bills, as distinguished from public bills, were expected to pay fees to the officers of the Commons when their bills had finally received approval. For the source of the passage as Hatsell phrased it, see JHC, I, 808.

PARAGRAPH [503]

1 This paragraph represents TJ's summary of what was said in a footnote in Hatsell (1785), II, 242. For the same footnote, see Hatsell (1818), II, 339-40. On Friday, January 29, 1768, the footnote declared, the king came to the House of Lords to endorse bills ready for his approval, and on that occasion the following serious question of parliamentary order arose. Some of the bills to be presented to the king had originated in the Commons, and had later been passed by the Lords, but they had then been sent for the king's approval without any intermediate word to anybody as to what had happened to them. The Commons were outraged, feeling that they should have had the usual notice of the Lords' action before anything further was done with their bills. Two eminent parliamentarians, Lord Marchmont and Lord Sandys, were summoned to decide whether the Commons had a just grievance or not, and their decision, which Hatsell stated in brief, furnished the basis of TJ's present paragraph. The Lords were in order in what they had done, it was ruled, but they had been lacking in respect and consideration for the Commons in the form which they allowed their conduct to take. TJ would have been aware, of course, that Hatsell was clerk assistant in the Commons during the period of the above episode and would therefore have

been close to what happened. Hatsell became clerk of the Commons later in the year 1768.

1 At this point, and thereafter for the next fourteen paragraphs, TJ, as he indicated, compiled his notes from Hatsell (1785), III, which devoted itself to the Lords, to Supply, and to an Appendix of seventeen separate sections. For TJ's only previous reference to this third volume, see above, par. [460].

2 This sentence was based by TJ upon an entry in Section I of Hatsell's chapter on the Lords, that section being devoted to the circumstances in which Lords may be admitted into the House of Commons. Hatsell noted that on March 2, 1548, the Commons, in considering the bill of attainder mentioned in TJ's sentence, resolved to proceed thereupon in an orderly fashion and thus to request that the Lords who had given evidence on that matter should come to the Commons' house and deliver their evidence "*vivâ voce.*" (TJ's single quotation mark at this point responds to the double quotation mark of his source, but the manuscript does not show where the quotation began.) Hatsell also noted that, on March 4, the Lords promised to answer the Commons' request if asked to do so, and that they were accordingly asked. See Hatsell (1785), II, 2; (1818), III, 2.

3 Had TJ chosen at once to answer this query, he might well have consulted JHL, I, 346, and JHC, I, 9, where entries show that this particular bill had been passed by the Lords on February 27 and had been received the next day by the Commons. Had he possessed Hatsell (1818), III, 2, he would have noticed a footnote making the query unnecessary, inasmuch as Hatsell there quoted from the Lords' Journal a passage describing their action in passing the bill on February 27.

1 Up to this point, the paragraph was transcribed by TJ from section II of the chapter devoted to the Lords, that section being made up not only of the record of thirty-two precedents wherein the Lords and Commons established procedures for attending each other's meetings, but also of observations by Hatsell upon some of those precedents. What must have particularly attracted TJ among the observations was one which identified itself as a summarizing statement of four conclusions developed upon these procedures by Hatsell himself "from the Journals, or from the History of the Proceedings in the House of Commons." Each of the conclusions is accurately condensed in this part of TJ's paragraph. See Hatsell (1785), III, 17; (1818), III, 20-1.

2 The rest of this paragraph represents TJ's precise condensation of Hatsell's footnote to the first of his four conclusions. See (1785), III, 17; (1818), III, 21.

1 Section III of Hatsell's chapter on the Lords discussed the procedures involved in exchanging messages between Lords and Commons, TJ's sentence having been drawn from a precedent established on February 15, 1743. TJ preferred "recieved" to the more usual form of his source. See Hatsell (1785), III, 22; (1818), III, 26, lines 15-18.

PARAGRAPH [507]

1 TJ compiled this sentence so as to make it partly a condensation and partly a verbatim transcription of Hatsell's report of a message sent by the Lords to the Commons on March 13, 1758. Hatsell (1785), III, 22; (1818), III, 26. For Hatsell's source, se JHC, XXVIII, 131. The "usual words" referred to by TJ, Hatsell, and JHC are "*soit baille aux seigneurs.*" See above, par. [252].

PARAGRAPH [508]

1 Based by TJ upon one of Hatsell's observations in Section III of his chapter on the Lords, this paragraph is at times a close paraphrase and at times a verbatim transcript of its source. See Hatsell (1785), III, 25; (1818), III, 29, lines 6-13.

PARAGRAPH [509]

1 TJ compiled this passage from another of Hatsell's observations in the section just identified. See Hatsell (1785), III, 25; (1818), III, 29-30. For Hatsell's source, see JHC, XIII, 267.

PARAGRAPH [510]

1 As TJ indicated in part, this sentence was closely based upon Hatsell (1785), III, 26. See also (1818), III, 30, lines 10-12. The question mentioned in TJ's last clause ordinarily received an affirmative vote, said Hatsell, but on July 1, 1717, it did not, and Hatsell added that the latter occurrence was the only one of its kind, so far as he knew. Had he explained its uniqueness, he would have introduced TJ to an important crisis in the relations between Lords and Commons—a crisis that involved impeachment proceedings against Robert Harley, first Earl of Oxford, and the refusal by the Lords, after the proceedings had begun, to accept the rules which the Commons wanted the prosecution to follow. When the Commons asked that the Lords reconsider their refusal, the Lords denied the request, whereupon the Commons voted 208 to 54 not to receive the messengers sent by the Lords to announce their decision. Despite that latter action by the Commons, the Lords opened the impeachment proceedings anyway, only to find that the Commons refused to take part. The Lords accordingly dismissed the charges filed by the Commons against the earl and ordered the earl's acquittal and release from imprisonment in the Tower. See JHC, XVIII, 612-15; also JHL, XX, 522-6. See also DNB, s.v. Harley, Robert, first Earl of Oxford.

PARAGRAPH [511]

1 A largely verbatim transcript by TJ of the essential core of a somewhat longer sentence in Hatsell (1785), III, 25. See also Hatsell (1818), III, 30, lines 5-7.

PARAGRAPH [512]

1 For the substance and much of the wording of this part of TJ's paragraph, see Hatsell (1785), III, 27-30. See also Hatsell (1818), III, 32 (lines 1-5), 33 (lines 12-13, and n., col. 1).

2 TJ canceled this phrase in his manuscript, recognizing no doubt that he had more accurately placed the same words in the concluding part of the sentence.

3 As TJ's note at the end of this passage indicated, he drew the last sentence from Hatsell (1785), II, 261. See also (1818), II, 265, lines 22-6; 253, n., col. 1. As for the authority behind TJ's statement that the Commons derives its status as a court of record from its having judicature in some things, see Hatsell (1818), II, 158, lines 12-16, where Sir Edward Coke was quoted as having spoken thus: "No question, but this [the Commons] is a court of Record,—and it hath power of Judicature in some Cases.—We have the power to judge of Returns, and Members of our House.—We make a warrant to the Great Seal; therefore a power of Record." See also above, par. 33.

PARAGRAPH [513]

1 This passage represents TJ's condensed version of Hatsell's quotation of the ancient rule governing requests for conferences by either Lords or Commons. See (1785), III, 31; (1818), III, 46, lines 11-18. As cited by Hatsell, this rule was incorporated in a message sent by the Commons to the Lords in answer to a request by the Lords that the Commons agree to a conference for the purpose of explaining their reasons for dealing "so hardly" with the Lords' bill to provide for "the Restitution in Blood of the Lord *Sturton*." The Commons had received that bill on March 7, 1575/76. They had read it twice on March 10 and a third time on March 12, while attaching to it a pair of provisos that Lord Sturton heard about and did not like. And they still had the bill in their possession. When the Lords sent the request mentioned above, the Commons coldly refused it by citing its parliamentary impropriety under the circumstances then prevailing; and that coldness still survived in TJ's condensation. In addition to Hatsell, see also JHC, I, 111, 113, 114, 115; also JHL, I, 743, 749; also above, par. [440].

PARAGRAPH [514]

1 In this thirty-word sentence, TJ, by using certain selected words of his source and by adding some of his own, stated the gist of an eighty-eight-word passage in Hatsell (1785), III, 51; (1818), III, 67, lines 5-13.

2 For the substance which TJ used as the basis of this forty-one-word sentence, see the much longer passage in Hatsell (1785), III, 51f.; (1818), 73, lines 1-3, 6-26. The phrase in parentheses is apparently shorthand for "as to the immediate taking down of words." See above, par. [501].

3 This fifty-five-word sentence follows the essential wording of an eighty-seven-word passage in Hatsell (1785), III, 51f.; (1818), III, 74, lines 12-21.

PARAGRAPH [515]

1 This sentence represents TJ's largely verbatim transcript of the essential line of meaning in a somewhat more elaborate passage in Hatsell (1785), III, 48; (1818), III, 70 (lines 4-8), 71 (lines 1-4).

PARAGRAPH [516]

1 As stated here, this rule is in part a paraphrase and in part a verbatim transcription by TJ of a passage in Hatsell (1785), III, 52; (1818), III, 74-5. Hatsell introduced the passage by emphasizing that neither House interferes with the other, whether under the Black Rod, acting for the Lords, or the serjeant, acting

for the Commons, but that each House may invoke the rule given here if it applies to its needs.

PARAGRAPH [517]

1 These notations were based by TJ upon Hatsell's account of an episode in which the Lords, while voting supplies to the king on June 19, 1661, decided themselves upon the amount to be granted, thus interfering at least nominally with the prerogative traditionally exercised by the Commons in that matter. In other words, this episode involved a voluntary transfer of power from the Commons to the Lords in a realm which the Commons had ruled as their own over the years to their great constitutional advantage. For Hatsell's account, which falls in his chapter on supply, and deals with occasional interferences by the Lords with the prerogatives of the Commons, see (1785), III, 83; (1818), III, 115, lines 12-19. See also JHC, VIII, 266-70, 275.

PARAGRAPH [518]

1 For these cases in TJ's source, see Hatsell (1785), III, 121, 122, 124, 126; (1818), III, 167, 169, 171-2, 174, 175. A rider is a clause added to a bill on its third reading to correct one of its shortcomings. The cases documented here concerned supply.

PARAGRAPH [519]

1 This rule appeared in George Petyt, p. 294, 310, 316, 326; and Petyt documented it by referring to Scobell's *Memorials*, p. 29, 45, and to Edward Coke's *Reports in Thirteen Parts*, Pt. 12, p. 116; but TJ's present wording is closer to that in the source indicated here than to that in the others. See also above, pars. 72, [442, Rule IV], [496].

PARAGRAPH [520]

1 The last three words of this rule TJ transcribed verbatim, and the other words represent his condensed paraphrase of a passage in the source indicated. His marginal inquiry suggests that, at the time when he made this particular entry, he doubted its universality but did not have at hand the facts to question it. Thus the entry may have been made far earlier than its present position in the Pocket-Book might imply. For TJ's definite awareness of the possibility of violating this rule on occasion, see above, pars. [440], [513, n.].

PARAGRAPH [521]

1 The *Arcana Parliamentaria*, p. 53-64, from which TJ derived this paragraph, introduced the case of Ferrers with this notation: "See *Hollinshed*, in his Cronicle, Fol. 1584." Thus the fourth figure given here is to be construed as a page number, not as a date.

2 That is, set at large, freed from bondage. See OED.

3 What TJ here calls a "very full report of this case" must be taken as a reference to *Arcana Parliamentaria*, p. 54-4. For previous mention of the same case, see above, pars. [350], [413], [414].

4 If this reference is to be taken at face value, it presents a real difficulty to an uninitiated reader. It would literally have to designate either Elsynge's *Method of Passing Bills* or his *Manner of Holding Parliaments*, his only two works on parliamentary matters. But the first of those works makes no reference to the case of Ferrers, while the second discusses that case on p. 203 in such a way as to make the reference inapplicable to TJ's paragraph. Even so, TJ's present reference ought not to be dismissed as a slapdash error on his part. In the five following paragraphs he cites Elsynge's *Memorials*, and that form of reference turns out demonstrably to designate the *Memorials* that Henry Scobell is known to have written. Did TJ intend his final documentation in paragraph [521] to refer to the latter work? There is a strong probability that he did. For one thing, a reference to Scobell's *Memorials*, p. 104, if intended at that point, would almost exactly fit into the context of TJ's paragraph, inasmuch as Scobell's *Memorials*, p. 105, mentioned the case of Ferrers and its part in Holinshed's *Chronicles*. For another thing, TJ may here have had in mind George Petyt's way, in the *Lex Parliamentaria*, of using the title of one work and the author's name of another to locate a quotation that he wanted to document. What Petyt did in this connection was to refer on many occasions to Hakewill's *Memorials* or *Memorials* in *Hakewill*, and it turned out each time that the reference in actual fact designated Scobell's *Memorials*, as that work appeared in a volume also devoted to one other work, Hakewill's *Modus tenendi Parliamentum*. Such a reference would be clear enough to the scholars and antiquarians who busied themselves with parliamentary law, and Petyt did not even think it necessary to specify openly what he was up to. See Lambert, *Bills and Acts*, p. 18. Also above, par. [189], n. 2. In all probability TJ's references in the present paragraphs to Elsynge or to Elsynge's *Memorials* simply follow the pattern that he had observed in Petyt's references to Hakewill's *Memorials*. Indeed, one of the volumes in TJ's library contained Scobell's *Memorials*, identified openly by title and obscurely by its author's initials and official status; and it also contained Elsynge's *Method of Passing Bills*, identified by title and by its author's full name. See Sowerby 2878, 2879, 2880 (III, 177-8). What more natural than for TJ to adopt for his citations of Elsynge's *Memorials* a method of reference paralleling that used by Petyt, and doubtless by other scholars, in citing "*Memorials* in *Hakewill*"? The idea is not preposterous. Indeed, it is quite possibly right. And, after all, TJ's references here were intended only for his own eyes.

PARAGRAPH [522]

1 Although TJ's documentation throughout this paragraph indicates that its source was Elsynge's *Memorials*, p. 53-4, its true source was Scobell's *Memorials*, p. 53-4, as is suggested in par. [521], n. 4, and as the following quotation from those pages of Scobell proves:

> All the Amendments reported by the Committee are to be proceeded in before any new Amendment or *Proviso* be admitted, unless it be amending the Amendments reported. . . .
>
> After the House hath proceeded upon all the Amendments reported, there have been sometimes offered other Amendments, Proviso's, or additional clauses written in paper. . . .
>
> But regularly, no such thing should be offered after a commitment, but the same should be offered to the Committee, where it may be first considered and prepared, and so the time of the House saved.

PARAGRAPH [523]

1 In compiling this paragraph, TJ reduced to twenty-eight words a passage of seventy-six words in Scobell's (not Elsynge's) *Memorials*, p. 59, lines 20-8. See above, pars. [521], n. 4, [523].

PARAGRAPH [524]

1 An accurate condensation by TJ of a passage in Scobell's *Memorials*, p. 62, lines 11-20. Scobell's source was the action of the Commons as recorded in JHC, I, 120-1, and in D'Ewes, p. 290, col. 1, but the date of the action was January 31 of the year in question, not January 20, as Scobell had it.

PARAGRAPH [525]

1 This sentence was TJ's somewhat condensed transcript of the following passage in Scobell's *Memorials*, p. 65 (not 95 as TJ mistakenly had it): "*It is no possession of a Bill, except the same be delivered to the Clerk to be read, or that the Speaker read the Title of it in the Chair.*" Italics are Scobell's. For Scobell's source, which he did not specify, see the resolutions adopted by the Commons on May 23, 1604 (JHC, I, 223).

2 This reference may have been intended by TJ to provide final authority for the present paragraph, inasmuch as his immediate source was silent on that matter. At any rate, these abbreviations designate the Commons' resolutions of May 23, 1604, as recorded in a volume called by short title, *Orders of the House of Commons*. TJ's library possessed a copy of the second edition (1756) of this work (Sowerby 2882; III, 178), and TJ's page references here, and in the paragraphs below, refer to it. The parallel page references refer to the first edition (1747). For the source of the present sentence, see *Orders of the House of Commons* (1756), p. 64, or (1747), p. 27. For the basic source, see JHC, I, 223 (May 23, 1604).

PARAGRAPH [526]

1 TJ here compiled a condensed paraphrase of a passage in Scobell's *Memorials*, p. 110. For the parliamentary action upon which Scobell based the passage, see JHC, I, 18.

2 See *Orders of the House of Commons* (1756), p. 122; (1747), p. 81.

PARAGRAPH [527]

1 At this point TJ's paragraph is based upon Elsynge's *Method of Passing Bills*, p. 23-7, a copy of which in his own library was bound with Scobell's *Memorials* and two other treatises. See above, par. [521], n. 4. For the location of the present paragraph in another edition of Elsynge's work, see *The Harleian Miscellany*, v, 216-17.

PARAGRAPH [528]

1 As he indicated in part, TJ based these two resolutions upon *Orders of the House of Commons* (1756), p. 67, 68; (1747), p. 30, where the two resolutions are stated as follows:

28 *May*, 1621.   An essential Order, that the Amendments be twice read.
30 *May*, 1621.   An essential Order, a Proviso from the Lords to be read thrice,

> tho' the Bill come from the lower House, and by Vote of the House to pass as a Law.

2 This rule was drawn by TJ from a passage on the indicated pages of the work just cited (March 26, 1626/27). See JHC, I, 841.

PARAGRAPH [529]

1 This sentence, which TJ framed and then partly corrected by the indicated cancellations as he went along, finally emerged with a conspicuous and surprising redundancy to mar it. It is based upon the following order of September 11, 1648: "That when Messengers are sent from the Lords to this House, as soon as the Business in Agitation, when the Messengers come, is ended, then the Messengers from the Lords to be called in." See *Orders of the House of Commons* (1756), p. 73; (1747), p. 55. See also JHC, VI, 18. For a somewhat opposed version of the rule stated here, see above, par. [506].

PARAGRAPH [530]

1 The rule given here represents TJ's condensation of the following entry in *Orders of the House of Commons*, (1756), p. 89; (1747), p. 51: "Mr. *Pym* went up to the Lords with this Message; Whereas this House has received a Message from their Lordships for a present Conference, without any Expression of the Subject or Matter of the Conference, which is contrary to the constant Course of either House, and therefore this House cannot yield to a present Conference." For the parallel entry in the official record of the Commons, see JHC, II, 232, under the date of August 2, 1641. Mr. Pym is of course the famous John Pym of the early days of the Long Parliament.

PARAGRAPH [531]

1 See *Orders of the House of Commons* (1756), p. 92; (1747), p. 123. See also JHC, I, 866 (June 2, 1626). See above, pars. 64, [362], [483], for other practices by the Commons on roll calls.

PARAGRAPH [532]

1 This forty-one-word passage accurately follows the essential wording and captures the essential meaning of a sixty-nine-word passage in TJ's source, *Orders of the House of Commons* (1756), p. 110; (1747), p. 82. See also JHC, I, 634, col. 2, under the date of June 1, 1621.

PARAGRAPH [533]

1 According to the original wording and subsequent interlineations in his manuscript, TJ seems to have started this sentence at a paragraph referring only to the privilege enjoyed by witnesses and to have asserted privilege for the two law officers when he noticed later that they enjoyed it too. See *Orders of the House of Commons* (1756), p. 119; (1747), p. 92-3. For separate reference to the privilege of witnesses, see (1747), p. 62; of solicitors, p. 86-7.

PARAGRAPH [534]

1 For TJ's source, see *Orders of the House of Commons* (1756), p. 121; (1747), p. 85-6.

PARAGRAPH [535]

1 TJ compiled this unit of the present paragraph from *Orders of the House of Commons* (1756), p. 122; (1747), p. 82, 86. TJ's first two dates in the margin are taken from that source, as indicated by the page numbers of the 1747 edition. See also JHC, I, 819; VIII, 665.

2 For this phrase, TJ drew upon *Orders of the House of Commons* (1756), p. 129; (1747), p. 81. See JHC, I, 18, where the date is given as February 22, not February 20.

3 For this rule, TJ depended upon *Orders of the House of Commons* (1756), p. 254. TJ's marginal reference at this point was designed to indicate the following resolution of the Commons on January 22, 1749/50: "That Mr. Speaker do issue his Warrant to the Clerk of the Crown, to make out a new Writ for the Electing of a Burgess to serve in this present Parliament for the Borough of *Dunbeved*, alias *Launceston*, in the County of *Cornwall* . . ." JHC, XXV, 945. The date of this action was of course too late for inclusion in the 1747 edition of *Orders of the House of Commons*.

PARAGRAPH [536]

1 TJ drew these rules from *Orders of the House of Commons* (1756), p. 131, 133, 134; (1747), p. 89-91. For their origin in the proceedings of the Commons, see JHC, XI, 751; XII, 349; XIII, 8; XX, 57. In connection with the first rule, the members of Commons acknowledged their own liability for payment of parish duties and taxes of all sorts, while asserting that suits designed to enforce such payments could properly be brought against themselves despite their immunity to most other kinds of legal proceedings during a session of Parliament. See JHC, XI, 751.

PARAGRAPH [537]

1 TJ's source for the wording of this cluster of rules, as he indicated in part, was *Orders of the House of Commons* (1756), p. 140; (1747), p. 108. For the ultimate source, see JHC, XII, 661 (April 22, 1699).

2 The culprit "committed to Newgate" was Thomas Colepepper, a member of the preceding Parliament, who, defeated for reelection in the autumn of 1701, charged his opponent with bribery at the polls, and, in the ensuing investigation, was found to have bribed voters on his side, and to have circulated a letter during the last session accusing some of his colleagues of being in the pay of France. Guided by these revelations, the Commons acquitted Colepepper's opponent of the charges against him, and proceeded then to imprison Colepepper for having made some of his colleagues appear to have been hirelings of England's implacable enemy. TJ's one-sentence account of this episode was compiled from *Orders of the House of Commons* (1756), p. 141; (1747), p. 108. See also JHC, XIII, 732-5.

3 This important rule grew out of an episode in which Lieutenant Colonel Copley, serving in 1689 as deputy governor of Kingston upon Hull, repeatedly seized the post mail when it arrived in that city and subjected it to personal examination at taverns or in his own home, opening some letters, assuming possession of others, and destroying still others, against the repeated official protests

of George Mawson, deputy postmaster. On August 13, 1689, Mawson petitioned Parliament, alleging that Copley's behavior worked great hardship upon
local traders, upon residents, and upon those members of Parliament who
chanced to have letters thus arbitrarily seized. Mawson's petition resulted in a
Commons' resolution on August 14, 1689, providing "That the breaking open
Letters directed to, or sent from any Member of this House, is a Breach of the
Privilege of this House." See *Orders of the House of Commons* (1756), p. 162;
(1747), p. 118. For further details, see JHC, x, 265.

PARAGRAPH [538]

1 Transcribed almost verbatim by TJ from his indicated source, *Orders of the
House of Commons* (1756), p. 223; (1747), p. 10. See also JHC, VIII, 95. (July
20, 1660)

PARAGRAPH [539]

1 This entire paragraph corresponds word for word with TJ's *Manual* (1801),
Sec. LIII, par. 6; (1812), p. 175-6, except that, in both printed versions, the penultimate number in the final reference to Selden's *Judicature* is 9, not 7. The
two marginal words are plainly intended to key the paragraph to Sec. LIII ("Impeachment") and par. 6 ("Jurisdiction").

2 The first clause in this sentence was drawn by TJ from a short passage in Selden's *Judicature*, p. 63, and the rest of the sentence from the same source, p. 12.

3 For TJ's source, see Selden's *Judicature*, p. 84.

4 Selden's *Judicature*, p. 6-7, provided TJ with the content and much of the
phraseology of his passage beginning, "The lords may not by the law try a commoner . . ." and ending "but not *try* the delinquent."

5 This reference means that, from this point to the end of the paragraph, TJ
depended for his material upon Wooddeson's *Laws of England*, II, 601, 576. The
Fitzharris case, which Wooddeson cited, involved a serious constitutional conflict between Lords and Commons in March 1681/82, and that conflict started
when, on March 25, the Commons decided to send next day to the Lords a resolution that Edward Fitzharris, Roman Catholic agitator of Irish birth, "be impeached of High Treason, in the Name of all the Commons of *England*." To this
resolution the Lords replied on March 26 by refusing to proceed with the impeachment, on the ground that the case against Fitzharris should be decided in
court under the common law. The Commons were outraged by this defiance of
the Lower House in a matter of this kind, and a confrontation between them and
the Lords would have been inevitable if Charles II had not dissolved Parliament
at once. In addition to Wooddeson's account of the case, see JHC, IX, 709-11.

6 In transcribing this reference to Grey's *Debates* as a source of the Fitzharris
case, TJ should not have copied the page numbers given here. He should instead
have followed his primary source, Wooddeson's *Laws of England*, II, 601, and
have written the page numbers as 332-8. What seems to have happened is that
TJ began to transcribe Wooddeson's reference to Grey, and during the process,
perhaps as the result of a momentary lapse of attention, he allowed his eyes to
skip forward to 325-7, which, as page numbers in Wooddeson's next reference,
had nothing to do with Grey or the Fitzharris case. Eye skips are common oc-

currences in the work of typesetters or typists, and errors caused thereby are discomforting to proofreaders. At this point in the Pocket-Book an error of that sort must be recorded against the normally careful TJ.

7 These references to Selden and Blackstone TJ transcribed from Wooddeson, II, 576, and they designate the following two works: 1) Selden's *Judicature* as contained in his *Opera Omnia*, III, 1610, 1619, 1641, 1604, 1618, 1654; 2) Blackstone's Commentaries, IV, 257.

PARAGRAPH [540]

1 This entire paragraph corresponds word for word with TJ's *Manual* (1801), Sec. LIII, par. 7; (1812), p. 176-7. The word in the margin appears also in the printed texts as if to set the theme for what follows.

2 TJ transcribed this sentence verbatim from Wooddeson's, *Laws of England*, II, 596-7.

3 Since Wooddeson did not mention this reference, it is probable that TJ supplied it from his own information, lending credit in the manuscript to this assumption by entering the citation as an interlineation above a caret.

4 From "The general course" to "the peers will take order for his appearance," TJ's wording is a close, almost verbatim transcription of Wooddeson's *Laws of England*, II, 603-4.

5 TJ transcribed these references from Wooddeson's *Laws of England*, II, 605, 606, except for the final one, which he doubtless added on his own. Wooddeson's reference to "Sachev. trial. 325" should have read "329," but TJ seems not to have noticed the error.

PARAGRAPH [541]

1 See TJ's *Manual* (1801), Sec. LIII, par. 8; (1812), p. 177, for the exact texts of the paragraph given here, with the marginal word added as a kind of paragraph title.

2 As TJ's documentation indicated in part, this paragraph was compiled from phrases and words scattered across the following pages of Selden's *Judicature*: 89, 90, 91, 98, 99.

PARAGRAPH [542]

1 With the marginal word as its title, this paragraph passed verbatim into TJ's *Manual* (1801), Sec. LIII, par. 9; (1812), p. 177.

2 This sentence TJ transcribed almost verbatim from Wooddeson's *Laws of England*, II, 602.

3 This sentence is a reduced version of Wooddeson's transcription of a ruling made by the Lords on March 14, 1709/10. See Wooddeson, *Laws of England*, II, 605. See also JHL, XVI, 718-19. See also above, par. [540].

4 These references were transcribed by TJ from Wooddeson, *Laws of England*, II, 605, 606.

1 Except for the absence of the marks of parentheses, and the presence of two words in the title of Clarendon's *History*, this paragraph, headed by the term in the left-hand margin, appears verbatim in TJ's *Manual* (1801), Sec. LIII, par. 10; (1812), p. 177-8.

2 As TJ indicated in part by this reference, he compiled the preceding passage by making an abstract of certain main points in the longer discussion in Selden's *Judicature*, p. 98, 99.

3 These references and the sentence to which they are here attached were based by TJ upon Wooddeson's *Laws of England*, II, 606. Wooddeson's more complete list of references reads thus: "T. Ray. 382. 1 Rush. 268. Fost. 232. 3 Seld. 1625. &c. (Wilk. ed.) 1 Clar. hist. rebell. 279, 280."

4 As TJ's annotation indicated, this statement was taken from Selden's *Judicature*, p. 100-1.

5 TJ constructed this general rule from the following passage in Selden's *Judicature*, p. 101: "At this Day, if the Commons accuse a Commoner of Misdemeanors in such a state of Liberty or restraint as he is in, when the Commons complain of him, in such he is to answer, *prout* 18 *Jac*."

6 See Selden's *Judicature*, p. 101: "Sir *Francis Michell*, and Sir *John Bennet* were both committed by the Commons before their complaint to the Lords, and so they answered as Prisoners: But that in a sort may be called *Judicium Parium suorum*." [That is, judgment of their peers.]

7 For TJ, this short sentence summarized Selden's four-page review of impeachment proceedings in which defendants were usually denied counsel in cases of treason or felony but were allowed counsel otherwise.

1 This entire paragraph, headed by the word in the left-hand margin, corresponds verbatim to TJ's *Manual* (1801), Sec. LIII, par. 11; (1812), p. 178-9, except that the text of the second sentence of the printed versions reads "plead guilty, as to part. . . ."

2 This passage as TJ framed it represents a drastically reduced but wholly correct statement of a much wordier passage in Wooddeson's *Laws of England*, II, 606-7.

3 TJ transcribed these references from footnotes in Wooddeson's *Laws of England*, II, 606-7. For the citation of the "Lords Journ. 13. Nov. 1643," see JHL, VI, 303.

4 See Wooddeson's *Laws of England*, II, 615. Also *State Trials*, II, 735.

1 This sentence, headed by the two marginal words, appears verbatim in TJ's *Manual* (1801), Sec. LIII, par. 12; (1812), p. 179, except that in the printed versions the reference to JHC is more completely stated, and the "&c" is entered there after the head words and again after their second appearance.

2 For this sentence and for all the references except that to Selden's *Judicature*, p. 114, TJ drew upon Wooddeson's *Laws of England*, II, 607. He evidently added the reference to Selden from his own information.

1 Headed by the word in the left-hand margin, this paragraph appears verbatim in TJ's *Manual* (1801), Sec. LIII, par. 13; (1812), p. 179.

2 In large part TJ transcribed this paragraph almost verbatim from Selden's *Judicature*, p. 120. TJ's following reference to Selden, p. 123, seems to have been intended as a reminder to himself that the indicated page dealt with a related procedure, as his next paragraph would show.

1 Headed by the word in the left-hand margin, this entire paragraph appears verbatim in TJ's *Manual* (1801), Sec. LIII, par. 14; (1812), p. 179-80, with the following emendations: 1) the spelling of "empannelled" was changed; 2) word order in two consecutive phrases was reversed; 3) Lord Berkeley "was arraigned for the murder of L. 2.," not "E. 2"; 4) "ex parte regis" was rendered "on the part of the king"; 5) the brackets around the last few sentences were removed; and 6) in the 1812 edition, a sentence was inserted from Hatsell (1796), IV, 73.

2 To put oneself on the trial of his country is to stand trial before a regular jury after renouncing whatever rights one might have to a special trial as a clergyman or peer.

3 That is, "in their own proper place (or court)." In other words, impeachments by the Commons have their own particular place in the world of legal jurisdiction. They may only be handled there, and not before regular juries in other courts of law. Properly, of course, "their own proper place" is Parliament.

4 This phrase means much the same thing as the one just above—impeachments have "their proper home" only within Parliament itself.

5 On April 4, 1327, Lord Berkeley was named joint custodian of Edward II when that king was deposed; and on the next day he courteously received his royal prisoner at Berkeley Castle. But when his fellow custodians, Sir John Mautravers and Sir Thomas Gurnay, demanded that the castle be placed under their command during Edward II's imprisonment there, Lord Berkeley sensed their murderous intention toward the king and withdrew himself to Bradley. True enough, Sir John and Sir Thomas put Edward to death, and their manner of doing so was probably no less savage than that which Christopher Marlowe dramatized in the penultimate scene of *Edward II*. As TJ's paragraph indicated, Lord Berkeley, having been suspected of complicity in Edward II's death, was arraigned on a charge of murder; but he was acquitted by a jury of twelve knights, after he had waived his rights to a trial by his peers. See Cokayne's *Peerage*, II, 129-30.

6 Up to this point, as his own documentation indicates in part, TJ compiled this paragraph from words, phrases, and observations appearing respectively in the following pages and lines of Selden's *Judicature*: p. 123 (lines 1, 24-6);

p. 163 (lines 20-4, 27-30); p. 148 (lines 5-8, 18-22); p. 188 (lines 1-3); p. 124 (lines 14-22); p. 125 (lines 6-16); p. 133 (lines 13-24).

7 In the bracketed passage, TJ cleared up a misconception arising from Selden's statements, p. 133 (lines 11-13), 125 (line 16), "That the Judgment belongeth to the Lords only" and that the Commons were the "*Patria sua*," "the proper home," of the prosecution in judicial proceedings in Parliament. Not at all, said TJ in effect. The Lords participate in every stage of the trials held before them—they order the proceedings, they examine witnesses, they rule on points of law, and at the end of the case, they acquit or condemn the defendant. TJ's paraphrased quotation from Sir Matthew Hale's *Historia Placitorum Coronae*, II, 275, was of course a direct refutation of Selden. But an even more impressive refutation, which TJ did not refer to, was contained in Sir Matthew's footnote reference to the Lords' trial in 1631 of Lord Audley on charges of rape and sodomy. Those who examine the procedure followed then by their Lordships will see that they participated in all aspects of it. For details, see *Cobbett's State Trials*, III, 401-18.

PARAGRAPH [548]

1 Headed by the phrase in the left-hand margin, this entire paragraph appears verbatim in TJ's *Manual* (1801), Sec. LIII, par. 15, except that the latter work did not repeat "Seld. Jud." at the end of the first sentence, and it referred to "*tr. of Straff.*," and "*Com. Journ.*," while, in a later citation of Selden, it made an error by recording "*id. 58, 159,*" (not "158, 159"). See also *Manual* (1812), p. 181-2.

2 As TJ's notes indicate in part, he drew these rules and procedures from two sources: 1) Selden's *Judicature*, p. 124 (lines 20, 22-6); 159 (lines 14-17); 158 (lines 16-18); 162 (lines 4-6); 167 (lines 21-5); and 2) Wooddeson's *Laws of England*, II, 614, 612. TJ's references to "Rushw. tr. Straff." and "Com. Jo. 4. Feb. 1709.10." came to him from Wooddeson, II, 614. The first of these references was to Rushworth's *Tryal of Strafford*, p. 37; the second, to a message from the Lords to the Commons appointing a date for the trial of impeachment proceedings against Henry Sacheverell in 1710. See JHC, XVI, 293. For earlier mention of the case of Henry Sacheverell, see par. [540].

PARAGRAPH [549]

1 Headed by the word in the left-hand margin, this entire paragraph appears verbatim in TJ's *Manual* (1801), Sec. LIII, par. 16, except that, in the latter text, the printer seems inadvertently to have dropped the "t" in "impeachments." But see *Manual* (1812), p. 182-3.

2 That is, "by the law of the land."

3 That is, "according to but never beyond the law."

4 As his own documentation indicates in part, TJ compiled this paragraph from the same two sources that supplied him with the subject matter of par. [548]. The following list shows from which of these sources the successive units of his present paragraph are drawn:

[322]

"Judgments in parliament . . ."   Selden, *Judicature*, p. 168, lines 7-13
"which they cannot alter . . ."   Selden, *Judicature*, p. 169, lines 18-19
"They can neither omit . . ."   Selden, *Judicature*, p. 170, lines 1-3
"Their sentence must be . . ."   Selden, *Judicature*, p. 173, line 15
"This trial, tho' it varies . . .   Wooddeson, *Laws of England*, II, 611-12
"The Chancellor gives . . ."   Selden, *Judicature*, p. 180, lines 19-22
"but now the Steward . . ."   Wooddeson, *Laws of England*, II, 612-13
"In misdemeanors . . ."   Selden, *Judicature*, p. 184, lines 3-5
"The king's assent . . ."   Selden, *Judicature*, p. 136, lines 15-23
"but 2. Woodd. 614. contra"   But Wooddeson, II, 614-15, took opposite view.

It should also be noted that TJ's references to "6. Sta. tr. 14" and "Fost. 144" were taken by him from Wooddeson, II, 611, 613. For the meaning of these short titles, see above, Jefferson's Abbreviations.

PARAGRAPH [550]

1 Headed by the word in the left-hand margin, this paragraph was entered verbatim by TJ as the last unit of the *Manual*. See (1801), Sec. LIII, par. 17; (1812), p. 183. In both printed versions, the citation of titles does not always follow the form used here.

2 TJ compiled this sentence and its documentation from two statements in Wooddeson's *Laws of England*, II, 617-18, the first being in Wooddeson's text, the second in a supporting footnote. For previous references to Raymond's *Reports*, see above, pars. 14, [543].

PARAGRAPH [551]

1 This uncompleted sentence is totally at odds with its immediate surroundings. Begun but not ended by a quotation mark, it may well have been intended by TJ to introduce in its complete form a quotation that would serve as an appropriate leading paragraph to the preceding twelve paragraphs on Impeachment. Thus it would have read, "The Senate shall have the sole power to try all impeachments," and in that form it would not only have been an excerpt from the Constitution of the United States, Art. 1, Sec. 3., but also the opening sentence of the second paragraph of the quotation from the Constitution at the head of TJ's *Manual* (1801), Sec. LIII. In other words, the uncompleted sentence that stands now as par. [551] of the Pocket-Book, may be misplaced in the present edition, solely on the strength of its position in TJ's manuscript; and it may have been intended in its complete form to be par. [539] and thus to serve to introduce the subsequent paragraphs on Impeachment in the Pocket-Book and in Sec. LIII of the *Manual*. At any rate, no other explanation of TJ's sudden entry of this sentence at this point in the Pocket-Book seems to make sense.

2 A partly obliterated reference at this point in TJ's manuscript may be "A13," but its actual identity and intended function are uncertain. Perhaps it designates Article 1, Sec. 3 of the Constitution.

PARAGRAPH [552]

1 As his reference indicates, TJ compiled this sentence from Grey's *Debates*, I, 88, 95, where, in one case, it was reported that a person was sent for "in custody

of the Serjeant at Arms, to answer the breach of privilege," and, in another, that a person was sent for, "but not by the Serjeant, only summoned." As Serjeant Maynard explained in Grey, I, 88-9, a person complained against in Commons and brought in custody of the serjeant to a hearing on his alleged offense was deemed guilty in advance.

PARAGRAPH [553]

1 This sentence, which figures almost verbatim in TJ's *Manual* (1801), Sec. xxxv, par. 3; (1812), p. 110, was drawn from the source indicated here, where it stood as a suggested amendment to a bill from the Lords "for taking away Privilege, and increasing the number of Peers upon tryals." That bill did not prove popular with the Commons, and the suggested amendment may well have been intended to make the bill so unpalatable to the Lords that they would withdraw it. In the *Manual* TJ's quotation from what the Commons said on that occasion was made to illustrate the intention just indicated, and that kind of interpretation, indeed, is not unreasonable, although it is not neatly supported by Grey's somewhat ambiguous record of the whole proceeding. See above, par. [462].

PARAGRAPH [554]

1 This marginal phrase ("Privile qu.") may well indicate that TJ meant to inquire at some later date whether it was proper in a parliamentary sense for either the Lords or the Commons to request a conference after the first reading of a bill. For other examples of his using "qu" in the margin to suggest that sentences in this manuscript needed further investigation, see pars. [475] and [520]. See below, n. 2., for comment upon what might have resulted from TJ's further investigation of the question raised by the sentence given here.

2 As TJ's notes indicated, this sentence came to him from Grey's *Debates*, I, 194-5. At that point a speech by Sir Philip Warwick to Commons in 1669 recalled that "In the Bill concerning the King's Judges, after once reading, the Lords desired a conference for explaining some things." Was it proper for the Lords (or the Commons) to request a conference with the other House after the first reading of any bill before them? TJ's marginal query seems to raise this question, and in his *Manual* (1801), Sec. xLVI, par. 7; (1812), p. 152, he answered it in the following passage: "A conference has been asked after the 1st reading of a bill. 1. *Grey*, 194. This is a singular instance." In other words, TJ found, between the writing of his marginal query in the Pocket-Book and the publishing of his *Manual* that, so far as he could discover, there was only one instance in parliamentary history of a conference being called by one House after it had given only one reading to a bill from the other House.

3 These two sentences, based by TJ upon Grey's *Debates*, I, 365, as his note indicated, figure in that source as part of an argument in the Commons on January 21, 1670/71; on the precise amount to be granted the king in a supply bill. The Commons' rule in an argument of that sort was to begin debating the lowest acceptable amount, and, if that failed to command assent, to propose successively higher amounts, until the House came to a final agreement upon the sum that seemed to them to extend their liberality to its farthest limit. See above, par. [441], n. 7. In a debate upon those sums, a point would be reached when the

amount to be granted seemed to satisfy the majority; and the proper question to be put to the House at that time, argued Mr. Attorney Finch, according to Grey's report, should propose that a higher sum be granted. Such a proposal, Finch said, would be fairer than one which mentioned the sum already established as the apparent consensus. And, of course, if the proposal lost, the apparent consensus could then fairly be actualized by vote. In his *Manual* (1801), Sec. XXXIII, par. 28; (1812), p. 102-3, TJ quoted Finch's words in part as a conclusion to his own discussion of the rule which in the U.S. Senate, made it necessary to begin a debate, say upon the budget, with a consideration of the largest sum, and to continue with lesser and lesser sums, until agreement upon a final amount was reached. TJ preferred the American rule on this subject to the British, but he was obviously interested in making his *Manual* represent both shades of opinion.

PARAGRAPH [555]

1 At the point indicated by TJ, Grey reported Sir Charles Harbord to have declared to the Commons on January 25, 1670/71, that "The Judges have determined that the Lords Journal is but a record *ad hoc propositum*." A later speaker explained that on occasion the Lords ordered parts of their Journal "to be enrolled," and those parts alone were regarded as a record.

PARAGRAPH [556]

1 In compiling this paragraph, TJ transcribed verbatim the first twelve words and supporting documentation from a speech by Mr. Williams in Commons on May 31, 1678; and he supplied the other words as his own supplemental summary of the surrounding debate. See Grey's *Debates*, VI, 44-6.

PARAGRAPH [557]

1 As TJ indicated in part, this sentence states the gist of two passages in Grey's *Debates*, X, 61-2. The first passage involved a resolution of the Commons on April 24, 1690, to the effect that a bill for restoring to the City of London its ancient privileges be committed "to a Committee of the whole House; and that Counsel be heard upon the said Bill, to such Points as the House shall direct." The second passage was from a speech by Sir William Pulteney upon the bill just mentioned, and it declared that "This Bill from *London, &c.* is not a General Bill, but a Private Bill; and to it any person may be heard by his Counsel." In addition to Grey's report upon these matters, see JHC, X, 384-5.

PARAGRAPH [558]

1 As TJ's documentation indicated, this sentence was based upon the following passage in Chandler, I, 300: "Mr. Coleman's Letters were then read; of which three were enter'd in the Journals by Order of the House, viz. one from Mr. Coleman to Father le Chaise, a second to the same, and a third from le Chaise, acknowledging the Receipt of the two former." This passage refers to Edward Coleman, executed December 3, 1678, after having been convicted of treason for his part in the conspiracy to assassinate Charles II and to place James, Duke of York, upon the English throne. The testimony of Titus Oates at Coleman's trial was largely responsible for Coleman's conviction, although the letters referred to above were counted as incriminating evidence against him, addressed

as two of them were to Père La Chaise, Louis XIV's confessor. See J. W. Ebsworth, "Coleman, Edward," in DNB; also JHC, IX, 523-5.

PARAGRAPH [559]

1 This sentence represents TJ's paraphrase of the following passage from Chandler, I, 303: "The 9th [November, 1678], Mr. Secretary Coventry inform'd the House, That his Majesty had been made acquainted that there is an Address depending before the House of Lords to be presented to his Majesty, for the Printing of Mr. Coleman's Letters. That these Letters have not as yet been read in the House of Lords, and that it was his Majesty's Pleasure (if this House has done with the Letters) that the same should be return'd, to the end they may be communicated to the Lords." For this passage in its parliamentary setting, see JHC, IX, 536. TJ's paraphrase of this passage appears verbatim in his *Manual* (1801), Sec. XLVII, par. 12, (1812), p. 156.

PARAGRAPH [560]

1 This sentence stands as TJ's paraphrase of a passage from a speech by Sir Thomas Clarges to the Commons on March 7, 1678/79, in a debate of protest against Charles II's refusal to accept the Commons' fully constitutional choice of Edward Seymour as their next Speaker. For the text of Clarges' speech, see Chandler, I, 331. The constitutiional crisis which Charles II precipitated by his arbitrary action, and by his subsequent recommendation of Sir Thomas Meers to be the next Speaker of the Commons, must have been of special interest to TJ. Chandler indicated on the pages surrounding Clarges' speech that the Commons were greatly affronted by what Charles II said and did on that occasion. They immediately shouted down the king's recommendation of Meers. They fell into a warm debate, during which Sir Thomas Clarges spoke. For the most part, the speeches expressed outrage that Charles II had disdained stating his objections to Seymour and had shown little or no respect for the traditions of Parliament. But next day the Commons modified their anger to the extent of asking the king for more time to consider the whole matter. Whereupon Charles II appointed Tuesday, March 11, for the Commons' reply. On that day, the Commons respectfully reminded the king of their traditional privileges in selecting their Speakers, and they reaffirmed Seymour as their considered present choice. The king responded by ordering the Commons to do what he had requested. In the debate in the Commons on the next day, Wednesday, March 12, the Commons drew up an address to the king, beseeching him to honor their traditions and their choice of Seymour. The king's answer was short. He would give a final answer to the Commons' address next day. And on the next day, he prorogued Parliament until Saturday, March 15. Prorogation meant, of course, that when Parliament came back into session, the act of the Commons in electing Seymour would have been erased from the record. The Commons would have to tackle the problem anew. So it turned out that the king on Saturday, speaking to the joint session of both Houses, reminded them of his opening speech on March 6, and through his deputy, the lord chancellor, requested the Commons to retire to their House and elect a Speaker. Once in their House, the Commons were advised that the king would find William Gregory acceptable as Speaker, and the Commons unanimously elected him, reporting their choice to the king on Monday, March 17. Thus the king won, in the sense that his recommendation of the next Speaker was endorsed by the Commons, as it usually was but did

not have to be. And thus the Commons also won, in the sense that the king did not get Meers as Speaker and had to understand that he could not repudiate the choice of the Commons for that post unless he made a good case against it. As for the contribution of this episode to TJ's parliamentary learning, he used a fragment of Clarges' speech to the Commons, and a summary of Chandler's surrounding explanation, to add detail in his *Manual* (1801), Sec. IX, par. 4, to his discussion of the office of the Speaker. See also (1812), p. 36.

2 This addendum came to TJ from Chandler, I, 334, line 43 (not 335).

PARAGRAPH [561]

1 As TJ specified in part, this sentence was based upon a passage in Chandler, I, 387, lines 30-3. See also JHC, IX, 643, under the date of October 30, 1680. See also JHC, IX, 708. TJ entered into his *Manual* (1801), Sec. XLIX, par. 9, an exact duplicate of this sentence, except that he there mistakenly gave the date as October 30, 1685. The same mistake appeared in the *Manual* (1812), p. 16.

PARAGRAPH [562]

1 This sentence is made up of TJ's summary of a fourteen-line passage in Chandler, I, 76-7. See also JHC, VIII, 536, 541-2, 560, 562, 563. The mentioned reprimand was delivered May 13, 1664, to William Prynne, for his having altered the wording of a bill between the time when the Commons assigned it to a committee and the time when the committee received it. The committee was not a committee of the whole, as TJ specified, but a special committee, of which Prynne was chairman. Confronted later with charges based upon what he had done, Prynne acknowledged his error in having tampered with the bill, and he asked pardon of the House. He then explained his conduct by saying that the Commons in their original discussion of the bill had noted certain defects in its wording, and that he himself had felt obliged to alter it by correcting those defects, before he turned it over to his committee for consideration. He stressed, however, that the committee had been informed of what he had done before they took the bill up. Having heard Prynne's account of his behavior, the Commons called attention to the gravity of his offense, and to the special necessity of adhering to the rule he had violated. But in the end they voted to excuse his improper conduct on that occasion. TJ considered Prynne's infraction important enough to serve as a warning against unauthorized interference with the wording of laws as they passed through the legislative process, and accordingly he entered into the *Manual* (1801), Sec. XVI, par. 2; (1812), p. 51, a verbatim transcript of the passage devoted here to Prynne.

PARAGRAPH [563]

1 As TJ's documentation indicated in part, he compiled these lines from a longer passage in Grey's *Debates*, IX, 523. See also JHC, X, 336-7. As if to call special attention to the orderly procedure which these lines recommend for the disciplining of a member by a legislative body, TJ entered them verbatim in the *Manual* (1801), Sec. XI, par. 4; (1812), p. 39. And indeed they deserve a place there. They grew out of what happened in the Commons on January 20, 1689/90, when Sir Robert Sawyer, a member, was found in a committee investigation conducted by his colleagues to have had a guilty connection six years earlier with the unfair prosecution and execution of Sir Thomas Armstrong on

a charge of high treason before the notorious Judge Jeffries in the Court of King's Bench. Under the rules of the Commons, the committee could not proceed directly to call Sir Robert to account for what he did in 1683. But they were entitled to make a special report upon his conduct in the Armstrong case. When the report was filed in 1689/90, the Commons proceeded to make charges against Sir Robert and to hear him out when he answered them "in his Place." Then, as TJ's sentence did not record, they requested Sir Robert to withdraw from the hearing; and forthwith they voted to expel him from his membership in the House. For additional details about this case, see Jennett Humphreys, "Armstrong, Sir Thomas (1624?-1684)," in DNB.

PARAGRAPH [564]

1 TJ adapted this sentence from the text of a short speech by Sir Thomas Lee as recorded in the following words in Grey's *Debates*, x, 147: "In ordinary course of Parliament, there are two free Conferences at least answered, and both Houses considered by adding and improving their Reasons, and then they come to adhering. This is the usual course, but, by this short way, all opportunity of an expedient is lost." A "free conference," it should be noted, allows a full oral debate between the two parties present, and it proceeds under the rule that neither party is permitted to announce its final stand upon the issue under examination until all arguments have been heard. The announcement of a final stand at an earlier time would constitute a denial of the value of keeping a question open until all considerations that might affect the final result have been stated. Moreover, an announcement of that sort would harden sentiment in the other party, it would make further discussion difficult, it would mean, in Sir Thomas Lee's words, that "all opportunity of an expedient is lost," and finally it would be, as Sir Thomas said, the "short way" of ending an otherwise time-consuming process. Sir Thomas' speech, as quoted above, was made in protest against the Lords' having opened a free conference on a poll tax bill by announcing what their final decision upon the issue was. In an address to the Commons on August 13, 1689, a committee of the Commons reported that that poll tax bill was now lost, "to the great Prejudice of the Crown, by your Lordships Adhering upon the First Free Conference." See JHC, x, 264. For other details concerning the whole episode of which Sir Thomas' speech was a part, see JHC, x, 122, 127, 133-4, 143-4, 153, 155, 160, 161. As for TJ's further use of the one-sentence paragraph given here, he included in the *Manual* (1801), Sec. XLVI, par. 3, a corollary of it from Grey, x, 147, to the effect that "an adherence is never delivered at a free conference, which implies debate;" and in the *Manual* (1812), p. 151, he gave an expanded version of the present one-sentence paragraph, relying on that occasion, however, not upon anything in Grey's *Debates*, but upon a passage from Hatsell (1796); IV, 330; (1818), IV, 356. The latter passage was not available to TJ when the first edition of the *Manual* was published. See below, pars. [583], [588].

PARAGRAPH [565]

1 The authorities cited by TJ in this paragraph accurately confirm his conclusion that joint committees in conferences between the two Houses sometimes voted as a unit and sometimes left no record as to whether they did or did not do so. For a verbatim reproduction of the text and documentation of this paragraph,

see TJ's *Manual* (1801), Sec. XI, par. 6. That Section is entitled "Committees."
See also (1812), p. 39-40.

PARAGRAPH [566]

1 As TJ indicated in part, this sentence was based upon the following note,
which Grey himself (*Debates*, VII, 353) inserted at the end of his report of a session of the Commons devoted on October 25, 1680, to the appointment of committees: "*N.B.* The Committee of Privileges is a standing Committee, and is
never adjourned." By "never" Grey meant "till the dissolution of that parliament." TJ entered the gist of Grey's note into his *Manual* (1801), Sec. XI, par.
1, as follows: "Standing committees as of Privileges and Elections, Uc. are usually appointed at the first meeting, to continue through the session." See also
(1812), p. 38.

PARAGRAPH [567]

1 TJ based the first part of the present paragraph upon the remark of Henry
Powle, Speaker of the Commons, in the course of a debate in that House on
March 20, 1688/89, upon a bill that had come from the Lords and had just been
read a first time. One member was for throwing the bill out, another for adopting
it, and still another for laying it aside. At that point, Mr. John Hampden proposed that it be neither thrown out nor read a second time—that "it lie upon the
Table." "To let the Bill lie upon the Table, and order it no second reading," remarked the Speaker, "I never saw." And then he added, "The proper Question
is, 'Whether you will read it a second time.' " Soon thereafter the debate was adjourned, and it was never resumed, although for the next six months the Lords
kept reminding the Commons that final action on the bill had not been taken.
For full details, see Grey, *Debates*, IX, 172-6; also JHC, X, 43, 53, 54, 117, 239,
258, 259. See TJ's *Manual* (1801), Sec. XXXIII, par. 11; (1812), p. 95.

2 TJ based this final sentence upon a remark by Sir Thomas Lee, on June 19,
1689, in the course of a debate in Commons on the Lord's amendment to the bill
of succession. Sir Thomas said on that occasion, "I think the Bill has lain too
long already, and shamefully too long upon the Table." Grey's *Debates*, IX, 346.

PARAGRAPH [568]

1 In a debate in Commons on November 9, 1680, Sir Edward Dering provided
TJ with a statement of the rule given here. Said Sir Edward on that occasion:
"A Motion relating to Privilege has the preference usually of other things."
Grey's *Debates*, VII, 433. For TJ's later recognition of this rule, see *Manual*
(1801), Sec. XXXIII, par. 3; (1812), p. 92.

PARAGRAPH [569]

1 As TJ's documentation indicated in part, the events mentioned here were set
forth at some length in Grey's *Debates*, IX, 148-53. The committee of the whole
to which TJ made reference was authorized by the Commons on March 11,
1688/89, to consider the king's speech of March 8 on the question of revenue.
The bill that came down from the Lords to interrupt the Commons was designed to annul William Russell's attainder, which had been voted in 1683 and
had been directly responsible for that influential Protestant statesman's death on

the gallows that same month. The importance attached to the Lords' bill of annulment is indicated by the willingness of the Commons to rise from the committee of the whole and to consider the Lords' bill at once by having it referred to a special committee, after being twice read and twice debated. TJ would of course have taken stock of these historical circumstances as he compiled his present paragraph. He may even have confirmed Grey's account by comparing it with the official account in the JHC, x, 45-6, 50-1. Thanks to the speedy action of the Lords and the Commons in rectifying the injustice done to William Russell, the bill to annul his attainder, after being considered by the Commons on March 11, was amended and passed by them on March 16, endorsed by the Lords the same day, and on that same day approved by William III. See also A. A. Ward, "Russell, William, Lord Russell (1639-1683)," in DNB.

PARAGRAPH [570]

1 TJ drew this sentence from Grey's record of John Hampden's short speech in Commons on March 26, 1688/89, during a debate on a proposal to provide a revenue for Princess Anne of Denmark. See Grey's *Debates*, IX, 199. Advising a cautious approach to the proposal, Hampden said, "In Motions of this nature, that are acceptable, we are most subject to errors in the management of it." And he added, "She may be in want of Money, but you cannot refer Money to a private Committee." See also JHC, x, 66. Princess Anne, daughter of James II and Anne Hyde, was later to be Queen Anne of England from 1702 to 1714. Her title in 1688/89 was in recognition of her marriage to Prince George of Denmark in 1683.

PARAGRAPH [571]

1 As TJ indicated in part, he drew this passage from the following editorial note at the head of Grey's text of the speeches made in the Commons on May 15, 1689: "A Bill, from the Lords, for exempting their Majesties Protestant Dissenting Subjects from the penalties of certain Laws, and the Commons Bill for Liberty and Indulgence to Protestant Dissenters, were both read the second time." Grey, *Debates*, IX, 252.

PARAGRAPH [572]

1 This rule was compiled by TJ from a remark made by Henry Powle, Speaker of the Commons, in the course of a debate upon the propriety of accepting a petition of protest against a tax bill at a time when the bill itself had not yet been formally introduced to the House. "I never knew a Petition against a Bill," said the Speaker on that occasion, "before the House was seized of it." Grey's *Debates*, IX, 438. A note in Grey said that the petition came from Jews, and the ensuing debate indicates that the Jews were petitioning to be exempted from certain taxes levied in the proposed bill, and that taxes were sometimes levied against a specific group within the kingdom. Practices of the latter sort were common enough in 1689, to be sure. For example a bill was amended in Commons on December 7 of that year so as to modify a clause requiring Quakers to pay a double tax; and, on the following December 30, a bill for levying a tax of £100,000 upon Jews was given a first reading. See JHC, x, 303, 319. This latter bill was undoubtedly the target of the petition mentioned above.

PARAGRAPH [573]

1 As his own annotations indicated in part, TJ based upon the following sources these notes concerning changes in the Speakership of the Commons: that from Job Charlton to Seymour, Chandler, I, 169 (lines 31-8); that from Seymour to Sawyer, Chandler, I, 276 (lines 45-9); that from Sawyer to Seymour, Chandler, I, 277 (lines 1-5); that from Thorpe to a new Speaker (Thomas Charlton), Grey's *Debates*, III, 11 (lines 3-9). It should be noted that TJ's *Manual* (1801), Sec. IX, pars. 6-7; (1812) p. 37, contains the exact text of the present table of changes from Speaker to Speaker in the Commons, except that "Apr. 29" is omitted from the third item. That omission corrects one of the two errors in the table as given here. Sawyer was elected to replace Seymour on April 11, 1678, (not April 15), and Seymour was elected to replace Sawyer, not on April 29, but on May 6 of the same year. In each case the incumbent reported himself too ill to continue in office. See JHC, IX, 463-4, 476.

PARAGRAPH [574]

1 According to Grey's *Debates*, III, 9-10, upon which TJ here relies, a bill to regulate the construction of buildings in London and Westminster was introduced in Commons on April 20, 1675, and, after being read once and debated, was ordered withdrawn in favor of a new bill on the same subject to be prepared and introduced by a special committee. See also JHC, IX, 319.

PARAGRAPH [575]

1 TJ based this observation upon a comment entered by Grey into his transcript of a debate in Commons on April 26, 1675, in the course of a move to impeach Sir Thomas Osborne, Earl of Danby, the Lord Treasurer. One of the speakers moved that the charges against Danby be postponed for two or three days, but this motion apparently received no second. At that point, Grey inserted an editorial comment, "This went off without a question." A previous speaker had referred to the debate as if it were to be regarded as a conversation. The attempt to impeach Danby ended on May 3, after all articles specified against him had been voted insufficient for their intended purpose. For details, see not only Grey's *Debates*, III, 40-5, but also JHC, IX, 324-9.

PARAGRAPH [576]

1 This sentence appears to be TJ's own observation after his having read in Grey's *Debates*, III, 51, that a witness at the door of Commons, ordered to testify on April 27, 1675, in the proceedings against Lord Danby, was not mentioned anonymously but was announced as "Mr *Mountenoy*, the Patentee." TJ's interest in this particular matter was indicated in his *Manual* (1801), Sec. XIII, par. 2; (1812), p. 45, by the following entry: "Witnesses are not to be produced but where the house has previously instituted an enquiry, 2 *Hats*. 102. nor then are orders for their attendance given blank, 3 Grey. 51."

PARAGRAPH [577]

1 On the pages of the source to which he here referred, TJ found the following statements to justify each of the two parts of this sentence: 1) on April 30, 1675, Sir Edward Seymour, Speaker of the Commons, referred to "the servants of the House, the Serjeant's men"; 2) on May 14 of the same year, Sir Thomas Meres

spoke in Commons as if the Serjeant was of course authorized to "make more deputies"; and 3) on June 4 of that year, Sir Edward Seymour, as Speaker, observed that "The deputies may go with the prisoners to the *Tower*, and the Serjeant stay with him [i.e., the lieutenant of the Tower]; which will prevent the Lords from taking the Serjeant, for the present." For the identity of the prisoners just mentioned, see JHC, IX, 353.

PARAGRAPH [578]

1 TJ drew this paragraph from an editorial footnote in Grey's *Debates*, III, 127. That note explained the meaning of a reference in a debate in the Commons on May 10, 1675, to "Lord *Arundel's* case, in the Lords House." Grey's footnote reads thus: "This was in the year 1626, when the Earl of *Arundel* was committed to the Tower for being too severe in language on Lord *Spencer*, concerning the marriage of his eldest son, *Henry*, Lord *Maltravers*, to the Lady *Elizabeth Stuart*, eldest daughter to the Duke of *Lenox*; which, it was alleged, was done contrary to the King's consent and knowledge, he having designed her for Lord *Lorn*. When the Parliament met, the Lords, being discontented, presented several petitions to the King, to preserve the privilege of Parliament, and, no cause of his commitment being expressed, at length refused to sit, until he was restored to them; which was ordered accordingly, in about three months." Grey indicated that he based his note upon Collins' *Peerage*, I, 139.

PARAGRAPH [579]

1 TJ derived his statement of this rule from the two following observations made by Sir Thomas Lee in a debate in Commons on May 14 and May 15, 1675, when that House was debating whether or not their privileges had been violated by actions taken just before by the Lords: 1) "If you ask for a Conference first, you may come to a free Conference on the Lords Answer; but, if they begin with Conference, we shall never have a free Conference" (Grey's *Debates*, III, 145); 2) "If you ask not the first Conference, you will never have a free Conference" (same, III, 151). For previous reference to the calling of conferences and to the distinction between conferences, see above, pars. [554], nn. 1, 2; [564], n 1.

PARAGRAPH [580]

1 "You cannot judge of the Lords Privileges, nor the Lords of yours," said Sir John Maynard on June 7, 1675, in the course of a debate in Commons on parliamentary privilege. That statement as recorded in Grey's *Debates*, III, 280, gave TJ authority for the present sentence.

PARAGRAPH [581]

1 "It is a rule," said Hatsell, (1818) II, 116, "that in a Committee of the House there can be no previous question." The present paragraph presents exceptions to this rule, and TJ found those exceptions in Grey's record of a meeting of the Commons in a committee of the whole on November 2, 1675. See Grey's *Debates*, III, 372-84. That particular meeting engaged itself in considering an appropriation for building ships for the Royal Navy, and, like all meetings of its kind, it was conducted without adherence to formal parliamentary rules and procedures. Thus there would have been no record of it in the *Journals* of that day,

and TJ's conclusions would have been impossible except for Grey's full and interesting report of who spoke and what was said.

One of the speakers, Sir Thomas Meres, thought that five new ships of eighty guns would be sufficient, in view of the smaller number of ships of that size in the Dutch navy. (Grey, III, 372). Sir Thomas Lee agreed, but he added that Britain really needed "only nimble sorts of ships, to catch them when they run away." (Grey, III, 373). Sir Charles Wheeler said that great ships had proved their value, and he moved "that two of the second rate ships may be built." At this point, Sir Henry Capel asked Samuel Pepys (diarist, naval expert, and member of Commons, 1673-1678, 1679, 1685-1687) for his opinion as to "why eleven of the second rate are requisite to two of the first rates." Pepys answered that the debate suggested the desirability of building forty new ships in the long run, twenty of which should be provided at once; that, in his opinion, the twenty should be of maximum force; and meanwhile fewer than "nine second rates" should not be proposed. Sir William Coventry said that he would be glad to see forty ships built, but that "five second rates" would be enough. (Grey, III, 374). This latter number seemed to gain acceptance. At any rate, Sir Thomas Meres said later that "five is your number proposed to the Question," (Grey, III, 375), although the record in Grey did not mention that a formal question had been proposed. Still later Sir Winston Churchill, assuming five rather than nine second rates to be the number most likely to meet approval, moved "for the previous Question." (Grey, III, 377). This motion, far from being challenged as improper in a committee of the whole, led to a vote which Grey characterized in the following words: "The Question was carried for five ships of the second rate, 182 to 170." (Grey, III, 378). Later that same day, the debate turned to the question of amounts of money to be appropriated for the building of new ships, and another call for the previous question was at length introduced, (Grey, III, 383-4), thus affording TJ with his second instance of the use of that device in the deliberations of a committee of the whole.

Despite these instances, TJ, in publishing his *Manual*, did not alter the usual rule that prohibited a call for the previous question in committee proceedings. In fact, he stated that prohibition without qualifying it in any way. "No Previous question," he declared, "can be put in a committee." See *Manual* (1801), Sec. XII, par. 4; (1812), p. 42-3. Perhaps he concluded after reading Grey that the calls for the previous question in the cases cited were not voted upon as a means of closing debate upon questions not yet proposed, but were merely regarded as ways to hasten the formulation of questions representing the consensus being reached in the debate. Thus calls for the previous question were not out of order, unless formal procedures were being observed. TJ's *Manual* (1801), Sec. xxx, par. 5; (1812), p. 86, repeats the prohibition against such calls in committee of the whole, as if to stress a second time their formal, but not their practical, lack of utility therein.

PARAGRAPH [582]

1 TJ did not document this distinction between Orders and Resolutions. He may have felt that it was so widely accepted in parliamentary circles as to make scholarly authentication unnecessary. In the *Journals of the House of Commons*, for example, all questions passed by affirmative vote were entered either as Orders or as Resolutions, and the difference between them is easily grasped from their content. "By its orders the House directs its committees, its members, its

officers, the order of its own proceedings and the acts of all persons whom they concern; by its resolutions the House declares its own opinions and purposes." May's *Treatise on Parliament*, p. 387. TJ considered the distinction important enough to be recommended to the U.S. Senate, and accordingly he entered it into his *Manual* (1801), Sec. XXI, par. 1; (1812), p. 68, using there the exact wording given here.

PARAGRAPH [583]

1 This and the following five paragraphs appeared in TJ's manuscript with a check mark in the left-hand margin, as indicated. All of the paragraphs were documented as having been derived from Hatsell's fourth volume, which TJ by his own testimony had not yet seen when the *Manual* was published in 1801. See his letter to Joseph Milligan, January 7, 1812 (Editor's Introduction). The Editor's present annotations on these six last paragraphs are obviously designed to show not only their precise origin in Hatsell's fourth volume, which TJ would have used in its 1796 edition, but also their direct contribution to TJ's *Manual* in its second (1812) edition.

2 The rule stated in this paragraph was brought out, not by Hatsell's direct statement of it on the indicated pages, but by his adverse comments upon two conspicuous violations of it, one by the Commons on April 13, 1614, and the other by the Lords on April 4, 1679. In each case, one of the houses amended a bill from the other house and asked for a conference upon the amendment, without waiting to see whether the other house felt a conference necessary or wanted to ask for one. See Hatsell (1796), IV, 4, 223; (1818), IV, 4, 242. For TJ's previous references to procedures governing conferences between the two houses, see above, pars. [513], [515], [520], [530]. For his later emphasis upon the rule stated here, see *Manual* (1801), Sec. XLVI, par. 1, and also *Manual* (1812), p. 147-8. In fact, in the latter work, TJ documented this rule by citing "4 *Hats.* 4, 223," as he did in the present paragraph, but not in the *Manual*'s first edition.

PARAGRAPH [584]

1 TJ formulated this paragraph from two passages in Hatsell (1796), IV, 31, 33; (1818), IV, 35, 37. The first passage stated the rule here given; and the second dealt with its enforcement in a specific case.

As adopted in Commons, the rule in Hatsell's version reads as follows:

On the 7th of February, 1580, upon motion made by Mr. Norton, it is ordered, "That such persons as shall be appointed by this House at any time to have Conference with the Lords, shall and may use any reasons or persuasions they shall think good in their discretions, so as it tend to the maintenance of any thing done or passed this House, before such Conference had, but not otherwise: But that any such person shall not in any wise yield or assent, at any such Conference, to any new thing there propounded, until this House be first made privy thereof, and give such order."

As for the second passage, which concerned the enforcing of the rule just given, it pointed to Sir Samuel Bernardiston, who, at a free conference between Lords and Commons on March 5, 1696/97, argued against a bill under consideration, even though his own house, the Commons, had originated it, and he was their appointed spokesman at the moment. For that breach of propriety, he was publicly reprimanded on March 20, and his punishent would certainly have extended further, had it not been for his great age, his infirmities, and his exemplary record in former times. For the sources of Hatsell's account of this episode, see JHC, XI, 695, 716, 720, 729, 749.

This rule did not appear in the *Manual* (1801), Sec. XLVI, par. 2, at the point where it would be expected. But it did appear in the *Manual* (1812), p. 149, as a sentence added by TJ to the text of his previous edition, its language being an almost verbatim transcription of the present paragraph in the Pocket-Book. See *Manual*, Sec. XLVI.

PARAGRAPH [585]

1 TJ based this paragraph upon an account by Hatsell of a simple conference requested by the Commons in order that they might deliver to the Lords an announcement of their vote upon the question of giving friendly assistance to the Scots. The date of the conference was February 4, 1640/41. After the Commons had announced their vote, the Lords requested that the Earl of Bristol be allowed to speak, despite the rule that made such a proposal improper in such a conference. The Commons turned the Lords down, as the rule stipulated. See Hatsell (1796), IV, 32; (1818), IV, 36. For TJ's later oblique reference to this rule, see the *Manual* (1801), Sec. XLVI, par. 2; (1812), p. 148.

PARAGRAPH [586]

1 Two passages in Hatsell, according to TJ's notes, provided him with authority for the rule given here. The first passage records that, on April 20, 1671, the Lords asked for a free conference on a bill which already had been the subject of one conference. The Commons agreed, but with the stipulation that the Lords should be notified of their error in asking for a free conference before two simple conferences had been held. Whereupon the Lords admitted their mistake. The second passage reads as follows: "A Free Conference is usually demanded after two Conferences have been holden without effect." See Hatsell (1796), IV, 37, 40; (1818), IV, 41, 54. An abbreviated statement of this rule appeared in the *Manual* (1812), p. 148, but reference to it was omitted in the first edition. Thus it must again be counted as one of the additions made to the *Manual* after 1801 from TJ's reading of Hatsell's fourth volume. See above, pars. [583], [584].

PARAGRAPH [587]

1 TJ based this paragraph upon Hatsell, as he indicated, and Hatsell based it upon the following direct quotation from Arthur Onslow. "During the time of a Conference, the House can do no business till the Conference is over; and the practice is, as soon as the names of all the Managers are called over, and they are gone to the Conference, for the Speaker to leave the Chair, without any question, and he resumes the Chair again, on the return of the Managers from the Conference. . . . It is the same whilst the Managers of an impeachment are at the House of Lords. . . ." Hatsell (1796), IV, 47, 209, 288; (1818), IV, 52 n., 225 n., 311 n. Onslow's words, as quoted by Hatsell, and as here edited and abridged in minor particulars by TJ, appear in TJ's exact present version in the *Manual* (1812), p. 152. And that passage represents one of the large additions made by TJ to the latter work in the years that followed the publication of its first edition.

1 This paragraph is TJ's somewhat abridged but otherwise largely verbatim transcript of a passage in Hatsell (1796), IV, 330; (1818), IV, 356. Hatsell based his text upon a report presented to the Commons on August 13, 1689, as a statement of some of their procedures in conducting conferences. The report, intended ultimately to reply to a message from the Lords, reads in part as follows: "The Commons find cause to be dissatisfied with the message; Because your Lordships have proceeded to adhere upon the first Free Conference: Which they look upon to be irregular; . . . it being well known to your Lordships, That it is usual to have two Free Conferences, or more, before either House proceeds to adhere . . . because, before that time, each House is not fully possessed of the reasons, upon which the other does proceed; nor have the Houses had the full opportunity of making replies to one another's arguments: And, to adhere sooner, is to exclude all possibility of offering expedients." TJ's shortened and yet quite accurate version of the words just quoted make up a full paragraph of the *Manual* (1812), p. 151. There indeed it stands as another of the most considerable additions which TJ made after 1801 to that volume. See above, par. [564], n., for a sketch of the circumstances surrounding this reply of the Commons to the Lords in 1689. See also JHC, X, 122, 127, 133-4, 143-4, 153, 155, 160, 161, 264.

A MANUAL OF
PARLIAMENTARY
PRACTICE

EDITOR'S INTRODUCTION

The Manuscript Problem

The manuscript used by Samuel Harrison Smith in printing the first edition of the *Manual* cannot now be located, although it may exist in some forgotten repository of documents belonging to his descendants. That particular manuscript, characterized by Smith's wife as having been written in TJ's "own neat, plain, but elegant hand writing," was delivered to the Smith home by TJ himself in early December 1800; and, according to Mrs. Smith's somewhat reverent later testimony, "It is still preserved by Mr. Smith and valued as a precious relique."[1] I would have welcomed the opportunity to examine this important document and to compare it with the first edition, so as to be sure that the new text is as close as it can be to TJ's original intentions. But that opportunity has not yet become available to modern scholarship.

We do know, however, that Smith's printed version of the *Manual* contains a few imperfections. Only the first of these would seem beyond question to have originated in Smith's failure to conform to TJ's final manuscript. The second is demonstrably the result of TJ's wish to add to Smith's text an item that came from his later recollection of something relevant to a point under discussion. And the third appears to have been caused by a lapse either in the printer's office when the final manuscript was being set into type, or in TJ's procedures when he was readying the final manuscript for the printer.[2] A list of these imperfections would possibly be increased if we could compare Smith's version with the copy text that he used, but as things stand at present, the printed edition cannot be faulted beyond the three blemishes just mentioned.

The first imperfection was pointed out by TJ himself. In his personal copy of the first edition of the *Manual*, TJ noticed that the last three lines of Section XXII did not conform in style to his original intention; and in the margin to their right he wrote, "these words should have been in Italics."[3] This correction, trifling as it may seem, corrects a practice that did not conform to similar passages in the printed text. No doubt at TJ's direct suggestion, Milligan's text printed these three lines in italics, as of course we do.[4]

The second imperfection in Smith's text consists in his omission of a sentence that TJ, perhaps only for the moment, regarded as important. That sentence appeared in TJ's handwriting as a footnote to the final sentence of the third paragraph of Section LII in his own copy of the *Manual*. The footnote, reads "The treaty of the Pardo between Spain & G. B. in 1739. being disapproved by parliament, was not ratified. In consequence whereof the war it was intended to prevent took place. Observns. of France on Memorial of England. pa. 107."[5] This

---

[1] See above, p. 24-5.

[2] See below, Editor's Notes, Sec. XLIX.

[3] TJ's copy of the first edition is now owned by Dr. Alfred J. Liebman, who kindly supplied Julian Boyd with a photocopy for use in the present edition.

[4] See below, *Manual*, Sec. XXII, and note.

[5] TJ's reference at the end of that note is to Gérard de Rayneval's *Observations on the Justificative Memorial of the Court of London* (Paris and Philadelphia, 1781). Sowerby, No. 3140 (III, 271), notes that the translation of this work is by Peter Stephen du Ponceau.

sentence may have occurred to TJ after he submitted his manuscript of the *Manual* to Smith, and thus its omission from the first edition could hardly be the publisher's fault. Milligan's second edition did not include it in the place where it should have been, however, and thus TJ may have changed his mind about the necessity of its being included in the work that carried his last additions. But we do not unequivocally know what his final intentions were, and the existence of the sentence in his own handwriting, coupled with the possibility of its having been overlooked in 1812, argues that it should now be given its place in the present edition.

The third imperfection in Smith's text, whether through the fault of publisher or author, is an omission from Section XLIX of Senate Rule 25. That rule contains the provision that executive meetings of the Senate must be recorded, not in the Senate's regular Journal, but in a separate record book. Milligan's edition also omitted this rule, and there is a strong possibility that TJ's final manuscript had inadvertently left it out. Thus it might be argued that TJ did not intend to include it in his final text. But there can be no doubt that the surrounding context of the *Manual* requires the presence of Rule 25, and that, in his Pocket-Book and in one of his early manuscripts of the *Manual*, TJ placed Rule 25 between Rule 24 and Rule 26.[6] Accordingly, it has now been restored to its rightful position.

These imperfections do not seriously undermine the assumption that the first edition is a reasonably accurate presentation of the final manuscript delivered by TJ to Smith's home in December 1800. There are at least three circumstances that strongly argue for that assumption. In the first place, when Joseph Milligan sought on January 3, 1812, to get TJ's permission to allow a second edition of the *Manual* to be published, TJ consented and supplied Milligan with a printed copy of additions to be inserted at designated places into Smith's original text.[7] Those additions were not presented as corrections to the 1801 edition, but as *new* passages, which TJ had come to know through his reading of the fourth volume of Hatsell's *Precedents of Proceedings*. In other words, Smith's text was a satisfactory transcription of what TJ had originally wanted the *Manual* to say. Secondly, when Smith printed the first edition, he and TJ were political and personal friends, and TJ, Vice President and favored to become the third President of the United States, was respected on all sides as author of the nation's hallowed political creed—incentives for his publisher to take extra care in transmitting his author's ideas to posterity. And thirdly, there was the uniqueness of the *Manual* itself—not only the first American guidebook to the practices of the U.S. Senate by the constitutionally appointed authority but also proof of the orderly proceedings of a democratic nation still viewed with condescension, skepticism, and even contempt by the aristocracies of the Old World. Six weeks after the *Manual* appeared in print, a review of it came out in Smith's newspaper, written no doubt by Smith himself, and that review, the first of its kind, expressed high regard for TJ's work and made a challenging assertion of its su-

---

Sowerby also suggests (II, 83; II, 372-3) that this work should not be confused with a work of similar title by Caron de Beaumarchais. In support of Sowerby's view, Beaumarchais's work fails to mention anywhere in it the treaty of the Pardo between Spain and Great Britain in 1739. Thus TJ could not have had Beaumarchais's work in mind.

[6] See below, *Manual*, Sec. XLIX, and note.

[7] See above, p. 32. TJ's additions included some that were not in Hatsell's fourth volume—for example, that involving the more extensive wording of Senate Rule 13. See below, note to Sec. XXII.

periority to tedious and incomprehensible foreign books in its field.[8] These sentiments, it must be admitted, would hardly be stressed by a publisher who thought himself careless and unprofessional in performing his important part in launching the *Manual* upon its historic mission.

Having established Smith's first edition of the *Manual* as the best available reproduction of TJ's final manuscript, we now must ask ourselves how that final manuscript came into existence. As we know, TJ's original plan was to deposit with the Senate at the end of his Vice Presidency a handwritten document that would show what his own standards had been as presiding officer and what guidelines should be followed in the future parliamentary conduct of the Senate and House.[9] We also know, from his own announcement of the plan, that he was at work on it before February 28, 1800, and that he meant to complete it the following summer. Thus, in all probability, he first formed the plan as early as 1797, when he began to preside over the Senate, and he worked upon it, as opportunity allowed, during the entire term of his Vice Presidency. The precise chronology of composition cannot be verified, of course, but TJ's efforts may be reconstructed with reasonable assurance from a second look at the manuscript of the Pocket-Book, and from an examination of his other handwritten parliamentary documents.

Quite possibly, TJ initially might have felt that his completed Pocket-Book might serve the Senate for its future guidance. TJ had found the Pocket-Book indispensable to his work as presiding officer—in fact, in that connection, he called the Pocket-Book his "pillar."[10] If it had been indispensable to him, the Senate might find it useful in the future. At any rate, there is distinct evidence that TJ may have toyed with this possibility.

In 1851, Henry Randall and Thomas Jefferson Randolph discovered a document at Edgehill, "a leather bound duodecimo," that Randall identified as the "Parliamentary Pocket Book."[11] The binding of the document suggests that TJ intended to make it useful as a guidebook to the Senate. The manuscript of the Pocket-Book also has a separate title page, as if for easy identification and use. No other handwritten document among TJ's parliamentary papers is identified like this, and thus the Pocket-Book seems to have been intended for something more than private use.

Still another piece of evidence is a fragment of two pages in one of TJ's parliamentary manuscripts. As we have noted, TJ numbered the opening paragraphs of the Pocket-Book from 1 to 145; and, in TJ's hand, the two-page fragment contains a list of thirty-four topics, each followed by numbers ranging between 1 and 94. The numbers seem to refer to paragraph numbers in the Pocket-Book, as if to direct a user to the place in the Pocket-Book where the indicated topic would be discussed.[12] In other words, the two-page fragment could well be an index to the first 94 numbered paragraphs of the Pocket-Book. That index, when completed, could be a way to make the Pocket-Book more useful as a parliamentary guidebook for the Senate.

The hypothetical guidebook, if it was ever visualized by TJ, came to naught,

---

[8] See above, p. 27.

[9] See ibid., p. 18-19.

[10] See ibid., p. 3.

[11] See above, p. 41.

[12] The two-page fragment in TJ's handwriting is now owned by Mr. Roger W. Barrett, who generously supplied Julian Boyd with a photocopy of it.

however; and indeed the difficulties involved in adapting the Pocket-Book for such a use would have been formidable. To begin with, an index that would have made the Pocket-Book a ready guide to the solution of problems in parliamentary procedure would have been almost impossible to construct and to use— shortcomings that TJ's experience with his "pillar" had doubtless made obvious to him. Moreover, the Pocket-Book in its original state, compiled over many years from TJ's wide reading in parliamentary law, was heavily weighted toward the doings and constitutional problems of the British House of Commons, with only an occasional glance at American practices, whereas the *Manual* would have that emphasis reversed. Reasons like these could well have led TJ to dismiss his Pocket-Book as a possible basis for a Senate manual.

He sought instead to compose an original document that would serve the purpose efficiently. Under the persuasions of George Wythe[13] and his own sense of practicality, he decided that the completed manuscript would best be printed. TJ worked upon that document in the summer of 1800, as he promised he would.[14] Its preliminary drafts are now fortunately available in large part to students of TJ's parliamentary writings. These provide clues to TJ's procedures in arriving at the final text that Smith put into type.

One draft, a nineteen-page document, devotes its entire first page to the following heading: "Parliamentary ⟨*Manual*⟩ rough notes, preserved, lest the fair digest should be lost."[15] The second word in the heading is obliterated, except for one or two scattered marks, and the word supplied in angle brackets is purely conjectural. In our judgment, the title of the document as a whole should be Rough Notes, more or less by the elimination of other possibilities, whereas Fair Digest should designate another document, still unidentified, which may in all likelihood be the final manuscript delivered by TJ to Smith.

On close inspection, the Rough Notes turn out to be made up of two separate documents, related only in that both deal with parliamentary procedure under the topics that were to be more systematically organized in the *Manual*. The longest of these two documents consists of thirteen pages, the first page of which, as we indicated above, is devoted solely to the half-obliterated heading. Ten of the remaining thirteen pages are closely written, each containing forty-five lines on the average, with each line 7 ½ centimeters in length. Six pages lead directly into the next following pages, but five do not, perhaps because the pages that followed them were dispersed before the present manuscript was made available for purchase. One page (p. 12) contains only four written lines.

[13] See above, p. 21, 32.

[14] See ibid., p. 19.

[15] The pages of our photocopy are numbered 1-19, and we cite the document by those numbers. The original manuscript is in the Library of Congress among the Thomas Jefferson Papers, vol. 233, p. 41793-41805. For other information, see *Index*, p. 76, col. 1, item 1. In addition to this nineteen-page document, the Library of Congress separately holds a two-page manuscript catalogued as "Notes on parliamentary procedures in the U.S. Senate in various matters, including the Alien Bill," and this fragment seems undoubtedly to have once belonged with what we are calling Rough Notes. What could have happened was that, when Henry Randall possessed the manuscripts of TJ's parliamentary writings, he detached this fragment and gave it to someone who later sold it. See below, *Manual*, Sec. xxxvi, par. 3, for a note on TJ's later use of this fragment. It may be inspected in the Library of Congress among the Thomas Jefferson Papers, vol. 82, p. 14221. For more information, see *Index*, p. 76, col. 1, item 61. For comments about Randall's dispersal of TJ's parliamentary manuscripts, see below, nn. 25-30.

One of the subjects treated on fourth page of these thirteen pages deserves special mention. It concerns the deliberations of the Senate in acting upon President Adams's appointment of his son John Quincy to be a commissioner with full power to negotiate a treaty of amity and commerce with the king of Sweden. We need not elaborate here upon what the Senate did on that occasion, the episode having been already covered.[16] But its inclusion here shows that, even though it was destined to be omitted from the *Manual*, it was still of interest to TJ at this point in the preparation of that work. His final decision to delete it from the published *Manual* was doubtless dictated by political considerations.

The thirteenth page of the first document in Rough Notes seems incorrectly to have been numbered 14. It is an important page in that it shows a tentative table of contents for the future *Manual*. The page contains a list of thirty-eight headings, several of which resemble the section titles of the *Manual*. Each of these headings is preceded by an Arabic numeral, and some headings are followed by one or more numerals of the same kind.[17] Twenty-three of the headings are followed by one or more Roman numerals, the highest of which is XXIX. Each one of these Roman numerals designates a Senate rule, and they were all to appear in the *Manual* in Arabic notation. For example, the heading labeled "admission within the house" is followed by XXIX, which in the *Manual* translates into Rule 29; the heading labeled "doors closed" is followed by XXVIII, which refers to Rule 28 in the *Manual*; the heading labeled "Exve" is followed by XXV, and in the present edition of the *Manual* that heading is explained by Rule 25;[18] the heading labeled "Journals" is followed by four Roman numerals—I, XXIV, XXVI, XXVII—and these respectively call attention to Rule 1, Rule 24, Rule 26, and Rule 27; the headings labeled "order in debate" and "right to speak" are designated II and III for the first, and IV and V for the second, these pairs of Roman numerals being respectively represented in the *Manual* as Rules 2 and 3, Rules 4 and 5. It is plain from these citations that the misnumbered page 14 of the longest of the two documents making up "Rough Notes" represents TJ in the act of visualizing the organization of the *Manual* in terms of major topics and the involvement of many of those topics with the relevant rule or rules of the Senate.

As for the other six pages, one is a seemingly complete page, one is half a page long, and four are made up of only a few written lines, as if they were separate notes intended for later expansion. The paragraphs on these six pages are written in lines measuring 13 centimeters in length, and thus these pages do not seem to belong to the same era of editorial activity as the earlier pages of the Rough Notes do. Moreover, the four pages of separate notes suggest that TJ, in compiling what was to be the *Manual*, jotted down paragraphs on separate sheets as they attracted his attention, and those sheets were later mingled indiscriminately, perhaps by dealers, with more complete sheets so as to create an assembled manuscript full of gaps, repetitions, and irregularities for future scholars to cope with.[19]

---

[16] See above, p. 13-14.

[17] I have not worked out the precise meaning attached by TJ to these Arabic numerals, but they seem to be intended as a bridge between an indicated topic and a manuscript page or numbered item where that topic would be discussed.

[18] See below, Sec. XLIX, and note.

[19] These four pages resemble in their complete discontinuty the five pages attached to CSMH 5986. See below.

The only competitor to Rough Notes among TJ's significant early drafts of what became his *Manual* is a manuscript of fifty-three pages in The Huntington Library, catalogued as CSmH 5986. Its first page is headed "A Manual of the Rules of proceeding in the Senate of the U.S." A second heading at the top of page 20 reads: "Rules of practice in the Senate of the U.S." Although there is no heading on page 42, a paragraph begins there with "Sec. 1" as a label in the margin, and what may be taken as the ensuing third part of the document goes on from there to end with page 48. The next five pages (49-53) are miscellaneous, two being devoted to treatment of bills in committee, one to conferences between the Houses of Parliament, and the last two to tables of topics. In sum, the entire manuscript is made up of four separate documents, one of which belongs to the first heading (pages 1-19), one to the second heading (pages 20-41), one to an unacknowledged third heading (pages 42-48), and the last one (pages 49-53) to disconnected items bearing upon parliamentary procedures and topics of parliamentary law.[20]

The page numbers affixed here to indicate the points of separation between each of these four documents are of course borrowed from the photocopy of the Huntington manuscript, and those numbers were devised by the cataloguers at the Huntington to make reference to the manuscript an easy matter. But it must be remembered that the numbers suggest a continuity that does not in fact exist from first to last among the pages of each of the four documents. Gaps in content, as indicated when the top lines of one page do not cohere with the bottom lines of its predecessor, occur frequently within each document, and each gap indicates that pages are missing, perhaps one page on some occasions, perhaps several on others. In the first document, for example, there are eight distinct gaps; and in each of the other documents, other gaps, the precise number being difficult to discover. But even if the gaps were accurately counted, it would be impossible to estimate the number of missing pages that each gap may originally have contained.

According to an officer of The Huntington Library, CSmH 5986 was purchased by Henry E. Huntington on December 6, 1921, at a sale conducted in

[20] The catalogue entry for CSmH 5986 reads: "Apparently two fragmentary drafts of Jefferson's 'Manual of Parliamentary Practise [sic]. . . .' Several disconnected leaves are included, and many strips have been pasted on." But it seems more likely that CSmH 5986 consists of four fragmentary documents, the last of which is made up of completely rather than partially disconnected leaves. That the first three of these documents are originally from separate preliminary drafts of the *Manual* is strongly suggested by the presence in this particular manuscript of three separate entries on pages 32, 37, and 38 concerning President Adams's appointment of his son John Quincy to be a trade commissioner to the king of Sweden. These entries are so much alike in wording and content as to raise the question whether they would all be likely to appear close together in the same document. The same question is raised not only by two separate entries on pp. 37 and 38 concerning the executive function of the Senate in approving or disapproving appointments by the President, but also by yet two more entries on pp. 39 and 40 concerning the ruling that a question interrupted by a motion to adjourn is removed from consideration and can be reinstated only by being introduced again. It is at least a plausible supposition that these various duplicate wordings of the same passages belonged originally to separate preliminary drafts of the *Manual* and were later dispersed, only to be carelessly reassembled by the dealer who subsequently sold them to Henry E. Huntington. For other details concerning TJ's discussion of the John Quincy Adams case, see above, p. 13-15.

New York by the American Art Association.[21] The catalogue of that sale listed this document as one of "a notable collection of rare manuscripts, books, and broadsides from a private collection, sold by order of Ashley T. Cole, Attorney, New York City." The catalogue also indicated that this document consisted of "ORIGINAL MANUSCRIPT NOTES ENTIRELY IN THE HANDWRITING OF JEFFERSON, 48, [sic] pp. 12 mo, closely written in his minute handwriting, with caption 'A MANUAL OF THE RULES OF PROCEEDING IN THE SENATE OF THE U. S.'" And it added: "THIS UNIQUE AND IMPORTANT MANUSCRIPT contains Jefferson's original draft of his celebrated 'Manual.'"

On page 48 of CSmH 5986 is found a table of contents for the emerging *Manual*. The middle column of this table lists the section titles that the *Manual* was to have, and in the left-hand column opposite the sequence of titles were Roman numerals running from I to LIV. This ordering of sections is plainly to be understood as TJ's outline for the final draft of the *Manual*.

Roman numerals that range from I to LV are distributed along the left-hand or the right-hand margins of thirty-eight of the first forty-eight pages of CSmH 5986. These numerals, in TJ's handwriting, correspond to the sections and titles of the table of contents just described.

Having thus established his main sections, their titles, and their order TJ would have been in a position to prepare his final manuscript. But he must soon have realized that certain corrections in his outline would have to be made. For one thing, he saw that he must cancel Section LIV from his table of contents, since it had originally been designed to deal with executive business, and what he wanted to say on that subject could be covered in Section XLIX.[22] For another thing, he saw that he must ignore Roman numeral LV as it appeared in the margins of pages 37, 38, and 43, inasmuch as it referred in those places to paragraphs either dealing with executive business (Sec. XLIX), or with treaties (Sec. LII). And for yet another thing, he discovered that some of his Roman numerals, as distributed in the margins of his manuscript drafts, were incorrect in identifying sections to which paragraphs belonged—on page 23, a paragraph should have been assigned to Sec. XLIV, not XLV, another to Sec. XLV, not to XLVI, and another to Sec. XLVI, not XLVII. But in the main TJ's directives in CSmH 5986 were dependable, and in all likelihood he followed them during the summer of 1800 in transcribing his final manuscript for delivery to Samuel Harrison Smith that December. In other words, that final manuscript may be judged to have been largely, but not completely, constructed from CSmH 5986, and if a reconstruction of the final manuscript were ever possible, it would turn out to be very close to the *Manual* of 1801.

The history of CSmH 5986 before it was sold to Henry S. Huntington cannot be traced in full detail, nor can all of its missing pages be confidently located in any modern collection of Jefferson manuscripts. But we do know with certainty that CSmH 5986 was in the hands of Henry Randall between 1851 and 1858, when he was writing the first comprehensive and still very useful biography of

---

[21] The editor gratefully acknowledges the generous assistance of Martha Briggs, Assistant Curator, American History, The Huntington Library, in researching the data in this paragraph. Ms. Briggs provided the detils concerning Henry Huntington's acquisition of this manuscript. Most helpfully of all, she sent me a photocopy of the catalogue in which the American Art Association offered this manuscript for sale.

[22] See below, note to Sec. XLIX.

Thomas Jefferson. In that biography, Randall described what he called "The first draft of the Parliamentary Manual," and there can be no doubt that he was speaking of CSmH 5986.[23] He said that his draft was "filled with interlineations and erasures, with 'riders' attached, and amended passages pasted over the original—stitched and folded so as to be carried within the more comprehensive Pocket Book"; and these words exactly describe the manuscript that we have just analyzed. He printed a facsimile page of it, and a glance at that page establishes its resemblance to the general run of pages in the Huntington manuscript. But what beyond question identifies Randall's "first draft" with CSmH 5986 is that the latter contains exactly the same table of contents which Randall described as being in the draft before him. Randall said of his document that "it corresponds very closely with the familiar published copy, except that it contains one more section (with a pen run through it, however), and the present order of arrangement is not observed except in the index." Randall's "index" is of course page 48 of CSmH 5986. What we call the table of contents contains fifty-four items designated by Roman numerals, and the last item is crossed out by a single line. Each Roman numeral and each title in Randall's "index" are identical with the elements of our table of contents, and the preceding pages of our manuscript could be described as Randall describes the draft he was looking at.

Of what happened to Randall's manuscript after 1858, we know only a few details, but they are interesting in themselves and also illustrate some of the difficulties confronting historical editors. As I said in the Introduction to the Parliamentary Pocket-Book, Randall and Thomas Jefferson Randolph came upon a large accumulation of TJ's "old books in manuscript" at Edgehill in 1851, among them not only the Parliamentary Pocket-Book and a draft of the Parliamentary *Manual*, but also other items, including in all probability the manuscript that TJ called Rough Notes. Randolph, TJ's legatee, turned over the manuscript of the Pocket-Book to his sister Ellen, who later gave it to her son Thomas Jefferson Coolidge, on its way to the archives of the Massachusetts Historical Society.[24] From a letter which Randall sent to James Parton on June 1, 1868, we know that Randolph gave Randall the other parliamentary manuscripts, with the stipulation that he keep some of them.[25] Randall fell into the habit of sending leaves from these manuscripts to friends interested in having samples of TJ's handwriting. For example, the letter just now mentioned indicated that Randall was sending to Parton some "characteristic" leaves of his remaining store of TJ's manuscripts, including "one from his draft of his Parliamentary law." For another example, Randall's letter of January 19, 1874, to Master Charlie Andrews reads in part: "My autographs of Mr Jefferson, as you would suppose, have been pretty well reduced, and there are none both *written* and *signed*, now within my reach. I enclose you a very curious and characteristic autograph, it being two leaves from Mr Jefferson's original draft of his parliamentary rules."[26]

Beyond question, therefore, Randall freely distributed pages of TJ's parliamentary manuscripts to those seeking specimens of TJ's handwriting, and by 1874 his store of such materials was severely reduced, perhaps even to the point

[23] Randall, *Life*, II, 356-7; also I, 16.   [24] See above, p. 41-2.
[25] For the text of this letter, see Flower, p. 236-9. Its final paragraph reads: "I must again express my regret that I cannot send you a fine autograph letter of Mr. Jefferson on some interesting topic—but I am stripped down to those his family expected me to keep."
[26] H. S. Randall to Charlie Andrew, 19 Jan. 1874 (Ralph G. Newman, Chicago: 1974).

where there remained in his possession only those pages which seemed to him to satisfy the restriction placed by the Jefferson family upon his disposal of TJ's papers. Perhaps he gave that residue to his children when he died in 1876, and perhaps it contained not only the attenuated remainder of Rough Notes but also a considerable number of leaves left over from what he had called the "first draft" of TJ's *Manual*. From that point on, what happened to those particular manuscripts is obscure, but it is clearly evident that what remained of the Rough Notes is now in The Library of Congress, and Randall's "first draft" is the nucleus of CSmH 5986. As for the leaves now obviously missing from those documents, we are for the most part at a loss. But the present whereabouts of some of them can be established, and one fragment proves on its face that it was at one time in the hands of Henry Randall.

Four handwritten pages of the "Manual of Parliamentary Practice" from the collection of David Gage Joyce were offered for sale at the Hanzel Galleries in Chicago on September 23-24, 1973, and they were purchased by Ralph G. Newman for Barron U. Kidd of Texas. Thanks to the kindness and courtesy of Mr. Kidd and Mr. Newman, these pages were made available in photostat to the Jefferson Papers office in Princeton. There can be little doubt that these pages once belonged to Randall's "first draft of the Parliamentary Manual." Like that draft, these pages contain cancellations of lines, interlineations, and marginal additions to certain paragraphs; titles identifying the subjects being treated to their right or left; and Roman numerals in the margins indicating to which section the adjacent paragraphs will belong in the *Manual*. We are at present unable to specify how these pages found their way from Randall to David Gray Joyce. But Randall's habit of distributing leaves of TJ's parliamentary writings hither and yon make it likely that he gave away to some interested friend the pages later purchased for Mr. Kidd.

The leaf that Randall printed in facsimile in his *Jefferson*[27] is now in The Library of Congress. It was acquired at an auction held on January 29, 1976, at Charles Hamilton Galleries in New York.[28] Through what intermediaries it got to that auction, we do not know. But we do know that it was found at Edgehill by Randall and Thomas Jefferson Randolph in 1851. Thus we may say that the Randall household has to assume responsibility in this case, too, for having failed to foresee the problems that future scholars would find in attempting to use dismembered manuscripts to measure the full extent of TJ's accomplishments as a scholar in parliamentary law.

One final example will lend additional support to the hypothesis that the key figure in the distribution of TJ's parliamentary manuscripts from a storage room in Edgehill to their present diverse locations was Henry Randall. This case concerns a fragment, not of the *Manual*, but of the Parliamentary Pocket-Book—a small but important fragment. It may have been compiled by TJ when he was thinking of the Pocket-Book as a possible parliamentary guide for the Senate's future use after his term as Vice President had ended; this fragment is now owned by Mr. Roger W. Barrett.[29] What follows is Mr. Barrett's account of the way in which this fragment came into his possession, provided by Mr. Barrett's personal letter of April 1, 1947, to Julian Boyd.

[27] See that work, II, insert at p. 256-7.
[28] The leaf immediately following the one represented in facsimile was acquired by The Library of Congress at the same auction.
[29] See above, p. 341, and n. 12.

a) Found, with other papers, by Col. Thomas J. Randolph in an old receptacle after Jefferson's death.
b) Given by Col. Thomas J. Randolph to Henry S. Randall, author of the Life of Jefferson.
c) Sold by Randall's Executor to Charles De F. Burns, a dealer in New York.
d) Sold by Burns to Charles F. Gunther in 1885.
e) Sold by Gunther to Oliver R. Barrett.
f) Given by Oliver R. Barrett to Roger W. Barrett about 16 years ago.[30]

The manuscripts now available to scholars have been helpful in establishing that TJ evolved his final but unavailable manuscript from a series of early drafts, best represented not only by what he called "Rough Notes" and by the various documents and miscellaneous leaves making up CSmH 5986, but also by fragments that once belonged to one or the other of those two sources. Even without the assistance of TJ's final manuscript, there seems to be a good case for believing that the printed text of the first edition of the *Manual* accurately represents, with insignificant exceptions, what TJ wanted that work to say. Perhaps it would not be out of order to stress by way of concluding this section that the compiling of the *Manual* from first to last involved TJ in several exacting tasks: that of wide reading in the source works available to him; that of accurate transcription of passages from those sources; that of revising the order of passages from one manuscript draft to another from an almost complete lack of coherent sequence in his notes to final consecutiveness in the *Manual*; that of making several versions of some passages, only to decide finally to omit them; that of making use of passages derived from his own experience as presiding officer of the Senate; and that of being attentive constantly to clarity and unaffectedness of style. His obvious success in performing these tasks with skill and grace gives me the opportunity to affirm with confidence that, among his many other distinctions, TJ must also be considered the foremost American scholar of his time in the field of parliamentary law.

The Basis of the Printed
Text of 1812

Joseph Milligan, a Georgetown publisher, must be credited with producing in 1812 the only genuine second edition of the *Manual*. TJ was fully aware of that enterprise from its very beginning and collaborated in it to the extent of providing Milligan with material not included in Samuel Harrison Smith's text of 1801.[31] Thus Milligan's text represents not only what TJ had originally intended the *Manual* to contain, but also what his later readings and reflections upon parliamentary law had induced him to add. Milligan's text is the basis for the present edition. The only changes made pertain to correcting its few typographical errors and to supplying the sole passage that both Smith and Milligan had omitted.

So far as we have been able to discover from a line-for-line, word-for-word comparison of Milligan's text with that of Smith, and from a careful examination of the passages that TJ wanted to add to what Smith had printed, there are in Milligan's text only six typographical errors, some of which are mistaken read-

[30] Quoted here with the kind permission of Mr. Roger W. Barrett.
[31] For details, see p. 32, 34.

ings of Smith's text, and some, inadvertent duplications of Smith's original errors. These are corrected in the notes to the sections concerned.[32]

Milligan's text has been followed in regard to printing style, where no issue is at stake beyond one printer's preference for a certain way of doing things. Thus this edition has preserved Milligan's manner of capitalizing certain words, of spelling out numbers, and of not abbreviating official titles of public documents, or the United States or public institutions, or months of the year.

Smith's text, except for three imperfections, is as accurate a version of TJ's original intentions for the *Manual* as we can at present hope to have.[33] But Smith's printing establishment allowed four typographical errors to appear in the first edition, and they should be mentioned in passing. At one point Smith did not notice that his text incorrectly read "almightly God"; at another he allowed "smalt" to stand for "small"; at still another, he printed "pro hac vice" for "pro hoc voce"; and at still another he allowed "pu" to represent "put."[34] Milligan's text silently corrects these errors, and indeed they deserve attention only to place the account of Milligan's own carelessness against a balancing account of his care in rectifying the mistakes of his predecessor whenever he became conscious of the need to do so.

Milligan's text omits a passage that TJ plainly intended the *Manual* to have.[35] Smith also omitted it, and there is a possibility that TJ's final manuscript did not include it, either. But it belongs to Section XLIX, and it is now printed there.

We have already recorded that, when Milligan asked TJ's permission to print the *Manual* in a second edition, TJ not only gave his consent but also supplied a printed document containing additions to be made in the new text.[36] For the most part these additions came from TJ's having read and reflected upon Hatsell's fourth volume, which had not been available to him in 1800; but they also came in part from his wish that the *Manual* of 1812 update obsolete or incomplete statements in the edition of 1801.[37] These additions, which in the aggregate amounted to seventy-four lines of type, or three new pages, are identified by notes affixed to the sections wherein they appear.[38]

TJ's *Manual* has been printed many times since it came out as a book,[39] and all of its printings that I have been able to examine seem ultimately to have been reproductions of its first edition. Perhaps, in the interest of completeness, future printings should depend upon Milligan rather than Smith.

TJ's Sources

So far as references to the sources of the *Manual* are concerned, Milligan's text differs in two ways from Smith's. In the first place, Milligan failed to register in

[32] See notes to Secs. III, XIII, XXXVI, LIII.

[33] See above, p. 339-40.

[34] For these four errors, see *Manual*, 1801, Sec. XVI, par. 3; Sec. XXVI, par. 12; Sec. XXXIII, par. 5; Sec. XXXIV, par. 3.

[35] See above, p. 340; also *Manual*, Sec. XLIX, and note.

[36] See above, TJ's Parliamentary Studies, p. 32.

[37] For examples of updated passages, see Secs. V and XXII. In the first section is a new list of Representatives; in the second, the new addition to Senate Rule 13.

[38] For these additions, see below, notes to Secs. I, XIII, XXII, XXVI, XXXV, XLVI, XLIX, LII, LIII.

[39] See p. 434-44.

full one of Smith's references to Grey's *Debates*, and thus he made a minor mistake; but the true mistake was that the reference itself is unjustifiable.[40] Secondly, Milligan's text contains all of TJ's citations of Hatsell's fourth volume added by TJ after Smith's edition was published.

In recording TJ's references to his sources, both Milligan and Smith used names of authors, or abbreviation of names, or short titles of works, or abbreviation of titles, even as TJ himself had done throughout his Pocket-Book and the preliminary drafts and the final draft of his *Manual*. A list of those abbreviations, alphabetically arranged, with identification of the works for which they stand, will be found in the front matter. For the most part, these constitute the sources from which the printed *Manual* emerged.

In addition to them, however, there are five other sources to be recorded here, if we would have a complete inventory of the works that lie behind the *Manual*. Although unacknowledged, one of them was the Pocket-Book, many of whose paragraphs bequeathed to the *Manual* their doctrine and wording.[41] Another source was the *Journal of the Senate*, and still another, a pamphlet entitled *Rules for Conducting Business in the Senate*.[42] From these TJ assembled the twenty-nine numbered rules that are distributed throughout the *Manual* in their proper context, except that one of them, the twenty-fifth, was inadvertently omitted by TJ or the publisher somewhere in the process of preparing the final manuscript or of getting it printed in 1801 and 1812.[43] The wording of the first nineteen rules suggests that TJ transcribed them from the *Journal*, and he probably drew the others from the pamphlet.[44] Still another source, this one fully acknowledged, was the Constitution of the United States. In the first nine sections of Article 1, that document laid down the guidelines which were to direct the parliamentary conduct of the legislative branch of the government, and TJ made frequent and effective use of them, even going so far as to have the printers call them to the readers' attention by visual means. "The rules and practices peculiar to the *Senate*," declares a note at the end of the Preface in Smith's and Milligan's texts of the *Manual*, "are printed in *Italic*. Those of Parliament are in the Roman letter."[45]

The same visual means were used to get readers to recognize that, in addition to the Constitution, the *Manual* had another important American source, this one acknowledged only indirectly—the procedural happenings during the conduct of legislative business in the Senate and to some extent in the House of Representatives. Thus it is that, wherever an italicized text does not identify itself as a Senate rule or as a direct offshoot of the Constitution, the passages concerned are TJ's own summary or digest of Senate happenings or practices.

[40] For details concerning this whole matter, see note to Sec. III.

[41] For details, see the notes to the following paragraphs of the Pocket-Book: [426], [441]-[442], [493]-[497], [539]-[550], [553]-[554], [559]-[562], [563], [565]-[568], [576], [581]-[588].

[42] The latter was published in 1797, probably in Philadelphia.

[43] See above, p. 340, 349 n. 35.

[44] See above, Parliamentary Pocket-Book, note to par. [442].

[45] Smith's edition has "Italics," Milligan's, "Italic." In compliance with the dictum here enunciated, Milligan's text italicizes all of the numbered Senate rules, except for the first sentences of Rule 13 and Rule 16. There seems to be no reason why Rule 13 should be treated as an exception to the dictum, and thus we here print it in italics. But a special consideration causes us to leave in Roman the first sentence of Rule 16. See notes to Secs. XVII and XXII.

One particular case will serve to illustrate the way TJ drew on his own observations as presiding officer of the Senate. In early 1800, Senate Federalists attempted to pass a bill giving a newly created committee of thirteen the power not only to validate each vote cast that autumn in the electoral college but also to decide by their own count who the next President of the United States would be. A distinguished historian of those events calls the Federalist bill "a bold attempt to alter by law rather than by amendment the constitutional system of counting the presidential electoral vote."[46] In view of what had happened in the vote of the electoral college in 1796, TJ would have had reason to see that the Federalist bill was designed to prevent his own party from gaining the Presidency in 1800. Republican opposition naturally mounted.

William Duane, editor of a Republican paper, the *Aurora*, published on February 19, 1800, a spirited attack upon the means used to bring the Federalist bill to the floor of the Senate; and at the same time Duane printed a copy of the bill, although it was still in its second reading and hence not yet ready in regular course for public comment. The Federalist senators successfully moved to require Duane to appear before their chamber to present what justification he could for his attack. But when, after some intermediate maneuvering, he finally did not show up on March 26, the day stipulated for his appearance, he was voted next day to be in contempt of the Senate and was ordered to be taken into custody by the sergeant-at-arms.[47] Duane evaded arrest, and the charge that he had defamed the Senate was never decided.[48]

Section III of the *Manual* contains TJ's report upon the debate over "the legality" of the order to have Duane taken into custody. That debate began on February 26, 1800, one week after the *Aurora* published its attack, and the question as to what to do about Duane occupied the Senate from then until the end of that session on May 14. In all probability TJ wrote his report during the summer of 1800, when he was putting into shape the final manuscript of the *Manual*. As it appeared in Smith's first edition, and later in Milligan's second, the report contains the arguments used in the debate upon Duane's alleged defamation of the Senate, there being some ten in favor of Duane's arrest, and some sixteen against. TJ's partisan sympathies would of course have lain with the opposition, but his report did not reveal this. It did reflect the high quality of the arguments on each side—arguments stressing historical, philosophical, and legal considerations.

TJ's report takes a place in the *Manual* as a record of senatorial deliberation at its best. He succeeded at times in making his treatise on parliamentary practice something more than a handbook of useful directions. To TJ's mind, a code of conduct for the Senate should not limit itself to the pots and pans of politics. Moreover, the report is one of many examples of TJ's use of his own observations as an important supplement to the parliamentary doctrines that he drew from years of reading standard British authorities.[49]

[46] Smith, *Freedom's Fetters*, p. 288-9.

[47] JS, III, 59-61.

[48] Smith, *Freedom's Fetters*, p. 300-6.

[49] For other conspicuous examples of TJ's anchoring of senatorial procedures to passages in the *Manual*, see Sec. XVIII (par. 9), Sec. XXV (par. 2) Sec. XXVI (pars. 12 and 14), Sec. XXVIII (par. 2), Sec. XXX (pars. 3-8), Sec. XXXI (par. 2), Sec. XXXII (par. 5), Sec. XXXIII (pars. 14-33), Sec. XXXV (par. 10), Sec. XXXVI (pars. 3-5), Sec. XL (pars. 2 and 5), Sec. XLI (pars. 5, 6, 9, and 15-17), Sec. XLIII (pars. 2 and 3), Sec. XLVII (pars. 2 and 8), Sec. LI (pars. 3 and 5), and Sec. LII (pars. 1-2, 4-11).

A MANUAL
OF
PARLIAMENTARY PRACTICE:
for the
Use of the Senate
of the
United States.

BY THOMAS JEFFERSON.

SECOND EDITION.

WITH THE LAST ADDITIONS OF THE AUTHOR

GEORGE TOWN:
PUBLISHED BY JOSEPH MILLIGAN; AND BY
WILLIAM COOPER, WASHINGTON.
1812.

TABLE OF CONTENTS.

Preface

THE Constitution of the United States establishing a legislature for the Union, under certain forms, authorises each branch of it "to determine the rules of its own proceedings." The Senate have accordingly formed some rules for its own government: but these going only to few cases, they have referred to the decision of their President, without debate and without appeal, all questions of order arising either under their own rules, or where they have provided none. This places under the discretion of the President a very extensive field of decision, and one which, irregularly exercised, would have a powerful effect on the proceedings and determinations of the House. The President must feel weightily and seriously this confidence in his discretion; and the necessity of recurring, for its government, to some known system of rules, that he may neither leave himself free to indulge caprice or passion, nor open to the imputation of them. But to what system of rules is he to recur, as supplementary to those of the Senate? To this there can be but one answer; to the system of regulations adopted for the government of some one of the Parliamentary bodies within these states, or of that which has served as a prototype to most of them. This last is the model which we have all studied, while we are little acquainted with the modifications of it in our several states. It is deposited too in publications possessed by many and open to all. Its rules are probably as wisely constructed for governing the debates of a deliberative body, and obtaining its true sense, as any which can become known to us; and the acquiescence of the Senate, hitherto, under the references to them, has given them the sanction of their approbation.

Considering therefore the law of proceedings in the Senate as composed of the precepts of the Constitution, the regulations of the Senate, and, where these are silent, of the rules of Parliament, I have here endeavored to collect and digest so much of these as is called for in ordinary practice, collating the Parliamentary with the Senatorial rules, both where they agree and where they vary. I have done this, as well to have them at hand for my own government, as to deposit with the Senate the standard by which I judge and am willing to be judged. I could not doubt the necessity of quoting the sources of my information; among which Mr. Hatsell's most valuable book is preeminent; but as he has only treated some general heads, I have been obliged to recur to other authorities in support of a number of common rules of practice to which his plan did not descend. Sometimes each authority cited supports the whole passage. Sometimes it rests on all taken together. Sometimes the authority goes only to a part of the text, the residue being inferred from known rules and principles. For some of the most familiar forms, no written authority is, or can be quoted; no writer having supposed it necessary to repeat what all were presumed to know. The statement of these must rest on their notoriety.

I am aware that authorities can often be produced in opposition to the rules which I lay down as Parliamentary. An attention to dates will generally remove their weight. The proceedings of Parliament in antient times, and for a long while, were crude, multiform and embarrassing. They have been, however, constantly advancing towards uniformity and accuracy; and have now attained a degree of aptitude to their object, beyond which, little is to be desired or expected.

Yet I am far from the presumption of believing that I may not have mistaken the Parliamentary practice in some cases; and especially in those minor forms, which, being practised daily, are supposed known to every body, and therefore have not been committed to writing. Our resources, in this quarter of the globe, for obtaining information on that part of the subject, are not perfect. But I have begun a sketch, which those who come after me will successively correct and fill up, till a code of rules shall be formed for the use of the Senate, the effects of which may be, accuracy in business, economy of time, order, uniformity, and impartiality.

NOTE. The rules and practices peculiar to the *Senate* are printed in *Italic*.

Those of Parliament are in the Roman letter.

IMPORTANCE OF RULES.

THE IMPORTANCE OF ADHERING
TO RULES.

MR. ONSLOW, the ablest among the Speakers of the House of Commons, used to say, 'it was a maxim he had often heard, when he was a young man, from old and experienced members, that nothing tended more to throw power into the hands of administration and those who acted with the majority of the House of Commons, than a neglect of, or departure from, the rules of proceeding: that these forms, as instituted by our ancestors, operated as a check and controul on the actions of the majority, and that they were in many instances, a shelter and protection to the minority, against the attempts of power.' So far the maxim is certainly true, and is founded in good sense, that as it is always in the power of the majority, by their numbers, to stop any improper measures proposed on the part of their opponents, the only weapons by which the minority can defend themselves against similar attempts from those in power, are the forms and rules of proceeding which have been adopted as they were found necessary from time to time, and are become the law of the House; by a strict adherence to which, the weaker party can only be protected from those irregularities and abuses which these forms were intended to check, and which the wantonness of power is but too often apt to suggest to large and successful majorities. 2 *Hats*. 171, 172.

And whether these forms be in all cases the most rational or not, is really not of so great importance. It is much more material that there should be a rule to go by, than what that rule is; that there may be an uniformity of proceeding in business, not subject to the caprice of the Speaker, or captiousness of the members. It is very material that order, decency and regularity, be preserved in a dignified public body. 2 *Hats*. 149.

And in 1698 the Lords say, "the reasonableness of what is desired is never considered by us, for we are bound to consider nothing but what is usual. Matters of form are essential to government, and 'tis of consequence to be in the right. All the reason for forms is custom, and the law of forms is practice; and reason is quite out of doors. Some particular customs may not be grounded on reason, and no good account can be given of them; and yet many nations are zealous for them; and Englishmen are as zealous as any others to pursue their old forms and methods." 4 *Hats*. 258.

SEC. II.
LEGISLATURE.

ALL Legislative powers herein granted, shall be vested in a Congress of the United States, which shall consist of a Senate and House of Representatives. Constitution of the United States, Art. 1, Sec. 1.

The Senators and Representatives shall receive a compensation for their services, to be ascertained by law, and paid out of the Treasury of the United States. Constitution of the United States, Art. 1. Sec. 6.

For the powers of Congress, see the following Articles and Sections of the Constitution of the United States. I. 4. 7. 8. 9. II. 1. 2. III. 3. IV. 1. 3. 5. and all the amendments.

SEC. III.
PRIVILEGE.

THE privileges of the members of Parliament, from small and obscure beginnings, have been advancing for centuries, with a firm and never yielding pace. Claims seem to have been brought forward from time to time, and repeated, till some example of their admission enabled them to build law on that example. We can only therefore state the point of progression at which they now are. It is now acknowledged, 1. That they are at all times exempted from question elsewhere for any thing said in their own house; that during the time of privilege, 2. Neither a member himself,* his wife, or his servants, (familiares sui) for any matter of their own, may be arrested,† on mesne process, in any civil suit: 3. Nor be detained under execution, though levied before time of privilege: 4. Nor impleaded, cited, or subpœnaed in any court: 5. Nor summoned as a witness or juror: 6. Nor may their lands or goods be distrained: 7. Nor their persons assaulted, or characters traduced. And the period of time covered by privilege, before and after the session, with the practice of short prorogations under the connivance of the crown, amounts in fact to a perpetual protection against the course of justice. In one instance, indeed, it has been relaxed by the 10. G. 3. c. 50, which permits judiciary proceedings to go on against them. That these privileges must be continually progressive, seems to result from their rejecting all definition of them; the doctrine being that "their dignity and independence are preserved by keeping their privileges indefinite;" and that "the maxims upon which they proceed, together with the method of proceed-

---

* Ord. of the H. of Com. 1663. July 16.
† Elsynge 217.1. Hats. 2 1.

ing, rest entirely in their own breast, and are not defined and ascertained by any particular stated laws." 1. *Blackst.* 163. 164.

It was probably from this view of the encroaching character of privilege, that the framers of our constitution, in their care to provide that the laws shall bind equally on all, and especially that those who make them shall not exempt themselves from their operation, have only privileged "Senators and Representatives" *themselves from the single act of* "arrest in all cases, except treason, felony and breach of the peace, during their attendance at the session of their respective Houses, and in going to and returning from the same, and from being questioned in any other place for any speech or debate in either House."* Const. U.S. Art. 1. Sec. 6. *Under the general authority* "to make all laws necessary and proper for carrying into execution the powers given them," Const. U.S. Art. 2. Sec. 8., *they may provide by law the details which may be necessary for giving full effect to the enjoyment of this privilege. No such law being as yet made, it seems to stand at present on the following ground: 1. The act of arrest is void ab initio.* 2. The member arrested may be discharged on motion.* 1. Bl. 166. 2. Stra. 990, *or by Habeas Corpus under the federal or state authority, as the case may be; or by a writ of privilege out of the Chancery,* 2 Stra. 989, *in those states which have adopted that part of the laws of England.* Orders of the H. of Commons. 1550. February 20. 3. *The arrest, being unlawful, is a trespass, for which the officer and others concerned are liable to action or indictment in the ordinary courts of justice, as in other cases of unauthorised arrest. 4. The court before which the process is returnable, is bound to act as in other cases of unauthorised proceeding, and liable also, as in other similar cases, to have their proceedings staid or corrected by the superior courts.*

The time necessary for going to and returning from Congress, not being defined, it will of course be judged of in every particular case by those who will have to decide the case.

While privilege was understood in England to extend, as it does here, only to exemption from arrest eundo, morando, et redeundo, the House of Commons themselves decided that "a convenient time was to be understood." (1580.) 1. *Hats.* 99, 100. Nor is the law so strict in point of time as to require the party to set out immediately on his return, but allows him time to settle his private affairs and to prepare for his journey; and does not even scan his road very nicely, nor forfeit his protection for a little deviation from that which is most direct; some necessity, perhaps, constraining him to it. 2. *Stra.* 986, 987.

---

* 2. Stra. 989.

This privilege from arrest, privileges of course against all process, the disobedience to which is punishable by an attachment of the person; as a subpœna ad respondendum, or testificandum, or a summons on a jury: and with reason; because a member has superior duties to perform in another place.

When a representative is withdrawn from his seat by summons, the 30,000 people whom he represents lose their voice in debate, and vote as they do on his voluntary absence: when a senator is withdrawn by summons, his state loses half its voice in debate and vote, as it does on his voluntary absence. The enormous disparity of evil admits no comparison.

So far, there will probably be no difference of opinion as to the privileges of the two Houses of Congress: but in the following cases it is otherwise. In December 1795, the H. of R. committed two persons of the name of Randall and Whitney, for attempting to corrupt the integrity of certain members, which they considered as a contempt and breach of the privileges of the House: and the facts being proved, Whitney was detained in confinement a fortnight, and Randall three weeks, and was reprimanded by the Speaker. In March 1796, the H. of R. voted a challenge given to a member of their House to be a breach of the privileges of the House; but satisfactory apologies and acknowledgments being made, no further proceeding was had. The editor of the Aurora having, in his paper of February 19, 1800, inserted some paragraphs defamatory of the Senate, and failed in his appearance, he was ordered to be committed. In debating the legality of this order, it was insisted, in support of it, that every man, by the law of nature, and every body of men, possesses the right of self defence; that all public functionaries are essentially invested with the powers of self-preservation; that they have an inherent right to do all acts necessary to keep themselves in a condition to discharge the trusts confided to them; that whenever authorities are given, the means of carrying them into execution are given by necessary implication; that thus we see the British Parliament exercise the right of punishing contempts; all the state legislatures exercise the same power; and every court does the same; that if we have it not, we sit at the mercy of every intruder, who may enter our doors or gallery, and, by noise, and tumult, render proceeding in business impracticable; that if our tranquillity is to be perpetually disturbed by newspaper defamation, it will not be possible to exercise our functions with the requisite coolness and deliberation; and that we must therefore have a power to punish these disturbers of our peace and proceedings. To this it was answered, that the Parliament and courts of England have cognisance of contempts by the express provisions of their law; that the state legislatures have equal authority, be-

cause their powers are plenary; they represent their constituents completely, and possess all their powers, except such as their constitutions have expressly denied them; that the courts of the several states have the same powers by the laws of their states, and those of the federal government by the same state laws, adopted in each state by a law of Congress; that none of these bodies therefore derive those powers from natural or necessary right, but from express law; that Congress have no such natural or necessary power, nor any powers but such as are given them by the constitution; that that has given them directly exemption from personal arrest, exemption from question elsewhere for what is said in their House, and power over their own members and proceedings; for these, no further law is necessary, the constitution being the law; that moreover, by that article of the constitution which authorises them "to make all laws necessary and proper for carrying into execution the powers vested by the constitution in them," they may provide by law for an undisturbed exercise of their functions, e.g. for the punishment of contempts, of affrays or tumult in their presence, &c. but, till the law be made, it does not exist; and does not exist, from their own neglect; that in the mean time, however, they are not unprotected, the ordinary magistrates and courts of law being open and competent to punish all unjustifiable disturbances or defamations, and even their own serjeant, who may appoint deputies ad libitum to aid him, 3 Grey. 59. 147. 255., is equal to small disturbances; that in requiring a previous law, the constitution had regard to the inviolability of the citizen as well as of the member; as, should one House, in the regular form of a bill, aim at too broad privileges, it may be checked by the other, and both by the President; and also, as, the law being promulgated, the citizen will know how to avoid offence. But if one branch may assume its own privileges without controul, if it may do it on the spur of the occasion, conceal the law in its own breast, and, after the fact committed, make its sentence both the law and the judgment on that fact; if the offence is to be kept undefined, and to be declared only ex re nata, and according to the passions of the moment, and there be no limitation either in the manner or measure of the punishment, the condition of the citizen will be perilous indeed. Which of these doctrines is to prevail, time will decide. Where there is no fixed law, the judgment on any particular case is the law of that single case only, and dies with it. When a new and even a similar case arises, the judgment which is to make, and at the same time apply the law, is open to question and consideration, as are all new laws. Perhaps, Congress, in the mean time, in their care for the safety of the citizen, as well as that for their own protection, may declare by law what is necessary and proper to enable them to carry into execution the powers vested in them, *and thereby hang up a rule for the inspection of all, which may direct the conduct of the citizen, and at the same time test the judgments they shall themselves pronounce in their own case.*

Privilege from arrest takes place by force of the election; and before a return be made, a member elected may be named of a committee, and is to every intent a member, except that he cannot vote until he is sworn. *Memor.* 107, 108. *Dewes* 642. *col.* 2, 643. *col.* 1. *Pet. Miscel. Parl.* 119. *Lex. Parl. c.* 23, 2. *Hats.* 22, 62.

Every man must, at his peril, take notice who are members of either House returned of record. *Lex. Parl.* 23, 4. *inst.* 24.

On complaint of a breach of privilege, the party may either be summoned, or sent for in custody of the serjeant. 1. *Grey,* 88, 95.

The privilege of a member is the privilege of the House. If the member waive it without leave, it is a ground for punishing him, but cannot in effect waive the privilege of the House. 3. *Grey* 140, 222.

For any speech or debate in either House, they shall not be questioned in any other place. *Const. U. S. I. 6. S. P. Protest of the Commons to James I.* 1621. 2. *Rapin, No.* 54. *pa.* 211, 212. But this is restrained to things done in the House in a Parliamentary course. 1. *Rush.* 663. For he is not to have privilege contra morem parliamentarium; to exceed the bounds and limits of his place and duty. *Com. P.*

If an offence be committed by a member in the House, of which the House has cognisance, it is an infringement of their right for any person or court to take notice of it, till the House has punished the offender, or referred him to a due course. Lex. Parl. 63.

Privilege is in the power of the House, and is a restraint to the proceeding of inferior courts; but not of the House itself. 2. *Nalson* 450. 2. *Grey,* 399. For whatever is spoken in the House is subject to the censure of the House; and offences of this kind have been severely punished, by calling the person to the bar to make submission, committing him to the tower, expelling the House, &c. *Scob.* 72. *L. Parl. c.* 22.

It is a breach of order for the Speaker to refuse to put a question which is in order. 2. *Hats.* 175. 6. 5. *Grey* 133.

And even in cases of treason, felony, and breach of the peace, to which privilege does not extend as to substance, yet in Parliament, a member is privileged as to the mode of proceeding. The case is first to be laid before the House, that it may judge of the fact and of the grounds of the accusation, and how far forth the manner of the trial may concern their privilege. Otherwise, it would be in the power of other branches of the government, and even of every private man, under pretences of treason, &c. to take any man from his service in the House, and so as many, one after another, as would make the House what he pleaseth. *Decl. of the Com. on the king's declaring Sir John Hotham a traitor. 4. Rushw.* 586. So when a member stood indicted of felony, it was adjudged that he ought to remain of the House till conviction. For it may be any man's case, who is guiltless, to be accused and indicted of felony, or the like crime. 23. *El.* 1580. *D'Ewes.* 283. *col.* 1. *Lex. Parl.* 133.

When it is found necessary for the public service to put a member under arrest, or when, on any public enquiry, matter comes out which may lead to affect the person of a member, it is the practice immediately to acquaint the House, that they may know the reasons for such a proceeding, and take such steps as they think proper. 2. *Hats.* 259. Of which see many examples. *Ib.* 256. 257. 258. But the communication is subsequent to the arrest. 1. *Blackst.* 167.

It is highly expedient, says Hatsell, for the due preservation of the privileges of the separate branches of the legislature, that neither should encroach on the other, or interfere in any matter depending before them, so as to preclude, or even influence that freedom of debate, which is essential to a free council. They are therefore not to take notice of any bills or other matters depending, or of votes that have been given, or of speeches which have been held, by the members of either of the other branches of the legislature, until the same have been communicated to them in the usual parliamentary manner. 2. *Hats.* 252. 4. *Inst.* 15. *Seld. Jud.* 53. Thus the king's taking notice of the bill for suppressing soldiers, depending before the House, his proposing a provisional clause for a bill before it was presented to him by the two Houses; his expressing displeasure against some persons for matters moved in Parliament during the debate and preparation of a bill, were breaches of privilege. 2. *Nalson,* 743. and in 1783, December 17, it was declared a breach of fundamental privileges, &c. to report any opinion or pretended opinion of the king on any bill or proceeding depending in either House of Parliament, with a view to influence the votes of the members. 2. *Hats.* 251, 6.

SEC. IV.
ELECTIONS.

THE times, places, and manner of holding elections for Senators and Representatives, shall be prescribed in each state by the legislature thereof; but the Congress may, at any time, by law, make or alter such regulations, except as to the places of chusing Senators. Constitution I. 4.

Each House shall be the judge of the elections, returns, and qualifications of its own members. Constitution I. 5.

SEC. V.

QUALIFICATIONS.

THE Senate of the United States shall be composed of two Senators from each state, chosen by the legislature thereof, for six years, and each Senator shall have one vote.

Immediately after they shall be assembled in consequence of the first election, they shall be divided as equally as may be into three classes. The seats of the Senators of the 1st class shall be vacated at the end of the 2d year; of the 2d class at the expiration of the 4th year; and of the 3d class at the expiration of the 6th year; so that one third may be chosen every second year; and if vacancies happen by resignation or otherwise, during the recess of the legislature of any state, the executive thereof may make temporary appointments, until the next meeting of the legislature, which shall then fill such vacancies.

No person shall be a Senator, who shall not have attained to the age of thirty years, and been nine years a citizen of the United States, and who shall not, when elected, be an inhabitant of that state for which he shall be chosen. Constitution I. 3.

The House of Representatives shall be composed of members chosen every second year by the people of the several states; and the electors in each state shall have the qualifications requisite for electors of the most numerous branch of the state legislature.

No person shall be a Representative who shall not have attained to the age of twenty-five years, and been seven years a citizen of the United States, and who shall not, when elected, be an inhabitant of that state in which he shall be chosen.

Representatives and direct taxes shall be apportioned among the several states which may be included within this Union, according to their respective numbers, which shall be determined by adding to the whole number of free persons, including those bound to service for a term of years, and including Indians not taxed, three fifths of all other persons. The actual enumeration shall be made within three years after the first meeting of the Congress of the United States, and within every subsequent term of ten years, in such manner as they shall be law direct. The number of Representatives shall not exceed one for every thirty thou-

sand, but each state shall have at least one Representative. Constitution of the United States I. 2.

The provisional apportionments of Representatives made in the constitution in 1787, and afterwards by Congress, were as follows:

	1787	1793	1801	1813
New Hampshire,	3	4	5	6
Massachusetts,	8	14	17	20
Rhode Island,	1	2	2	2
Connecticut,	5	7	7	7
Vermont,		2	6	6
New-York,	6	10	17	27
Jersey,	4	5	6	6
Pennsylvania,	8	13	18	23
Delaware,	1	1	1	2
Maryland,	6	8	9	9
Virginia,	10	19	22	23
Kentucky,		2	3	10
Tennessee,			1	6
N. Carolina,	5	10	12	13
S. Carolina,	5	6	8	9
Georgia,	3	2	4	6
Ohio,				6

When vacancies happen in the representation from any state, the executive authority thereof shall issue writs of election to fill such vacancies. Constitution I. 2.

No Senator or Representative shall, during the time for which he was elected, be appointed to any civil office under the authority of the United States which shall have been created, or the emoluments whereof shall have been increased, during such time; and no person holding any office under the United States, shall be a member of either House during his continuance in office. Constitution I. 6.

SEC. VI.
QUORUM.

A MAJORITY of each House shall constitute a quorum to do business: but a smaller number may adjourn from day to day, and may be authorised to compel the attendance of absent members, in such manner, and under such penalties as each House may provide. Constitution I. 5.

In general, the chair is not to be taken till a quorum for business is present; unless, after due waiting, such a quorum be despaired of; when the chair may be taken and the House adjourned. And whenever, during business, it is observed that a quorum is not present, any member may call for the House to be counted, and being found deficient, business is suspended. 2. *Hats.* 125. 126.

The President having taken the chair, and a quorum being present, the journal of the preceding day shall be read, to the end that any mistake may be corrected that shall have been made in the entries. Rules of Senate 1.

SEC. VII.
CALL OF THE HOUSE.

ON a call of the House, each person rises up as he is called, and answereth. The absentees are then only noted, but no excuse to be made till the House be fully called over. Then the absentees are called a second time, and if still absent, excuses are to be heard. *Ord. H. Com.* 92.

They rise that their persons may be recognized; the voice, in such a crowd, being an insufficient verification of their presence. But in so small a body as the Senate of the United States, the trouble of rising cannot be necessary.

Orders for calls on different days may subsist at the same time. 2. *Hats.* 72.

SEC. VIII.
ABSENCE.

NO member shall absent himself from the service of the Senate, without leave of the Senate first obtained. And in case a less number than a quorum of the Senate shall convene, they are hereby authorised to send the serjeant at arms, or any other person or persons by them authorised, for any or all absent members, as the majority of such members present shall agree, at the expense of such absent members respectively, unless such excuse for non-attendance shall be made, as the Senate, when a quorum is convened, shall judge sufficient: and in that case, the expense shall be paid out of the contingent fund. And this rule shall apply as well to the first convention of Senate, at the legal time of meeting, as to each day of the session, after the hour is arrived to which the Senate stood adjourned. Rule 19.

SEC. IX.
SPEAKER.

THE Vice-President of the United States shall be President of the Senate, but shall have no vote, unless they be equally divided. Constitution I. 3.

The House of Representatives shall chuse their Speaker and other officers. Constitution I. 2.

When but one person is proposed, and no objection made, it has not been usual in Parliament to put any question to the House; but without a question, the members proposing him conduct him to the chair. But if there be objection, or another proposed, a question is put by the clerk. 2. *Hats.* 158. As are also questions of adjournment. 6 *Grey.* 406. Where the House debated and exchanged messages and answers with the king for a week, without a Speaker, till they were prorogued. They have done it de diem in diem for fourteen days. 1. *Chand.* 331. 335.

In the Senate, a President pro tempore in the absence of the Vice-President is proposed, and chosen by ballot. His office is understood to be determined on the Vice-President's appearing and taking the chair, or at the meeting of the Senate after the first recess.

Where the Speaker has been ill, other Speakers pro tempore have been appointed. Instances of this are 1. *H.* 4. Sir John Cheyney, and so Sir William Sturton, and in 15. *H.* 6. Sir John Tyrrel, in 1656, January 27. 1658, March 9. 1659, January 13

Sir Job Charlton ill. Seymour chosen, 1673, February 18. }
Seymour being ill, Sir Robt. Sawyer chosen, 1678, April 15. } Not merely pro tem. 1 *Chand.* 169. 276, 277.
Sawyer being ill, Seymour chosen. }

Thorpe in execution, a new Speaker chosen, 3 *H.* VI. 3 *Grey* 11. and March 14, 1694, Sir John Trevor chosen. There have been no later instances 2 *Hats.* 161. 4 inst. 8 *L. Parl.* 263.

A Speaker may be removed at the will of the House and a Speaker pro tempore appointed. 2 *Grey* 186. 5 *Grey* 134.

SEC. X.
ADDRESS.

THE President shall from time to time give to the Congress information of the state of the Union, and recommend to their consideration such measures as he shall judge necessary and expedient. Constitution II. 3.

A joint address of both Houses of Parliament is read by the Speaker of the House of Lords. It may be attended by both Houses in a body, or by a committee from each House, or by the two Speakers only. An address of the House of Commons only, may be presented by the whole House, or by the Speaker, 9 *Grey* 473. 1 *Chandler*, 298, 301. or by such particular members as are of the Privy Council. 2 *Hats.* 278.

SEC. XI.

COMMITTEES.

STANDING committees, as of privileges and elections, &c. are usually appointed at the first meeting, to continue through the session. The person first named is generally permitted to act as chairman. But this is a matter of courtesy; every committee having a right to elect their own chairman, who presides over them, puts questions, and reports their proceedings to the House. 4 inst. 11, 12, *Scob.* 9. 1 *Grey* 122.

At these committees the members are to speak standing, and not sitting: though there is reason to conjecture it was formerly otherwise. *D'Ewes* 630. *col.* 1. 4. *Parl. Hist.* 440. 2 *Hats.* 77.

Their proceedings are not to be published, as they are of no force till confirmed by the House. *Rushw. Parl.* 3. *vol.* 2. 74. 3 *Grey* 401. *Scob* 39. Nor can they receive a petition but through the House. 9 *Grey* 412.

When a committee is charged with an enquiry, if a member prove to be involved, they cannot proceed against him, but must make a special report to the House, whereupon the member is heard in his place, or at the bar, or a special authority is given to the committee to enquire concerning him. 9 *Grey* 523.

So soon as the House sits, and a committee is notified of it, the chairman is in duty bound to rise instantly, and the members to attend the service of the House. 2 *Nals.* 319.

It appears that on joint committees of the Lords and Commons, each committee acted integrally in the following instances. 7 *Grey* 261, 278, 285, 338. 1 *Chandler* 357, 462. In the following instances it does not appear whether they did or not. 6 *Grey* 129. 7 *Grey* 213, 229, 321.

SEC. XII.
COMMITTEE OF THE WHOLE.

THE speech, messages and other matters of great concernment, are usually referred to a committee of the whole House. 6 *Grey* 311. Where general principles are digested in the form of resolutions, which are debated and amended till they get into a shape which meets the approbation of a majority. These being reported and confirmed by the House, are then referred to one or more select committees, according as the subject divides itself into one or more bills. *Scob.* 36, 44. Propositions for any charge on the people are especially to be first made in a committee of the whole. 3 *Hats.* 127. The sense of the whole is better taken in committee, because in all committees every one speaks as often as he pleases. *Scob.* 49. They generally acquiesce in the chairman named by the Speaker: but, as well as all other committees, have a right to elect one, some member, by consent, putting the question. *Scob.* 36. 3 *Grey* 301. The form of going from the House into committee, is, for the Speaker, on motion, to put the question that the House do now resolve itself into a committee of the whole, to take under consideration such a matter, naming it. If determined in the affirmative, he leaves the chair, and takes a seat elsewhere, as any other member; and the person appointed chairman seats himself at the clerk's table. *Scob.* 36. Their quorum is the same as that of the House; and if a defect happens, the chairman, on a motion and question, rises, the Speaker resumes the chair, and the chairman can make no other report than to inform the House of the cause of their dissolution. If a message is announced during a committee, the Speaker takes the chair, and receives it, because the committee cannot. 2 *Hats.* 125, 126.

In a committee of the whole, the tellers on a division, differing as to the numbers, great heats and confusion arose, and danger of a decision by the sword. The Speaker took the chair, the mace was forcibly laid on the table, whereupon, the members retiring to their places, the Speaker told the House "he had taken the chair without an order, to bring the House into order." Some excepted against it; but it was generally approved as the only expedient to suppress the disorder. And every member was required, standing up in his place, to engage that he would proceed no further in consequence of what had happened in the grand committee, which was done. 3 *Grey* 128.

A committee of the whole being broken up in disorder, and the chair resumed by the Speaker without an order, the House was adjourned. The next day the committee was considered as thereby dissolved, and the subject again before the House; and it was decided in the House, without returning into committee. 3 *Grey* 130.

No previous question can be put in a committee; nor can this committee adjourn as others may; but if their business is unfinished, they rise, on a question, the House is resumed, and the chairman reports that the committee of the whole have, according to order, had under their consideration such a matter and have made progress therein; but not having had time to go through the same, have directed him to ask leave to sit again. Whereupon a question is put on their having leave, and on the time when the House will again resolve itself into a committee. *Scob.* 38. But if they have gone through the matter referred to them, a member moves that the committee may rise, and the chairman report their proceedings to the House; which being resolved, the chairman rises, the Speaker resumes the chair, the chairman informs him that the committee have gone through the business referred to them, and that he is ready to make report when the House shall think proper to receive it. If the House have time to receive it, there is usually a cry of "now, now," whereupon he makes the report: but if it be late, the cry is "to-morrow, to-morrow," or "on Monday, &c," or a motion is made to that effect, and a question put that it be received to-morrow, &c. *Scob.* 38.

In other things the rules of proceeding are to be the same as in the House. *Scob.* 39.

SEC. XIII.
EXAMINATION OF WITNESSES.

COMMON fame is a good ground for the House to proceed by enquiry, and even to accusation. *Resolution House Commons* 1. *Car.* 1. 1625. *Rush. L. Parl.* 115. 1 *Grey* 16. . . . 22. 92. 8 *Grey* 21, 23, 27, 45.

As the heads of impeachment were severally read against the Lord Clarendon in 1667, some member in his place, stated to the House, "that several persons had undertaken to make that head good." Or, "that the member had heard this from a certain great lord." Or, "that this was too public to stand in need of proof." Or, in one instance, "that the member did not doubt that it will be made out." *St. Tr.* 558. 4 *Hats.* 137.

Witnesses are not to be produced but where the House has previously instituted an enquiry. 2 *Hats.* 102. nor then are orders for their attendance given blank. 3 *Grey* 51. The process is a summons from the House. 4. *Hats.* 255, 258.

When any person is examined before a committee, or at the bar of the House, any member wishing to ask the person a question, must address it to the Speaker or Chairman, who repeats the question to the person, or says to him, "you hear the question, answer it." But if the propriety of the question be objected to, the Speaker directs the witness, counsel and parties, to withdraw; for no question can be moved or put, or debated while they are there. 2 *Hats.* 108. Sometimes the questions are previously settled in writing before the witness enters. *Ib.* 106, 107. 8 *Grey* 64. The questions asked must be entered in the Journals. 3 *Grey* 81. But the testimony given in answer before the House is never written down; but before a committee it must be, for the information of the House, who are not present to hear it. 7 *Grey* 52, 334.

If either House have occasion for the presence of a person in custody of the other, they ask the other their leave that he may be brought up to them in custody. 3 *Hats.* 52.

A member, in his place, gives information to the House of what he knows of any matter under hearing at the bar. *Jour. H. of C. January* 22, 1744 . . . 5.

Either House may request, but not command the attendance of a member of the other. They are to make the request by message to the other House, and to express clearly the purpose of attendance, that no improper subject of examination may be tendered to him. The House then gives leave to the member to attend, if he chuse it; waiting first to know from the member himself whether he chuses to attend, till which, they do not take the message into consideration. But when the peers are sitting as a court of criminal judicature, they may order attendance; unless where it be a case of impeachment by the Commons. There it is to be a request. 3 *Hats.* 17. 9 *Grey* 306, 406. 10 *Grey* 133.

Counsel are to be heard only on private, not on public bills, and on such points of law only as the House shall direct. 10 *Grey* 61.

SEC. XIV.
ARRANGEMENT OF BUSINESS.

THE Speaker is not precisely bound to any rules as to what bills or other matter shall be first taken up, but is left to his own discretion, unless the House on a question decide to take up a particular subject. *Hakew.* 136.

A settled order of business is, however, necessary for the government of the presiding person, and to restrain individual members from calling up favorite measures, or matters under their special patronage, out of their just turn. It is useful also for directing the discretion of the House, when they are moved to take up a particular matter, to the prejudice of others having priority of right to their attention in the general order of business.

In Senate, the bills and other papers which are in possession of the House, and in a state to be acted on, are arranged every morning, and brought on in the following order.

1. Bills ready for a second reading are read, that they may be referred to committees, and so be put under way. But if, on their being read, no motion is made for commitment, they are then laid on the table in the general file, to be taken up in their just turn.

2. After twelve o'clock, bills ready for it are put on their passage.

3. Reports in possession of the House, which offer grounds for a bill, are to be taken up, that the bill may be ordered in.

4. Bills or other matters before the House and unfinished on the preceding day, whether taken up in turn, or on special order, are entitled to be resumed and passed on through their present stage.

5. These matters being dispatched, for preparing and expediting business, the general file of bills and other papers is then taken up, and each article of it is brought on according to its seniority, reckoned by the date of its first introduction to the House. Reports on bills belong to the dates of their bills.

In this way we do not waste our time in debating what shall be taken up: we do one thing at a time; follow up a subject while it is fresh, and till it is done with; clear the House of business gradatim as it is brought on, and prevent, to a certain degree, its immense accumulation towards the close of the session.

Arrangement however can only take hold of matters in possession of the House. New matter may be moved at any time, when no question is before the House. Such are original motions, and reports on bills. Such are bills from the other House, which are received at all times, and receive their first reading as soon as the question then before the House is disposed of; and bills brought in on leave, which are read first whenever presented. So messages from the other House respecting amendments to bills, are taken up as soon as the House is clear of a question, unless they require to be printed, for better consideration. Orders of the day may be called for, even when another question is before the House.

SEC. XV.
ORDER.

EACH House may determine the rules of its proceedings; punish its members for disorderly behaviour, and, with the concurrence of two thirds, expel a member. Constitution I. 5.

In Parliament "instances make order" per Speaker Onslow, 2 *Hats*. 141. but what is done only by one Parliament, cannot be called custom of Parliament, by Prynne. 1 *Grey* 52.

SEC. XVI.
ORDER RESPECTING PAPERS.

THE clerk is to let no journals, records, accounts, or papers be taken from the table, or out of his custody. 2 *Hats*. 193, 194.

Mr. Prynne having at a committee of the whole amended a mistake in a bill without order or knowledge of the committee, was reprimanded. 1 *Chand*. 77.

A bill being missing, the House resolved that a protestation should be made and subscribed by the members "before Almighty God and this honorable House, that neither myself nor any other to my knowledge, have taken away, or do at this present conceal a bill entitled, &c." 5 *Grey* 202.

After a bill is engrossed, it is put into the Speaker's hands, and he is not to let anyone have it to look into. *Town. col.* 209.

SEC. XVII.
ORDER IN DEBATE.

WHEN the Speaker is seated in his chair, every member is to sit in his place. *Scob.* 6. 3 *Grey* 403.

When any member means to speak, he is to stand up in his place, uncovered, and to address himself, not to the House, or any particular member, but to the Speaker, who calls him by his name, that the House may take notice who it is that speaks. *Scob.* 6. *D'Ewes* 487. *Col.* 1. 2 *Hats*. 77. 4 *Grey* 66. 8 *Grey* 108. But members who are indisposed may be indulged to speak sitting. 2 *Hats*. 75, 77. 1 *Grey* 195.

In Senate, every member, when he speaks, shall address the chair, standing in his place, and when he has finished shall sit down. Rule 3.

When a member stands up to speak, no question is to be put, but he is to be heard, unless the House overrule him. 4 *Grey* 390. 5 *Grey* 6, 143.

If two or more rise to speak nearly together, the Speaker determines who was first up, and calls him by name, whereupon he proceeds, unless he voluntarily sits down and gives way to the other. But sometimes the House does not acquiesce in the Speaker's decision, in which case the question is put "which member was first up?" 2 *Hats.* 76. *Scob.* 7. *D'Ewes* 434. *col.* 1, 2.

In the Senate of the United States, the President's decision is without appeal. Their rule is in these words: When two members rise at the same time, the President shall name the person to speak; but in all cases, the member first rising, shall speak first. Rule 5.

No man may speak more than once to the same bill on the same day; or even on another day if the debate be adjourned. But if it be read more than once in the same day, he may speak once at every reading. *Co.* 12, 116. *Hakew.* 148. *Scob.* 58. 2 *Hats.* 75. Even a change of opinion does not give a right to be heard a second time. *Smyth Comw. L.* 2. *c.* 3. *Arcan. Parl.* 17.

The corresponding rule of Senate is in these words: No member shall speak more than twice in any one debate on the same day, without leave of the Senate. Rule 4.

But he may be permitted to speak again to clear a matter of fact. 3 *Grey* 357, 416. Or merely to explain himself, 2 *Hats.* 73. in some material part of his speech, *ib.* 75. or to the manner or words of the question, keeping himself to that only and not travelling into the merits of it; *Memorials in Hakew.* 29. or to the orders of the House if they be transgressed, keeping within that line, and not falling into the matter itself. *Mem. in Hakew.* 30, 31.

But if the Speaker rises to speak, the member standing up ought to sit down, that he may be first heard. *Town col.* 205. *Hale Parl.* 133. *Mem. in Hakew.* 30, 31. Nevertheless, though the Speaker may of right speak to matters of order and be first heard, he is restrained from speaking on any other subject, except where the House have occasion for facts within his knowledge; then he may, with their leave, state the matter of fact. 3 *Grey* 38.

No one is to speak impertinently or beside the question, superfluously or tediously. *Scob.* 31, 33. 2 *Hats.* 166, 168. *Hale Parl.* 133.

No person is to use indecent language against the proceedings of the House, no prior determination of which is to be reflected on by any member, unless he means to conclude with a motion to rescind it. 2 *Hats.* 169, 170. *Rushw. P. 3. v. 1. fol. 42.* But while a proposition is under consideration, is still in fieri, though it has even been reported by a committee, reflections on it are no reflections on the House. 9 *Grey* 508.

No person in speaking, is to mention a member then present by his name; but to describe him by his seat in the House, or who spoke last, or on the other side of the question, &c. *Mem. in Hakew.* 3 *Smyth's Comw. L. 2. c. 3.* nor to digress from the matter to fall upon the person, *Scob.* 31. *Hale Parl.* 133. 2 *Hats.* 166. by speaking reviling, nipping, or unmannerly words against a particular member. *Smyth's Comw. L. 2. c. 3.* The consequences of a measure may be reprobated in strong terms; but to arraign the motives of those who propose or advocate it, is a personality, and against order. Qui digreditur a materia ad personam, Mr. Speaker ought to suppress. *Ord. Com.* 1604. *Apr.* 19.

When a member shall be called to order, he shall sit down until the President shall have determined whether he is in order or not. Rule 16.

No member shall speak to another, or otherwise interrupt the business of the Senate, or read any printed paper while the Journals or public papers are reading, or when any member is speaking in any debate. Rule 2.

No one is to disturb another in his speech by hissing, coughing, spitting, 6 *Grey* 332. *Scob.* 8. *D'Ewes* 332. *col.* 1. 640. *col.* 2. speaking or whispering to another; *Scob.* 6. *D'Ewes.* 487. *col.* 1. nor to stand up or interrupt him; *Town. col.* 205. *Mem. in Hakew.* 31. nor to pass between the Speaker and the speaking member, nor to go across the House; *Scob.* 6. or to walk up and down it, or to take books or papers from the table, or write there. 2 *Hats.* 171.

Nevertheless, if a member finds that it is not the inclination of the House to hear him, and that by conversation or any other noise they endeavour to drown his voice, it is his most prudent way to submit to the pleasure of the House, and sit down; for it scarcely ever happens that they are guilty of this piece of ill manners without sufficient reason, or inattentive to a member who says any thing worth their hearing. 2 *Hats.* 77, 78.

If repeated calls do not produce order, the Speaker may call by his name any member obstinately persisting in irregularity, whereupon the House may require the member to withdraw. He is then to be heard in exculpation, and to withdraw. Then the Speaker states the offence committed, and the House considers the degree of punishment they will inflict. 2 *Hats.* 167, 7, 8, 172.

For instances of assaults and affrays in the House of Commons, and the proceedings thereon, see 1. *Pet. Misc.* 82. 3 *Grey* 128. 4 *Grey* 328. 5 *Grey* 382. 6 *Grey* 254. 10 *Grey* 8. Whenever warm words, or an assault, have passed between members, the House, for the protection of their members, requires them to declare in their places not to prosecute any quarrel; 3 *Grey* 128, 293. 5 *Grey* 289. or orders them to attend the Speaker, who is to accommodate their differences and report to the House: 3 *Grey* 419. and they are put under restraint if they refuse, or until they do. 9 *Grey* 234, 312.

Disorderly words are not to be noticed till the member has finished his speech. 5 *Grey* 356. 6 *Grey* 60. Then the person objecting to them, and desiring them to be taken down by the clerk at the table, must repeat them. The Speaker then may direct the clerk to take them down in his minutes. But if he thinks them not disorderly, he delays the direction. If the call becomes pretty general, he orders the clerk to take them down, as stated by the objecting member. They are then part of his minutes, and when read to the offending member, he may deny they were his words, and the House must then decide by a question whether they are his words or not. Then the member may justify them, or explain the sense in which he used them, or apologize. If the House is satisfied, no farther proceeding is necessary. But if two members still insist to take the sense of the House, the member must withdraw, before that question is stated, and then the sense of the House is to be taken. 2 *Hats.* 199. 4 *Grey* 170. 6 *Grey* 59. When any member has spoken, or other business intervened after offensive words spoken, they cannot be taken notice of for censure. And this is for the common security of all, and to prevent mistakes which must happen if words are not taken down immediately. Formerly they might be taken down any time the same day. 2 *Hats.* 196. *Mem. in Hakew.* 71. 3 *Grey* 48. 9 *Grey* 514.

Disorderly words spoken in a committee must be written down as in the House; but the committee can only report them to the House for animadversion. 6 *Grey* 46.

The rule of the Senate says, if a member be called to order for words spoken, the exceptionable words shall be immediately taken down in writing, that the President may be better enabled to judge. Rule 17.

In Parliament, to speak irreverently or seditiously against the king is against order. *Smyth's Comw. L.* 2. c. 3. 2 *Hats.* 170.

It is a breach of order in debate to notice what has been said on the same subject in the other House, or the particular votes or majorities on it there: because the opinion of each House should be left to its own independency, not to be influenced by the proceedings of the other; and the quoting them might beget reflections leading to a misunderstanding between the two Houses. 8 *Grey* 22.

Neither House can exercise any authority over a member or officer of the other, but should complain to the House of which he is, and leave the punishment to them. Where the complaint is of words disrespectfully spoken by a member of another House, it is difficult to obtain punishment, because of the rules supposed necessary to be observed (as to the immediate noting down of words) for the security of members. Therefore it is the duty of the House, and more particularly of the Speaker, to interfere immediately, and not to permit expressions to go unnoticed which may give a ground of complaint to the other House, and introduce proceedings and mutual accusations between the two Houses, which can hardly be terminated without difficulty and disorder. 3 *Hats*. 51.

No member may be present when a bill or any business concerning himself is debating, nor is any member to speak to the merits of it till he withdraws. 2 *Hats*. 219. The rule is, that if a charge against a member arise out of a report of a committee, or examination of witnesses in the House, as the member knows from that to what points he is to direct his exculpation, he may be heard to those points, before any question is moved or stated against him. He is then to be heard, and withdraw before any question is moved. But if the question itself is the charge, as for breach of order, or matter arising in the debate, there the charge must be stated, that is, the question must be moved, himself heard, and then to withdraw. 2 *Hats*. 121, 122.

Where the private interests of a member are concerned in a bill or question, he is to withdraw. And where such an interest has appeared, his voice has been disallowed, even after a division. In a case so contrary not only to the laws of decency, but to the fundamental principle of the social compact, which denies to any man to be a judge in his own cause, it is for the honor of the House that this rule, of immemorial observance, should be strictly adhered to. 2 *Hats*. 119, 121. 6 *Grey* 368.

No member is to come into the House with his head covered, nor to remove from one place to another with his hat on, nor is to put on his hat in coming in, or removing, until he be set down in his place. *Scob.* 6.

A question of order may be adjourned to give time to look into precedents. 2 *Hats*. 118.

In the Senate of the United States, every question of order is to be decided by the President, without debate: but if there be a doubt in his mind, he may call for the sense of the Senate. Rule 16.

In Parliament, all decisions of the Speaker may be controuled by the House. 3 *Grey* 319.

SEC. XVIII.
ORDERS OF THE HOUSE.

OF right, the door of the House ought not to be shut, but to be kept by porters, or serjeants at arms, assigned for that purpose. *Mod. Ten. Parl.* 23.

By the rules of the Senate, on motion made and seconded, to shut the doors of the Senate on the discussion of any business which may in the opinion of a member require secrecy, the President shall direct the gallery to be cleared, and during the discussion of such motion, the doors shall remain shut. Rule 28.

No motion shall be deemed in order, to admit any person or persons whatever, within the doors of the Senate Chamber, to present any petition, memorial, or address, or to hear any such read. Rule 29.

The only case where a member has a right to insist on any thing is, where he calls for the execution of a subsisting order of the House. Here, there having been already a resolution, any member has a right to insist that the Speaker, or any other whose duty it is, shall carry it into execution; and no debate or delay can be had on it. Thus any member has a right to have the House or gallery cleared of strangers, an order existing for that purpose; or to have the House told when there is not a quorum present. 2 *Hats.* 87, 129. How far an order of the House in binding, see *Hakew.* 392.

But where an order is made that any particular matter be taken up on a particular day, there a question is to be put when it is called for, whether the House will now proceed to that matter? Where orders of the day are on important or interesting matter, they ought not to be proceeded on till an hour at which the House is usually full, *(which in Senate is at noon.)*

Orders of the day may be discharged at any time, and a new one made for a different day. 3 *Grey* 48, 313.

When a session is drawing to a close, and the important bills are all brought in; the House, in order to prevent interruption by further unimportant bills, sometimes come to a resolution that no new bill be brought in, except it be sent from the other House. 3 *Grey* 156.

All orders of the House determine with the session; and one taken under such an order may, after the session is ended, be discharged on a habeas corpus. *Raym.* 120. *Jacob's L. D. by Ruffhead. Parliament,* 1 *Lev.* 165. *Prichard's case.*

Where the constitution authorises each House to determine the rules of its proceedings, it must mean in those cases legislative, executive or judiciary, submitted to them by the constitution, or in something relating to these, and necessary towards their execution. But orders and resolutions are sometimes entered in the journals, having no relation to these, such as acceptances of invitations to attend orations, to take part in processions, &c. These must be understood to be merely conventional among those who are willing to participate in the ceremony, and are therefore, perhaps, improperly placed among the records of the House.

SEC. XIX.
PETITIONS.

A PETITION prays something. A remonstrace has no prayer. 1 *Grey* 58.

Petitions must be subscribed by the petitioners, *Scob.* 87. *L. Parl. c.* 22. 9 *Grey* 362. unless they are attending, 1 *Grey* 401. or unable to sign, and averred by a member. 3 *Grey* 418. But a petition not subscribed, but which the member presenting it affirmed to be all in the hand writing of the petitioner, and his name written in the beginning, was on the question (Mar. 14, 1800) received by the Senate. The averment of a member, or of somebody without doors, that they know the hand writing of the petitioners is necessary if it be questioned. 6 *Grey* 36. It must be presented by a member, not by the petitioners, and must be opened by him, holding it in his hand. 10 *Grey* 57.

Before any petition or memorial addressed to the Senate, shall be received and read at the table, whether the same shall be introduced by the President or a member, a brief statement of the contents of the petition or memorial shall verbally be made by the introducer. Rule 21.

Regularly a motion for receiving it must be made and seconded, and a question put whether it shall be received? But a cry from the House of "received," or even its silence, dispenses with the formality of this question. It is then to be read at the table and disposed of.

SEC. XX.
MOTIONS.

WHEN a motion has been made, it is not to be put to the question or debated until it is seconded. *Scob.* 21.

The Senate say no motion shall be debated until the same shall be seconded. Rule 6.

It is then and not till then in possession of the House, and cannot be withdrawn but by leave of the House. It is to be put into writing, if the House or Speaker require it, and must be read to the House by the Speaker as often as any member desires it for his information. 2 *Hats*. 82.

The rule of the Senate is, when a motion shall be made and seconded, it shall be reduced to writing, if desired by the President, or any member, delivered in at the table, and read by the President before the same shall be debated. Rule 7.

It might be asked whether a motion for adjournment or for the orders of the day can be made by one member while another is speaking? It cannot. When two members offer to speak, he who rose first is to be heard, and it is a breach of order in another to interrupt him, unless by calling him to order, if he departs from it. And the question of order being decided, he is still to be heard through. A call for adjournment, or for the order of the day, or for the question, by gentlemen from their seats, is not a motion. No motion can be made without rising and addressing the chair. Such calls are themselves breaches of order, which though the member who has risen may respect, as an expression of the impatience of the House against further debate, yet, if he chuses, he has a right to go on.

SEC. XXI.
RESOLUTIONS.

WHEN the House commands, it is by an "order." But facts, principles, their own opinions, and purposes, are expressed in the form of Resolutions.

A Resolution, for an allowance of money to the clerks, being moved, it was objected to as not in order, and so ruled by the chair. But on an appeal to the Senate (i.e. a call for their sense by the President on account of doubt in his mind according to Rule 16.) the decision was overruled. Journ. Sen. June 1, 1796. *I presume the doubt was, whether an allowance of money could be made otherwise than by bill.*

SEC. XXII.
BILLS.

EVERY bill shall receive three readings, previous to its being passed; and the President shall give notice at each whether it be the first, second, or third; which readings shall be on three different days, unless the Senate unanimously direct otherwise, or, unless by a joint vote of both Houses, or the expiration of their term, the session is to be closed within three days. Rule 13.

SEC. XXIII.
BILLS, LEAVE TO BRING IN.

ONE day's notice at least shall be given of an intended motion for leave to bring in a bill. Rule 12.

When a member desires to bring in a bill on any subject, he states to the House in general terms the causes for doing it, and concludes by moving for leave to bring in a bill intituled, &c. Leave being given, on the question, a committee is appointed to prepare and bring in the bill. The mover and seconder are always appointed of this committee, and one or more in addition. *Hakew.* 132. *Scob.* 40.

It is to be presented fairly written, without any erasure or interlineation, or the Speaker may refuse it. *Scob.* 41. 1 *Grey* 82, 84.

SEC. XXIV.
BILLS, FIRST READING.

WHEN a bill is first presented, the clerk reads it at the table, and hands it to the Speaker, who rising, states to the House the title of the bill, that this is the first time of reading it, and the question will be whether it shall be read a second time? Then sitting down to give an opening for objections, if none be made, he rises again and puts the question whether it shall be read a second time? *Hakew.* 137, 141. A bill cannot be amended at the first reading. 6 *Grey* 286. nor is it usual for it to be opposed then: but it may be done and rejected. *D'Ewes* 335, col. 1. 3 *Hats.* 198.

SEC. XXV.
BILLS, SECOND READING.

THE second reading must regularly be on another day. *Hakew.* 143. It is done by the clerk at the table, who then hands it to the Speaker. The Speaker, rising, states to the House the title of the bill, that this is the second time of reading it, and that the question will be whether it shall be committed, or engrossed and read a third time? But if the bill came from the other House, as it always comes engrossed, he states that the question will be whether it shall be read a third time? and before he has so reported the state of the bill, no one is to speak to it. *Hakew.* 143, 146.

In the Senate of the United States, the President reports the title of the bill, that this is the second time of reading it, that it is now to be considered as in a Committee of the Whole, and the question will be, whether it

[381]

shall be read a third time? or, that it may be referred to a special committee.

SEC. XXVI.

BILLS, COMMITMENT.

IF on motion and question it be decided that the bill shall be committed, it may then be moved to be referred to a committee of the whole House, or to a special committee. If the latter, the Speaker proceeds to name the committee. Any member also may name a single person, and the clerk is to write him down as of the committee. But the House have a controuling power over the names and number, if a question be moved against any one, and may in any case put in and put out whom they please.

Those who take exceptions to some particulars in the bill are to be of the committee. But none who speak directly against the body of the bill. For he that would totally destroy, will not amend it. *Hakew.* 146. *Town. coll.* 208. *D'Ewes.* 623. *col.* 2 *Scob* 47. or as is said, 5 *Grey* 145. the child is not to be put to a nurse that cares not for it. 6 *Grey* 373. It is therefore a constant rule "that no man is to be employed in any matter who has declared himself against it." And when any member who is against the bill hears himself named of its committee, he ought to ask to be excused. Thus March 7, 1606, Mr. Hadley was, on the question's being put, excused from being of a committee, declaring himself to be against the matter itself. *Scob.* 46.

No bill shall be committed or amended until it shall have been twice read, after which it may be referred to a committee. Rule 14.

All committees shall be appointed by ballot, and a plurality of voices shall make a choice. Rule 15.

The clerk may deliver the bill to any member of the committee. *Town. col.* 138. But it is usual to deliver it to him who is first named.

In some cases, the House has ordered a committee to withdraw immediately into the committee chamber, and act on, and bring back the bill, sitting the House. *Scob.* 48.

A committee meets when, and where they please, if the House has not ordered time and place for them. 6 *Grey* 370. But they can only act when together, and not by separate consultation and consent; nothing being the report of the committee but what has been agreed to in committee actually assembled.

A majority of the committee constitutes a quorum for business. *Elsynge's Method of passing Bills.* 11.

Any member of the House may be present at any select committee,

[382]

but cannot vote, and must give place to all of the committee, and sit below them. *Elsynge* 12. *Scob.* 49.

But in 1626, April 24, the House of Commons resolved, that though any members may be present at the examination of witnesses, they may not be at the debate, disposition or penning of the business by the select committee. 4 *Hats.* 124.

The committee have full power over the bill, or other paper committed to them, except that they cannot change the title or subject. 8 *Grey* 228.

The paper before a committee, whether select, or of the whole, may be a bill, resolutions, draught of an address, &c. and it may either originate with them, or be referred to them. In every case, the whole paper is read first by the clerk, and then by the chairman, by paragraphs, *Scob.* 49. pausing at the end of each paragraph, and putting questions for amending, if proposed. In the case of resolutions on distinct subjects, originating with themselves, a question is put on each separately, as amended, or unamended, and no final question on the whole: 3 *Hats.* 276. but if they relate to the same subject, a question is put on the whole. If it be a bill, draught of an address, or other paper originating with them, they proceed by paragraphs, putting questions for amending, either by insertion or striking out, if proposed: but no question on agreeing to the paragraphs separately. This is reserved to the close, when a question is put on the whole, for agreeing to it as amended, or unamended. But if it be a paper referred to them, they proceed to put questions of amendment, if proposed, but no final question on the whole: because all parts of the paper having been adopted by the House, stand of course, unless altered, or struck out by a vote. Even if they are opposed to the whole paper, and think it cannot be made good by amendments, they cannot reject it, but must report it back to the House without amendments, and there make their opposition.

The natural order in considering and amending any paper is, to begin at the beginning, and proceed through it by paragraphs; and this order is so strictly adhered to in Parliament, that when a latter part has been amended, you cannot recur back and make any alteration in a former part. 2 *Hats.* 90. In numerous assemblies this restraint is doubtless important. *But in Senate of the United States, though in the main we consider and amend the paragraphs in their natural order, yet recurrences are indulged: and they seem on the whole, in that small body, to produce advantages overweighing their inconveniences.*

To this natural order of beginning at the beginning, there is a single exception found in Parliamentary usage. When a bill is taken up in committee, or on its second reading, they postpone the preamble, till the other parts of the bill are gone through. The reason is, that on consideration of the body of the bill, such alterations may therein be made as may also occasion the alteration of the preamble. *Scob.* 50. 7 *Grey* 431.

On this head the following case occurred in Senate, March 6, 1800. A resolution, which had no preamble, having been already amended by the House, so that a few words only of the original remained in it, a motion was made to prefix a preamble, which having an aspect very different from the resolution, the mover intimated that he should afterwards propose a correspondent amendment in the body of the resolution. It was objected that a preamble could not be taken up till the body of the resolution is done with. But the preamble was received: because we are in fact through the body of the resolution, we have amended that as far as amendments have been offered, and indeed till little of the original is left. It is the proper time, therefore, to consider a preamble: and whether the one offered be consistent with the resolution, is for the House to determine. The mover indeed, has intimated, that he shall offer a subsequent proposition for the body of the resolution; but the House is not in possession of it; it remains in his breast, and may be withheld. The rules of the House can only operate on what is before them. *The practice of the Senate too, allows recurrences backwards and forwards, for the purposes of amendment, not permitting amendments in a subsequent, to preclude those in a prior part, or e converso.*

When the committee is through the whole, a member moves that the committee may rise, and the chairman report the paper to the House, with, or without amendments, as the case may be. 2 *Hats.* 289, 292. *Scob.* 53. 2 *Hats.* 290. 8 *Scob.* 50.

When a vote is once passed in a committee, it cannot be altered but by the House, their votes being binding on themselves. 1607, *June* 4.

The committee may not erase, interline, or blot the bill itself; but must in a paper by itself, set down the amendments, stating the words which are to be inserted or omitted; *Scob.* 50. and where, by references to the page, line and word of the bill. *Scob.* 50.

18 SEC. XXVII.
REPORT OF COMMITTEE.

THE chairman of the committee, standing in his place, informs the House, that the committee, to whom was referred such a bill, have, according to order, had the same under consideration, and have directed him to report the same without any amendment, or with sundry amendments, (as the case may be,) which he is ready to do, when the House pleases to receive it. And he, or any other, may move that it be now received. But the cry of "now, now," from the House, generally dispenses with the formality of a motion and question. He then reads the amendments with the coherence in the bill, and opens the alterations, and the reasons of the committee for such amendments, until he has gone through the whole. He then delivers it at the clerk's table, where the amendments reported are read by the clerk, without the coherence, whereupon the papers lie on the table, till the House at its convenience, shall take up the report. *Scob.* 52. *Hakew.* 148.

The report being made, the committee is dissolved, and can act no more without a new power. *Scob.* 51. But it may be revived by a vote, and the same matter recommitted to them. 4 *Grey* 361.

SEC. XXVIII.
BILL, RECOMMITMENT.

AFTER a bill has been committed and reported, it ought not, in an ordinary course, to be recommitted. But in cases of importance, and for special reasons, it is sometimes recommitted, and usually to the same committee. *Hakew.* 151. If a report be recommitted before agreed to in the House, what has passed in committee is of no validity; the whole question is again before the committee, and a new resolution must be again moved, as if nothing had passed. 3 *Hats.* 131. *note.*

In Senate, January 1800, the salvage bill was recommitted three times after the commitment.

A particular clause of a bill may be committed without the whole bill; 3 *Hats.* 131. or so much of a paper to one, and so much to another committee.

SEC. XXIX.
BILL, REPORT TAKEN UP.

WHEN the report of a paper originating with a committee, is taken up by the House, they proceed exactly as in committee. Here, as in committee, when the paragraphs have, on distinct questions, been agreed to seriatim, 5 *Grey* 366. 6 *Grey* 368. 8 *Grey* 47, 104, 360. 1 *Torbuck's Deb.* 125. 3 *Hats.* 348. no question needs be put on the whole report. 5 *Grey* 381.

On taking up a bill reported with amendments, the amendments only are read by the clerk. The Speaker then reads the first, and puts it to the question, and so on, till the whole are adopted or rejected, before any other amendment be admitted, except it be an amendment to an amendment. *Elsynge's Mem.* 53. When through the amendments of the committee, the Speaker pauses, and gives time for amendments to be proposed in the House to the body of the bill: as he does also if it has been reported without amendments; putting no questions but on amendments proposed: and when through the whole, he puts the question whether the bill shall be read a third time?

SEC. XXX.
QUASI-COMMITTEE.

IF on the motion and question, the bill be not committed, or if no proposition for commitment be made, then the proceedings in the Senate of the United States, and in Parliament, are totally different. The former shall be first stated.

The 20th rule of the Senate says, "All bills, on a second reading, shall first be considered by the Senate in the same manner as if the Senate were in a committee of the whole, before they shall be taken up and proceeded on by the Senate agreeably to the standing rules, unless otherwise ordered:" that is to say, unless ordered to be referred to a special committee.

The proceeding of the Senate as in a committee of the whole, or in quasi-committee, is precisely as in a real committee of the whole, taking no questions but on amendments. When through the whole, they consider the quasi-committee as risen, the House resumed, without any motion, question, or resolution to that effect, and the President reports that "the House acting as in a committee of the whole, have had under their consideration the bill intituled, &c. and have made sundry amendments, which he will now report to the House." The bill is then before them as it would have been if reported from a committee, and questions are regularly to be put again on every amendment: which being gone through, the President pauses to give time to the House to propose amendments to the body of the bill, and when through, puts the question whether it shall be read a third time?

After progress in amending a bill in quasi-committee, a motion may be made to refer it to a special committee. If the motion prevails, it is equivalent in effect to the several votes that the committee rise, the House resume itself, discharge the committee of the whole, and refer the bill to a special committee. In that case the amendments already made fall. But if the motion fails, the quasi-committee stands in statu quo.

How far does this 20th rule subject the House when in quasi-committee, to the laws which regulate the proceedings of committees of the whole?

The particulars in which these differ from proceedings in the House, are the following.

1. In a committee, every member may speak as often as he pleases. 2. The votes of a committee may be rejected or altered when reported to the House. 3. A committee, even of the whole, cannot refer any matter to another committee. 4. In a committee, no previous question can be taken. The only means to avoid an improper discussion is, to move that the committee rise: and if it be apprehended that the same discussion will be attempted on returning into committee, the House can discharge them, and proceed itself on the business, keeping down the improper discussion by the previous question. 5. A committee cannot punish a breach of order, in the House, or in the gallery. 9 *Grey* 113. It can only rise and report it to the House, who may proceed to punish.

The 1st and 2d of these peculiarities attach to the quasi-committee of the Senate, as every day's practice proves; and seem to be the only ones to which the 20th rule meant to subject them. For it continues to be a House, and therefore, though it acts in some respects as a committee, in others it preserves its character as a House. Thus 3. It is in the daily habit of referring its business to a special committee. 4. It admits the previous question. If it did not, it would have no means of preventing an improper discussion; not being able as a committee is, to avoid it by returning into the House: for the moment it would resume the same subject there, the 20th rule declares it again a quasi-committee. 5. It would doubtless exercise its powers as a House on any breach of order. 6. It takes a question by yea and nay, as the House does. 7. It receives messages from the President and the other House. 8. In the midst of a debate it receives a motion to adjourn, and adjourns as a House, not as a committee.

SEC. XXXI.
BILL, SECOND READING IN THE HOUSE.

IN Parliament, after the bill has been read a second time, if, on the motion and question, it be not committed, or if no proposition for commitment be made, the Speaker reads it by paragraphs, pausing between each, but putting no question but on amendments proposed; and when through the whole, he puts the question whether it shall be read a third time? if it came from the other House; or, if originating with themselves, whether it shall be engrossed and read a third time? The Speaker reads sitting, but rises to put questions. The clerk stands while he reads.

But the Senate of the United States is so much in the habit of making many and material amendments at the third reading, that it has become the practice not to engross a bill till it has passed. An irregular and dangerous practice; because, in this way, the paper which passes the Senate is not that which goes to the other House; and that which goes to the other House as the act of the Senate, has never been seen in Senate. In reducing numerous, difficult, and illegible amendments into the text, the Secretary may, with the most innocent intentions, commit errors, which can never again be corrected.

The bill being now as perfect as its friends can make it, this is the proper stage for those fundamentally opposed, to make their first attack. All attempts at earlier periods are with disjointed efforts; because many who do not expect to be in favor of the bill ultimately, are willing to let it go on to its perfect state, to take time to examine it themselves, and to hear what can be said for it; knowing that, after all, they will have sufficient opportunities of giving it their veto. Its two last stages therefore are reserved for this, that is to say, on the question whether it shall be read a third time? And lastly, whether it shall pass? The first of these is usually the most interesting contest; because then the whole subject is new and engaging, and the minds of the members having not yet been declared by any trying vote, the issue is the more doubtful. In this stage, therefore, is the main trial of strength between its friends and opponents: and it behoves every one to make up his mind decisively for this question, or he loses the main battle; and accident and management may, and often do, prevent a successful rallying on the next and last question whether it shall pass?

When the bill is engrossed, the title is to be endorsed on the back, and not within the bill. *Hakew.* 250.

SEC. XXXII.
READING PAPERS.

WHERE papers are laid before the House, or referred to a committee, every member has a right to have them once read at the table, before he can be compelled to vote on them. But it is a great, though common error, to suppose that he has a right, *toties quoties*, to have acts, journals, accounts, or papers on the table read independently of the will of the House. The delay and interruption which this might be made to produce, evince the impossibility of the existence of such a right. There is indeed so manifest a propriety of permitting every member to have as much information as possible on every question on which he is to vote, that when he desires the reading, if it be seen that it is really for information, and not for delay, the Speaker directs it to be read without putting a question, if no one objects. But if objected to, a question must be put. 2 *Hats.* 117, 118.

It is equally an error, to suppose that any member has a right, without a question put, to lay a book or paper on the table, and have it read, on suggesting that it contains matter infringing on the privileges of the House. *Ib.*

For the same reason, a member has not a right to read a paper in his place, if it be objected to, without leave of the House. But this rigour is never exercised, but where there is an intentional or gross abuse of the time and patience of the House.

A member has not a right even to read his own speech, committed to writing, without leave. This also is to prevent an abuse of time; and therefore is not refused, but where that is intended. 2 *Grey* 227.

A report of a committee of the Senate on a bill from the House of Representatives, being under consideration, on motion that the report of the committee of the House of Representatives on the same bill be read in Senate, it passed in the negative; February 28, 1793.

Formerly when papers were referred to a committee, they used to be first read: but of late, only the titles: unless a member insists they shall be read, and then nobody can oppose it. 2 *Hats.* 117.

SEC. XXXIII.
PRIVILEGED QUESTIONS.

WHILE a question is before the Senate, no motion shall be received unless for an amendment, for the previous question, or for postponing the main question, or to commit it, or to adjourn. Rule 8.

It is no possession of a bill, unless it be delivered to the clerk to be read, or the Speaker reads the title. *Lex. Parl.* 274. *Elsynge Mem.* 95. *Ord. House of Commons* 64.

It is a general rule, that the question first moved and seconded, shall be first put. *Scob.* 28, 22. 2 *Hats.* 81. But this rule gives way to what may be called privileged questions; and the privileged questions are of different grades among themselves.

A motion to adjourn simply takes place of all others; for otherwise, the House might be kept sitting against its will, and indefinitely. Yet this motion cannot be received after another question is actually put, and while the House is engaged in voting.

[389]

Orders of the day take place of all other questions, except for adjournment. That is to say, the question which is the subject of an order, is made a privileged one pro hac voce. The order is a repeal of the general rule as to this special case. When any member moves therefore for the orders of the day to be read, no further debate is permitted on the question which was before the House; for if the debate might proceed, it might continue through the day, and defeat the order. This motion, to entitle it to precedence, must be for the orders generally, and not for any particular one; and if it be carried on the question, "Whether the House will now proceed to the orders of the day," they must be read and proceeded on in the course in which they stand. 2 *Hats.* 83. For priority of order gives priority of right, which cannot be taken away but by another special order.

After these, there are other privileged questions which will require considerable explanation.

It is proper that every Parliamentary assembly should have certain forms of question so adapted, as to enable them fitly to dispose of every proposition which can be made to them. Such are 1. The previous question. 2. To postpone indefinitely. 3. To adjourn a question to a definite day. 4. To lie on the table. 5. To commit. 6. To amend. The proper occasion for each of these questions should be understood.

1. When a proposition is moved, which it is useless or inexpedient now to express or discuss, the previous question has been introduced for suppressing for that time the motion and its discussion. 3 *Hats.* 188, 189.

2. But as the previous question gets rid of it only for that day, and the same proposition may recur the next day, if they wish to suppress it for the whole of that session, they postpone it indefinitely. 3 *Hats.* 183. This quashes the proposition for that session, as an indefinite adjournment is a dissolution, or the continuance of a suit sine die is a discontinuance of it.

3. When a motion is made which it will be proper to act on, but information is wanted, or something more pressing claims the present time, the question or debate is adjourned to such day within the session as will answer the views of the House. 2 *Hats.* 81. And those who have spoken before may not speak again when the adjourned debate is resumed. 2 *Hats.* 73. Sometimes, however, this has been abusively used, by adjourning it to a day beyond the session, to get rid of it altogether, as would be done by an indefinite postponement.

4. When the House has something else which claims its present attention, but would be willing to reserve in their power to take up a

proposition whenever it shall suit them, they order it to lie on their table. It may then be called for at any time.

5. If the proposition will want more amendment and digestion than the formalities of the House will conveniently admit, they refer it to a committee.

6. But if the proposition be well digested and may need but few and simple amendments, and especially if these be of leading consequence, they then proceed to consider and amend it themselves.

The Senate, in their practice, vary from this regular gradation of forms. Their practice, comparatively with that of Parliament stands thus:

For the Parliamentary,		The Senate uses,
Postpmt. indefinite	=	Postp. to a day beyond the session.
Adjournment	=	Postp. to a day within the session.
Lying on the Table	=}	Postpmt. indefinite. Lying on the table.

In their 8th rule therefore, which declares that while a question is before the Senate, no motion shall be received unless it be for the previous question, or to postpone, commit, or amend the main question, the term postponement must be understood according to their broad use of it, and not in its Parliamentary sense. Their rule then establishes as privileged questions, the previous question, postponement, commitment and amendment.

But it may be asked, have these questions any privilege among themselves? Or, are they so equal, that the common principle of the "first moved, first put" takes place among them? This will need explanation. Their competitions may be as follow:

1. Prev. Qu. and Postpone, Commit, Amend

2. Postpone and Prev. Qu. Commit, Amend.

3. Commit and Prev. Qu. Postpone, Amend.

4. Amend and Prev. Qu. Postpone, Commit.

In the 1st, 2d and 3d classes and the 1st member of the 4th class, the rule "first moved first put" takes place.

In the first class, where the previous question is first moved, the effect is peculiar. For it not only prevents the after motion to postpone or commit from being put to question before it, but also, from being put after it. For if the previous question be decided affirmatively, to wit, that the main question shall now be put, it would of course be against the decision to postpone or commit. And if it be decided negatively, to wit, that the main question shall not now be put, this puts the House out of possession of the main question, and consequently there is nothing before them to postpone or commit. So that neither voting for, or against the previous question, will enable the advocates for postponing or committing to get at their object. Whether it may be amended, shall be examined hereafter.

2d Class. If postponement be decided affirmatively, the proposition is removed from before the House, and consequently there is no ground for the previous question, commitment, or amendment. But, if decided negatively, that it shall not be postponed, the main question may then be suppressed by the previous question, or may be committed, or amended.

The 3d class is subject to the same observations as the 2d.

The 4th class. Amendment of the main question first moved, and afterwards the previous question, the question of amendment shall be first put.

Amendment and postponement competing, postponement is first put, as the equivalent proposition to adjourn the main question would be in Parliament. The reason is, that the question for amendment is not suppressed by postponing or adjourning the main question, but remains before the House whenever the main question is resumed: and it might be that the occasion for other urgent business might go by, and be lost by length of debate on the amendment, if the House had it not in their power to postpone the whole subject.

Amendment and commitment. The question for committing, though last moved, shall be first put: because, in truth, it facilitates and befriends the motion to amend. *Scobell* is express. "On a motion to amend a bill, any one may notwithstanding, move to commit it, and the question for commitment shall be first put." *Scob.* 46.

We have hitherto considered the case of two or more of the privileged questions contending for privilege between themselves, when both were moved on the original or main question; but now let us suppose one of them to be moved, not on the original primary question, but on the secondary one: *e.g.*

Suppose a motion to postpone, commit or amend the main question, and that it be moved to suppress that motion by putting a previous question on it. This is not allowed: because it would embarrass questions too much to allow them to be piled on one another several stories high; and the same result may be had in a more simple way, by deciding against the postponement, commitment or amendment. 2 *Hats*. 81, 2, 3, 4.

Suppose a motion for the previous question, or commitment, or amendment of the main question, and that it be then moved to postpone the motion for the previous question, or for commitment, or amendment of the main question. 1. It would be absurd to postpone the previous question, commitment or amendment alone, and thus separate the appendage from its principal. Yet it must be postponed separately from its original, if at all: because the 8th rule of Senate says, that when a main question is before the House, no motion shall be received but to commit, amend, or pre-question the original question, which is the Parliamentary doctrine also. Therefore the motion to postpone the secondary motion for the previous question, or for committing or amending, cannot be received. 2. This is a piling of questions one on another, which, to avoid embarrassment, is not allowed. 3. The same result may be had more simply, by voting against the previous question, commitment or amendment.

Suppose a commitment moved of a motion for the previous question, or to postpone or amend. The 1st, 2d and 3d reasons before stated, all hold good against this.

Suppose an amendment moved to a motion for the previous question. Answer. The previous question cannot be amended. Parliamentary usage, as well as the 9th rule of the Senate has fixed its form to be "Shall the main question be now put?" *i.e.* at this instant. And as the present instant is but one, it can admit of no modification. To change it to to-morrow, or any other moment, is without example, and without utility. But suppose a motion to amend a motion for postponement; as to one day instead of another, or to a special, instead of indefinite time. The useful character of amendment, gives it a privilege of attaching itself to a secondary and privileged motion. That is, we may amend a postponement of a main question. So we may amend a commitment of a main question, as by adding, for example, "with instructions to enquire, &c." In like manner, if an amendment be moved to an amendment, it is admitted. But it would not be admitted in another degree: to wit, to amend an amendment to an amendment, of a main question. This would lead to too much embarrassment. The line must be drawn somewhere, and usage has drawn it after the amendment to the amendment. The same result must be sought by deciding against the amendment to the amendment, and then moving it again as it was wished to be amended. In this form it becomes only an amendment to an amendment.

In filling a blank with a sum, the largest sum shall be first put to the question by the 18th rule of the Senate, contrary to the rule of Parliament which privileges the smallest sum and longest time. 5 *Grey* 179. 2 *Hats*. 81, 83. 3 *Hats*. 132, 133. And this is considered to be not in the form of an amendment to the question; but as alternative, or successive originals. In all cases of time or number, we must consider whether the larger comprehends the lesser, as in a question to what day a postponement shall be, the number of a committee, amount of a fine, term of an imprisonment, term of irredeemability of a loan, or the terminus in quem, in any other case. Then the question must begin a maximo. Or whether the lesser concludes the greater, as in questions on the limitation of the rate of interest, on what day the session shall be closed by adjournment, on what day the next shall commence, when an act shall commence, or the terminus a quo in any other case, where the question must begin a minimo. The object being not to begin at that extreme, which, and more, being within every man's wish, no one could negative it, and yet, if he should vote in the affirmative, every question for more would be precluded: but at that extreme which would unite few, and then to advance or recede, till you get to a number which will unite a bare majority. 3 *Grey* 376, 384, 385. "The fair question in this case is not that to which and more all will agree, but whether there shall be addition to the question." 1 *Grey* 265.

Another exception to the rule of priority is, when a motion has been made to strike out, or agree to a paragraph. Motions to amend it are to be put to the question before a vote is taken on striking out, or agreeing to the whole paragraph.

But there are several questions, which being incidental to every one, will take place of every one, privileged or not; to wit, a question of order arising out of any other question, must be decided before that question. 2 *Hats*. 88.

A matter of privilege arising out of any question, or from a quarrel between two members, or any other cause, supersedes the consideration of the original question, and must be first disposed of. 2 *Hats*. 88.

Reading papers relative to the question before the House. This question must be put before the principal one. 2 *Hats*. 88.

Leave asked to withdraw a motion. The rule of Parliament being, that a motion made and seconded is in possession of the House, and cannot be withdrawn without leave, the very terms of the rule imply that leave may be given, and consequently may be asked and put to the question.

SEC. XXXIV.
THE PREVIOUS QUESTION.

WHEN any question is before the House, any member may move a previous question "Whether that question (called the main question) shall now be put?" If it pass in the affirmative, then the main question is to be put immediately, and no man may speak any thing further to it, either to add or alter. *Memor. in Hakew.* 28. 4 *Grey* 27.

The previous question being moved and seconded, the question from the chair shall be, "Shall the main question be now put?" and if the nays prevail, the main question shall not then be put. Rule 9.

This kind of question is understood by Mr. Hatsell to have been introduced in 1604. 2 *Hats.* 80. Sir Henry Vane introduced it. 2 *Grey* 113, 114. 3 *Grey* 384. When the question was put in this form, "Shall the main question be put?" a determination in the negative suppressed the main question during the session; but since the words "now put" are used, they exclude it for the present only. Formerly indeed, only till the present debate was over; 4 *Grey* 43. but now, for that day and no longer. 2 *Grey* 113, 114.

Before the question "whether the main question shall now be put?" any person might, formerly, have spoken to the main question, because otherwise he would be precluded from speaking to it at all. *Mem. in Hakew.* 28.

The proper occasion for the previous question is, when a subject is brought forward of a delicate nature, as to high personages, &c. or the discussion of which may call forth observations which might be of injurious consequences. Then the previous question is proposed: and, in the modern usage, the discussion of the main question is suspended, and the debate confined to the previous question. The use of it has been extended abusively to other cases: but in these it is an embarrassing procedure: its uses would be as well answered by other more simple Parliamentary forms, and therefore it should not be favoured, but restricted within as narrow limits as possible.

Whether a main question may be amended after the previous question on it has been moved and seconded? 2 *Hats.* 88. says, If the previous question has been moved and seconded, and also proposed from the chair, (by which he means stated by the Speaker for debate) it has been doubted whether an amendment can be admitted to the main question. He thinks it may, after the previous question moved and seconded; but not after it has been proposed from the chair. In this case he thinks the friends to the amendment must vote that the main question be not now put; and then move their amended question, which being made new by the amendment, is no longer the same which has been just suppressed, and therefore may be proposed as a new one. But this proceeding certainly endangers the main question, by dividing its friends, some of whom may chuse it unamended, rather than lose it altogether: while others of them may vote, as Hatsell advises, that the main question be not now put, with a view to move it again in an amended form. The enemies to the main question, by this manœuvre of the previous question, get the enemies to the amendment added to them on the first vote, and throw the friends of the main question under the embarrassment of rallying again as they can. To support his opinion too, he makes the deciding circumstance, whether an amendment may or may not be made, to be that the previous question has been proposed from the chair. But as the rule is that the House is in possession of a question as soon as it is moved and seconded, it cannot be more than possessed of it by its being also proposed from the chair. It may be said indeed, that the object of the previous question being to get rid of a question, which it is not expedient should be discussed, this object may be defeated by moving to amend, and, in the discussion of that motion, involving the subject of the main question. But so may the object of the previous question be defeated by moving the amended question, as Mr. Hatsell proposes, after the decision against putting the original question. He acknowledges too, that the practice has been to admit previous amendment, and only cites a few late instances to the contrary. On the whole, I should think it best to decide it ab inconvenienti, to wit, which is most inconvenient, to put it in the power of one side of the House to defeat a proposition by hastily moving the previous question, and thus forcing the main question to be put unamended; or to put it in the power of the other side to force on, incidentally at least, a discussion which would be better avoided? Perhaps the last is the least inconvenience; inasmuch as the Speaker, by confining the discussion rigorously to the amendment only, may prevent their going into the main question, and inasmuch also as so great a proportion of the cases in which the previous question is called for, are fair and proper subjects of public discussion, and ought not to be obstructed by a formality introduced for questions of a peculiar character.

SEC. XXXV.
AMENDMENTS.

ON an amendment being moved, a member who has spoken to the main question may speak again to the amendment. *Scob.* 23.

If an amendment be proposed, inconsistent with one already agreed to, it is a fit ground for its rejection by the House; but not within the competence of the Speaker to suppress as if it were against order. For were he permitted to draw questions of consistence within the vortex of order, he might usurp a negative on important modifications, and suppress, instead of subserving, the legislative will.

Amendments may be made so as totally to alter the nature of the proposition; and it is a way of getting rid of a proposition, by making it bear a sense different from what was intended by the movers, so that they vote against it themselves. 2 *Hats.* 79, 4, 82, 84. A new bill may be ingrafted by way of amendment, on the words "Be it enacted, &c." 1 *Grey* 190, 192.

If it be proposed to amend by leaving out certain words, it may be moved as an amendment to this amendment, to leave out a part of the words of the amendment, which is equivalent to leaving them in the bill. 2 *Hats.* 80, 9. The Parliamentary question is always, whether the words shall stand part of the bill?

When it is proposed to amend by inserting a paragraph, or part of one, the friends of the paragraph may make it as perfect as they can by amendments, before the question is put for inserting it. If it be received, it cannot be amended afterwards, in the same stage; because the House, has on a vote, agreed to it in that form. In like manner, if it is proposed to amend by striking out a paragraph, the friends of the paragraph are first to make it as perfect as they can by amendments, before the question is put for striking it out. If, on the question, it be retained, it cannot be amended afterwards: because a vote against striking out, is equivalent to a vote agreeing to it in that form.

When it is moved to amend, by striking out certain words, and inserting others, the manner of stating the question is, first to read the whole passage to be amended as it stands at present, then the words proposed to be struck out, next those to be inserted, and lastly, the whole passage as it will be when amended. And the question, if desired, is then to be divided, and put first on striking out. If carried, it is next on inserting the words proposed. If that be lost, it may be moved to insert others, 2 *Hats.* 80, 7.

A motion is made to amend by striking out certain words, and inserting others in their place, which is negatived. Then it is moved to strike out the same words, and to insert others, of a tenor entirely different from those first proposed. It is negatived. Then it is moved to strike out the same words and insert nothing, which is agreed to. All this is admissible; because to strike out and insert A, is one proposition. To strike out and insert B, is a different proposition. And to strike out and insert nothing, is still different. And the rejection of one proposition does not preclude the offering a different one. Nor would it change the case were the first motion divided, by putting the question first on striking out, and that negatived. For as putting the whole motion to the question at once, would not have precluded, the putting the half of it cannot do it.*

But if it had been carried affirmatively to strike out the words, and to insert A, it could not afterwards be permitted to strike out A and insert B. The mover of B should have notified while the insertion of A was under debate, that he would move to insert B. In which case, those who preferred it, would join in rejecting A.

After A is inserted, however, it may be moved to strike out a portion of the original paragraph, comprehending A, provided the coherence to be struck out, be so substantial as to make this effectively a different proposition. For then it is resolved into the common case of striking out a paragraph after amending it. Nor does any thing forbid a new insertion, instead of A and its coherence.

In Senate, January 25, 1798, a motion to postpone until the 2d Tuesday in February some amendments proposed to the constitution. . . . The words "until the 2d Tuesday in February," were struck out by way of amendment. Then it was moved, to add "until the 1st day of June." Objected that it was not in order, as the question should be first put on the longest time; therefore, after a shorter time decided against, a longer cannot be put to question. It was answered, that this rule takes place only in filling blanks for time. But when a specific time stands part of a motion, that may be struck out as well as any other part of the motion; and when struck out, a motion may be received to insert any other. In fact, it is not till they are struck out, and a blank for the time thereby produced, that the rule can begin to operate, by receiving all the propositions for different times, and putting the questions successively on the longest. Otherwise, it would be in the power of the mover, by inserting originally a short time, to preclude the possibility of a longer. For till the short time is struck out, you cannot insert a longer; and if, after it is struck out, you cannot do it, then it cannot be done at all. Suppose the first motion had been to amend by striking out "the 2d Tuesday of February," and inserting instead thereof "the 1st of June." It would have been regular then to divide the question, by proposing first the question to strike out, and

---

* In the case of a division of the question, and a decision against striking out, I advance doubtingly the opinion here expressed. I find no authority either way; and I know it may be viewed under a different aspect. It may be thought that having decided separately not to strike out the passage, the same question for striking out cannot be put over again, though with a view to a different insertion. Still I think it more reasonable and convenient, to consider the striking out and insertion, as forming one proposition; but should readily yield to any evidence that the contrary is the practice in Parliament.

then that to insert. Now this is precisely the effect of the present proceeding; only instead of one motion and two questions, there are two motions and two questions, to effect it; the motion being divided as well as the question.

When the matter contained in two bills might be better put into one, the manner is to reject the one, and incorporate its matter into another bill by way of amendment. Or, both may be referred to a committee to be made into one bill. 4 *Hats.* 319. So if the matter of one bill would be better distributed into two, any part may be struck out by way of amendment, and put into a new bill. If a section is to be transposed, a question must be put on striking it out where it stands, and another for inserting it in the place desired.

A bill passed by the one House with blanks. These may be filled up by the other; by way of amendments, returned to the first as such and passed. 3 *Hats.* 83.

The number prefixed to the section of a bill, being merely a marginal indication, and no part of the text of the bill, the clerk regulates that, the House or committee is only to amend the text.

SEC. XXXVI.
DIVISION OF THE QUESTION.

IF a question contain more parts than one, it may be divided into two or more questions. *Mem. in Hakew.* 29. But not as the right of an individual member, but with the consent of the House. For who is to decide whether a question is complicated or not? where it is complicated? into how many propositions it may be divided? The fact is, that the only mode of separating a complicated question is, by moving amendments to it; and these must be decided by the House on a question, unless the House orders it to be divided: as on the question December 2, 1640, making void the election of the knights for Worcester, on a motion, it was resolved, to make two questions of it, to wit, one on each knight. 2 *Hats.* 85, 86. So wherever there are several names in a question, they may be divided and put one by one. 9 *Grey* 444. So 1729, April 17, on an objection that a question was complicatd, it was separated by amendment. 2 *Hats.* 79, 5.

The soundness of these observations will be evident from the embarrassments produced by the 10th rule of the Senate, which says, *"if the question in debate contain several points, any member may have the same divided."*

1798, May 30, the Alien Bill in quasi-committee. To a section and proviso in the original, had been added two new provisoes by way of amendment. On a motion to strike out the section as amended, the question was desired to be divided. To do this, it must be put first on striking out either the former proviso, or some distinct member of the section. But when nothing remains but the last member of the section, and the provisoes, they cannot be divided so as to put the last member to question by itself; for the provisoes might thus be left standing alone, as exceptions to a rule, when the rule is taken away; or the new provisoes might be left to a second question, after having been decided on once before at the same reading; which is contrary to rule. But the question must be on striking out the last member of the section as amended. This sweeps away the exceptions with the rule, and relieves from inconsistence. A question to be divisible, must comprehend points so distinct and entire, that one of them being taken away, the other may stand entire. But a proviso or exception, without an enacting clause, does not contain an entire point or proposition.

May 31. The same bill being before the Senate. . . . There was a proviso that the bill should not extend, 1. To any foreign minister; nor, 2. to an person to whom the President should give a passport; nor, 3. to any alien merchant conforming himself to such regulations as the President shall prescribe, and a division of the question into its simplest elements, was called for. It was divided into four parts, the 4th taking in the words "conforming himself, &c." It was objected that the words "any alien merchant," could not be separated from their modifying words "conforming, &c." because these words, if left by themselves, contain no substantive idea, will make no sense. But admitting that the divisions of a paragraph into separate questions must be so made as that each part may stand by itself, yet, the House having, on the question, retained the two first divisions, the words "any alien merchant" may be struck out, and their modifying words will then attach themselves to the preceding description of persons, and become a modification of that description.

When a question is divided, after the question on the 1st member, the 2d is open to debate and amendment: because it is a known rule, that a person may rise and speak at any time before the question has been completely decided, by putting the negative, as well as affirmative side. But the question is not completely put, when the vote has been taken on the first member only. One half of the question, both affirmative and negative, remains still to be put. See Execut. Journ. June 25, 1795. *The same decision by President Adams.*

SEC. XXXVII.
CO-EXISTING QUESTIONS.

IT may be asked, whether the House can be in possession of two motions or propositions at the same time? So that, one of them being decided, the other goes to question without being moved anew? The answer must be special. When a question is interrupted by a vote of adjournment, it is thereby removed from before the House, and does not stand ipso facto before them at their next meeting: but must come forward in the usual way. So, when it is interrupted by the order of the day. Such other privileged questions also as dispose of the main question (e.g. the previous question, postponement or commitment,) remove it from before the House. But it is only suspended by a motion to amend, to withdraw, to read papers, or, by a question of order or privilege, and stands again before the House when these are decided. None but the class of privileged questions can be brought forward, while there is another question before the House, the rule being that when a motion has been made and seconded, no other can be received, except it be a privileged one.

SEC. XXXVIII.
EQUIVALENT QUESTIONS.

IF, on a question for rejection, a bill be retained, it passes of course to its next reading. *Hakew.* 141. *Scob.* 42. And a question for a second reading, determined negatively, is a rejection without farther question. 4 *Grey* 149. And see *Elsynge's Memor.* 42. in what cases questions are to be taken for rejection.

Where questions are perfectly equivalent, so that the negative of the one amounts to the affirmative of the other, and leaves no other alternative, the decision of the one concludes necessarily the other. 4 *Grey* 157. Thus the negative of striking out amounts to the affirmative of agreeing; and therefore, to put a question on agreeing after that on striking out, would be to put the same question in effect twice over. Not so in questions of amendments between the two Houses. A motion to recede being negatived, does not amount to a positive vote to insist, because there is another alternative, to wit, to adhere.

A bill originating in one House, is passed by the other with an amendment. A motion in the originating House to agree to the amendment is negatived. Does there result from this a vote of disagreement, or must the question on disagreement be expressly voted? The questions respecting amendments from another House are, 1. To agree. 2. Disagree. 3. Recede. 4. Insist. 5. Adhere.

1st.　To agree.

2nd.　To disagree. Either of these concludes the other necessarily: for the positive of either is exactly the equivalent of the negative of the other, and no other alternative remains. On either motion amendments to the amendment may be proposed, e.g. if it be moved to disagree, those who are for the amendment have a right to propose amendments, and to make it as perfect as they can, before the question of disagreeing is put.

3d.　To recede. You may then either insist or adhere.

4th.　To insist. You may then either recede or adhere.

5th.　To adhere. You may then either recede or insist.

Consequently the negative of these is not equivalent to a positive vote the other way. It does not raise so necessary an implication as may authorise the secretary by inference to enter another vote: for two alternatives still remain, either of which may be adopted by the House.

SEC. XXXIX.
THE QUESTION.

THE question is to be put first on the affirmative, and then on the negative side.

After the Speaker has put the affirmative part of the question, any member who has not spoken before to the question, may rise and speak before the negative be put. Because it is no full question till the negative part be put. *Scob.* 23. 2 *Hats.* 73.

But in small matters, and which are of course, such as receiving petitions, reports, withdrawing motions, reading papers, &c. the Speaker most commonly supposes the consent of the House, where no objection is expressed, and does not give them the trouble of putting the question formally. *Scob.* 22.2 *Hats.* 79, 2, 87. 5 *Grey* 129. 9 *Grey* 301.

SEC. XL.
BILLS, THIRD READING.

TO prevent bills from being passed by surprise, the House, by a standing order, directs that they shall not be put on their passage before a fixed hour, naming one at which the House is commonly full. *Hakew.* 153.

The usage of the Senate is not to put bills on their passage till noon.

A bill reported and passed to the third reading cannot on that day be read the third time and passed. Because this would be to pass on two readings in the same day.

At the third reading, the clerk reads the bill and delivers it to the Speaker, who states the title, that it is the third time of reading the bill, and that the question will be whether it shall pass? Formerly, the Speaker, or those who prepared a bill, prepared also a breviate or summary statement of its contents, which the Speaker read when he declared the state of the bill, at the several readings. Sometimes however, he read the bill itself, especially on its passage. *Hakew.* 136, 137, 153. *Coke* 22, 115. Latterly, instead of this, he, at the third reading, states the whole contents of the bill verbatim, only instead of reading the formal parts, "Be it enacted, &c." he states that "the preamble recites so and so. . . . the 1st section enacts that, &c. the 2d section enacts, &c."

But in the Senate of the United States, both of these formalities are dispensed with; the breviate presenting but an imperfect view of the bill, and being capable of being made to present a false one: and the full statement being an useless waste of time, immediately after a full reading by the clerk; and especially as every member has a printed copy in his hand.

A bill on the third reading, is not to be committed for the matter or body thereof; but to receive some particular clause or proviso, it hath been sometimes suffered, but as a thing very unusual. *Hakew.* 156. thus 27 *El.* 1584. a bill was committed on the third reading, having been formerly committed on the second, but is declared not usual. *D'Ewes 337. col. 2, 414, col. 2.*

When an essential provision has been omitted, rather than erase the bill, and render it suspicious, they add a clause on a separate paper, engrossed and called a ryder, which is read and put to the question three times. Elsynge's Memorials 59. 6 Grey 335. 1 Blackst. 183. For examples of ryders see 3 *Hats.* 121, 122, 124, 126. Every one is at liberty to bring in a ryder without asking leave. 10 *Grey* 52.

It is laid down as a general rule, that amendments proposed at the second reading shall be twice read, and those proposed at the third reading thrice read; as also all amendments from the other House. *Town. col.* 19, 23, 24, 25, 26, 27, 28.

It is with great, and almost invincible reluctance, that amendments are admitted at this reading, which occasion erasures or interlineations. Sometimes a proviso has been cut off from a bill; sometimes erased. 9 *Grey* 513.

This is the proper stage for filling up blanks; for if filled up before, and now altered by erasure, it would be peculiarly unsafe.

At his reading the bill is debated afresh, and for the most part is more spoken to, at this time, than on any of the former readings. *Hakew.* 153.

The debate on the question whether it should be read a third time? has discovered to its friends and opponents the arguments on which each side relies, and which of these appear to have influence with the House; they have had time to meet them with new arguments, and to put their old ones into new shapes. The former vote has tried the strength of the first opinion and furnished grounds to estimate the issue; and the question now offered for its passage, is the last occasion which is ever to be offered for carrying or rejecting it.

When the debate is ended, the Speaker, holding the bill in his hand, puts the question for its passage, by saying, "Gentlemen, all you who are of opinion that this bill shall pass, say aye," and after the answer of the ayes, "All those of the contrary opinion say no." *Hakew.* 154.

After the bill is passed, there can be no further alteration of it in any point. *Hakew.* 159.

SEC. XLI.
DIVISION OF THE HOUSE.

THE affirmative and negative of the question having been both put and answered, the Speaker declares whether the yeas or nays have it by the sound, if he be himself satisfied, and it stands as the judgment of the House. But if he be not himself satisfied which voice is the greater, or if, before any other member comes into the House, or before any new motion made (for it is too late after that) any member shall rise and declare himself dissatisfied with the Speaker's decision, then the Speaker is to divide the House. *Scob.* 24. 2 *Hats.* 140.

When the House of Commons is divided, the one party goes forth, and the other remains in the House. This has made it important which go forth, and which remain; because the latter gain all the indolent, the indifferent and inattentive. Their general rule therefore is, that those who give their votes for the preservation of the orders of the House, shall stay in, and those who are for introducing any new matter or alteration, or proceeding contrary to the established course, are to go out. But this rule is subject to many exceptions and modifications. 2 *Hats.* 134. 1 *Rush. p.* 3, *fol.* 92. *Scob.* 43, 52. *Co.* 12, 116. *D'Ewes.* 505. *col.* 1. *Mem. in Hakew.* 25, 29. as will appear by the following statement of who go forth.

Petition that it be received,* Read.	} Ayes.	
Lie on the table, Rejected after refusal to lie on table,	} Noes.	
Referred to a committee, or farther proceeding,	} Ayes.	
Bill, that it be brought in, Read 1st or 2d time, Engrossed, or read 3d time, Proceeding on every other stage, Committed,	} Ayes.	
To committee of the whole,	Noes.	
To a select committee,	Ayes.	
Report of bill to lie on table,	Noes.	
Be *now* read, Be taken into consideration 3 months hence,	} Ayes.	30 P. J. 251.
Amendments be read a 2d time,	Noes.	
Clause offered on report of bill be read 2d time,	} Ayes.	
For receiving a clause,		334.
With amendments be engrossed,		395.
That a bill be *now* read a 3d time,	Noes.	398.
Receive a ryder,		260.
Pass,	} Ayes.	259.
Be printed,		
Committees. That A take the chair, To agree to the whole or any part of report, That the H. do *now* resolve into committee, Speaker. That he now leave the chair, after order to go into committee, That he issue warrant for a new writ, Member. That none be absent without leave,	} Noes.	291.
Witness. That he be further examined,	Ayes.	344.
Previous question,	Noes.	
Blanks. That they be filled with the largest sum, Amendments. That words stand part of	} Ayes.	

* Noes 9 *Grey* 365.

Lords. That their amendment be read a 2d time,	} Noes.
Messenger be received,	
Orders of day to be now read, if before 2 o'clock,	} Ayes.
If after 2 o'clock,	Noes.
Adjournment, till the next sitting day, if before 4 o'clock,	} Ayes.
if after 4 o'clock,	Noes.
Over a sitting day (unless a previous resolution,)	} Ayes.
Over the 30th of January,	Noes.
For sitting on Sunday or any other day, not being a sitting day,	} Ayes.

The one party being gone forth, the Speaker names two tellers from the affirmative, and two from the negative side, who first count those sitting in the House, and report the number to the Speaker. Then they place themselves within the door, two on each side, and count those who went forth, as they come in, and report the number to the Speaker. *Mem. in Hakew.* 26.

A mistake in the report of the tellers may be rectified after the report made. 2 *Hats.* 145. *note.*

But in both Houses of Congress, all these intricacies are avoided. The Ayes first rise and are counted, standing in their places, by the President or Speaker. Then they sit, and the Noes rise and are counted in like manner.

In Senate, if they be equally divided, the Vice-President announces his opinion, which decides.

The constitution however has directed that "the Yeas and Nays of the members of either House on any question shall, at the desire of one fifth of those present, be entered on the journal." And again, that in all cases of reconsidering a bill, disapproved by the President, and returned with his objections, "the votes of both Houses shall be determined by Yeas and Nays, and the names of the persons voting for and against the bill, shall be entered on the journals of each House respectively."

By the 11th rule of the Senate, when the Yeas and Nays shall be called for by one fifth of the members present, each member called upon, shall, unless for special reasons he be excused by the Senate, declare openly and without debate, his assent or dissent to the question. In taking the Yeas and Nays, and upon the call of the House, the names of the members shall be taken alphabetically.

When it is proposed to take the vote by Yeas and Nays, the President or Speaker states, that "the question is, whether e.g. the bill shall pass? that it is proposed that the Yeas and Nays shall be entered on the journal. Those therefore who desire it will rise." If he finds and declares that one fifth have risen, he then states that "those who are of opinion that the bill shall pass are to answer in the affirmative, those of the contrary opinion in the negative." The clerk then calls over the names alphabetically, notes the Yea or Nay of each, and gives the list to the President or Speaker, who declares the result. In Senate, if there be an equal division, the secretary calls on the Vice-President, and notes his affirmative or negative, which becomes the decision of the House.

In the House of Commons, every member must give his vote the one way or the other. *Scob.* 24. As it is not permitted to any one to withdraw who is in the House when the question is put, nor is any one to be told in the division who was not in when the question was put. 2 *Hats.* 140.

This last position is always true when the vote is by Yeas and Nays; where the negative as well as affirmative of the question is stated by the President at he same time, and the vote of both sides begins and proceeds pari passu. It is true also when the question is put in the usual way, if the negative has also been put. But if it has not, the member entering, or any other member, may speak, and even propose amendments, by which the debate may be opened again, and the question be greatly deferred. And as some who have answered aye, may have been changed by the new arguments, the affirmative must be put over again. If then the member entering may, by speaking a few words, occasion a repetition of the question, it would be useless to deny it on his simple call for it.

While the House is telling, no member may speak, or move out of his place; for it any mistake be suspected, it must be told again. *Mem. in Hakew.* 26. 2 *Hats.* 143.

If any difficulty arises in point of order during the division, the Speaker is to decide peremptorily, subject to the future censure of the House if irregular. He sometimes permits old experienced members to assist him with their advice, which they do, sitting in their seats, covered, to avoid the appearance of debate; but this can only be with the Speaker's leave, else the division might last several hours. 2 *Hats.* 143.

The voice of the majority decides. For the lex majoris partis is the law of all councils, elections, &c. where not otherwise expressly provided. *Hakew.* 93. But if the House be equally divided, "semper presumatur pro negante;" that is, the former law is not to be changed but by a majority. *Town. col.* 134.

But in the Senate of the United States, the Vice-President decides, when the House is divided. Constitution United States I. 3.

When from counting the House on a division, it appears that there is not a quorum, the matter continues exactly in the state in which it was before the division, and must be resumed at that point on any future day. 2 *Hats.* 126.

1606, May 1, On a question whether a member having said yea, may afterwards sit and change his opinion? a precedent was remembered by the Speaker, of Mr. Morris, attorney of the wards in 39 *Eliz.* who in like case changed his opinion. *Mem. in Hakew.* 27.

SEC. XLII.
TITLE.

AFTER the bill has passed, and not before the title may be amended, and is to be fixed by a question; and the bill is then sent to the other House.

SEC. XLIII.
RECONSIDERATION.

WHEN a question has been once made and carried in the affirmative, or negative, it shall be in order for any member of the majority, to move for the reconsideration thereof. Rule 22.

1798, January. A bill on its second reading, being amended, and on the question whether it shall be read a third time negatived, was restored by a decision to reconsider that question. Here the votes of negative and reconsideration, like positive and negative quantities in equation, destroy one another, and are as if they were expunged from the journals. Consequently the bill is open for amendment, just so far as it was the moment preceding the question for the third reading. That is to say, all parts of the bill are open for amendment, except those on which votes have been already taken in its present stage. So also it may be recommitted.

The rule permitting a reconsideration of a question affixing to it no limitation of time or circumstance, it may be asked whether there is no limitation? If, after the vote, the paper on which it is passed has been parted with, there can be no reconsideration: as if a vote has been for the passage of a bill, and the bill has been sent to the other House. But where the paper remains, as on a bill rejected; when, or under what circum-

stances does it cease to be susceptible of reconsideration? This remains to be settled; unless a sense that the right of reconsideration is a right to waste the time of the House in repeated agitations of the same question, so that it shall never know when a question is done with, should induce them to reform this anomalous proceeding.

In Parliament, a question once carried, cannot be questioned again at the same session; but must stand as the judgment of the House. *Town. col.* 67. *Mem. in Hakew.* 33. And a bill once rejected, another of the same substance cannot be brought in again the same session. *Hakew.* 158. 6 *Grey* 392. But this does not extend to prevent putting the same question in different stages of a bill; because every stage of a bill submits the whole and every part of it to the opinion of the House, as open for amendment, either by insertion or omission, though the same amendment has been accepted or rejected in a former stage. So in reports of committees, e.g. report of an address, the same question is before the House, and open for free discussion. *Town. col.* 26. 2 *Hats.* 98, 100, 101. So orders of the House, or instructions to committees may be discharged. So a bill, begun in one House, sent to the other, and there rejected, may be renewed again in that other, passed and sent back. *Ib.* 92. 3 *Hats.* 161. Or if, instead of being rejected, they read it once and lay it aside, or amend it, and put it off a month, they may order in another to the same effect, with the same or a different title. *Hakew.* 97, 98.

Divers expedients are used to correct the effects of this rule; as by passing an explanatory act, if any thing has been omitted or ill expressed, 3 *Hats.* 278. or an act to enforce, and make more effectual an act, &c. or to rectify mistakes in an act, &c. or a committee on one bill may be instructed to receive a clause to rectify the mistakes of another. Thus, June 24, 1685, a clause was inserted in a bill for rectifying a mistake committed by a clerk in engrossing a bill of supply. 2 *Hats.* 194, 6. Or the session may be closed for one, two, three or more days, and a new one commenced. But then all matters depending must be finished, or they fall, and are to begin de novo. 2 *Hats.* 94, *to* 98. Or a part of the subject may be taken up by another bill, or taken up in a different way. 6 *Grey* 304, 316.

And in cases of the last magnitude, this rule has not been so strictly and verbally observed as to stop indispensable proceedings altogether. 2 *Hats.* 92, 98. Thus when the address on the preliminaries of peace in 1782 had been lost by a majority of one, on account of the importance of the question, and smallness of the majority, the same question in substance, though with some words not in the first, and which might change the opinion of some members, was brought on again and carried; as the motives for it were thought to outweigh the objection of form. 2 *Hats*. 99, 100.

A second bill may be passed to continue an act of the same session; or to enlarge the time limited for its execution. 2 *Hats*. 95, 98. This is not in contradiction to the first act.

SEC. XLIV.
BILLS SENT TO THE OTHER HOUSE.

ALL bills passed in Senate shall, before they are sent to the House of Representatives, be examined by the committees respectively, who brought in such bills, or to whom the same have been last committed in Senate. Rule 23.

A bill from the other House is sometimes ordered to lie on the table. 2 *Hats*. 97.

When bills passed in one House and sent to the other, are grounded on special facts requiring proof, it is usual either by message, or at a conference, to ask the grounds and evidence; and this evidence, whether arising out of papers, or from the examination of witnesses, is immediately communicated. 3 *Hats*. 48.

SEC. XLV.
AMENDMENTS BETWEEN THE HOUSES.

WHEN either House, e.g. the House of Commons, sends a bill to the other, the other may pass it with amendments. The regular progression in this case is, that the Commons disagree to the amendment; the Lords insist on it; the Commons insist on their disagreement; the Lords adhere to their amendment; the Commons adhere to their disagreement. The term of insisting, may be repeated as often as they choose, to keep the question open. But the first adherence by either, renders it necessary for the other to recede or adhere also; when the matter is usually suffered to fall. 10 *Grey* 148. Latterly however, there are instances of their having gone to a second adherence. There must be an absolute conclusion of the subject somewhere, or otherwise transactions between the Houses would become endless. 3 *Hats*. 268, 270. The term of insisting, we are told by Sir John Trevor, was then (1679) newly introduced into Parliamentary usage, by the Lords. 7 *Grey* 94. It was certainly a happy innovation, as it multiplies the opportunities of trying modifications which may bring the Houses to a concurrence. Either House however is free to pass over the term of insisting, and to adhere in the first instance.

10 *Grey* 146. But it is not respectful to the other. In the ordinary Parliamentary course, there are two free conferences at least before an adherence. 10 *Grey* 147.

Either House may recede from its amendment and agree to the bill; or recede from their disagreement to the amendment, and agree to the same absolutely, or with an amendment. For here the disagreement and receding destroy one another, and the subject stands as before the disagreement. *Elsynge* 23, 27. 9 *Grey* 476.

But the House cannot recede from, or insist on its own amendment, with an amendment: for the same reason that it cannot send to the other House an amendment to its own act after it has passed the act. They may modify an amendment from the other House by ingrafting an amendment on it, because they have never assented to it; but they cannot amend their own amendment, because they have, on the question, passed it in that form. 9 *Grey* 353. 10 *Grey* 240. In Senate, March 29, 1798. Nor where one House has adhered to their amendment, and the other agrees with an amendment, can the first House depart from the form which they have fixed by an adherence.

In the case of a money bill, the Lords proposed amendments, become by delay, confessedly necessary. The Commons however, refused them, as infringing on their privilege as to money bills; but they offered themselves to add to the bill a proviso to the same effect, which had no coherence with the Lords' amendments; and urged that it was an expedient warranted by precedent, and not unparliamentary, in a case become impracticable and irremediable in any other way. 3 *Hats.* 256, 266, 270, 271. But the Lords refused, and the bill was lost. 1 *Chand.* 288. A like case, 1 *Chand.* 311. So the Commons resolve that it is unparliamentary to strike out at a conference any thing in a bill which hath been agreed and passed by both Houses. 6 *Grey* 274. 1 *Chand.* 312.

A motion to amend an amendment from the other House, takes precedence of a motion to agree or disagree.

A bill originating in one House, is passed by the other with an amendment. The originating House agrees to their amendment with an amendment. The other may agree to their amendment with an amendment; that being only in the second and not the third degree. For as to the amending House, the first amendment with which they passed the bill, is a part of its text; it is the only text they have agreed to. The amendment to that text by the originating House, therefore, is only in the first degree, and the amendment to that again by the amending House is only in the second, to wit, an amendment to an amendment, and so admissible. Just so when, on a bill from the originating House, the other, at its second reading, makes an amendment; on the third reading, this amendment is become the text of the bill, and if an amendment to it be moved, an amendment to that amendment may also be moved, as being only in the second degree.

SEC. XLVI.
CONFERENCES.

IT is on the occasion of amendments by one House disagreed to by the other, that conferences are usually asked; but they may be asked 4 *Hats.* 4, 223, in all cases of difference of opinion between the two Houses, on matters depending between them. 4 *Hats.* 4, 5, 7. The request of a conference, however, must always be by the House which is possessed of the papers. 3 *Hats.* 31. 1 *Grey* 425. 4 *Hats.* 3, 43.

Conferences may be either simple or free. At a conference simply, written reasons are prepared by the House asking it, and they are read and delivered, without debate, to the managers of the other House at the conference; but are not then to be answered. 3 *Grey* 144. The other House then, if satisfied, vote the reasons satisfactory, or say nothing; if not satisfied, they resolve them not satisfactory, and ask a conference on the subject of the last conference, where they read and deliver in like manner written answers to those reasons. 3 *Grey* 183. They are meant, chiefly, to record the justification of each House to the nation at large, and to posterity, and in proof that the miscarriage of a necessary measure is not imputable to them. 3 *Grey* 255. At free conferences, which are asked after two conferences, 4 *Hats.* 37, 40. the managers discuss viva voce and freely, and interchange propositions for such modifications as may be made in a Parliamentary way, and may bring the sense of the two Houses together. The conferees may argue in support of what is done in their House, but not against it, nor assent to any new thing there propounded, till their House be informed and agree to it. 4 *Hats.* 31, 33. And each party reports in writing to their respective Houses, the substance of what is said on both sides, and it is entered in their journals. 9 *Grey* 220. 3 *Hats.* 280. 4 *Hats.* 48. This report cannot be amended or altered, as that of a committee may be. *Journ. Sen. May 24, 1796.*

A conference may be asked before the House asking it has come to a resolution of disagreement, insisting or adhering. 3 Hats. 269, 341. In which case the papers are not left with the other conferees, but are brought back to be the foundation of the vote to be given. And this is the most reasonable and respectful proceeding. For, as was urged by the Lords on a particular occasion, "it is held vain and below the wisdom of Parliament to reason or argue against fixed resolutions, and upon terms of impossibility to persuade." 3 *Hats.* 226. So the Commons say "an adherence is never delivered at a free conference, which implies debate." 10 *Grey* 147. And on another occasion, the Lords made it an objection that the Commons had asked a free conference after they had made resolutions of adhering. It was then affirmed, however, on the part of the Commns, that nothing was more Parliamentary than to proceed with free conferences after adhering; 3 *Hats.* 269. and we do in fact see instances of conference, or of free conference, asked after the resolution of disagreeing, 3 *Hats.* 251, 253, 260, 286, 291, 316, 239; of insisting, *ib.* 280, 296, 299, 319, 322, 355; of adhering, *ib.* 269, 270, 283, 300; and even of a second or final adherence, 3 *Hats.* 270. And in all cases of conference asked after a vote of disagreement, &c. the conferees of the House asking it, are to leave the papers with the conferees of the other: and in one case, where they refused to receive them, they were left on the table in the conference chamber. *Ib.* 271, 317, 323, 354. 10 *Grey* 146.

The Commons affirm that it is usual to have two free conferences or more, before either House proceeds to adhere: because, before that time, the Houses have not had the full opportunity of making replies to one another's arguments; and to adhere so suddenly and unexpectedly, excludes all possibility of offering expedients. 4 *Hats.* 330.

After a free conference, the usage is to proceed with free conferences, and not to return again to a conference. 3 *Hats.* 270. 9 *Grey* 229.

After a conference denied, a free conference may be asked. 1 *Grey* 45.

When a conference is asked, the subject of it must be expressed, or the conference not agreed to. *Ord. H. Commons* 89. 1 *Grey* 425. 7 *Grey* 31. 4 *Hats.* 20, 46. They are sometimes asked to enquire concerning an offence, or default of a member of the other House. 6 *Grey* 181. 1 *Chandler* 304. Or the failure of the other House to present to the king a bill passed by both Houses. 8 *Grey* 302. Or on information received, and relating to the safety of the nation. 10 *Grey* 171. Or, when the methods of Parliament are thought by the one House to have been departed from by the other, a conference is asked to come to a right understanding thereon. 10 *Grey* 148. So when an unparliamentary message has been sent, instead of answering it, they ask a conference. 3 *Grey* 155. Formerly, an address, or articles of impeachment, or a bill with amendments, or a vote of the House, or concurrence in a vote, or a message from the king, were sometimes communicated by way of conference. 6 *Grey* 128, 300, 387. 7 *Grey* 80. 8 *Grey* 210, 255. 1 *Torbuck's Deb.* 278. 10 *Grey* 293. 1 *Chandler* 49, 287. But this is not the modern practice. 8 *Grey* 255.

A conference has been asked after the first reading of a bill. 1 *Grey* 194. This is a singular instance.

During the time of a conference the House can do no business. As soon as the names of the managers are called over, and they are gone to the conference, the Speaker leaves the chair, without any question, and resumes it on the return of the managers. It is the same while the managers of an impeachment are at the House of Lords. 4 *Hats.* 47, 209, 288.

SEC. XLVII.
MESSAGES.

MESSAGES between the Houses are to be sent only while both Houses are sitting. 3 *Hats.* 15. They are received during a debate, without adjourning the debate. 3 *Hats.* 22.

In Senate the messengers are introduced in any state of business, except, 1. While a question is putting. 2. While the Yeas and Nays are calling. 3. While the ballots are calling. The first case is short: the second and third are cases where any interruption might occasion errors difficult to be corrected. So arranged June 15, 1798.

In the House of Representatives, as in Parliament, if the House be in committee when a messenger attends, the Speaker takes the chair to receive the message, and then quits it to return into committee, without any question or interruption. 4 *Grey* 226.

Messengers are not saluted by the members, but by the Speaker for the House. 2 *Grey* 253, 274.

If messengers commit an error in delivering their message, they may be admitted, or called in, to correct their message. 4 *Grey* 41. Accordingly, March 13, 1800, the Senate having made two amendments to a bill from the House of Representatives, their secretary, by mistake, delivered one only; which being inadmissible by itself, that House disagreed, and notified the Senate of their disagreement. This produced a discovery of the mistake. The secretary was sent to the other House to correct his mistake, the correction was received, and the two amendments acted on de novo.

As soon as the messenger who has brought bills from the other House, has retired, the Speaker holds the bill in his hand, and acquaints the House "that the other House have, by their messenger, sent certain bills," and then reads their titles, and delivers them to the clerk to be safely kept, till they shall be called for to be read. *Hak.* 178.

It is not the usage for one House to inform the other by what numbers a bill has passed. 10 *Grey* 150. Yet they have sometimes recommended a bill, as of great importance to the consideration of the House to which it is sent. 3 *Hats.* 25. Nor when they have rejected a bill from the other House, do they give notice of it; but it passes sub silentio, to prevent unbecoming altercations. 1 *Blackst.* 183.

But in Congress, the rejection is notified by message to the House in which the bill originated.

A question is never asked by the one House of the other by way of message, but only at a conference: for this is an interrogatory, not a message. 3 *Grey* 151, 181.

When a bill is sent by one House to the other, and is neglected, they may send a message to remind them of it. 3 *Hats.* 25. 5 *Grey* 154. But if it be mere inattention, it is better to have it done informally, by communications between the Speakers, or members of the two Houses.

Where the subject of a message is of a nature that it can properly be communicated to both Houses of Parliament, it is expected that this communication should be made to both on the same day. But where a message was accompanied with an original declaration, signed by the party to which the message referred, its being sent to one House was not noticed by the other, because the declaration, being original, could not possibly be sent to both Houses at the same time. 2 *Hats.* 260, 261, 262.

The king having sent original letters to the Commons, afterwards desires they may be returned, that he may communicate them to the Lords. 1 *Chandler* 303.

SEC. XLVIII.
ASSENT.

THE House which has received a bill and passed it, may present it for the king's assent, and ought to do it, though they have not by message notified to the other, their passage of it. Yet the notifying by message is a form which ought to be observed between the two Houses from motives of respect, and good understanding. 2 *Hats.* 242. Were the bill to be withheld from being presented to the king, it would be an infringement of the rules of Parliament. *Ib.*

When a bill has passed both Houses of Congress, the House last acting on it, notifies its passage to the other, and delivers the bill to the joint com-

mittee of enrollment, who see that it is truly enrolled in parchment. When the bill is enrolled, it is not to be written in paragraphs, but solidly and all of a piece, that the blanks between the paragraphs may not give room for forgery. 9 *Grey* 143. *It is then put into the hands of the clerk of the House of Representatives to have it signed by the Speaker. The clerk then brings it by way of message to the Senate to be signed by their President. The secretary of the Senate returns it to the committee of enrollment, who present it to the President of the United States. If he approves, he signs and deposits it among the rolls in the office of the secretary of state, and notifies by message the House in which it originated, that he has approved and signed it; of which that House informs the other by message. If the President disapproves, he is to return it, with his objections, to that House in which it shall have originated; who are to enter the objections at large on their journal, and proceed to reconsider it. If after such reconsideration, two thirds of that House shall agree to pass the bill, it shall be sent, together with the President's objections, to the other House, by which it shall likewise be reconsidered; and if approved by two thirds of that House, it shall become a law. If any bill shall not be returned by the President within ten days (Sunday excepted) after it shall have been presented to him, the same shall be a law, in like manner as if he had signed it, unless the Congress, by their adjournment, prevent its return; in which case it shall not be a law.* Constitution United States, I. 7.

Every order, resolution, or vote, to which the concurrence of the Senate and House of Representatives may be necessary, (except on a question of adjournment,) shall be presented to the President of the United States, and before the same shall take effect, shall be approved by him, or being disapproved by him, shall be repassed by two thirds of the Senate and House of Representatives, according to the rules and limitations prescribed in the case of a bill. Constitution United States, I. 7.

SEC. XLIX.
JOURNALS.

EACH House shall keep a journal of its proceedings, and from time to time publish the same, excepting such parts as may, in their judgment, require secrecy. Constitution I. 5.

Every vote of Senate shall be entered on the journals, and a brief statement of the contents of each petition, memorial or paper, presented to the Senate, be also inserted on the journals. Rule 24.

The proceedings of Senate, when they shall act in their Executive capacity shall be kept in separate & distinct books. Rule 25.

The proceedings of the Senate, when not acting as in a committee of the House, shall be entered on the journals, as concisely as possible, care being taken to detail a true account of the proceedings. Rule 26.

The titles of bills, and such parts thereof only as shall be affected by proposed amendments, shall be inserted on the journals. Rule 27.

If a question is interrupted by a vote to adjourn, or to proceed to the orders of the day, the original question is never printed in the journal, it never having been a vote, nor introductory to any vote: but when suppressed by the previous question, the first question must be stated, in order to introduce and make intelligible the second. 2 *Hats.* 83.

So also when a question is postponed, adjourned, or laid on the table, the original question, though not yet a vote, must be expressed in the journals; because it makes part of the vote of postponement, adjourning, or laying it on the table.

Where amendments are made to a question, those amendments are not printed in the journals separated from the question; but only the question as finally agreed to by the House. The rule of entering in the journals only what the House has agreed to, is founded in great prudence and good sense; as there may be many questions proposed which it may be improper to publish to the world, in the form in which they are made. 2 *Hats.* 85.

In both Houses of Congress all questions whereon the Yeas and Nays are desired by one fifth of the members present, whether decided affirmatively or negatively, must be entered in the journals. Constitution I. 5.

The first order for printing the votes of the House of Commons, was October 30, 1685. 1 *Chandler* 387.

Some judges have been of opinion, that the journals of the House of Commons are no records, but only remembrances. But this is not law. *Hob.* 110, 111. *Lex. Parl.* 114, 115. *Journ. H. C. Mar. 17, 1592. Hale Parl.* 105. For the Lords in their House have power of judicature, the Commons in their House have power of judicature, and both Houses together have power of judicature; and the book of the clerk of the House of Commons is a record, as is affirmed by act of Parliament; 6 *H.* 8. *c.* 16. 4 *Inst.* 23, 24. and every member of the House of Commons hath a judicial place. 4 *Inst.* 15. As records, they are open to every person, and a printed vote of either House is sufficient ground for the other to notice it. Either may appoint a committee to inspect the journals of the other, and report what has been done by the other in any particular case. 2 *Hats.* 261. 3 *Hats.* 27, 30. Every member has a right to see the journals, and to take and publish votes from them. Being a record, every one may see and publish them. 6 *Grey* 118, 119.

On information of a misentry or omission of an entry in the journal, a committee may be appointed to examine and rectify it, and report it to the House. 2 *Hats*. 194, 5.

SEC. L.
ADJOURNMENT.

THE two Houses of Parliament have the sole, separate, and independent power of adjourning each their respective Houses. The king has no authority to adjourn them; he can only signify his desire, and it is in the wisdom and prudence of either House to comply with his requisition, or not, as they see fitting. 2 *Hats*. 232. 1 *Blackstone* 186. 5 *Grey* 122.

By the Constitution of the United States, a smaller number than a majority may adjourn from day to day. I. 5. But "neither House, during the session of Congress, shall, without the consent of the other, adjourn for more than three days, nor to any other place than that in which the two Houses shall be sitting." I. 5. And in case of disagreement between them with respect to the time of adjournment, the President may adjourn them to such time as he shall think proper. Constitution II. 3.

A motion to adjourn simply, cannot be amended as by adding "to a particular day." But must be put simply "that this House do now adjourn?" and if carried in the affirmative, it is adjourned to the next sitting day, unless it has come to a previous resolution "that at its rising it will adjourn to a particular day," and then the House is adjourned to that day. 2 *Hats*. 82.

Where it is convenient that the business of the House be suspended for a short time, as for a conference presently to be held, &c. it adjourns during pleasure. 2 *Hats*. 305. Or for a quarter of an hour. 5 *Grey* 331.

If a question be put for adjournment, it is no adjournment till the Speaker pronounces it. 5 *Grey* 137. And from courtesy and respect, no member leaves his place till the Speaker has passed on.

SEC. LI.
A SESSION.

PARLIAMENT have three modes of separation, to wit, by adjournment, by prorogation, or dissolution by the king, or by the efflux of the term for which they were elected. Prorogation or dissolution constitutes there what is called a session, provided some act has passed. In this case, all matters depending before them are discontinued, and at their next meeting are to be taken up de novo, if taken up at all. 1 *Blackst.* 186. Adjournment, which is by themselves, is no more than a continuance of the session from one day to another, or for a fortnight, a month, &c. ad libitum. All matters depending remain in statu quo, and when they meet again, be the term ever so distant, are resumed without any fresh commencement, at the point at which they were left. 1 *Lev.* 165. *Lex. Parl. c.* 2. 1 *Ro. Rep.* 29. 4 *Inst.* 7, 27, 28. *Hutt.* 61. 1 *Mod.* 252. *Ruffh. Jac. L. Dict. Parliament.* 1 *Blackst.* 186. Their whole session is considered in law but as one day, and has relation to the first day thereof. *Bro. Abr. Parliament* 86.

Committees may be appointed to sit during a recess by adjournment, but not by prorogation. 5 *Grey* 374. 9 *Grey* 350. 1 *Chandler* 50. Neither House can continue any portion of itself in any Parliamentary function beyond the end of the session, without the consent of the other two branches. When done, it is by a bill constituting them commissioners for the particular purpose.

Congress separate in two ways only, to wit, by adjournment, or dissolution by the efflux of their time. What then constitutes a session with them? A dissolution certainly closes one session, and the meeting of the new Congress begins another. The constitution authorises the President "on extraordinary occasions, to convene both Houses or either of them." I. 3. If convened by the President's proclamation, this must begin a new session, and of course determine the preceding one to have been a session. So if it meets under the clause of the constitution which says, "the Congress shall assemble at least once in every year, and such meeting shall be on the first Monday in December, unless they shall by law appoint a different day," I. 4. this must begin a new session. For even if the last adjournment was to this day, the act of adjournment is merged in the higher authority of the constitution, and the meeting will be under that, and not under their adjournment. So far we have fixed land marks for determining sessions. In other cases, it is declared by the joint vote authorising the President of the Senate and the Speaker to close the session on a fixed day, which is usually in the following form, "Resolved by the Senate and House of Representatives, that the President of the Senate and the Speaker of the House of Representatives, be authorised to close the present session, by adjourning their respective Houses on the———— day of————."

When it was said above, that all matters depending before Parliament were discontinued by the determination of the session, it was not meant for judiciary cases, depending before the House of Lords, such as impeachments, appeals, and writs of error. These stand continued of course, to the next session. *Raym.* 120, 381, *Ruffh. Jac. L. D. Parliament.*

Impeachments stand in like manner continued before the Senate of the United States.

SEC. LII.

TREATIES.

THE President of the United States has power, by and with the advice and consent of the Senate, to make treaties, provided two thirds of the Senators present concur. Constitution United States II. 2.

Resolved that all confidential communications, made by the President of the United States to the Senate, shall be, by the members thereof, kept inviolably secret; and that all treaties, which may hereafter be laid before the Senate shall also be kept secret until the Senate shall, by their resolution, take off the injunction of secrecy. December 22, 1800.

Treaties are legislative acts. A treaty is a law of the land. It differs from other laws only as it must have the consent of a foreign nation, being but a contract with respect to that nation. In all countries, I believe, except England, treaties are made by the legislative power: and there also, if they touch the laws of the land, they must be approved by Parliament. *Ware v. Hylton. 3 Dallas Rep.* 273. It is acknowledged, for instance, that the king of Great Britain cannot by a treaty make a citizen of an alien. *Vattel. B.* 1. *c.* 19. *sec.* 214. An act of Parliament was necessary to validate the American treaty of 1783. And abundant examples of such acts can be cited. In the case of the treaty of Utrecht in 1712, the commercial articles required the concurrence of Parliament. But a bill brought in for that purpose was rejected. France, the other contracting party, suffered these articles, in practice, to be not insisted on, and adhered to the rest of the treaty. 4 *Russel's Hist. Mod. Europe* 457. 2 *Smollet* 242, 246.†

By the Constitution of the United States, this department of legislation is confided to two branches only of the ordinary legislature; the President originating, and the Senate having a negative. To what subjects this power extends, has not been defined in detail by the constitution; nor are we entirely agreed among ourselves. 1. *It is admitted that it must concern the foreign nation party to the contract, or it would be a mere nullity, res inter alios acta.* 2. *By the general power to make treaties, the constitution must have intended to comprehend only those subjects which*

† The treaty of the Pardo between Spain & G.B. in 1739. being disapproved by parliament, was not ratified. In consequence whereof the war it was intended to prevent took place. Observns. of France on Memorial of England. pa. 107.

[420]

are usually regulated by treaty, and cannot be otherwise regulated. 3. It must have meant to except out of these the rights reserved to the states; for surely the President and Senate cannot do by treaty what the whole government is interdicted from doing in any way. 4. And also to except those subjects of legislation in which it gave a participation to the House of Representatives. This last exception is denied by some, on the ground that it would leave very little matter for the treaty power to work on. The less the better, say others. The constitution thought it wise to restrain the Executive and Senate from entangling and embroiling our affairs with those of Europe. Besides, as the negotiations are carried on by the Executive alone, the subjecting to the ratification of the Representatives such articles as are within their participation is no more inconvenient than to the Senate. But the ground of this exception is denied as unfounded. For examine, e.g. the treaty of commerce with France, and it will be found that out of thirty one articles, there are not more than small portions of two or three of them which would not still remain as subjects of treaties, untouched by these exceptions.

Treaties being declared, equally with the laws of the United States, to be the supreme law of the land, it is understood that an act of the legislature alone can declare them infringed and rescinded. This was accordingly the process adopted in the case of France in 1798.

It has been the usage for the Executive, when it communicates a treaty to the Senate for their ratification, to communicate also the correspondence of the negotiators. This having been omitted in the case of the Prussian treaty, was asked by a vote of the House of February 12, 1800, and was obtained. And in December 1800, the convention of that year between the United States and France, with the report of the negotiations by the envoys, but not their instructions, being laid before the Senate, the instructions were asked for and communicated by the President.

The mode of voting on questions of ratifications is by nominal call.

Resolved, as a standing rule, that whenever a treaty shall be laid before the Senate for ratification, it shall be read a first time for information only; when no motion to reject, ratify or modify the whole or any part shall be received.

That its second reading shall be for consideration; and on a subsequent day, when it shall be taken up as in a committee of the whole, and every one shall be free to move a question on any particular article in this form, "Will the Senate advise and consent to the ratification of this article?" or to propose amendments thereto, either by inserting or by leaving out words, in which last case the question shall be, "Shall the words stand part of the article?" And in every of the said cases, the concurrence of two thirds of the Senators present shall be requisite to decide affirma-

[421]

tively. And when through the whole, the proceedings shall be stated to the House, and questions be again severally put thereon for confirmation, or new ones proposed, requiring in like manner a concurrence of two thirds for whatever is retained or inserted.

That the votes so confirmed shall, by the House, or a committee thereof, be reduced into the form of a ratification, with or without modifications, as may have been decided, and shall be proposed on a subsequent day, when every one shall again be free to move amendments, either by inserting or leaving out words; in which last case the question shall be, "Shall the words stand part of the resolution?" And in both cases the concurrence of two thirds shall be requisite to carry the affirmative; as well as on the final question to advise and consent to the ratification in the form agreed to. Rule of January 6, 1801.

Resolved, that when any question may have been decided by the Senate, in which two thirds of the members present are necessary to carry the affirmative, any member who voted on that side which prevailed in the question, may be at liberty to move for a reconsideration: and a motion for reconsideration shall be decided by a majority of votes. Rule of February 3, 1801.

SEC. LIII.

IMPEACHMENT.

THE House of Representatives shall have the sole power of impeachment. Constitution United States, I. 3.

The Senate shall have the sole power to try all impeachments. When sitting for that purpose, they shall be on oath or affirmation. When the President of the United States is tried, the chief justice shall preside: and no person shall be convicted without the concurrence of two thirds of the members present. Judgment in cases of impeachment shall not extend further than to removal from office, and disqualification to hold and enjoy any office of honor, trust, or profit under the United States. But the party convicted shall nevertheless be liable and subject to indictment, trial, judgment and punishment, according to law. Constitution, I. 3.

The President, Vice-President, and all civil officers of the United States, shall be removed from office on impeachment for, and conviction of treason, bribery, or other high crimes and misdemeanors. Constitution, II. 4.

The trial of crimes, except in cases of impeachment, shall be by jury. Constitution, III. 2.

These are the provisions of the Constitution of the United States on the subject of impeachments. The following is a sketch of some of the principles and practices of England on the same subject.

Jurisdiction. The Lords cannot impeach any to themselves, nor join in the accusation, because they are the judges. *Seld. Judic. in Parl.* 12, 63. (A work of doubtful authority.) 4 *Hats.* 153, 186. Nor can they proceed against a Commoner but on complaint of the Commons. *Ib.* 84. The Lords may not, by the law, try a Commoner for a capital offence, on the information of the king, or a private person; because the accused is entitled to a trial by his peers generally; but on accusation by the House of Commons, they may proceed against the delinquent of whatsoever degree, and whatsoever be the nature of the offence; for there they do not assume to themselves trial at common law. The Commons are then instead of a jury, and the judgment is given on their demand, which is instead of a verdict. So the Lords do only judge, but not try the delinquent. *Ib.* 6, 7. But Wooddeson denies that a Commoner can now be charged capitally before the Lords, even by the Commons; and cites Fitzharris's case, 1681, impeached of high treason, where the Lords remitted the prosecution to the inferior court. 8 *Grey's Deb.* 325 . . . 7. 2 *Wooddeson* 601, 576. 3 *Seld.* 1610, 1619, 1641. 4 *Blacks.* 257. 3 *Seld.* 1604, 1618, 9, 1656. 4 *Hats.* 200. *et passim contra.*

Accusation. *The Commons, as the grand inquest of the nation, become suitors for penal justice.* 2 *Wood.* 597, 6 *Grey* 356. The general course is, to pass a resolution containing a criminal charge against the supposed delinquent, and then to direct some member to impeach him by oral accusation at the bar of the House of Lords, in the name of the Commons. The person signifies that the articles will be exhibited, and desires that the delinquent may be sequestered from his seat, or be committed, or that the peers will take order for his appearance. *Sachev. Trial.* 325. 2 *Wood.* 602, 605. *Lords' Journ.* 3 *June,* 1701. 1 *Wms.* 616. 6 *Grey* 324.

Process. If the party do not appear, proclamations are to be issued, giving him a day to appear. On their return they are strictly examined. If any error be found in them, a new proclamation issues, giving a short day. If he appear not, his goods may be arrested, and they may proceed. *Seld. Jud.* 98, 99.

Articles. The accusation (articles) of the Commons is substituted in place of an indictment. Thus, by the usage of Parliament, in impeachment for writing or speaking, the particular words need not be specified. *Sach. Tr.* 325. 2 *Wood.* 602, 605. *Lords' Journ.* 3 *June,* 1701. 1 *Wms.* 616.

Appearance. If he appears, and the case be capital, he answers in custody; though not if the accusation be general. He is not to be committed but on special accusations. If it be for a misdemeanor only, he answers a Lord in his place, a Commoner at the bar, and not in custody, unless, on the answer, the Lords find cause to commit him, till he finds sureties to attend, and lest he should fly. *Seld. Jud.* 98, 99. 4 *Hats.* 176, 185. A copy of the articles is given him, and a day fixed for his answer. *T. Ray.* 1 *Rushw.* 268. *Fost.* 232. 1 *Clar. Hist. of the Reb.* 379. On a misdemeanor, his apperance may be in person, or he may answer in writing, or by attorney. *Seld. Jud.* 100. The general rule on an accusation for a misdemeanor is, that in such a state of liberty or restraint as the party is when the Commons complain of him, in such he is to answer. *Ib.* 101. If previously committed by the Commons, he answers as a prisoner. But this may be called in some sort judicium parium suorum. *Ib.* In misdemeanors, the party has a right to counsel by the common law; but not in capital cases. *Seld. Jud.* 102 . . . 5.

Answer. The answer need not observe great strictness of form. He may plead guilty as to part, and defend as to the residue; or, saving all exceptions, deny the whole, or give a particular answer to each article separately. 1 *Rush.* 274. 2 *Rush.* 1374. 12 *Parl. Hist.* 442. 3 *Lord's Journ.* 13 *Nov.* 1643. 2 *Wood.* 607. But he cannot plead a pardon in bar to the impeachment. 2 *Wood.* 615. 2 *St. Tr.* 735.

Replication, Rejoinder, &c. There may be a replication, rejoinder, &c. *Seld. Jud.* 114. 8 *Grey's Deb.* 233. *Sachev. Tr.* 15. *Journ. H. of Commons*, 6 *March*, 1640 . . . 1.

Witnesses. The practice is to swear the witnesses in open House, and then examine them there: or a committee may be named, who shall examine them in committee, either on interrogatories agreed on in the House, or such as the committee in their discretion shall demand. *Seld. Jud.* 120, 123.

Jury. In the case of Alice Pierce, 1 *R.* 2. a jury was impanelled for her trial before a committee. *Seld. Jud.* 123. But this was on a complaint, not on impeachment by the Commons. *Seld. Jud.* 163. It must also have been for a misdemeanor only, as the Lords spiritual sat in the case, which they do on misdemeanors, but not in capital cases. *Ib.* 148. The judgment was a forfeiture of all her lands and goods. *Ib.* 188. This, Selden says, is the only jury he finds recorded in Parliament for misdemeanors: but he makes no doubt, if the delinquent doth put himself on the trial of his country, a jury ought to be impanelled, and he adds, that it is not so on impeachment by the Commons; for they are in loco proprio, and there no jury ought to be impanelled. *Ib.* 124. The Ld. Berkeley, 6 *E.* 3. was arraigned for the murder of E. 2. on an information on the part of the king, and not on impeachment of the Commons; for then they had been patria sua. He waived his peerage, and was tried by a jury of Gloucestershire and Warwickshire. *Ib.* 125. But 4 *Hats.* 73, says he was a Commoner, and that there was no waiver of privilege. In 1 *H.* 7. the Commons protest that they are not to be considered as parties to any judgment given, or hereafter to be given in Parliament. *Ib.* 133. They have been generally, and more justly, considered, as is before stated, as the grand jury. For the conceit of Selden is certainly not accurate, that they are the patria sua of the accused, and that the Lords do only judge, but not try. It is undeniable that they do try. For they examine witnesses as to the facts, and acquit or condemn, according to their own belief of them. And Lord Hale says, "the peers are judges of law as well as of fact." 2 *Hale P. C.* 275. Consequently of fact as well as of law.

Presence of Commons. The Commons are to be present at the examination of witnesses. *Seld. Jud.* 124. Indeed they are to attend throughout, either as a committee of the whole House, or otherwise, at discretion, appoint managers to conduct the proofs. *Rush. Tr. of Straff.* 37. *Com. Journ.* 4 *Feb.* 1709 . . . 10. 2 *Wood.* 614. And judgment is not to be given till they demand it. *Seld. Jud.* 124. But they are not to be present on impeachment when the Lords consider of the answer or proofs, and determine of their judgment. Their presence however is necessary at the answer and judgment in cases capital, *ib.* 158, 159, as well as not capital. 162. The Lords debate the judgment among themselves. Then the vote is first taken on the question of guilty or not guilty: and if they convict, the question, or particular sentence, is out of that which seemeth to be most generally agreed on. *Seld. Jud.* 167. 2 *Wood.* 612.

Judgment. Judgments in Parliament for death have been strictly guided per legem terræ, which they cannot alter: and not at all according to their discretion. They can neither omit any part of the legal judgment, nor add to it. Their sentence must be secundum, non ultra legem. *Seld. Jud.* 168, 171. This trial, though it varies in external ceremony, yet differs not in essentials from criminal prosecutions before inferior courts. The same rules of evidence, the same legal notions of crimes and punishments prevail. For impeachments are not framed to alter the law, but to carry it into more effectual execution against two powerful delinquents. The judgment therefore is to be such as is warranted by legal principles or precedents. 6 *Sta. Tr.* 14. 2 *Wood.* 611. The Chancellor gives judgments in misdemeanors; the

Lord High Steward formerly in cases of life and death. *Seld. Jud.* 180. But now the Steward is deemed not necessary. *Fost.* 144. 2 *Wood.* 613. In misdemeanors, the greatest corporal punishment hath been imprisonment. *Seld. Jud.* 184. The king's assent is necessary in capital judgments, (but 2 *Wood.* 614, contra) but not in misdemeanors. *Seld. Jud.* 136.

Continuance. An impeachment is not discontinued by the dissolution of Parliament; but may be resumed by the new Parliament. *T. Ray.* 383. 4 *Com. Journ.* 23 *Dec.* 1790. *Lords' Journ. May* 16, 1791. 2 *Wood.* 618.

THE END.

EDITOR'S NOTES

PREFACE

Pars. 1 and 2 are based upon a passage in CSmH 5986, p. 38-39, which reads as follows:

> . . . But what is the law on the floor of Congress which is to govern the proceedings of the two houses? As to the Senate it stands on the following ground. The Constitution says 'each house may determine the rules of it's proceedings. And the Senate have accordingly established certain rules for conducting their business. One of these rules refers the decision of every question of order to the President, with authority to call for the sense of the Senate whenever there is a doubt in his mind. As far then as the rules as established by the Senate provide, the President is to decide according to those rules; and in all other cases according to his own discretion. The President, in his discretion, thinks, and ought to think, that it will be more satisfactory & expedient to the Senate, and safer for himself, instead of leaving himself free to indulge caprice or passion, or open to the imputation of it, to adopt known rules of decision: and accordingly, in all cases not provided for by the Rules of the Senate, regulates his decisions by the law of parliament. The constant acquiescence of the Senate has added to this practice the weight of their authority. But it would be better that they should make the adoption their own act, and allow an appeal to themselves from the decision of the President, on it's being claimed by a member, or some given number of members.

SEC. I, PAR. 1.

Except for differences in the use of abbreviations, capitalization, contractions, and punctuation, this paragraph appears verbatim in CSmH 5986, p. 42. In the margin of the manuscript is the section title, "Rules, importance of," followed by Roman numeral I. The three words after "power of the Majority" in the eleventh line are underscored for emphasis. After the reference to "2. *Hats*. 171.172." are "§. no. and whether" to indicate TJ's intention to add a section number and to continue the discussion of rules. The next paragraph in the manuscript, however, deals with the subject of privilege, which is treated in Section III of the printed *Manual*.

PAR. 3.

These lines represent the first of the additions that TJ wanted Milligan to include in the new second edition of the *Manual*. See p. 32; also p. 340. The other additions are identified below in our notes to the pertinent sections.

SEC. III, PAR. 1

Milligan's second footnote concluded with "Grey's deb. 133," thus omitting the reference to Vol. 1 in Smith's otherwise parallel directive. By this omission Milligan's text may be held accountable for a minor typographical error, but even Smith's full reference did not support the rule to which his text affixed it, nor does page 133 of any other volume of Grey's *Debates*. Thus I have deleted this part of the footnote altogether, on the ground that TJ's original intention cannot here be established or productively guessed at. Perhaps his final manuscript supported this part of his text by a valid reference to some other page of some other volume of Grey's *Debates*, and perhaps Smith's printing office misprinted the valid reference in putting it into type. These things we simply do not know. But we do know that Smith's error has been reproduced time after time in subsequent printings of his text of the *Manual*, even unto its latest official appearance as a congressional document.

PAR. 7.

Milligan's text misspells "necessary" at one point, and I have corrected the error.

PAR. 12.

This entire passage appears in CSmH 5986, p. 1, in the following words:

> For any speech or debate in either house, they shall not be questioned in any other place. Constn. U.S. S. P. Protestation of the Commons to Jac. I. 1621. 2. Rapin No. 54. pa. 211.212. but this is restrained to things done in the house in a parliamentary course. 1. Rush. 663. for he is not to have privilege contra morem parliamentarium, to exceed the bounds & limits of his place & duty. Com. p. §113.

The final words of this passage are exactly the same as those in the concluding part of the first sentence of par. [397] of the Pocket-Book. See the note thereon. As for the abbreviation "*Com. P.*," it is plainly intended to stand for *Commons Protest* and to recall in short form TJ's earlier reference in this passage to "*S. P. Protest of the Commons to James I.* 1621." It was usual practice in eighteenth-century legal scholarship for works to be cited first by the more complete title and later by short title or abbreviation. In adopting the practice here, TJ did what Rapin, that is, Rapin-Thoyras, also did. Rapin-Thoyras used a short form, *The Commons Protestation*, when he printed that document in his *History of England*, and later, when he made reference to it, he called it "*Protestation*." In citing that same document in the Pocket-Book, par. [215], TJ called it "Protestation of Comm. to Jac. I. 1621." For a more extended note on the meaning of "*Com. P.*," see my article, "The Abbreviation 'Com. P.' in Jefferson's *Manual*: An Explanation," *Parliamentary Journal* 21 (January 1980), 17-22, 26-30. For an opposing explanation by Bernard J. Sussman, see ibid., p. 22-5.

SEC. V, PAR. 7.

Smith's table of Representatives lists sixteen states and gives the number of Representatives for each in 1787 and 1793, so far as the state concerned had representatives in those years. Milligan's similar table lists seventeen states and adds two new columns for representatives, one for 1801 and the other for 1813. The new state in Milligan's table is Ohio. See above, p. 365.

EDITOR'S NOTES

SEC. XIII, PAR. 2.

These lines represent the second of the additions made by TJ to Milligan's new edition. See above, p. 32; also note to Sec. i, par. 3.

PAR. 3.

The final sentence and its documentation represent the third of TJ's additions to Milligan's new edition.

PAR. 7.

In reproducing Smith's text, Milligan put "may be tended to him." I restore Smith's reading by substituting "tendered" for "tended."

SEC. XVI, PAR. 3.

Smith's text read "almightly God," and Milligan corrected the error.

SEC. XVII, PARS. 14, 30.

Par. 14 printed in Roman type the first sentence of Rule 16, and par. 30 printed its second sentence in italics. Both sentences were combined into a single resolution when Rule xvi was adopted by the Senate on April 16, 1789, and TJ treated it as a single resolution when he transcribed it in his Pocket-Book, par. [442]. It would be normal to expect that both sentences would be printed as a single resolution in the *Manual*, and that both would be italicized. But TJ evidently decided otherwise. Perhaps he wanted the second sentence to proclaim its importance by being separated from the first, and the first sentence to suggest its unimportance by being denied italics. That line of reasoning would receive support from TJ's remark in the Preface of the *Manual* that the Senate originally adopted a few rules for their own guidance and then "referred to the decision of their President, without debate and without appeal, all questions of order arising either under their own rules, or where they have provided none." At any rate, we have preserved Milligan's differentiation between the two sentences in regard to type, although he elsewhere used italics in printing the Senate rules, except (by inadvertence?) for the first twenty-seven words of Rule 13. See Sec. xxii.

SEC. XXII, PAR. 1.

As printed in Roman type in Smith's text, Rule 13 made up the whole of Section xxii, and it read as follows:

> Every bill shall receive three readings, previous to its being passed; and the President shall give notice at each whether it be the 1st. 2nd. or 3d. which readings shall be on three different days, unless the Senate unanimously direct otherwise. *Rule* 13.

The first forty-one words of Rule 13, as printed by Milligan, constitute only the first part of his version of Section xxii, but he followed Smith verbatim in that part, except for his use of italics and his manner of printing ordinal numbers. After finishing Smith's version, however, Milligan added the following clause:

. . . or, unless by a joint vote of both Houses, or the expiration of their term, the session is to be closed within three days. Rule 13.

Where this addition came from is a matter of doubt and conjecture. It was not a part of the original rule as passed by the Senate on April 16, 1789. It did not figure in the Pocket-Book, par. [442], when TJ entered Rule 13 therein. It was not mentioned on either of the two occasions when TJ's preliminary drafts of the final manuscript of the *Manual* recorded the text of what he there called Rule XIII. (See CSmH 5986, p. 21, 22.) And the Senate Journals contain no reference to this particular addition whenever it gives the original text of the rule concerned. (See JS, II, 346, 541; IV, 66.) What might have happened is that TJ himself made this addition after the first edition of the *Manual* appeared in 1801, remembering it as a necessary restriction which he had applied to Rule 13 in practice. In that form he may have passed the addition on to Milligan in 1812, along with the other additions from Hatsell's fourth volume, not being aware that the Senate, on March 26, 1806, had changed the number of Rule 13 to 12, and had added to the original wording a lengthy resolution having nothing whatever to do with three readings of bills on three different days. (See JS, IV, 66.) Despite my uncertainties on this matter, however, I feel obliged to prefer Milligan's text to Smith's at this point, since it obviously represents what TJ wanted, and since the addition itself does no violence to TJ's other known versions of the rule here discussed. But I have italicized the entire text of the rule, as Milligan's usual practice would dictate.

SEC. XXVI, PAR. 10.

These lines represent the fifth of the additions that TJ wanted Milligan to include in his second edition of the *Manual*.

SEC. XXXII, PAR. 1.

Toties quoties is a legal expression meaning "as often as it shall happen."

SEC. XXXIV, PAR. 3.

Sir Thomas Littleton, as quoted in Grey's *Debates*, II, 113, intimated in Commons in 1672 that Sir Henry Vane was the first to make the call for the previous question into an accepted parliamentary form. Hatsell, after having authoritatively established May 25, 1604, as the date when that form was first used, denied the correctness of Littleton's attributing it to Sir Henry Vane. *Precedents of Proceedings* (1785, II, 80; 1818, II, 111). What TJ apparently did was to accept the date of the call as given by Hatsell, and the name of its first user as claimed by Littleton, without becoming aware of the anachronism hidden in those two pronouncements. Sir Henry Vane, father or son, could not have been in Commons in 1604, the elder having been planning to matriculate in Brasenose College in June of that year, and the younger not yet born. For an analysis of TJ's error in this matter, see Robert W. Smith, "Jefferson's *Manual* Corrected," *Parliamentary Journal*, 21 (January 1980), 30-4. Smith's analysis seems designed to make TJ's error consist in his having mistakenly connected Sir Henry Vane's alleged action with the 1604 date, and in his having written 1604 instead of 1640, when both Vanes could have been in parliament. But TJ accepted the 1604 date on Hatsell's authority, as he explicitly showed. His mistake was in saying, against the explicit warning brought to his attention by Hatsell, that Sir

Henry Vane was the first to use that particular parliamentary maneuver. The error is regrettable, to be sure, but it is difficult to regard it as anything more than an uncharacteristic lapse of attention on the part of the notably careful TJ.

SEC. XXXV, PAR. 11.

Three lines in this paragraph, identified as having come from "4 *Hats*. 319," represent the sixth of the additions made by TJ to this edition of the *Manual*.

SEC. XXXVI, PAR. 1.

In the fifth line, Milligan's text read "Ut" when it should have read "but."

PAR. 3.

The second page of the two-page fragment mentioned above, Editor's Introduction to *A Manual*, n. 15, contains a rough draft of this passage.

SEC. XLVI.

The following clauses, paragraphs, or separate references in the present text are additions that TJ provided for inclusion in Milligan's edition:

PAR. 1.

... by one House disagreed to by the other ... 4 *Hats*. 4, 223 ... 4 *Hats*. 4, 5, 7 ... 4 *Hats*. 3, 43.

PAR. 2.

... which are asked after two conferences, 4 *Hats*. 37, 40.

PAR. 2.

The conferees may argue in support of what is done in their House, but not against it, nor assent to any new thing there propounded, till their House be informed and agree to it. 4 *Hats*. 31, 33. . . . 4 *Hats*. 48.

PAR. 4.

The Commons affirm that it is usual to have two free conferences or more, before either House proceeds to adhere: because, before that time, the Houses have not had full opportunity of making replies to one another's arguments; and to adhere so suddenly and unexpectedly, excludes all possibility of offering expedients. 4 *Hats*. 330.

PAR. 7.

4 *Hats*. 20, 46.

PAR. 9.

During the time of a conference the House can do no business. As soon as the names of the managers are called over, and they are gone to the conference, the Speaker leaves the chair, without any question, and resumes it on the return of the managers. It is the same while the managers of an impeachment are at the House of Lords. 4 *Hats*. 47, 209, 288.

SEC. XLIX, PAR. 3.

Rule 25 did not appear in Smith's or Milligan's text of the *Manual*, but it must have been omitted in each case by inadvertence; or TJ himself, also by inadvertence, may perhaps have omitted it when he was preparing his final manuscript in the summer of 1800. Nevertheless, the reasons why it is being restored to its proper position in this edition seem compelling. In the first place, the presence of Rule 25 is made imperative by the necessity of having a rule with this number to fit into the sequence of numbered rules in the *Manual*. Secondly, there can be no doubt that TJ's own intention was to have Rule 25 appear in the *Manual* at this point. He indicated as much in the Pocket-Book, par. [442], where his list of Senate Rules contains Rule xxv, worded there exactly as it is worded here, and positioned there, as here, between Rule xxiv and Rule xxvi. He also indicated that intention in his manuscript titled "Rough Notes," where, on page 14 (or perhaps more correctly 13), he listed some of the topics that were to appear in the *Manual*, and after one of them, called "Exve business," he placed the numeral xxv, which in that context could only designate Rule 25. (See p. 340). Moreover, he also indicated the same thing in CSmH 5986, p. 15, l. 10, where his notes specified the presence of Rule xxv between Rule xxiv and Rule xxvi.

What may have happened was that, when TJ was preparing his final manuscript for the printer, he planned to have his *Manual* extend to fifty-four sections, with the last section to deal with executive business and to contain Rule 25 as pertinent to that very topic. But when he later changed that plan, and canceled out the final section, as he did in CSmH 5986, he may have neglected to remind himself that Rule 25 should not therefore be overlooked but should be relocated in Sec. xlix, where it also would belong. Or, as another possibility, he may have included Rule 25 in his final manuscript, only to have Smith's printer skip over it in setting type. But in any case there can be no doubt that TJ's intention was to have Rule 25 included in his own final version of the *Manual*.

SEC. LII, PAR. 3.

The footnote attached to the final sentence is not in Milligan's or Smith's text, but it is added here on the authority of TJ, who wrote it at the foot of the page in his own personal copy of the first edition of the *Manual*. See above, p. 420. It should not be counted here, however, as an addition proposed by TJ for inclusion in Milligan's second edition.

SEC. LIII, PAR. 6.

The parenthetical note and added reference to Hatsell, iv, 153, 186, are not in Smith's text, and thus they are to be counted as TJ's thirteenth and fourteenth additions to Milligan's present work.

PAR. 14.

Milligan's text erred by doubling the n in printing "impanelled."

PAR. 14.

Smith and Milligan both erred in saying that Lord Berkeley was arraigned "for the murder of L. 2," and the mistake is plainly theirs, not TJ's. In the Pocket-Book, par. [547], TJ noted that Lord Berkeley was arraigned "for the murder of E. 2," that is, Edward II. For details, see the Pocket-Book, par. [547] and note 4.

PAR. 14.

"But 4 *Hats*. 73, says that he was a Commoner, and that there was no waiver of privilege." These words, which are not in Smith's text, constitute the fifteenth of TJ's contributions to Milligan's second edition.

LIST OF EDITIONS

This list is arranged in the following categories: mistaken editions; editions for the Senate; editions for the House of Representatives; other legislative editions; editions for citizens; and editions in other languages.

Our list does not claim to be definitive. As a matter of fact, a truly definitive list would probably be out of the question. This list represents a reasonably thorough gathering of titles of editions recorded in such standard sources as these: *The National Union Catalog* (NUC); *British Museum General Catalogue of Printed Books* (*B.M. Cat*); *Catalogue Général des divres Imprimés de la Bibliothèque Nationale* (*B.N. Cat*); card catalogue of the Princeton University Library; and so on. As far as the NUC is concerned, TJ's *Manual* is listed not only by its own author and title, but also under the following heads: U.S. Congress Constitution; U.S. Congress House; U.S. Congress Senate, Constitution, Rules, Manual; John M. Barclay; Joel B. Sutherland, Joseph Bartlett Burleigh; Thomas V. Cooper; Bennett Champ Clark; and Dodson E. Griffith.

This gathering shows that, so far as the number of its printings may attest, the *Manual* is qualified to be regarded as a major influence in its field and as the most enduring of any book by any American President or Vice President.

MISTAKEN EDITIONS

[XXIX] Rules for Conducting Business in the Senate. By Thomas Jefferson. [Philadelphia: Printed by John Fenno, 1797.]

This title is hailed by Evans, XI, 319, as heralding "The first publication of his frequently reprinted Manual of Parliamentary Practice." Doubtless on the strength of Evans's authority, Campion, p. xvii, dates the first edition of the *Manual* in 1797. But in reality this seven-page pamphlet contains twenty-nine rules adopted by the Senate in the period between Apr. 16, 1789, and June 25, 1798. See JS, I, 13, 14, 27, 28, 116, 398, 407, 408; II, 34, 481. These rules were entered by TJ into the Parliamentary Pocket-Book, par. [442], and they appear in his *Manual*, to be sure. But they constitute only a small part of the latter, and Evans' characterization of them is quite insufficient.

Rules for Conducting Business in the Senate. [Philadelphia, 1800.]

This entry may well have led Sabin (IX, 238) to say that there was an 1800 edition of the *Manual*, and indeed Sabin's authority is cited by Johnston to justify such an identification. But there was in fact no edition of the *Manual* in that year.

Manual of Parliamentary Practice. New York, 1808.

NUC, Vol. 278, p. 679, lists this title and places at the Illinois State Library the sole existing copy. The published catalogue of that library recorded its copy under Jefferson's name as having been published in 1808, but under Parliamentary Law and again under Manual, the catalogue listed the copy's publication date as 1868. Unfortunately, this item has been missing since 1965. Inasmuch as the *Manual* was published by Clark and Maynard at New York in 1868, and inasmuch as no copy of an 1808 edition was recorded anywhere but at Illinois, the Jefferson listing could have been a cataloguing error, especially since it contradicts two other entries in the same catalogue. Therefore, an 1808 edition of the *Manual* at New York cannot be accepted as a valid entry into this critical bibliography.

EDITIONS FOR THE SENATE

A Manual of Parliamentary Practice. For the Use of the Senate of the United States. By Thomas Jefferson. Washington City: Printed by Samuel Harrison Smith, MDCCCI.

For further details, see above, p. 24-7. This edition has regularly been reprinted except for that which appeared at Georgetown and Washington in 1812. Shaw and Shoemaker record a second impression of the first edition in 1803.

A Manual of Parliamentary Practice, for the Use of the Senate of the United States. By Thomas Jefferson. Second Edition. Lancaster, Pennsylvania: Printed and published by William Dickson, North Queenstreet, 1810.

For a dismissal of the publisher's claim that this work is a true second edition, and for other details, see above, p. 31.

A Manual of Parliamentary Practice: for the Use of the Senate of the United States. By Thomas Jefferson. Second Edition. With the last additions of the author. George Town: Published by Joseph Milligan; and by William Cooper, Washington, 1812.

This important work must be called the true second edition. As its title page indicates, it contains material added by TJ to his original text of 1801, and thus it measurably extends what he had said before on its subject. Its text is the basis of our edition, and it should by rights have been the basis of all texts printed after 1812. For an account of its origin and publication, see above, p. 32-5.

A Manual of Parliamentary Practice. For the Use of the Senate of the United States. By Thomas Jefferson. 3rd edition. Lancaster, Pa: Printed and published by William Dickson, 1813.

This so-called third edition is in fact a reprint of the text used by Dickson for his "second" edition, even as the latter was a reprint of Smith's first edition. See above, p. 32.

A Manual of Parliamentary Practice. For the Use of the Senate of the United States. By Thomas Jefferson. To which is added, the Rules and Orders of the Senate and House of Representatives of the United States, and Joint Rules of the two Houses. Washington city: Printed by David & Force, 1820.

A Manual of Parliamentary Practice. 1824.

An edition under this date is recorded in NUC, vol. 278, p. 680, with indication of a sole American copy at the University of Virginia. We are informed, however, that no such copy is now registered at that institution.

The Constitution of the United States of America: the Rules of the Senate, and of the House of Representatives: with Jefferson's Manual. Printed by order of the Senate of the United States. Washington: Printed by Duff Green, 1828.

In the edition printed by Milligan and Cooper in 1812, TJ's *Manual* is bound with the Constitution (separately paged), with the Rules of the Senate (separately paged), and with the Rules of the House and Joint Rules of both

MANUAL OF PARLIAMENTARY PRACTICE

Houses (paged together in sequence). In 1828 the Senate decided to have Duff Green print a volume devoted to the documents that they particularly wanted to have at hand in doing their daily work, and the Milligan-Cooper edition, its contents rearranged, became their model. That model, sometimes with other items added, has been used over and over again by the Senate to make legislative principles and procedures available to their changing membership, and thus the publishing life of TJ's *Manual* has been constantly renewed. A somewhat similar model was borrowed by the House of Representatives as they began to provide their membership with needed procedural information, and in the latter milieu the *Manual* has flourished down to the present. Meanwhile, it has had other legislative editions, and citizens' editions, both domestic and foreign, to satisfy American and international needs for rules to govern orderly deliberations in all sorts of public meetings.

Constitution of the United States with the amendments thereto, the rules of the Senate, the joint rules of the two Houses, Jefferson's Manual of Parliamentary practice, with some general laws of useful reference and other matter. Washington: Govt. Print. Off., 1868.

Constitution of the United States of America, with the amendments thereto; to which are prefixed the Declaration of Independence, the Articles of Confederation, and the Ordinance of 1787; and to which are added the rules of the Senate, the joint rules of the two houses, and Jefferson's Manual of Parliamentary Practice; with some general laws of useful reference in legislation, and other interesting matter, from authentic sources. Compiled by W. J. McDonald . . . Printed for the use of the Senate. Washington: Govt. Print. Off., 1871. Reprinted 1873, 1877, and 1881.

Constitution of the United States of America with the amendments thereto: to which are prefixed The Declaration of Independence, The Articles of Confederation, and the ordinance of 1787; to which are added the Standing Rules of the Senate . . . and Jefferson's Manual of Parliamentary Practice . . . Revised in accordance with the resolution of the Senate of July 1, 1884, By Charles B. Reede, . . . Washington: Govt. Print. Off., 1885.

—Second Edition. Washington: Govt. Print. Off., 1886.

Senate Manual. Fiftieth Congress, First Session. Embracing The Standing Rules and Orders of the Senate; the Constitution of the United States; Declaration of Independence; Articles of Confederation, and the Ordinance of 1787; Jefferson's Manual, etc. Revised under the direction of the Committee on Rules, United States Senate. Washington: Govt. Print. Off., 1886.

Senate Manual. Fifty-first Congress, First Session . . . Jefferson's Manual; etc. Revised to Mar. 1, 1890, under the direction of the Committee on Rules, United States Senate. Washington: Govt. Print. Off., 1890.

Senate Manual. Containing the Standing Rules and Orders of the United States Senate, the Constitution of the United States, Declaration of Independence . . . Jefferson's Manual, etc. . . . . [Edition of April 14, 1896.] Washington: Govt. Print. Off., 1896.

The Princeton copy contains the name of Grover Cleveland in gold lettering on the outside of the cover.

Senate Manual. Containing the Standing Rules and Orders of the United States

Senate, the Constitution . . . Jefferson's Manual, etc. Revised under the direction of the Senate's Committee on Rules, fifty-fifth Congress. Ed. of March 2, 1899. Washington: Govt. Print. Off., 1899.

Senate Manual. Containing . . . Jefferson's Manual, etc. . . . Edition of February 11, 1901. Washington: Govt. Print. Off., 1901.

Senate Manual, containing . . . Jefferson's Manual, etc. Revised under the direction of the Senate Committee on Rules, fifty-ninth Congress. Edition of February 14, 1907. Washington, Govt. Print. Off., 1907.

Senate Manual . . . Washington: Govt. Print. Off., 1911.

Senate Manual, containing . . . Jefferson's Manual, etc. Prepared under the direction of the Senate Committee on Rules, sixty-sixth Congress. Washington: Govt. Print. Off., 1921.

Senate Manual, containing . . . Jefferson's Manual, etc. Prepared under the direction of the Senate Committee on Rules, sixty-seventh Congress. Washington: Govt. Print. Off., 1923.

Senate Manual, containing . . . Jefferson's Manual, etc.; prepared under the direction of the Senate Committee on Rules . . . Washington: Govt. Print. Off., 1941.

Senate Manual, containing . . . Jefferson's Manual, etc. . . . Washington: Govt. Print. Off., 1949. [832 pp.]

Senate Procedure: Precedents and Practices. By Floyd M. Riddick, Parliamentarian, Washington: U.S. Senate: for sale by the Supt. of Docs., U.S. Govt. Print. Off., 1974. [1076 pp.]

EDITIONS FOR THE HOUSE OF REPRESENTATIVES

Constitution of the United States of America: Rules of the House of Representatives. Joint Rules of the two Houses. And Rules of the Senate, with Jefferson's Manual . . . Washington: T. Allen, printer to the House. 1837.

This volume is listed in NUC, vol. 613, p. 352, as having been "Printed by order of the House of representatives," and it marks what appears to be the earliest appearance of TJ's *Manual* within a collection of documents specifically requested by the Lower House. TJ, who on occasion had spoken unfavorably of the parliamentary conduct of the Representatives (see p. 13, 17-18, 29), would doubtless have welcomed this development.

Constitution of the United States of America, with the amendments thereto: to which are added Jefferson's Manual of Parliamentary Practice and the standing rules and orders for conducting business in the House of Representatives and Senate of the United States . . . Washington: A.O.P. Nicholson, public printer, 1854.

"Printed for the Use of the House of representatives," notes the NUC, vol. 613, p. 352.

Constitution of the United States of America, with the Amendments thereto: to which are added Jefferson's Manual of Parliamentary Practice, and the standing rules and orders for conducting business in the House of Representatives and Senate of the United States . . . Whashington: C. Wendell, public printer, 1856.

"Printed for the use of the House of representatives," notes the NUC, vol. 613, p. 352.

Constitution of the United States of America, with the amendments thereto: to which are added Jefferson's Manual of Parliamentary Practice, and the standing rules and orders for conducting business in the House of Representatives and Senate of the United States. Printed for use of the House of Representatives. Washington: C. Wendell, public printer, 1857.

Constitution of the United States of America, with the amendments thereto: to which are added Jefferson's Manual of Parliamentary Practice, and the standing rules and orders for conducting business in the House of Representatives and Senate of the United States . . . Washington: J. B. Steedman, printer, 1859.

"Printed for use of the House of Representatives." (NUC, vol. 613, p. 352)

Manual of the House of Representatives U.S.: being a digest of the Rules of the House, the joint rules of the two houses, and of so much of Jefferson's Manual as under the rules governs the House . . . Arranged alphabetically. Washington, 1859.

For this entry, see NUC, vol. 613, p. 603.

Constitution of the United States of America, with the Amendments thereto: to which are added Jefferson's Manual of Parliamentary Practice, the standing rules and orders for conducting business in the House of Representatives and Senate of the United States, and Barclay's Digest of the rules of proceeding in the House of Representatives of the United States. Compiled by John M. Barclay . . . Washington, 1860-1861.

Digest of the rules of the House of Representatives, U.S. the joint rules of the two houses, and of so much of Jefferson's Manual as . . . governs the House . . . Arranged alphabetically. Washington, 1861.

Constitution of the United States of America, with the amendments thereto; to which are added Jefferson's Manual of Parliamentary practice, and the standing rules and orders for conducting business in the House of Representatives and Senate of the United States. Washington: Govt. Print. Off., 1863.

Digest of the rules of the House of Representatives, U.S. the joint rules of the two houses, and of so much of Jefferson's Manual as . . . governs the House. Arranged alphabetically. Washington: 1863-1864.

Digest of the rules of the House of Representatives U.S., the joint rules of the two Houses, and of so much of Jefferson's Manual as under the rules governs the House; of precedents of order and usages of the House; together with such portions of the Constitution . . . , laws of Congress, and resolutions of the House as relate to the proceedings of the House, and the rights and duties of its members. Compiled and published by John M. Barclay . . . Arranged alphabetically. Washington: 1865-1866.

This entry as somewhat condensed here is taken from NUC, vol. 35, p. 163, s.v. Barclay, John M. Other separate editions of Barclay's *Digest*, in addition to those noted above under the dates 1859, 1861, and 1863-1864, were published at Washington in 1867, 1869, 1871, 1872, and 1875.

Constitution of the United States of America, with the amendments thereto: to which are added Jefferson's Manual of Parliamentary Practice, and the standing rules and orders for conducting business in the House of Representatives and Senate of the United States. Washington: Govt. Print. Off., 1865.

—Another Edition. With Barclay's Digest. Washington: Govt. Print. Off., 1867.

—Another Edition. With Barclay's Digest. Washington: Govt. Print. Off., 1868.

—Another Edition. (With Declaration of Independence and Articles of Confederation included.) Compiled by W. J. McDonald. Washington: Govt. Print. Off., 1868.

Constitution of the United States of America, with the amendments thereto: to which are added Jefferson's Manual of Parliamentary Practice, the standing rules, joint rules, and orders for conducting business in the House of Representatives of the United States, and Barclay's Digest. Washington: Govt. Print. Off., 1871.

—Another Edition. 3d sess. 42d Cong. Washington: [Govt. Print. Off., 1872]

—Another Edition. 1st sess. 43d Cong. Washington: [Govt. Print. Off., 1873]

—Another Edition. 2d sess. 43d Cong. Washington: [Govt. Print. Off., 1874]

—Another Edition. 1st sess. 44th Cong. Washington: [Govt. Print. Off., 1875]

—Another Edition. Washington: [Govt. Print. Off., 1876]

Constitution of the United States of America with the amendments thereto: to which are added Jefferson's Manual . . . , the standing rules and orders for conducting business in the House of Representatives . . . , the joint rules in force at the close of the 43d Congress, and a digest thereof . . . Compiled by Henry Harrison Smith. [Washington: Govt. Print. Off., 1877]

—Second Edition. [Washington: Govt. Print. Off., 1877]

Constitution of the United States of America, with the amendments thereto: to which are added Jefferson's Manual . . . , the standing rules and orders for conducting business in the House of Representatives . . . , the joint rules in force at the close of the 43d Congress, and Jefferson's Manual as under the rules governs the House . . . Compiled by Henry H. Smith. 4th ed. [Washington: Govt. Print. Off., 1880]

—Fifth Edition. [Washington: Govt. Print. Off., 1882]

—Sixth Edition. [Washington: Govt. Print. Off., 1883]

Digest and Manual of the Rules and practices of the House of Representatives, to which are added the Constitution of the United States . . . with the amendments thereto, and so much of Jefferson's Manual of Parliamentary Practice as under rule XLIV governs the House . . . 2d ed. Washington: Govt. Print. Off., [1884].
  This volume went through other editions in [1887], [1889], [1890], and [1897].

Constitution of the United States . . . with the amendments thereto: to which are added Jefferson's Manual . . . the standing rules . . . and Barclay's Digest. Washington: [Govt. Print. Off., 1884]

—Ninth Edition. [Washington: Govt. Print. Off., 1886]

—Tenth Edition. [Washington: Govt. Print. Off., 1886]

—Twelfth Edition. (Compiled by John C. Robinson) [Washington: Govt. Print. Off., 1889]

Constitution of the United States, Jefferson's Manual, the rules of the House of Representatives of the fifty-second Congress, and also a digest and manual of the rules and practice of the House of Representatives . . . with an appendix. Prepared by Nathaniel T. Crutchfield. . . . Washington: Govt. Print. Off., 1893.

—Another Edition. Fifty-third Congress. Washington: Govt. Print. Off., 1893.

—Another Edition. Fifty-fourth congress. Washington: 1896.

Constitution of the United States, Jefferson's Manual, the rules of the House of Representatives of the Fifty-fourth Congress, and a digest and manual of the rules and practice of the House of Representatives. . . . Prepared by Thomas H. McKee. Washington: Govt. Print. Off., 1897.

—Another Edition. Fifty-fifth Congress. Washington: Govt. Print. Off., 1898.

—Another Edition. Fifty-fifth Congress. Washington: Govt. Print. Off., 1899.

Constitution . . . Jefferson's Manual, the rules of the House of Representatives . . . and a digest and manual of the rules and practice of the House. Prepared by Asher C. Hinds, Washington: Govt. Print. Off., 1900.
    Other editions under this title and auspices appeared under the following dates: 1901, 1902, 1903, 1904, 1905, 1906, 1908, 1909, and 1910.

Constitution, Jefferson's Manual and rules of the House of Representatives . . . with a digest of the practice, Sixty-second Congress, first session. By Charles R. Crisp, clerk at the Speaker's table. Washington: Govt. Print. Off., 1911.

—Another Edition. Crisp. Washington: Govt. Print. Off., 1912.

Constitution, Jefferson's Manual and rules of the House of Representatives . . . , with a digest of the practice, sixty-third Congress, by Bennet Champ Clark. Washington: Govt. Print. Off., 1915.

Constitution, Jefferson's Manual, and Rules of the House of Representatives . . . with a digest of the practice, Sixty-fifth Congress, second sess. by Clarence A. Cannon. Washington: Govt. Print. Off., 1918.

—Another Edition. Lehr Fess. Washington: Govt. Print. Off., 1921.

—Another Edition. Fess. Washington: Govt. Print. Off., 1923.

—Another Edition. Fess. Washington: Govt. Print. Off., 1927.

Constitution, Jefferson's Manual, and Rules of the House of Representatives of the United States, Seventy-first Congress. Washington: Govt. Print. Off., 1929.
    Listed under the name of Lewis Deschler, NUC, vol. 613, p. 594.

—Another Edition. Lewis Deschler. Washington: Govt. Print. Off., 1937.

—Another Edition. Deschler. Washington: Govt. Print. Off., 1961.

—Another Edition. Deschler. Washington: Govt. Print. Off., 1971.

—Another Edition. Deschler. Washington: Govt. Print. Off., 1973.

Constitution, Jefferson's Manual, and Rules of the House of Representatives of the United States, Ninety-fifth Congress, by Wm. Holmes Brown. Washington: Govt. Print. Off., 1977.

Constitution, Jefferson's Manual, and rules of the House of Representatives of the United States. Washington: Govt. Print. Off., [1980].
NUC, 1980, v. 15, p. 891.

OTHER LEGISLATIVE EDITIONS

A Manual of Legislative Practice and Order of Business in Deliberative Bodies. Second Edition. By Joel B. Sutherland. Philadephia: Printed by P. Hay & Co., 1830.
The first edition (Philadelphia, 1827) did not contain TJ's *Manual*, but later editions (Philadelphia, 1840, 1852, 1853, 1855, 1860) did. See NUC, vol. 577, p. 337. This work contains the Pennsylvania Constitution, the rules of Pennsylvania's House of Representatives, the legislative manual of Pennsylvania, the joint rules of Pennsylvania's House and Senate; the rules of Pennsylvania's Senate, the Declaration of Independence, and the U.S. Constitution, as well as TJ's *Manual*.

Reference Book, Virginia House of Delegates. Rules of the House of Delegates, Jefferson's Manual, Code of Virginia sections, Constitution of Virginia. Index compiled by E. Griffith Dodson, Clerk of the House of Delegates. [Richmond, Division of Purchases and Printing] 1942.
See NUC, vol. 145, p. 617. Also vol. 639, p. 173; and vol. 278, p. 681.

EDITIONS FOR CITIZENS

A Manual of Parliamentary Practice, Composed originally for the Use of the Senate of the United States. By Thomas Jefferson. To which are added, the Rules and Orders of both Houses of Congress. Washington: Gales & Seaton, 1822.
This edition is the earliest to appear with the words "Composed originally" in the title, and thus it seems to be the first to invite use by citizens in general.

A Manual of Parliamentary Practice. Composed originally for the Use of the Senate of the United States. By Thomas Jefferson. To which are added, the Rules and Orders of both Houses of Congress. Concord: G. Hough & J. B. Moore, 1823.

A Manual of Parliamentary Practice, composed originally for the Use of the Senate of the United States. To which are added, the Rules and Orders of both Houses of Congress. Cincinnati: Drake and Conclin, 1828

A Manual of Parliamentary Practice, composed originally for the use of the Senate of the United States. By Thomas Jefferson. With References to the Practice and Rules of the House of Representatives. The whole brought down to the practice of the present time; to which are added The Rules and Orders of Both Houses of Congress. Philadelphia: Hogan & Thompson, Pittsburgh: D. M. Hogan, 1834.
Hogan & Thompson brought out other editions in 1837, 1840, 1843, 1848, and 1850.

A Congressional Manual; or, Outline of the Order of Business in the House of

[441]

Representatives of the United States. With copious indexes. By Joel B. Sutherland. Philadelphia: P. Hay & Co., Printers, 1839.

Later editions appeared in 1841 (P. Hay & Co.) and in 1846 (Barrett & Jones).

Manual of Parliamentary Practice, composed originally for the Senate of the United States. By Thomas Jefferson. The Constitution of the United States, and the Rules for conducting business in both Houses of Congress; with all the amendments, erasures, and additions, down to the year 1842 . . . Columbus, Ohio: Jonathan Phillips, 1842.

—Another Edition updated. Columbus, Ohio: J. Phillips, 1848.

The Legislative Guide, containing all the Rules for conducting business in Congress: Jefferson's Manual; and the Citizens' Manual, including a concise System of Rules of Order founded on congressional proceedings; with copious notes and marginal references . . . by Joseph Bartlett Burleigh, LL.D. Philadelphia: Lippincott, Grambo & Co., 1852.

Later editions appeared in 1853, 1854, 1856, 1858, 1860, 1861, and 1865. See NUC, vol. 85, p. 441-2, s.v. Burleigh, Joseph Bartlett.

A Manual of Parliamentary Practice: Composed originally for the use of the Senate of the United States. By Thomas Jefferson. With References to the Practice and Rules of the House of Representatives. The Whole brought down to the Practice of the Present Time; To which are added the Rules and Orders, Together with the Joint Rules of Both Houses of Congress. And accompanied with copious indices. Philadelphia: Parrish, Dunning & Mears, No. 30, North Fourth Street, 1853.

A Manual of Parliamentary Practice: Composed originally for the use of the Senate of the United States. With References to the Practice and Rules of the House of Representatives. The whole brought down to the Practice of the present time; to which is added the Rules and Orders, together with the joint Rule of both Houses of Congress. And accompanied by copious indices. New York: Clark, Austin & Smith, 1854.

Later editions under this imprint came out in 1856, 1857, 1858, 1859, 1860, and 1862.

A Manual of Parliamentary Practice: Composed originally for the use of The Senate of the United States. By Thomas Jefferson. With References to the Practice and Rules of the House of Representatives. The whole brought down to the present time; to which are added The Rules and Orders, together with The Joint Rules of both Houses of Congress. And accompanied with Copious Indices. New York: Clark & Maynard, Publishers, No. 5 Barclay Street. 1864.

Under this imprint later editions appeared in 1866, 1867, 1868, 1870, 1871, 1873, 1874, and 1876.

American Politics (non-partisan) from the beginning to date. Embodying a History of all Political Parties, with their views and records on all important questions. Great Speeches on all great Issues. The text of all existing political laws. A complete tabulated history of American Politics . . . Parliamentary practice from Jefferson's Manual with complete References, U.S. Constitution, Articles of Confederation, Declaration, etc. . . . By Hon. Thomas V. Cooper . . .

and Hector T. Fenton, Esq. Eighth and Revised Edition. Chicago, Ill.: C. R. Brodix, 1884.

In Bk. IV, pp. 22-55, this vast work contains TJ's *Manual* without TJ's Preface. First published in Boston by B. A. Fowler & Co. in 1870, it had many printings in Chicago, New York, Philadelphia, and Springfield, by such other publishers as C. R. Blackall & Co. (New York), C. R. Brodix (Chicago), Fireside Publishing Co. (Philadelphia), Russell & Henderson (Boston), and Baird & Dillon (Chicago).

EDITIONS IN OTHER LANGUAGES

Manuel du droit parlementaire, ou Précis des règles suivies dans le Parlement d'Angleterre et dans le Congrès des États-Unis, pour l'introduction, la discussion et la décision des affaires; compilé à l'usage du Sénat des États-Unis, par Thomas Jefferson, Ancien Président des États-Unis. Traduit de l'Anglais, par L. A. Pichon, Ancien agent diplomatique; ancien conseiller d'état, et intendant-général du trésor en Westphalie. A Paris, chez H. Nicolle, à la Librairie Stéréotype, Rue de Seine, No 12., 1814.

For a note on Pichon and this translation, see above, p. 35-6.

Handbuch des Parlamentarrechts; oder, Darstellung der Verhandlungsweise und des Geschäftsganges beim Englischen Parlament und beim Congress der Vereinigten Staaten von Nordamerika. Ubers. und mit Anmerkungen begleitet von Leopold von Henning. Berlin, F. Dümmler, 1819.

For a note on this translator and his translation, see above, p. 36-7.

Manual de Practica Parlamentaria, para el Uso del Senado de los Estados Unidos. Por Tomas Jefferson. Al cual se han agregado el Reglamento de Cada Camara y el Comun a Ambas. Traducido del Ingles y Anotado por Felix Varela. Nueva-York: Por Henrique Newton, *Calle de Chatham, No.* 157. 1826.

This translation is based upon the text of Harrison Smith's first edition (1801), not upon Milligan's more complete text of 1812. But it contains fifty-three sections, as did the original printing, and it includes notice that it was copyrighted in New York Oct. 27, 1826. Its Spanish rendering of TJ's English is markedly different from that of the Manila translation of 1909.

Manual del derecho parlamentario, Ó Resumen de las reglas que se observan en el parlamento de Inglaterra y en el Congress de los Estados Unidos para la proposicion, discusion y decision de los negocias; recopilado por Tomas Jefferson, Presidente que fue de los Estados Unidos, con notas por L. A. Pichon, Del Consejo de S. M. el rey de Francia, antiquo agente diplomático cerca del gobierno de los mismos, etc.; Traducido de la ultima edicion Por Don Joaquin Ortega, Profesor de Jurisprudencia. Paris, Libreria Americana calle del Temple, No 69. 1827.

This Spanish translation was based upon the text and notes of Pichon's French translation, and it followed that source in omitting Sections II and VIII of TJ's original work. Sabin did not list the 1827 edition but did list an edition at Paris in 1837.

Rules and Practice of the United States Senate and House of Representatives. *Manuel de pratique parlementaire* de Thomas Jefferson. Édition française avec un avant-propos et des notes de références, et, en appendice, les réglements des chambres Américaines, par Joseph Delpech . . . et Antoine Marcaggi . . . Paris: Fontemoing [etc., etc.], 1905.

Joseph Delpech and Antoine Margaggi were connected with the Faculty of Law and Letters of the University of Aix-Marseille. The title given above is from NUC, vol. 278, p. 681.

Government of the Philippine Islands. Philippine Assembly. Manual de práctica parlamentaria, de Jefferson. Manila: Bureau of Printing, 1909.

This work bears witness to the influence of TJ's *Manual* in the historic process by which the Republic of the Philippines developed from a Spanish colony to a territory of the United States and onward to independent nationhood. For a good statement of that influence, see Aruego, *Philippine Government*, p. 213. See also Rivera, *Congress of the Philippines*, pp. 283-292. Rivera, p. 812, quotes Senate Rule Ch. LI, Sec. 120, of the Philippine Congress as follows:

> If there be no rule applicable to a specific case, the precedents of the legislative bodies of the Philippines shall be resorted to, and as a supplement to these, the rules contained in Jefferson's Manual.

And the same work, p. 842, quotes Rule xxv of the Philippine House of Representatives in similar but more dramatic words, thus:

> The following shall govern in the House in a supplementary manner and in so far as they are not incompatible with the Rules and Standing Orders thereof:
> (a) The parliamentary practices of the Philippine Assembly and of the House of Representatives and Senate of the Philippines;
> (b) The parliamentary practices of the House of Representatives and Senate of the United States of America;
> (c) Jefferson's Manual.

For additional comments upon the Manila edition of the *Manual*, see above, p. 38.

INDEX

INDEX

Hale, Sir Matthew, 115

Hall, Arthur: proceedings against, 55; case of, 78, 81, 130, 173, 201-3, 206-7, 281

Hall, Sir Francis, 130

Hampden, John: case of, 214, 261; debates rule for tabling bills, 329; and revenue for Princess Anne, 330

Harbord, Sir Charles, 203, 325

Harcourt, Sir Walter: case of, 125

Harley, Robert: impeachment of, 311

Harris, Dr., 79

Harrison, Mr.: and case of Lanckton's servant, 268

Harrison, Thomas: trial of, 77-8, 200

Hartgill, William: murder of, 284

Hastings, Sir Francis: and rules of speaking in Commons, 217; and Kendall's case, 269

Hatsell, John: *Precedents* purchased by TJ, 6; influence on TJ, 8, 33-4, 43, 340, 355; fourth volume quoted in Pocket-Book, 160-1, 334-5

Hatton, Sir Christopher: and privacy of debate, 219

Hatton, Lady Elizabeth: and Charles I's attempt to exclude Coke from Commons, 289

Hengham, Sir Ralph: *Registrum Brevium* as source for Pocket-Book, 44

Henning, Leopold Dorotheus von: translates *Manual* into German, 36-7

Herbert, Sir William, 209, 228

Hesslerig, Sir Arthur: case of, 214

Hide, Lawrence: case of, 83, 207, 211

Hilary Term: defined, 163

Hillhouse, James: serves as president pro tempore of Senate, 17, 25

An Historical Review of the Constitution and Government of Pennsylvania. See Franklin, Benjamin; Franklin, William; and Jackson, Richard

Hobart, Sir Henry: case of, 283

Hobby (Hoby), Sir Edward: and privacy of debate, 218-19; and King James' injury, 222; speech in Commons, 234; mentioned, 107, 212

Hogan, Henry, 119

Holcroft, Sir Thomas: case of, 267

Holland, Mr.: case of, 78, 202

Holland, John: and case of John Asgyll, 290

Holland, Sir Thomas: election of, 224

Holles (Hollis), Denzil: case of, 214, 220

Hollis, Jervis: case of, 82-3, 207, 208, 210

Hotham, Sir John: case of, 121, 126, 262, 274-5, 363

House of Commons: rules of membership in, 47-9, 96; cannot convene without Lords, 49; composition of, 51; choosing Speaker of, 52-3, 326-7; committees of, 53; and revenue, 54, 116, 171-2, 255-6; nature of representation in, 54; judicial role of members, 55; notice of proceedings, 55; witnesses before, 55, 160, 331; not prorogued separately, 57; attendance at, 58, 77; removal of member from, 62, 117-18; journals of, 70, 77-8, 102, 417; and writs of quo warranto, 80; freedom of speech limited in, 81, 82-4; rules of debate in, 93-5; and arrest of members, 95-6, 116-17, 229, 256; sending bills to Lords, 103; elections to, 114, 125-6; role of in impeachments, 156-7; origins of, 168, 169; wages of members, 177; conflict with Charles I, 247, 270-72; conflict with Charles II, 326-7. *See also* Parliament

House of Lords: cannot convene without Commons, 49-50; and use of proxies, 54, 171; not prorogued separately, 57; attendance at, 58-9; and election of commoners, 72; and revenue bills, 116, 255-6; journals of, 158, 417. *See also* Parliament

Howard, Mr., 301

Hulme, Obadiah, 194

Hume, David: essays of recommended by TJ, 8

Hungerford, Mr.: case of, 84, 207; and case of Sir John Trevor, 211

Hungerford, Sir Thomas: as speaker of Commons, 169

Huntington, Henry E.: purchases TJ's manuscript copy of *Manual*, 344

impeachment: and Senate, 11, 157, 323; TJ on, 11-12; pardon for prohibited,

Library of Congress Cataloging-in-Publication-Data

Jefferson, Thomas, 1743-1826.
Jefferson's parliamentary writings.

(The Papers of Thomas Jefferson. Second series)
Includes index.
1. United States. Congress. Senate—Rules and practice. 2. Parliamentary practice.
I. Howell, Wilbur Samuel, 1904- . II. Jefferson, Thomas, 1743-1826. Manual of
parliamentary practice. 1987. III. Title. IV. Series: Jefferson, Thomas,

1743-1826. Selections. 1983.

KF4982.J44   1987   328.73'05   87-45522
ISBN 0-691-04713-8 (alk. paper)